GLENCOE
INTRODUCTION TO
Web Design
Using Microsoft® FrontPage®

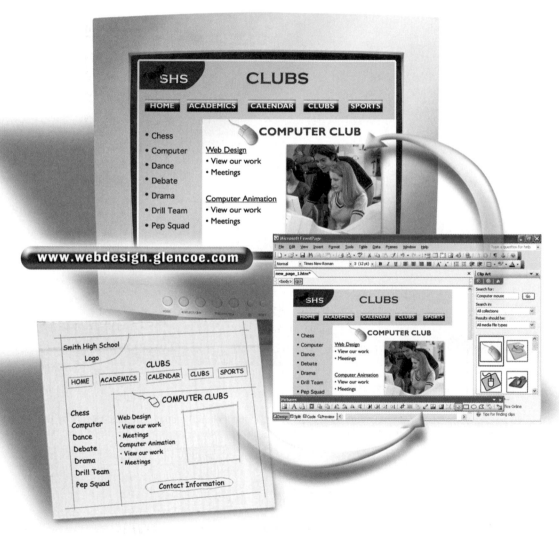

James Renner

Mariemont City School District
Cincinnati, Ohio

New York, New York   Columbus, Ohio   Chicago, Illinois   Peoria, Illinois   Woodland Hills, California

The McGraw·Hill Companies

About the Author

James Renner is principal of Mariemont High School, a three-time National Blue Ribbon High School located just outside of Cincinnati, Ohio. He is also the Regional Director of Cisco Networking Academy, which delivers an on-line curriculum sponsored by Cisco Systems. Jim has made numerous presentations at state-wide and national conferences on such topics as Technology in the Comprehensive High School, Wireless Technology in the Classroom, and Authentic Integration of Technology. He received his B.A. in Geology from Hanover College in Hanover, Indiana, and his M.Ed. in Educational Administration from Xavier University in Cincinnati, Ohio. He will soon complete his Ph.D. in Educational Leadership at Miami University, Oxford, Ohio. James lives in Milford, Ohio, with his wife and three young children.

Academic Review Board

Douglas M. Bergman
Computer Science Instructor,
    Webmaster
Porter-Gaud School
Charleston, South Carolina

Kim Garcia
Webmastering and Computer Science
    Instructor
Georgetown High School
Georgetown, Texas

Dr. Linda Mallinson
Digital Design Instructor
Mid Florida Tech Center
Orlando, Florida
Nova University
Fort Lauderdale, Florida

Scott Whittle
Technology Coordinator
Lincoln High School
Tallahassee, Florida

Academic Reviewers

Tammy Bradley
Chapel Hill High School
Chapel Hill, North Carolina

Danna A. Cusick
Port Richmond High School
Staten Island, New York

Steve Feld
John F. Kennedy High School
Bronx, New York

Nancy Ford
Freer High School
Freer, Texas

Nancy Mack
Booker T. Washington School
Dallas, Texas

Jim Marshall
Winter Springs High School
Winter Springs, Florida

Regiena Maxwell
Osceola High School
Kissimmee, Florida

Michael Wade Perry
Chapel Hill High School
Douglasville, GA
Kennesaw State University
Kennesaw, Georgia

Margaret Roberts
Fort Pierce Central High School
Fort Pierce, Florida

Kathleen Schrock
Administrator for Technology
Nauset Public Schools
Orleans, Massachusetts

Annet Stein
University High School
Orlando, Florida

Brian Thomas
James Wood High School
Winchester, Virginia

Gary M. Vale
Technology Department Chair
Santa Susana High School
Simi Valley, California

Tom Vogelgesang
Lincoln High School
Tallahassee, Florida

Donna Yencer
Highland School of Technology
Gastonia, North Carolina

Technical Reviewers

Bernice Glenn
Web Site Structure Design Instructor
Saddleback College
Mission Viejo, CA

Charles Robert Paige
Computer Science Instructor
Globe College
Oakdale, Minnesota

Jennifer Shiman
Multimedia Designer
Los Angeles, California

Table of Contents

Table of Contents

Table of Contents

Table of Contents

Table of Contents

You Try It Activity Contents

Features Contents

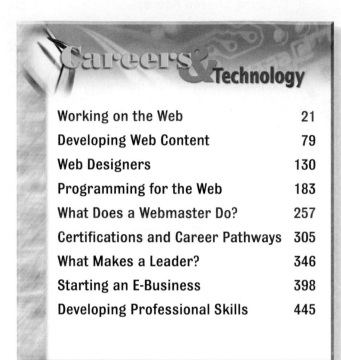
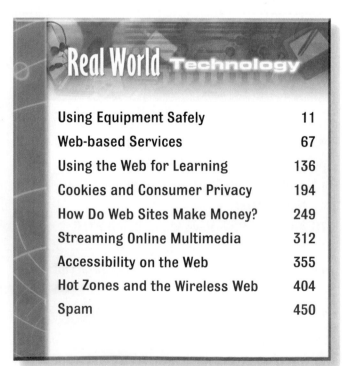
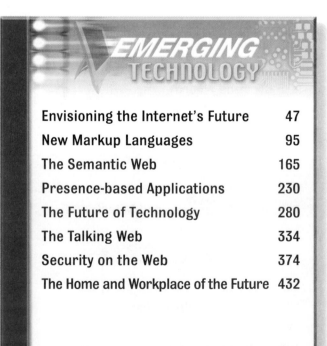

Why Study Web Design?

By understanding how the Web works and how we communicate through the Web, you will learn how to create effective Web sites.

This book can help you develop skills needed to become a Web designer. It can also help you develop skills that will allow you to succeed in any subject area and throughout your life. This textbook was written and designed to help you achieve each of the following goals:

Become a 21st Century Citizen

◆ Use technology wisely and safely

◆ Understand how the Web works

◆ Evaluate the accuracy and usefulness of information on the Web

◆ Find and share information quickly, safely, and ethically

Become an Effective Web Designer

◆ Demonstrate your understanding of fundamental Web design principles

◆ Become a skilled and creative user of Web design technology

◆ Create your own unique, functional Web sites that engage your clients and your audience

◆ Become an expert at evaluating Web sites

◆ Offer constructive feedback to improve your own and others' sites

Develop Learning and Study Skills for All Subjects

◆ Improve reading comprehension with both guided and independent reading strategies

◆ Develop critical thinking skills

◆ Build teamwork skills

◆ Integrate technology skills across the curriculum

BE AN ACTIVE READER!

When you read this textbook, you are gaining insights into technology and how it is used in the world around you. This textbook is an example of non-fiction writing—it describes real-world ideas and facts. It is also an example of technical writing because it tells you how to use technology.

Here are some reading strategies that will help you become an active textbook reader. Choose the strategies that work best for you. If you have trouble as you read your textbook, look back at these strategies for help.

Before You Read

SET A PURPOSE
- ◆ Why are you reading the textbook?
- ◆ How might you be able to use what you learn in your own life?

PREVIEW
- ◆ Read the chapter title to find out what the topic will be.
- ◆ Read the subtitles to see what you will learn about the topic.
- ◆ Skim the photos, charts, graphs, or maps.
- ◆ Look for vocabulary words that are boldfaced. How are they defined?

DRAW FROM YOUR OWN BACKGROUND
- ◆ What do you already know about the topic?
- ◆ How is the new information different from what you already know?

As You Read

QUESTION
◆ What is the main idea?
◆ How well do the details support the main idea?
◆ How do the photos, charts, graphs, and maps support the main idea?

CONNECT
◆ Think about people, places, and events in your own life. Are there any similarities with those in your textbook?

PREDICT
◆ Predict events or outcomes by using clues and information that you already know.
◆ Change your predictions as you read and gather new information.

VISUALIZE
◆ Use your imagination to picture the settings, actions, and people that are described.
◆ Create graphic organizers to help you see relationships found in the information.

IF YOU DON'T KNOW WHAT A WORD MEANS...
◆ think about the setting, or context, in which the word is used.
◆ check if prefixes such as *un-*, *non-*, or *pre-* can help you break down the word.
◆ look up the word's definition in a dictionary or glossary.

READING DOs

Do...
✓ establish a purpose for reading.
✓ think about how your own experiences relate to the topic.
✓ try different reading strategies.

READING DON'Ts

Don't...
⊘ ignore how the textbook is organized.
⊘ allow yourself to be easily distracted.
⊘ hurry to finish the material.

After You Read

SUMMARIZE
◆ Describe the main idea and how the details support it.
◆ Use your own words to explain what you have read.

ASSESS
◆ What was the main idea?
◆ Did the text clearly support the main idea?
◆ Did you learn anything new from the material?
◆ Can you use this new information in other school subjects or at home?

Take the Web Design Challenge!

Many features in this text—such as colored headings, illustrations with captions, tables and charts—have been carefully constructed to help you read, understand, and remember key ideas and concepts. Taking advantage of these features can help you improve your reading and study skills.

Get Started

The scavenger hunt on these pages highlights features that will help you get the most out of your textbook. Collect points as you complete each step.*

1 What are the major topics you expect to learn about in Unit 1? [4 points. *Hint: The Table of Contents gives you at-a-glance information about the major divisions and topics in the book.*]

2 How many times does the **Glencoe Online URL** webdesign.glencoe.com appear in the Chapter 1? [8 points]

3 What is the purpose of the **Think About It** activity on page 3? Why is it important? [6 points]

4 What is the best way to get an overview of what you will learn in Chapter 1? [6 points]

5 What are two study tips you learned from the **Read to Succeed** activity on page 5? [4 points]

6 What type of **Reading Strategy** graphic organizer is found in the Section 2 Guide to Reading? [6 points]

7 What three **key terms** are explained on the first page of Section 1.1? [3 points. *Hint: Key terms stand out from the rest of the text because they are printed in bold, bright blue letters.*]

8 How many **Read Me!** margin features are found Chapter 1? What topics do they discuss? [6 points]

* When finished, see page xx for Web Design Challenge answers and scoring rubric.

9 What is the main heading on page 8 and what are the two sub-headings? [5 points]

10 What margin feature sends you to the Web to learn more about special topics? [4 points]

11 What interpersonal skills are needed to successfully complete the **Building 21st Skills** project on page 206? [7 points]

12 How many steps will it take you to complete **You Try It Activity** 1B? *[4 points. Hint: You Try It Activities can be found easily by looking for the bright yellow arrow in the margin.]*

13 Which **Student Data File** will be used in You Try It Activity 1B? [5 points]

14 Why is it important to read the **Section Assessments** before you read the section? [5 points]

15 What are the four different types of full-page **feature articles**? [4 points. *Hint: Each chapter has two different full page features.*]

16 On what page of each chapter will you find **Reviewing Key Terms, Understanding Main Ideas,** and **Critical Thinking**? [6 points]

17 What online study tools will help you check your comprehension of key ideas in the chapter? [4 points]

18 Which of the **Activities and Projects** on page 29 show you how standards relate to real-world situations? [3 points]

19 On which page will you find an activity that reviews the skills you learned in a You Try It Activity? [4 points]

20 Where can you find projects that will allow you to work on **Building Your Portfolio** of Web sites? [6 points]

What's Your Score?

POINTS	CHALLENGE RATING
90 to 100	You really know how to let your textbook work for you!
70 to 89	Researching and organizing are skills you possess!
Less than 70	Consider working with your teacher or classmates to learn how to use your book more effectively—you will gain skills you can use your whole life.

1. Web Basics, Computer Basics, Online Basics, and HTML Basics
2. Eight times
3. The importance of planning in advance. Each Think About It helps you connect what you will read to real-world situations. Reading experts have discovered it is easier to understand what you are reading if you first set a purpose for reading.
4. Look at pages 3–4, and note the chapter title, objectives, and activities listed. Or, read the main ideas from the Guide to Reading at the start of each section.
5. First, do a quick survey of the content by reading the colored headings. Second, jot down words you do not recognize so that you can look them up later.
6. The graphic organizer is a Venn diagram.
7. Internet, World Wide Web, and file
8. Three Read Me's. *Jargon* defines Internet versus the Web. *Caution* tells how to find Student Data Files. *Tech Tip* refers to Microsoft toolbars.
9. The main heading is Types of Web Sites. The sub-heads are Commercial Sites and Portal Sites. (Did you notice that main topics use a large red font, but subheads use a smaller blue font?)
10. Go Online activities direct you to more activities on the Glencoe Web site.
11. Communication and teamwork skills
12. Five steps
13. The GardenCo student data file
14. By reading the questions first, you can focus on what to look for as you read.
15. Real World Technology, Careers and Technology, Emerging Technology, and Ethics and Technology
16. The Chapter Review and Assessment page
17. Study with PowerPoint and Online Self Check
18. Standards at Work
19. The You Try It Skills Studio on page 30
20. At the end of each unit

Using Microsoft® FrontPage®

The hands-on activities in this textbook can be easily completed using Microsoft FrontPage 2002 or 2003. Activities are written to be used with either version of the software and variations are noted in parentheses where needed.

Recommended Hardware and Software

Access to Microsoft FrontPage and an Internet *browser* are required for this course. Internet *access* is *not* required, but it will make the course more rewarding.

Equipment Needs

Required	Hardware	Software
	Computer	Microsoft Windows
	Color monitor	Microsoft FrontPage
	(make sure your equipment meets the minimum system requirements of your software)	Microsoft Notepad
		Internet browser
Recommended	CD or DVD drive	Internet access software
	CD burner or other storage drive	Word processing software
	Printer	Presentation software
	Scanner	Spreadsheet software
	Microphone	Graphics software
	Video camera	Audio/video player or editing software
	Digital camera	
	Audio/video editing equipment	

Using Student Data Files

To complete some activities and projects in this book, Student Data Files are required.

◆ When you see the Student Data File icon, locate needed files before beginning the activity.

◆ Student Data Files are available on the Teacher Resource CD and on the book Web site at **webdesign.glencoe.com**.

◆ Your teacher will tell you where to find these files.

Saving Your Work

You may need to save your projects while working with Microsoft FrontPage or other applications.

◆ Your teacher will let you know where to save your work.

◆ Always double check to make sure you save to the correct location. Otherwise, you may not be able to find your work later.

◆ Do not ever overwrite or delete others' work. Think about how you would feel if someone did this to you.

Technology Standards

Most educators today believe that in order to live, learn, and work successfully in an increasingly complex society, students must be able to use technology effectively.

ISTE and NETS

The International Society for Technology in Education (ISTE) has developed National Educational Technology Standards to define educational technology standards for students NETS-S. The activities in this book are designed to meet ISTE standards. For more information about ISTE and the NETS, please visit **www.iste.com**.

Standards at Work

The ISTE standards identify skills that students can practice and master in school, but the skills are also used outside of school, at home, and at work. To reinforce how these standards are related to real-world situations, refer to the Standards at Work activities in each Chapter Review. Each activity emphasizes one of the six NETS student standards. Refer back to these pages for a full listing of all the standards and performance indicators for students.

Technology Standards

Technology Foundation Standards for Students

The NETS are divided into six broad categories that are listed below. Activities in the book are specifically designed to meet the standards within each category.

1. Basic operations and concepts
◆ Students demonstrate a sound understanding of the nature and operation of technology systems.
◆ Students are proficient in the use of technology

2. Social, ethical, and human issues
◆ Students understand the ethical, cultural, and societal issues related to technology.
◆ Students practice responsible use of technology systems, information, and software.
◆ Students develop positive attitudes toward technology uses that support lifelong learning, collaboration, personal pursuits, and productivity.

3. Technology productivity tools
◆ Students use technology tools to enhance learning, increase productivity, and promote creativity.
◆ Students use productivity tools to collaborate in constructing technology-enhanced models, prepare publications, and produce other creative works.

4. Technology communications tools
◆ Students use telecommunications to collaborate, publish, and interact with peers, experts, and other audiences.
◆ Students use a variety of media and formats to communicate information and ideas effectively to multiple audiences.

5. Technology research tools
◆ Students use technology to locate, evaluate, and collect information from a variety of sources.
◆ Students use technology tools to process data and report results.
◆ Students evaluate and select new information resources and technological innovations based on the appropriateness of specific tasks

6. Technology problem-solving and decision-making tools
◆ Students use technology resources for solving problems and making informed decisions.
◆ Students employ technology in the development of strategies for solving problems in the real world.

Technology Standards

Educational Technology Performance Indicators for Students

In this text, all students should have opportunities to demonstrate the following performance indicators for technological literacy. Each performance indicator refers to the NETS Foundation Standards category or categories (listed on previous page) to which the performance is linked.

1. Identify capabilities and limitations of contemporary and emerging technology resources and assess the potential of these systems and services to address personal, lifelong learning, and workplace needs. (2)

2. Make informed choices among technology systems, resources and services. (1, 2)

3. Analyze advantages and disadvantages of widespread use and reliance on technology in the workplace and in society as a whole. (2)

4. Demonstrate and advocate for legal and ethical behaviors among peers, family, and community regarding the use of technology and information. (2)

5. Use technology tools and resources for managing and communicating personal/professional information (e.g. finances, schedules, addresses, purchases, correspondence). (3, 4)

6. Evaluate technology-based options, including distance and distributed education, for lifelong learning. (5)

7. Routinely and efficiently use online information resources to meet needs for collaboration, research, publications, communications, and productivity. (4, 5, 6)

8. Select and apply technology tools for research, information analysis, problem-solving, and decision-making in content learning. (4, 5)

9. Investigate and apply expert systems, intelligent agents, and simulations in real-world situations. (3, 5, 6)

10. Collaborate with peers, experts, and others to contribute to content-related knowledge base by using technology to compile, synthesize, produce, and disseminate information, models, and other creative works. (4, 5, 6)

Technology Handbook

Contents

Ethical Computer Use

Computers are more common than ever before—almost every office desk in the country has a computer of some sort, and most schools have them in classrooms. The number of computers in the home is growing, too.

Computers can be used to do wonderful things, but they can also be misused. Knowing some simple ethical guidelines will ensure that you are always doing the right thing.

Using Computers at School

Whether in the classroom or at the library, you likely spend time working at a computer. Remember that the computer is there to help you get your work done. If you instead use the computer to play games, check your personal e-mail, or look at offensive material on the Internet, you are inappropriately using the resource that is being provided for you.

Many institutions are taking action to prevent such misuse. Hidden software applications watch everything users do while they are on a machine, including which Web sites they visit, what e-mails they send, even what keystrokes they type. If you are engaging in inappropriate activity on a school computer, you could be suspended from school, or perhaps even prosecuted.

> A good guideline to keep in mind: **Do not do anything on a computer that you would not do if your teacher or parents were standing behind you, watching.**

Using Computers at Work

While it might seem harmless to do a few small personal tasks while you are at work, the costs really do add up. According to the organization SurfControl, American businesses waste $54 billion every year due to personal use of company computers.

Plagiarism and Copying

Plagiarism is the act of taking somebody else's ideas and passing them off as your own, whether it be one or two sentences or an entire term paper. The "cut-and-paste" feature built into modern operating systems makes a lot of mundane tasks, like moving a paragraph of text, quick, and easy—but also makes plagiarism all too easy. Be on guard against falling into this trap.

It is acceptable to quote sources in your work, but you must make sure to identify those sources and give them proper credit. Also, some Web sites do not allow you to quote from them. Be sure to check each site or resource you are quoting to make sure you are allowed to use the material.

Tip

Using Internet Connections Responsibly

- Because your school may have a fast Internet connection, you may be tempted to use these connections to download large files. Check with your teacher first, as there may be policies forbidding this.
- E-mail systems leave a "digital paper trail." This means that what you type into an e-mail can be found by a system administrator. Be sure not to abuse company or school e-mail systems—it may come back to haunt you!
- If you download any files or applications, be sure to check with your system administrator before using them. Downloaded files are one of the chief sources of viruses, which cause millions of dollars in damages to computer networks every year.
- You would not steal office supplies from your office or school, so make sure you do not take home computer-related resources like CD-ROMs or floppy disks.

Copyright Laws

A copyright protects someone who creates an original work. When you create something—a book, a play, or a single sentence—you can copyright it, thereby claiming that you created it, and you are the owner. The goal is to prevent unauthorized copying of that work by another party.

Copyright protection is provided by the Copyright Act of 1976, a federal statute. At one time, if you wanted to copyright something you had to fill out a form, file your work with the Copyright Office in the Library of Congress, and pay a fee. Today, this is no longer the case. If you create an original work, it is automatically protected by copyright law—even if you forget to put the "© 2004" marker on the document. However, registering a copyright with the office does provide some additional protections, should you ever have to go to court over your creation.

Obtaining Permission

So what do you do if you want to use a portion of a copyrighted work in your own work? In order to do this, you need to obtain permission from the copyright holder.

Obtaining permission depends on the work in question. If you want to use an excerpt from a book, you will need to write a letter to the publisher, since they are the owner of the copyright.

(Sometimes the author, or an organization other than the publisher, owns the copyright. Check the copyright page in the front of the book to make sure.) Each instance is different, but many publishers are willing to grant permissions to individuals for educational purposes. If you want to reproduce information you found on the Web, contact the Webmaster or author of the article to request permission.

Duration and Public Domain

So once a copyright is in place, how long before it expires? The answer depends on when the work was created. For all works created since January 1, 1978, copyright lasts until 70 years after the creator's death. For works created before that date, the answer is considerably more complex. The copyright would last anywhere from 28 to 67 years from the date of creation, with possible options for renewal.

Once a work's copyright has expired, that work is considered to be in the public domain, meaning that nobody owns it and anybody can reprint it as they please. This is why you can find so many different printed versions of classic literature from writers like Dickens, Shakespeare, and the like—the publishers do not have to pay any fees for the right to print those books.

Some Common Misconceptions About Copyrights

- "If it does not say it is copyrighted, it is not copyrighted." Original work published after March of 1989 is copyrighted, whether it says so or not.
- "I found it on the Internet, therefore it is okay for me to copy it." Most of the text on the Internet is indeed copyrighted. Copying information from the Internet is a serious breach of copyright, and can result in prosecution.
- "It is okay to put copyrighted material on my Web site, because I do not charge people to look at it." It does not matter whether you are making a profit from the reuse of copyrighted material—you are distributing it, and that is illegal.
- "I have changed the material, so it is no longer copyrighted." Copyright law says that only the owner of the copyright can make "derivative works"— that is, new works based on the existing material.
- "I can reprint the material, because it is considered fair use." Be careful! "Fair use" refers to the right to reprint brief excerpts from copyrighted works. However, there are no clear definitions on how much of a work can be used. Some examples of fair use include quoting a book in a book report or parodying a work.

Word Processing Tips and Tools

One of the most common types of application software used in both business and school is the word processor. Word processing software allows you to create and edit documents such as reports, term papers, and essays. Many word processing programs will even allow you to create documents in HTML, which can be posted to the Web. To make the most of word processing, you will need to learn some of the features many of these programs offer.

Checking for Errors

Many people have come to depend on the spell-checker feature of word processing programs. Inside each word processor is a large file called the *dictionary.* Unlike the dictionaries that you will find on your bookshelf or online, this file does not contain any information about the meanings or pronunciations of words; instead, it knows how to spell them.

As you type into a word processor, the program constantly scans the dictionary. Every time you tap the space bar, the program knows you have just completed a word, so it looks up that word in the dictionary. If it cannot find it, the program will let you know, usually by

placing a red line underneath the word.

Depending on the program, you may have a variety of options—for instance, looking at other words that the program thinks you meant to type, adding the word you typed into the dictionary so the program will recognize it, or telling the program to ignore it.

> Remember that spell-checkers and grammar-checkers are not perfect.

For instance, if you meant to type the word *stay* but accidentally typed *sty,* the program will not alert you to the error, because *sty* is a valid word. It is important to proofread each of your documents.

Many programs now also include grammar-checkers. Grammar-checkers compare sentence structures in documents to a file of common errors.

Tracking Changes

Sometimes, more than one person will need to work on a single document. Using the Versions feature (or Tracking feature) of a word processing program makes this easy. The program keeps copies of different versions of the document as changes are made, so you can refer back to earlier versions.

Another helpful feature is Comments. Comments allow you to make remarks about the document for other group members to see. They can make changes based on your comments, revise the comments, or leave more comments in return.

Tip

Online Calendars

Keeping track of all the work you need to do can be difficult—it is easy to get overwhelmed when you are faced with a mountain of books and papers and are not sure where to start. In cases like this, you might find that using an online calendar will help you get organized and handle your work efficiently.

Online calendars work much like paper day-planners that you buy at the office supply store, but instead of writing out tasks by hand, you type them into your Web browser. The calendar site keeps track of appointments, due dates, and to-do lists. Keeping all your tasks entered into an online calendar is one way of making certain you are accomplishing them in the smartest order.

You might also want to use the reminders feature; these are alarms that tell you when something must be done. The reminder might be a sound, a pop-up box, or an e-mail sent to you by the calendar site.

Also, since the information is stored online, you can check your calendar from anywhere—from home, school, or any place that has an Internet connection.

Etiquette for Digital Communication

New rules of etiquette have evolved for the new communication media provided by the Internet—e-mail, chat rooms, and newsgroups. Nicknamed "netiquette," these basic guidelines are important to keep in mind whenever you are communicating with someone online.

E-mail

Of all the conveniences provided by the Internet, e-mail is the most widely used. It has changed how people live, work, and socialize. Letters that used to take days to arrive in the mail now take mere seconds. Business communication has become much more efficient thanks to e-mail. Here are a few things to keep in mind when sending e-mail:

✔ Do not send large attachments, unless the recipient is expecting them.

✔ When forwarding e-mails, be sure to trim off unnecessary information like old headers and quotes—these can build up quickly!

✔ Keep your communication appropriate, and do not say anything about someone that you would not want them to hear. Even after you click Delete, e-mail records stay in the system for a long time, and can even be found years later.

✔ Never send or forward chain letters. Even if they seem like a good idea, they are often fraudulent—and will likely anger the people you are sending them to.

Chat Rooms

Chat rooms can be useful communication tools, but they can also be raucous free-for-alls. Some things to keep in mind:

✔ Choose the chat room wisely. Some chat rooms are populated with questionable people, so do some research first.

✔ For your safety, always remain anonymous.

✔ Take turns with the conversation. Just like in a real conversation, allow people to finish their thoughts, and do not interrupt.

✔ Be aware of "lurkers," people who are reading the conversation but not taking part. Try not to say anything that might hurt somebody's feelings.

Newsgroups

The Usenet system is made up of thousands of discussion groups, each on a particular topic. Having a rewarding newsgroup experience requires some basic netiquette, including the following guidelines:

✔ Stay on topic. Most Usenet groups are very specific, and readers do not appreciate posts that do not fit the topic.

✔ Avoid flaming. Newsgroups are particularly ripe for flaming—people tend to get passionate in these conversations. Never type something that you would not want to say out loud.

✔ Know your facts. There is no fact-checking process in Usenet—anybody can say anything he or she wants. Just because somebody says something in a newsgroup does not mean it is true—remember this when quoting or replying to someone.

Tip

General Netiquette Guidelines

- Behave as though you were communicating face-to-face.
- Remember that your words can be misinterpreted, and things like sarcasm, body language, and irony may not come across.
- Do not "flame." A flame is an aggressive or insulting letter.
- Do not "spam." Spam, or junk e-mail, is a billion-dollar problem, clogging mail systems and wasting time. Do not add to the problem.
- Do not SHOUT. Make sure your Caps Lock key is off.
- Do not distribute copyrighted information. Just because something is on the Internet does not mean it is free.
- Do not hide behind a screen name. Behave online as you would in the real world—honestly, ethically, and wisely.

Online Resources

One of the most useful elements of the Internet is the World Wide Web (also called "the Web"), which allows documents to be viewed by anyone anywhere in the world. This is particularly helpful when it comes to documents that are normally expensive or hard to find. For instance, many families do not own an encyclopedia, so a student who needs to do research would normally have to make a trip to the library. The Web makes it possible for documents like encyclopedias and dictionaries to be accessed by many people.

Dictionaries

There are hundreds of online dictionaries. Some specialize in certain types of information, such as law, medicine, or technology.

● **Dictionary.com** The name makes it easy to remember; this site also contains a fully searchable thesaurus. (**www.dictionary.com**)
● **OneLook Dictionaries** A "meta-dictionary," this site lets you type in a word once to search across more than 840 dictionaries. (**www.onelook.com**)
● **Merriam-Webster** A Web version of one of the best-known print dictionaries, this site includes a "word of the day" feature, a thesaurus, and links to other research sites. (**www.m-w.com**)

Encyclopedias

Encyclopedias need to be updated often, making them a perfect choice for online delivery. Online encyclopedias are searchable, and many contain photos and illustrations.

● **Brittanica Online** The online version of one of the most respected print encyclopedias offers both free and premium access, with more content and fewer ads in the premium version. (**www.britannica.com**)

● **World Book Online** The online version of World Book does not offer any free information; you have to pay a monthly fee to access the entries, which include all the contents of the print versions dating back to 1922. (**www.worldbook.com**)

● **Encarta** A popular encyclopedia by Microsoft, the Encarta Web site offers lots of free content, but to access all their information you will need to buy either a subscription or a copy of the CD-ROM. (**www.encarta.msn.com**)

Other Resources

While dictionaries and encyclopedias offer lots of useful information, other specialized resource sites can give you information about other subjects.

● **Roget's Thesaurus** The online version of the definitive thesaurus lets you search for words or browse them alphabetically or by category. The site also offers plug-ins that put dictionary and thesaurus buttons right in your browser window. (**www.thesaurus.com**)
● **RefDesk** A comprehensive site with links to every kind of information imaginable. If you do not know where to start looking for a particular fact or statistic, start here. (**www.refdesk.com**)
● **Bartleby** Bartleby is fully searchable and contains the complete text of Bartlett's Quotations, Simpson's Quotations, the Columbia World of Quotations, as well as dozens of biographies, articles, and books. (**www.bartleby.com**)

Safe Surfing

The Internet can be a wonderful place. There is much to learn, explore, and discover. You can find the answers to many of your questions on the Internet, often much more quickly than at the local library. And the Internet can put you in touch with people you might never have met—experts, writers, or just other students from around the world.

But the Internet can also be a dangerous place. There are Web sites that you would freely visit, and many others that you will want to avoid.

Privacy and Personal Information

Information is valuable. Companies that operate on the Internet are constantly seeking more information about customers, as well as potential customers. By building vast databases of names, addresses, and information about buying habits, those companies can market their products and services with increased efficiency, thereby increasing sales.

But in addition to legitimate sites that ask you for information like name, address, or age, there are many questionable sites that are looking for data as well. Before you type any

information into an online form or in a chat room, be sure to evaluate to whom you are sending that information, and why you are sending it.

Here are some things to keep in mind:

✔ Know to whom you are giving the information. Check the URL in your browser—does it match the domain you visited? Or were you "redirected" to another site without your knowledge?

✔ Why are you giving the information? If, for example, you are ordering something online, you will need to give your address in order for the product to be shipped. There should always be a good reason for all information you provide. Never give out your social security number, your birth date, or your mother's maiden name without adult consent. These are often used to secure credit reports, and giving these to a dishonest source could ruin your credit.

✔ Never give personal information of any sort to someone you meet in a chat room. Always remain anonymous.

✔ If you are still unsure whether it is safe to give the information, check with a parent or other trusted adult.

Tip

Avoiding Physical Stress at the Computer

If you are going to be spending time in front of a computer, it is important that you minimize stress to your body. Here are some important things to keep in mind:

● Make sure you use a chair that provides strong back support. Be sure to keep your back straight while working, and keep your feet flat on the floor.

● Keep your wrists straight while you are typing. If your keyboard includes a "wrist rest," be sure not to use it while typing. Resting your hands while typing causes the wrists to bend, which causes muscle fatigue and can put you at risk for injuries.

● Position the monitor so that it is just a little below eye level and about two feet away. This will prevent strain on your neck muscles.

● Make sure there is enough light in the room so that you can easily see the monitor without straining your eyes.

● Keep your monitor's resolution set to a comfortable level. The highest possible resolution setting is not necessarily the best. Choose a resolution that displays images and text at a size that is comfortable to view.

Tips for Using the Internet for Research

The Internet is probably the single most important new tool for research since the public library. However, the advantage provided by the Internet can also be its greatest challenge: There is so much information out there that it is difficult to know where to begin.

Where to Start

A good place to begin work regardless of your research topic is Google. Arguably the most useful search engine, Google is an enormous "spider" (an automated piece of software that "crawls" the Web looking for information) that keeps an index of over three billion URLs.

Simply type your topic into Google's search bar. By default, Google looks for sites that contain every word you type. For instance, if you enter the words *sports medicine,* you will see a list of sites that contain both of those words, not just one or the other. To get better results, here are a few tips:

✔ Place quotes around your topic. Searching for **"sports medicine"** will find sites where that exact phrase appears.
✔ Use NEAR. Entering **sports NEAR medicine** will return sites that contain both words, and have the two words close to one another.

✔ Exclude unwanted results. Simply use a minus sign to indicate the words you do not want: **"sports medicine" - baseball**

When conducting a search online, be sure to spell all your search words correctly. Incorrect spellings can prevent you from getting good results.

✔ Stick to a single domain. If you only want to find information from a specific site, just add the domain after the search term along with the "site" tag, and Google will only look for documents on that site: **"sports medicine" site: www.espn.com**

Refining the Search

Your Google searches will likely give you page after page of hits, each with a brief summary of some of the text from that page. Some things to think about while browsing your Google results:
✔ Links on the right hand side of the page (and sometimes at the top, in a colored box) are sponsored links—this means that the

company in question has paid to have their link show up. While this does not necessarily mean that the link is not worth exploring, it is usually an indicator that the site is selling a product or service, and might not be valuable for pure research.
✔ Google displays a few lines of text from each page and shows your search phrase in bold. Read the sentence surrounding the bold information to see if it is appropriate for your work.
✔ After you have entered your search phrase and have finished looking at the results, click on the "News" tab near the top of the page. This will show you recent news stories about your topic from a number of news services and wires.

Unique Online Research Tools

● **iTools** This "meta-research" tool lets you search not only the Web, but also discussion groups, dictionaries, and other sources. (**www.itools.com**)
● **RefDesk** This site contains links to hundreds of different Web resources, each designed for a very specific purpose. (**www.refdesk.com**)
● **eLibrary** This premium site searches the full text of hundreds of periodicals, newswires, books, maps, and more. (**www.elibrary.com**)

How to Evaluate Web Sites

While there is a lot of valuable information online, there is also a lot of information that can be deceptive and misleading. The books in your library have been evaluated by scholars and publishers; Web sites, however, are not verified. Learning to evaluate Web sites will make you a more savvy surfer and enable you to gather the information you need quickly and easily.

When you are trying to decide whether a Web site provides trustworthy information, there are a number of components to consider.

Authorship

When dealing with information from a Web site, the first and most important question to ask is "Who wrote this information?"

Once you have found the name of the author (usually located near the top or bottom of the page), do a quick Web search to see what else that author has written. Typing the author's name into Google will often return not only pages by that author, but also pages about that author, such as reviews of his or her work.

Check to see if the author has published in print. Search online for books that he or she has written. All this information will help you decide whether you should consider the person's information trustworthy.

Sponsorship/Publishing

Take a look at the domain that is offering the information. Why have they published this article? Are they trying to sell a product or service, or are they an impartial organization providing unbiased information?

Determining sponsorship or the publishing body will help you decide whether the information is biased. For instance, if an article that suggests a certain pesticide is very effective is posted on the Web site of a company that sells that pesticide, it is probably biased.

Accuracy

When you write a term paper, you are expected to provide sources for each of your facts. Look for Web sites that do the same thing by providing footnotes containing bibliographical information or references.

Also, look for clues that the information was written by someone knowledgeable. Spelling errors and grammatical mistakes are warning signs that the information provided may not be accurate.

Timeliness

Most articles will contain information about when it was written and when it was last updated. Recent update information normally appears at the very bottom of a Web site's main page, while date of authorship information usually appears near the title of the specific article.

The more recently something was written, the more likely it is to be accurate. An article from 1995 about "Internet trends," for instance, probably does not contain up-to-date information.

One Final Guideline

When using information from a Web site, remember to treat it just as you would print information. Never use information that you cannot verify with another source.

Visit *Glencoe Online*

Go to this book's Web site at **webdesign.glencoe.com.**

Click on **Unit Activities** and select **Unit 1 Internet Scavenger Hunt.** Complete the online scavenger hunt to learn how to use the Internet safely and how to use this Web site.

Think About It

Be Prepared!

When you travel, do you pack ahead of time or at the last minute? With careful planning, you can make sure you have everything you need for a successful trip.

Planning Activity

Planning to build a Web site is a lot like preparing for a trip. How do you think Web designers make sure their sites are successful? List ten things you think Web designers need to do *before* they begin to create a site. As you read this unit, compare your list to what you learn.

Web Basics

YOU WILL LEARN TO...

WHY IT MATTERS......................................

Every day, millions of people connect to the Internet to access information they need. Whether they use it to shop, pay bills, or check the local news, many people make the Internet an essential part of their daily routine. As the Internet's role in communications, entertainment, commerce, and work increases, so does the need for people with Web skills. The information in this chapter provides the foundation on which you can build these necessary skills.

Quick Write Activity

Think about the Web sites you visit most often. What types of sites do you like to visit? Why do you use these sites? Summarize how the Internet is (or is not) an important part of your daily routine.

WHAT YOU WILL DO...

READ TO SUCCEED

Survey Before You Read

Before starting the chapter, do a quick survey of the content by reading the colored headings. Think about what you already know about the topic. Look for the bolded terms and jot down words you do not recognize. Study the pictures and the charts. Do they help you predict what information will appear in the chapter? Finally, read the chapter summary and the review questions. This will help you pay attention to important concepts in the reading.

Section 1.1 Introduction to the Web

Guide to Reading

Main Ideas

The Internet is a worldwide network of hardware. The World Wide Web is part of the Internet. Web sites are divided into categories that meet particular needs.

Key Terms

Internet
World Wide Web
file
Web browser
Web site
Web page
home page

Reading Strategy

Identify and describe the five components of a Web browser. Use a table like this one (also available online).

Components	Description

Most people use the Internet without even thinking about how it works. Now that you will be creating your own Web pages, you will need to consider how your pages will work best on the Web.

THE INTERNET AND THE WORLD WIDE WEB

Web design involves creating a Web site that meets a specific goal. When designing a site, you must determine how the site will be structured, what information it will contain, and how this information will appear on screen. Before you create a Web site, you must first understand the Internet and the World Wide Web.

The Internet Is Hardware

The **Internet** (often called the Net) is hardware—lots of hardware—connected together to create a massive worldwide network. The Internet's hardware consists of those components that you can physically touch, such as computers, cables, telephone wires, and high-speed communication lines. A network is a group of computers and related devices that can communicate, or "talk," with one another. The Internet is thus an *inter*-linked collection of many smaller *net*works.

The Web Is Software

The part of the Internet we are most familiar with is the **World Wide Web,** often referred to as the WWW, or the *Web,* for short. The Web includes software that sends information along the Internet's hardware. The information on the Web is stored in individual files. A **file** contains information such as text, graphics, video, or animation, that is stored on computer hardware. Each file on the Web has a specific name. Web files are joined together somewhat like a giant spider web—hence the name Web. These files are stored on special computers called Web servers.

READ ME!

Jargon Although the terms are used interchangeably, the Web and the Internet do not mean the same thing. The World Wide Web provides the information that a user wants to know. The Internet provides access to the World Wide Web.

HOW THE WEB WORKS

The basic component of a Web page is a text document. A text document contains words, letters, numbers, and other unique characters. Special software called a **Web browser** interprets these files to display Web pages on your computer screen.

Web Sites versus Web Pages

A **Web site** is a group of related files organized around a common topic. These files include individual Web pages, graphics, and other multimedia elements such as audio and video. A **Web page** is a single file within a Web site, which has a unique name. The pages in a Web site are linked so that you can move (or navigate) from one to another. A Web site's main page is typically called the home page. The **home page** usually contains general information about the Web site. This page is almost always the first page a user sees when visiting a Web site, so it is important that it gives a good first impression.

Browser Functions

Hypertext Markup Language, or *HTML,* is the code used to create Web pages. The function of a Web browser is to translate the text-based HTML code into a graphical Web page. Your Web browser also lets you navigate from one Web page to another. Figure 1.1 shows the Microsoft Internet Explorer browser with some of its main components labeled. Some of the major components of any Web browser are:

◆ The title bar tells you the name of the current Web page
◆ Menus allow you to select from lists of commands
◆ The Web address displays the address of the current Web page
◆ Navigation buttons help you move from one page to another
◆ The viewing area displays the current Web page

● Figure 1.1

Web browsers such as Internet Explorer make it easy to move from one Web site to another. How can you determine the address of the Web page shown here?

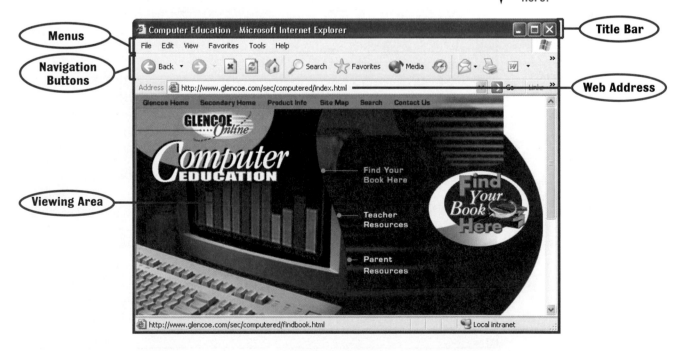

TYPES OF WEB SITES

Most Web sites can be placed into particular categories based on their purposes or main goals. Five major types of Web sites are: commercial sites, portal sites, informational sites, educational sites, and personal sites.

Commercial Sites

The primary purpose of a commercial site is to sell or promote a company's products or services.

E-commerce Sites Buying and selling goods and services over the Internet is called electronic commerce, or e-commerce. Shopping at an e-commerce site is different from going to a traditional store. Consumers expect a complete description of the item. Photographs are often used to encourage the consumer to buy the item.

Corporate Presence Sites Some commercial Web sites do not sell anything. Their job is to promote a positive image for the company. These types of sites are often referred to as corporate presence Web sites. For example, a pharmaceutical (drug) company would probably not sell any medications on its Web site. However, it might discuss the research it is doing to improve the treatment of people with certain diseases.

Portal Sites

A Web portal is a Web site that provides a variety of services that people use every day. As shown in Figure 1.2, most portals provide general news and business information. Portals often provide access to items such as telephone directories, maps, travel services, and shopping directories. Many people use portals because they can easily get a variety of information in a single location.

Activity 1.1 Identify Web Sites Visit various categories of Web sites by connecting to the links available at **webdesign.glencoe.com**.

Figure 1.2 Many Web portals let users search the Web for needed information. What are three features that you find useful in a Web portal?

Informational Sites

Informational sites serve one purpose—to provide people with useful information. One advantage that Web sites have over other informational sources such as magazines and books is that they are relatively easy to update.

News Sites News sites often contain up-to-the-minute local, national, and international news. They also feature business news, stock market reports, weather forecasts, and sports updates. Many of these sites are associated with specific newspapers or television networks such as CNN.

Government Sites Government Web sites tell us about the activities of our federal, state, and local governments. They also provide an easy way to find current government information and regulations. Many foreign governments have Web sites that provide information on current events, the country's economy and population, and so forth.

Public Interest Sites A public interest site is a Web site that focuses on certain problems or situations and suggests how individuals might respond. Public interest Web sites span a wide range of topics from animal rights to helping others in need (see Figure 1.3).

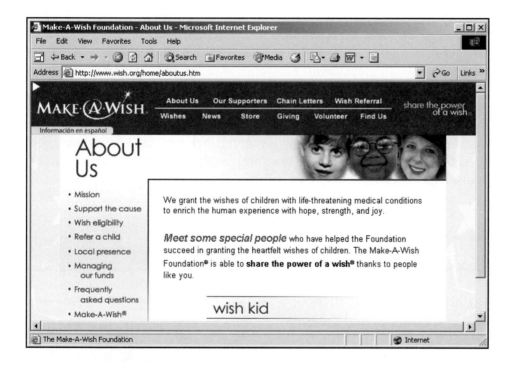

► ● Figure 1.3
Public interest sites make people aware of a particular situation and often encourage them to take specific actions. What public interest Web sites would you be likely to visit?

Educational Sites

Educational sites often provide information about a school or university. Some even offer online courses or teach specific skills.

School and University Sites Many schools and universities have educational Web sites that contain general information about the school, class schedules, and courses offered. Some sites let you access homework assignments, view your grades, and even e-mail questions to your teacher.

Tutorials and Distance Learning Many educational sites offer interactive tutorials that let students learn by doing. For example, some tutorials teach students to use computer software such as word processors and graphics programs.

Through distance learning, students take classes over the Internet. In some situations, classes meet at a specific time, and students use their keyboards to discuss topics with one another or to ask the teacher questions. In other situations, students work independently and use e-mail to submit assignments or to interact with their teacher.

Museums and Other Institutions Many museums have Web sites that provide information about their exhibits. Some Web sites have "virtual tours" in which a visitor can move from one Web page to another, similar to how they might actually walk through the museum's exhibits.

Personal Sites

Personal Web sites are maintained by individuals. These sites allow people to share their interests with others, or to share news with family members who live far away.

Individuals, especially children and young adults, should always be careful when posting personal information on the Internet. Online information is available to anyone with an Internet connection, and posting personal information can lead to dangerous situations. To remain safe, never post personal contact information on a Web site, and avoid describing how you look or where you live in great detail. Furthermore, never post similar information about other people, especially if they are very young.

Another use of a personal Web site is to display a portfolio. A portfolio is a collection of work created by an individual. Web site developers often maintain portfolios showing examples of the Web sites they have developed. Potential clients can look at the portfolio to learn about the Web site developer's experience and skills.

Section 1.1 Assessment

Concept Check

1. **Define** Internet, World Wide Web, file, Web browser, Web site, Web page, home page.

2. **Summarize** the difference between the Internet and the World Wide Web.

3. **Explain** the function of a Web browser.

Critical Thinking

4. **Compare and Contrast** How is a public interest site different from and similar to an educational site?

5. **Draw Conclusions** Why do you think companies are using the Internet to train employees?

Applying Skills

Categorize Web Sites Make a list of five Web sites that you have visited recently. Beside each site, write the category to which you think this site belongs.

Real World Technology

USING EQUIPMENT SAFELY

Any school or workplace can pose potential dangers. To keep yourself and others safe, you should learn how to recognize and avoid these hazards.

Using an ergonomically designed keyboard can help you avoid common computer-related injuries.

Avoiding Computer Injuries

Computers can cause injuries if they are not used correctly. Some results of improper use are:

◆ Repetitive strain injuries (RSIs) from using a keyboard and a mouse for long periods
◆ Eyestrain resulting from staring at a monitor for too long without a break
◆ Backaches from sitting improperly or in the same position for too long

To avoid these problems, make sure your workstation is ergonomically correct. Always readjust your seat if your workstation is used by many people. Make sure your feet are flat on the floor and your wrists are straight. The monitor should be about two feet away from you, at a height that lets you look at it without bending or twisting your neck.

Take periodic breaks from the computer, so you can get up and move around. Look away from the monitor frequently. Adjust the resolution and brightness of your monitor to avoid eyestrain.

Safety-Conscious Attitudes

A good attitude can lead to a safer work environment:

◆ Know how to use equipment properly.
◆ Stay alert for safety hazards such as loose cords that can make you trip or frayed wires that can shock.
◆ Stack or store equipment properly.
◆ Avoid horseplay. It can cause accidents and damage.

Fire Safety

Electrical fires are possible where a lot of computer equipment is running, because circuits can become overloaded or wiring can be faulty or outdated. Learn the location of fire alarms in your school or workplace. Know the procedures to follow in case a fire breaks out. Take fire drills seriously. They could save your life.

Avoiding Common Injuries

Be aware of common school or workplace injuries. Shock results from touching electrical components or handling damaged wiring. Never stick your hand or any object into an open piece of equipment. Make sure wiring is not broken before handling it. Always turn off equipment before working on it.

Tech Focus

1. Make a presentation about your school's emergency evacuation plan or one you create with the other students in your class.

2. Research a common school or workplace injury. Demonstrate ways to avoid such an injury, including proper use of equipment.

Section 1.2 Elements of a Web Page

Guide to Reading

Main Ideas

Web pages are composed of many different elements, including text, graphics, animation, and hyperlinks. Hyperlinks link Web pages together and help a user navigate through a Web site.

Key Terms

text
graphics
multimedia
audio
animation
video
hyperlink

Reading Strategy

Identify the similarities and differences between internal and external hyperlinks. Use a Venn diagram like this one (also available online).

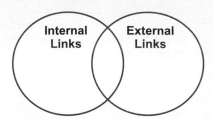

Web pages are made up of individual parts, or elements. When a Web page is developed, each element is created individually. and then combined into a finished page. Common Web page elements include:

◆ Text
◆ Graphics
◆ Multimedia, including audio and video
◆ Animation
◆ Hyperlinks

Figure 1.4 (shown on the next page) illustrates the different elements, including text, graphics, multimedia, and hyperlinks that make up a NASA (National Aeronautics and Space Administration) Web page.

TEXT AND GRAPHICS

Text consists of words, letters, numbers, and other symbols. Text might be in the form of paragraphs, just as in books and other printed media, or it might glide across the screen. Text can be used to label pictures, describe the buttons used for navigation, and provide links to other screen displays.

Text in Web pages can be of different sizes and may be underlined, or in bold or italics. The viewer is more likely to read text that is in large letters than in hard-to-read small letters. Color can also be used to emphasize text.

Web sites often contain colorful images or graphics. **Graphics** include drawings, charts, diagrams, paintings, and photographs. Even the buttons, arrows, and other visual elements that help users navigate through a site are graphic elements.

Graphics are an important part of Web pages. They can be used to attract the viewers' attention or explain things that might be difficult to describe with words. In this book, you will learn how to insert attractive and useful graphics into your Web pages.

webdesign.glencoe.com

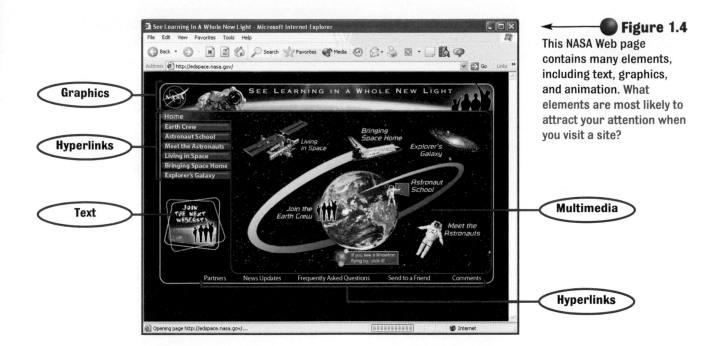

Figure 1.4
This NASA Web page contains many elements, including text, graphics, and animation. What elements are most likely to attract your attention when you visit a site?

MULTIMEDIA

Many Web sites feature multimedia elements. The term **multimedia** refers to the integration of elements such as graphics, text, audio, video, animation, and interactivity by means of computer technology.

Audio

Sound can add interest and appeal to a Web site. In Web site development, live or recorded sound is referred to as **audio.** Audio can be in the form of speech, such as a voice-over or a narration. Another form of audio is sound effects—sounds that emphasize the information being presented. A zoo's Web site might have animal sounds in the background. A catchy tune can capture an audience for an advertisement that might otherwise be ignored. Many countries' Web sites let you hear their national anthems.

Animation

Animation refers to the movement of text or graphics. Some news Web sites use animated text so that major news announcements move across the screen. Sometimes text appears to grow larger or bounce. Simple animation can be achieved by drawing a series of graphics in such a way that the object to be animated is in a slightly different position in each subsequent graphic. If these graphics are quickly displayed one after the other, it will appear as if the object is moving. This is similar to the way in which some television cartoons are created.

Video

Video consists of live or recorded *moving* images. Like sound, video attracts interest in your Web site. You can see video clips of recent stories on news sites like CNN. Some sites let you view short clips from current movies or the latest music video from your favorite musical group. The terms *video* and *animation* are often used interchangeably, but they really mean two different things. Video captures live motion and breaks it up into separate pieces, called frames. Animation, on the other hand, takes separate images and puts them all together so the finished product looks like continuous motion.

HYPERLINKS

Web pages are linked together through **hyperlinks,** which allow users to move from one online location to another. A hyperlink, or *link,* can be a word, phrase, or graphic. You can recognize a text link because the words are usually underlined and in a different color. Graphics links are usually in the form of buttons.

When you position your mouse pointer on a link, the cursor changes shape. For example, the cursor may take the shape of a hand with an upward-pointing finger. This change helps users identify hyperlinks on a page.

There are three kinds of links:

 ◆ Internal links
 ◆ External links
 ◆ Intrapage links

An internal link takes you to another page on the same Web site, while an external link takes you to a page on a different Web site. Some Web pages have intrapage links. These links move you to a different spot on the same page. Intrapage links are useful for locating specific topics within long pages. For example, clicking an intrapage link at the bottom of a page may take you to the top of the page. In the following You Try It activity, you will use internal links to move around a Web site.

YOU TRY IT

ACTIVITY 1A Viewing a Web Site in a Web Browser

1 Open your Web browser.

Student Data File

2 Select the **File** menu, and click **Open** (your program may use **Open File**).

3 In the dialog box, browse to the DataFile folder. Open the folder. Open the **Examples** folder. Then select the **GardenCo** folder and click the **Open** button. The Garden Company files and folders appear.

4 Open the **index.htm** file. The Garden Company home page appears on your screen. Read the page's text to learn about The Garden Company.

5 The left side of the screen contains internal links to several pages, such as Products, Class Offerings, and Press Releases. Click the **Products** link. A list of products is displayed as shown in Figure 1.5.

6 Click the **Plants for hobbyists!** link. A screen appears containing a photograph and a description of a carnivorous (animal-eating) plant.

7 At the bottom of the screen is a section titled Other Resources. It contains links to related Web sites. (You may need to scroll down a little to see this section.) These are examples of external links—they lead to Web sites that are outside the current one. Click your browser's **Back** button to return to the Products page.

8 At the top of the Products page, click **The Garden Company** logo. You will return to the home page. Regardless of where you are in this site, clicking the logo takes you home.

9 Continue navigating to different areas of the site until you feel comfortable with its structure. Close the Web browser.

You should have a good reason for including each individual element on your Web page. Some reasons include presenting information, attracting viewer attention, and letting the viewer navigate to different locations.

Section 1.2 Assessment

Concept Check

1. **Define** text, graphics, multimedia, audio, animation, video, hyperlink.

2. **Identify** the basic parts of a Web page.

3. **Describe** how to use a Web browser to navigate around a Web site.

Critical Thinking

4. **Analyze** Why might a Web designer choose to include more graphics than text on a Web page?

5. **Draw Conclusions** Both Web sites and books have pages. How do hyperlinks make using the Web different from reading a book?

Applying Skills

Identify Hyperlinks
Visit a Web site and identify an example of an internal link and an external link. Write down the text that serves as each link. Beside each link, write the web address, or URL, to which it takes you.

Section 1.3 Web Site Development

Web site development offers a variety of career opportunities. Companies and organizations develop Web sites, add features to existing Web sites, and maintain their sites to keep the information current. Each new Web site goes through a development process. Software tools aid the people who design, create, and maintain Web sites.

THE WEB SITE DEVELOPMENT PROCESS

Developing a Web site is a complex task. Web developers use a series of steps to break the task into manageable parts. There are five basic steps in Web site development:

1. Determine the purpose and goal of the Web site
2. Design and implement the Web site
3. Evaluate and test the Web site
4. Publish the Web site
5. Maintain the Web site

These steps are illustrated in Figure 1.6. We will take a brief look at these steps here. You will learn more about each of them throughout this book.

Figure 1.6
There are five steps in Web site development. How might you divide a task such as studying for a final exam into smaller steps?

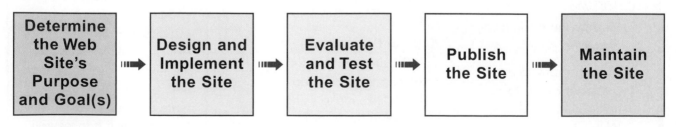

| Determine the Web Site's Purpose and Goal(s) | ⇒ | Design and Implement the Site | ⇒ | Evaluate and Test the Site | ⇒ | Publish the Site | ⇒ | Maintain the Site |

webdesign.glencoe.com

Step 1: Determining Purpose and Goals

It is important to determine your Web site's purpose and goals before beginning to design it. Questions you will want to ask include:

- **What is the site's purpose?** You may want to inform, educate, or sell a product.
- **What are the site's goals?** It might be to increase sales of your products, or teach the viewer how to throw a curve ball.
- **What tools do you need to reach your goals?** For example, if you want to use video to teach people how to play table tennis, you will need special hardware and software to create and edit the video.
- **Who is your primary (target) audience?** Who will visit the site? A Web site about Washington, D.C., for elementary students will probably be quite different than one for retired adults.
- **What kinds of hardware and software are visitors likely to be using?** You should think about the capabilities of the typical visitor's computer system as you create your site. For example, not all computer systems are capable of producing audio and video output.

As you continue to work on developing your site, always keep your site's purpose and goals in mind.

Step 2: Designing and Implementing a Web Site

Once you have determined your Web site's purpose, you can draw a rough diagram of the pages you will need. Figure 1.7 shows a diagram of the pages that might be needed in a garden company Web site.

● **Figure 1.7**
When developing a Web site, begin by creating a basic plan. How is this chart similar to an outline you might create before writing a history report?

```
                    Welcome
                    to Our
                     Site

  Products   Class      Press     Contact   Questions   Specials
             Offerings  Releases    Us       and
                                            Answers
```

After you have created a diagram of your site, you are ready to decide how your Web pages will look and interact with each other. The design process can be divided into three categories: interaction design, information design, and presentation design.

Interaction Design In **interaction design,** you determine how hyperlinks will help the user navigate through the site. When working on interaction design, you need to:

- Determine where the user needs to go.
- Determine the order in which the user is likely to move through the site.
- Make certain that each link's purpose is clear to the viewer.

Information Design In **Information design,** you determine the content that will appear on each page. Content is the text and graphics that will be included on the site. Web text must be concise (contain a minimum number of words). Graphics should reflect the purpose of the site.

Presentation Design In **Presentation design,** you focus on the physical appearance of the site's pages. Your plans for the presentation include:

◆ What look and feel the site will have
◆ What color scheme will be used
◆ What text sizes will be used
◆ Where graphics and text appear
◆ How hyperlinks will be positioned

Many sites contain the same elements on every page. For example, as shown in Figure 1.8, The Garden Company Web site has the company's logo at the top of every page (a logo is an image that identifies a company). This graphic is also a hyperlink to the home page.

Figure 1.8 ●———▶
Clicking a logo will often return a user to a company's home page. Why is this feature useful to people visiting a company's Web site?

Implementing the Design Once you have a satisfactory design, you are ready to implement your site. This step involves using the design to create an actual Web site. You use a software application to implement your plans. For most of the activities in this book, you will be using the Web development tool Microsoft FrontPage. Other popular development tools include Macromedia Dreamweaver and Adobe GoLive.

Step 3: Evaluating and Testing a Web Site

When evaluating the site, you confirm that the completed site meets your intended purpose and goals.

Testing the site involves making sure that everything works and displays correctly. Test all the hyperlinks, navigating among them and back to the home page to make certain they work correctly. If there are any problems, they must be corrected before continuing to Step 4.

Because different browsers can display the same Web site in slightly different ways, you should view your site using various browsers. You should also test your site on different computers. If possible, look at it on both a Macintosh computer and on a Windows computer.

Step 4: Publishing a Web Site

After a site has been evaluated and tested, it is ready to be published. Publishing a Web site means copying it to a Web server. This process is often referred to as "going live." Anyone with Internet access can use a Web browser to view your site once it is published on the Web. Publishing a Web site is discussed in more detail in Chapter 14.

Step 5: Maintaining the Site

If they are to remain useful to viewers, Web sites need to be maintained. Information that is out-of-date should be removed and replaced with current information. You should periodically check all hyperlinks to make certain they work properly. If your site links to an external site that is removed, you must remove the link. If you add new pages to your site, they will need to be properly linked to existing pages. For large companies, site maintenance requires a great deal more time and money than creating new sites.

WEB SITE DEVELOPMENT SKILLS

Developing a Web site requires a variety of skills including writing skills, design skills, and programming skills.

When creating a Web page, you must write clearly and concisely. If the content of your page is too wordy or boring, you will quickly lose the viewer's attention.

Design skills require an eye for attractive layout of text and graphics. You must learn how to use color effectively. The viewer's eye should be attracted to the important parts of the page. The purpose of each page should be clear. Links should be used to let site visitors find what they want quickly.

Finally, you must be able to use a tool that will let you actually implement your Web site. In the past, people needed to program or write instructions in HTML. HTML is the code used to create Web pages. Today, Web development tools make this job considerably easier.

WEB SITE DEVELOPMENT CAREERS

Developing a Web site requires a variety of skills including writing skills, design skills, and programming skills. In most companies, a variety of professionals work together to create Web sites (see Figure 1.9).

Web Authors

The **Web author** writes the actual text that will appear on each page. A Web author must be able to write clearly and concisely. Viewers quickly lose interest in a page that is too wordy or boring. You will learn more about writing good Web content in Chapter 6.

Web Designers

A **Web designer** focuses on the look and feel of the Web site. He or she determines such things as a site's page layout, color theme, and graphic elements. The Web designer makes certain that pages are visually engaging, and that they present information in an easy-to-use format. Some Web designers learn the programming skills needed to develop portions of a Web site. However, they generally leave complex programming tasks to Web developers.

● Figure 1.9
It often takes a team of people with diverse skills to create a Web site. What types of careers are available to people interested in Web site development?

Activity 1.2 View Professional Web Pages View examples of Web portfolios and good Web design by connecting to the links available at **webdesign.glencoe.com**.

Web Developers

A **Web developer** uses programming skills to develop entire Web sites. The developer knows how to program HTML, which is the code used to create Web pages. He or she makes sure that the site functions properly and meets its goals.

Web professionals often use the terms *Web development* and *Web design* interchangeably. However, these terms are not identical. Web development refers to the entire process of determining a site's goals, and designing, publishing, and maintaining a site. Web design, on the other hand, refers specifically to the process of determining a site's content, appearance, and navigational scheme.

Webmasters

The **Webmaster** manages and maintains the Web site. Some Webmasters develop Web sites, while others maintain sites that were developed by other professionals. Webmasters are responsible for the overall quality and usefulness of Web sites. They make certain that sites function properly and are kept up-to-date. Many Web sites allow you to e-mail the Webmaster. You may want to e-mail the Webmaster if a site is not working properly or if some of its content is outdated.

Web site development is a constantly changing field. Web sites are becoming increasingly complex and contain more multimedia features such as audio and video. Because of this constant change, Web site development professionals are always improving their skills and learning new ones.

Section 1.3 Assessment

Concept Check

1. **Define** interaction design, information design, presentation design, Web author, Web designer, Web developer, Webmaster.

2. **Summarize** the three categories of the Web design process.

3. **Describe** the tasks involved in the five basic steps of Web development.

Critical Thinking

4. **Compare and Contrast** How is the job of a Web author different from that of a Web designer?

5. **Synthesize** How do interaction design, information design, and presentation design work together to create a functional Web site?

Applying Skills

Identify Career Skills Make a list of skills that each of the following professionals would need to perform his or her job: Web designer, Web developer, Web author, and Webmaster. Identify which of those skills you have, and which you would need to develop.

Careers & Technology

WORKING ON THE WEB

The World Wide Web employs people in a wide range of fields from creative arts to programming to business administration.

Online classified ads are a good place to look for job opportunities in the World Wide Web.

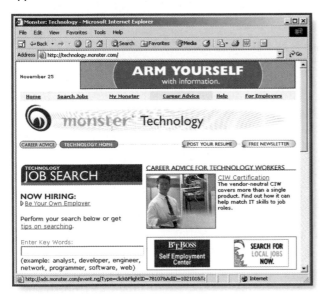

Finding Jobs Using the Web

To see career opportunities on the Web, spend some time surfing through Web sites. Some are designed to entertain, with brilliant graphics and clever interactive elements. Others provide training and educational content, including exams and chat rooms. There are also e-commerce sites for all sorts of complex business transactions.

The Web has created its own specific jobs, too:

◆ **Web designers** create the look of a site, its content, and the ways users will interact with its elements.

◆ **Webmasters** administer the Web site, making sure information is up to date and trouble-shooting any problems. Some are also responsible for developing and designing the Web site.

Preparing for a Web Career

The training you need to work on the Web depends on the type of job that interests you and how specialized it is. A graphic designer might need a strong art background and experience using Web design software. On the other hand, a webmaster might need to have skills in design, programming, and administration.

Many colleges offer degrees in computer or Web-related careers. Technical schools and software companies have courses for specific Web certifications. School programs and job experience will expose you to the various career paths you can choose.

Mapping a Career Path

Even if you are uncertain of your goals, it is helpful to map out a career path, marked by short- and long-term expectations. Where would you like your career to begin and end, and what jobs do you hope to have during your career?

You can find many resources for Web-related jobs, including job centers, newspapers, online classified ads, and corporate sites. Job descriptions will help you determine what type of education and experience you will need for various types of Web careers.

Tech Focus

1. Research Web career opportunities. Identify your career goals and create a career plan.

2. Participate in a career-related activity. In a short report, describe the activity and what you learned.

Section 1.4 An Introduction to FrontPage

Guide to Reading

Main Ideas

FrontPage is similar to other application programs. FrontPage provides many features, such as task panes, toolbars, and different page views that simplify creating a Web site.

Key Terms

interface
task pane
Folder List
Navigation Pane

Reading Strategy

Identify the four major elements of the FrontPage interface. Use a diagram like the one below (also available online).

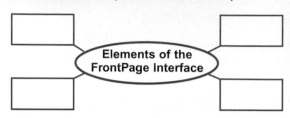

Elements of the FrontPage Interface

Microsoft FrontPage is a Web site development tool. You can use FrontPage to create pages that contain text, graphics, hyperlinks, and multimedia elements—all without writing a single line of HTML code. In this section, you will use FrontPage to examine an existing Web site.

THE FRONTPAGE INTERFACE

One of the main features of FrontPage is that it is easy to use. Many of its features are similar to other applications you have used. For example, it contains elements such as drop-down menus and toolbars with buttons.

Depending on which version of FrontPage you are using, your display may look different from what is described in this section. All of the illustrations and activities in this text use FrontPage 2003. If you are using an earlier version of FrontPage, you can still complete all the activities. Major differences between versions are noted where they apply. If you have difficulty completing an activity, ask your teacher for additional help.

Toolbars

Figure 1.10 (shown on next page) illustrates major elements in the FrontPage interface. An **interface** is the means by which a user interacts with a computer or a computer program. The Title bar at the top of the screen displays the version of FrontPage that you are using. The current document is in the main display area. The Menu bar contains drop-down menus that contain lists of related options. For example, the File menu contains options such as New, which lets you create a new Web site or Web page, and Open Site, which lets you open an existing site.

The Standard and Formatting toolbars give you access to most menu items by simply clicking an icon. The main display area shows the current content that you are working on.

READ ME!

Tech Tip The toolbars used in FrontPage are the same toolbars used in other Microsoft applications. This similarity makes it easier for users to move between applications.

---

 webdesign.glencoe.com

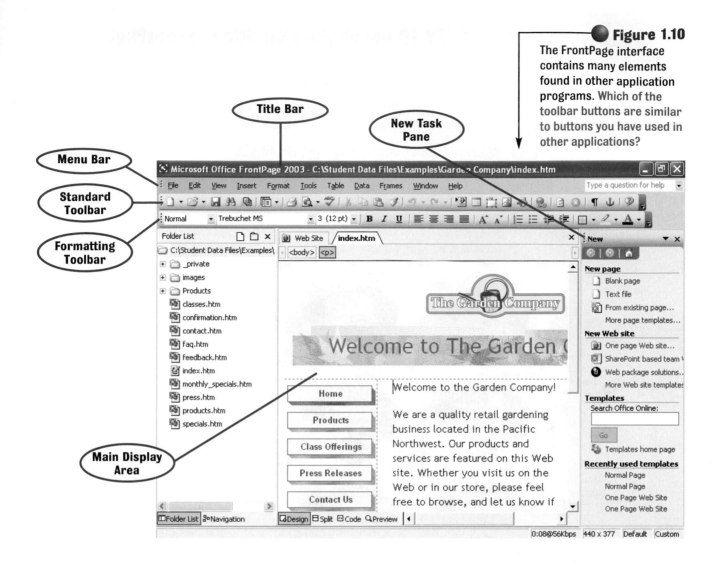

Figure 1.10
The FrontPage interface contains many elements found in other application programs. Which of the toolbar buttons are similar to buttons you have used in other applications?

The Task Pane

Task panes provide convenient access to the typical tasks performed when creating a Web site. For example, the New task pane contains links to help users create a new Web page or site (see Figure 1.10).

The Folder List and Navigation Pane

When a Web site is open, two different panes can appear at the left side of the screen: the Folder List and the Navigation Pane. While both are located at the left side of the screen, only one of these panes can appear at a time. The **Folder List** displays the folders and files that you can access in the current Web site. You can open the folders on the Folder List by double-clicking them.

The **Navigation Pane** displays the page titles of all the files that have been added to the Web site. The navigational structure is usually shown as a map of connected pages within the site and what routes you can take from one page to another (you will learn more about navigational structure in Chapter 5).

As you develop Web sites, you will find that you can "toggle" or move between these two panes by clicking the Folder List and Navigation buttons at the bottom of the pane. In addition, the Toggle Pane button on the Standard toolbar lets you open or close the current pane.

ACTIVITY 1B Opening a Web Site in FrontPage

Student Data File

❶ From your desktop, click the **Start** button at the bottom-left of your screen. Choose **Programs,** and click **Microsoft FrontPage.**

❷ Select the **File** menu, and click **Open.** Browse to and open the **DataFile\Examples** folder. Click **GardenCo,** and then click **Open.**

❸ In the Open File dialog box, double-click the **index.htm** file and click **Open.** The Garden Company home page appears. The Folder List should be open (see Figure 1.11). If it is not open, click the **Toggle Pane** button.

Figure 1.11
The Web site's home page is labeled index.htm.

Toggle Pane Button

index.htm Tab

Open Folder List

Folder List Button

❹ Click the **Navigation** button to switch to the Navigation Pane, as shown in Figure 1.12.

Figure 1.12
The Navigation button is at the bottom of the Navigation Pane.

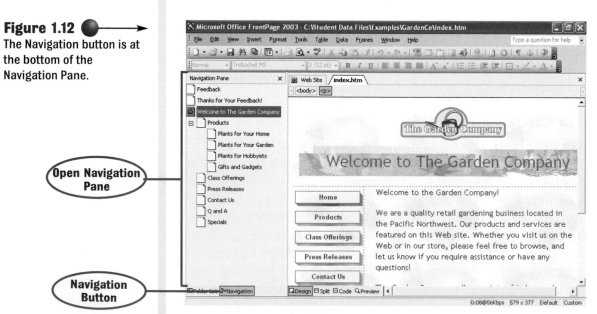

Open Navigation Pane

Navigation Button

❺ Click the **Toggle Pane** button's drop-down arrow and select **Folder List** to switch back to the Folder List pane.

VIEWING WEB PAGES IN FRONTPAGE

A Web site's home page is typically named either index.htm or default.htm. You can identify a site's home page in the Folder List by looking for these names.

You can open other individual pages in a site by double-clicking their names in the Folder List. The name of each currently opened page is listed on a tab at the top of the window.

An open Web page is usually viewed in the Page View window. Front-Page lets you look at an individual page in different ways when you are in Page View mode. Table 1.1 shows the Page View options available in Front-Page 2002 and 2003.

Page View Options

In FrontPage 2002	In FrontPage 2003	Function
Normal	Design	Lets you modify a page
HTML	Code	Lets you examine the HTML code for the page and make changes to it, if necessary.
View Not Available in 2002	Split	Shows Code View at the top of the screen and Design View at the bottom. Allows you to compare the actual page with the HTML code used to create it.
Preview	Preview	Lets you see the page approximately as it will appear in a Web browser.

Table 1.1
FrontPage provides different options for viewing an individual Web page. How are the options available in FrontPage 2003 different from those available in 2002?

In this activity, you will practice using different page views in The Garden Company Web site.

ACTIVITY 1C Using Different Views and Closing FrontPage

YOU TRY IT

❶ Make certain that The Garden Company Web site is open and the home page is displayed.

❷ Click the **Preview** button at the bottom of the screen. This shows the home page approximately as it will appear in a Web browser.

❸ Click the **Code** button (click **HTML** if you are using 2002). This will show the HTML code for the home page on the screen.

❹ If you are using FrontPage 2003, click the **Split** button. Now the screen is divided, as shown in Figure 1.13. The top half of the screen shows the HTML code, while the bottom half shows the page in Design view. If you are using a different version of FrontPage, you will need to move between HTML and Normal view to see the code and the Web page.

Figure 1.13
FrontPage 2003 provides
four different page views.

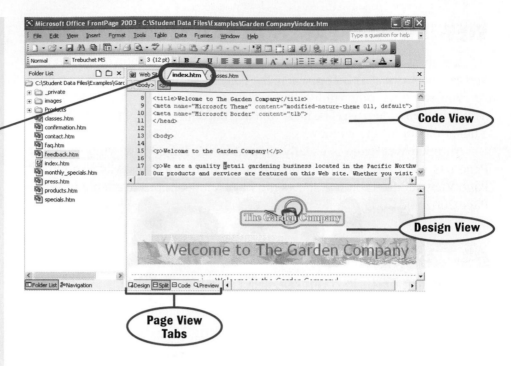

**Tab indicates
an open page**

Code View

Design View

**Page View
Tabs**

❺ Click the **Design** (in 2002, **Normal**) button. You can only modify a page when it is open in Design view.

❻ Practice switching among the different views. When you are done, return to **Design** (in 2002, **Normal**) view.

❼ From the **File** menu, click **Close Site** (in 2002, **Close Web**). The Garden Company site closes, but FrontPage remains open.

❽ Click the **Close** button in the top-right corner of the window to close FrontPage.

Section 1.4 Assessment

Concept Check

1. **Define** interface, task pane, Folder List, Navigation Pane.

2. **Identify** the parts of the FrontPage interface.

3. **Explain** how to switch between the Folder List and the Navigation Pane.

Critical Thinking

4. **Analyze** Why might an individual need to use Code view when creating a Web site?

5. **Draw Conclusions** Why do you think Web developers need to view Web pages in different views?

Applying Skills

View Web Pages Use Code view to view three pages of The Garden Company Web site. Locate each Web page's title in the HTML code. Write the title of each page on a separate piece of paper.

SECTION 1.1 Introduction to the Web

Key Terms

Internet, 6
World Wide Web, 6
file, 6
Web browser, 7

Web site, 7
Web page, 7
home page, 7

Main Ideas

- Web design focuses on creating Web sites that meet specific goals.
- The Internet consists of all the hardware that connects computers around the world.
- The World Wide Web (the Web) is the software that allows users to access information stored on the Internet.
- Web browsers interpret and display information found on Web pages and Web sites.
- Web sites are composed of Web pages.
- The major types of Web sites are commercial sites, portal sites, informational sites, educational sites, and personal sites.

SECTION 1.2 Elements of a Web Page

Key Terms

text, 12
graphics, 12
multimedia, 13
audio, 13

animation, 13
video, 13
hyperlink, 14

Main Ideas

- Text consists of words, letters, numbers, and symbols.
- Graphics can be used to attract a viewer's attention and to explain difficult concepts.
- Multimedia elements capture viewers' attention and add interactivity to a Web site.
- Hyperlinks tell the Web browser to move to a different location on the page, on the site, or on the Web.
- A Web browser can be used to view and navigate around a Web site.

SECTION 1.3 Web Site Development

Key Terms

interaction design, 17
information design, 18
presentation design, 18
Web author, 19

Web designer, 19
Web developer, 20
Webmaster, 20

Main Ideas

- The specific purpose and goals for a Web site should be determined before the site is designed.
- Interaction design focuses on how the user will navigate through the site.
- Information design concentrates on the specific content that will appear on the site.
- Presentation design focuses on the physical appearance of the Web site.
- Publishing a Web site means copying it to a Web server.
- Careers in Web site development include Web designer, Web developer, Web author, and Webmaster.

SECTION 1.4 An Introduction to FrontPage

Key Terms

interface, 22
task pane, 23

Folder List, 23
Navigation Pane, 23

Main Ideas

- Microsoft FrontPage is a Web site development tool that helps you create Web pages and Web sites.
- The FrontPage interface is similar to other Microsoft software applications.
- Task panes give access to many FrontPage features.
- The Folder List displays the folders and files that can be accessed in the current Web site.
- The Navigation Pane displays the navigational structure of the current Web site.
- Page views allow you to see a Web page in different ways.

READ TO SUCCEED PRACTICE

Survey Skills Develop a personal study tool by modifying the survey strategy introduced on page 5. Use the section and paragraph headings to create a topic outline, leaving enough room between topics to add key items. Then close your textbook and fill in as much information as you can remember about these topics. This is a good way to help you determine which topics you understand and which topics need the most additional review.

Reviewing Key Terms

1. What type of software is used to view Web pages on a computer screen?
2. Which FrontPage pane displays the folders and files that you can access in the current Web site?
3. What do you use to move from one location to another on the World Wide Web?
4. What is the purpose of presentation design?
5. Which page in a Web site do viewers usually see first?

Understanding Main Ideas

6. **Identify** three things that you must determine when designing a Web site.
7. **Summarize** how a Web site is different from a Web page.
8. **Identify** the types of multimedia elements that may be featured on Web pages.
9. **Describe** the three types of links found on Web pages.
10. **Summarize** the three categories of the design process for a Web site.
11. **Describe** the steps that should be used to evaluate a Web site.
12. **Explain** how a Webmaster differs from a Web author.
13. **Explain** how FrontPage is similar to other software applications.
14. **Describe** the purpose of the following FrontPage page views: Design view, Code view, and Preview view.

Critical Thinking

15. **Evaluate Decisions** You are planning to purchase a snowboard. You have located several e-commerce sites that sell snowboards. There is only one retailer in your community that stocks snowboards. What factors should you consider when deciding whether to buy a snowboard from an e-commerce site or from the local retailer? Explain the reasons behind your decision.

16. **Make Inferences** Which of the two sentences below would be easier to read on a Web page? Explain your reasoning.

   Ⓐ According to our surveys, which were conducted under the most stringent conditions to ensure their accuracy, it is estimated that at least five million people (in both the United States and abroad) accessed this Web site last year.

   Ⓑ Five million people accessed this Web site last year.

17. **Make Predictions** Your school has a Web site that contains a calendar of upcoming events, pictures of recent school events, links to scholarship offerings, information about courses and profiles of teachers. What parts of the site will require the most maintenance? Explain your reasoning.

e-Review
webdesign.glencoe.com

Study with PowerPoint
Go to the book Web site shown above to review the main points in this chapter. Then select **e-Review** > **PowerPoint Outlines** > **Chapter 1**.

Online Self Check
Test your knowledge of the material in this chapter by selecting **e-Review** > **Self Checks** > **Chapter 1**.

Making Connections

Math—Create a Graph Find five different news organization home pages that you think are well designed. Count the number of words you can see on the opening screen (without scrolling) of each site. Calculate the average number of words that are used for each of the five examples. Plot your results for each site on a bar graph. What is the average number of words used on all five sites? Write a brief report noting the patterns you noticed and how they can help you use text on a Web page.

STANDARDS AT WORK

Students use technology tools to enhance learning, increase productivity, and promote creativity. (NETS-S 3)

Use Productivity Tools

FrontPage is a productivity tool for creating Web pages and managing Web site development. Although beginners can use it immediately, it also contains many advanced features for professionals. If you design a site for a business, you may find that you have to use FrontPage or other software applications in more creative and complex ways.

One of the most useful (and underused) tools in computer applications is the Help feature. It can provide you with instructions on how to get the most out of the software you are using. It can also guide you through tasks you may be expected to do on the job.

Explore the features available to you in Front-Page by accessing its Help Contents. Choose five topics that relate to features you learned about in the chapter. Make a chart that describes each feature, how to access it, and why you would want to use it.

TEAMWORK SKILLS

Group Planning

Working in a small group, plan a Web page about a national park. You have only one Web page, but may plan links to other relevant Web sites about the park. As you plan the page, answer the following questions:

1. What are the purpose and goals of the page?
2. What information will the page include?
3. What Web page elements will best convey the information?
4. What hyperlinks will we include?
5. What look and feel should the page have?
6. What color scheme will we use?

Write a summary of your answers to the questions. Draw a sketch of what you plan for the page. The sketch should show the placement of elements and the basic look and feel that you have planned.

CHALLENGE YOURSELF

Identify Web Sites

There are many types of Web sites, though most can be placed into one of five major categories: commercial, portal, informational, educational, and personal.

Surf the Web to find examples of one Web site category. Try to find two sites that are different from each other even though they fit into the same category. For example, e-Bay and Microsoft's Web sites are both commercial, but one is a retail site and the other is corporate.

Print out the home page of each Web site you have chosen. Then write a brief description for each page explaining:

- What category the Web site fits into
- What subcategory it can be classified as
- How they are the same
- How they are different

YOU TRY IT

Skills Studio

These exercises reinforce the skills you learned in this chapter's You Try It activities. Refer back to the You Try It activities if you need extra guidance.

1. Using Hyperlinks

Explore the hyperlinks at a major online newspaper such as USA Today, the New York Times, the Chicago Tribune, or the Los Angeles Times.

Ⓐ Write the name and Web address of the newspaper you have chosen.

Ⓑ Use a hyperlink to find the job listings on the site. Write the Web address the link takes you to.

Ⓒ Find a hyperlink on the page that takes you to the Job Search page. Describe the information you find.

Ⓓ Find Information Technology jobs. (Hint: On some sites you may have to scroll through a "Job Type" list to find the category, then click **Search.**)

Ⓔ Write down five different jobs listed in the Information Technology jobs page.

Ⓕ Return to the home page, using either the logo or a home page link.

2. Switching Views and Using the Folder List

Display a Web page using different FrontPage views.

Ⓐ Open The Garden Company Web site home page in FrontPage.

Ⓑ Double-click **products.htm** in the Folder List. Examine the page carefully.

Ⓒ Switch to **Preview** view. What changes did you notice between Design (in 2002, Normal) view and Preview view?

Ⓓ Double-click **feedback.htm** in the Folder List. This action should return you to Design (in 2002, Normal) view. Read the comment at the top of the page.

Ⓔ Switch to **Preview** view. What happens to the comment? Why do you think this happens?

Ⓕ Close FrontPage without saving your changes.

Web Design Projects

1. Evaluate Web Site Design

Locate five different Web sites. Print out the home page for each Web site that you choose. Evaluate the five sites and make a table that identifies:

◆ The site's category (e.g., commercial, informational, personal)
◆ The purpose of the site
◆ The target audience (consider age, gender, interests, economic levels)
◆ Key elements that "jump out at you" on the home page

You may want to use the example below as a model for evaluating the Web sites you visit, or develop your own.

SITE	CATEGORY	PURPOSE	AUDIENCE	KEY ELEMENTS
Nickelodeon (www.nick.com)	Commercial (corporate presence site)	Entertain and introduce viewers to Nickelodeon products	Children/ teenagers between ages 8 and 14	Animation, games, fun activities to do with friends

2. Research Web Development Careers

Select one of the following career opportunities:

◆ Web developer
◆ Web designer
◆ Webmaster

Conduct research to answer the following questions:

Ⓐ What types of specialized skills does the job require?
Ⓑ What types of leadership skills does the job require?
Ⓒ What preparations would you need to make for this job?
Ⓓ What are some of the job responsibilities?

Organize your information into a one-page report about the career.

Computer Basics

YOU WILL LEARN TO...

WHY IT MATTERS....................................

It is almost impossible to imagine a world without computers. When you get money from an automatic teller machine, you are using a computer. When you pump gas at the gas station, a computer scans your purchase. Computers are the visible—and invisible—helpers that have become an integral part of our daily lives.

Quick Write Activity

Think about ten tasks you perform every day. Then note which of these tasks involves a computer. Write a brief paragraph that answers the following questions. Which tasks could you not complete without a computer? How would your daily routine be different if computers did not exist?

WHAT YOU WILL DO...

ACTIVITIES AND PROJECTS

Applying Skills

You Try It Activities

Chapter Assessment

You Try It Skills Studio

Web Design Projects

IN THE WORKBOOK

Optional Activities and Projects

Guided Reading
Web Design Projects

ON THE WEB

Activities at webdesign.glencoe.com

Reading Strategy Organizers
Go Online Activities
Study with PowerPoint
Self-Check Assessments

READ TO SUCCEED

Key Terms
Knowing the dictionary definition of a word does not always help you understand the word's full meaning. To gain a more complete understanding and to help you recall the meaning, create a Key Term Journal. Divide a piece of paper into four columns. Label the first column *Key Term*. Then, label the other columns: *What is it? What else is it like?* and *What are some examples?* Write down each key term and answer the questions as you read the chapter.

Section 2.1 Computer Hardware

Guide to Reading

Main Ideas

Computer systems are composed of users, hardware, software, and data. The four basic categories of computer hardware are processing components and input, output, and storage devices.

Key Terms

hardware
software
central processing unit (CPU)
random-access memory (RAM)
keyboard
mouse
monitor
printer

Reading Strategy

Categorize the four types of computer hardware. Use a diagram like the one below (also available online).

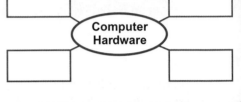

When you create a Web site for the first time, the task may seem overwhelming. However, if you have a basic understanding of the tools you will be using, the task will become more manageable. One of the most important tools you will use to create a Web site is the computer itself.

COMPUTERS AND THE COMPUTER SYSTEM

A computer is an electronic device that processes data. Computers are categorized as either PCs or Macs. A PC (sometimes referred to as an IBM-compatible computer) is a computer that runs the Windows operating system (OS). A Mac is a Macintosh computer that runs the Macintosh OS.

A computer system consists of four parts: users, hardware, software, and data.

- A user is a person who is working on or using the computer.
- **Hardware** is the physical components of the computer.
- **Software** is the instructions that tell the computer what to do.
- Data are individual bits of information.

PROCESSING COMPONENTS

Hardware's purpose is to get data into the computer, process the data, and produce results. Processing components convert raw data into information.

Central Processing Unit

Inside every computer is a **central processing unit (CPU),** or processor. The CPU is like the "brain" of the computer. For example, the CPU can add groups of numbers, and change the color of graphics. In most computers, the CPU is a single chip, called a microprocessor (see Figure 2.1).

 webdesign.glencoe.com

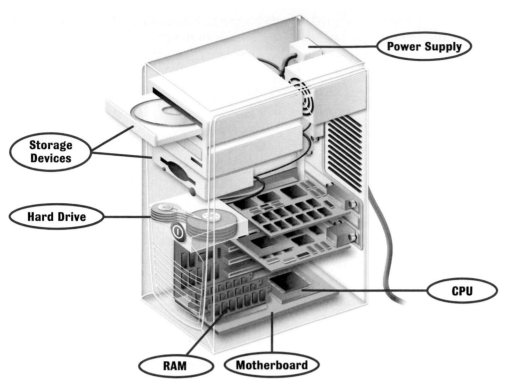

Figure 2.1
The CPU is usually located on the motherboard, which is a computer's main circuit board. What is the function of the CPU?

Memory

The computer stores data it is currently processing in **random-access memory,** or **RAM.** The more RAM a computer has, the faster it can process data. RAM is also called primary storage because it is where the computer first processes data. However, data are only stored in RAM temporarily. When the computer is turned off, or the power is interrupted, anything stored in RAM is lost. It is extremely important that you save your work frequently to avoid losing important data.

INPUT DEVICES

Data must be entered into a computer to be processed. Different kinds of devices allow you to enter text, commands, images, or audio.

Keyboards and Pointing Devices

The most commonly used input device is the **keyboard,** which lets you enter text into the computer. You use pointing devices such as the **mouse** to enter commands.

Graphic and Video Devices

You can use a variety of input devices to create and edit graphic and video elements for your Web pages.

Scanners A scanner lets you convert printed images or documents into digital files. Scanners come in many sizes, from small hand-held scanners, to flat-bed scanners that look like copy machines, to large drum scanners used by professionals for high resolution images.

Digital Cameras A digital camera allows you to capture photographs as digital files. Once you transfer the images from the camera to your computer's hard drive, you can use them in your Web pages just as you would any other image.

Digital Camcorders and Webcams To get original video into your Web pages, you can use a digital camcorder, as shown in Figure 2.2. The video can then be copied to a hard drive so that you can use it on a Web page. A Webcam lets you broadcast live video over the Web.

Audio Devices

You can record original audio such as speech, music, or special effects using microphones or digital recorders.

Microphones A microphone connects directly to your computer and lets you save audio right to your hard drive. If you have voice recognition software, you can "type" text by speaking into the microphone. These programs are especially useful for people who have difficulty using keyboards or other input devices.

Digital Recorders A digital recorder lets you create audio files when you are away from your computer. You have to transfer the audio files to the computer's hard drive.

OUTPUT DEVICES

Output devices let users examine the results of processed data. Commonly used output devices are monitors, printers, and speakers.

Monitors

A **monitor,** also known as a display screen, shows output in a quick, readable form. The monitor, along with your computer's graphics card, determines the screen's resolution and the color quality of its images. There are two common types of monitors, as shown in Figure 2.3.

- ◆ CRT (cathode ray tube) monitors resemble traditional television sets and are large and heavy.
- ◆ LCD (liquid crystal display) monitors are lightweight and have thin screens.

Figure 2.3 ●——→
The LCD monitor shown on the right is much thinner than the CRT monitor shown on the left. How have LCD monitors helped computers become more portable?

Printers

While a monitor produces soft copy, a **printer** produces hard copy, or output that is permanent. Most of today's printers are either laser printers or ink-jet printers. Ink-jet printers are inexpensive and lightweight, but do not produce as high-quality output as laser printers do.

Speakers

Through the computer's speakers, you can hear audio, such as music, speech, and sound effects. On laptops, the speakers are usually built into the computer. On desktop computers, they may be in separate units or built into the monitor.

STORAGE DEVICES

While RAM is the computer's primary storage, it only saves data temporarily. You need to use a secondary storage device to save your data longterm.

Storage capacity is usually measured either in megabytes (MB) or gigabytes (GB). A megabyte is about one *thousand* bytes, while a gigabyte is about one *million* bytes. A byte is the amount of storage space required to store a single character, such as the letter "d."

Hard Drives

The most widely used secondary storage is the hard drive. The hard drive (also called the hard disk) is where all your programs, files, and folders are permanently stored. As shown in Figure 2.4, hard drives can be either internal or external.

Removable Storage Devices

Removable storage disks are used to transfer files between computers. They also are used to install new software applications on a computer's hard drive.

Floppy Disks A floppy disk stores only about 1.4 MB of data. The disks are inexpensive and can be used to move documents from one computer to another.

Zip Disks Zip disks, developed by Iomega Corporation, store a lot more data than floppy disks. They can store 100 MB, 250 MB, or 750 MB of data.

● Figure 2.4
Hard drives can be either internal (shown left) or external (shown right). Is the hard drive on your computer system internal or external?

Activity 2.1 Investigate Storage Devices Explore the characteristics of common types of storage devices at webdesign.glencoe.com.

Optical Disks Hard drives, floppy drives, and Zip drives have one thing in common: they all use magnetic fields to store data. Optical drives, on the other hand, use lasers to store data. Optical storage devices are often categorized as read only, recordable, or rewritable.

◆ **Read only** You cannot record new data to the disk. Examples include CD-ROMs (compact disc read-only memory) and DVD-ROMs (digital versatile disc read-only memory).

◆ **Recordable** Data can be recorded to the disk only one time. Examples include CD-Rs (CD recordable) and DVD-Rs and DVD+Rs (DVD recordable).

◆ **Rewritable** Data can be recorded, or written, to the disk as many times as needed. Examples include CD-RWs (CD rewritable), DVD-RWs and DVD1RWs (DVD rewritable), and DVD-RAMs (DVD random-access memory).

One CD can store over 600 MB of data, about as much as over 400 floppy disks. Some DVDs have a capacity of 17 GB, which is enough room to hold several full-length movies.

Flash Memory Increasingly, people want easier and smaller ways to store and move large amounts of data from one device to another. Flash memory technology provides a way to store over 200 MBs of data in the palm of your hand or even on a keychain!

Tape Backups Data can be lost if the storage device is damaged or fails. One way to avoid data loss is to back up the data, or copy it to another location. Most removable storage devices can be used to back up data, but tapes can store even more information than other removable disks.

Section 2.1 Assessment

Concept Check

1. **Define** hardware, software, central processing unit (CPU), random-access memory (RAM), keyboard, mouse, monitor, printer.

2. **Compare and Contrast** the input devices discussed in this section.

3. **Summarize** the reasons why computer systems need hardware.

Critical Thinking

4. **Compare and Contrast** List the capacity and general uses for primary and secondary storage devices.

5. **Evaluate Hardware** Create a list of input, output, and storage devices you would include in a computer system for Web designers. Explain why you chose specific devices.

Applying Skills

Research Computer Systems Research the current prices for computer systems. Find at least three quotes from online or retail sources. Evaluate each quote and recommend the system that offers the most value. Explain why you chose this system.

webdesign.glencoe.com

Ethics & Technology

COMPUTERS AND POLLUTION

Do you leave your computer running when you are not using it? Do you print out lots of hard copies? Multiply these habits by millions of users to imagine the amount of electricity and paper being wasted daily.

Every year, people discard millions of tons of out-of-date hardware, but proper recycling can reduce the environmental threat.

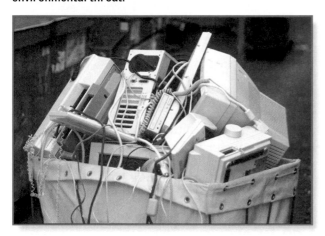

Paper Waste

Computers were supposed to produce a "paperless society." Unfortunately, they have not reduced paper use at all. In fact, computer printing is so easy and inexpensive that more documents are created than ever. The trillions of hard copies printed every year contribute to deforestation, pollution from paper manufacturing, lots of trash, and wasted electricity.

Computer Waste

Computers themselves can be an ecological problem. Millions of tons of computers and other electrical devices are thrown out every year, taking up landfill space. Computers also contain many toxic materials that can harm the environment.

New laws are under consideration requiring manufacturers to reduce the use of dangerous materials and provide recycling for their products. If these laws are passed, companies will have to meet environmental requirements in order to sell their products.

Protecting the Environment

What can you do to protect the environment?

◆ Find recycling programs that collect older computers and donate them to organizations like schools or nonprofit groups.
◆ Before printing, think about whether you need a hard copy. Use both sides of the paper whenever possible.
◆ Buy computer equipment with low-power mode. Turn off your computer or monitor even if it has energy-saving features.
◆ If possible, try to upgrade your computer instead of buying a new one. If you do buy a new computer, reuse components like the monitor and keyboard.

Tech Focus

1. Make a chart showing how computers affect the environment. Discuss each example's importance, its environmental impact, and possible solutions.

2. Write a report or create a presentation about a specific computer recycling topic or effort. Analyze how the widespread use of technology has made the issue you have selected important.

Section 2.2 Computer Software

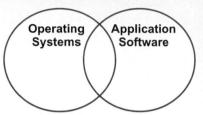
Computer software gives instructions to the computer's hardware to make it work. Software can be divided into two main categories: operating systems and application software.

OPERATING SYSTEM SOFTWARE

Every time you start, or "boot up," your computer, a small program called the **basic input/output system (BIOS)** starts. The BIOS activates the computer's operating system and stops functioning once the operating system takes over. An **operating system (OS)** specifies how the computer receives and processes input, and delivers it as output.

Responsibilities of an Operating System

The responsibilities of an OS can be divided into four major categories. The OS must do all these for the computer system to work properly.

- ◆ **Task management** Keeps track of everything the computer does.
- ◆ **Memory management** Moves data between RAM and other storage devices.
- ◆ **Input and output management** Keeps track of input from devices like the keyboard, and sends output to devices like the monitor and printer.
- ◆ **User interface** Provides an interface through which a user gives commands to the computer.

Commonly Used Operating Systems

The two most common OSs are Microsoft Windows (for PCs) and the Macintosh OS (for Apple Computers). Unix and Linux are two other flexible operating systems that are found primarily on networks.

webdesign.glencoe.com

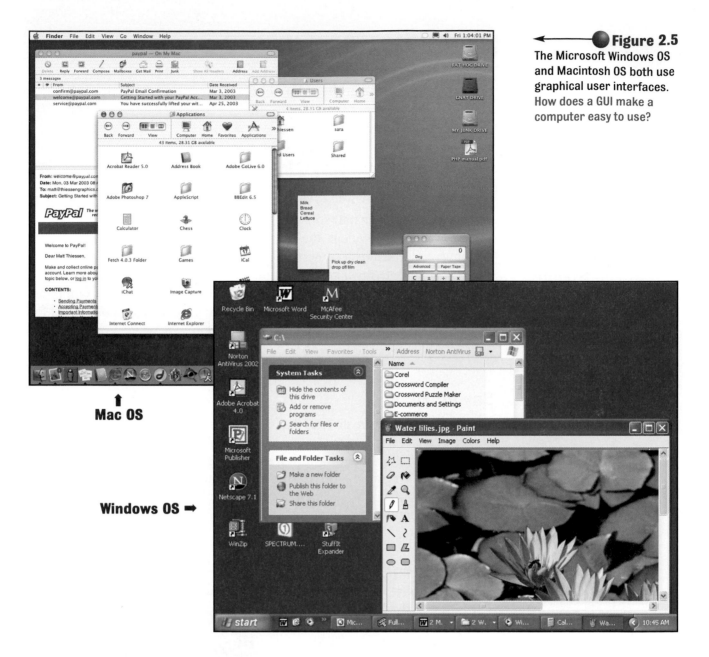

Figure 2.5
The Microsoft Windows OS
and Macintosh OS both use
graphical user interfaces.
How does a GUI make a
computer easy to use?

Mac OS

Windows OS ➡

Graphical User Interfaces

Early computers were mainly text-based. Today's operating systems and applications, however, use a **graphical user interface,** or **GUI** (pronounced "goo-ee"). A GUI allows users to select words, symbols, or graphics from a desktop. A desktop displays the files, folders, menus, and programs available. Both the Windows and the Mac OS desktops are shown in Figure 2.5.

APPLICATION SOFTWARE

Most of the time when you use a computer, you are using **application software.** Common application software includes word processing, spreadsheet, database, presentation, and utility applications.

Today's operating systems are capable of **multitasking.** This allows you to work with more than one application or document at a time.

CROSS-PLATFORM ISSUES

Your computer's hardware, operating system, and application programs must all work together in order for your computer to function properly.

Compatibility

When computer components work together properly, they are said to be compatible. The Windows and Macintosh OSs are generally incompatible. This means that you cannot run the Windows XP operating system on a Macintosh computer, nor can you run the Mac OS on a Windows computer. Although some users install software on Macs that allow them to work in a Windows-like environment, the Mac OS is still running in the background. Windows and Macintosh computers sometimes cannot share hardware without the help of intermediary devices or software.

In addition, applications must be compatible with both the computer hardware and the OS. Some applications come in several versions, each for a different operating system. For example, Microsoft Word is available for both Windows and Mac OS. However, there is no version of FrontPage for the Macintosh.

Saving Files

Some programs create files that can be opened on either a Mac or a Windows OS. Other applications let you save your document in a format that a different operating system or a different version of the program can use. For example, if you create a Word document in Windows, you can save it in many formats—in a Macintosh Word format, in earlier versions of Word, or even in a format for another program, such as Corel WordPerfect.

Section 2.2 Assessment

Concept Check

1. **Define** basic input/output system (BIOS), operating system (OS), graphical user interface (GUI), application software, multitasking.

2. **Explain** the difference between operating system software and application software.

3. **Identify** three types of operating system software.

Critical Thinking

4. **Predict Outcomes** You need to purchase software for your Macintosh, but your computer store only has the Windows version of the software. Should you purchase the application? Explain your reasoning.

5. **Evaluate Software** Why is the ability to multitask an important advancement in OS software?

Applying Skills

Categorize Applications List the names of software applications that you use regularly. Beside each name, categorize the application as word processing, spreadsheet, database, graphics, presentation, browser, Web site development, or utility.

Section 2.3 Networks

Guide to Reading

Main Ideas

Networks allow computers to share information, messages, and software. Dial-up, broadband, and wireless are three types of network connections.

Key Terms

network
local area network (LAN)
wide area network (WAN)
server
client
network interface card (NIC)
modem

Reading Strategy

List facts about the three types of network connections. Use a table like the one below (also available online).

Dial-up	Broadband	Wireless

In the early days of computing, computers could not communicate directly with one another. Data had to be copied onto secondary storage to be transferred between computers, much as you might copy a document onto a floppy disk to share it with a friend.

Today, most computers are networked. In a **network,** communication lines or wireless connections are used to connect computers together. Once connected to each other, computers can easily share information, communications such as e-mail, and resources such as software. Networks also allow users to access the Internet.

TYPES OF NETWORKS

Networks come in many configurations. A configuration refers to how a system of computers is arranged or set up. For instance, a network can connect two computers in a home or millions of computers around the world, as in the case of the Internet. Regardless of their size, networks can be divided into two basic categories: local area networks and wide area networks.

A **local area network (LAN)** connects computers in a single location, such as a single department within a company. A LAN can also connect computers within a building or complex of buildings. Schools use LANs to circulate information about classes and schedules. Businesses use LANs to help employees share information and resources more easily. Individual departments often have their own LANs, which can be networked to allow different departments to share information.

A **wide area network (WAN)** connects computers across a wider geographical area, such as a region of the United States. The major difference between a LAN and a WAN is the size of the area that the network covers. While a LAN is restricted to a relatively small geographic location, a WAN may include computers in multiple blocks, cities, states, or even continents. The Internet is often considered to be a gigantic WAN, which connects thousands of smaller LANs and WANs together.

Activity 2.2 Explore Networks Learn more about various types of networks at **webdesign.glencoe.com**.

TYPES OF CONNECTIONS

Computers and other network components communicate using different types of connections. The following discussion focuses on the methods used to connect to the Internet because this is critical for Web designers to understand. Cost, speed, and convenience are three of the factors that many people consider when choosing how to connect to the Internet.

Dial-up Connections

Dial-up connections require a modem and a standard telephone line. This method is inexpensive and usually requires no additional hardware. However, dial-up connections are slow and relatively unreliable. Users may get unexpectedly disconnected and have to dial in again to reestablish their connection. It also takes a long time to transfer files between computers when using a dial-up connection.

Broadband Connections

Table 2.1

There are advantages and disadvantages to using different types of broadband connections. What are the advantages to using a T3 line over a cable connection?

A broadband connection uses cable television equipment or a dedicated telephone line to connect computers together. With broadband, your computer is always connected to the network or Internet. Bandwidth determines the amount of data that can be transmitted. Since it uses more bandwidth, broadband transfers more data at a faster rate than dial-up connections. The different types of broadband connections are shown in Table 2.1.

Types of Broadband Connections

Type of Connection	Equipment Used	Advantage(s)	Disadvantage(s)
Cable	Cable equipment	Transmits data several hundred times faster than dial-up.	Transmission rates can vary depending on network activity. Typically more expensive than dial-up.
DSL (Digital Subscriber Line)	High-capacity telephone lines	Different services available offer a variety of capabilities and rates.	Often more expensive than dial-up. Not as widely available as dial-up.
ISDN, T1, T3 Lines	High-capacity telephone lines	Provide multiple channels to transmit data. T3 line (672 channels) transmits data about one thousand times faster than dial-up.	Cost of service increases as the transmission rate increases.

Wireless Connections

Instead of cable or phone lines, wireless connections use infrared waves, radio waves, or microwaves to transmit data between computers. Wireless connections provide a great deal of flexibility.

Wireless connections are most reliable over a small area. Users may get cut off unexpectedly, similar to using a cell phone. However, the wireless industry continues to grow and become more reliable.

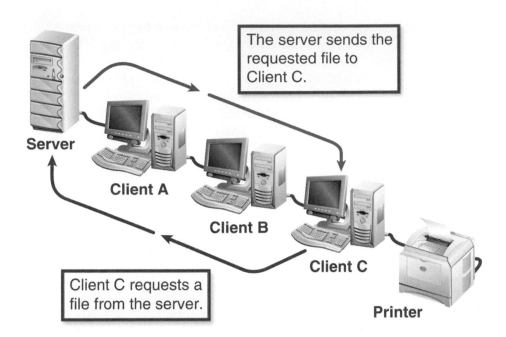

The server sends the requested file to Client C.

Server

Client A

Client B

Client C

Client C requests a file from the server.

Printer

Figure 2.6

In a client/server network, the server responds to the requests of client computers. How does a client/server network help to make good use of a company's hardware?

NETWORK HARDWARE

Network hardware is the physical components that connect computers to one another. For a network to function properly, all the hardware components must be compatible.

Client/Server Networks

Most LANs used by businesses today are client/server networks. These networks have a powerful central computer called a **server.** The job of the server is to respond to requests from individual computers, called **clients.** For example, a user may need information that is stored on the server. As shown in Figure 2.6, the client computer requests this information from the server, which locates the information and sends it to the client. Client/server networks are important to large companies because they efficiently share the processing and storage workloads among the server and the individual clients.

Network Interface Cards

To connect to the network, the client computer needs a **network interface card,** or **NIC.** The NIC provides the place to plug the network cable into the computer, and it creates and sends the signal from one network component to another. The NIC allows the computer to "talk" the same language as the other hardware devices on the network. One popular type of NIC, the Ethernet card, is widely used on LANs.

Modems

A **modem** is a hardware component that enables a computer to send and receive signals through telephone wires or cable. To establish a dial-up connection, your computer must have a modem. The modem translates the digital computer signals into analog, or voice, signals that can be transmitted over standard telephone lines. The speed of a modem is important, especially when working on the Web. Many sites contain large multimedia files with video, sound, and animation. At slow transmission speeds, a page can take a long time to load. Most dial-up modems are capable of transmitting data at 56 K (kilobytes) per second.

To use a cable connection, you need a cable modem. Cable modems connect computers to the Internet through the cable television system. Much faster than dial-up connections, cable modems can transmit at speeds measured in megabytes per second, such as 2 MB.

Routers

Companies often want to connect two or more LANs so that employees using different networks can share e-mail and data. A special hardware device called a router is used to join LANs. Computers on a LAN can also access the Internet using routers.

NETWORK SOFTWARE

As discussed in Section 2.2, individual computers are controlled by operating systems. Networks are controlled by a specific group of software called a *network operating system,* or *NOS.* The NOS is responsible for managing network resources, controlling who can access different network components, and keeping the network running smoothly. Some popular network operating systems are Novell NetWare, Microsoft Windows 2000 Server, Microsoft Windows 2003 Server, and Linux. While a server runs a network operating system, each client computer on the network runs its own operating system. For example, a server might run Windows 2000 Server while the client computers run Windows XP.

Section 2.3 Assessment

Concept Check

1. **Define** network, local area network (LAN), wide area network (WAN), digital subscriber line (DSL), server, client, network interface card (NIC), modem.

2. **Identify** the basic hardware components needed to connect a computer to the Internet.

3. **Describe** the difference between a client and a server.

Critical Thinking

4. **Compare and Contrast** What are the primary differences between dial-up and broadband connections?

5. **Predict Outcomes** Your job provides you a computer with wireless connection capability. What advantages and disadvantages do you see in having this technology?

Applying Skills

Research Network Connections Use the Internet or other resources to learn more about one type of network connection. Write a paragraph evaluating whether the usage of this network connection will increase or decrease in the next few years.

EMERGING TECHNOLOGY

ENVISIONING THE INTERNET'S FUTURE

Even though Tim Berners-Lee is credited with creating the Web, you might be surprised to learn that no one person or organization is responsible for running it.

The Web "runs itself" by means of standardized technologies, protocols, and rules. These allow all types of computers to interact and exchange data, despite constant changes. Who creates these standards? The World Wide Web Consortium (W3C).

The World Wide Web Consortium strives to keep the Web vibrant and accessible to everyone.

What Is the W3C?

The W3C is a global organization started by Tim Berners-Lee. It oversees the development of new technologies and standards that keep the Web functional and open to everyone.

Today, the organization includes representatives from hundreds of universities, corporations, and governments. These people contribute their time and expertise to developing the technological, social, and legal aspects of the Web.

So far, the W3C has published over 50 specifications for Web technologies, including Hypertext Markup Language (HTML), Cascading Style Sheets (CSS), and Extensible Markup Language (XML).

Developers rely on these specifications to create Web-based products that are fully compatible with one another. But the W3C focuses on more than just technology. It is also concerned with legal and ethical questions, such as universal access to technology and privacy.

Shaping the Web's Future

The W3C is shaping the Web's future as well by focusing on a number of emerging technologies that will change the way the Web works. The following list summarizes a few of the W3C's exciting projects.

◆ The **semantic Web** will use deductive tools that give search agents artificial "reasoning" abilities. This will make it easier for users to access any type of information from any computer system.
◆ The **talking Web** will be based on the W3C's developing standards for VoiceXML and other tools that will enable people to use their voice to navigate the Web. The talking Web will accept voice input and will be able to deliver data in audio format.
◆ The **multimodal Web** will accept input from every type of source, including keyboards, mice, voice, and even eye movements.

Tech Focus

1. Research either the semantic, talking, or multimodal Web. How is that technology being developed, how will it be used on the Web, and what is its importance?

2. Find out how to become a member of the W3C. What you would have to do once you become a member?

Section 2.4 Creating a One Page Web Site

In Chapter 1, you opened a Web site in FrontPage and examined several of its pages. Now you will get a chance to create your own Web page.

CREATING AND SAVING A WEB PAGE

One of the most important things to learn is how and where to save your files. While this text provides general instructions, you must always check with your teacher to learn how you should save and store any files that you create.

Saving Files

When saving your Web sites, you need a plan. Develop a system of folders and subfolders to locate your Web pages easily. A **folder** helps you organize files in a single place. A **subfolder** further organizes files.

An easy way to locate your work is to create a folder and name it with your initials. If your initials are MPB, you might name your folder *MPB Webs* to store all the Web pages or sites that you create. You can then store each individual Web page or site in its own subfolder.

When you save a new Web site using FrontPage, it saves the site to the location, or path, that you specify. The path identifies the drive, folder, and subfolder where the site is being saved as shown below. Always select meaningful names for your folders. Names may include letters, numbers, and some symbols. The following symbols may *not* be used: ? \ * " < > / |.

READ ME!

Caution Remember to save your Web pages frequently. You do not want to lose your work if the computer shuts down unexpectedly.

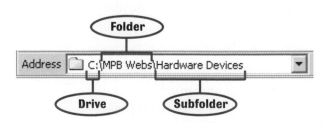

Templates

FrontPage offers templates that simplify creating Web sites. A **template** is a reusable pattern that helps you place information quickly and efficiently on a Web page. Some templates contain **placeholder text** that you simply replace with your own content.

In the following activity, you will use a FrontPage template to create an empty one page Web site. Before you begin, you must create the general folder in which you will save all your Web sites. Ask your teacher how to do this. Unless directed differently by your teacher, name the folder *XYZ Webs,* but replace *XYZ* with your initials.

ACTIVITY 2A Using a Template and Saving Files

1 Start FrontPage. Select the **File** menu, and click **New** (in FrontPage 2002, click **New** and then **Page or Web**) to open the New task pane.

2 Select **One page Web site** (in 2002, **Web Site Templates**) to open the Web Site Templates dialog box (see Figure 2.7).

YOU TRY IT

Figure 2.7
The Web Site Templates dialog box lists the templates available.

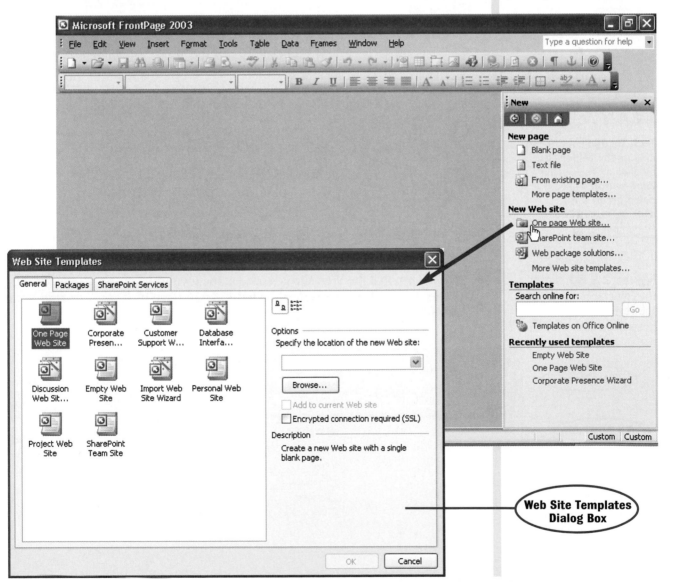

Web Site Templates Dialog Box

3 Click **Browse** to open the New Web Site Location dialog box (in 2002, New Web Location). Using the Look in box (see Figure 2.8), browse to the general folder that you have created to store all your Web sites (*XYZ Webs*). Double-click the folder to open it.

Figure 2.8
Use the New Web Site Location dialog box to specify a location to store your Web sites.

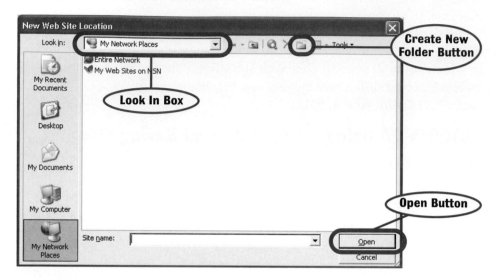

4 Click the **Create New Folder** button at the top of the dialog box (see Figure 2.8). The New Folder dialog box opens. With your teacher's permission, type Hardware Devices in the Name window. This is the name of your Web site. Click **OK.** The New Folder dialog box will close.

READ ME!

Tech Tip You can display the Folder List by clicking the Toggle Pane button's drop-down arrow and clicking Folder List.

5 In the New Web Site Location (in 2002, New Web Location) dialog box, click **Open** (see Figure 2.8). The dialog box will close.

6 In the Web Site Templates dialog box, click **One page Web Site** (in 2002, **One Page Web**), and then click **OK.** A new one page site is created and stored in the folder you have specified.

7 You should now be in Folders view with the Folder List open. Notice that the new site contains a single page, index.htm.

Figure 2.9
The Folders view shows each folder related to a Web site.

8 Confirm that the Web site is stored at the location you specified (see Figure 2.9). Ask your teacher for help if you have difficulty storing your folder.

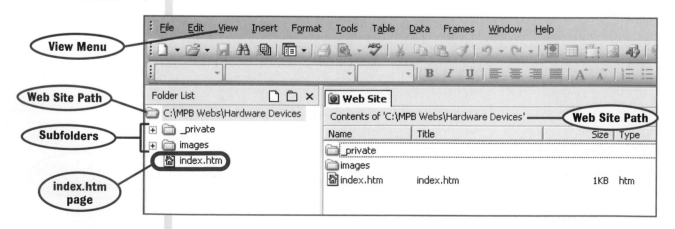

Themes

A **theme** is a collection of design elements, graphics, and colors that help maintain a consistent appearance throughout your Web site.

ACTIVITY 2B Applying a Theme

YOU TRY IT

1 Open the Hardware Devices Web site. Make sure the page is open in Folder view with the Folder List showing.

2 In the Folder List, double-click **index.htm** to open the home page. Make certain that the Design (in 2002, Normal) view button is selected.

3 Click **Format** on the menu bar and select **Theme.** The Theme task pane appears, as shown in Figure 2.9 (in 2002, the Themes dialog box will open, which looks different from the 2003 Theme task pane).

4 Scroll down the list of themes to examine the different options (themes may be slightly different, depending on the version of Front-Page you are using). Notice that the task pane displays a preview of each theme. Click a theme and see it applied to the page.

5 Click two more themes to see how the page changes. Finally, select the **Network Blitz** theme—themes are listed alphabetically. (If you are using 2002, click **OK** to apply the theme to your page, and skip step 6.)

6 If you are using FrontPage 2003, click the Theme task pane's **Close** button to close the pane. Be careful not to close the Web site by mistake!

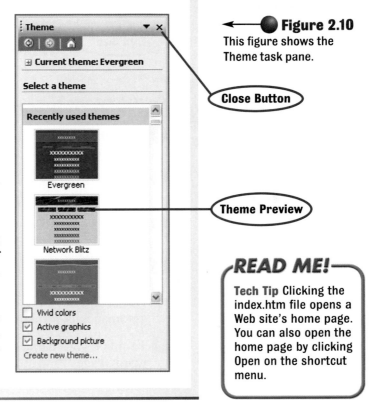

● Figure 2.10
This figure shows the Theme task pane.

Close Button

Theme Preview

┌READ ME!─┐

Tech Tip Clicking the index.htm file opens a Web site's home page. You can also open the home page by clicking Open on the shortcut menu.

ADDING TEXT TO A WEB PAGE

You are now ready to place text and graphics on your Web page. After you enter text onto a page, you need to format it. When you format text, you specify how text characters will look on your page. To format Web text, follow the same basic rules that you would follow when creating a report in a word processor. For example, make headings larger and bolder than the paragraphs below the heading. Determine whether to align the text to the left, to the right, or in the center of a page.

Formatting text also involves choosing the fonts you will use. A **font** is a family of letters, numbers, and other symbols that share a consistent style. Examples of commonly used fonts include Times New Roman, Arial, and Verdana. You can increase or decrease the size of text and make it bold, italic, or underlined. The Style box on the Formatting toolbar lets you choose from a list of predefined styles.

The Formatting toolbar contains buttons that allow you to format text quickly. The buttons on the Formatting toolbar in FrontPage are similar to the formatting tools available in other applications, such as Microsoft Word. Figure 2.11 shows the FrontPage Formatting toolbar and some of its commonly used buttons.

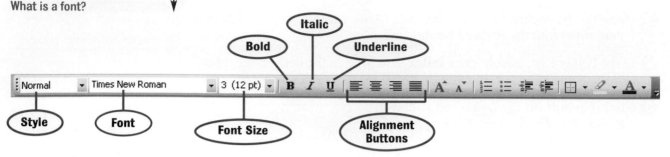

YOU TRY IT

ACTIVITY 2C Inserting and Formatting Text

❶ Open the Hardware Devices Web site. Make sure the home page is displayed in the Page window in Design (in 2002, Normal) view.

❷ Make sure the insertion point is in the upper-left corner of the page. Type Hardware Devices Used in My Pages. This is the title of your Web page.

❸ Select the **View** menu, and click **Toolbars.** Make certain there is a check mark beside the word "Formatting." If not, click **Formatting.**

Figure 2.12 ●
The drop-down list shows the styles available.

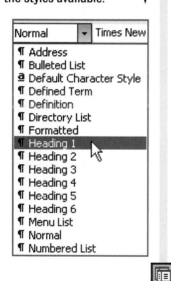

❹ Click anywhere in the title you just typed to position the insertion point. On the Formatting toolbar, click the Style box's drop-down arrow. Click **Heading 1** on the drop-down list, as shown in Figure 2.12. The title is automatically formatted according to the theme you have chosen.

❺ To place your name on the page, position the insertion point after the word "Pages" and press **Enter.** Type by and then your name. (For this activity, we are using the name Matt Baumann.)

❻ Make certain the insertion point is on the line you just typed. Click the Style button's drop-down arrow. Click **Address.** The text is automatically formatted.

❼ If necessary, click the **Toggle Pane** button to close the Folder List. Your page now should look similar to Figure 2.13.

❽ Notice that an asterisk appears in the tabs next to the page name (index.htm*). This asterisk means that the page has been edited, but not saved. On the Standard toolbar, click the **Save** button. Your page is now specified, and the asterisk vanishes.

Figure 2.13 ●
An asterisk shows that a change has been made to the page since the last time the site was saved.

As you work on your Web sites, be sure to save the pages often. The You Try It activities will remind you to save from time to time, but you should get in the habit of saving your work every few minutes.

ADDING GRAPHICS TO A WEB PAGE

One easy way to add graphics to a Web page is to use a pre-made graphic. In the following activity, you will use graphics files that can be found in the Student Data Files. Ask your teacher how to store and use the Student Data Files for this book.

ACTIVITY 2D Inserting Graphics

1 Open your Web site with the home page displayed.

2 Position the insertion point at the end of the line containing your name. Press **Enter** twice.

3 On the Standard toolbar, click the **Insert Picture From File** button. The Picture dialog box opens, as shown in Figure 2.14.

YOU TRY IT

Student Data File

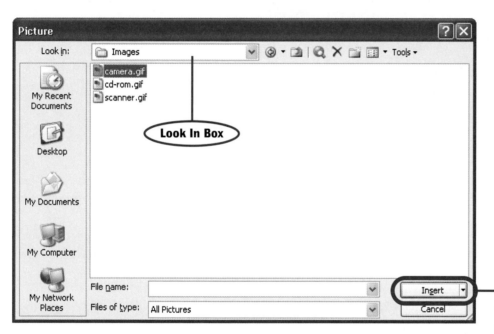

● **Figure 2.14**
You can access graphics from the Picture dialog box.

4 In the Picture dialog box, use the Look in box to browse to the DataFile\Ch02\Images.

5 In this folder, locate the file named camera.gif. Click **camera.gif** and then click **Insert.** FrontPage inserts the image of a digital camera into your page.

6 Press **Enter** to move the insertion point to the next line. Type This is a digital camera. I can download pictures from my camera to my computer and insert them into my Web pages.

7 Make certain that the insertion point is at the end of the text you just typed. Press **Enter** twice. Repeat steps 3 and 4, but click the file named **cd-rom.gif** to insert a graphic of a CD-ROM into your page.

Hardware Devices Used in My Web Pages

by Matt Baumann

This is a digital camera. I can download pictures from my camera to my computer and insert them into my Web pages.

This is a CD-ROM. I can copy text, pictures, sound, and video stored on CD-ROMs into my Web pages.

This is a scanner. The scanner creates digital files of the images it scans. I can insert these files into my Web pages.

8 Press **Enter** and type This is a CD-ROM. I can copy text, pictures, sound, and video stored on CD-ROMs into my Web pages.

9 Make certain that the insertion point is at the end of the text you just typed. Press **Enter** twice.

10 Repeat steps 3 and 4, but insert the graphic of a scanner by clicking the file named **scanner.gif.**

11 Press **Enter** and type This is a scanner. The scanner creates digital files of the images it scans. I can insert these files into my Web pages.

12 Click **Save** to save your modified Web page. When the Save Embedded Files dialog box appears, click **OK.** Your page should now look similar to Figure 2.15.

13 On the **File** menu, click **Exit.**

Figure 2.15
All the changes you have made to the site appear on the page.

You have created your first Web page using FrontPage. In the next few chapters you will learn many tools and techniques that will help you build on the basic skills that you learned in this chapter.

Section 2.4 Assessment

Concept Check

1. **Define** folder, subfolder, template, placeholder text, theme, font.

2. **Describe** how to use a template to create a Web site.

3. **Explain** why Web designers use themes.

Critical Thinking

4. **Draw Conclusions** Why do you need a plan when saving Web site files?

5. **Analyze Text** Why is it helpful to use different fonts and sizes for text headings?

Applying Skills

Review Themes Apply two different themes to the Hardware Devices page and print each page. Evaluate each theme. Close the Web site without saving it.

SECTION 2.1 Computers and Computer Hardware

Key Terms

hardware, 34
software, 34
central processing unit (CPU), 34
random-access memory (RAM), 35
keyboard, 35
mouse, 35
monitor, 36
printer, 37

Main Ideas

- A computer is an electronic device that converts raw data into useful information.
- Computer systems consist of hardware, software, one or more users, and data.
- Input devices include keyboards, mice, graphic, audio, and video devices.
- Common output devices are monitors, printers, projection systems, and speakers.

SECTION 2.2 Computer Software

Key Terms

basic input/output system (BIOS), 40
operating system (OS), 40
graphical user interface (GUI), 41
application software, 41
multitasking, 41

Main Ideas

- An operating system acts as an interface between a user and the computer hardware.
- Commonly used operating systems include Microsoft Windows, Mac OS, Unix, and Linux.
- Application software performs specific tasks, such as word processing and Web page creation.
- A graphical user interface (GUI) allow users to interact with software by selecting words, symbols, or graphics from the screen.
- For a computer system to function properly, all parts of the system must be compatible.

SECTION 2.3 Networks

Key Terms

network, 43
local area network (LAN), 43
wide area network (WAN), 43
server, 45
client, 45
network interface card (NIC), 45
modem, 45

Main Ideas

- LANs and WANs are two basic types of networks.
- Dial-up connections use modems and standard telephone lines.
- Bandwidth determines the amount of data that can be transmitted over a broadband connection.
- Broadband connections can use cable television lines, DSLs, and ISDN, T1, and T3 lines.
- Wireless connections use infrared waves, radio waves, or microwaves to transmit data.
- Client/server networks have a powerful central computer known as a server.
- Network hardware components include servers, network interface cards, modems, and routers.

SECTION 2.4 Creating a One Page Web Site

Key Terms

folder, 48
subfolder, 48
template, 49
placeholder text, 49
theme, 51
font, 51

Main Ideas

- You should use a consistent plan for saving the files associated with Web sites.
- Templates are reusable patterns that simplify the creation of Web sites.
- Themes are collections of design elements that can be applied to Web sites.
- A font is a family of letters, numbers, and symbols that share a consistent style.

READ TO SUCCEED PRACTICE

Key Term Journal Working in pairs or in small groups, compare entries in your Key Term Journal with those of the other students. How are the answers in the *What else is it like?* column similar or different? Note in your own journal examples suggested by other students that you find helpful.

Reviewing Key Terms

1. Where does the computer store data that it is currently processing?
2. What is the output device used to produce soft copy?
3. What do you call working with several applications or documents at the same time?
4. What is the purpose of a server?
5. What FrontPage tool allows you to maintain a consistent layout and design for all pages on a Web site?

Understanding Main Ideas

6. **Identify** the four main parts of all computer systems.
7. **List** two examples of tasks performed by the central processing unit (CPU).
8. **Describe** the two main processing components.
9. **Describe** three types of application software.
10. **Explain** how a user interacts with a GUI (graphical user interface).
11. **Identify** the two basic categories of networks.
12. **Identify** the primary responsibilities of the network operating system (NOS).
13. **Describe** the role of the network interface card (NIC).
14. **Describe** the different ways you can connect to the Internet.
15. **Explain** the purpose of placeholder text in a Web site template.
16. **Explain** why it is very important to save your work frequently.

Critical Thinking

17. **Analyze Software** Why was the invention of a graphical user interface a major innovation in computer technology?
18. **Make Recommendations** The owner of a small business with ten full-time employees is deciding what type of connection the business will use to connect to the Internet. All the employees need access to the Internet, but only three of them need daily access. All three of these employees spend only a few hours a day on the Internet. What type of Internet connection would you recommend? Why?
19. **Research Information** Use the Internet or catalogs to find computer product descriptions. These are available at many retail stores or online computer stores. Identify the current operating systems available for different computer systems. Using a spreadsheet, make a chart that lists the features of each system.
20. **Identifying Graphics** Your school district is planning a new Web site. Each school in the district will be featured. The site will be used as a way to communicate with parents, students, and the community. What type of graphics, audio, and video do you think the site should include?

e-Review ················

webdesign.glencoe.com

Study with PowerPoint

To review the main points in this chapter select **e-Review > PowerPoint Outlines > Chapter 2**.

Online Self Check

Test your knowledge of the material in this chapter by selecting **e-Review > Self Checks > Chapter 2**.

Making Connections

Language Arts — Write a Report Linux is an operating system used on many Web servers. The Linux system is available without charge. Research the interesting story of the development of Linux. How has Linux evolved since it was first developed? How is it being used today? Write a two-page report (approximately 500 words), summarizing your findings. For tips on using online resources, refer to the Technology Handbook in the front of this book.

STANDARDS AT WORK

Students evaluate and select new information resources and technological innovations based on the appropriateness of specific tasks. (NETS-S 5.)

Evaluate Digital Cameras

In digital cameras, the higher the number of megapixels, the higher the quality of the images produced by the camera. Image quality is a primary factor in the price of digital cameras, as are the camera's features, size, and memory capacity.

A friend who collects and sells props from movies is preparing a brochure and planning a Web site. It will feature some of her most interesting finds.

Your friend asks you to recommend a digital camera for the photos. She needs to ensure that the details in her props are clearly visible. She also wants to keep a digital archive of her best pieces.

Research the features, quality, and prices of digital cameras on the Internet, in retail catalogs, or by visiting camera retailers. List your top three choices. Explain your reasons for making these choices.

TEAMWORK SKILLS

Understand Computer Terms

Form small groups following your teacher's instructions. As a group, develop a dictionary of computer terms.

First, make a master list of terms. Divide the terms among group members. Have each group member find definitions of the terms using dictionaries and online reference resources. Using word processing software, key in all the terms and definitions. Place the terms in alphabetical order. All group members should:

1. Read the terms and definitions.
2. Mark any errors for correction.
3. Make sure all terms are in alphabetical order.
4. Suggest improvements to the definitions.
5. List any additional terms that should be added.

Have the group continue reviewing the dictionary until all corrections have been made and all terms and definitions have been added.

CHALLENGE YOURSELF

Explore Networks

Client/server networks are widely used in businesses and schools. They allow many people to access information stored on a server.

Interview the network administrator at your school or for your district to learn about the network used in the school or district. Before the interview, write the questions that you want to ask. The questions should help you learn about the network components, how the components work together, what network operating system is used, and what safeguards the network components from power surges and viruses. Write a summary of your interview.

YOU TRY IT

Skills Studio

These exercises reinforce the skills you learned in this chapter's You Try It activities. Refer back to the You Try It activities if you need extra guidance.

1. Applying a Template and Theme

Create a new one page Web site to advertise a street fair.

Ⓐ Create a new one page Web site named *Street Fair*. Use your teacher's instructions to store the site's files in the proper location.

Ⓑ Open the **index.htm** page.

Ⓒ Select the **Bold Stripes** theme.

Ⓓ Add the following text, each on its own line:

Main Street Fair
August 2 and 3
11 a.m. to 11 p.m.
Featuring live music…
Treats from local restaurants…
Games for all ages…
Come join the fun!

Ⓔ Format the name of the fair as Heading 1. Format the date and time information as Address. Format the remaining text as Heading 3. Your screen should look similar to the one shown here.

Main Street Fair

August 2 and 3
11 a.m. to 11 p.m.

Featuring live music…

Treats from local restaurants…

Games for all ages…

Come join the fun!

2. Adding Graphics and a List to a Web Site

Enhance the street fair Web site by adding a graphic. Then add the list of local restaurants to the page.

Student Data File

Ⓐ Open the Street Fair Web site.

Ⓑ Make a list of local restaurants. Use this list to add details to your site.

Ⓒ Position the insertion point at the top of your Web page. Insert the fair.gif from the DataFile\Ch02\Images folder. Press **Enter** one or two times after inserting the clip art to get the text to align properly.

Ⓓ Position the insertion point after "Treats from local restaurants…" Press **Enter.**

Ⓔ Type the list of local restaurants into the page.

Ⓕ Format the list by selecting **Menu** (in 2002, **Directory**) **List** from the Style box on the Formatting toolbar.

Ⓖ Save the Web site and close FrontPage.

Web Design Projects

1. Create Inventory Sheets

With your teacher's approval, create an inventory of hardware and software components in your computer lab or at home. The table below shows some of the information you may want to gather about the computer hardware. If possible, use database or spreadsheet software to organize this information.

Computer Hardware

COMPUTER ID	INPUT DEVICES	OTHER STORAGE DEVICES	OPERATING SYSTEM	NETWORK CONNECTION (Yes or No)
Lab01	Mouse, Keyboard	ZIP250	Windows XP Pro	Yes

The table below shows some information you can gather about software.

Computer Software

SOFTWARE NAME	VENDOR	TYPE (Application or OS)	VERSION	PRIMARY USE
Word	Microsoft	Application	2002	word processing

2. Prepare a Presentation

Create a presentation about computer systems. If possible, create this presentation using a productivity tool, such as word processing or presentation software. Your audience will be elementary school students. Your presentation should explain what a computer system is and what parts are included. Use illustrations to add interest. If possible, have a computer system available so that you can point to items as you talk about them.

Give your presentation to two classmates. Have them recommend ways to improve it. If possible, give your presentation to elementary students or even to other students in your school.

YOU WILL LEARN TO...

Section 3.1

- Describe Internet hardware and software
- Explain Internet protocols
- Compare intranets, extranets, and the Internet

Section 3.2

- Identify URL components
- Compare Web browsers
- Use search engines

Section 3.3

- Describe Web development applications and hardware
- Describe connectivity components
- Insert external hyperlinks

Section 3.4

- Explain how to download files responsibly
- Summarize copyright and fair use laws
- Cite digital sources
- Evaluate Web site content

WHY IT MATTERS.....................................

The Internet has changed the way we research topics, play games, get our news, and buy products. The ease with which users can obtain information has led to unique online social, ethical, and legal issues. For example, anyone with a computer and Internet access can easily download music files. Many people do not know that copying music from the Internet often violates copyright law. Users need to be aware of ethical, legal, and social issues when using online materials.

Quick Write Activity

Write a paragraph describing how you use materials that you download from the Web on a regular basis (pictures, music, information, etc.). Note any ethical or legal issues that you think you need to consider when using these online resources.

WHAT YOU WILL DO..

ACTIVITIES AND PROJECTS

Applying Skills

You Try It Activities

Chapter Assessment

You Try It Skills Studio

Web Design Projects

IN THE WORKBOOK

Optional Activities and Projects

Guided Reading
Web Design Projects

ON THE WEB

Activities at webdesign.glencoe.com

Reading Strategy Organizers
Go Online Activities
Study with PowerPoint
Self-Check Assessments

READ TO SUCCEED

Adjust Reading Speed
Effective readers not only think about what they are reading, they think about the process of reading. One action you can take to improve your comprehension is to adjust your speed of reading to match the difficulty of the text. As you read this chapter, slow down your reading speed when you have difficulty understanding a concept. If needed, re-read the text to give yourself enough time to absorb the material. It may take longer to read the assignment, but you will understand and remember more.

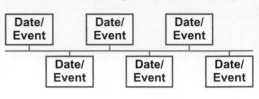

Guide to Reading

Main Ideas

Protocols allow computers to communicate. People often use the Internet to communicate with other users. Intranets and extranets are networks that are protected from unauthorized access.

Key Terms

Internet service provider (ISP)
protocol
Transmission Control Protocol/
 Internet Protocol (TCP/IP)
Hypertext Transfer Protocol (HTTP)
File Transfer Protocol (FTP)
intranet
extranet

Reading Strategy

List important dates in Internet history. Use a time-line like the one below (also available online).

Date/ Event		Date/ Event		Date/ Event	
	Date/ Event		Date/ Event		Date/ Event

The Internet originated in the late 1960s. It is only since the early 1990s, however, that the Internet has been commonly used in homes, schools, and businesses.

ORIGINS OF THE INTERNET

In 1969, the U.S. government began developing a network of computers with various universities and defense contractors. This network was called ARPANET after its developer, the Advanced Research Projects Agency of the U.S. Department of Defense.

ARPANET grew rapidly as scientists began using it to share information and hold online discussions. In 1980, the National Science Foundation (NSF) made ARPANET available to computer science departments for research purposes. As demand grew, NSF added to the existing network, calling the new network the Internet. Soon, several private companies got together to create their own network. These private networks were eventually joined to the Internet, and in 1995, the government discontinued Internet funding.

ARPANET, and later the Internet, were used to share text messages, articles, and other resources. During these early days, the average computer did not have the power or ability to transmit graphics, audio, or video. In addition, these files did not contain hyperlinks, so files could not be linked together.

In 1990, scientist Tim Berners-Lee created the first GUI (graphical-user interface) browser, which he named *WorldWideWeb*. This GUI browser allowed users to view graphic, audio, and video files located on the Internet. Berners-Lee also wrote a software program that could link computer files. When his Web technology became freely available to anyone in 1993, Web sites started appearing at a rapid pace. In 1994, the Web's governing body, the World Wide Web Consortium, or W3C, was founded. The W3C establishes standards for the various protocols and languages used on the Web. For example, if you want to know the current standards for HTML, you can get them on the W3C Web site.

Activity 3.1 Explore Online History Find out more about the history of the Internet and the Web by visiting the book's Web site at **webdesign.glencoe.com**.

webdesign.glencoe.com

HOW THE INTERNET WORKS

While the terms are often used interchangeably, the Internet and the Web are two separate things. The Internet is a large collection of networks, and the Web is just one part of this larger network. Every time you are on the Web, you are also on the Internet. However, you can use the Internet without being connected to the Web.

Hardware and Software Components

Internet hardware consists of the computers and servers connected to the Internet and the communication lines over which files are transmitted. The files are stored on servers that send the files to individual computers. Software applications allow you to use these files after your computer receives them from a particular server. For example, a Web browser allows you to view multimedia files stored on Web servers. (Web servers are discussed further in Chapter 14).

Internet Service Providers

You must be connected to the Internet to use its resources. To do this, most people use a communication line, such as a telephone line or a cable connection, to access an Internet service provider. An **Internet service provider (ISP)** is a business that allows its customers' computers to access the Internet through its own network. An ISP typically charges its customers a monthly fee for ongoing Internet access. Some examples of ISPs include AOL, Earthlink, AT&T, and Time-Warner.

ISPs have one or more Internet servers that link together local and regional networks and control the way data is routed over the Internet. As discussed in Chapter 2, most schools, businesses, and organizations use LANs or WANs to connect their computers to one another. Most of these networks use a gateway to access the Internet, as shown in Figure 3.1. A *gateway* is an Internet server that allows the LAN to communicate with the Internet.

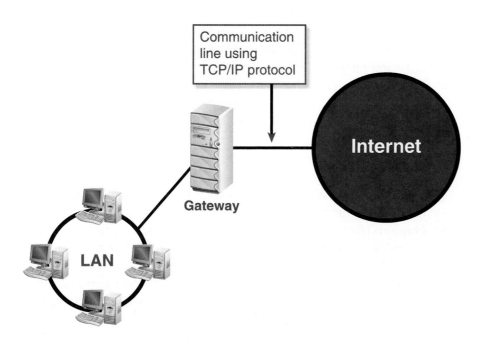

Figure 3.1
Most networks use gateways to access the Internet. What is a gateway?

Internet Protocols

All of the different computers on the Internet must communicate with each other to share information and resources by using protocols. A **protocol** is a set of rules and procedures that specify how data are formatted and transmitted between computer systems. Computers must follow the same protocol in order to "talk" to each other.

TCP/IP The basic Internet protocol is **Transmission Control Protocol/Internet Protocol,** or **TCP/IP.** TCP/IP protocol contains the specific information that allows computers to identify each other and exchange data. Using TCP/IP gives all computers on the Internet a common "language."

Each computer on the Internet has a four-part numeric address, called the *Internet protocol address,* or *IP address.* An IP address allows other computers to send messages to a specific computer. While servers can efficiently use an IP address to locate a specific computer, strings of numbers are difficult for humans to remember. To solve this problem, most people use domain names. Each domain name is just a nickname for an IP address. For example, the domain name address for the Yahoo Web site is www.yahoo.com, while its IP address is 216.109.118.70 (as shown in Figure 3.2). Typing in either address will send you to the Yahoo site, but most people find the domain name address easier to remember than the IP address.

Figure 3.2
You can access Web pages by typing in a URL or an IP address, as shown here. What is the domain name for this Web site?

IP Address

Reproduced with permission of Yahoo! Inc. ©2004 by Yahoo! Inc. YAHOO! and the YAHOO! logo are trademarks of Yahoo! Inc.

Other Internet Protocols TCP/IP is the main Internet protocol. Other protocols, however, are often used with this basic protocol to accomplish specific tasks. The list below describes some commonly used protocols.

- ◆ **HTTP** The protocol that underlies the Web is **Hypertext Transfer Protocol,** or **HTTP.** The Web uses HTTP protocol to transfer files from a Web server to a Web browser. HTTP also interprets hyperlinks and jumps to the specified location.
- ◆ **FTP** The **File Transfer Protocol,** or **FTP,** provides a standardized method of uploading and downloading files on the Internet. Files for FTP sites are stored on FTP servers. Today, people often use Web browsers to access FTP sites.
- ◆ **Telnet** The Telnet protocol allows you to use your computer to access another computer from a remote location. Telnet allows users to connect to databases, library catalogs, and similar information resources around the world.
- ◆ **Gopher** The Gopher protocol uses the software applications Veronica and Jughead to let users search indices of text-based resources located on Gopher servers around the world.
- ◆ **WAIS** Wide area information servers (WAIS) use their own protocol to access servers that store specialized databases organized by subject. All WAIS documents are text based.

INTERNET RESOURCES

Internet protocols allow users to access specific Internet resources, such as FTP, Telnet, Gopher, or the Web. While the Web is probably the best-known component of the Internet, you should also be familiar with the other resources that are available. FTP sites, for example, are often used in businesses where people need to use and share large files. You may also use an FTP site to upload Web site files to a Web server.

Communication on the Internet

People can use the Internet to communicate with other people. The most common way to communicate over the Internet is by using electronic mail, or *e-mail*. To receive e-mail messages, you need a unique e-mail address that will route your messages directly to you. In order to actually type in, send, and receive e-mail messages, you need an e-mail application, such as Microsoft Outlook, Netscape Messenger, and Eudora. You typically access an e-mail application through a Web browser. Table 3.1 lists other ways that people communicate over the Internet.

Types of Internet Communications	
Communication Type	**Function**
Listserv	Users post group messages. Users can access and respond to messages at their convenience.
Newsgroups or Forums	Users post articles on a topic that other subscribers to the newsgroup can read. Many of these newsgroups reside on USENET, a worldwide bulletin board system.
Chat Rooms	A group of users converse in real time about particular subjects, such as hobbies or special interests. Users need no special software to access a chat room.
Internet Relay Chat (IRC)	Users communicate with one another in real time by typing messages back and forth. Conversations may be public or private.
Instant Messaging (IM)	Instant messaging works like IRC communication. Unlike IRC, many private companies have developed IM applications.

Table 3.1
The Internet is commonly used for communications. Why is the Internet a useful tool for communicating with others?

Entertainment on the Internet

The Internet also offers online gaming, in which users play games, such as chess, in real time with people in other locations. *Multiuser domain games* (MUDs) and *MUD object-oriented games* (MOOs) let users experience a virtual universe where they interact with other users. While most of these games are adventure oriented, some have educational uses, such as allowing users to re-create historical sites or reenact historical events.

OTHER NETWORKS

The Internet is useful for exchanging information, but it is also accessible to everyone. Other networks allow users to control access to their content.

Intranets and Extranets

An **intranet** is a LAN or WAN that is designed to make it easy to share information within an organization, such as a business or a school. Intranets typically allow users to access company databases, set up meetings, and send e-mail. Their primary purpose is to share information within the organization while protecting this information from outsiders, particularly competitors.

An **extranet** is similar to an intranet, but extranets can be accessed by outside or remote users who are authorized to use the network. Outside users typically must enter an identification or account number and a password to gain access.

Comparing Networks

There is basically no technical difference between the Internet, intranets, and extranets. All three networks use TCP/IP and require the same hardware, including communication lines, servers, and routers. All three can be accessed using standard Web browsers, and e-mail can be sent using a standard e-mail application, such as Microsoft Outlook.

The differences between the Internet, extranets, and intranets lie in the way these networks are used, who owns them, and who is allowed to access them. Intranets are designed to meet the internal needs of a specific organization. Extranets are designed for a similar purpose, but authorized outside users can access them over the Internet. While the Internet is public and anyone with the required hardware and software can access it, intranets and extranets are privately owned by the organizations that create and maintain them.

Section 3.1 Assessment

Concept Check

1. **Define** Internet service provider (ISP), protocol, Transmission Control Protocol/Internet Protocol (TCP/IP), Hypertext Transfer Protocol (HTTP), File Transfer Protocol (FTP), intranet, extranet.

2. **Summarize** the six types of Internet protocols discussed in this section.

Critical Thinking

3. **Draw Conclusions** Why do you think the development of protocols has been so important in the history of the Internet?

4. **Compare and Contrast** How are the Internet, intranets, and extranets the same and how do they differ?

Applying Skills

Communicate on the Internet List the six types of Internet communications discussed in this section. Identify which of these methods are available in your classroom or lab. With your teacher's supervision, try using one or more methods to communicate with other students.

Real World Technology

WEB-BASED SERVICES

You know that you can buy all kinds of products online, but did you know you can shop for services there, too? Whether you need a lawyer, a bank, or an accountant, the Web can help you find one.

You can find information about many online products and services at the Federal Citizen Information Center's Web site.

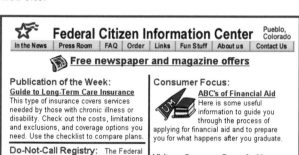

Federal Citizen Information Center Pueblo, Colorado

| In the News | Press Room | FAQ | Order | Links | Fun Stuff | About us | Contact Us |

Free newspaper and magazine offers

Publication of the Week:
Guide to Long-Term Care Insurance
This type of insurance covers services needed by those with chronic illness or disability. Check out the costs, limitations and exclusions, and coverage options you need. Use the checklist to compare plans.

Do-Not-Call Registry: The Federal Trade Commission has launched a **nationwide do-not-call registry** for residents who want to block unsolicited advertising via their home and cellular telephones.

Consumer Action Website:

Want your money back because your parrot doesn't talk? The **Consumer Action Website** is now available. Based on the 2003 Consumer Action Handbook, the

Consumer Focus:
ABC's of Financial Aid
Here is some useful information to guide you through the process of applying for financial aid and to prepare you for what happens after you graduate.

Visit our **Consumer Focus Archive**

FirstGov.gov: The "Front Door" where citizens can get easy-to-understand information and services from the government. **FirstGov.gov** pulls together more than 26 million state and local government pages.

Federal Information in Other Languages: For many Americans, English is their second language—check out: our **Spanish resources page** and our **multi-language gateway.**

Online Personal Services
Here are just a few of the services provided online:

◆ **Job Hunting** Many job hunters use online career services to get detailed information tailored to their needs and location.
◆ **Banking** Most banks offer online services that allow customers to manage their accounts, pay bills online, apply for loans, and much more. There are also "Internet-only" banks, such as NetBank.
◆ **Real Estate** House hunters can find a realtor on the Web and even do a simulated "walk through" of a house. They can also compare interest rates through online mortgage lenders.

◆ **Insurance** Most major insurance companies can give online quotes for cars, homes, or life insurance policies. Potential customers provide Information through a secure form, and then receive quotes that allow them to compare services and prices.
◆ **Taxes** Taxpayers can fill out and file their tax forms online through the Internal Revenue Service's (IRS) site. The site also offers advice and resources. Companies such as H&R Block offer online tax preparation services.

Business Services
Many companies use the Web to provide services to other companies. Many companies handle their orders, billing, and shipment details online. This process saves businesses millions of dollars every year.

Government Services
Many government agencies offer information online to help consumers find trustworthy services, products, and information on the Web. Two popular government sites for consumers are the Federal Citizen Information Center and the FirstGov for Consumers site.

Tech Focus

1. Use the Web to locate a bank with online services. Compare the personal and business services available on the site.

2. Use the Internet to search for three government agencies (local, state, or federal) that assist consumers or businesses. What kinds of information and services are available at these sites?

Section 3.2 The Web

The Web is probably the Internet's most widely used component. As you learned, the Web uses HTTP (Hypertext Transfer Protocol), which allows pages to be interlinked. This interlinking lets users move easily from page to page. It is this ability to browse through pages that sets the Web apart from other Internet components, such as FTP sites and newsgroups.

UNIFORM RESOURCE LOCATORS (URLS)

Every Web page has a unique address known as a **uniform resource locator,** or **URL.** URLs enable a browser to locate specific page files on the Web. Without URLs, users would not be able to browse between Web pages.

URL Components

HTTP requires Web page URLs to be in a standard format that browsers know how to interpret. Most Web addresses consist of four main parts: protocol://address/directory path/retrieved file.

◆ The protocol indicates the type of server where the file is stored.
◆ The address is the server's address.
◆ The directory path is the file's location within the file structure of that particular server.
◆ The retrieved file is the name of the specific Web page file being accessed.

Together, these four components form a URL that specifies a single page on the Web. No other Web page has this exact address.

Figure 3.3 on page 69 shows the URL for the corporate history page on the McGraw-Hill Web site: http://www.mcgraw-hill.com/about/history.html. The letters "http" specify that this page is stored on an HTTP, or Web, server. The HTTP protocol must be used to access this server.

The address component of the URL is the Web server's address. The letters "www" indicate that the server is part of the World Wide Web. Next comes the site's domain name, "mcgraw-hill.com." A site's **domain name** identifies the entity (such as a university, individual, or business) that sponsors the site. This URL tells users that McGraw-Hill owns the site. The extension ".com" indicates that this is a commercial site.

The next part of the URL, "about," tells users the directory path they need to follow to find a specific page. The final part of the URL, "history.html," is the name of the file that contains the Web page the user is viewing. The "html" indicates that this page is written in HTML code.

● **Figure 3.3**
Each component of a URL has a specific meaning. How can you tell that this URL specifies a file on the World Wide Web?

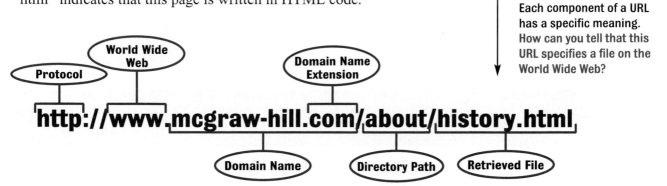

Domain Name Extensions

A domain name typically ends with a dot followed by letters. These letters identify the URL's **domain name extension.** A domain name extension tells users what type of organization uses the address. For example, government sites use a .gov extension. Table 3.2 lists some commonly used domain name extensions.

Common Domain Name Extensions

Extension	Type of Organization
.com	Commercial business
.edu	Educational institution
.gov	Government
.org	Nonprofit organization
.mil	Military
.net	Network
.biz	Commercial business
.info	Information

◀———● **Table 3.2**
URLs contain domain name extensions. What information can you learn from a domain name extension?

USING A WEB BROWSER

You need a Web browser to request, retrieve, and view Web pages. A browser is a software application. You can delete, install, and customize your browser just as you might any other application. When you view a Web page in your browser, the toolbars and menu bars are part of the browser application. The content within the browser's main window comes from the Internet.

Platform Differences

Not all Web browsers interpret HTML identically. Margin spacing around the edges of a page often varies in different browsers. Text may wrap at different places. Font sizes and colors may vary. Text that is dark blue in one browser may appear purple in another. The appearance of hyperlinks may also vary. For example, with some browsers, hyperlinks may not always be underlined.

You must preview your Web pages in as many different browsers as you can. Most people use Microsoft Internet Explorer and Netscape Navigator. Other available browsers include America Online, Opera, Mozilla, Lynx, and Safari.

Browser Restrictions Not every browser will support all of the features that you may want to use in your Web pages. Some browsers, for example, do not support frames, a feature that will be covered later in this book. Also, some older operating systems may not be able to run newer browsers.

Browsers and Accessibility Many browsers include accessibility options. An **accessibility option** is a feature that allows differently abled individuals to access and use Web pages. For example, most browsers let users increase the size of text on the screen. This option helps users with impaired vision read text more easily.

Retrieving a Web Page

The Web is based on the client/server model. A Web server runs special server software designed to respond to client (in this case, browser) requests. When you type a URL into your browser and press Enter, a specific Web page is retrieved through the following process:

1. Your browser (the client) sends the URL to an Internet domain name server. The domain name server uses the URL to determine the IP address of the Web server that maintains the requested page.
2. Your browser uses this IP address to locate the needed Web server.
3. Your browser requests the specific page you want, and the Web server returns that page information to your computer.
4. Your browser interprets the HTML code and displays the page in your browser window.

Previewing a Web Page

Most Web designers make certain that their pages display properly in Microsoft Internet Explorer and Netscape Navigator. You also need to consider your audience. If you know your audience uses the Opera browser, you want to make certain that your pages look good in Opera. FrontPage allows you to preview your pages in several different browsers.

ACTIVITY 3A Preview a Web Page

❶ Open FrontPage. Close the task pane if it is open.

❷ On the **File** menu, click **Open Site** (in FrontPage 2002, **Open Web**).

❸ In the dialog box, browse to the **DataFile\Examples\GardenCo** folder. Open the Garden Company Web site.

❹ In Folders View, double click **faq.htm** to open the Q and A page.

❺ Click the **Preview** button. On the **File** menu, click **Preview in Browser.** The browsers listed in your program will vary, depending on the browsers installed on your computer.

6 Select a browser, such as Internet Explorer 6.0, as shown in Figure 3.4. (In 2002, click **Preview** again to view the page in your selected browser.)

Web Browser

Web Page Viewed in Web Browser

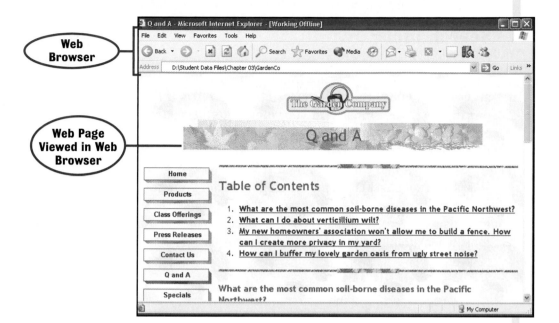

◄━━●**Figure 3.4**
The page is viewed in the Microsoft Internet Explorer 6.0 Web browser.

7 Leave the browser window open. In FrontPage, repeat steps 5 and 6 but select a different browser option, such as Netscape Navigator 7.1, as shown in Figure 3.5.

Web Browser

Web Page Viewed in Web Browser

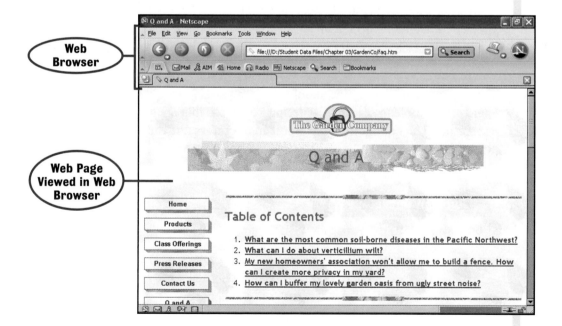

◄━━●**Figure 3.5**
The page is viewed in the Netscape Navigator 7.1 Web browser.

8 Compare how the two screens look in the different browsers. For example, the color of the text links is different. Preview the page in as many different browsers as you can. Close each browser and exit FrontPage.

LOCATING INFORMATION ONLINE

The vast number of pages on the Web can make it hard to find specific resources. Using search tools can help you locate online information.

Search Tools

A **search engine** is an application that locates information about Web pages and then stores this information in searchable databases that you can access from your browser. You search for specific information by entering one or more words related to your topic into the search engine. The search engine then displays a list of Web pages that are relevant to these selected words. Popular search engines include Google, Alta Vista, and Excite.

Search engines catalog individual Web pages. A **Web directory** catalogs Web sites (not pages) by topic or category. After you choose the category, the directory displays a list of sites related to that category. Since databases tend to contain different information, it can be a good idea to use at least two search tools when attempting to locate online information.

Using Search Tools

To use a search engine, you make a search query. Keyword and Boolean searches are two types of search queries.

Keyword Searches A search query is one or more keywords that you enter into the search engine. A **keyword** is an important word related to the specific topic you are trying to locate. For example, if you are looking for a Web site that contains information on HTTP, you would enter the keyword "HTTP." When you enter a keyword into the search engine, the engine searches its indices for possible matches. The search engine then returns the results or hits to you.

Boolean Searches When you want a more precise search than a keyword search, you may want to perform a Boolean search. A **Boolean search** specifies how the search engine should use keywords to locate specific pages. You perform a Boolean search by entering keywords that are separated by Boolean operators. The commonly used Boolean operators and their function are listed in Table 3.3.

Table 3.3

Using Boolean operators will help you perform a more precise search. What are the three most commonly used Boolean operators?

Boolean Operators	
Operator	**Function**
AND	The search engine locates only those pages containing both keywords. Many search engines use the plus sign (+) in place of AND.
OR	The search engine locates pages containing one or both of the keywords.
NOT	The search engine locates pages that contain the first keyword but not the keyword after the NOT operator. Many search engines use the minus sign (−) in place of NOT.

ACTIVITY 3B Performing a Boolean Search

1 Open your Web browser. With your teacher's permission, type the following URL into the address box at the top of the browser window: www.google.com. Press **Enter.** The Google search engine appears.

2 Start with a simple keyword search. Type squash into the search box and press **Enter.** Write down the number of results (displayed on the blue bar near the top of the page).

3 Type the phrase squash+vegetable into the search box and press **Enter** [Note that most search engines require that there be no space between the symbol (+ or -) and the keyword]. Write down the number of results you receive.

4 Type squash OR vegetable and press **Enter.** Write down the number of results.

5 Type squash-game. Again, write down the number of results.

6 Compare the number of results that you received for each of these four searches. Note which search produced the most results and which search produced the fewest results.

Using the OR search should result in many more "hits" than the AND search. While the AND search only finds pages that contain both the word *squash* and *vegetable,* the OR search finds pages that contain the word *squash* and pages that contain the word *vegetable* (the two words do not have to appear together on the same page). The search using the NOT operator should eliminate many Web sites that are about the game of squash rather than the vegetable.

Section 3.2 Assessment

Concept Check

1. **Define** uniform resource locator (URL), domain name, domain name extension, accessibility option, search engine, Web directory, keyword, Boolean search.

2. **Explain** ways in which Web pages may vary when viewed in different browsers.

Critical Thinking

3. **Apply Knowledge** What domain name extension would be used for the official site of the U.S. Supreme Court?

4. **Compare and Contrast** Give an example where it would be better to use the Boolean operator AND rather than OR when querying a search engine. Explain your answer.

Applying Skills

Perform a Keyword Search Use three search engines to conduct a keyword search for the population of the town where you live. Evaluate which search engine helped you to locate the information the quickest and write a summary of your findings.

Section 3.3 Web Site Development Tools

You need certain hardware and software tools to create a Web site. Because the hardware requirements often depend on the chosen software, this section will begin by discussing software needs.

SOFTWARE NEEDS

The software tools you need to create Web sites can be divided into two broad categories:

1. The applications required to create the Web pages themselves
2. The applications required to create individual Web page components, such as graphics, video, and audio

Applications for Creating Web Pages

Two types of applications are used to create Web pages: text editors and WYSIWYG editors.

Text Editors The simplest type of application for creating a Web page is a **text editor.** A text editor (also known as an HTML editor) is used to enter and edit the HTML code in a Web page. When you use a text editor, you manually type all the HTML commands and your Web page text into a blank document. The most basic text editor is Notepad, which comes with the Microsoft Windows operating system. Other text editors include Microsoft WordPad, Allair HomeSite, HotDog Professional, Simpletext, and BBEdit.

Web Site Development Applications Many Web professionals prefer to use more sophisticated packages, called **Web site development applications,** to create Web sites. Unlike text editors, you do not have to manually type HTML code into a Web site development application. Instead, you use a graphical user interface (GUI) in these applications to create your pages. What you see on the screen is very similar to the appearance of the final page. This feature is commonly referred to as **WYSIWYG,** which stands for "what you see is what you get." These applications will also allow you to view and edit the HTML source code. Microsoft FrontPage and Macromedia Dreamweaver are examples of Web site development applications.

Text Editors versus Web Site Development Applications Many people like text editors because they are simple to learn, relatively inexpensive, and require minimal hardware and storage space. On the other hand, users must know HTML, and it is difficult to add features such as animation.

Web site development applications have the advantage of providing WYSIWYG interfaces, simple ways to insert features, and users do not need to know HTML. They do, however, take more time to learn how to use, require significant hard drive space and powerful computers, and can be costly.

Web Page Component Applications

Besides HTML code, Web pages often contain graphics, video, and audio. The Web designer's toolbox should include applications for creating and modifying all of these components.

Text Applications You can enter text into a Web page by simply typing it in with your keyboard. However, some pages contain a great deal of text that often must be formatted in complex ways. In these situations, it can be easier to use a word processing program, such as Microsoft Word or Corel WordPerfect. You can then insert the document file created in the word processing program into your Web page.

Graphics Applications Graphics are vital to most Web pages. Although you may often use premade graphics, you will also want to create your own original graphics or edit existing ones. To accomplish these tasks, you will need a graphics application. Graphics packages let you resize, crop, and change the color of an image. Popular graphics applications include Microsoft Paint, Microsoft Photo Editor, Macromedia Fireworks, Jasc Software Paint Shop Pro, Mac iPhoto, and Adobe® Photoshop®, which is shown in Figure 3.6.

Adobe product screen shot reprinted with permission from Adobe Systems Incorporated.

● Figure 3.6
Adobe Photoshop is one popular graphics application. Why do Web designers use graphics applications?

Video and Audio Applications You need special applications to manipulate, edit, and play video and audio files. Most recent versions of the Windows and Mac operating systems provide applications, such as Windows Media Player, that you can use to play video and audio files. You can download other players from the Internet. Video editing software includes Adobe Premiere, Quicktime, iMovie, and Apple Final Cut Pro. Audio applications, such as SoundEdit, allow you to edit audio files, increase speed and volume, and filter out background noise.

HARDWARE AND CONNECTIVITY NEEDS

A computer, a monitor, and a mouse are the basic hardware that you need to create any Web site. Your other hardware needs depend on the types of software tools you use and the complexity of your site.

General System Requirements

Working with graphics and multimedia files can put a significant strain on a computer's resources. Table 3.4 shows the general system requirements needed to run most graphics software.

Table 3.4
When you use FrontPage or any other software, make sure that your computer meets that software's minimum system requirements. Why is it important in Web design to have enough video RAM?

Overview of General System Requirements		
Component	**Minimum Requirements**	**Description**
Processor	Pentium II 233 MHz chip or faster	Determines how quickly your computer system can carry out commands
RAM (memory)	128–256 MB of memory	Enable your computer to perform high-level graphics tasks
Hard Drive	245 MB of free space	Extra storage space available in case the RAM supply gets low.
Video Capabilities	32 MB of video RAM	Determines the speed at which your monitor displays images.

Input and Output Devices

Most Web developers use a few standard input and output devices when creating sites. These devices include:

◆ A monitor with a resolution of at least 800 x 600 that is capable of displaying at least 256 colors
◆ A mouse or similar pointing device
◆ A color printer to get hard copies of Web pages
◆ A scanner to get printed images and photographs into the computer
◆ A digital still camera for photos that can go directly into the computer
◆ A camcorder to obtain video images
◆ A microphone to capture audio and speakers to output audio
◆ A CD-ROM drive to install applications and access resources

Connectivity Needs

While you are creating your Web site, you will probably store it on your computer's hard drive or on a network server. When you publish your Web site, you will copy the site's files from your local hard drive or server to a Web server. Many people use a **Web hosting service** to gain access to a Web server. Web hosting services sell server space, usually for a monthly fee. When choosing a Web host, make certain that it has appropriate high-speed lines, such as T1 or T3, to upload your Web files. Check the amount of storage space you will be allotted and make sure the space is sufficient to hold all your Web site files. Also ask about the service's technical support in case you run into problems with your Web site.

LINKING TO ONLINE RESOURCES

As you learned in Section 3.2, hyperlinks set Web pages apart from other Internet documents. Because they allow users to quickly jump from page to page, hyperlinks make it easy to access the Web's varied resources.

In this activity, you will add external hyperlinks to the Hardware Devices site you created in Chapter 2. An **external hyperlink** takes users to a page on a different Web site. The hyperlinks you insert will allow users to access additional information on each of the three devices noted on your Web page.

ACTIVITY 3C Inserting External Hyperlinks

1 Make certain that the Hardware Devices Web site home page is open in Design (in FrontPage 2002, Normal) view.

2 Locate the text below the digital camera image. Position the insertion point after the second sentence. Press **Enter**.

3 Type Learn more about digital cameras. Double-click the words **digital cameras** to highlight them.

4 Click the **Insert Hyperlink** button on the Standard toolbar. The Insert Hyperlink dialog box opens, as shown in Figure 3.7. The word "digital cameras" will be the link in your page to an external URL.

YOU TRY IT

READ ME!

Tech Tip You can also open the Insert Hyperlink dialog box in FrontPage by pressing Ctrl K.

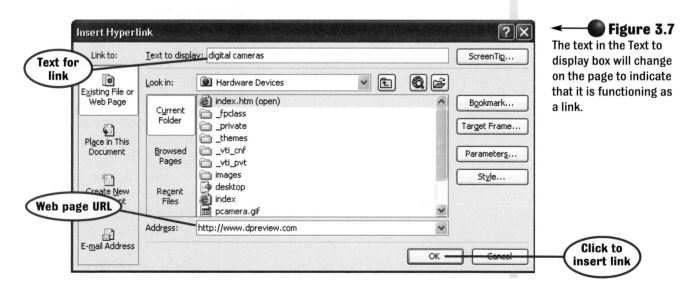

Figure 3.7
The text in the Text to display box will change on the page to indicate that it is functioning as a link.

Text for link

Web page URL

Click to insert link

Hardware Devices
Used in My Web Pages

by Matt Baumann

This is a digital camera. I can download pictures from my camera to my computer and insert them into my Web pages.
Learn more about <u>digital cameras</u>.

This is a CD-ROM. I can copy text, pictures, sound, and video stored on CD-ROMs into my Web pages.
Learn more about <u>CD-ROMs</u>.

This is a scanner. The scanner creates digital files of the images it scans. I can insert these files into my Web pages.
Learn more about <u>scanners</u>.

Figure 3.8
The text link appears in color and underlined.

5 Type the URL that you want users to link to in the Address box. For this exercise, we will type the URL www.dpreview.com into the Address box. Click **OK.**

6 Repeat steps 2 through 5 to create a hyperlink to Learn more about CD-ROMs. Type the URL www.cdrom-guide.com.

7 Repeat steps 2 through 5 to create a hyperlink to Learn more about scanners. Type the URL www.imaging-resource.com. Save the Web page.

8 Click the **Preview** button at the bottom of the window. Your page will appear as it will look in a Web browser (see Figure 3.8).

9 If you are connected to the Web, you can test your hyperlinks by clicking on them. If they work, you should be sent to the Web site you specified.

10 If the links do not work, repeat steps 4 and 5.

Always check to make sure that every external link you add to your Web site is active and current.

Section 3.3 Assessment

Concept Check

1. **Define** text editor, Web site development application, WYSIWYG, Web hosting service, external hyperlink.

2. **Describe** some of the hardware needs for creating a Web site.

3. **List** the steps in using FrontPage to insert a hyperlink into a Web page.

Critical Thinking

4. **Compare and Contrast** Explain the differences between a text editor and a Web site development application.

5. **Evaluate Resources** If you created a Web site about Japan, what three external hyperlinks would you include on your home page?

Applying Skills

Identify Hardware
With your teacher's help, explore your computer's System Properties to find out what kind of hardware is available on your computer. Make a list of the major hardware devices available, such as the hard drive, monitor, and modem.

Careers & Technology

DEVELOPING WEB CONTENT

All the Web's navigational tools, players, and other gadgets would be meaningless without the words, pictures, video, and other content you find on a Web site. After all, people do not go online simply to use a browser. They go online to find information, to be entertained, or to do business.

Web sites are often designed by teams of people, many of whom focus on the site's content rather than its technical elements.

What kinds of people develop content for the Web? Here is a handful of examples:

Writers and Editors

Most Web sites use text in some manner, whether to provide video game instructions or describe the rings of Saturn. Often professional writers and editors create the online text.

Web-based writers must be able to write content that is easy to read on a monitor and appropriate for a site's target audience. They often work with subject matter experts, instructional designers, and programmers. This teamwork allows writers to see how their content fits into the overall design of the Web site.

Graphic Designers

These professionals give Web sites their appeal by creating icons, backgrounds, illustrations, and other graphic elements. Graphic artists may work with photographs or use sophisticated programs to create original art. These designers use a wide range of tools, such as Adobe Photoshop, Corel-Draw, and many others.

Subject Matter Experts (SME)

These professionals are experts in their field and often have worked in a particular industry for a long time. A subject matter expert may write content. Often they provide technical information for a writer who develops the material. Organizations use SMEs to ensure that the content on their sites is as accurate and up-to-date as possible.

Instructional Designers

Computer-based training (CBT) and distance learning use instructional designers to create computer-based teaching materials. Instructional designers may be teachers, trainers, or curriculum specialists. They create the curriculum and teaching tools, such as tests, presentations, and record-keeping tools.

Tech Focus

1. Search a Web site for Web-related job openings. Create a résumé to apply for one of those positions. In your résumé, note the education, training, and experience that you would need for this job.

2. Write a brief essay that compares and contrasts the content requirements of different types of Web sites. Use examples from at least four different sites.

Section 3.4   Social, Ethical, and Legal Issues

Guide to Reading

Main Ideas

Ethical, social, and legal guidelines govern the use of online resources. Users must respect copyright law and trademark rules when using digital resources and cite their sources whenever possible.

Key Terms

Internet Use Agreement
Netiquette
commercial software
shareware
freeware
copyright

Reading Strategy

Identify how the software listed can be used. Use a table like the one below (also available online).

Commercial Software	Shareware	Freeware

The Internet has influenced the way we communicate, learn, do business, and lead our daily lives. While the Internet offers many benefits to society, it has also created many new ethical and legal issues.

THE INTERNET AND SOCIETY

Online communications enable you to share all kinds of information instantly with people around the world. Through the Internet, you can stay in touch with friends and relatives who live far away and meet new friends who share your interests and hobbies. While the Internet helps communications, spending a lot of time at computers can also isolate people. Be sure to balance the time you spend online with other activities.

ETHICAL INTERNET USE

The Internet is widely used in personal, school, and business settings. In each of these settings, there is a set of rules that online users must follow. Some of these rules are formalized into written contracts. Others are guidelines for good online behavior.

Internet Use Agreements

Many organizations, such as schools and businesses, have an **Internet Use Agreement** (also called an Acceptable Use Policy or AUP) that regulates online use. Always read such an agreement carefully before signing it. Some common rules include:

- Always check with an authorized individual, such as your teacher, before downloading files.
- Do not abuse an organization's e-mail system. Understand which Web sites you are allowed to access. Do not access forbidden sites.
- Do not use the Internet for personal reasons if the organization forbids this practice.

webdesign.glencoe.com

Netiquette

While there is no fixed set of rules for interacting over the Internet, general guidelines, called **Netiquette,** have developed over the years. Netiquette encourages users to respect each other when interacting online. This involves treating other online users with courtesy and respecting their privacy. For more Netiquette guidelines, read *Etiquette for Digital Communication* in the Technology Handbook at the front of this book.

Protecting Your Privacy

You cannot always be sure who you are dealing with when you are online. When online, remember that people may not be who they seem. Keep your personal identity private. Do not tell others anything that would allow them to determine your name or where you live. If an individual makes you feel uncomfortable, for example, by asking for your name or sending overly personal messages, tell a parent or other trusted adult.

DOWNLOADING AND COPYING FROM THE INTERNET

Many Web sites allow you to copy or download graphics and other multimedia files or even software to your computer. Laws govern what you can legally download and how you can use these files. Many Web sites have Terms of Use (TOU) agreements that you must follow when downloading files. Always check these rules before you download and use files from a site. Most software can be categorized as **commercial software, shareware,** or **freeware.** These three types of software are described in Table 3.5.

Downloading Graphic Files

Many TOUs grant permission to use graphics for personal and not commercial use (for example, in a personal Web site). Under this agreement, it is illegal to sell documents containing graphics that are meant only for personal use. Always check site rules before downloading graphic files.

Activity 3.2 Use Online Resources Ethically Examine the ethics of using online information by visiting the book's Web site at **webdesign.glencoe.com.**

Types of Software

	Description	Examples
Commercial	Copyrighted and intended to be sold for a profit. **Cannot** be copied or sold to others.	Microsoft Word and most video games
Shareware	Can be downloaded or copied if you pay a small fee to the copyright holder.	WinZip
Freeware	Can be freely downloaded, copied, and used for any legal purpose.	Linux OX

Table 3.5
Most software can be categorized into one of these three types of software. What is the difference between shareware and freeware?

USING INFORMATION FROM THE WEB

While it may be easy to copy material from a Web site, it is not always legal. Many online resources are protected by law from unauthorized use.

Copyright and Fair Use Laws

A **copyright** asserts that only the copyright's owner has the right to sell his or her work or to allow someone else to sell it. Authors, software developers, and musicians all "own" their creative works, which are often referred to as *intellectual property*. You cannot claim a copyrighted work as your own or use it without permission in a Web site. One important instance in which you may legally use an excerpt from a work involves the *fair use doctrine.* The fair use doctrine allows for small portions of a work to be used for educational purposes. Generally, a "small portion" means a few paragraphs from a book or a short excerpt from a song or video. However, even when you use copyrighted material for educational purposes, you must cite the source in your work.

A copyright notice typically contains the copyright symbol (©) followed by the year and the copyright holder's name. Just because an item does not display a copyright notice does not mean that it is not copyrighted. A work is automatically copyrighted as soon as it is created. Many people also register their works with the U.S. Copyright Office. This registration process can provide additional protections in certain situations. In the following activity, you will add a copyright notice to the Hardware Devices Web site.

YOU TRY IT

ACTIVITY 3D Adding a Copyright Notice

❶ Make certain that your Hardware Devices Web site home page is open in Design (in 2002, Normal) view.

❷ Press **Ctrl + End** (hold down the **Control** key while pressing the **End** key). This will take you to the bottom of the page.

❸ On the **Insert** menu, click **Symbol.** The Symbol dialog box opens. Select the copyright (©) symbol, as shown in Figure 3.9, and then click **Insert.** Click **Close** to close the Symbol dialog box.

Figure 3.9 ●
Use the Symbol dialog box to insert symbols into a Web page.

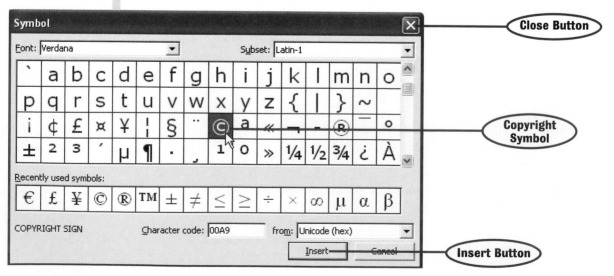

4 Locate the copyright symbol that you inserted into your page (it should be in the lower-left corner of your page). Type the rest of the copyright information using this format: © <year> <your name>. For this activity, we will type 2004 Matt Baumann.

5 Select the entire copyright line. On the formatting toolbar click the **Center** button.

6 Make certain that the line is still selected. Click the **Font Size** down arrow and select **2 (10 pt)**. Save and close the Web site.

After you add the copyright notice, your Web site should look similar to Figure 3.10. This Web page contains the basic elements that most Web pages contain— text, graphics, and hyperlinks. However, the page is very basic and probably looks a little "undone" to you. In future chapters, you will learn how to enhance a basic page such as this to produce professional-looking sites.

Hardware Devices Used in My Web Pages

by Matt Baumann

This is a digital camera. I can download pictures from my camera to my computer and insert them into my Web pages.
Learn more about digital cameras.

This is a CD-ROM. I can copy text, pictures, sound, and video stored on CD-ROMs into my Web pages.
Learn more about CD-ROMs.

This is a scanner. The scanner creates digital files of the images it scans. I can insert these files into my Web pages.
Learn more about scanners.

© 2004 Matt Baumann

Figure 3.10
The copyright notice appears at the bottom of the Web page. Why do you think it is important to claim a copyright for your work?

Evaluating Online Resources

Anyone with the proper skills and equipment can publish a Web site. Many Web sites contain incorrect, misleading, and out-of-date information. To evaluate the quality of a Web site's information, ask yourself the following questions:

◆ **Who are the site's authors?** Find out who wrote the information on a site. Then, use a search engine to see what other works they have written and organizations they belong to.

◆ **What is the site's purpose?** Knowing a site's purpose can help you to detect bias in the site's content. Is it maintained by a company that is trying to sell something? Is it sponsored by a particular organization?

◆ **Is the Web site current?** Check to see when the site was last updated. If the site contains information that changes over time, then it should be updated frequently.

◆ **Is the Web site accurate?** Web sites should cite sources to support their content. Verify a site's accuracy by looking at other reliable resources, including print books or related Web sites. Use information that you can verify from several sources.

Citing Digital Sources

When you use information from a Web site, you must cite the source of the information. To use an author's work without giving that person credit is plagiarism.

Because Web sites are constantly being updated, moved, and even eliminated, the method for citing them is somewhat different than with print material. List items in the citation as follows (see Figure 3.11):

- The author's name, if given
- The title of the article or Web page, placed in quotes
- The Web site's title, underlined
- The name of the organization responsible for the Web site
- The copyright date or the date the site was last revised (if available)
- The date you visited the site, placed in parentheses
- The site's URL, placed in angle brackets

Sometimes you may not be able to locate all of the information needed for a citation. For example, many Web sites do not include author names. Always include as much information as you possibly can in your citations.

Figure 3.11 ●
Citing sources allows your readers to know that your information is reliable. Why do you think it is important to include the date you visited the site?

Wallace, Scott. "Into the Amazon." nationalgeographic.com. **National Geographic Society. 2003 (accessed July 30, 2003).** <http://magma.nationalgeographic.com/ngm/0308/feature1/index.html>.

Section (3.4) Assessment

Concept Check

1. **Define** Internet Use Agreement, Netiquette, commercial software, shareware, freeware, copyright.

2. **Explain** the differences among the three types of software: commercial software, shareware, and freeware.

Critical Thinking

3. **Analyze Issues** Describe at least two negative issues connected to Internet use.

4. **Evaluate Ethics** A friend says that it is not illegal to download music off the Internet. If it were illegal, music would not be available for free online. Evaluate this argument. Why do you agree or disagree with your friend?

Applying Skills

Cite Digital Sources
Assume you are doing a written report on Antarctica. Locate three Web sites that you would use to write this report. Write the citations for each of the sites. Include as much information as you can and cite your sources using established methods.

SECTION 3.1 The Internet

Key Terms

Internet service provider (ISP), 63
protocol, 64
Transmission Control Protocol/Internet Protocol (TCP/IP), 64
Hypertext Transfer Protocol (HTTP), 64
File Transfer Protocol (FTP), 64
intranet, 66
extranet, 66

Main Ideas

■ Tim Berners-Lee created the first GUI browser, leading to the development of the Web.

■ The main Internet protocol, TCP/IP, provides a common language for all computers.

■ The Web uses HTTP protocol. Other Internet protocols include FTP, Telnet, Gopher, and WAIS.

■ E-mail, listservs, newsgroups or forums, chat rooms, Internet relay chat, and instant messaging are forms of Internet communication.

■ Intranets and extranets are privately owned networks.

SECTION 3.2 The Web

Key Terms

uniform resource locator (URL), 68
domain name, 68
domain name extension, 69
accessibility option, 70
search engine, 72
Web directory, 72
keyword, 73
Boolean search, 72

Main Ideas

■ Most URLs consist of a protocol, an address, a directory path, and a retrieved file.

■ The exact appearance of a Web page varies, depending on the browser that displays it.

■ Examples of Web browsers include Microsoft Internet Explorer, Netscape Navigator, America Online, Opera, Mozilla, Lynx, and Safari.

■ If you enter keywords or phrases into a search engine, it will return a list of related Web pages.

SECTION 3.3 Web Site Development Tools

Key Terms

text editor, 74
Web site development application, 74
WYSIWYG, 74
Web hosting service, 77
external hyperlink, 77

Main Ideas

■ Text editors allow you to enter and edit HTML code.

■ Web site development applications provide a WYSIWYG environment.

■ Word processors, graphics applications, and audio and video applications are used to create Web page elements.

■ Web hosting services allow you to publish your site to their Web servers.

■ External links allow users to jump from one Web site to a different Web site.

SECTION 3.4 Social, Ethical, and Legal Issues

Key Terms

Internet Use Agreement, 80
Netiquette, 81
commercial software, 81
shareware, 81
freeware, 81
copyright, 82

Main Ideas

■ Businesses, schools, and organizations may require individuals to sign an Internet Use Agreement.

■ Software can be categorized as commercial software, shareware, or freeware.

■ Copyright law protects intellectual property from being used without author compensation.

■ Always cite the source of online information.

READ TO SUCCEED PRACTICE

Reading Speed Turn back to Section 1.1. Make a note on a separate piece of paper of those sections or paragraphs that took you longer to read or that you read twice. Make brief notes about the content. As you study for a quiz or test, give the noted sections extra attention. If you still feel you do not understand the material, ask your teacher or a classmate for more explanation.

Reviewing Key Terms

1. Which of these is NOT a protocol used on the Internet: TCP/IP, FTP, HTML, Telnet?
2. Rewrite the following sentence to make it true: *In the URL www.uiowa.edu, the .edu portion of the domain name is the domain name index.*
3. What does the abbreviation "URL" stand for?
4. Explain how a search engine differs from a Web directory.
5. What two categories of application software are used in developing Web sites?

Understanding Main Ideas

6. **Identify** each component of the following URL and explain each one's purpose: http://www.redcross.org.
7. **Compare and contrast** domain name addresses and IP addresses.
8. **Describe** situations in which each of the following might be useful: an FTP site, a listserv, a newsgroup.
9. **Summarize** how the TCP/IP protocol works on the Internet.
10. **Explain** the function of the Boolean operators AND, OR, and NOT.
11. **Describe** intellectual property and plagiarism, and their relationship to copyright laws and fair use laws.
12. **Explain** why it is important to test a Web page in different browsers.
13. **Describe** at least three ways you can protect your privacy while you are online.

Critical Thinking

14. **Evaluate Information** Why is it important to include the date on which you accessed a Web site in the site's citation?
15. **Draw Conclusions** If the URL http://www.noaa.gov/satellites takes you to the National Oceanic and Atmospheric Administration's Satellite page, where do you suppose the URL http://www.noaa.gov/ takes you? Explain your answer.
16. **Make Predictions** Do you think the illegal downloading of music without paying for it will increase or decrease over the next few years? Explain your answer.
17. **Cause and Effect** What difficulties might you have creating a Web site if you had a slow processor, low RAM, or limited hard drive space?
18. **Analyze Information** In what situation might you choose to use a text editor instead of a Web site development application to create a Web site? Explain your reasoning.
19. **Evaluate Information** How can identifying the author and/or sponsor of a site help you determine whether or not information on that site is biased?
20. **Draw Conclusions** Why might some users prefer to use shareware instead of commercial software?

e-Review ················· webdesign.glencoe.com

Study with PowerPoint

To review the main points in this chapter, select **e-Review > PowerPoint Outlines > Chapter 3**.

Online Self Check

Test your knowledge of the material in this chapter by selecting **e-Review > Self Checks > Chapter 3**.

Making Connections

Social Studies — Perform an Online Search
Use the Internet to research the history of a telecommunications technology that is an important part of your life (the Internet, the Web, cell phones, personal computers, e-mail, etc.)

Describe the history of the technology. Begin with how and why it was created. End with a description of the product and its importance today. Include at least six significant dates. You can create your history as a timeline or a short chronological essay. To locate information, use a keyword or Boolean search on at least two different search engines. Evaluate and cite your sources.

STANDARDS AT WORK

Students practice responsible use of technology systems, information, and software. (NETS-S 2)

Understand Copyrights and Trademarks
The software you use has both trademarks and copyrights. A trademark protects the brand name of the product. Microsoft is a trademarked name and if you use it for commercial reasons, you must get permission.

Microsoft also has copyrights on its software and software code. You must get the company's permission to use or copy its software. When you purchase a program like Word, you are getting permission to use the software, but you do not actually own it.

Read the Terms of Use Web page of any large software company. Write down one item from the Terms of Use that you think is important for responsible users to know. Explain why this particular rule is important to both the company and its customers.

TEAMWORK SKILLS

Evaluate Internet Service Providers
Working in a small group, contact three Internet service providers (ISPs) to learn about the services that they offer to individuals and businesses and the prices they charge for these services. If possible, contact an ISP in your local community so that you can compare their services to larger regional or national services. Create a chart based on the information that you learn. The chart should be similar to the one shown below.

ISP Name	Services for Individuals	Services for Business	Prices for Services

CHALLENGE YOURSELF

Internet Puzzler
Use Boolean and keyword searches to find the answers to the following clues. Then, use the first letter of each answer to solve the riddle below.

1. This era of human history is usually divided into the Paleolithic, the Mesolithic, and the Neolithic periods.
2. This country in South America is bordered by Colombia, Peru, and the Pacific Ocean.
3. This is the Spanish word for the color red.
4. A peace treaty ending World War I was signed in this French castle.
5. The land between this river and the Tigris River is often referred to as "the cradle of civilization."
6. The lead singer of this popular sixties rock group is Mick Jagger.

RIDDLE: What is the name of a type of powerful computer?

YOU TRY IT
Skills Studio

These exercises reinforce the skills you learned in this chapter's You Try It activities. Refer back to the You Try It activities if you need extra guidance.

1. Searching for Information Online

Find information about famous people who have the same birthday as you.

Ⓐ With your teacher's permission, perform a Boolean search to identify three well-known people who share your birthday.

Ⓑ Perform another Boolean or keyword search to find an informative Web site about each person.

Ⓒ Make a list of the people and URLs that you have located. For each URL, cite your digital source using established methods.

2. Creating a Web Page with External Links

Use the information gathered in Exercise 1 to create a Web page about your birthday.

Ⓐ Open FrontPage. Choose a template to create a Web page. Apply a theme.

Ⓑ Type What happened on <insert your birthday date>? at the top of your page.

Ⓒ Write a short description (two to three sentences) for each person born on your birthday. Add this information to your page under Famous Birthdays. If possible, illustrate this information with graphics.

What happened on April 3?

Famous Birthdays

Washington Irving

:: **Born 1783. Famous author who wrote the short story** The Legend of Sleepy Hollow.

Jane Goodall

:: **Born 1934. Famous animal researcher who studied** chimpanzees.

© 2004 Mary Smith

Ⓓ Use the URLs you located in step C of You Try It Skills Studio Exercise 1 to create external links on your page. Link each person discussed on your page to an external Web site that provides additional information.

Ⓔ Add a copyright notice to the bottom of the page. Proofread your work to find and correct any errors.

Ⓕ View your page in at least two browsers to make sure it displays properly in both.

Web Design Projects

1. Use Online Resources

Research the history of the Internet and the Web. Write a report or create a presentation based on your findings. Summarize how the Internet and the Web have evolved. Then, identify one current issue related to the use of online resources (for example, the issue of online privacy). Evaluate how the issue has affected society either positively or negatively. Describe potential solutions to reduce the negative effects of the issue.

2. Evaluate Software

Research the Web site development applications that are currently available. For example, use the Web or software catalogs to learn more about the following software:

- Microsoft FrontPage
- Macromedia Dreamweaver
- Adobe GoLive
- HoTMetaL Pro

Create a table like the one below to compare and contrast these different applications. In your table, note the system requirements, features, and price for each specific application. Compare and contrast your findings. Finally, predict which individuals or organizations might choose to use each application to complete specific tasks.

WEB SITE DEVELOPMENT APPLICATION	SYSTEM REQUIREMENTS	FEATURES	PRICE

YOU WILL LEARN TO...

Section 4.1
- Format HTML tags
- Identify HTML guidelines

Section 4.2
- Organize Web site files and folder
- Use a text editor
- Use HTML tags and attributes
- Create lists using HTML
- View an HTML document

Section 4.3
- Insert images using HTML
- Insert links using HTML
- Debug and test a Web page

Section 4.4
- Re-create an existing HTML document in FrontPage
- Test a Web page in FrontPage

WHY IT MATTERS....................................

Many people drive their cars every day without knowing exactly how the car works. While you can drive a car without understanding its mechanics, it is useful to understand what is happening under the hood—especially if the car breaks down. Likewise, while HTML code is the basis of all Web pages, you can create a Web site without knowing any HTML at all. Still, knowing HTML is useful—especially if you need to correct or modify the code used to create your page.

Quick Write Activity

Think about a mechanical object that you use every day. Do you understand how it works? If so, summarize how it works and explain how this understanding helps you use the object. If you do not understand how it works, then evaluate how developing this understanding could help you use it.

WHAT YOU WILL DO...

READ TO SUCCEED

Create Memory Tools

Successful readers use "mind tricks" to help them remember. An old—but proven—strategy is to make associations with new ideas you are learning. For example, the term WYSIWYG (wiz-zee-wig) stands for "**W**hat **Y**ou **S**ee **I**s **W**hat **Y**ou **G**et" and illustrates the concept of a computer application that lets you see on the monitor exactly what appears when the document is printed. As you read the chapter, look for opportunities to make up your own memory tools.

Guide to Reading

Main Ideas

An HTML document is composed of instructions, or tags. These tags tell Web browsers how to display the content contained in a Web page. The World Wide Web Consortium establishes guidelines and standards for using HTML.

Key Terms

Hypertext Markup Language (HTML)
HTML tag
starting tag
ending tag
nested tag
empty tag
source code

Reading Strategy

List four types of tags and give examples of each. Use a table like the one below (also available online).

Types of Tags	Example

Hypertext Markup Language, or **HTML,** is the code used to create Web pages. Knowing HTML will help you understand how Web site development applications like FrontPage work. And it will help you customize pages created in FrontPage.

HTML TAGS

You can use a text editor to enter HTML code into a text document, or you can use a Web site development application like FrontPage to automatically create the HTML code for you.

You create Web page documents by inserting HTML tags into a text document. An **HTML tag** consists of text that appears between two angle brackets (< >). This text tells the Web browser how to display a page's content.

Tag Sets

HTML tags often come in pairs that are called tag sets. Each pair includes a **starting tag** (also called an opening tag) and an **ending tag** (also called a closing tag). These tag sets tell a browser where formatting should start and end. A forward slash in the brackets indicates an ending tag. This example shows a tag set that makes text bold.

Starting Tag   `<b> very </b>`   Ending Tag

The HTML tags below format the sentence as a paragraph, display the word "very" in italics, and format the word "HTML" in bold:

```
<p>It is <i>very</i> important to carefully
proofread your <b>HTML</b> code.</p>
```

 webdesign.glencoe.com

If this were placed in an HTML document and displayed in a Web browser, it would appear as shown in Figure. 4.1. You do not see the HTML tags in the browser. They tell the browser how to display the information between the tags, but the tags themselves are not shown.

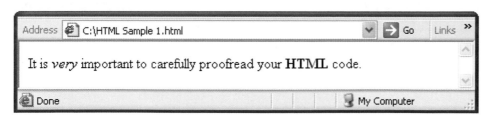

Address   C:\HTML Sample 1.html   Go   Links »

It is *very* important to carefully proofread your **HTML** code.

Done   My Computer

● Figure 4.1

This example shows text that was formatted using several HTML tags. How would you alter the code to make the word "very" bold?

Nested Tags

Nesting refers to the order in which HTML tags appear. A **nested tag** is a tag enclosed inside another set of tags. In the example above, the italic tag set (`<i></i>`) and the boldface tag set (`<b></b>`) are nested within the paragraph tag set (`<p></p>`).

When you nest tags, make sure you close the tag when you want that formatting to stop. In the example below, the Web browser will keep formatting text as bold `<b>` until it comes to an end tag that tells it to stop `</b>`.

```
<html><p><b>very</b></p></html>
```

Empty Tags

While most HTML tags are used in pairs, some are not. A tag that requires only an opening tag is called an **empty tag** (sometimes referred to as an orphan tag). There is no closing tag. For example, to add a line break, enter `<br>`. Or insert a horizontal line with the `<hr>` tag.

You will use some HTML tags over and over again when creating Web pages. These common tags are listed in Appendix B. Refer to these tags as you create HTML and FrontPage documents.

HTML GUIDELINES

Understanding basic guidelines for using HTML code will help you see the relationship between the code you write and what you see in the Web browser.

HTML and Spacing

HTML documents display a single space between words. If you use the space bar, Tab key, or Enter key to add spaces between words, you will not necessarily see those spaces in a Web browser. Look at the following lines of HTML code. Notice how the space between the words "HTML" and "code" is different in each line.

TECH TRIVIA

HTML Doctor HTML and TIDY are programs that can find and fix obvious problems with HTML code.

```
<b>HTML code</b>
<b>HTML                              code</b>
<b>            HTML code</b>
```

However, when displayed in a browser, each line of code looks the same, as shown in Figure 4.2.

Figure 4.2 ●
Extra spaces between elements in an HTML document will not necessarily display in a Web browser. How would the text in the third line of code display if you added a space between the words "HTML" and "code"?

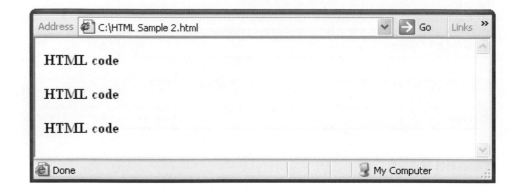

Activity 4.1 Use HTML Tutorials Learn more about HTML guidelines by accessing online tutorials at **webdesign.glencoe.com**.

HTML and Case Sensitivity

HTML tags are not case sensitive. This means that browsers do not care whether a tag is in uppercase or lowercase letters. A browser reads <B> and <b> the same way. In this book, we use lowercase tags.

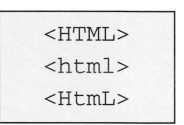

```
<HTML>
<html>
<HtmL>
```

Viewing Source Code

You can see the HTML commands used to create any Web page by viewing its source code. A Web page's **source code** is the text and HTML commands used to create that page. In most browsers, you can see the source code by selecting either Source or Page Source from the View menu.

In FrontPage you can see the source code by opening the page in Code view (or in 2002, in HTML view). FrontPage 2003 also offers Split view, which allows you to see both the Web page and its source code on the same screen.

Section 4.1 Assessment

Concept Check

1. **Define** Hypertext Markup Language (HTML), HTML tag, starting tag, ending tag, nested tag, empty tag, source code.

2. **Name** four types of HTML tags and explain each one's purpose.

Critical Thinking

3. **Evaluate** Why is a basic understanding of HTML an important skill for a Web designer?

4. **Analyze Tags** Why must you be careful to include all end tags when using HTML?

Applying Skills

Write HTML Code
Write the HTML code to display the following sentence in a Web browser. Be sure your code formats the sentence as shown: **HTML code** allows information to be displayed in a *Web browser.*

NEW MARKUP LANGUAGES

HTML is adequate for formatting Web pages, but beyond its formatting capabilities, HTML is limited.

VRML can create all sorts of intriguing virtual "worlds."

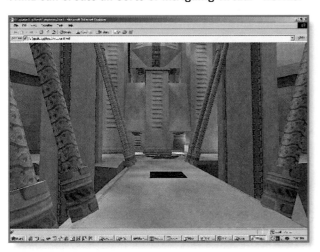

Beyond HTML

Many Web pages must perform actions beyond simply displaying text and graphics. Web designers need other tools besides HTML to create these kinds of functionality.

Extensible Markup Language (XML)

New markup languages like XML allow designers to create Web pages that can perform complicated tasks. Whereas HTML tags only format documents, XML tags can give meaningful descriptions to the parts of a document.

For example, a product listing in a toy maker's on-line catalog might look like this:

```
<product>Zany Bear</product>
<price>$19.99</price>
<manufacturer>Todd's Toys,
Inc.</manufacturer>
```

The descriptive tags in this code specify the product, price, and manufacturer of a toy. Using these tags, an XML application can automatically locate, interpret, and exchange data about toys such as the Zany Bear. This ability means XML documents function more like databases than like traditional documents.

Virtual Reality Markup Language (VRML)

VRML lets designers create online "virtual worlds" made from three-dimensional (3D) shapes and environments.

Using special browsers, viewers can move through these worlds, manipulate objects, and interact visually with one another.

Most people see VRML as a basis for online games, but it may someday be used to provide three-dimensional training for soldiers, surgeons, and drivers. City planners may use it to create 3D views of urban designs.

VRML environments are easy to create and do not consume much disk space. However, the constantly changing scenes in VRML worlds require a great deal of Internet bandwidth. For this reason, many experts believe VRML will not reach its potential until broadband Internet access becomes universally available.

Tech Focus

1. Research an emerging Web language and compare and contrast it with HTML.

2. Why do you think new markup languages are constantly being developed?

Section 4.2 Using a Text Editor

Guide to Reading

Main Ideas

You can use a text editor to create text documents that can be displayed in a Web browser. These documents must contain HTML commands. Always organize your folders and files carefully when creating a Web site.

Key Terms

file name extension
attribute
ordered list
unordered list

Reading Strategy

Compare and contrast ordered and unordered lists. Use a Venn diagram like the one below (also available online).

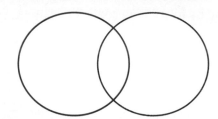

In this section, you will use the text editor Microsoft Notepad to create an HTML document (Notepad is part of the Microsoft Windows OS).

ORGANIZING FILES AND FOLDERS

Every Web site is composed of folders and files. When you create a new Web site in FrontPage, the program automatically creates several folders for you. Under that folder it creates subfolders. When you use a text editor, you must manually create the folders that will hold your Web site's components.

Whether you use a text editor or a Web site development application, you must keep your files organized. When you add graphics and create hyperlinks in an HTML document, you must include instructions that tell the Web browser which file to access and where to find it. Having well organized files makes it easier to add this information to your HTML document.

YOU TRY IT

ACTIVITY 4A Creating Folders to Organize a Site

Student Data File

❶ Identify the location where you are storing your Web sites. Ask your teacher for help if needed.

❷ In your general folder, create a new folder named **MySkills1.**

❸ In the MySkills1 folder, create a folder named **images.** You will store the images for the MySkills1 Web site in this folder.

❹ Copy the **p_border.gif** file from the DataFile\Ch04\Images folder into the images folder you just created.

USING NOTEPAD

Using Notepad is like using a word processing application, but it does not contain toolbars and other features available in word processors.

Creating an HTML Document in Notepad

The first step to creating an HTML document is to enter HTML tags into your text editor. Most HTML documents have a structure like the one in Figure 4.3. The first tag is typically <html>. This tells the browser that it is reading an HTML document and to interpret every tag as HTML code, until it reaches the </html> ending tag.

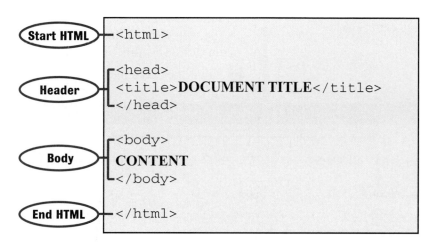

Figure 4.3
Most HTML documents have a basic structure similar to the one shown here. When this document is opened in a Web browser, where will the text contained within the <title> </title> tags appear?

An HTML document has two main parts: the header and the body. Most HTML documents only contain one header tag set, and one body tag set.

The <head></head> tag set, or header, provides information to the browser about your Web page, such as its title, author, and keywords. This is used by the Web browser to catalog the page and is not shown on the page. The Web page title is displayed in the browser title bar, and not on the Web page itself. The <body></body> tag set encloses the rest of the Web page code including all links, text, and images. The body of the Web page is what you see in the browser window.

Saving an HTML Document in Notepad

When you save a file for the first time in Notepad, use the Save As dialog box to navigate to the folder where you want to store your HTML document.

Naming the File Some Web servers do not recognize file names with more than eight characters, or names with spaces. So, keep your file names to eight or less characters when possible. Use the underscore character to indicate a blank space. For example, name a file ask_us.html, rather than ask us.html.

Choosing File Extensions The three or four characters after a period in a file name are the **file name extension.** It tells the computer what type of file it is reading. Notepad automatically saves all files as text files with the text file extension .txt.

Web browsers cannot open a file with the .txt extension. You must change the .txt extension to an .html or .htm extension when saving your HTML document in Notepad so that a Web browser will open it.

READ ME!

Tech Tip To enter a left angle bracket < press Shift + the comma key. For a right angle bracket > press Shift + the period key.

ACTIVITY 4B Creating and Saving an HTML Document

1 From the **Start** menu, select **All Programs** (or **Programs**), then **Accessories,** then **Notepad.**

2 In Notepad, type the text shown in Figure 4.4. Leave blank lines as indicated so you can easily add more HTML code later.

Figure 4.4 ●
These tags form the basic structure of an HTML document.

3 Click the **File** menu, and choose **Save.** The Save As dialog box appears.

4 Browse to the **MySkills1** folder and open it.

5 Type skills1.html in the File name box (see Figure 4.5). In the Save as type drop-down list, select **All Files** (this allows you to save an .html or .htm file in Notepad).

6 Click the **Save** button to save your file.

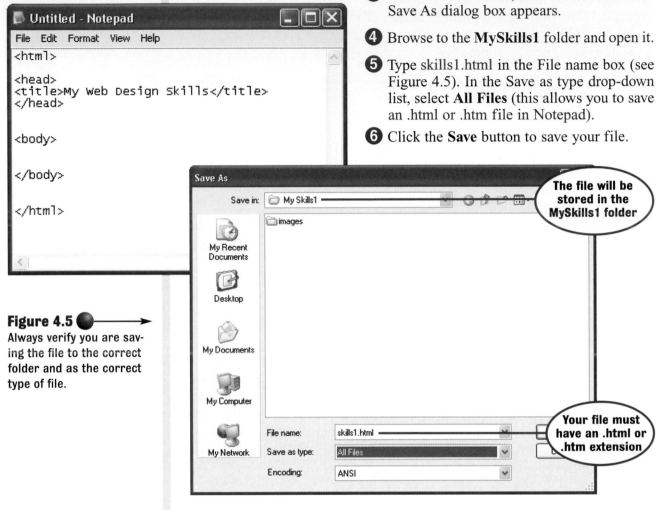

Figure 4.5 ●
Always verify you are saving the file to the correct folder and as the correct type of file.

ADDING ATTRIBUTES USING HTML

Some HTML tags can contain properties, or attributes. An **attribute** is an instruction that further specifies a tag's characteristics, such as the color and font for a heading or the background color on a page. Attributes allow you to assign colors, styles, and alignment. Attributes appear within opening tags. The attribute has a name, an equal sign (=), and a descriptor that appears in quotes. In this example, the attribute color="green" will make the word *grass* appear green in a browser.

```
<font color="green">grass</font>
```

Font Color Attributes

In HTML, you use the attribute `color` to change the text color. The descriptor then specifies which color to use. The easiest way to specify a color is to use one of 16 named colors, such as red, blue, white, or green (see Appendix C). In this example, the attribute `color` and the descriptor `green` make one word in the sentence green.

```
<p>They say the <font color="green">grass</font>
is greener over there.</p>
```

If you insert this code into an HTML document, the text displays in a browser as shown in Figure 4.6.

The other way to specify a color is to use one of the 216 hexadecimal colors. In this system, each color is represented by a 6-character number/letter combination (see Appendix C for a complete list). While the 16 named colors are easy to remember, the 216 hexadecimal colors offer a greater variety of color choices. In this example, the descriptor `#33cc33` is the hexadecimal color of a shade of green.

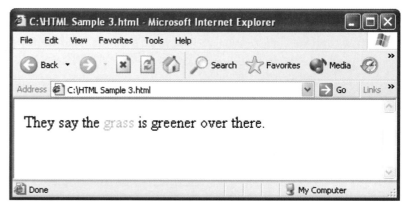

Figure 4.6
The browser interprets the HTML code and places the word "grass" in green. What would happen if the `</font>` tag were moved after the word "greener"?

```
<p>They say the <font color="#33cc33">grass</font>
is greener over there.</p>
```

Background Color Attributes

You specify a page's background color by adding attributes to the `<body>` tag. You can use one of the 16 named colors or a hexadecimal color. The following tag uses the attribute `bgcolor` to make the background color green.

```
<body bgcolor="#33cc33">
```

Heading Attributes

In HTML coding, you can define six heading levels by using the tag sets `<h1></h1>`, `<h2></h2>`, and so on to `<h6></h6>`. The `<h1>` tag indicates the largest heading size and `<h6>` indicates the smallest heading size. Headings break the text into short, readable sections. In this book, you will notice different sized headings. These headings also have attributes, such as color and alignment.

Alignment Attributes

By default, all text on a Web page aligns to the left margin. You may want to change the alignment of some headings to center them on the page. You would add the `align` attribute to achieve this result, as follows:

```
<h1 align="center">
```

YOU TRY IT

ACTIVITY 4C Adding Color and Formatting Text Using HTML

1 Open the **skills1.html** document in Notepad. To add the background color yellow to the page, edit the opening `<body>` tag so that it appears as follows: `<body bgcolor="#ffffcc">`

2 Move the insertion point to the line below the body tag. Type the following to create the blue heading for the page: `<h1 align="center"><font color="#6666ff">Web Design Skills</font></h1>`

3 Press **Enter.** Type the following to create the first dark blue subheading: `<h2><font color="#000099">Skills I Already Have </font></h2>`

4 Press **Enter** twice. Type the following to create the second dark blue subheading: `<h2><font color="#000099">Skills That I Will Learn</font></h2>`

5 Click the **File** menu and choose **Save** to save your document.

READ ME!

Tech Tip You can also press Ctrl + S to save your document.

CREATING LISTS USING HTML

Lists help make text easier to read and add visual interest to a page. Lists can also help readers identify key points on a page more quickly.

Types of Lists

There are two types of lists: ordered lists and unordered lists. An **ordered list** features items that must appear in a particular sequence, such as the steps required to complete a task. Because numbers precede each item in an ordered list, these lists are often called numbered lists. An **unordered list** contains items that can appear in any order. A bulleted list is an example of an unordered list.

Figure 4.7 Lists can be ordered or unordered. Which type of lists should you use for a series of steps?

Ordered List
1. Open Notepad.
2. Enter HTML code.
3. Save the file.

Unordered List
■ Starting Tags
■ Ending Tags
■ Nested Tags

ACTIVITY 4D Creating an Unordered List Using HTML

1 Open the **skills1.html** document in Notepad. Position the insertion point at the end of "Skills I Already Have". Press **Enter.** Type <ul>. Press **Enter.**

2 Enter each bulleted item. Press **Enter** after typing each item. Type:

```
<li> I can operate my computer's hardware.</li>
<li>I can use FrontPage to create simple Web
sites.</li>
<li> I can insert previously made graphics into
my Web pages.</li>
<li> I can insert links into my Web pages.</li>
```

3 Type </ul> to indicate the end of the first unordered list.

4 Position the insertion point at the end of "Skills That I Will Learn". Press **Enter.** Type <ul>. Press **Enter.**

5 Enter each bulleted item. Press **Enter** after typing each item. Type:

```
<li> I will learn to use Notepad to create HTML
documents.</li>
<li>I will learn to create Web pages that are
well designed.</li>
<li> I will learn to use color and images
appropriately.</li>
<li> I will learn to create and modify
graphics.</li>
```

6 Type </ul>. Choose **File** menu and **Save.** Your document should look similar to Figure 4.8.

READ ME!

Tech Tip As you enter code into Notepad, be sure to proofread your work carefully. Make sure all angle brackets, slash marks (/), and quotation marks are present. Missing elements or misspelled HTML tags can cause your Web page to display incorrectly or not at all.

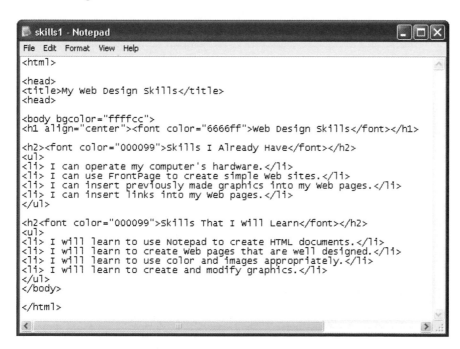

```
skills1 - Notepad
File Edit Format View Help
<html>

<head>
<title>My Web Design Skills</title>
<head>

<body bgcolor="ffffcc">
<h1 align="center"><font color="6666ff">Web Design Skills</font></h1>

<h2><font color="000099">Skills I Already Have</font></h2>
<ul>
<li> I can operate my computer's hardware.</li>
<li> I can use FrontPage to create simple Web sites.</li>
<li> I can insert previously made graphics into my Web pages.</li>
<li> I can insert links into my Web pages.</li>
</ul>

<h2<font color="000099">Skills That I Will Learn</font></h2>
<ul>
<li> I will learn to use Notepad to create HTML documents.</li>
<li> I will learn to create Web pages that are well designed.</li>
<li> I will learn to use color and images appropriately.</li>
<li> I will learn to create and modify graphics.</li>
</ul>
</body>

</html>
```

● **Figure 4.8**
Make sure that each item in the unordered lists has an opening and ending tag.

7 Click the **File** menu and select **Print.** In the Print dialog box, click **Print.** Carefully proofread the printed document. Pay attention to matching up tags. Make needed corrections and save again.

VIEWING AN HTML PAGE

With text editors you cannot see how your page will appear in a Web browser while you are creating it. Instead, you must save the HTML document and then view it in a browser. Always examine your page carefully in a browser. If you need to make changes, reopen the page in Notepad, make corrections, and re-save the file. Open the file in the browser to see if it now displays properly.

YOU TRY IT

ACTIVITY 4E Viewing HTML in a Browser

1 Start your Web browser. Choose **File** menu and **Open** (or **Open File**).

2 Browse to the **MySkills1** folder. Select the **skills1.html** file and click the **Open** button.

3 Click **OK.** Examine the page. It should look like Figure 4.9.

READ ME!

Tech Tip Easily reopen the Notepad file in your browser by clicking the browser's Refresh (Internet Explorer) or Reload current page (Netscape Navigator) button.

Figure 4.9
Viewing an HTML document in a Web browser is a good way to identify coding errors.

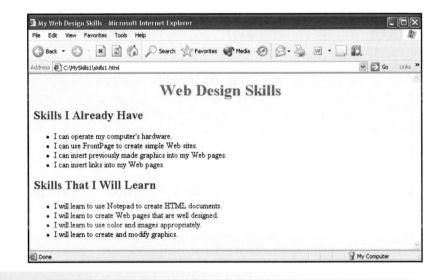

Section 4.2 Assessment

Concept Check

1. **Define** file name extension, attribute, ordered list, unordered list.

2. **Discuss** two guidelines for naming files.

3. **Explain** why it is important to use an .html or .htm extension when saving HTML documents in Notepad.

Critical Thinking

4. **Analyze** Why should you have a specific plan when organizing your Web site's files and folders?

5. **Compare and Contrast** When is it better to use an unordered list? An ordered list? Give examples and explain your choices.

Applying Skills

Create an Ordered List Using Notepad, create an ordered list of HTML attributes that you can display in a Web browser. With your teacher's permission, print your Notepad document and print the page from a browser.

Guide to Reading

Main Ideas

Use image tags to insert graphics using HTML. You can create links by using an anchor tag to specify the clickable area. A link can be absolute or relative. Web pages must be tested.

Key Terms

text link
graphic link
anchor tag
absolute link
relative link
debugging
testing

Reading Strategy

Compare and contrast absolute and relative links. Use a chart like the one below (also available online).

Absolute Links	Relative Links

You create Web pages in stages. Adding new components in increments allows you to correct errors as you go, rather than waiting until you finish the entire page.

ADDING IMAGES USING HTML

You can insert images into pages using the `<img>` tag called the image tag. The `<img>` tag is an empty tag. This means that there is a starting tag but no ending tag.

Using Image Tags

When a browser loads a Web page, the `<img>` tag finds the image from the specified location and displays it in the browser. For example, you want to add an image of books to your page. This image is stored in your Web site's subfolder and it is named books.gif. The image tag might look like this:

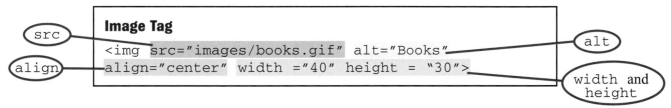

Image Tag

src
align

```
<img src="images/books.gif" alt="Books"
align="center" width ="40" height = "30">
```

alt
width and height

Common Attributes

The image tag above includes five common attributes. You should always use the `src` and `alt` attributes. The `align`, `width`, and `height` attributes are optional.

The `src` attribute specifies the source location of the image. In our example, the browser loads the books.gif file, which is stored in the images subfolder.

If the browser cannot load the image file, the `alt` attribute gives the browser an alternative text message to display in place of the missing image.

If the Web browser cannot locate the books.gif file, the `alt` attribute instructs the browser to display the text "Books" instead.

The `align` attribute is used to wrap text around an image. The image could be in the center, to the right, or to the left of the text.

The `height` and `width` attributes specify the image's height and width pixels (you will learn more about pixels in Chapter 6). Our `<img>` tag displays the books.gif image with a width of 40 pixels and a height of 30 pixels.

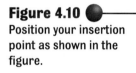

ACTIVITY 4F Inserting an Image Using HTML

❶ Open the **skills1.html** page in Notepad.

❷ Position the insertion point at the end of the `<h1>` heading and press **Enter.** The insertion point should be positioned as shown in Figure. 4.10.

Figure 4.10 ●
Position your insertion point as shown in the figure.

❸ Type the following to insert the border graphic stored in your Web site's images subfolder: `<img src="images/p_border.gif" alt="Border">`

❹ Save your document.

INSERTING LINKS USING HTML

As you learned in Chapter 1, hyperlinks can be categorized as external, internal, or intrapage, depending on where they send the user. You use anchor tags to insert links into an HTML document.

Using Anchor Tags

An **anchor tag** identifies what is clicked on and where it takes the user. The `<a></a>` tag set is used to create all links. It uses the `href` attribute to tell the Web browser where it needs to link to.

Text and Graphic Links

Hyperlinks can be categorized according to how users activate the link. Sometimes users click text to access a link (text link), and sometimes they click an image (graphic link). You can make any text or any image into a hyperlink. In Figure 4.11 on the next page, both the text link and the graphic link will take you to the Coralville Public Library home page.

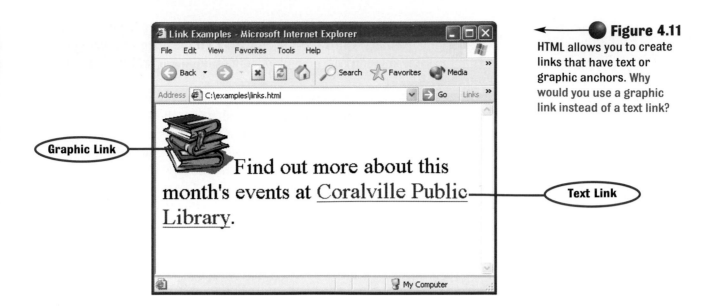

Text Links A **text link** specifies what text on a page will be a hyperlink. This example tells the browser to display the text "Coralville Public Library" as a hyperlink:

```
<a href="http://www.coralvillepubliclibrary.org/">
Coralville Public Library</a>
```

Graphic Links The anchor tag for a **graphic link** identifies the image users must click to activate a link. To activate the following link, users click the books.gif graphic, as shown in Figure 4.11. The anchor tag for this link contains a nested image tag:

```
<a href="http://www.coralvillepubliclibrary.org/">
<img src="images/books.gif" alt="Books" width
="40" height = "30"></a>
```

Absolute Versus Relative Links

Text and graphic links can be categorized as either absolute or relative.

Absolute Links The code used to create an **absolute link** contains the complete URL or path of the file being linked to. External links are often absolute links. For example, the links to the Coralville Public Library are absolute links. They contain the complete URL for the library's Web site: http://www.coralvillepubliclibrary.org/

Relative Links The code used to create a **relative link** contains the name of the file being linked to:

```
<a href="design_tips.html">More Design Tips</a>
```

Activity 4.2 Identify Absolute and Relative Links Learn more about absolute and relative links by visiting webdesign.glencoe.com.

In this relative link, users click the text More Design Tips to go to the page design_tips.html. A relative link only works if the document being linked to is in the same folder as the document containing the link. Internal links are often relative links.

Relative links have an important advantage when linking to documents in your Web site. For example, when you publish a site, the site moves to a Web server. As long as the folder structure remains the same, the Web browser will still be able to locate files as needed. If you use absolute links, the links would no longer work because they would not identify the new location. Remember, an absolute link contains the complete path of the file being linked to. If files change location, you would have to update the paths in the absolute links.

YOU TRY IT

ACTIVITY 4G Inserting Absolute Links Using HTML

1 Open the **skills1.html** page in Notepad.

2 Place the insertion point at the beginning of the line `</body>`. Press **Enter.** Move the insertion point up one line so that it is on the blank line you just created.

3 Type the following: `<p><b> Here are some additional links to Web sites with more information about Web design:</b></p>`

4 Press **Enter.** Insert this link: `<a href="http://www.w3.org/"> World Wide Web Consortium</a><br>`

5 Press **Enter.** Insert this link: `<a href="http://webmaster. indiana.edu/">University of Indiana Webmaster</a>`

6 Save your Web page. It should look similar to Figure 4.12.

Figure 4.12
The links appear at the bottom of the Web page.

Links Inserted Here

TESTING A WEB PAGE

Debugging refers to locating and correcting any obvious errors in your code. You should try to debug your work regularly as you build your sites.

A number of applications have been developed to debug HTML code. These applications are called HTML validators. Basically, you submit your HTML file to the validator and, if the code contains errors, the validator generates an error list. The World Wide Web Consortium Web site offers a validator for checking Web page code. With your teacher's permission, you can use this validator to check your own HTML documents.

Testing involves checking the page to make certain that it displays as designed. Test your site in both Internet Explorer and Netscape Navigator and in any other browser you think your audience may use. Always double check that links work properly. External links are particularly important to check because sometimes pages get removed from the Web or their URLs change.

ACTIVITY 4H Testing an HTML Document

YOU TRY IT

1 Open the **skills1.html** file in your browser. The page should look similar to Figure 4.13. The exact appearance of your page may vary.

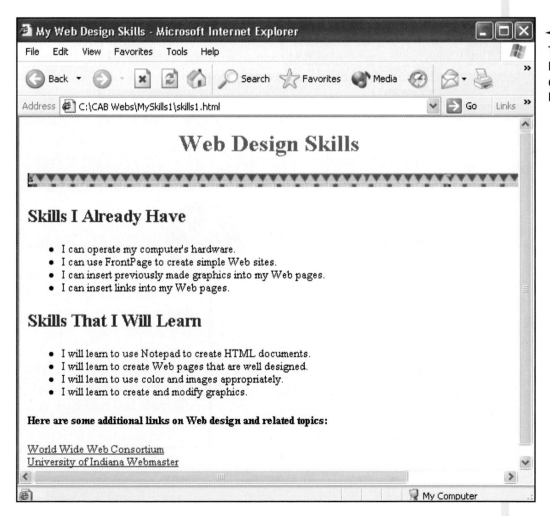

Figure 4.13
The finished Web Design Skills page as displayed in Microsoft Internet Explorer 6.0.

2 Check the following items:

- ◆ Does the text contain any spelling errors?
- ◆ Do the headings display properly?
- ◆ Does the image appear in the correct location?
- ◆ Do bullets appear in front of each item in the unordered lists?
- ◆ Does each link work properly?

3 If needed, make corrections.

4 Save the file, and test the page again.

5 Open your page in other browsers if possible. Check the items in step 2. Make any corrections.

6 Save the file, and test the page again.

7 Be sure to view the page in as many browsers as possible.

HTML AND THE W3C

The World Wide Web Consortium (W3C) releases specifications, called recommendations, on HTML. At the W3C Web site, you can read the complete specifications for the most recent version of HTML. The specifications developed by this governing body help ensure that Web designers create pages that follow specific standards and can be displayed by any browser that also follows these specifications.

Section 4.3 Assessment

Concept Check

1. **Define** text link, graphic link, anchor tag, absolute link, relative link, debugging, testing.

2. **List and describe** the two attributes that you should use with every `<img>` tag.

3. **Describe** the process of testing a Web site.

Critical Thinking

4. **Analyze Links** Does the following HTML statement contain an absolute link or a relative link? Explain your answer.
   ```
   <a href=
   "products.html">
   Product List</a>
   ```

5. **Evaluate Links** When should you use an absolute link? A relative link? Give examples and explain your choices.

Applying Skills

Insert an Image Write the HTML code to insert an image named frame.gif into a Web page. The image file is stored in the site's images folder. Center the image and include an alternate text message to display.

Ethics & Technology

RESPECTING INTELLECTUAL PROPERTY

Many people do not understand that online resources are protected by law.

The Department of Justice's Cybercrime site provides information about protecting intellectual property.

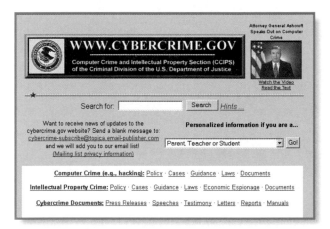

Understanding Intellectual Property

The term "intellectual property" refers to something that is a product of a person's intellect and creativity. Intellectual property can be:

◆ Text, such as books, plays, and articles
◆ Photographs and illustrations
◆ Songs
◆ Software programs

The Importance of Copyright Protection

Copyright laws guarantee a work's creator the right to determine where and how the work is used. If you download a copyrighted work without paying for it or getting permission from the copyright holder, you may be breaking the law.

Similarly, trademark laws protect "marks," such as company and product names and logos. These should never be used without their owner's consent.

Intellectual property is automatically copyrighted as soon as it is complete, but registering the work with the U.S. Government's Copyright Office secures certain rights. Trademarks are secured through the government's Trademark Office.

Using Resources Ethically

Because it is easy to copy materials from the Internet, it is easy to violate someone's copyright or trademark. Avoid this problem by following these guidelines:

◆ Never copy text or graphics from a Web site without getting permission from the original author. If you use the material, acknowledge the source.
◆ Do not copy songs through file-sharing services. This is stealing. Download only from services that compensate the songs' creators.
◆ Never copy software programs to give away or sell, and never accept a copied software program. Distributing copied software is piracy and is illegal.

You can use copyrighted materials in limited ways called "fair use." For instance, it is legal and ethical to copy small portions of a writer's work, as long as you quote the material and attribute it to its source.

Tech Focus

1. Compare and contrast copyright and trademarks?

2. What are the consequences of illegal use of digital information? How can people be convinced to use the Internet's resources legally?

Section 4.4 FrontPage versus Notepad

Guide to Reading

Main Ideas

A Web site development application allows you to create Web sites by clicking buttons instead of typing HTML commands into a text document.

Key Terms

border
embedded file

Reading Strategy

Identify the steps involved in testing a Web page. Use an organizer like the one below (also available online).

In the previous section, you used Notepad to create a single Web page named Web Design Skills. In this section, you will re-create this page using FrontPage. While both versions are composed of HTML commands, you will see that creating the page in FrontPage is much different from creating it in Notepad.

ADDING COLOR AND FORMATTING TEXT IN FRONTPAGE

A major advantage to using FrontPage is that you can see approximately how your final page will appear while you are working on it. This allows you to make adjustments, such as changing the size of a font or the color of the background, as you go.

Selecting a Background Color in FrontPage

FrontPage provides different ways for selecting background colors for Web pages. You can either enter hexadecimal numbers to select a color, or choose a color from a color hexagon. In the next activity, you will create an empty Web site and set the background color of a page in that site. This will provide the basic framework in which to build your Web site.

YOU TRY IT

ACTIVITY 4I Creating and Formatting a Page in FrontPage

❶ Start FrontPage. Click **File** menu and **New** to open the New task pane. Under New Web site, select **More Web site templates** (in FrontPage 2002, select **File>New>Page or Web>Web Site Templates**).

❷ Select **Empty Web Site** (in 2002, **Empty Web**).

❸ Browse to the location where you are storing your Web sites and open your general file. Name the new Web site **MySkills2.** Click **OK.**

─READ ME!─

Tech Tip It is common convention for path names to be indicated by a > symbol, as shown here.

 webdesign.glencoe.com

4 Click the **Create a new normal page** button. A new empty page opens. Make certain that you are in Design (in 2002, Normal) view.

5 Right-click anywhere in the page and select **Page Properties** from the Shortcut menu. The Page Properties dialog box opens. In the Title box, enter My Web Design Skills. Click **OK** to close the dialog box.

6 Click the **Format** menu and select **Background.**

7 In the Page Properties dialog box, select the **Formatting** (in 2002, **Background**) tab. Under Colors, open the drop-down list in the Background box and select **More Colors** to open the More Colors dialog box.

8 In the More Colors dialog box, position the insertion pointer in the Value box and type Hex={FF,FF,CC}, as shown in Figure 4.14. This will specify a light yellow background. (Note that you can also click on a color in the color hexagon to select a color. This is useful if you do not know the hexadecimal value of the color.)

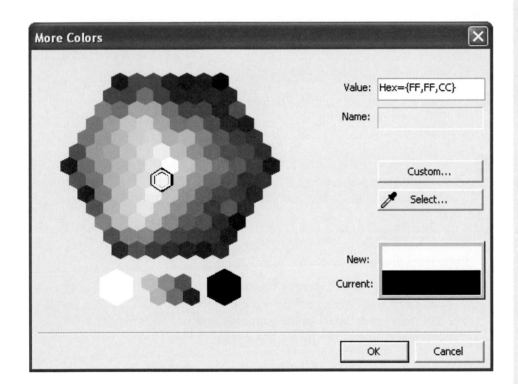

Figure 4.14
You can use the Value box or the color hexagon to select a background color for your Web site.

9 Click **OK** to close the More Colors dialog box. Click **OK** to close the Page Properties dialog box. The background of the Web page changes to light yellow.

10 Click the **Save** button on the Standard toolbar and type skills2.html in the File name box. Click **Save.**

Creating Headings and Lists in FrontPage

Because of the ease with which you can create pages in FrontPage, you will be adding both the headings and the unordered lists in a single activity. Creating an unordered list is as simple as clicking the Bullets button on the Formatting toolbar. To create an ordered list, click the Numbering button on the Formatting toolbar.

YOU TRY IT

ACTIVITY 4J Adding Headings and Unordered Lists in FrontPage

1 Make certain that the **skills2.html** page is open in Design (in 2002, Normal) view. The insertion point should appear at the top of the page. Type Web Design Skills.

2 Select the heading **Web Design Skills.** Open the Style drop-down list on the Formatting toolbar and select **Heading 1**. Click the **Center** button to center the heading.

3 Make certain that the entire heading is still selected. Open the Font Color drop-down list. Select **More Colors.** In the More Colors dialog box, change the Hex value from {00,00,00} to {66,66,FF}. Click **OK.** Position the insertion point at the end of the heading and press **Enter.**

4 Type the subheading Skills I Already Have. Select the entire subheading. Click the **Align Left** button to align the heading at the left margin. Open the Style drop-down list and select **Heading 2.**

5 Make certain that the Skills I Already Have subheading is still selected. Change the Hex value to {00,00,99}. Click **OK.** Position the insertion point at the end of the subheading and press **Enter.**

6 Click the **Bullets** button in the Formatting toolbar. Type the first bulleted item in the list below. Press **Enter** to create the next bulleted item. Continue until you have entered all the items.

> I can operate my computer's hardware.
> I can use FrontPage to create simple Web sites.
> I can insert previously made graphics into my Web pages.
> I can insert links into my Web pages.

7 The insertion point should appear on the blank line immediately below the bulleted list. Click the **Bullets** button to deselect it. Type Skills That I Will Learn for the second subheading. Select the entire subheading and repeat steps 5 and 6 to change the subheading's font color.

8 Repeat step 7 to create the bulleted list of skills that you will learn.

> I will learn to use Notepad to create HTML documents.
> I will learn to create Web pages that are well designed.
> I will learn to use color and images appropriately.
> I will learn to create and modify graphics.

9 Save your Web page.

READ ME!

Tech Tip When entering hexadecimal numbers, remember that they may contain the number zero (0). However, they will never contain the letter O.

ADDING GRAPHICS AND LINKS

In the following activity, you will again add a **border** to your page. A border is a visual break on the page. It adds visual interest and helps separate items on a page.

When you save a page in FrontPage after inserting a graphic, the program will ask you where to save embedded files. **Embedded files** are files that you have added to your FrontPage document from other applications. Examples of embedded files include graphics and word processing files.

ACTIVITY 4K Inserting a Graphic and Links in FrontPage

YOU TRY IT

Student
Data File

❶ Make certain that the **skills2.html** page is open in Design (in 2002, Normal) view. Position the insertion point at the end of the Web Design Skills heading. Press **Enter.**

❷ Click the **Insert Picture From File** button. The Picture dialog box opens. Browse to the **DataFile\Ch04\Images** folder. Click the **p_border.gif** file and then click **Insert.**

❸ Save your Web page. When the Save Embedded Files dialog box appears, click **Change Folder.** Double-click the **images** subfolder to open it and click **OK** to save the graphic file in this folder. Click **OK.**

❹ Position the insertion point at the end of the last bulleted item on your page. Press **Enter.** Click the **Bullets** button to deselect it.

❺ Click the **Bold** button on the Formatting toolbar. Open the Font Size drop-down list and select **4 (14 pt).** Type the following: Here are some additional links to Web sites with more information about Web design: **B**

❻ Press **Enter.** Open the Font Size drop-down list and select **Normal.** Click the **Bold** button to deselect it.

❼ Click the **Insert Hyperlink** button. Type World Wide Web Consortium into the Text to display box and http://www.w3.org into the Address box, as shown in Figure 4.15. Click **OK.**

● Figure 4.15
In the Insert Hyperlink dialog box, enter both the address of the hyperlink and the text to display as the link on the Web page.

❽ Press **Enter.** Click the **Insert Hyperlink** button. Type University of Indiana Webmaster into the Text to display box and http://webmaster.indiana.edu into the Address box. Click **OK.**

❾ To view the source code, switch from **Design** to **Code** view (in 2002, from **Normal** to **HTML** view). FrontPage automatically entered the HTML code you created in Notepad. Switch back to **Design** (in 2002, **Normal**) view. Save the page.

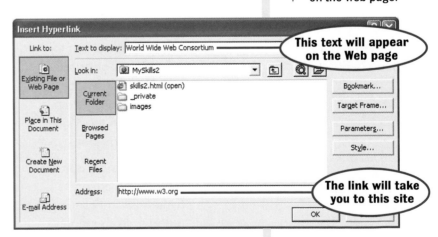

This text will appear on the Web page

The link will take you to this site

TESTING A WEB PAGE

Whether you use Notepad or FrontPage to create your HTML document, you must test your page. Carefully, proofread and spell check your Web page. Always examine your page in more than one browser to make sure each line works properly.

YOU TRY IT

ACTIVITY 4L Testing a Web Page in FrontPage

 ❶ Make certain that the **skills2.html** page is open in Design (in 2002, Normal) view. Click the **Spelling** button to spell check your page. The Spelling dialog box opens if spell check detects an error. Type the correct spelling into the Change To box and click the **Change** button.

 ❷ Click the **Print** button. Proofread and correct your page.

❸ Open the **File** menu. Choose **Preview in Browser** and select a browser to preview your page in. It should look similar to the HTML page you created earlier (turn back to Figure 4.14 on page 111).

❹ Test your hyperlinks to be sure they take you to the correct Web pages. Make certain the page components, such as the headings, bullets, and hyperlinks, display properly. View your page in different browsers.

❺ Save your Web page and close the Web site.

You now know the basic HTML coding that defines the various elements on the pages you will create. Knowing HTML will allow you to make minor changes to your pages by viewing and updating the page's source code.

Section 4.4 Assessment

Concept Check

1. **Define** border, embedded file.

2. **Describe** each alignment button available in FrontPage.

3. **Explain** how you would create an unordered list in FrontPage.

Critical Thinking

4. **Analyze** What are the advantages of using hexadecimal numbers for colors rather than the colors in the More Colors dialog box?

5. **Compare and Contrast** How was creating hyperlinks in FrontPage different from creating them in Notepad?

Applying Skills

Change Colors In FrontPage, open MySkills2. Find three colors in the hexadecimal chart in Appendix C. Enter each color in the More Colors box. Which background color looks best? Why? Do not save your changes.

SECTION 4.1 HTML Coding

Key Terms

Hypertext Markup Language
(HTML), 92
HTML tag, 92
starting tag, 92
ending tag, 92

nested tag, 93
empty tag, 93
source code, 94

Main Ideas

- HMTL tags tell the Web browser how to display a Web page's content.

- You can use tags such as <b>, <i>, and <p> to format text.

- You can nest tags within one another.

- While most tags, such as <body> </body>, are used in pairs, some tags, such as <br> and <hr>, are empty tags.

- The World Wide Web Consortium provides specifications for various Web-based technologies, including HTML.

SECTION 4.2 Using a Text Editor

Key Terms

file name extension, 97
attribute, 98

ordered list, 100
unordered list, 100

Main Ideas

- When creating a Web site, organize its files and folders so that you can easily locate various page components.

- You must save a Web page file with an .html or .htm extension so that browsers can identify it as an HTML document.

- Attributes within HTML tags specify characteristics such as background and font color and font size.

- Ordered (or numbered) lists contain sequential items, while unordered (or bulleted) lists contain items that can appear in any order.

- To view the Web page you created in a text editor, you must open it in a Web browser.

SECTION 4.3 Enhancing and Testing Your Page

Key Terms

anchor tag, 104
text link, 105
graphic link, 105
absolute link, 105

relative link, 105
debugging, 107
testing, 107

Main Ideas

- The <img> tag inserts a graphic into a page. The src attribute specifies the graphic's file location.

- The <a> tag inserts a link. The href attribute specifies the location (or object) being linked to.

- A link's anchor can be either text or an image.

- An absolute link lists the complete URL or path of the linked file. A relative link is used with local files and contains only a partial URL or folder location.

- You must test a newly created Web page in several browsers to make certain it displays properly and all of its links work correctly.

SECTION 4.4 FrontPage versus Notepad

Key Terms

border, 113

embedded file, 113

Main Ideas

- A Web page that was created using Notepad can also be created using FrontPage.

- Because FrontPage provides a WYSIWYG editor, you do not need to enter HTML tags.

- You can use the Page Properties dialog box to set a page's background color.

- You can apply styles to text, such as font color and font size, to change its appearance.

- You can insert graphics and links by entering the Web page or file location into a dialog box.

- Careful proofreading and testing are a vital part of creating a Web page.

Reviewing Key Terms

1. Which of the following is NOT an HTML tag:

   a. `<img>`   **c.** `<alt`

   b. `</p>`   **d.** `<body>`

2. Explain how nested tags are different from empty tags.

3. What is the purpose of an attribute?

4. Describe the tag sets that are used to create ordered and unordered lists.

5. Rewrite this statement to make it true:
   When a link statement contains the complete URL of the site being linked to, it will create a relative link.

Understanding Main Ideas

6. **Describe** the basic structure of an HTML document.

7. **Discuss** the purpose of the `<title>` tag.

8. **Explain** the need for starting and ending tags.

9. **Identify** which of the following is NOT a way of formatting text:

   a. placing it in italics

   b. spell checking it

   c. centering it

   d. increasing its size

10. **Explain** the difference between an unordered list and an ordered list.

11. **Discuss** why you should include the `alt` attribute when creating an `<img>` statement.

12. **Explain** the difference between testing a Web page and debugging it.

13. **Summarize** how Web browsers read spacing and case sensitivity in HTML documents.

Critical Thinking

14. **Analyze HTML** The W3C Web site states that "HTML is the common language for publishing on the World Wide Web." What does this statement mean?

15. **Evaluate Applications** Create a table with two columns labeled "Notepad" and "FrontPage." In the first column, list any advantages you found when creating a Web page in Notepad. In the second column, list any advantages you found when creating the same Web page in FrontPage. Below the table, write a few sentences summarizing what you discovered.

16. **Predict Outcomes** A Web site's image files are stored in the images folder. What would happen if you created a link to an image file that was not stored in the images folder?

17. **Write HTML** Write the HTML code to display the following sentences:

> The American flag is **red**, white, and **blue**. It has *thirteen stripes* and *fifty stars*.

Make sure your sentences are formatted as shown. Add a background color to your page so all the text will display properly.

e-Review
webdesign.glencoe.com

Study with PowerPoint
To review the main points in this chapter select **e-Review** > **PowerPoint Outlines** > **Chapter 4**.

Online Self Check
Test your knowledge of the material in this chapter by selecting **e-Review** > **Self Checks** > **Chapter 4**.

Making Connections

Language Arts–Research and Write a Report
Time Magazine Online voted Tim Berners-Lee (the creator of HTML) into the category of the top 100 Thinkers and Scientists.

Research the contributions that Berners-Lee has made to the development of the Web. Then, write a two-page paper on how his work has changed the world we live in.

STANDARDS AT WORK

Students use a variety of media and formats to communicate information and ideas effectively to multiple audiences. (NETS-S 4)

Create an HTML Quick Reference Table
Create a quick reference guide for your computer lab or classroom. The guide should describe common HTML tags and should include an example showing how each tag is used.

Make of list of tags to be included. Organize the tags into the following categories:

- Structure
- Headings (assume six levels of headings)
- Paragraph and character formats
- Lists (both ordered and unordered)
- Links (absolute and relative)
- Images

Create a table similar to the one below. If you have word processing software, use the table feature. Proofread your work carefully.

Tag Name	Description	Example
Structure		
`<html>...</html>`		

With your teacher's permission, prepare several copies of the reference table for your computer lab or classroom.

TEAMWORK SKILLS

Create Web Design Biographies
With your teacher's permission, gather the following information from each member of your team:

- Name
- E-mail address
- A short biography

As a team, use HTML to create a Web page that includes this information. Separate each team member's information with a horizontal rule.

As your team selects background and font colors, font sizes, and so on, write a specification sheet describing the formats you have chosen. This specification sheet will help you in the future as you build and improve the page.

CHALLENGE YOURSELF

Create a Table Using HTML
Type the following code in Notepad.

```
<table height="200" border="2">
<tr>
<td width="100" height="200">
<p><b><font size="2">Width 100 x
Height 200 </font></b></p></td>
<td width="100" height="200"
bgcolor="#ff00ff"></td>
<td width="350" height="200"><h3>
<font color="#cc0000">
Width 350 x Height 200
</font></h3></td>
</tr>
</table>
```

Save the code and view the results in a browser. Change the text in the first and third cells. View the changes in a browser.

YOU TRY IT

Skills Studio

These exercises reinforce the skills you learned in this chapter's You Try It activities. Refer back to the You Try It activities if you need extra guidance.

1. Creating a Home Page Using HTML

Create a home page using HTML that lists three books you have read and would recommend for others to read.

Ⓐ Create a folder named **Books_Read**. Use Notepad to create a basic HTML document. The page's main head will be "Books I Recommend."

Ⓑ Save the file as **index.htm** in the **Books_Read** folder.

Ⓒ Create an unordered list of the three books that you have read.

Ⓓ Select appropriate colors for the background and fonts. Change fonts as needed.

Ⓔ Save your page.

Ⓕ View the results in a browser. Make any changes needed. View the results after making the changes.

2. Creating a Links Page Using HTML

Create a second page that will link to your home page.

Ⓐ Use Notepad to create a second page titled "Book Summaries." Save the file as **links.htm** in the **Books_Read** folder.

Ⓑ List each book's title as a heading. Type a brief paragraph summarizing each book. Select appropriate colors for the background and fonts. Change fonts as needed. Save your page.

Ⓒ Open the **index.htm** page. Add relative links to the **links.htm** page. Use the following format:

```
<a href="links.htm">book title</a>
```

Ⓓ Open the **index.htm** page in the browser. Test all links, making changes as needed.

Web Design Projects

1. Create a Home Page Using HTML

You have been assigned to develop a Web site for a cross-cultural travel club. You decide that the club's home page will have a light yellow background with a large red heading that reads: Cross-Cultural Travel Club. You plan to add a travel-related image to the page. The page also will contain a short sentence describing the club's purpose and an unordered list highlighting the following upcoming events:

◆ **Meeting:** Wednesday, October 5 from 3:30 to 5:00 p.m., *Xavier Jiminez* as guest speaker

◆ **Meeting:** Wednesday October 19 from 3:30 to 5:00 p.m., *Barbara Lin* to show slides of her trip to Taiwan

Create the page using HTML (you can use FrontPage as your text editor). Test the page in a browser and make any changes to improve the look of the page. Also print the final HTML code for your page.

2. Add Pages in FrontPage

Use FrontPage to add a Meetings page to your cross-cultural travel club Web site. The Meetings page should have a light green background. On the Meetings page:

◆ Add a large heading in red:
CROSS-CULTURAL TRAVEL CLUB CALENDAR

◆ Find an appropriate graphic for this page and insert it below the main heading.

◆ Add the subheading: **Meeting:** Wednesday, October 5 from 3:30 to 5:00 p.m. *Xavier Jiminez* will talk about a conversation he had with his grandmother from *Guatemala.* He will describe the village where she was born, the life of the people there, and her experiences after moving to a large city in the United States.

◆ Add the subheading: **Meeting:** Wednesday, October 19 from 3:30 to 5:00 p.m. *Barbara Lin* will present a slide show on *Taiwan.* She will talk about her experiences on this trip and her visit with her parents' relatives. She will show slides of the major cities as well as the countryside.

Add a link from each event on the Cross-Cultural Travel Club home page to the Meetings page. On the Meetings page, add a link to the government sites for Guatemala and Taiwan. Test the site in a browser and make any necessary changes.

Building 21st Century Skills

Critical Thinking: Evaluate Technology Resources

A friend is starting a graphic design business. She asks you to recommend a computer that she can use for her business. In particular, she needs a computer that:

◆ is portable, so she can take it on client visits.
◆ has a lot of memory to support graphics software and other programs.
◆ has a hard drive with a large capacity.
◆ can function without wires.
◆ is made by a well-known, reliable manufacturer.

1. Use the Web or catalogs to research products that meet your friend's requirements.

2. Prepare a table like the one below to organize your research. List the information for three computers, each from a different manufacturer.

MANUFACTURER	MODEL #	PRICE	FEATURES	OPTIONAL FEATURES

3. Recommend one computer to your friend and give reasons for your choice.

Use Technology Tools: Create a Web Page Using HTML

Use HTML to create a Web page called Reference Web Sites for Online Research. Include the following elements on your page:

◆ A page title
◆ A graphic
◆ An unordered list of three Web sites that you frequently use to research school projects online

When planning and creating your Web page, follow these steps:

1. Choose colors for your page, including the background color and the font colors. Choose appropriate font sizes.

2. Select a graphic element such as a border that will work on your page.

3. Plan the content for your page. Write a short description of each research site you have chosen. Note why you think each site is a reliable resource.

4. Write the HTML code for the page. Include a link to each research site.

5. View your completed page in a browser. Check spelling and proofread your page. Test your links. Revise the HTML code to correct errors as needed.

6. Have a peer review your finished Web page, and revise your page as needed.

Building Your Portfolio

Create a Community Web Site

The Internet can be a powerful tool for social change. In 1997, Jody Williams won a Nobel Prize for her work to outlaw land mines. Using e-mails and the World Wide Web, she organized citizen's groups around the world and helped forge a coalition among the world's nations.

Select a community or national issue that is important to you. Create a one page Web site that tells other teens about this issue, and lets them know what actions they can take to become more involved.

When creating your Web site, follow these steps:

1. Plan the site's content. Research the issue using reliable resources. Try to locate different perspectives on the issue and identify possible solutions.

2. Summarize your research. Describe the issue and how it affects your community, the nation, or the world. Include a list of steps that your audience can take to address the issue. You will include this information on your Web site, so be brief.

3. Write down the URLs of links where people can learn more about the issue.

Community Web Site

Summary of the Issue

Steps to Address the Issue

Learn More About the Issue

- Link
- Link
- Link

4. Use FrontPage to create a one page Web site about your issue. On this site, include:

   ◆ the summary of your research
   ◆ the list of steps needed to address the issue
   ◆ links to sites related to the issue

5. Select appropriate background and font colors for your site. Add a graphic such as a border to the site.

6. Test your site in a browser. Be sure to test all the hyperlinks. Spell check and proofread the site and make changes as needed.

7. Optional (with your teacher's permission)—publish the finished Web site on your school or class Web site.

8. For your portfolio, include a screen shot and an electronic copy of your finished product.

UNIT

2

Designing Web Sites

 Visit *Glencoe Online*

Go to this book's Web site at webdesign.glencoe.com.

Click on **Unit Activities** and select **Unit 2 Internet Research Tips.** Practice skills and strategies that will help you quickly find what you are looking for on the Internet.

Think About It

Know Your Strengths!
Building a Web site requires many different talents and strengths. You will find that some aspects of Web design are easy for you while others may be hard. Knowing what you enjoy doing can help focus your learning of new or difficult tasks.

Evaluate Yourself Activity
Write down the top two tasks you have enjoyed most during your study of Web design so far. Then, write down your two least favorite tasks. What characteristics do the tasks you enjoy have in common? How are these different from your least favorite tasks?

Planning a Web Site

YOU WILL LEARN TO...

WHY IT MATTERS.....................................

Benjamin Franklin wrote, "By failing to prepare, you are preparing to fail." Planning is always the first step in any successful project. Failing to plan can lead to wasted time, wasted resources, and wasted energy. Developing a Web site is a lot like planning a road trip. Where do you want to "go" first? What is your final destination? How many stops along the way can you afford?

Quick Write Activity

President Dwight Eisenhower once said, "Plans are nothing, but planning is everything." What do you think he meant by that? In what way is the process of planning a Web site be more important than the actual plan for the Web site?

WHAT YOU WILL DO ....

ACTIVITIES AND PROJECTS

Applying Skills

You Try It Activities

Chapter Assessment

You Try It Skills Studio

Web Design Projects

IN THE WORKBOOK

Optional Activities and Projects

Guided Reading
Web Design Projects

ON THE WEB

Activities at webdesign.glencoe.com

Reading Strategy Organizers
Go Online Activities
Study with PowerPoint
Self-Check Assessments

READ TO SUCCEED

Reading for a Purpose
Just as the author's purpose helped him or her determine what content to put in and what to leave out, your purpose for reading helps you decide what is most important to remember. Write down and complete this sentence for each section *before* you read: My purpose for reading this section is to _____. (Hint: You may want to use each section's Guide to Reading and the colored headings to help you finish the sentence.)

Guide to Reading

Main Ideas

Before you create a Web site, you should identify the purpose and audience of the site. Once these are known, you will be able to write a mission statement for your site.

Key Terms

mission statement
target audience

Reading Strategy

Identify the steps in planning a Web site. Use a flowchart like the one below (also available online).

Determine Purpose and Goals ⟹ ☐ ⟹ ☐

How you design your Web site depends upon your purpose and your audience. To clarify why you are creating a Web site, you should create a **mission statement,** a brief statement that describes the purpose and audience of your Web site.

DETERMINING PURPOSE AND GOALS

Before you create a Web site, consider the site's purpose and goals. For example, determine whether your site informs, entertains, serves as a Web portal (such as a search site or a directory of links), addresses a particular group of people (such as hobbyists, activists, employees, or customers), provides a personality profile (such as a personal page or résumé), or fulfills another specific purpose.

Identifying Your Purpose

To determine the purpose of your site, ask yourself the following questions:

◆ Why do I want a Web site?
◆ What are my immediate goals for the Web site?
◆ What are my long-term goals for the Web site?
◆ What is my budget?
◆ What is my time line?

Thinking about the answers to these questions will help you determine goals that you can work toward. For example, how might your long-term goals vary from your immediate ones? Suppose you develop a site for a local theater. When you first develop the site, it might simply provide a list of upcoming plays. However, over the next year, you might expand it to include a synopsis of each play, biographies of the actors, and even allow visitors to purchase tickets online.

Refining Your Topic

After you define the overall goal of your site, consider whether the goal can be reasonably achieved. If your topic is too broad, your site will lack

 webdesign.glencoe.com

focus. For example, imagine you decide to create a site that contains information about pets. Pets is a broad topic. You could narrow your goal further by providing information about the care and feeding of pet lizards.

DETERMINING THE AUDIENCE

After you have outlined the goals for your site, determine who will be your target audience. Your **target audience** includes all of the people that you want to visit your Web site. You need to consider your target audience early in the planning process because the content and design should appeal to them. To help analyze your audience, answer the questions presented in Table 5.1.

Identifying a Target Audience

Question	Purpose
Who is my target audience?	Be as specific as possible when defining your audience, including the typical age group. Age specifics, or demographics, can help you determine the information you will include on your Web site.
Who am I?	Determine how you want to present yourself to your target audience. Do you want to present yourself as professional or casual? Choosing how you want to communicate with your audience can prevent inappropriate content or design decisions.
What does my target audience already know about my topic?	Defining an audience's knowledge base will help determine how general or specific the information will be that you provide. If the audience knows nothing about a topic, then you need to provide introductory information. If most of your audience knows a lot about your topic, then consider what specific information you can provide that they will find useful and interesting.
What does my target audience want to learn from my site?	Consider what your target audience wants or needs to know about your topic. If possible, try to talk to potential visitors and include information that meets their needs.
How will my target audience access my site?	Think about how a typical person within your audience will access your site. Does your intended audience use high-bandwidth networks, dial-up connections, or a combination of both? You want to create a site that everyone in your audience can access and use easily.

Table 5.1
Identifying your target audience can help you determine what content you want to include on your site. Why is it important to consider how people will access your site?

WRITING A MISSION STATEMENT

Once you have determined your Web site's purpose and target audience, you are ready to write your mission statement. Creating a mission statement helps you determine what content is essential to your Web site. Refer to your mission statement frequently as you continue the planning and development process. This will encourage you to stay "on target."

To demonstrate this process, we will use the Garden Company Web site that you examined earlier in Chapter 1. This site provides information about the Garden Company's products and services. Assume that this Web site has not yet been developed and it is our job to build it. To create a mission statement, ask yourself a series of questions like those listed below. Your answers to these questions will help you develop the mission statement shown in Figure 5.1.

◆ **What is the purpose of the Web site?** The site will provide general information about gardening, along with specific information about products and classes offered by the Garden Company.

◆ **What are the site's immediate goals?** The site will answer visitor questions, supply general gardening information, and provide information about the Garden Company's location and its products and services.

◆ **What are the site's long-term goals?** The goal is to expand the gardening information offered at the site and to allow visitors to make online purchases.

◆ **Who is the target audience and what are they looking for?** The audience consists of anyone interested in gardening. This could include anyone from beginners to seasoned gardeners. Most of the audience will be adults who will access the site from home. Graphics should be kept simple to speed up download time and accommodate dial-up connections.

Figure 5.1
A mission statement helps you remember the purpose of the site as you develop it. How might the mission statement differ if the Garden Company was developing a site to sell plants to other garden centers?

Garden Company Mission Statement

The Garden Company Web site will promote the hobby of gardening by providing useful gardening information and will encourage customers to visit the Garden Company's store by describing the products and services available there.

YOU TRY IT

YOU TRY IT 5A Creating a Mission Statement

❶ At the top of a page, write or type this title: Astronomy Club Mission Statement.

2 Use the information in Table 5.2 and write a mission statement below the title. The statement should be relatively short (less than 50 words).

Astronomy Club Purpose and Audience

Question	Answer
Who is the audience?	High-school students, members and nonmembers of the club.
What does the audience already know about this topic?	The level of knowledge varies. Some individuals are new to the subject.
What does the audience want to find out from the site?	Meeting times, locations, and topics. Upcoming guest speakers and fundraisers.
How will the audience access the site?	The site will be accessed from the school's high-speed Internet connection, or from home, where most students have dial-up connections.

Table 5.2
The Astronomy Club Web site is being developed for high school students.

3 Proofread the mission statement. If you are using word processing software, use the spell check tool.

4 Save your document to use later. If using word processing software, name the file Astronomy Mission. Ask your teacher where to save the file.

Section 5.1 Assessment

Concept Check

1. **Define** mission statement, target audience.

2. **Explain** why it is often necessary to refine a Web site's topic when planning a site.

3. **List** four things you should know about the audience to write a mission statement.

Critical Thinking

4. **Analyze Goals** How might the immediate goals of the Astronomy Club Web site be different from its long-term goals?

5. **Compare and Contrast** How would a movie Web site for very young children differ from a movie site for teenagers?

Applying Skills

Write a Mission Statement Write a mission statement for a Web site you would like to develop for one of your hobbies. Describe the purpose of your Web site and your target audience.

WEB DESIGNERS

Most Web designers are involved in creating the look and feel of a Web site. They are concerned with page layout, color themes, and graphic elements. Web designers are often part of a development team that includes experts in graphics, markup languages, programming, multimedia, networking, or databases.

Complex Web sites, like the CNN site, have features that require the efforts of a large team of professional designers.

Interface Design

One of the designer's most important tasks is creating the Web site's interface. The interface contains the navigation tools and information that make the site attractive and interactive. To build an interface, the designer creates and positions each tool, icon, and menu, making sure that it looks and works right.

E-Commerce Design

Usability is the key to any Web site. This is especially true for e-commerce sites, such as Amazon.com or eBay. If you want to buy something, you caneasily find information about it, check prices, and order it. If a Web site makes any of these steps difficult, you will probably do your shopping elsewhere.

Security is another challenge facing e-commerce Web designers. Customer information must always be kept safe. Designers may work with security specialists to integrate security technology into the site. Designers may also need to work with constantly changing databases of information about products, prices, and customers.

Game Design

Game designers are responsible for developing a game's objectives and rules. They also design characters and scenery, and determine how players interact with the game.

Programming is usually not required of Web designers, but they should at least understand technologies such as Macromedia Flash and Shockwave. Game designers often work with programmers and graphic artists to create an exciting multimedia experience.

Preparing for a Career in Web Design

To qualify for an entry-level job in Web design, you should have graphic design experience and basic knowledge of Web design tools and languages such as HTML, DHTML, and XML. Successful designers work well as part of a team. Many colleges and technical schools offer certification and degree programs in Web design or related fields.

Tech Focus

1. What education and training would you need to be a Web designer?

2. Find a postsecondary school that offers a program that fits your career plans. Create a multimedia presentation showing how education fits into your career path.

Section 5.2 Navigation Schemes

Guide to Reading

Main Ideas

Navigation schemes define the structure for Web sites. The navigation scheme should enhance the purpose of the site and help visitors find the information they seek.

Key Terms

navigation scheme
hierarchical navigation scheme
top-level page
parent-child relationship
peer-to-peer relationship
linear navigation scheme
random-access navigation scheme

Reading Strategy

Compare and contrast the hierarchical and linear navigation schemes. Use a Venn diagram like the one below (also available online).

In the early days of Web design, designers often began building a Web site by creating the individual Web pages that they needed. Once the pages were done, they were linked together. As sites became larger and more complex, they often became disorganized and difficult to navigate. Web designers soon realized that they needed to plan the relationships among a site's pages before building the site.

TYPES OF NAVIGATION SCHEMES

The plan that determines how Web pages will relate to each other within a Web site is often referred to as a **navigation scheme.** Once you have written the mission statement, you can begin to determine how your Web site will be structured. A Web site's structure should support the site's purpose and appeal to its target audience. As discussed in Chapter 1, developing a site's navigation scheme is part of interaction design. When choosing a navigation scheme, think about how visitors will interact with your site. Will your visitors go directly to specific topics or will they access the pages sequentially? Viewing your site from the audience's perspective can help you develop a site it will enjoy using.

There are many different navigation schemes:

♦ The hierarchical navigation scheme is used by the majority of Web sites.

♦ The linear navigation scheme is often used with a hierarchical scheme.

♦ The random-access navigation scheme is rarely used.

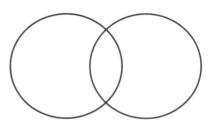

Activity 5.1 Explore Navigation Schemes Learn more about different navigation schemes by visiting the book's Web site at **webdesign.glencoe.com.**

Hierarchical Navigation Scheme

In a **hierarchical navigation scheme,** pages are arranged in levels from top to bottom. At the topmost level is the Web site's home page. The home page contains links to the second-level pages below it. In turn, these second-level pages contain links to third-level pages. A hierarchical site can contain as many page levels as needed to present the site's content. As you move down the chart, the pages at lower levels typically contain increasingly specific information related to the Web site's topic. Figure 5.2 illustrates how the Web pages in a hierarchical site can be organized.

Figure 5.2
Web pages in a hierarchical scheme are arranged in levels. Which page is always at the topmost level in a hierarchical navigation scheme?

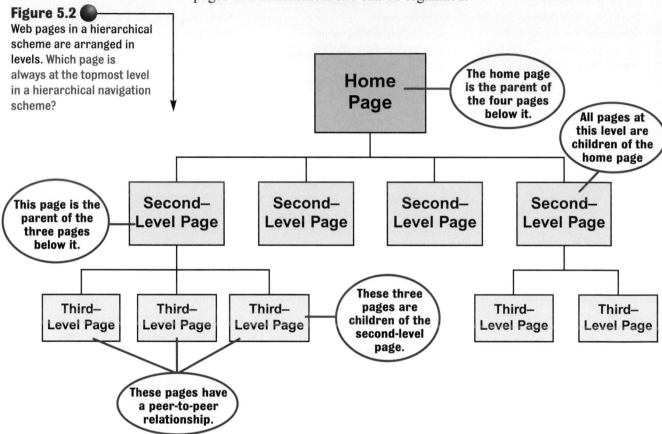

Relationships in the Hierarchical Scheme A hierarchical site's home page is often referred to as a **top-level page** because it is at the highest level in the structure. Pages that are all on the same level are often referred to as same-level pages. As shown in Figure 5.2, you can access any of the second-level pages from the home page. However, you can only access third-level pages from a second-level page.

A page that is connected to a page one level below has a **parent-child relationship** with that page. In this relationship, the page that is on the level above is the parent, and the page that is on the level below is the child. A parent may have many children, but in a hierarchical scheme, each child may have only one parent. Two or more child pages with the same parent have a **peer-to-peer relationship,** also called a "sibling" relationship. These relationships are shown in Figure 5.2.

A hierarchical navigation scheme can also be thought of as an upside down tree, with the home page being the main trunk and each of the subsequent pages creating its branches. These branches can create their own subtrees. A subtree is one part of the larger tree that consists of a parent and its children (and any subsequent children below them).

Advantages of a Hierarchical Site The hierarchical navigation scheme has specific advantages. Visitors can get a site overview quickly by examining the home page. Once visitors know what type of information the site contains, they can select the pages they want to see. Visitors can choose pages that cover particular material in more detail, and skip those pages that do not interest them. This freedom to "click around" allows them to avoid becoming overwhelmed by irrelevant information. This scheme also makes it relatively easy for visitors to keep track of where they are on the site.

Linear Navigation Scheme

In a **linear navigation scheme,** every page exists at the same level. Each Web page in this scheme is accessed from the previous page and then is linked to the next page. When we read a book, we read in linear order. A visitor navigates a linear site in the same way, moving through a line of pages, one after another.

Advantages of a Linear Site Like the hierarchical scheme, the linear scheme typically has a single home page that the visitor must access first (see Figure 5.3). However, unlike the hierarchical scheme, the visitor then must access each page in a specific order. There are situations in which a linear scheme is useful. For example, if you created a Web site in which you listed the steps in making cinnamon rolls, you might use a linear structure. To make the rolls, it would be necessary to begin with the first step and continue on until the last step was reached.

● **Figure 5.3**
The linear navigational scheme directs visitors to view the site page by page. What page do visitors view first when they use a linear site?

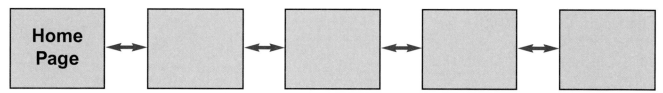

Combination Schemes Many Web sites use both hierarchical and linear navigation schemes. For example, a Web site containing photographs from a vacation might let the visitor go directly to a specific photo (hierarchical), or it may let the visitor see the photos in the order in which they were taken (linear).

Random-Access Navigation Scheme

In a **random-access navigation scheme,** the pages are not organized in any particular order. They are linked randomly to each other. This scheme makes it difficult for visitors to locate what they need quickly, especially in a Web site of any significant size. Therefore, the random-access scheme is not used by professional Web designers.

VIEWING A WEB SITE'S NAVIGATION SCHEME

The Garden Company Web site uses a hierarchical structure. In You Try It Activity 5B, you will use FrontPage's Navigation view to examine the navigation structure of this Web site.

YOU TRY IT 5B Viewing a Web Site in Navigation View

1 Open FrontPage, and then open the Garden Company Web site. It is located in the DataFile\Examples\GardenCo folder.

2 If the Folder List pane is open on the left side of the screen, click the **Toggle Pane** button on the Standard toolbar to close it. You can close the Task Pane (if it is open) to get more viewing room.

3 Click the **View** menu and select **Navigation.** FrontPage displays the Navigation toolbar and the navigation structure of the Garden Company Web site. In 2003, the Navigation toolbar appears at the top of the Navigation view window, as shown in Figure 5.4 (in 2002, the Navigation toolbar appears under the Formatting toolbar).

Figure 5.4
The Garden Company Web site is shown in Navigation View.

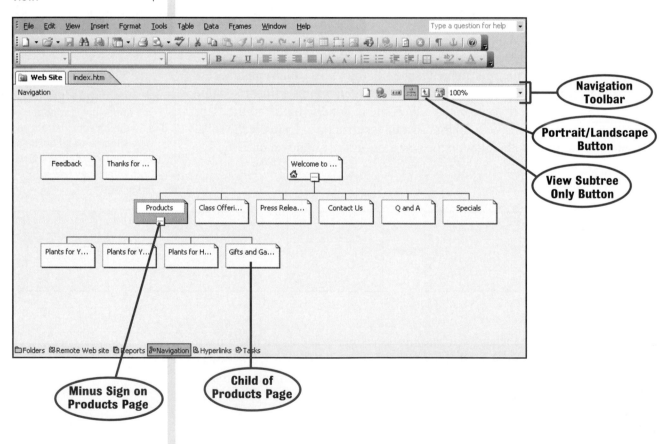

4 Locate the Products page box. You will see either a plus (+) or a minus (−) sign at the bottom of this box. Click whichever sign is there. Clicking a plus sign will open the Products subtree. This subtree contains all of the Products page's children, as shown in Figure 5.5. Clicking a minus sign will close the subtree. Practice opening and closing the subtree. When you are done, leave the subtree open.

⑤ Click the **Products** page to select it. On the Navigation toolbar, click the **View Subtree Only** button. Only the Products subtree should be displayed, as shown in Figure 5.5.

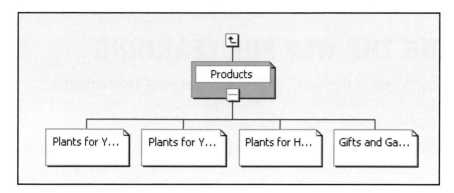

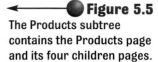

● Figure 5.5
The Products subtree contains the Products page and its four children pages.

⑥ Click the **View Subtree Only** button again to go back to displaying the entire Web site.

⑦ On the Navigation toolbar, click the **Portrait/Landscape** button. The orientation of the chart is changed. Click the button again to return to Landscape orientation. Close the Web site and exit FrontPage.

┌─*READ ME!*─┐

Tech Tip Individual page titles may be "cut off" when you view a Web site in Navigation view. If you position the mouse pointer over a specific page, the ScreenTip displays the Web page's complete title.

Section **5.2** Assessment

Concept Check

1. **Define** navigation scheme, hierarchical navigation scheme, top-level page, parent-child relationship, peer-to-peer relationship, linear navigation scheme, random-access navigation scheme.

2. **List** two factors to consider when choosing a navigation scheme for a Web site.

Critical Thinking

3. **Draw Conclusions** Can a Web page be both a parent page and a child page? Explain your answer.

4. **Compare and Contrast** Explain the similarities and differences between a hierarchical and a linear navigation scheme.

Applying Skills

Create a Hierarchical Chart Assume you have read seven books in the past month. Four were fiction and three were non-fiction. Create a chart that places the books you have read into a hierarchical structure. Include the titles of all seven books in your chart.

USING THE WEB FOR LEARNING

People have been studying at home for decades by using mail, educational television, audiotapes, and videotapes. The term "distance learning," however, has only recently become commonplace, thanks to the growth of the Internet.

Many companies use distance learning to train their employees.

Uses for Distance Learning

Distance learning refers to education that takes place outside the classroom. Technology makes it possible to take classes from home or nearby computer centers. People can use distance learning to take a single course or even earn college degrees or technical certifications.

Many companies use computer-based training (CBT) and Web-based training (WBT) to teach workers about their products, policies, and customers. This option allows busy professionals to train from the own desks and study at their own pace.

The Internet also brings the classroom to people who cannot easily attend classes. This is especially true for people who live in rural areas, who work during regular class times, or who are homebound due to health or transportation problems.

Distance-Learning Technologies

The most common technologies used for distance learning are:

◆ **The Internet** The Internet allows students to register for a class, view prerecorded or live lectures, complete assignments, interact with teachers and other students, and take tests.

◆ **Videoconferences** Videoconferencing provides a "virtual classroom" where students can gather online. Using microphones, video cameras, and software, students and teachers can see and hear each other to participate in real-time lectures and discussions online.

◆ **E-Mail** Students can use e-mail to participate in discussions, receive homework assignments, and deliver completed assignments to the instructor.

◆ **Chat** Many schools set up private, Web-based chat rooms for students and teachers to engage in real-time instant message sharing.

◆ **Discs** Computer-based training uses compact discs (CD-Roms) or digital video discs (DVDs). CBT programs can offer customized study for each student, and provide feedback on student performance. Many printed textbooks have companion discs that act as CBT, offering online tests and other features.

Tech Focus

1. Research how people around the world benefit from distance-learning technologies. Prepare a report about your findings.

2. Use the Internet to find two schools that offer classes through distance learning. Compare the courses, costs, and types of technologies used by each school.

Section 5.3 Storyboarding Your Site

Guide to Reading

Main Ideas

Storyboarding your site includes drawing a chart illustrating its navigation structure and creating sketches of what content the main pages will include. These graphics provide a basic overview of the site you will create.

Key Terms

storyboard
page name
file name

Reading Strategy

Identify the two processes involved in storyboarding. Under each process, list one fact about the process. Use a diagram like the one below (also available online).

STORYBOARDING

Many Web design professionals use storyboarding when they are designing a Web site. A **storyboard** is a visual representation of the Web site. Storyboarding involves illustrating your organizational ideas by roughly sketching the relationships among elements on each page, as well as the relationships among the Web site's pages. This process helps Web designers determine whether their ideas will work well before they begin creating the actual pages. Storyboarding has a number of advantages:

- It helps you visualize the basic structure of the Web site.
- It graphically illustrates the links between individual Web pages.
- It provides a brief look at the contents of each Web page.

Not everyone approaches storyboarding in the same way. Some use formal drawing tools to create their storyboards. Others use presentation software to create a working model of the site. Many Web designers, however, find it most helpful to sketch their concepts with paper and pencil.

Two tasks need to be accomplished during the storyboarding process. One is to identify the navigation structure of the site using one of the navigational schemes discussed in Section 5.2. The other is to create a brief summary of each page's contents.

DRAWING A WEB SITE'S NAVIGATION STRUCTURE

To develop the navigation structure of the Astronomy Club Web site, we need a list of its major pages. A basic list of the Web site's pages is contained

GO Online

Activity 5.2 Storyboarding a Web Site Learn more about various storyboarding methods by visiting the book's Web site at **webdesign.glencoe.com**.

TECH TRIVIA

Origins of Storyboarding
The term storyboarding originally came from the film industry. Film makers use storyboards to visualize how each frame of a film will look before it is shot.

Table 5.3

Astronomy Club Web Site Pages

Page Name	Brief Description
Home	Welcomes the visitor and serves as a jumping-off point to other pages
About Us	Describes the purpose of the club and lists its officers
Meetings & Activities	Lists meetings and other special activities, such as lectures
Sky Guide	Contains information (and possibly photos) on the nine planets, with a separate subpage for each item
Astronomy Links	Links to related astronomy sites

in Table 5.3. At this point in the process, these page titles and descriptions are tentative. We are merely trying to get a basic idea of the pages the Web site will contain. As we continue, we may find it necessary to add additional pages, or perhaps combine two pages into one.

Charting the Astronomy Club Web Site

The Astronomy Club Web site will have a hierarchical structure, which will make it easy for users to access the information. For example, if a visitor is only interested in finding out the time of the next meeting, he or she can go directly to the Meetings & Activities page. In You Try It Activity 5C, you will chart the hierarchical structure of this site.

YOU TRY IT

YOU TRY IT 5C Charting Navigation Structure

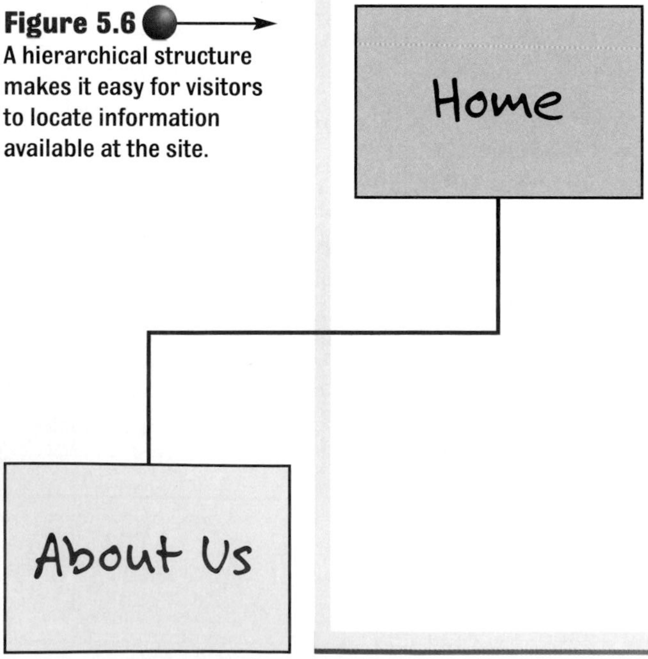

Figure 5.6
A hierarchical structure makes it easy for visitors to locate information available at the site.

Home

About Us

❶ At the top of a page, write or type Astronomy Club Site Navigation Structure in large type. This is the title of your chart.

❷ Create a chart that shows the structure of the proposed Astronomy Club site. It should use a hierarchical structure with the home page at the top. Figure 5.6 shows part of this chart. Be sure to include each page's name in the corresponding box and to draw lines showing the relationships among the pages.

❸ Add subpages under the Sky Guide page. Write appropriate page names for these subpages.

❹ Proofread your chart. Save your document for later use. If you are using word processing software, save your document under the name Astronomy Chart. Ask your teacher where you should save your document.

Page Names Versus File Names

You have now determined the major pages for the Astronomy Club site. At this point, it is a good idea to think of appropriate names for your files. In your navigation chart, you specified the title of each page. However, the file in which each page is stored must also be specified.

Choosing a Page Name A page name is not the same thing as a file name. A Web page's **page name** appears in the title bar when the page is displayed in a browser. The terms *page name* and *page title* can be used interchangeably.

You should choose logical names for your pages—names that visitors will understand when they notice it on the title bar. For example, a name like change_password.htm would suggest that users should go to this page if they want to change their password.

Page names should be short and descriptive, and you should be consistent with your naming scheme. For instance, on a Web site about Shakespeare's plays, you name one of the pages Hamlet.htm. To be consistent, you should name a second page MacBeth.htm and not, for example, ScottishPlay.htm or Tragedy2.htm.

Choosing a File Name A **file name** is the name of the HTML document that makes up the Web page itself. When choosing file names, try to select names that make sense and are easy to remember. For example, assume that you are creating a library's site that contains thousands of pages. It would be difficult to find the file that corresponds to the book *Emma* if that book's Web file was named x52h61aw.htm. A file name such as Emma.htm would make it much easier to locate that book's file.

Use Save As instead of Save when you first save your Web page, and select a good file name. As you know, each file name must have an .htm or .html extension so that Web browsers will recognize it as an HTML page. In addition, you should keep file names short, and omit blanks.

Page names and file names usually are not the same. For example, in the Astronomy Club Web site, the home page will have the file name index.htm. Table 5.4 contains a list of the file names for the individual pages in this Web site.

READ ME!

Read Me Jargon A Web page's page name appears in the Web browser when users view the page. A Web page's file name, on the other hand, is the name of the HTML document that makes up that Web page. A Web page's page name usually differs from its file name.

Astronomy Club Page Names and File Names

Page Name	File Name
Home	index.htm
About Us	about_us.htm
Meetings & Activities	meetings.htm
Sky Guide	sky_guide.htm
Astronomy Links	links.htm
Mars, Neptune, Saturn, and so on	mars.htm, neptune.htm, saturn.htm, and so on

Table 5.4
Specify the file names for your Web pages so that you will have a record of file names used in the site. How is a page name different from a file name?

YOU TRY IT 5D Specifying File Names

❶ Insert the file name assigned to each page on the Astronomy Club navigation chart. Write the file name under the page title, as shown in Figure 5.7.

Figure 5.7
You can keep track of file names by recording them in your navigation chart.

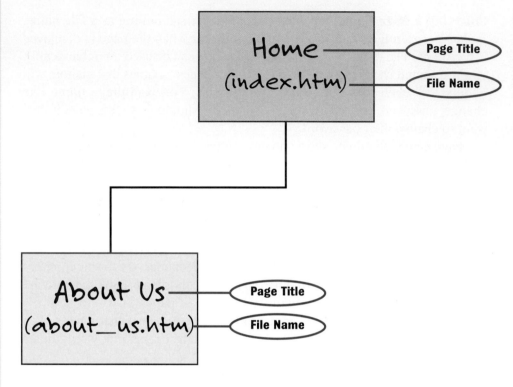

Home
(index.htm)

Page Title

File Name

About Us
(about_us.htm)

Page Title

File Name

❷ Proofread the file names, verifying that each name is used only once and that there are no spaces in the file names.

❸ If you are using a word processing application, print a copy of the chart and save the revised version of your document.

CREATING SKETCHES OF INDIVIDUAL PAGES

Before you start to build a Web site, you should create a simple drawing of each page. This drawing is a basic sketch of the Web page you are going to create. This sketch identifies the text and graphics you plan to use on a page, and roughly shows where you plan to place these elements. Sketches serve several purposes:

◆ They help make certain that all the goals of the Web site are met.
◆ They provide guidelines for developing Web page content.
◆ They are useful when you create the page template.

You do not have to be an artist to create sketches of your Web pages. At this point, only a brief overview of the site's pages is required. You need not worry about the specific text or graphics that will appear on each page—just keep your eye on the overall purpose of the page. In You Try It Activity 5E, you will create a sketch for the About Us page in the Astronomy Club Web site.

YOU TRY IT 5E Sketching a Web Page

❶ Create a sketch for the About Us page. Identify the content you want to include. For this page, you want to state the purpose of the club, and a list of the individuals who run the club.

❷ Sketch the content for this page. Estimate where you would place the elements you want to include. Also estimate the space needed for the different elements.

❸ Review your work to make sure the sketch contains the needed elements. Your sketch should look similar to Figure 5.8. If you are using application software to create the sketches, save the document as Astronomy Sketches.

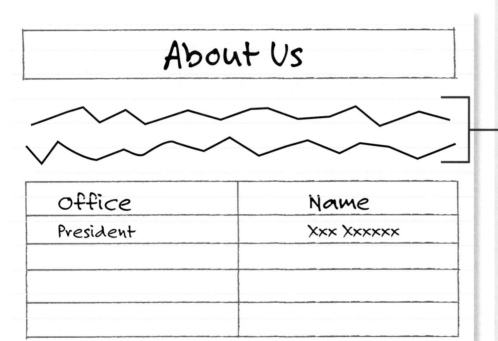

● **Figure 5.8**
A sketch like this shows how elements will appear on the page.

Statement of Club's Purpose

❹ Create a second sketch for the same Web page. Keep the same content, but create a different arrangement for your items. Save your document as before.

❺ Compare your sketches with those of other students. Explain why you decided to place items where you did. Evaluate which sketches you prefer and explain why.

WEB SITE PLANNING CHECKLIST

Planning a Web site carefully will help you create a well-designed site that people enjoy using. There is a lot to think about before you start creating your Web pages. That is why you should always use a checklist. A checklist helps you keep track of your planning tasks. In this checklist, the planning steps need to be completed before the storyboarding process begins. Determining a Web site's purpose and audience is always the first step to creating a successful site, as shown in Table 5.5.

Table 5.5
A planning checklist helps you manage the details of creating Web sites. Why do you think planning should be completed before storyboarding begins?

Steps in Planning a Web Site

STEP COMPLETED	STEP
☑	1. The site's purpose is clearly stated.
☑	2. Both immediate and long-term goals are specified.
☑	3. The audience for the site is specified.
☑	4. A clear and specific mission statement is written.
☑	5. An appropriate navigation scheme is chosen.
☑	6. A chart is created showing the navigation scheme, including each page's title and file name.
☑	7. Sketches of the major pages are drawn.

We have completed the steps for planning the Astronomy Club Web site. Following all the planning steps carefully will help you determine whether your plan will succeed when it is implemented as a Web site. The planning process is designed to help you identify any potential problems before you actually begin to build your site. It is much easier to correct problems at this stage than later on, when you may have to alter an existing Web page or change the structure of an existing Web site.

Section 5.3 Assessment

Concept Check

1. **Define** storyboard, page name, file name.

2. **Discuss** three advantages to storyboarding a Web site.

3. **List** the items that should be included in a Web page sketch. Explain the importance of each item.

Critical Thinking

4. **Analyze Navigation** What might be an advantage to a Web site having a linear navigation scheme? What might be an advantage to a hierarchical scheme?

5. **Draw Conclusions** What problems could be avoided by completing a Web site planning checklist before creating a site?

Applying Skills

Create a File Name List Create a table that lists appropriate file names for the following pages that are part of the Garden Company Web site: Welcome to the Garden Club, Products, Class Offerings, Press Releases, Contact Us, Q and A.

SECTION 5.1 Creating a Mission Statement

Key Terms

mission statement, 126   target audience, 127

Main Ideas

- Before building a Web site, you must spend some time planning it.
- It is important to determine the purpose of your Web site before building it.
- Characteristics of the site's audience must be identified, including how much it already knows about the site's topic and what it wants to learn from the site.
- A mission statement describes the purpose and audience of the Web site.

SECTION 5.2 Navigation Schemes

Key Terms

navigation
    scheme, 131
hierarchical navigation
    scheme, 132
top-level page, 132
parent-child
    relationship, 132

peer-to-peer
    relationship, 132
linear navigation
    scheme, 133
random-access
    navigation scheme,
    133

Main Ideas

- A navigation scheme specifies the organization of a site and how its pages are related to one another.
- Examples of navigation schemes include hierarchical, linear, and random-access.
- A page that is connected to a page one level below it has a parent-child relationship with that page.
- Children of the same parent have a peer-to-peer relationship.
- A Web site's home page is a top-level page.

SECTION 5.3 Storyboarding Your Site

Key Terms

storyboard, 137   file name, 139
page name, 139

Main Ideas

- Storyboarding involves drawing a site's navigation structure and creating sketches of the major pages.
- A Web page's sketch outlines the major content that will be included on that page.
- A page name is not the same as a file name.
- The Web site planning checklist can help you determine whether you have completed every step in the planning process.

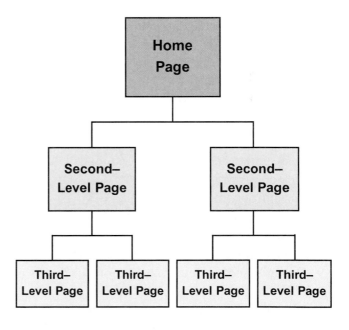

READ TO SUCCEED PRACTICE

Reviewing the Purpose Go back to the Reading for a Purpose sentences you completed before you read each section. Did you succeed in your stated purpose? Use your Key Term Journal, class notes, and your memory to write down a brief explanation for each purpose sentence. This exercise will help you determine what you need to review.

Reviewing Key Terms

1. What is a mission statement?
2. Which of the following is NOT a type of navigation scheme: hierarchical, oval, linear, random-access.
3. Rewrite this statement to make it true: *Each child page can only have a single parent whereas a parent page can only have up to three child pages.*
4. Why is there always a single page at the top of a hierarchical navigation scheme?
5. What are the two main items that are created when storyboarding a site?

Understanding Main Ideas

6. **Explain** the purpose of a mission statement.
7. **Discuss** why it is important to be familiar with what your audience already knows about a particular topic when you are developing a mission statement.
8. **Summarize** the differences and similarities between the immediate and the long-term goals of a Web site you might develop.
9. **Describe** how a linear navigation scheme is different from a hierarchical one.
10. **Identify** advantages and disadvantages of the linear and hierarchical navigation structures.
11. **Explain** the difference between a page name and a file name.
12. **Discuss** the purpose of creating sketches.
13. **Discuss** the advantages of using a Web site planning checklist.

Critical Thinking

14. **Analyze a Web Site's Audience** Some Web sites, such as the National Aeronautics and Space Administration (NASA) site, try to appeal to a broad range of visitors. For example, the NASA site's audience could include both adults and children, in addition to people who are very knowledgeable about the space program and those who have a minimum of previous knowledge. What are some of the ways such a Web site might deal with such a broad audience? Give specific suggestions in your answer.
15. **Create Navigation Schemes** In the Astronomy Club Web site, explain how you might make the About Us page a parent page.
16. **Draw Conclusions** In the Garden Company Web site, what would happen if the Products page were removed, and all of the pages under it linked directly to the home page? How would this affect how visitors accessed these pages? Do you think this would be a good change? Explain your answer.
17. **Analyze Navigational Schemes** Why is a drawing of a hierarchical navigation scheme often called a tree diagram?

e-Review ··················

webdesign.glencoe.com

Study with PowerPoint

To review the main points in this chapter select **e-Review > PowerPoint Outlines > Chapter 5.**

Online Self Check

Test your knowledge of the material in this chapter by selecting **e-Review > Self Checks > Chapter 5.**

Making Connections

Social Studies—Create a Time Line The invention of the printing press in the mid-15th century started a revolution involving access to and communication of information throughout Europe. The World Wide Web created a similar information revolution.

Create a time line that identifies five important dates in the history of communications. In your time line, include dates for when the printing press and the Internet were invented. Finally, create a storyboard that places the dates from your time line into a linear navigational scheme.

STANDARDS AT WORK

Students use technology to locate, evaluate, and collect information from a variety of sources. (NETS-S 5)

Analyze Web Sites

Locate two Web sites in one of the following categories: Corporate presence, portal, informational, or educational. Try to locate two Web sites that are very different from each other. For each site, answer the following questions:

1. What is the purpose of the Web site?
2. What is the goal of the Web site?
3. Who is the Web site's target audience?
4. What is the target audience seeking from the site?
5. Is the content of the site easy to scan?
6. What type of navigation scheme does the site use?

Use your answers to develop a chart that compares and contrasts the two Web sites. If possible, use either a word processing application or a spreadsheet to create your chart.

TEAMWORK SKILLS

Create a Storyboard

You have been asked to create a Web site for Services for Seniors, a local group serving senior citizens in your community. This group provides seniors with information about health care, adult education programs, and other services. Work as a team to research similar sites. Conduct interviews with the site's potential audience (your grandparents, other family members, and friends). Based on your research, prepare a mission statement and site goals.

Brainstorm a list of pages to include in the site such as housing, medical, legal, and education. Create an index card for each page showing the page and file names. Organize the index cards on a piece of paper and draw lines to indicate the navigation scheme that you will use. This will serve as your storyboard for the site. Explain to the class the reasoning behind your navigation scheme.

CHALLENGE YOURSELF

Plan a Web Site

Assume you have been hired to create a Web site for your local aquarium. The aquarium is a major attraction in your town, and it wants a site that will highlight its many activities and exhibitions.

Based on planning you have done with the client, you determine that the site will have 20 pages arranged in four levels. It will use a hierarchical navigation scheme. The following topics need to be covered: general information, types of exhibitions, special attractions, and gift shop merchandise.

Create a storyboard for the aquarium Web site that fits the noted requirements. Brainstorm what type of parent and child pages will need to be included in the site. Determine how you want visitors to navigate the site. When you have completed your storyboard, create a sketch for the Web site's home page.

YOU TRY IT

Skills Studio

These exercises reinforce the skills you learned in this chapter's You Try It activities. Refer back to the You Try It activities if you need extra guidance.

1. Creating a Mission Statement

Create a mission statement for a group or club which you belong to.

Ⓐ At the top of a page, write or type the name of the group, organization, or club you will be creating a mission statement for. Add the words "Mission Statement" after the group's name.

Ⓑ Answer the questions to identify your target audience.

IDENTIFYING YOUR TARGET AUDIENCE
Who is the audience?
What does the audience already know about this topic?
What does the audience want to learn from the site?
How will the audience access the site?

Ⓒ Use your answers and your knowledge of what belongs in a mission statement to write or type a mission statement for the group's Web site.

Ⓓ Proofread your mission statement. If you are using word processing software, use the spell check feature. Save your document for future use.

2. Planning a Web Site

Create a storyboard for your chosen organization's Web site.

Ⓐ Brainstorm a list of pages to include in your site. Write down your ideas.

Ⓑ Create a chart showing the site's hierarchical structure. Include each page's name and draw lines showing parent-child and peer-to-peer relationships.

Ⓒ Under each page name, add the file name. Proofread your chart. Save your document for later use.

Ⓓ Create a sketch of the home page and one other page planned for your site. Estimate where you would place the content you want to include.

Ⓔ Review your work to make sure the sketches contain the needed elements. Save your sketches for later use.

Web Design Projects

1. Create a Storyboard

Assume that a travel bookstore has hired you to create their Web site. The store wants its site to include a home page, pages for virtual trips, and a currency conversion page. The virtual trips will visit a wide range of locations and include historical and geographical data, as well as links to other items of interest.

Create a storyboard for the bookstore's Web site. In addition to the home page, your storyboard should include pages for two virtual trips and the currency conversion page. When planning your virtual trips pages, consider the fact that the bookstore plans to introduce new virtual trips every six months. Since the number of virtual trips will grow over time, you will want to include a general Virtual Trips page that contains introductory information about this feature. Each individual trip will be a child page connected to this general parent page.

2. Create Sketches

Use the information from Web Design Project 1 and the information below to create sketches of the general Virtual Trips page and the first two virtual trip pages.

Parent Page: Introduction to Virtual Trips
a. What is a virtual trip?
b. How do I take a virtual trip?
c. Where will these virtual trips go?

Child Page 1: Nome, Alaska
a. Location: Alaska map
b. History:
   ◆ Gold discovered and Nome becomes a boom town.
   ◆ The Iditarod, a famous Alaskan dog race, ends in Nome.

Child Page 2: Grand Canyon
a. Location: topographical map of the Grand Canyon
b. History: [research and fill in appropriate information]

Research the information needed to add history to the Grand Canyon page. Also locate one hyperlink to be added to each of the virtual trip child pages. The links should allow the visitor to find out more about one of the historical points mentioned on the page.

CHAPTER 6 Developing Content and Layout

WHY IT MATTERS.....................................

People today are surrounded by information. We see billboards on our streets, listen to radios in our cars, and watch TV or access the Web at home. Various media are always competing to capture an audience's attention. In this chapter, you will learn how to create Web content that will catch—and hold—your viewers' interest.

Quick Write Activity

Think about all the ways you get information throughout the day. Write down everything you can think of and compare your results with the rest of the class. Which medium (magazine, Web site, etc.) best captures your attention, and which do you find easiest to ignore?

WHAT YOU WILL DO..

ACTIVITIES AND PROJECTS

Applying Skills

You Try It Activities

Chapter Assessment

You Try It Skills Studio

Web Design Projects

IN THE WORKBOOK

Optional Activities and Projects

Guided Reading
Web Design Projects

ON THE WEB

Activities at webdesign.glencoe.com

Reading Strategy Organizers
Go Online Activities
Study with PowerPoint
Self-Check Assessments

READ TO SUCCEED

Stay Engaged
You are an active reader when you stay engaged in the material. One way to stay engaged is to turn each of the colored section heads into questions, then read the section to find the answers. When you can think of a good question and find complete answers, you will be engaged in learning.

Section 6.1 Creating Web Site Content

Guide to Reading

Main Ideas

Many specific strategies can help you write interesting content for the Web. You must write your Web content clearly and concisely.

Key Terms

content
inverted pyramid

Reading Strategy

Identify the steps you use to generate and organize ideas for the content of your Web pages. Use a flow diagram like the one below (also available online).

As you learned in Chapter 1, the Web design process can be divided into three categories:

- Interaction design
- Information design
- Presentation design

In Chapter 5, you created a navigation chart for the Astronomy Club Web site. This chart is a component of interaction design. Now you are going to look more closely at information design.

Information design involves determining what content will appear on a particular page. **Content** is the text and graphics included on a Web page. When people consider creating Web pages, they usually think first about how the page will look rather than what it should say.

To be successful, your Web page must provide information that captures viewers' attention by using words as well as graphics. Text should be short and easy to read. Graphics should be both visually appealing and informative. For example, you could include a photograph of an airplane on a Web page about travel. Including a map of a country discussed on the page, however, would both provide visual interest and help viewers understand where that country is located.

WRITING FOR THE WEB

Good Web writing shares some basic principles with good print writing. For example, Web text should be clear, grammatically correct, and written for a specific audience. Web text, however, is not the same as printed text. Reading off a monitor is not as straightforward as reading off a printed page. There can also be a lot of visual information on a Web page that you do not see in a book or newspaper. Text must stand out from graphics, animation, navigation buttons, and other elements. You need to keep your online readers in mind when developing content.

TECH TRIVIA

Reading Online Web experts have found that reading a block of text online takes approximately 25 percent longer than reading the same text on a printed page. In other words, in the amount of time you spend reading 100 words online, you could read 125 words on a printed page.

Online Text

Users do not generally read through Web pages as they would a novel or other printed item. Instead, they scan a page, read a couple snippets of text that interest them, click a link to check out a photograph, and click again to move to another page or site. Online users usually look for key words or phrases instead of reading every word on the screen. If a Web page buries information, then users will probably move on to another page or site. Using headings, short paragraphs, and bulleted lists helps readers locate information on a page quickly and easily.

Web Text Guidelines Use the following guidelines to help you write effective online text:

◆ Introduce one idea per paragraph.
◆ Limit paragraphs to about 75 words or fewer.
◆ Keep sentences short.
◆ Use simple sentence structures.
◆ Use bulleted lists when you can.
◆ Use numbered lists only when presenting a series of steps.
◆ Insert headings and subheadings to break up text and highlight key points.
◆ Make sure your headings follow a logical and clear hierarchy.
◆ Format main headings larger than subheadings or place them in a unique color or typeface.

Comparing Web Text To understand these concepts, compare the two screen shots in Figure 6.1. The top image shows a Web page that does not adhere to good online-text practices. The information is presented as one large block of text. Finding information requires a close reading.

The bottom image, on the other hand, follows the guidelines presented in this section. Notice how much faster you can identify the text's main points in the bottom image than in the top image. The bottom image presents information in short sections, and heading helps the reader identify the main topics. The bulleted list presents a compact summary of the key points.

● **Figure 6.1**
Text should be broken into small pieces on the Web page. How does reading the top screen differ from reading the bottom screen?

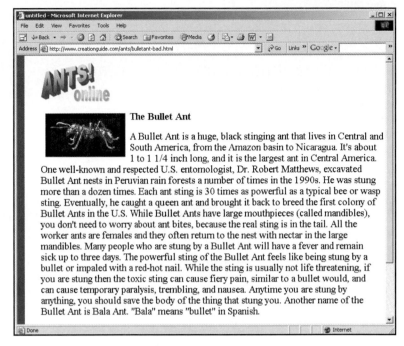

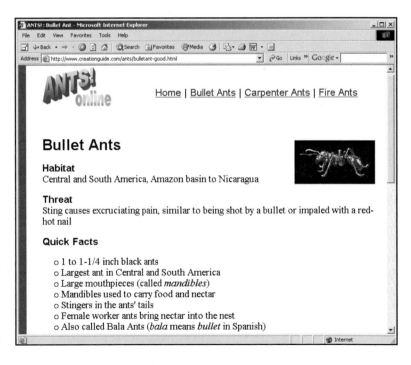

Figure 6.2

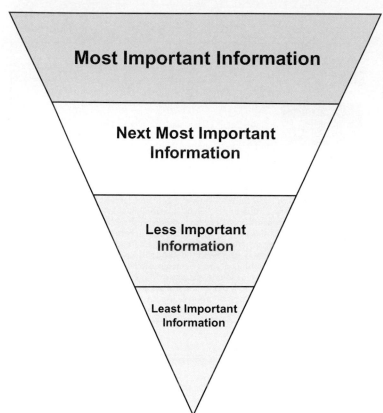

Figure 6.2
An inverted pyramid structure places the most important information first. Why should important information appear first on a Web page?

Most Important Information

Next Most Important Information

Less Important Information

Least Important Information

Organizing Web Text

Many professional Web designers agree that, like newspaper text, Web text should be organized in an inverted pyramid form, as shown in Figure 6.2. An **inverted pyramid** approach places the most important information at the beginning of a story, where it will best catch an online reader's attention. In traditional news writing, a good story answers the questions Who? What? Where? When? Why? and How? as briefly as possible in order of importance.

After the key points appear at the beginning of the story, the remainder of the article serves to fill in the details, with the least important information at the end.

Using the Mission Statement

As you develop content, remember to refer back to your mission statement so you do not forget your site's purpose and audience. Use both the mission statement and your storyboarding items to keep yourself "on target."

Revising Your Text

You have not completed the writing process until you have revised your text. On Web pages, conciseness—saying exactly what you mean in as few words as possible—is key. Take time to review your text to include strong verbs and nouns, eliminate the passive voice and wordiness, and check your spelling and grammar.

Activity 6.1 Evaluate Writing Styles Learn more about writing for the Web at **webdesign.glencoe.com**.

DEVELOPING CONTENT FOR A WEB PAGE

Now that you have learned some guidelines for writing online text, you are ready to look at some practical ideas to get you started writing.

Generating and Organizing Ideas

Brainstorming is a technique that can help you generate ideas. Write down every topic you want to include in your Web page, then write a keyword next to each one. Each keyword should be a word or phrase that identifies the topic's core content. For example, here are a few keywords that you could use to develop a Web page on the planet Saturn:

- Position in relation to Sun
- Atmosphere
- Planet's surface

After you create your list, review your keywords and determine which ones you want to use in headings. Identifying your headings will help you group your information on the page.

 webdesign.glencoe.com

Developing a Web Page

In the next activity, you will develop content for the Saturn Web page in the Astronomy Club Web site. This page presents facts about the planet Saturn. Keep in mind the points you learned about content development. Remember, Web content should be concise—write no more than 200 words for this page.

ACTIVITY 6A Creating Content for a Web Page

YOU TRY IT

1 Write a brief document outlining the purpose and audience of the Saturn page. Place the title Our Solar System: Saturn at the top of your page.

2 Brainstorm ideas for your content. Make a list of the text and graphics you want to include on the page.

3 Write keywords next to your list of ideas.

4 Determine which keywords to use in headings.

5 Use the inverted pyramid style to organize your brainstormed ideas. Place the topic you want to emphasize at the top of your page. Then list the rest of your topics in order of decreasing importance. The least important topic should be at the bottom of your page.

6 Create the content of the Saturn page (if possible, use a word processing application). Refer back to your notes as you write.

7 Proofread and spell check the document. Correct the errors.

8 If using a word processing application, save your work as **saturn.doc.** You will use this document in a later activity.

Section 6.1 Assessment

Concept Check

1. **Define** content, inverted pyramid.

2. **Summarize** how reading a Web page is different from reading a printed page.

3. **Identify** the initial factors you need to consider when planning a Web page's content.

Critical Thinking

4. **Draw Conclusions** Why might a reader not want to read a Web page that contains too much content?

5. **Analyze** Assume you have developed a list of keywords for a family vacation Web site. What factors determine which keywords you will use as headings in the final Web site?

Applying Skills

Determine Content
Write a mission statement for a Web site about classes at your school. Determine the content you would include on one page of this site.

Ethics & Technology

THE DIGITAL DIVIDE

Although it seems like computers are everywhere, many people worldwide do not own computers or have access to the Internet.

Technology skills can help lessen the digital divide.

The Technology Gap

The gap between people who use technology and those who do not is often referred to as the "digital divide." Computer literacy is rapidly increasing in the United States. But the digital divide remains a global problem. According to The Digital Divide Network, only about six percent of the world's population has Internet access.

Computer Literacy

Computers and the Internet give you access to job skills, educational opportunities, information, opinions, and more. In many poor American areas, children have limited access to computers. It is also hard for adults to get ahead without computers, since many jobs require some computer proficiency.

Although most Americans can find a way to access a computer if they need to, technology is simply out of reach for most people in developing nations. Many of these countries are more concerned with finding adequate nutrition, medical care, and jobs for their citizens.

Closing the Gap

A huge public and private effort is underway to close the digital divide. Organizations have donated millions of dollars worth of training, hardware, and software to communities in need all around the world.

In developing countries in Africa, Asia, and elsewhere, small computer centers are being set up in isolated towns and villages. These give people access to better communication and education. They also provide job training and small business opportunities.

Organizations like Boys and Girls Clubs and the YMCA provide computers and training for people who cannot afford computers in their homes. They often need used hardware or software and volunteers to teach computer skills.

Tech Focus

1. Use classified ads or the Web to look at job listings. Estimate the percentage of jobs that require computer skills. Discuss the impact of computer access on job opportunities.

2. Contact a charitable organization in your area that either donates used computers or needs volunteers to teach computer skills. Write a brief summary of the program and its results.

Section 6.2 Placing Items on a Page

Guide to Reading

Main Ideas

The best Web pages have clear, attractive layouts, which you can achieve by understanding simple Web design guidelines.

Key Terms

pixel
screen resolution
safe area
white space
proximity

Reading Strategy

Identify and summarize three guidelines for Web page layout. Use a table like the one below (also available online).

Layout/Design Guidelines	How It Helps

The size of a Web page affects its readability. If Web pages are too wide or too long, then online readers have to scroll to locate information. Too much scrolling can annoy users and cause them to surf to other Web sites.

WEB PAGE DIMENSIONS

A Web page's dimensions are defined by the width and height of the page. To prevent scrolling, a Web page's width and height should roughly match the width and height of the viewer's monitor screen. A screen's viewing area is measured in pixels. A **pixel** (short for **pic**ture **el**ement) is a single point in a graphic image. Thousands of pixels combine to display an image on a monitor's screen.

Page Dimension Guidelines

Most early computer monitors had a screen area of 640 pixels wide by 480 pixels high (referred to as 640 x 480). Today, computer monitors typically have a screen area of 800 x 600 or higher. Most new monitors also allow users to choose between at least two different screen area sizes. Users can make content appear smaller or larger by changing their **screen resolution,** which is the amount of pixels that a monitor can display. Some users prefer a 640 x 480 display because everything on the screen appears larger. Other users prefer a 1024 x 768 display because it allows more information to fit on the screen.

The perfect page dimension cannot be precisely defined. There is, however, a certain amount of space available on every Web browser/system combination. This area, called the **safe area,** is generally defined as 640 x 480 pixels, the size of the smallest monitor available. Viewers usually see the content included in the safe area first. When designing pages (especially your home page), try to place your most important and eye-catching information in this area. Placing items in the safe area also keeps users from having to scroll to locate vital information and links.

The ideal spot within the safe area is the upper-left corner. No matter how much a user resizes the browser window, the upper-left corner remains in view. Therefore, the upper-left corner is prime property—the ideal place to insert a company's logo or other key information.

Screen Resolution

Preview your Web pages at various screen resolutions to make sure the important content displays in your target audience's screen area. The lowest possible screen resolution available on most modern monitors is 800 x 600. Since your audience's computer equipment will vary, preview your pages in the lowest and highest resolutions available on your computer system to see how your page looks at each extreme. FrontPage allows you to preview pages in different Web browsers at different screen resolutions.

YOU TRY IT

ACTIVITY 6B Viewing a Page at Various Resolutions

1 Open the **Garden Company** home page in FrontPage (browse to the DataFile\Examples\GardenCo folder in the Student Data Files).

2 Click the **File** menu and choose **Preview in Browser.**

3 Select the lowest screen resolution available on your computer system (Web browser/screen resolution pairings will vary). For this activity, we selected **Microsoft Internet Explorer 6.0 (640 x 480),** as shown in Figure 6.3.

Figure 6.3
This figure shows the Garden Company home page viewed at a 640 x 480 screen resolution.

4 Repeat step 3 but select the highest screen resolution available on your computer system. For this activity, we selected **Microsoft Internet Explorer 6.0 (1024 x 768),** as shown in Figure 6.4.

◀——————●**Figure 6.4**
This figure shows the Garden Company home page viewed at a 1024 x 768 screen resolution.

5 Compare the different screen resolutions. Close the **Garden Company** Web site when finished.

PAGE LAYOUT GUIDELINES

Some common design principles can guide you in laying out Web pages. Following these principles will help you create a site that is user-friendly.

Eliminate Clutter

One of the biggest mistakes people make when creating Web pages is placing too much content on a page. Too much content can confuse a visitor, and cause him or her to surf to a different site.

Remove Unnecessary Content Delete unnecessary content. Or, if you still have too much information for one page, expand your page into a Web site. Divide information into logical sections and place each section on a separate subpage linked to your home page. Also, remember that you do not have to use all the text and graphics you have. Web pages are dynamic, which means you can selectively update and modify information on a regular basis. For example, if you want to publicize the birthdays of your friends and family, you can update the page monthly.

Activity 6.2 Evaluate Page Layouts Learn more about layout guidelines at **webdesign.glencoe.com**.

Choose Function over Form When deciding what to include, choose function over form. Keep elements that fill a need and discard elements that just add visual interest. If you are not sure whether a design element is functional, temporarily remove the element from the page and analyze the page without it. If your page works as well (or better) without it, the element can be deleted. Avoid using too much of any element or technique, including links, colors, scrolling, and so forth. Also avoid blinking text and unnecessary animation. Many people find these effects annoying and meaningless.

Create Visual Rest Stops

Long, unbroken blocks of text tire the eye. One way to ease eyestrain is to include plenty of white space. **White space** is an area without content—an area where the eye can take a break as it scans the page. Use white space to create visual breaks between and around images and body text. Using white space in this manner helps frame and draw attention to your content.

Emphasize Important Content

When laying out content, size elements on your page in proportion to their importance. In the design world, a bigger design indicates more important information. Similarly, a smaller design sends the message that the item is less important. Most users look first at the largest or boldest element on the page. Next they scan the page quickly, noticing the general design created by the text and graphics. Finally, they begin to read the actual words on the page. Remember the inverted pyramid rule and place your most important content at the top of your page.

Group Related Items

The **proximity** (closeness) of elements on a page can cause readers to make assumptions about how elements relate to each other. If a block of text refers to an image, then that image should appear next to the text. Remember, if items are grouped closely together, people will assume that these items are related. Try not to create false impressions by closely grouping unrelated items.

Figure 6.5, an online version of a small newspaper, illustrates a page where it is difficult to determine the purpose of individual items. The page is filled with so many graphics and ads that the news—the main content on the site—gets lost in the clutter. The headlines are not even visible in the first screen that loads. Worst of all, the ad for the scuba store dominates the page. Most people look first at the most colorful element on the page, so the visitor's first impression may be that this is a site for a diving shop, not a newspaper!

Figure 6.5
This newspaper home page is so cluttered that viewers cannot determine which information is important. When you first look at this page, to what spot is your eye first drawn and why?

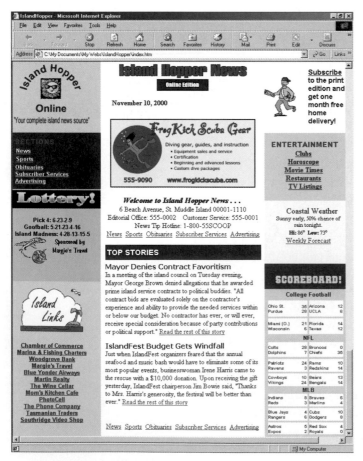

Figure 6.6 shows the redesigned Island Hopper News site. The eye is now drawn to the logo, which is the largest element on the page. The less-important scuba store ad has been moved to the bottom of the page, where it cannot confuse visitors. The site's layout has been revised to resemble a traditional newspaper, which further reinforces the site's purpose. In this layout, news that is of most interest—the day's top story, the weather, and sports scores—are all positioned near the top of the page. Colored bands emphasize important content and help group related items together. Links to other parts of the site are provided at both the top and bottom of the page so that people can surf the site with minimal scrolling.

Align Text Consistently

When laying out your page, line up items with each other. Text can be aligned to the left, to the right, or to the center. Try not to mix alignments on a page. Having to switch from right-aligned to left-aligned text can confuse your reader. Since English speakers read from left to right, paragraphs of text should be left aligned, which is the default alignment in HTML.

Keep Download Time Short

Because every text or graphic item you add to a page increases that page's download time, you should not cram too much content into a single page. You only have a few seconds to catch a viewer's attention, so make sure your page downloads as quickly as possible.

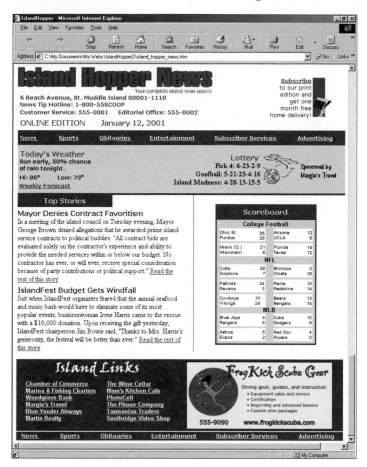

Figure 6.6
The redesigned site draws the eye to important news. What are some differences between this page and the one in Figure 6.5?

Section 6.2 Assessment

Concept Check

1. **Define** pixel, screen resolution, safe area, white space, proximity.

2. **Identify** where important content should be placed on a Web page.

3. **Explain** why it is important to include white space on a Web page.

Critical Thinking

4. **Analyze** Why might some viewers use a resolution of 640 x 480, while others use 1024 x 768?

5. **Cause and Effect** Why might too much clutter cause a visitor to leave the Web site quickly?

Applying Skills

Compare Web Designs Find two examples of Web pages in this book. Compare the two layouts and determine which one you believe is more effective. Explain your reasoning.

Section 6.3 Creating a Page Template

Guide to Reading

Main Ideas

Creating a custom template provides consistency among the pages on a site and simplifies creating the individual pages. The template can contain the elements that will appear on every page.

Key Terms

logo
title graphic
table
column
row
cell

Reading Strategy

Describe the following parts of a table: column, row, cell, header row, and header column. Use a table similar to the one below (also available online).

Part	Description

As discussed in Chapter 2, using a template is an easy way to create a new Web page or site. A template provides a grid that you can use to lay out your page elements.

DESIGNING A TEMPLATE

Most Web pages contain a title area, a logo, navigation links, a body (where the majority of content is located), and a footer. FrontPage provides pre-made templates with placeholders for these basic page elements. However, a pre-made template may not always meet your needs. In these situations, you can create a custom template that fits the design structure you want for your site. In Chapter 5, you planned pages for the Astronomy Club Web site. Now you will create a basic template for those pages. You will use this template for every page except the home page, which will have a special design. Figure 6.7 shows the common elements of this template.

Figure 6.7
Each page in the Astronomy Club site will follow a similar format. Why is the logo in the upper-left corner of the page?

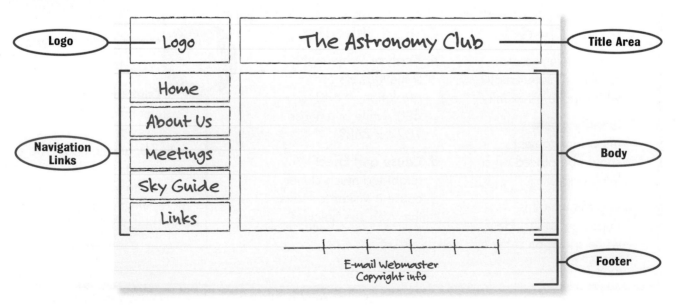

In the following activity, you will begin creating the Astronomy Club site's basic template. You will also insert the site's background graphic. This graphic will give the pages a standard appearance throughout the Web site.

ACTIVITY 6C Creating a Page Template

❶ Start FrontPage. Create a new empty Web site. Name the Web site **Astronomy Club**. Store the site in the location specified by your teacher.

❷ Click the **Create a new normal page** button on the Standard toolbar to create a blank page. Make certain the page is open in Design (in 2002, Normal) view. Close the task pane and Folder List pane if they are open.

❸ Right-click a blank area on the page. Select **Page Properties** to open the Page Properties dialog box. In the Title text box on the General tab, type The Astronomy Club.

❹ Click the **Formatting** (in 2002, **Background**) tab. Click the **Background picture** check box to specify that you want the page to use a background picture, and then click **Browse.**

❺ Browse to the DataFile\Ch06\Images folder. Double-click **bg.gif** to open the background file.

❻ Continuing on the Formatting (in 2002, Background) tab, click the **Background** drop-down arrow and click the **black** color box. Then click the **Text** drop-down arrow and click the **black** color box. Click **OK.** The background image (black with white stars) should appear on your page.

❼ Click the **Save** button. In the Save As dialog box, click the **Change Title** button (located in the lower-right portion of the dialog box) to open the Set Page Title dialog box. Change the text to The Astronomy Club: Generic Page, as shown in Figure 6.8. Click **OK.**

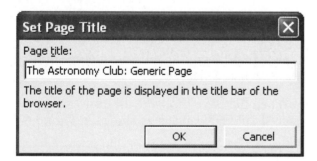

Figure 6.8
The text that you insert in the Page title box will display in a Web browser's title bar.

❽ Type ac_template.htm in the File Name text box. Click **Save.**

❾ The Save Embedded Files dialog box appears. Click **Change Folder.** Double-click the **images** folder to open it, and click **OK.** In the Save Embedded Files dialog box, click **OK** to save the **bg.gif** file in the images folder.

You may be wondering why we set both the background and the text colors to black. Most of the text in this Web site will display on a white (and not a black) background. Setting the default text color to black now will save you time later.

THE ASTRONOMY CLUB LOGO AND TITLE GRAPHIC

A **logo** is a symbol used to represent a business or an organization. On many Web sites, clicking the logo will return users to the site's home page. A **title graphic** is an image that appears at the top of every page on a Web site. You will place the Astronomy Club logo in the template's most visible spot—the upper-left corner of the page. You will position the title graphic immediately to the right of it.

You will add alternative text to both the logo and the title graphic. Alternative text is text that appears on the screen if the image is not available. Even though you have not yet created the home page, you will link the template's logo to it now. Adding the link to the template saves you the trouble of inserting this link later when you create each individual page.

YOU TRY IT

Student Data File

ACTIVITY 6D Adding a Logo and Title Graphic

① Open the **ac_template.htm** page in Design (in 2002, Normal) view.

② Position the insertion point in the upper-left corner of the page. Click the **Insert Picture From File** button.

③ In the Picture dialog box, browse to the DataFile\Ch06\Images folder. Double-click the **logo.gif** file to open the logo file.

④ Click the **Insert Picture From File** button. In the dialog box, double-click the **titlebar.gif** file to open the title bar file.

⑤ Right-click the **logo.gif** image (the planet image). Select **Picture Properties** and click the **General** tab. Under Alternative representations, click **Text.** In the corresponding text box, type Astronomy Club Logo. Click **OK.**

⑥ Right-click the **titlebar.gif** image. Repeat step 5, typing Astronomy Club as your alternative text. Click **OK.**

⑦ Right-click the **logo.gif** image again. Select **Hyperlink.** Type index.htm in the Address text box. Click **OK.**

⑧ Click **Save.** When the Save Embedded Files dialog box appears, click **OK.** Your page should now appear as shown in Figure 6.9.

Figure 6.9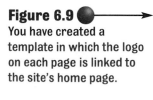
You have created a template in which the logo on each page is linked to the site's home page.

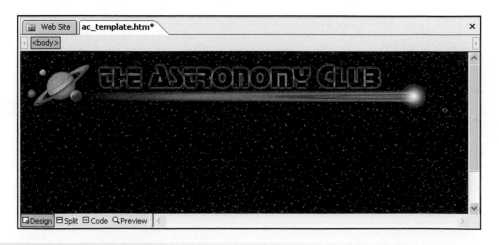

TABLES

Many designers use tables to organize a Web page's content. A **table** consists of vertical **columns** and horizontal **rows.** Each individual square within a table is called a **cell** (see Figure 6.10).

● **Figure 6.10**

A table consists of vertical columns and horizontal rows. How could you quickly determine the number of cells in this table?

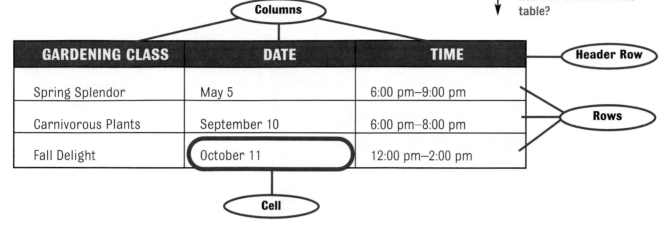

GARDENING CLASS	DATE	TIME
Spring Splendor	May 5	6:00 pm–9:00 pm
Carnivorous Plants	September 10	6:00 pm–8:00 pm
Fall Delight	October 11	12:00 pm–2:00 pm

Columns — Header Row — Rows — Cell

ACTIVITY 6E Creating a Table

YOU TRY IT

① Open the Astronomy Club's **ac_template.htm** page in Design (in 2002, Normal) view. Position the insertion point below the logo.

② On the **Table** menu, select **Insert > Table** to open the Insert Table dialog box. Type 6 in the Rows text box and 2 in the Columns text box. Type 600 in the Specify width text box. Click **In pixels.** Set Cell padding to 4 and Cell spacing to 0 (see Figure 6.11). Click **OK.**

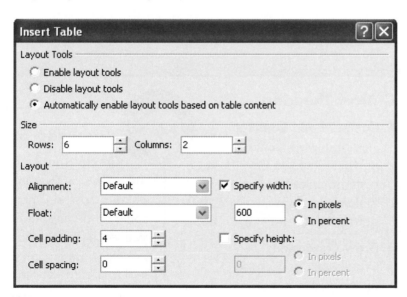

● **Figure 6.11**

Fill in the Insert Table dialog box as shown in this figure.

③ Move the mouse pointer over the table's first column so that it changes to a downward-pointing arrow. Click to select the entire first column. Right-click anywhere in the column, and choose **Cell Properties** to open the Cell Properties dialog box.

READ ME!

Tech Tip The Insert Table dialog box is identical to the Table Properties dialog box. You can open the Table Properties dialog box by right-clicking in any existing table.

④ Set Horizontal alignment to **Left.** Set Vertical alignment to **Middle.** Ensure that the Specify width check box is selected. Type 150 in the Specify width text box and select the **In pixels** option.

⑤ Ensure that the Specify height check box is selected. Type 30 in the Specify height text box and select the **In pixels** option. Click **OK.**

⑥ Repeat step 3 with the second column. Set Horizontal alignment to **Left,** and Vertical alignment to **Baseline.** Type 450 in the Specify width text box and 30 in the Specify height text box (make sure all boxes are checked as in steps 4 and 5).

⑦ Under Background (near the bottom of the Cell Properties dialog box), open the **Color** drop-down list and select the **white** color box (only apply the white background to the second column). Click **OK** to activate the settings.

⑧ Your template should now look like Figure 6.12. Save your work.

Figure 6.12
The right column's white background will allow content to remain visible on the screen.

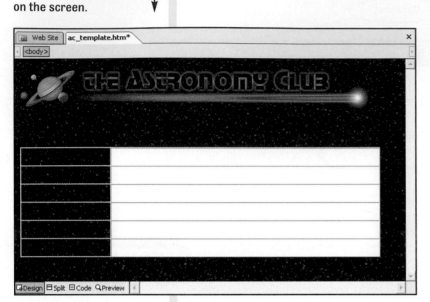

Section 6.3 Assessment

Concept Check

1. **Define** logo, title graphic, table, column, row, cell.

2. **Explain** how a custom template differs from a pre-made template.

3. **List** three properties that can be set in the Cell Properties dialog box. Explain the function of these three properties.

Critical Thinking

4. **Compare and Contrast** Describe two situations in which it would be better to enter text in a table rather than in paragraph form.

5. **Draw Conclusions** What would a user see on the screen if the graphic were not available and no alternative text had been included?

Applying Skills

Create a Table Review the notes you took in one of your classes. Organize some of the information you learned into a table. If possible, use a technology tool to create your table.

EMERGING TECHNOLOGY

THE SEMANTIC WEB

Imagine that you are planning to take a trip to Alaska, and you want to visit its most scenic natural wonders, go when the weather is best, and stay at inexpensive, yet interesting, hotels. You would have to surf from Web site to Web site to collect the information you needed and then book reservations. What if your computer could do all this for you?

Tim Berners-Lee, the inventor of the Web, envisions new ways to increase the potential of the Internet.

The Intelligent Web

Tim Berners-Lee, the inventor of the World Wide Web, wants to make the Web more "intelligent." He calls this new model the "Semantic Web." "Semantics" refers to the meaning or relationships among words or signs. The Semantic Web is intended to help computers understand relationships among various types of data. Researchers at the World Wide Web Consortium (W3C) are already beginning to incorporate this new, powerful functionality into the existing Web.

Finding Relationships

The Semantic Web would allow computers to recognize content by using a common set of rules that make any data meaningful. For example, when you look for information on the "Visit Alaska!" Web site, you know that clicking on a "lodging" hyperlink will take you to a list of hotels with descriptions and prices.

A computer program does not understand the word "lodging" or the hotel price and rating system on the site. It will, however, understand rules that define the relationships between Alaska, lodging, hotels, prices, and hotel amenities. These rules will allow the computer to link "inexpensive hotel" to descriptions such as "mountain view," and find hotels that cost between $60 to $85.

Developing Rules

The Semantic Web is a long way in the future. Computers still need user input to make reasonable choices or find the best solutions. Semantic Web researchers are trying to add rules and logic that will make it possible for computers to interpret information on the Web without human help.

Tech Focus

1. Why do you think Berners-Lee believes the Semantic Web is an important development? Write a one-page report, assessing the potential of this emerging technology.

2. Create a timeline that shows the development of the World Wide Web, from the initial concept of using hyperlinks up to present-day advances.

Section 6.4 Enhancing the Template

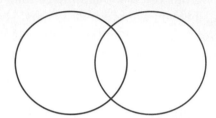
The Astronomy Club template is almost complete. In this section, you will add navigation buttons and insert the template's footer information.

NAVIGATION BUTTONS

A **navigation link** is a button that users click to locate additional information and to navigate to other Web pages. There are different types of navigation buttons. A **hover button** is a navigation button that changes appearance when touched by a mouse pointer. For example, a hover button may change from dark blue to light blue when touched by a mouse pointer. Clicking the button may change its appearance yet again. A clicked button is referred to as an **active button,** because it is in the process of doing something, such as transferring the user to another Web page.

A hover button is a type of **interactive button** (sometimes called a dynamic button). An interactive button lets users know that an action has taken place. These cues increase the user-friendliness of your site. FrontPage provides many different styles of pre-made interactive buttons, and it also allows you to create custom buttons.

All navigation buttons in the Astronomy Club Web site will be vertically aligned at the left side of the template. A related group of horizontally or vertically aligned links is called a **link bar** (also referred to as a navigation bar). Placing a link bar in a Web page template helps users in several ways:

◆ The bar acts as a map to the site's main pages.
◆ The bar is easy to locate because it is always in the same position on every page.
◆ Users can quickly find links because they are in the same order on every page.

ACTIVITY 6F Adding Navigation Buttons

1 Open the Astronomy Club's **ac_template.htm** page in Design (in 2002, Normal) view. Click in the first row of the first column.

2 If you are using 2003: On the **Insert** menu, click **Interactive Button.** In the dialog box, click the **Button** tab. Under Buttons, click **Border Bottom 1.**

3 If you are using 2002: Click **Insert>Web Component.** In the dialog box, double-click **Hover Button.** Select **Navy** for Button color, and **Blue** for Effect color.

4 In the Text (in 2002, Button Text) box, type Home. In the Link (in 2002, Link To) box, type index.htm.

5 Click the **Image** tab (in 2002, there is no tab to click). For Width, type 125. For Height, type 25. In 2003, make certain that the three check boxes below Width are selected. Click **OK.**

6 Use Table 6.1 to create four more buttons.

Navigation Buttons

Button	Text Box	Link Box
1	Home	index.htm
2	About Us	about_us.htm
3	Meetings	meetings.htm
4	Sky Guide	sky_guide.htm
5	Links	links.htm

7 Right-click anywhere in the onscreen table and select **Table Properties.** Under Borders, set Size to **0** and click **OK.** The borders now appear as dotted lines. These dotted lines allow you to see where you are in the table, but they are only visible in Design view.

8 Save your work. Click **OK** in the Save Embedded Files dialog box.

9 Switch to **Preview** view. Notice there are no borders around the table, as shown in Figure 6.13. Switch back to **Design** view and save your work.

Table 6.1
Change the information in the Text and Link boxes for each new button.

READ ME!

Tech Tip Rather than re-create the same button four times, you may choose to copy and paste the original button. Then all you need to do is open each button's Interactive Button dialog box and change the Text box and Link box as indicated in Table 6.1.

Figure 6.13
In Preview view, your Astronomy Club template should look similar to this illustration.

FOOTER INFORMATION

A Web page's **footer** usually contains date information, copyright information, contact information, and text links. The Astronomy Club Web pages will have the following:

- Text links
- A link that allows visitors to e-mail the Webmaster
- Copyright information

You will center each of these items horizontally on a separate line at the bottom of the template.

YOU TRY IT

ACTIVITY 6G Adding Footer Information

1 Open the **ac_template.htm** page in Design (in 2002, Normal) view.

 2 Position the insertion point below the table, at the left margin. Click the drop-down arrow on the Font Color button in the Formatting toolbar and click the **white** color box.

3 Type the following, including the vertical line between each link. (To create the vertical line, hold down **Shift** while pressing the **backslash key** [\]). Place a space between each item you type: Home | About Us | Meetings | Sky Guide | Links.

4 Press **Enter** and then type: Questions or comments about the Web site? E-mail the Webmaster.

5 Press **Enter.** Open the **Font Size** drop-down list and choose **1 (8 pt)**. Type the following: Copyright 2004 – Astronomy Club.

6 Select all three lines of text you have typed. Click the **Center** button to center the lines. Proofread your work and make any needed corrections. Save your work.

Text Links

You should always include text links in your footer. Some people hide graphics so they can download pages more quickly. Including text links in the footer allows viewers who do not have graphic capabilities to navigate the site.

Like interactive buttons, text links often change colors to show whether the link has been clicked. Even if you use FrontPage's default settings, you should always set your hyperlink colors to make sure that they work well with your site and do not blend into the background. Also confirm that the colors assigned to nonvisited, visited, and active links are consistent throughout your site.

YOU TRY IT

ACTIVITY 6H Adding Text Links

1 Open the Astronomy Club's **ac_template.htm** page in Design (in 2002, Normal) view.

2 Select the word **Home** in the text links at the bottom of the page. Right-click the selected text, and click **Hyperlink.** The Insert Hyperlink dialog box opens.

❸ Make certain that the Look in text box contains the location of your Web site.

❹ In the Address text box, type index.htm. Click **OK.**

❺ Repeat steps 2 through 4 for each text link. Use the information shown in Table 6.2.

Text Links

Select	Enter in the URL Text Box
About Us	about_us.htm
Meetings	meetings.htm
Sky Guide	sky_guide.htm
Links	links.htm

Table 6.2
Each text link connects to a specific URL.

❻ Right-click anywhere on the page and click **Page Properties.** In the Page Properties dialog box, click the **Formatting** (in 2002, **Background**) tab. Under Colors, set Hyperlink to **blue,** Visited hyperlink to **purple,** and Active hyperlink to **red.** The dialog box appears as shown in Figure 6.14. Click **OK** and save your work.

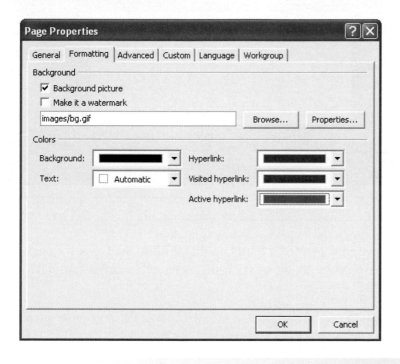

Figure 6.14
Some Web browsers may use default settings if you do not specify your hyperlink colors.

Links to E-mail Windows

The last step in creating the Astronomy Club template is to create a link to an e-mail window (also referred to as an e-mail hyperlink). When visitors click the Webmaster link at the bottom of the page, an e-mail window will pop up that contains the Webmaster's e-mail address. This feature allows visitors to send messages to the Webmaster.

ACTIVITY 6I Adding a Link to an E-mail Window

YOU TRY IT

❶ Open the **ac_template.htm** page in Design (in 2002, Normal) view.

❷ Select the **E-mail the Webmaster** text. Right-click the selected text and click **Hyperlink** to open the Insert Hyperlink dialog box.

3 In the Insert Hyperlink dialog box, click the **E-mail Address** button in the lower-left corner. In the E-mail address text box, enter your e-mail address (or another address, as instructed by your teacher). Notice that the text "mailto:" is automatically inserted at the beginning of the line. Click **OK** and save your work.

4 Spell check and proofread your template. Since you will build your Web pages on this template, you want to make certain everything is correct. If you make any changes, be sure to re-save the page.

5 Switch to **Preview** view. Your template should now appear similar to Figure 6.15. Preview the page in several different browsers at several different resolutions. Make any needed corrections and re-save your work.

Figure 6.15
Be sure to carefully proofread and test your final template.

You have now created a template that will be the basis for each Astronomy Club Web page. In the next chapter, you will use this template to create pages for the Web site.

Section 6.4 Assessment

Concept Check

1. **Define** navigation link, hover button, active button, interactive button, link bar, footer.

2. **Identify** at least two ways that you can control a navigation button's appearance.

3. **Explain** the purpose of an e-mail window.

Critical Thinking

4. **Analyze** What are the primary advantages of interactive buttons on Web pages?

5. **Synthesize** Besides using interactive buttons, how else can a Web designer make a site more user-friendly?

Applying Skills

Create a Footer Open the MySkills page you created in Chapter 4. Add a footer to the page that contains an e-mail contact and a copyright notice.

SECTION 6.1 Creating Web Site Content

Key Terms

content, 150   inverted pyramid, 152

Main Ideas

- Users typically scan text for keywords.
- Use an inverted pyramid to organize Web text.
- Group online text into smaller topics with concise heads.
- Place items in a clear hierarchy and use bulleted lists to make text easy to read.
- Brainstorming is a useful technique for generating and organizing online content.

SECTION 6.2 Placing Items on a Page

Key Terms

pixel, 155   white space, 158
screen resolution, 155   proximity, 158
safe area, 155

Main Ideas

- To prevent scrolling, a Web page's width and height should roughly match the width and height of the viewer's monitor screen.
- View your Web pages in various browsers and at various screen resolutions to see how they will appear to different users.
- Place important content, such as logos, in a screen's safe area.
- Do not place too much content on a Web page. Instead, include enough white space to keep the page from looking too cluttered and confusing.

SECTION 6.3 Creating a Page Template

Key Terms

logo, 162   column, 163
title graphic, 162   row, 163
table, 163   cell, 163

Main Ideas

- Templates help designers organize common Web page items such as logos, title graphics, navigation links, and footers.
- Designers can create custom templates to meet the needs of a specific site.
- Logos and title graphics help give each Web page in a site a consistent visual appearance.
- Tables help organize a page's content into rows and columns.

SECTION 6.4 Enhancing the Template

Key Terms

navigation link, 166   interactive button, 166
hover button, 166   link bar, 166
active button, 166   footer, 168

Main Ideas

- A hover button changes its appearance when users position the mouse pointer over it.
- A related group of horizontally or vertically aligned links forms a link bar.
- Including both text links and graphical links makes a site more user-friendly.
- Visited text links are typically a different color from nonvisited and active links.
- Including a link to an e-mail window helps users contact the site's Webmaster or owner.

Reviewing Key Terms

1. What items make up a Web page's content?
2. Which of the following items should be placed in a page's safe area: footer, logo, title graphic?
3. What should you use to create visual space between images and body text?
4. True or false: A table consists of vertical rows and horizontal columns.
5. Rewrite this statement to make it true: *A navigation button is a symbol used to identify a business or an organization and typically is linked to the site's home page.*

Understanding Main Ideas

6. **Identify** techniques you can use to create a well-written Web site.
7. **Discuss** how you can use an inverted pyramid to organize your ideas.
8. **Describe** how the size of an element affects a user's perception of Web page content.
9. **Explain** why it is important to keep vital elements within certain areas of the Web page.
10. **Explain** how table rows, columns, and cells are related to one another.
11. **List** four properties that can be set in the Table Properties dialog box.
12. **Describe** three situations in which an interactive button's appearance might change.
13. **Discuss** ways in which link bars make Web pages more user-friendly.
14. **Describe** two situations in which you might want to include links to an e-mail window.

Critical Thinking

15. **Compare and Contrast** Do you prefer reading a magazine in print or online form? Why do you prefer one over the other? Analyze how online magazines present their articles compared to the print editions. How do these magazines adapt their content to suit online readers?
16. **Analyze Content** Imagine designing a Web site for your favorite movie. Following the rule of using function over form, identify the elements that you would include on your home page and those you would resist including. Explain why you would not include these items on your page.
17. **Evaluate Layout** Give an example of a situation in which it would be more appropriate to use a pre-made template than a custom template. Give an example of a situation in which it would probably be more appropriate to use a custom template. Explain the reasons behind your decisions.
18. **Analyze Design** Describe ways in which a well-designed Web page provides visual cues to help users navigate the site. Explain how these visual clues help make a site more user-friendly.

e-Review

webdesign.glencoe.com

Study with PowerPoint

To review the main points in this chapter, select **e-Review** > **PowerPoint Outlines** > **Chapter 6**.

Online Self Check

Test your knowledge of the material in this chapter by selecting **e-Review** > **Self Checks** > **Chapter 6**.

Making Connections

Language Arts—Write Web Text Rewrite the following text for use on a Web page. Use headings and bulleted lists to break the text into smaller sections.

Cape Cod, Massachusetts, is a popular vacation destination. In the summer, you can swim in the ocean, go on a whale-watching expedition, or walk the beach on Cape Cod Bay. In the fall, you can take nature walks at the National Seashore, attend cranberry harvest festivals, or visit Plymouth Plantation to learn how the pilgrims lived. Many people also visit Cape Cod in the winter to enjoy the snow and to attend the holiday festivals.

STANDARDS AT WORK

Students use telecommunications to collaborate, publish, and interact with peers, experts, and other audiences. (NETS-S 4)

Evaluate Layout

Print out the home page of a Web site you visit often. Assume you need to evaluate the page's layout and send the Web designer an e-mail with your comments.

1. Evaluate the Web page's layout using the following questions:

   ◆ Where does your eye go first?
   ◆ Is important content emphasized?
   ◆ Is there enough white space on the page?
   ◆ Are related items grouped together?
   ◆ Is text aligned consistently?

2. Write an e-mail that summarizes your evaluation. Be sure to include the link to the page you reviewed. With your teacher's permission, exchange e-mails with another student. Review each other's evaluations. Reply to the e-mail explaining why you agree or disagree with the other student's evaluation.

TEAMWORK SKILLS

Evaluate Content

Select one Web page you have created and have it reviewed by your peers. Following your teacher's instructions, form a team with three other students. Make sure that no one in the team has seen each other's pages.

Look at the first Web page for ten seconds. As a group, discuss the following:

1. What is the Web page about?
2. What information could you determine from the viewing area?
3. Was information easy to see and understand? Why or why not?
4. How can the page be improved? The team must agree on how the page should be revised.

Repeat this for each member's Web page. Make any needed changes to your page, and share the pages again as a group. Point out how you improved your page and see if your team members agree.

CHALLENGE YOURSELF

Create a Template

Use FrontPage to design a template based on the diagram below. This template can be used as a photo gallery. Include placeholder text as appropriate. The text can describe the expected content for the page. Save the template and give it an appropriate name.

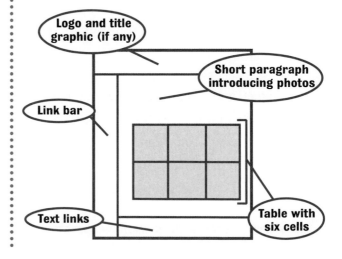

Logo and title graphic (if any)

Short paragraph introducing photos

Link bar

Text links

Table with six cells

YOU TRY IT
Skills Studio

These exercises reinforce the skills you learned in this chapter's You Try It activities. Refer back to the You Try It activities if you need extra guidance.

1. Creating Web Content

Family friends have just opened an Italian restaurant. They want you to design a Web site that contains their menu, phone number, and e-mail so that customers can make reservations or call in for take-out orders.

A Make a list of keywords that apply to the restaurant.

B Use the information from their advertisement (shown right) to write the content for the site's home page.

C Write the content for the restaurant's menu page.

2. Creating a Template

Create a template for the restaurant site in You Try It Skills Studio 1.

A Sketch a layout for the home page that uses a two-column table. The template must also include a logo, a title, a footer, and navigation buttons. Place the navigation buttons in the table's left column and the page's content in the right column.

B Create a template in FrontPage for the site's home page based on your sketch.

C Add the home page content you wrote in You Try It Skills Studio 1.

D Add navigation buttons for other pages in the site: Menu page, Restaurant Events page, and Employee of the Month page.

E Add text links and "E-mail the Webmaster" in the footer.

F Add a link from "E-mail the Webmaster" in the footer to an e-mail window.

G Save your work.

Giovanni's

Featuring the best pasta in town, outstanding pizza, and terrific panini sandwiches!

At Giovanni's, we offer the finest food at reasonable prices! Our chef brings his authentic family recipes direct from Italy.

Come dine with us at 1234 Riverview Avenue.

Call in advance for reservations or takeout orders. We also deliver.

Reach us by phone 323-555-5555 or e-mail at contactus@pasta.com

Web Design Projects

1. Develop Content for a Template

In Chapter 5, you created a storyboard and thumbnails for a Web site for a travel bookstore. Use the storyboard and thumbnails to plan the content for the home page and create the Web site.

First, write the content for the home page. Then, create a template for the site. The template should include a title bar, navigation buttons, and a footer. Plan a table for the template that places navigation links and content in appropriate places.

Enter the content information for the home page. Create the additional pages in the Web site, but do not add content to them. Link all pages using the navigation structure shown in your storyboard.

2. Create a Personal Web Site

Plan and create a personal Web site. The home page should describe who you are, what your interests are, and what can be found at your site. Use appropriate keywords on your home page. Your site should also include at least three other pages. Ideas for pages include a portfolio page showing work you are proud of, an interests page describing your hobbies, pages for one or more of the classes you are taking, a creativity page for ideas you want to explore further or use later, or a résumé page.

Sketch a storyboard for your site. Then, write the content for your home page. Based on your sketch, use FrontPage to create the home page for your site. Be sure to include appropriate navigation. Add the content that you have written. Create the remaining pages for your site, but do not add content at this time. Save your work.

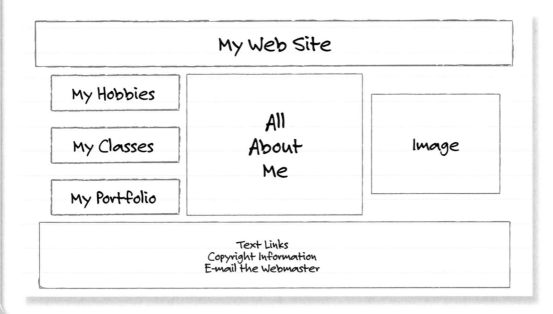

CHAPTER 7

Selecting Color and Design

YOU WILL LEARN TO...

Section 7.1
- Identify presentation design principles
- Use a custom template
- Add pages to a navigation structure

Section 7.2
- Identify color scheme guidelines
- Use Web-safe colors

Section 7.3
- Identify text properties
- Summarize formatting guidelines
- Format text

Section 7.4
- Insert a text document
- Create an image map
- Define a hotspot
- Use a checklist

WHY IT MATTERS.....................................

Consistency of design helps you use tools more effectively. For example, every car has the steering wheel, brakes, and other important controls in about the same place. You expect each of these controls to work in the same way. This consistency enables you to drive different cars without having to relearn their basic parts every time. In this chapter, you will learn how to design consistent Web sites that are equally user-friendly.

Quick Write Activity

Think about a tool that you use every day (a stove, television set, toothbrush, etc.). Write a short paragraph identifying the features or controls that make this tool easy to use. What would happen if you used a similar tool that did not have these features? How easy or hard would it be to relearn how to use this tool if it were redesigned?

176 Chapter 7

WHAT YOU WILL DO...

READ TO SUCCEED

Get Creative
An excellent way to stay engaged in your reading is to make associations while you read. For example, drawing an image of a piece of computer hardware and labeling it reinforces your memory. Thinking of an easy-to-remember rhyme or setting a series of short steps to music is another way to help your brain make associations for easier recall. Your memory trick does not have to be beautiful or impressive—it only has to mean something to you.

Section 7.1 Principles of Presentation Design

Main Ideas

Well-designed Web pages follow the guidelines of consistency and repetition. Using consistent visual elements and placing key items in the same place from page to page makes a site user-friendly.

Key Terms

consistency
repetition
page banner

Reading Strategy

Identify five presentation design principles. Use a web diagram similar to the one below (also available online).

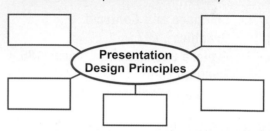

Presentation Design Principles

A user-friendly Web site is a site that visitors feel comfortable navigating. Two features that make Web sites user-friendly are consistency and repetition. These are important elements of presentation design.

CONSISTENCY AND REPETITION

Presentation design focuses on the physical appearance of a Web site's pages. You learned some presentation design guidelines in Chapter 6. Aligning text and images consistently, grouping related items, and including plenty of white space on a page are all principles of good presentation design. Following these principles helps you create pages that are visually appealing.

Consistency and repetition are two more presentation design guidelines. **Consistency** is a logical coherence among parts. If key elements on your pages are consistent, users will recognize that they are on the same site as they navigate it. Using the same color palette and visual style throughout a site helps maintain this feeling of consistency. For example, if your home page uses pastel colors, then the other pages in the site also should use pastel, and not primary, colors. Applying a theme also helps to create consistency. Logos, title bars, and graphic navigation buttons should look the same from page to page. These visual clues let users know when they have surfed to a page that is not part of your site.

Repetition is the duplication of specific elements on all (or most) of a site's pages. The same navigation buttons should appear in the same order on all of the main pages. Text-based links should appear at the bottom of each page. The logo should always be in the same spot so users can easily find their way back to the home page. Repetition helps users quickly find the buttons and links they need to navigate through the site. The principles of consistency and repetition make a Web site more user-friendly.

Activity 7.1 Explore Presentation Design Find out more about presentation design by visiting **webdesign.glencoe.com**.

CREATING WEB PAGES

You are now ready to use the template you made in Chapter 6 to create the Astronomy Club site's individual Web pages. Because you are using a template, the position and appearance of main elements, such as the site's logo, title graphic, and navigation buttons, will be the same on each page. The template helps the site follow the presentation guidelines of consistency and repetition.

Assigning File Names and Page Titles

In the following activity, you will create the five main pages in the Astronomy Club Web site. You will then assign file names and page titles to each of these pages.

ACTIVITY 7A Using a Template to Create New Pages

YOU TRY IT

❶ Start FrontPage. Open the Astronomy Club Web site. If the Folder List is not open, click **View** and choose **Folder List.**

❷ In the Folder List, right-click **ac_template.htm.** On the shortcut menu, click **Copy.**

❸ Right-click an empty area of the Folder List and click **Paste.** Repeat this process four times to create a total of five copies. When you finish, the Folder List should look similar to Figure 7.1.

❹ Right-click the **ac_template_copy(1).htm** file, and click **Rename.** Rename the file index.htm. Repeat this process for the remaining four copies. Use the file names shown in the left column of Table 7.1.

❺ In the Folder List, right-click the **index.htm** file, and click **Properties.** Type Astronomy Club Home in the Title box on the General tab. Click **OK.** Repeat this step for the remaining four files. Use the page titles shown in the right column of Table 7.1.

❻ When you copy and rename pages this way, your changes are saved automatically. You do not need to click Save.

READ ME!

Tech Tip You can also open the Folder List by pressing Alt + F1.

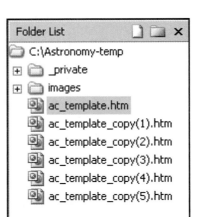

● **Figure 7.1**
The folder list has five copies of the original page.

● **Table 7.1**
Assign each page the file name and page title shown here.

File Names and Page Titles

File Name	Page Title
index.htm	Astronomy Club Home
about_us.htm	About Us
meetings.htm	Meetings & Activities
sky_guide.htm	Sky Guide
links.htm	Astronomy Links

Pages and Navigation Structure

Now that you have created the five main pages and given them titles, you need to add them to the site's navigation structure. In the next You Try it, you will follow the navigation scheme developed in Chapter 5 and make the About Us, Meetings & Activities, Sky Guide, and Astronomy Links pages into child pages of the home page.

YOU TRY IT ▶ **ACTIVITY 7B Adding Pages to the Navigation Structure**

❶ Open the Astronomy Club Web site.

❷ On the **View** menu, click **Navigation.** Notice that only the home page is currently part of the navigation structure.

❸ Drag the **about_us.htm** file from the Folder List to the Navigation view window. Drop the file below the home page.

❹ Repeat this process for the **meetings.htm, sky_guide.htm,** and **links.htm** pages. Your pages should look like Figure 7.2. Note that Navigation view displays the page title, not the file name. To view the full title, place your pointer over the page.

Figure 7.2 ●
This figure shows the basic navigation structure for the Astronomy Club Web site. ▼

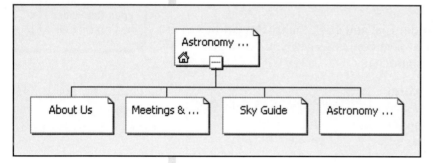

❺ On the View menu, click **Hyperlinks.** This view shows how each main page links to the site's home page (see Figure 7.3). The arrows indicate the direction of each link. Click **View** and choose **Navigation** to return to Navigation view.

❻ Because you are modifying the structure of your site, and not making changes to individual pages, you do not need to save your work. The modifications are automatically saved for you.

Figure 7.3 ●
The Hyperlinks view displays the links to the site's home page.

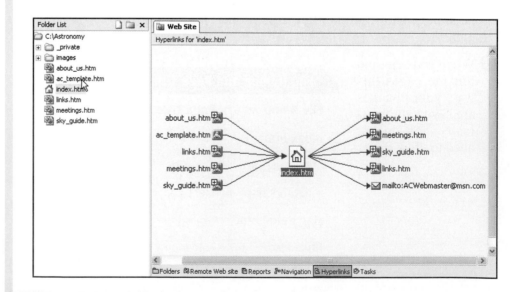

Page Banners

A **page banner** contains graphics and/or text that help users identify where they are in a Web site. A site's logo and title graphic are usually part of the page banner, which can run across the top or down the side of a Web page. Page banners usually also contain the page title. Page banners help give a site a consistent look.

In the Astronomy Club Web site, the home page has a slightly different banner than the other pages. Both the title graphic for the entire site and the Welcome message are contained in a single graphic. The banners on the other pages are somewhat different from each other. They consist of the title graphic for the site (which is part of the template) and a title graphic for each individual page.

In the following activity, you will add a page banner to each page in the Astronomy Club Web site. The title graphic tells viewers the name of the Web site they are currently visiting. Additional text identifies each individual Web page.

ACTIVITY 7C Inserting Page Banners

1 In the Folder List, double-click **index.htm** to open the home page.

2 Click the logo (planet graphic) in the upper-left corner. Right-click and click **Cut.** The logo is removed. Click the title graphic. Right-click and click **Cut.**

3 Make certain that the insertion point is positioned in the upper-left corner of the page. Click the **Insert Picture From File** button. Browse to the DataFile\Ch07\Images folder. Double-click the file named **titlebar_home.gif** to insert it into the page. Notice that this file contains the logo, the title graphic, and the home page's specific welcome message, as shown in Figure 7.4.

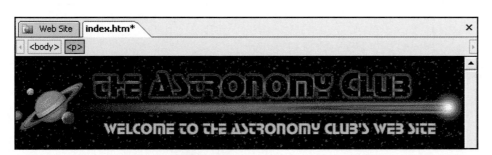

4 Right-click the **titlebar_home.gif** image. Select **Picture Properties.** On the General tab, click **Text** under Alternative representations. Type Astronomy Club Home in the text box. Click **OK.**

5 Save the page. In the Save Embedded Files dialog box, make certain the files will be saved in the **images** folder. Click **OK.**

6 In the Folder List, double-click **about_us.htm** to open the About Us page. Position the insertion point at the right edge of the title graphic and press **Shift + Enter** to insert a blank line. Click the **Insert Picture From File** button. Browse to the DataFile\Ch07\Images folder. Double-click **t_aboutus.gif.**

● **Figure 7.4**
This figure shows the page banner for the home page.

READ ME!

Tech Tip If the logo and the Web site title cannot both fit on the top line, use the mouse pointer to make the Folder List pane narrower. However, be careful that your page still displays well at different resolutions!

Figure 7.5
The text on this page banner is different from the text on the home page banner.

READ ME!

Tech Tip A quick way to save a Web page is to press Ctrl + S.

Table 7.2
Insert the graphic and alternative text for the remaining three pages.

⑦ The page should now look like Figure 7.5. Repeat steps 4 and 5 with the **about_us.gif** image. Type About Us for the alternative text.

⑧ Repeat steps 4 and 5 for each of the remaining pages. For each page, insert the graphic and the alternative representation name as listed in Table 7.2.

Page Banner Information

Page Title	Graphic	Alternative Representations
Meetings	t_meetings.gif	Meetings
Sky Guide	t_skyguide.gif	Sky Guide
Astronomy Links	t_links.gif	Astronomy Links

You have now completed the basic framework for all of the Astronomy Club pages. In the next section, you will add content to these pages.

Section 7.1 Assessment

Concept Check

1. **Define** consistency, repetition, page banner.

2. **Explain** why consistency and repetition are important design principles.

3. **List** three items that are typically repeated on a Web site's main pages.

Critical Thinking

4. **Analyze** In this section, you altered the home page banner so that the logo no longer contained a link to the home page. Why is a link not needed on this page?

5. **Synthesize** Discuss several ways in which you rely on consistency and repetition in your daily life.

Applying Skills

Compare and Contrast Graphics Each Astronomy Club Web page has a graphic that identifies the entire site and a graphic that identifies each individual page. How are these two graphics different from one another? How are they alike?

Careers & Technology

PROGRAMMING FOR THE WEB

Most computer users believe Web sites consist of nothing more than text, images, and HTML tags that anyone can create in a few minutes. Look behind the scenes at a feature-rich Web site such as CNN.com, however, and you will get a different picture.

Sites that include many different features often require more complex programming.

Programming Complex Sites

Many Web sites go far beyond standard text-and-graphics pages. Many e-commerce sites, for example, incorporate advanced databases, transaction processing, and security elements along with their text and graphics. To see examples, go shopping at a site such as Amazon.com, or design a custom-built computer with Dell's on-line "configurator."

Common Languages of the Web

What tools do programmers use to develop Web pages? Here are just a few:

- Java
- JavaScript
- CGI
- Visual Basic
- VBScript
- C++

Programmers use different languages to produce different results. Streaming technologies, such as those developed by Real Networks, enable Web-masters to serve audio and video content from their sites. This type of content, along with animations supported by Macromedia's Flash, Shockwave, and Director, requires developers to use sophisticated authoring environments.

Many sites also use databases to create and manage customer, inventory, and transaction information. Catalog and shopping sites may use database management systems such as Oracle, Sybase, SQL Server, and others.

Training for Web Programmers

Every Web programmer must be proficient in common Web tools such as HTML and XML. Perl and CGI are two basic languages that all Web programmers should know. Experts also recommend that people who are interested in becoming Web programmers should study as many visual programming languages as they can. If database or multimedia programming is your interest, then focus on the languages required for those disciplines. Many colleges and technical schools offer certification or degree programs in computer programming.

Tech Focus

1. Explain why is it important to understand programming languages when creating complex Web sites.

2. Go online and research Web-related programming and the training and educational opportunities available in this field. Create a multimedia Web page describing the career path that interests you.

Guide to Reading

Main Ideas

A Web site's color scheme should both appeal to visitors and create a sense of continuity among the pages. Using Web-safe colors helps ensure that pages will appear the same to all viewers, regardless of the systems and browsers they are using.

Key Terms

color scheme
Web-safe color

Reading Strategy

Identify three color scheme guidelines. Use a web diagram similar to the one below (also available online).

Color Scheme Guidelines

Color attracts attention. You should consider a number of factors when choosing a color scheme for a Web site.

Activity 7.2 Select Color Schemes Find out more about using color in your Web pages by visiting **webdesign.glencoe.com**.

COLOR SCHEME GUIDELINES

A **color scheme** is a set of selected colors used consistently for your Web site's interface elements, such as title graphics, navigation buttons, and background. Ideally, you should limit the number of colors used in your Web site's interface to three or four. Limiting the number of colors helps create a sense of unity throughout a site.

You can use colors to draw attention to important items on a page, such as navigation links, logos, headings, key content, and so forth. When choosing a scheme, it is also important to select colors that are appropriate for your message. The Astronomy Club Web pages, for example, have a black background filled with stars, evoking the image of the night sky. The colors in its buttons and banners are primarily blue and gold. Limiting the pages to these colors with a consistent background creates a strong sense of unity among the pages.

TECH TRIVIA

Pixel Values Each pixel on a computer screen is defined as some amount of red, green, and blue. White appears when a pixel is assigned the maximum value of red, green, and blue. Black appears when a pixel is assigned no red, green, or blue.

USING WEB-SAFE COLORS

Not all colors will display exactly the same way on every screen. Colors can look different depending on the computer platform, monitor type, or Web browser visitors use to view the page.

Only 216 of the many colors available will display consistently from computer to computer. Using these colors, which are commonly referred to as **Web-safe colors,** gives Web designers some control over their pages' appearance. Appendix C contains a chart showing these 216 colors along with their corresponding hexadecimal values. When choosing colors, confirm that your choices appear on the Web-safe color chart. Choose hexidecimal numbers that contain the following character pairs: 00, 33, 66, 99, CC, and FF.

Numbers that contain these character pairs are Web-safe colors, as illustrated in Appendix C. In addition, the color palette contained in FrontPage's More Colors dialog box only features Web-safe colors. In the following activity, you will use Web-safe colors to add colored text to your home page.

ACTIVITY 7D Adding Content and Color to the Home Page

YOU TRY IT

❶ Open the Astronomy Club home page in Design (in FrontPage 2002, Normal) view.

❷ Click in the table's bottom row. From the Table menu, select **Insert>Rows or Columns.** In the dialog box, click **Rows** and type 2 in the Number of Rows text box. Click **OK.** Repeat the process but click **Columns** and type 1 in the Number of Columns text box. Click **OK.**

❸ Select the entire middle column. Right-click anywhere in the column and click **Merge Cells.** The entire column becomes a single cell.

❹ Repeat step 3 for the third column in the table. Click outside the table to deselect it. Your page should resemble Figure 7.6.

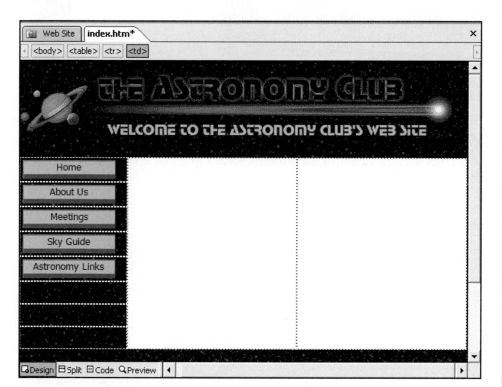

Figure 7.6
The cells have been merged in the table's second and third columns.

❺ Click in the first white cell. Type Photo of the Month. Press **Shift + Enter.**

❻ Click the **Insert Picture From File** button. Browse to the DataFile\Ch07\Images folder. Double-click **home_photo.gif.**

❼ Position the insertion point in the last column of the table. Type This photo captures matter and antimatter being propelled by the Crab pulsar, a neutron star about the size of Manhattan. Press **Enter** twice. Type Photo Credit: NASA.

8 Right-click anywhere on the page and click **Page Properties.** Click the **Formatting** (in 2002, **Background**) tab. Under Colors, click the **Text** drop-down arrow. Click **More Colors.** Type Hex={00,00,99} in the Value text box. Click **OK.** Click **OK** again to close the Page Properties dialog box. All of the text on the home page becomes dark blue, as shown in Figure 7.7.

Figure 7.7
Your Astronomy Club home page now includes a photo and a caption.

9 Click **Save.** In the Save Embedded Files dialog box, make certain the files will be saved in the **images** folder and click **OK.** Proofread and spell check your work. Resave your page as needed.

Section 7.2 Assessment

Concept Check

1. **Define** color scheme, Web-safe color.

2. **List** the steps in specifying a Web-safe color for a page's text.

3. **Explain** why you should only use Web-safe colors on your pages.

Critical Thinking

4. **Draw Conclusions** Describe a color scheme for a Web site about tropical islands. Explain your answers.

5. **Analyze** What factors might a company selling sports clothing online take into consideration when choosing a color scheme for its site?

Applying Skills

Explore Background Colors Experiment with three different background colors for the Astronomy Club home page. What effect do these changes have on the look of the page? (Do not save your changes.)

Section 7.3 Fonts and Typography

In this section, we will discuss **typography,** which is the style, arrangement, and appearance of text. Well-designed text will make your page more readable. It will also call attention to important information and present it clearly and logically.

TEXT PROPERTIES

Presentation design also involves the physical appearance of text on a page. Web designers select the text's type, size, style, alignment, and color. All of these properties affect how text displays on the screen. The process of selecting specific properties is referred to as formatting text. In FrontPage, you use the Formatting toolbar to format text.

Font Types

A **font** is a set of characters that have a specific shape and style. Each font is assigned a name, such as Arial, Times Roman, or Courier. In FrontPage, you select fonts using the Font menu on the Formatting toolbar. The Font menu displays the fonts that are available for you to use, as shown in Figure 7.8.

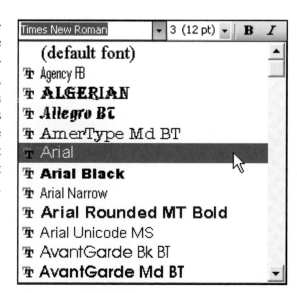

● Figure 7.8
Scroll down the Font menu to view all the fonts that are available on your computer system. What are some of the fonts available on your system?

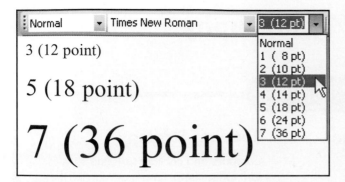

3 (12 point)

5 (18 point)

7 (36 point)

Font Size

You use the Font Size menu on the formatting toolbar to select font sizes (see Figure 7.9). In FrontPage, font sizes are specified by the numbers 1 through 7. Number 1 is the smallest font size and 7 is the largest. Each font size has a point size associated with it. A **point** is a traditional unit of type measurement. The larger the point size, the bigger the text appears on the screen.

Figure 7.9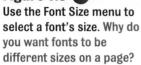
Use the Font Size menu to select a font's size. Why do you want fonts to be different sizes on a page?

Bold, Italic, and Underline

Text can be bold, italic, or underlined. To apply these styles to text, use the bold, italic, or underline buttons on the Formatting toolbar (see Figure 7.10). It is poor design practice to underline Web text. On Web pages, underlined text usually indicates a hyperlink. If you underline text that is not a hyperlink, users will click on it and get frustrated when they think the link is broken. Instead of underlining, emphasize text by making it **bold** or *italic*.

Figure 7.10
You apply styles using buttons on the Formatting toolbar. Why do Web designers avoid underlining text on Web pages?

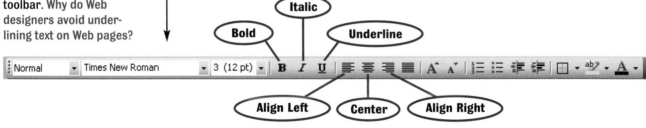

Font Alignment

Figure 7.11
Text can be left-aligned, centered, right-aligned, or justified. When might you want to center text?

Alignment is the position of text on a page. You use the alignment buttons on the Formatting toolbar to align text on a page (see Figure 7.10). Figure 7.11 contains examples of the four types of alignment.

Left-aligned text is positioned flush with the left edge of the page. Text is usually left-aligned automatically when you enter it on a page.	**Centered text is positioned in the middle of the page.**	**Right-aligned text is positioned flush with the page's right edge.**	**Justified text is positioned so that all lines have the same left and right margins.**

Font Color

You can use the Font Color menu on the Formatting toolbar to make fonts different colors (see Figure 7.12). Color can help draw attention to important text. Many Web designers use a single color for most text, and then use one or two additional colors to attract a reader's attention to key content. Always use Web-safe colors, even for fonts.

● **Figure 7.12**
Use the Font Color menu to make your fonts different colors. Why might you make a font a different color on a page?

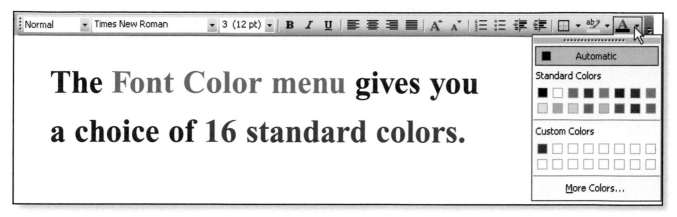

Formatting Style Menu

As you learned in Chapter 2, FrontPage lets you use a number of predefined styles. These styles are listed on the Style menu on the Formatting toolbar. As shown in Figure 7.13, this list provides a Normal style, six levels of headings (Heading 1 through Heading 6), and a number of other styles. Heading 1 uses a large font size (size 6) while Heading 6 uses a small font style (size 1). These predefined styles help you format text quickly.

● **Figure 7.13**
This figure shows the predefined styles available on the FrontPage formatting toolbar's Style drop-down list. What is the advantage to using these styles?

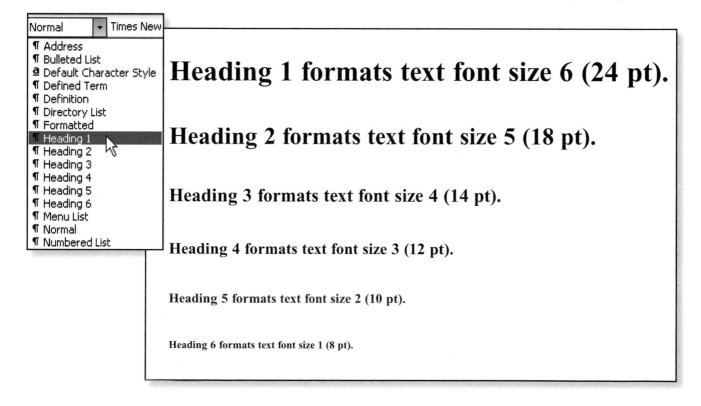

FORMATTING GUIDELINES

All the text on your page should be:

◆ Readable
◆ Consistent
◆ Attractive

Readability

If the text on your page is difficult to read, visitors will surf elsewhere. All text on the page, including headings and captions, should be legible on the monitor. By following some basic guidelines you can make your text more readable.

Use Sans Serif Fonts Fonts can be divided into two broad categories: serif and sans serif. A **serif** font has an extra line or curve on the ends of certain letters or numbers. A **sans serif** font does not have this adornment, as shown in Figure 7.14. ("Sans" is a French word that means "without.")

Figure 7.14 ●—→
Most people find sans serif fonts easier to read on the screen than serif fonts. How is a serif font different from a sans serif font?

Serif Fonts	Sans Serif Fonts
Times New Roman	Arial
Courier New	Futura
Garamond	Helvetica

It is generally accepted that serif fonts are easier to read on paper. For example, Times New Roman is often used in newspapers and other print documents. However, most people find on-screen text more legible when a sans serif font is used. Most Web designers use sans serif fonts such as Arial for online text.

Choose High-Contrast Fonts and Backgrounds You must always consider your page's background when choosing font colors. Make certain that there is enough contrast between your text color and your background to make the text readable. Users find it difficult to read text that blends into the page's background (see Figure 7.15). Black text on a white background, for example, is always readable. Preview your page in a browser to make certain your text is easy to read.

Figure 7.15 ●
Make sure there is enough contrast between your text color and your background color. Which example do you find easier to read?

Text is easier to read when it is used with an appropriate background. The color and size of the text as well as the color and pattern of the background influence readability. Is this text easy to read?

Text is easier to read when it is used with an appropriate background. The color and size of the text as well as the color and pattern of the background influence readability. Is this text easy to read?

Use Styles and Colors Sparingly Too much bold or italic makes text difficult to read. Using too many different font colors on a page can also confuse readers. Use different styles and colors to emphasize important items, but do not emphasize too many items on the page.

Consistency

No matter what formatting you choose, you should use the same formatting throughout the site.

Align Text Consistently As you learned in Chapter 6, you should be consistent when aligning text on your Web pages. If you center the headings in a table on one page, then center the headings in every table throughout the site.

Limit the Number of Fonts You should also limit the number of fonts that you use. A page that contains many different fonts can look disjointed, and the fonts draw attention to themselves and away from your message. For a professional look, use a maximum of three fonts per site. Use one font for logo and banner text, a second font for headings, and a third font for body text. In Web design, a serif font is often used for headings and a sans serif font for body text.

Appearance

As with your color scheme, the fonts you use should visually support the message of your site and page.

Use Formatting to Emphasize Text The formatting you use should also reflect the item's importance. Generally, the more important the page element, the larger its size should be. Items such as titles and table headings are often larger than body text, as shown in Figure 7.16. Copyrights and footer information are usually smaller than body text. As noted, you can also use color to highlight important content.

> **READ ME!**
>
> **Tech Tip** Style sheet help keep formatting consistent. See Appendix D for more information about using style sheets.

● **Figure 7.16**
The size of text reflects the item's importance. What is the most important element on this page?

Hardware Devices Used in My Pages — **Title: 6 (24pt)**

By Matt Baumann — **Author: 4 (14pt)**

This is a digital camera. I can download pictures from my camera to my computer and insert them into my Web pages. — **Body: 3 (12pt)**

© 2004 Matt Baumann — **Copyright: 2 (10 pt)**

Use Standard Fonts Like colors, fonts can display differently depending on the computer platform or browser settings visitors use to view a page. A font change can cause your text to reflow and significantly alter your page's appearance.

You can reduce the risk of having your fonts reformatted by using standard fonts. A standard font is a font that is found on most computer systems.

Computers running the Windows operating system typically have at least three installed fonts: Arial, Times New Roman, and Courier New. Macintosh systems typically have three similar fonts: Helvetica, Times, and Courier. When a Macintosh user views a page that contains Arial font, this font is automatically replaced with Helvetica font, as shown in Table 7.3. The differences between these two fonts are so slight that the substitution does not significantly change the page's appearance.

Table 7.3
Computers come with different fonts on their hard drives. Which of the fonts below are serif fonts?

Mac OS and Windows Font Substitutions	
Mac OS System Font	**Windows System Font**
Courier	Courier New
Helvetica	Arial
Times	Times New Roman
New York	MS Serif

Web designers often use other fonts that are available on most, but not all, computer systems. Two of these fonts, Verdana and Georgia, were specifically designed for display on computer screens.

Use Default Font Sizes Different Web browsers, monitor resolutions, and computer platforms affect the size at which a font displays on the screen. The same-size fonts on the Macintosh will usually appear about one or two points smaller when viewed on the Windows OS. To minimize resizing problems, most Web designers use the default font size (size 3, 12 points) for body text. Using the default setting tells a browser to keep different font sizes relative to each other. Consequently, regardless of how size 3 displays on the screen, sizes 1 and 2 will still be smaller than 3, and sizes 4, 5, 6, and 7 will still be progressively larger than 3.

FORMATTING TEXT IN FRONTPAGE

Because FrontPage provides a WYSIWYG editor, you can immediately see how text is formatted on your pages. In the following activity, you will format text on the Astronomy Club's home page.

YOU TRY IT

ACTIVITY 7E Formatting Text

1 Open the Astronomy Club home page in Design (in 2002, Normal) view.

2 Select the title **Photo of the Month**. On the Formatting toolbar, click the **Font** drop-down arrow and click **Verdana.**

3 Click the **Font Size** drop-down arrow and click **4 (14 pt).**

4 Click the **Center** button to center the text. Click the **Bold** button.

5 Select the caption text in the third column. Click the **Font** drop-down arrow and click **Verdana.** Click the **Center** button to center the caption. Select **Photo Credit: NASA** and format it font size **2 (10pt).**

6 Right-click in the right column and select **Cell Properties.** In the Cell Properties dialog box, under Layout, open the Vertical Alignment drop-down list and click **Middle.** Click **OK.** The caption is now centered vertically in the cell.

7 Position the insertion point on the boundary between the second and third columns. It turns into a two-headed arrow. While holding down the mouse button, drag the boundary about one-half inch to the left.

READ ME!

Tech Tip You can also click the Increase Font Size button on the Formatting toolbar to increase the font by one size.

8 Click the **Save** button. Go to **Preview** view. The home page should now appear as shown in Figure 7.17. Go back to **Design** (in 2002, **Normal**) view.

● **Figure 7.17**
You have changed the style and alignment of elements on the home page.

The Astronomy Club's home page is now complete. In the next section, you will continue adding pages and features to the Web site.

Section 7.3 Assessment

Concept Check

1. **Define** typography, font, point, alignment, serif, sans serif.

2. **Discuss** two reasons why the on-screen size of a font can vary from one computer system to another.

3. **Identify** the four types of alignments.

Critical Thinking

4. **Evaluate** Describe a situation in which you might NOT want to use Justify to align a block of text.

5. **Make Decisions** In Web site design, the principles of readability and appearance are often at odds. For example, the colors of a company's logo may clash with the page background. How should this conflict be handled?

Applying Skills

Evaluate Fonts Apply three different types of fonts to the photo caption on the Astronomy Club home page. Evaluate each font. Close the site without saving your changes.

Real World Technology

COOKIES AND CONSUMER PRIVACY

Online merchants often use cookies to track online customers. A "cookie" is a text file that a Web server places on a visitor's computer. This file stores information that the server can use the next time that person visits the site.

If you use the Web a lot, there may be hundreds of cookies stored on your computer's hard disk.

- Cookie: ask.com
- Cookie: brittanica.com
- Cookie: cbs.com
- Cookie: clrn.org
- Cookie: microsoft.com

Tracking Consumers Online

Cookies can collect many kinds of online information. For example, cookies often create lists of the Web sites you visit and pass this information to the Web server. Using this list, the merchant can choose to display ads on your screen that match the interests revealed by your surfing habits.

When you shop online, cookies may store your name and the type of items you search for. The next time you log on to the site, the site will greet you by name and perhaps offer you a list of items related to your previous purchase.

Many e-commerce sites also use cookies to automate the log-on procedure. After logging on for the first time, a cookie saves your user ID and password, so you will not have to type them again.

Privacy Concerns

Businesses can use cookies to gather enormous databases of information about consumers. Much of this information is personal, such as Social Security numbers, income data, phone numbers, passwords, and credit card data.

Privacy advocates argue that companies gather too much information about consumers and use it inappropriately. For example, a company may sell this information (without its customers' consent) to marketing agencies, which use it to target advertising or telemarketing campaigns.

Reputable online merchants use cookies only for legitimate reasons, and not as "spyware." Unfortunately, you cannot trust all Webmasters to use cookies in an ethical way.

Controlling Cookies

You can manage the cookies on your computer by setting your browser to reject cookies or to prompt you before accepting a cookie. This, however, greatly slows down browsing. Some Web sites will not work unless you accept their cookies.

You can use your browser and file manager to manually remove cookies from your system, but you may find it hard to get rid of all of them. Many users now rely on cookie-management software to control cookies. These programs can automatically delete unwanted cookies while keeping ones from your favorite Web sites.

Tech Focus

1. Cookie files end with the .txt extension. Search your hard disk for files in this format. How many appear to be cookies? What Web sites are they associated with?

2. Visit an e-commerce Web site and analyze its privacy policy and use of cookies. What conclusions can you draw about the site's integrity and ethical use of cookies?

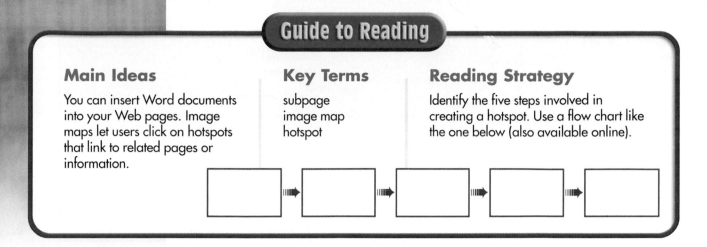

Main Ideas

You can insert Word documents into your Web pages. Image maps let users click on hotspots that link to related pages or information.

Key Terms

subpage
image map
hotspot

Reading Strategy

Identify the five steps involved in creating a hotspot. Use a flow chart like the one below (also available online).

In this section, you will add a child page to the Sky Guide main page. You will then insert an image map into the Sky Guide page that contains a link to this child page.

CREATING SUBPAGES

According to the Astronomy Club Web site's navigation scheme, the Sky Guide page is the parent to several child pages. These child pages each contain information about a particular planet. Often the term **subpage** is used when referring to a page that is a child of another page. In the following activity, you will create the subpage for the planet Saturn and add that subpage to the site's navigation structure.

ACTIVITY 7F Adding a Subpage to the Sky Guide Page

YOU TRY IT

❶ Open the Astronomy Club Web site. In the Folder List, right-click **ac_template.htm.** On the shortcut menu, click **Copy.** Right-click an empty area of the Folder List and click **Paste.** A copy of the template page is created.

❷ Right-click the **ac_template_copy(1).htm** file in the Folder List and click **Rename.** Rename the file saturn.htm.

❸ In the Folder List, double-click **saturn.htm** to open the Saturn page. Right-click anywhere on the page and click **Page Properties.** Under Title, change the title to Saturn Informational Page. Click **OK.**

❹ Click in the table's bottom row. From the **Table** menu, select **Insert>Rows or Columns.** In the dialog box, click **Rows** and type 6 in the Number of Rows text box. Click **OK.**

❺ Select the entire second column. Right-click anywhere in the column and click **Merge Cells.** The column becomes a single cell.

❻ Click the **Save** button to save the Saturn page.

7 On the **View** menu, click **Navigation.** Drag the **saturn.htm** file from the Folder List to the Navigation view window and drop it below the Sky Guide page, as shown in Figure 7.18. Return to **Page** view.

Figure 7.18
The Saturn page is a child (or subpage) of the Sky Guide page.

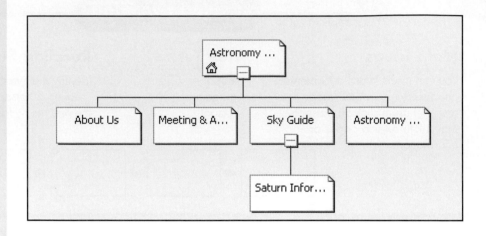

Using Word Documents in FrontPage

Now that you have created the Saturn page, you are ready to insert its contents. In the following activity, you will insert a Word document from the Student Data Files. With your teacher's permission, you can instead insert the document that you created in You Try It Activity 6A in Chapter 6.

YOU TRY IT

ACTIVITY 7G Inserting a Document File into a Web Page

1 Click the tab for the Saturn page (**saturn.htm**) to make it visible.

2 Click anywhere in the white table to position the insertion point. On the **Insert** menu, click **File.** Browse to the DataFile\Ch07\Text folder. Double-click the **saturn.doc** file to open it.

3 Select the text for the entire document. Change the document's font to **Verdana.** Make the title "Our Solar System: Saturn" font size **5 (18 pt).** Bold both this title and the title "Planetary Data."

4 Position the insertion point at the upper-left corner of the document, in front of any text. Click the **Insert Picture From File** button. Browse to the DataFile\Ch07\Images folder. Double-click **saturn.jpg** to insert the image of Saturn.

5 Right-click the Saturn image and click **Picture Properties.** In the Picture Properties dialog box on the Appearance tab, set Wrapping style to **Right.** Click **OK.**

6 Proofread and spell check the text. Save the Saturn page. In the Save Embedded Files dialog box, make certain the file will be saved in the **images** folder and click **OK.** The Saturn page should now look similar to Figure 7.19 on page 197.

READ ME!

Tech Tip Sometimes spell check will place a squiggly red line below a word it thinks is spelled incorrectly. To get rid of this red line, right-click it and click Ignore All.

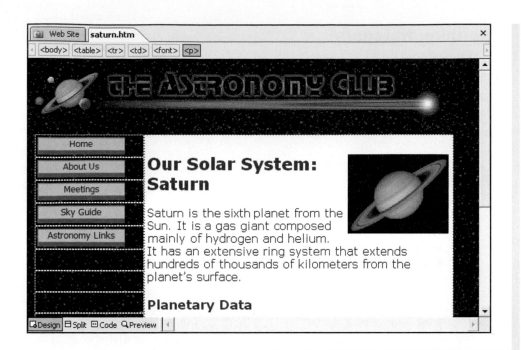

Figure 7.19
The Saturn page's content is consistent with other content on the site.

IMAGE MAPS

An **image map** is a graphic with clickable areas called hotspots. A **hotspot** provides a graphic link to related pages or other areas on the current page. For example, an image map of the United States might contain fifty hotspots, one for each state. If you clicked on Texas, you would be taken to a page containing additional information on that state.

Preparing the Image Map

The Sky Guide page will contain an image map. When users click a planet on this image map, they will be taken to an information page about that planet. In the next You Try It, you will insert the graphic that will be used for the image map.

ACTIVITY 7H Inserting a Graphic for an Image Map

YOU TRY IT

❶ Double-click **sky_guide.htm** in the Folder List to open the Sky Guide page.

❷ Change the number of rows in the table from 6 to 8.

❸ Select the entire second column. Right-click anywhere in the column and click **Merge Cells.** The entire column becomes a single cell.

❹ Click anywhere in the column. Click the **Insert Picture From File** button. Browse to the DataFile\Ch07\Images folder. Double-click **solarsystem.gif** to insert it into the page.

❺ Save the Sky Guide page. Make certain the solarsystem.gif file will be saved in the **images** folder and click **OK.**

Defining Hotspots

To create an image map in FrontPage, you draw outlines to define the clickable hotspots. You can use different tools to create hotspots with different shapes. Hotspots can be rectangular, circular, or polygonal, as described in Table 7.4. In the following activity, you will use the polygon tool to create a hotspot for the planet Saturn.

Table 7.4
The Picture toolbar contains three tools that you can use to create hotspots. Why do you need hotspots that are different shapes?

Hotspot Tools

Picture Toolbar Button	Name	Description
▢	Rectangular Hotspot	Drag the mouse pointer over the portion of the image that should be a hotspot. The hotspot will have a rectangular shape.
⬭	Circular Hotspot	Drag the mouse pointer over the portion of the image that should be a hotspot. The hotspot will have a circular shape.
◺	Polygon Hotspot	Click the mouse pointer around the edges of the shape you want. When you are ready to close the shape, click the starting point.

YOU TRY IT

ACTIVITY 7I Creating a Hotspot

❶ Open the **Sky Guide** page in Design (in 2002, Normal) view.

❷ Click anywhere in the Solar System graphic to select it. Click **View > Toolbars > Pictures** to open the Pictures toolbar.

 ❸ On the Pictures toolbar, click the **Polygon Hotspot** button. Click around the Saturn image as shown in Figure 7.20. The Insert Hyperlink dialog box appears when your ending point joins the starting point.

Figure 7.20
Use the Polygon tool to draw a hotspot around Saturn.

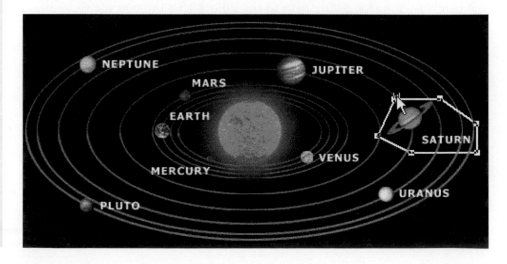

4 In the Insert Hyperlink dialog box, click the **Existing File or Web Page** button on the left side. In the Address text box, type saturn.htm. Click **OK.**

5 Close the Pictures toolbar. Save the Sky Guide page.

6 Switch to **Preview** view. The pointer should become a hand when it passes over the hotspot to indicate a link.

7 Close the Astronomy Club Web site. If possible, open the Sky Guide page in a browser and test the hotspot. It should take you to the Saturn Informational Page as shown in Figure 7.21. Correct and retest the hotspot as needed.

READ ME!

Tech Tip Alternatively, you can click saturn.htm in the file list to insert the file name into the Address text box.

● **Figure 7.21**
Use hotspots to create links between pages.

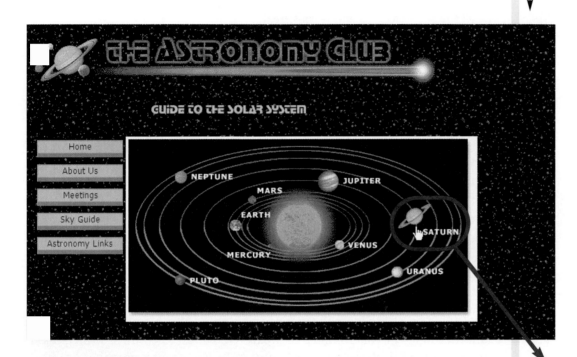

Click the Saturn hotspot and the Saturn page opens.

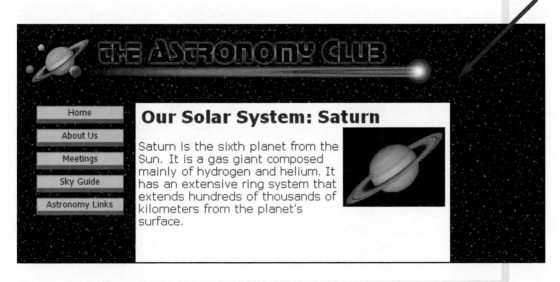

Our Solar System: Saturn

Saturn is the sixth planet from the Sun. It is a gas giant composed mainly of hydrogen and helium. It has an extensive ring system that extends hundreds of thousands of kilometers from the planet's surface.

CHECKLISTS

You have now learned many important guidelines concerning how to use text, images, and color on your Web sites. Checklists can be useful in determining whether your pages conform to these guidelines. Table 7.5 contains a sample checklist that you can use to evaluate both a Web site and a Web page.

Table 7.5
The Web site checklist helps you verify that your site meets its design goals. Why is consistency important in a Web site?

Evaluation Checklist

Web Site Evaluation

☑ The site's content, formatting, and color scheme support the mission statement.

☑ The site's color scheme is consistent.

☑ The site's formatting is consistent.

☑ Text is readable against the background.

☑ Page elements such as link bars and page banners are placed consistently throughout the site.

Web Page Evaluation

☑ Text is presented in short sections.

☑ Graphics support the page's purpose.

☑ All content is proofread and spell checked.

☑ The page contains sufficient white space.

☑ Important content is emphasized.

☑ Related items are grouped together.

☑ All hyperlinks have been tested.

In this unit, you learned the basic principles of information and presentation design. As you continue to create Web sites, keep these principles in mind. Following these principles will help you create sites that are both attractive and user-friendly.

Section 7.4 Assessment

Concept Check

1. **Define** subpage, image map, hotspot.

2. **List** the steps in creating a hotspot.

3. **Discuss** the advantages of using an evaluation checklist.

Critical Thinking

4. **Evaluate** Why might a Web designer decide to use an image map as opposed to a navigation button or a text link?

5. **Compare and Contrast** How is the Web site checklist different from the Web page checklist? How are they similar?

Applying Skills

Evaluate a Web Site
Use a checklist similar to the one in Table 7.5 above to evaluate the Astronomy Club Web site as a whole and its individual pages. Identify and explain any changes you would make to the site.

SECTION 7.1 Principles of Presentation Design

Key Terms

consistency, 178   page banner, 181
repetition, 178

Main Ideas

■ Two characteristics of most well-designed Web sites are consistency and repetition.

■ Elements such as banners, logos, and link bars should be repeated on the site's main pages.

■ A universal color scheme contributes to consistency across the site.

■ A page banner helps users identify where they are in a Web site.

SECTION 7.2 Choosing Web-safe Colors

Key Terms

color scheme, 184   Web-safe color, 184

Main Ideas

■ A Web site's color scheme is a set of selected colors used consistently in elements such as title graphics, navigation buttons, and backgrounds.

■ The color scheme should be compatible with the Web site's purpose.

■ You can use color to emphasize important content.

■ Colors can look different depending on the computer platform, monitor type, or Web browser.

■ Only 216 colors will display the same way on all computers.

■ Use Web-safe colors to ensure that the colors on your Web site will display consistently on different computer systems.

■ The color palette in FrontPage only features Web-safe colors.

SECTION 7.3 Fonts and Typography

Key Terms

typography, 187   alignment, 188
font, 187   serif, 190
point, 188   sans serif, 190

Main Ideas

■ A text's properties include its font type, size, styles, alignment, and color.

■ A font is a set of characters that have a specific shape and style.

■ Font size varies from 1 (the smallest) to 7 (the largest).

■ Most people find it easier to read san serif fonts online.

■ It is best to stick with standard fonts that are found on most computer systems.

■ Limit the number of fonts you use on a Web page to no more than three.

■ Do not underline text on a Web page.

■ Text alignments include left-aligned, centered, right-aligned, and justified.

■ Text should be consistently formatted, readable, and attractive.

SECTION 7.4 Image Maps and Checklists

Key Terms

subpage, 195   hotspot, 197
image map, 197

Main Ideas

■ You can insert Word documents into Web pages.

■ An image map has areas called hotspots that, when clicked, take the user to another location.

■ Hotspots can be rectangular, circular, or polygonal.

■ Checklists are useful tools for evaluating Web sites and pages.

Reviewing Key Terms

1. Give three examples of ways in which repetition is commonly used in Web sites.
2. What is a font? Give examples of three standard fonts.
3. How many Web-safe colors are available?
4. Change the following sentence to make it true: *Image maps contain fonts that you click to go to related information.*
5. Identify the four types of alignment.

Understanding Main Ideas

6. **Discuss** ways in which the Astronomy Club Web site exhibits the characteristics of consistency and repetition.
7. **Explain** the factors that you should consider when choosing a color scheme.
8. **Explain** the meaning of the term "standard font." Discuss the main reason why you should use standard fonts on a Web site.
9. **List** five ways in which text can be formatted.
10. **Describe** the difference between serif and sans serif fonts. Which type is considered most readable in printed text? on a computer screen?
11. **Discuss** the factors that influence the type of font a Web designer uses on a particular page.
12. **Describe** an advantage of an image map over text-based links.
13. **Explain** why it is important to use checklists when evaluating the Web sites and Web pages you create.

Critical Thinking

14. **Make Predictions** This chapter discusses why you should use Web-safe colors. Do you think this guideline will change in the future? Explain your answer.
15. **Analyze** Discuss two ways that the hardware and software used by Web site visitors affect the Web designer.
16. **Draw Conclusions** Which font would you use in a site about a children's zoo? Which font would you use in a site about gourmet cooking classes in Italy? Explain your answers.
17. **Synthesize** Select another medium with which you are familiar, such as newspapers or television. Are principles such as consistency and repetition applied in this medium? How are the ways in which they are applied similar to Web design principles? How are they different?
18. **Analyze** Which formatting features would you use to create titles? Which would you use to call out important passages of text?
19. **Compare and Contrast** Identify five valid reasons a Web site might use many colors and unusual fonts. Then give five reasons a site would use limited colors and traditional fonts. Think of examples for both types of sites.

e-Review ....
webdesign.glencoe.com

Study with PowerPoint

To review the main points in this chapter, select **e-Review** > **PowerPoint Outlines** > **Chapter 7**.

Online Self Check

Test your knowledge of the material in this chapter by selecting **e-Review** > **Self Checks** > **Chapter 7**.

Making Connections

Science—Demonstrate Color Differences

The human eye views color differences based on their wavelengths. Colors with a long wave length, such as blue, indigo, and violet, appear to come forward when viewed on a computer screen. Colors with a shorter wave length, such as red and orange, appear to recede or go backward when viewed on a computer screen.

Create a Web page that demonstrates this concept. Place a red circle on a blue background and a blue circle on a red background. Compare and contrast these two color combinations. Identify which combination is easier to read and explain why.

STANDARDS AT WORK

Students use technology tools to enhance learning, increase productivity, and promote creativity. (NETS-S 3)

Analyze Text Styles and Color

Create a Web page in FrontPage that contains a one-column table with four rows. Color the rows from top to bottom as follows: white, black, light blue, and dark red. Use hexadecimal values to create the colors. Type the following text in the top cell:

> This is a Heading 1.
> This is a Heading 2.
> This is a Heading 3.
> This is a paragraph size 2.
> This is a paragraph size 3.

Style each line of text as described by the text. For example, use the Heading 1 style for the line "This is a Heading 1." Use a serif font for all lines of text. All text should be black. Copy the text to the other rows. Change the text color so that the text is legible and easy to read.

Write a paragraph that compares and contrasts the legibility of text in each cell of the tables.

TEAMWORK SKILLS

Create Web Content

Your team is creating a Web Design Tips and Resources "e-zine" for your school. You plan to include the following pages: home page, FrontPage Tips and Tricks, Graphics Resources, Reviews, Equipment Information.

1. Write the content for the site home page, including a short paragraph about the site and a bulleted list with details of the site.

2. Research Web sites that could be used as sources of images. You will use this research to create links on the Graphics Resources page. Write the content for the Graphics Resources page, which will contain links to graphics resources. Each link should include a short paragraph describing what the site contains, the type of images available, and terms of use (if any).

3. Write a brief content summary for each of the other pages in the site.

CHALLENGE YOURSELF

Create a Color Scheme

Create a color scheme for a resort specializing in winter sports. Locate a graphic that best represents the products and images of the resort. The graphic you choose will be the starting point for your color scheme.

Select Web-safe colors that coordinate with the graphic for each of the following page elements:

- Background
- Logo
- Heading 1
- Heading 2
- Bulleted list
- Buttons
- Unvisited links
- Visited links

Use FrontPage to create a sample of the elements listed above, using the colors you have selected. Refine your choices as needed until you are satisfied with your overall color scheme.

YOU TRY IT
Skills Studio

These exercises reinforce the skills you learned in this chapter's You Try It activities. Refer back to the You Try It activities if you need extra guidance.

1. Formatting Text in Tables

Add content to the About Us page in the Astronomy Club Web site.

Ⓐ Insert a third column into the About Us page.

Ⓑ Merge the top two rows in the second and third columns. The entire area will become a single cell.

Ⓒ Change the text color on the page to hexadecimal number 00,00,99.

Ⓓ Use the Verdana font, size 4, and add the following text to the merged cell: The Astronomy Club is dedicated to learning about our universe.

Ⓔ Enter the text shown in the table on this page into the second and third columns of the Web page's table (do not enter the text Astronomy Club Officers into the online table). Add rows as needed to fit the content. Use Verdana as the font, and make the column headings ("Office" and "Name") bold as shown. Proofread and save your work.

Astronomy Club Officers	
Office	**Name**
President	Mannie Sanchez
Vice President	Tina Ling
Secretary	Dave Weinstein
Treasurer	Eric Robinson

2. Creating a Hotspot

Add a Mars subpage to the Astronomy Club Web site.

Ⓐ Use the ac_template to add a subpage to the Sky Guide page. Name the subpage's file mars.htm. Make its page title Mars Informational Page. Add the page to the site's navigation structure.

Ⓑ Add two rows to the table on the page. Merge the cells in the second column. Use the Saturn page you created in You Try It Activity 7F (page 195) as a model.

Ⓒ Insert the **mars.doc** located in the DataFile\Ch07\Text folder. Change the document's font to Verdana. Make the document's title font size 5 (18 pt). Format the rest of the text as needed.

Ⓓ With your insertion point in the upper left corner of the document, insert the **mars.jpg** file from the DataFile\Ch07\Images folder. Wrap text to the left of the image.

Ⓔ On the Sky Guide page, create a hotspot around Mars. Insert a hyperlink to the Mars informational page. Save the file. Test the hotspot in a browser.

Student Data File

Web Design Projects

1. Add a Meeting and Activities Page

A Meetings and Activities page is planned for the Astronomy Club Web site. You have already created a link to the page. In this activity, you will add content to this page. The list of meetings and activities will appear in a two-column table. The left column will list the meeting name (monthly meeting, lecture on quasars, and so on). The right column will list the meeting's date, time, and location.

◆ Plan and schedule four meetings for the club over the next two months.

◆ Two of the meetings will be regular monthly meetings and two will be special meetings with guest speakers.

◆ Decide on the topics for the special meetings.

◆ Include all the information on the Meetings and Activities page.

Meetings and Activities

Activity	Time and Place		
Quasars and Waves (guest speaker: Prof. Steven Lightman, State University)	January 8	3:30 p.m.	Rm. 105
Monthly Meeting	January 15	3:00 p.m.	Cafeteria

2. Refine Your Personal Web Site

In Chapter 6 you created a storyboard for a personal Web site and the content for the home page (see page 175). Refine the home page now. Select the fonts to use for your headings, paragraph text, bulleted lists, and so on. Create a color scheme for the entire Web site, including background color and color for all type.

◆ Design a banner for the home page and a smaller banner for other pages.

◆ Revise your home page to apply the selected style sheet and color scheme.

◆ Add a photo to your home page layout. Add a caption such as "More about who I am." Apply an image map to photo. Link it to your personal interests page.

◆ Add content to the personal interest page. Remember to protect your personal identity. Don't give out your address or phone number.

◆ Apply the color scheme to all pages, so the entire site has a consistent look.

Building 21st Century Skills

Communication Skills: Write for a Web Audience

Find a short printed document such as a brochure, advertisement, or book excerpt and adapt the material for a Web page.

1. Draw a sketch of the Web page.

2. Rewrite the print content for a Web audience. Use bulleted lists, headings, subheadings, or links to secondary pages if needed.

3. Use a FrontPage template or design a custom template to create your page.

4. Have classmates review your work.

5. If you agree with their assessment, revise your Web page. Good Web designers continually assess and revise their sites, even after they are up and running.

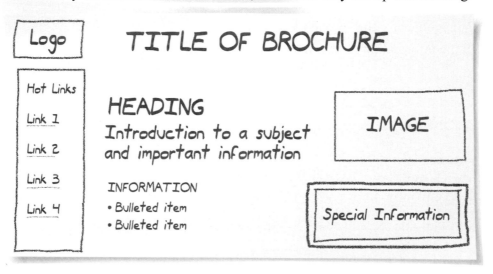

Teamwork: Create a Web Site About Your Town

Work with three other people to create a Web site about one specific feature of your town, such as a favorite hangout, a famous resident, or an historical site.

1. As a team, decide on a purpose and target audience.

2. Brainstorm content and draw a diagram of how the home page and subpages should look. Determine the layout and color scheme.

3. Assign one person to write the text, one to find graphics, one to find sites for hyperlinks, and one to write, test, and debug any HTML code you may use.

4. Work together to create the final Web site and present it to the class.

Building Your Portfolio

Create a School Web Page

For this project, you will create a Web page for your school's Web site. Choose one of the following topics for your page:

(A) A profile of one of the teachers or administrators in your school.

(B) An important issue that the school's PTA or teachers are trying to resolve.

(C) A description of a local organization that provides social or recreational resources for high school students.

When creating your Web page, follow these steps:

1. Determine your mission statement and audience.

2. Do research and interviews to find the information you need for the content. Identify block quotes from your interview to use on the Web page.

3. Determine how visitors will navigate to your page from the Web site's home page.

4. Determine the elements to include on the page, including title, text, visuals, navigation elements, themes, and colors. Locate any images you might need.

5. Create a sketch showing how the page will be laid out to include all the necessary elements.

6. Use a FrontPage template or design a custom template to produce the Web page.

7. Add hyperlinks to other pages on the school Web site or to other relevant Web sites.

8. Use the checklist (shown right) to evaluate the items on your site.

9. Present your finished page to your teacher and peers for their review. Have them evaluate it based on the checklist.

10. Revise your Web page based on the evaluations.

11. Optional (with your teacher's permission)—publish the finished Web page on your school or class Web site. On the home page, write a brief text that directs visitors to your page. Include a link to your page.

12. For your portfolio, include a screen shot and an electronic copy of your finished product.

Web Page Checklist

OVERALL APPEARANCE & CONTENT

☑ The subject of the Web page is clearly identified.

☑ The design is consistent and uncluttered.

☑ Most important elements are visible on the screen without scrolling.

☑ Images and links relate to the text on the page.

ORGANIZING TEXT

☑ Content is organized logically.

☑ Text is broken into small blocks or "chunks."

☑ The fonts are easy to read.

☑ Key points are highlighted effectively.

☑ Headings and subheadings follow a logical hierarchy.

☑ Paragraphs or text blocks are separated by white space.

LANGUAGE

☑ Sentences are short and simple.

☑ Bulleted or numbered lists are used effectively.

☑ Grammar, punctuation, and spelling are correct.

☑ Language is concise.

☑ Text uses effective style such as active voice, strong verbs and nouns, etc.

UNIT
3

Enhancing a Web Site

Visit *Glencoe Online*

Go to this book's Web site at **webdesign.glencoe.com.**

Click on **Unit Activities** and select **Unit 3 Evaluating Web Sites.** Learn how to evaluate Web sites to make sure the information is reliable.

Think About It

Hooking the Audience
Entertainment sites such as boardwalks and amusement parks often use light, sound, and animation to attract visitors. These dynamic elements help make the location interesting and exciting.

Design Evaluation Activity
Books and magazines also use visual elements to attract readers. Look at some books or magazines. Jot down the elements that attract you and those that make you want to put the publication down. Then describe how some of the same design principles might apply to Web pages.

YOU WILL LEARN TO...

Section 8.1

- Create a custom theme
- Design a color scheme
- Use shared borders

Section 8.2

- Identify types of graphics
- Identify and compare graphic formats
- Describe compression schemes

Section 8.3

- Identify image sources
- Use graphics ethically
- Use clip art
- Describe graphic input tools
- Create WordArt

Section 8.4

- Crop, resize, and resample a graphic
- Create a photo gallery
- Create a thumbnail

WHY IT MATTERS.....................................

Images can convey feelings and meaning in ways that words cannot. Have you ever seen a painting or photo and imagined what the person in the painting or photo must have felt? Images are *evocative*—they make us react intensely and immediately. Using images effectively can help you create a powerful Web site.

Quick Write Activity

Think of a powerful image you have seen in the last few weeks. It could have been a piece of artwork, a newspaper photograph, or an image on television. Write a paragraph about how that image made you feel. Describe the characteristics of the image that you think caused this emotional reaction.

WHAT YOU WILL DO...

READ TO SUCCEED

Prior Knowledge
Imagine some friends are talking about a new movie you have not seen. You soon lose interest. However, when they talk about your favorite movie, you become interested. Reading works much the same way. The more you know about a subject, the more you understand. That makes it easier to be an active, interested participant. Look over the "You Will Learn To" at the beginning of the chapter. Write down what you already know about each objective and what you want to find out by reading the chapter. As you read, find examples for both categories.

Section 8.1 Using Custom Themes and Shared Borders

Guide to Reading

Main Ideas

You can create custom themes that reflect your site's purpose. Using shared borders allows page components such as banners and link bars to appear on all pages of your site.

Key Terms

external style sheet
embedded style sheet
cascading style sheet
shared border

Reading Strategy

Compare external and embedded style sheets. Use a Venn diagram similar to the one below (also available online).

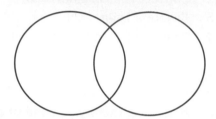

Creating a good graphic foundation greatly enhances the design of your site. In this section, you will learn more about two FrontPage features that simplify this task: custom themes and shared borders. Both themes and borders are part of a Web site's graphic foundation.

CREATING A GRAPHIC FOUNDATION

In this unit, you will create a Web site that promotes a community event. The Cedar Valley Ecology Walk is an annual event. The money raised by this walk is used to support local environmental causes. The committee creating the site determined that the site's audience will include people of all ages. The committee developed the following mission statement for the site:

> **The Web site will promote environmental responsibility by informing visitors about the local projects supported by the Cedar Valley Ecology Walk. It will encourage all visitors to participate in this walk.**

As part of the planning process, the committee outlined the basic navigation structure of the site. The site contains a home page and three main pages:

◆ A page that tells visitors when the walk is and how to register. This page links to a registration form.
◆ A page that explains the projects supported by the walk.
◆ A page that lists the walk's sponsors.

All of these pages will work together to fulfill the site's mission.

 webdesign.glencoe.com

CUSTOM THEMES

The purpose of the Cedar Valley site is to promote an outdoor event, and you want the look of the site to reflect this fact. Because the walk takes place in the fall, you decide to use a color scheme that incorporates the greens, golds, and browns of the changing leaves.

Since FrontPage does not provide a theme that exactly matches your intended color scheme, you will create a custom theme. Because a theme contains so many different elements, it is generally easier to modify an existing theme than to start from scratch.

Customizing Graphics and Colors in a Theme

In the following You Try It, you will change the colors in an existing Front-Page theme and save this customized theme under a new name. You will use this theme for the Cedar Valley Ecology Walk Web site.

ACTIVITY 8A Creating a Custom Theme

1 Browse to the DataFile\Ch08\Web Examples folder. Select the **CV Walk Basic** folder. On the **Edit** menu, select **Copy To Folder.** Copy the CV Walk Basic folder to the general folder where you store your Web sites. Save the folder as **CV Walk.**

2 Open the CV Walk Web site in FrontPage. Open the **index.htm** page in Design (in FrontPage 2002, Normal) view.

3 On the **Format** menu, click **Theme** to open the Theme task pane (in 2002, the Themes dialog box).

4 Place the pointer over the **Expedition** theme and click the drop-down arrow. Select **Customize.** The Customize Theme dialog box appears (in 2002, select the **Expedition** theme and click **Modify**). As shown in Figure 8.1, only **Active graphics** should be selected in the Customize Theme (in 2002, Themes) dialog box.

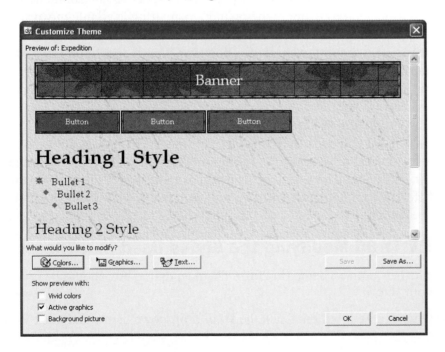

Figure 8.1
Use the Customize Theme dialog box to create a custom theme for your Web site.

READ ME!

Tech Tip When entering hexadecimal numbers, remember that they may contain the number zero (0). However, they will never contain the letter O.

Custom Theme Colors

Item	Value Text Box
Body	Hex={99,33,00}
Heading 1	Hex={66,33,00}
Heading 2	Hex={CC,33,00}

5 Click the **Graphics** button. On the **Picture** tab, delete **exptextb.jpg** from the Background Picture text box. Click **OK.**

6 Click the **Colors** button. Click the **Custom** tab.

7 Click the **Item** drop-down arrow and click **Background.** Click the **Color** drop-down arrow and click **More Colors.** In the More Colors dialog box, type Hex={FF,CC,00} in the Value box. Click **OK.**

8 Repeat step 7 for each item listed in Table 8.1.

9 Click **OK.** Your screen should now display the main Customize Theme (in 2002, Themes) dialog box.

Specifying Fonts in a Theme

A style sheet stores format and layout settings, such as fonts, colors, and alignments, for the elements of a Web page. The style sheet applies the settings to all Web pages you create with it. Using a style sheet helps you create a consistent look without having to constantly redefine your settings.

An **external style sheet** is a style sheet that is stored in a separate file. You can link this file to multiple Web pages to create a consistent look across both individual pages and the entire Web site.

An **embedded style sheet** is a style sheet that only applies to the current Web page. To create an embedded style sheet, click Style on the Format menu and then define your own styles. These definitions are saved in the HTML code for that page.

A **cascading style sheet** consists of code that defines formatting and layout settings for HTML tags in a single location. Cascading style sheets allow you to place elements on the page using specific horizontal and vertical coordinates and to apply the refined formatting available in word processing programs. You can identify a cascading style sheet file by its .css extension. It is important to know, however, that while Internet Explorer 4.0 and above supports cascading style sheets, not all browsers support cascading style sheets. See Appendix D for more information on cascading style sheets.

The FrontPage themes use style sheets to define the formatting used in specified Web pages. In the following You Try It, you will choose the fonts for several of your theme's components. You will choose Verdana as your primary font. However, because you cannot control the fonts installed on different computer systems, you will also list two alternate fonts: Arial and Helvetica.

YOU TRY IT

ACTIVITY 8B Modifying the Styles Used in a Theme

1 The Customize Theme (in 2002, Themes) dialog box should be open on your screen.

2 Click the **Text** button. Click the **Item** drop-down arrow and click **Body.**

3 In the Font text box, replace the existing text with Verdana, Arial, Helvetica (see Figure 8.2). Click **OK.**

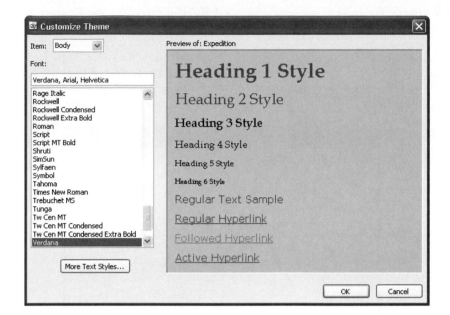

Figure 8.2
You can modify a theme's font in the Customize Theme dialog box.

4 Repeat steps 2 and 3 for Heading 1 and Heading 2.

5 Click **Graphics.** Click the **Item** drop-down arrow and click **Banner.**

6 Click the **Font** tab. In the Font text box, type Verdana, Arial, Helvetica. Click the **Style** drop-down arrow and click **Bold.** Click **OK.**

7 Repeat step 5 and click **Vertical Navigation** in the **Item** drop-down list. Repeat step 6.

8 Click **Save As.** In the Save Theme dialog box, type Ecology Walk. Click **OK.** Click **OK** to close the Customize Theme (in 2002, Themes) dialog box. (If using 2002, make sure **All pages** is selected under **Apply Theme.** Skip step 9 and save your work.)

9 In 2003, in the Theme task pane, open the **Ecology Walk** drop-down arrow and click **Apply as default theme.** Click **Yes** when the warning message appears. You have now applied your custom theme to all pages on the Web site. Close the Theme task pane. Save your work.

READ ME!

Tech Tip After entering the font names for the first time, copy them by pressing **Ctrl + C**. You can then paste them into the Font text box when needed by pressing **Ctrl + V**.

SHARED BORDERS

A **shared border** is an area that remains the same on all (or some) of the pages on the Web site. When you change the information on one shared border, every shared border on the site changes.

Adding Shared Borders in FrontPage

In the next activity, you will add three shared borders to your Cedar Valley Ecology Walk Web site. Later, you will add a page banner, a link bar, and footer information to these borders.

ACTIVITY 8C Creating Shared Borders

1 Open the CV Walk home page in Design (in 2002, Normal) view.

2 On the **Format** menu, click **Shared Borders** to open the Shared Borders dialog box.

3 Under Apply to, click the **All pages** option. Click the **Top, Left,** and **Bottom** check boxes. Under **Left,** click the **Include navigation buttons** check box (see Figure 8.3). Click **OK.** Save your work.

Figure 8.3
Check the boxes in the Shared Borders dialog box as shown here.

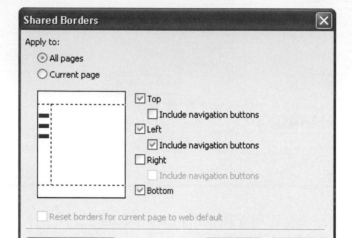

Adding Elements to Shared Borders

In the following You Try It, you will insert navigation links and a page banner to your Web site. You will specify that the link bar will list only the site's main pages (that is, the home page and the children of the home page).

ACTIVITY 8D Inserting a Banner and Link Bar

1 Open the CV Walk home page in Design (in 2002, Normal) view.

2 Position the insertion point in the top shared border. On the **Insert** menu, click **Page Banner** to open the Page Banner Properties dialog box.

3 Under Properties, select **Picture.** The home page's title, Cedar Valley Ecology Walk, should appear in the text box under Page banner text (in 2002, Page banner). Click **OK.** A banner appears at the top of the page.

4 Click anywhere in the left shared border. On the **Insert** menu, click **Web Component** to open the Insert Web Component dialog box.

5 Under Component type, click **Link Bars.** Under Choose a bar type, click **Bar based on navigation structure.** Click **Next.**

6 Under Choose a bar style, select **Use Page's Theme.** Click **Next.**

7 Under Choose an orientation, choose the vertical orientation on the right. Click **Finish.** The Link Bar Properties dialog box appears.

8 On the General tab, under Hyperlinks to add to page, select **Child pages under Home.** Under Additional pages, select **Home page.** Click **OK.**

9 As shown in Figure 8.4, the link bar appears along the left side of the page. Delete any remaining placeholder text from the top and left shared borders. Save your work. If possible, test your links in Preview view. When you finish, return to **Design** (in 2002, **Normal**) view.

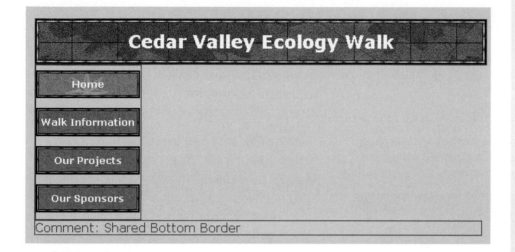

Figure 8.4
Shared borders make it easy to add page banners and link bars to a Web site.

READ ME!

Tech Tip To test a link in Design view, hold down Ctrl and click the link. You will go to the linked-to page.

You now have much of the CV Walk Web site's basic structure established. You placed banners on each page, along with navigation bars. Shared borders enabled you to do all of this in just a few steps.

Section 8.1 Assessment

Concept Check

1. **Define** external style sheet, embedded style sheet, cascading style sheet, shared border.

2. **Identify** three advantages of creating a custom theme rather than using one of FrontPage's built-in themes.

3. **Explain** how shared borders help provide consistency to a Web site.

Critical Thinking

4. **Make Decisions** What kind of custom theme might you create for a Web site about one of your school's sports teams? Explain your choices.

5. **Analyze** Web designers rarely use shared borders on the right side of a page. Why do you think this is so?

Applying Skills

Add Shared Borders
Open a multiple-page Web site that you have created. Add a top shared border to the site that includes a page banner and a link bar. If necessary, these elements can replace existing elements.

Ethics & Technology

VERIFYING YOUR SOURCES

The Internet is a rich resource for information. Unfortunately, you cannot trust everything you read online.

Online information is only as good as its source. Look for reputable sources that check facts, identify authors and sources, and post unbiased information.

Misinformation at Your Fingertips

For every trustworthy information source online, you can find an untrustworthy one. Some examples:

- The Securities and Exchange Commission has sued chat room participants for lying about various companies in order to drive stock prices up or down.

- Many people use the Internet to look up symptoms and treatments for illnesses. The information they find, however, may not be valid or up to date and could even be harmful.

- Some search engines post "sponsored links" without telling users. This means that some companies pay the search engine to post their links at or near the top of the list of search results.

Avoiding Misinformation Pitfalls

When doing serious research online, be a smart information consumer. Learn to find reliable sources and to verify information you find online:

- **Remember that site owners do not always check their facts.** This is especially true of information posted in informal settings, such as chat rooms or personal "Web logs." Be prepared to check facts yourself. Also, check to see when the site was last updated.

- **Look for reputable sources.** Start with the Web sites of major news organizations, encyclopedias, government, and professional organizations. Ask people you trust which sites they prefer.

- **Learn to evaluate.** View online information with a critical eye, and ask questions. Is the author identified? Might the organization that sponsors the site have biased interests? Is the information attributed to another source? Can you find the same information elsewhere?

Finally, trust your instincts. If you feel uncomfortable with any information you find online, discard it and keep digging until you find reliable facts.

Tech Focus

1. Log on to a medical Web site to evaluate its reliability. What are the positive and negative consequences of accessing medical information on the Web?

2. Bias is a well-known factor in the spread of misinformation, especially online. Search the Internet to find one example of bias-based information. Report your findings.

Section 8.2 Web Graphic Types and File Formats

Guide to Reading

Main Ideas

The two basic types of graphics are raster and vector. The two most common graphic file formats are GIF and JPEG.

Key Terms

raster graphic
paint program
vector graphic
draw program
GIF (Graphic Interchange Format)
JPEG (Joint Photographic Experts Group)
lossless compression
lossy compression

Reading Strategy

Compare and contrast GIF files and JPEG files. Use a Venn diagram like the one below (also available online).

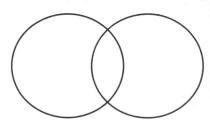

Web designers have two major concerns when using graphics on a Web site. The first concern is how good the image will look on the screen. The second concern is how quickly the image will download. In this section, you will learn how Web designers must constantly balance these two concerns when choosing graphic file formats.

TYPES OF GRAPHICS

How a graphic is created determines its type. There are two basic types of graphics: raster graphics and vector graphics.

Raster Graphics

A **raster graphic,** also called a bitmapped graphic, is made up of pixels. Pixels are tiny squares of color arranged on a rectangular grid like tiles in a mosaic. The human eye reads collections of pixels as a seamless image. Designers use **paint programs** to create raster graphics. Popular paint programs include Microsoft Paint, Adobe Photoshop, Macromedia Fireworks, and Jasc Software Paint Shop Pro. Macromedia Fireworks was specifically developed to create Web graphics.

Vector Graphics

A **vector graphic** is composed of simple lines defined by mathematical equations. Designers use **draw programs,** such as PhotoDraw, to create vector graphics. A draw program automatically calculates the equations used to produce a vector graphic. These applications work well for creating logos, text banners, 3D Web buttons, and other illustrations that feature simple shapes.

GRAPHIC FILE FORMATS

All files are stored in specific formats. For example, Web pages are saved in HTML format. Once you create a graphic, you must save it in a graphic file format. The format that you choose to save a graphic affects both the graphic's quality and its download time.

Most Web browsers only display images saved in the GIF or JPEG graphic file formats. Consequently, these are the two most popular file formats used in Web design. Both of these formats are based on pixels, so most images on the Web are raster graphics. If you save a vector graphic as a GIF or JPEG file, it also gets converted into pixels.

GIF

The **GIF (Graphic Interchange Format)** graphic format can save only a maximum of 256 colors. Because they can save only a limited number of colors, GIF files tend to be small and download quickly. The format's limited color range makes it good for saving images such as line drawings, simple graphics, and text objects that feature large areas of solid color (see Figure 8.5). You must use this format if you want to create a transparent GIF (an image that allows a Web page's background color to show through) or you want to apply animation effects to the image. Windows uses the .gif file name extension for GIF files.

Figure 8.5
The GIF file format works well for saving simple line drawings. Why would a GIF format not work well for photographs?

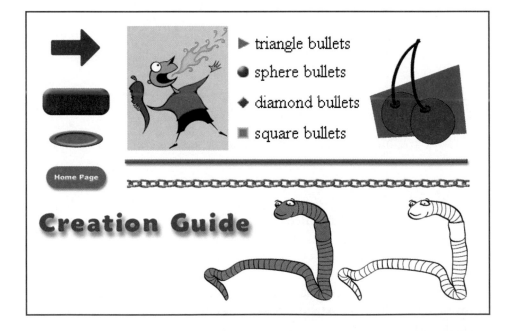

JPEG

Unlike GIF files, the **JPEG (Joint Photographic Experts Group)** graphic file format can support millions of colors. Because it can support many colors, JPEG is a better format than GIF for saving photographs. Because they save more colors, however, JPEG files are generally larger than GIF files and download more slowly. On Windows-based systems, JPEG files have either a .jpg or a .jpe file name extension.

Other Graphic File Formats

Some Web designers also use the BMP and PNG file formats to save graphics. BMP (bitmap) is a full-color format with good image quality. However, since BMP files tend to be quite large and download very slowly, they are not the best choice for Web pages. Windows uses the .bmp file name extension for BMP files.

Like GIF files, PNG (Portable Network Graphics) files are small and download quickly. Unlike GIF files, PNG files can support more than 256 colors. However, not every browser supports the PNG (pronounced "ping") file format. For this reason, you should avoid using PNG files on your Web pages. The file name extension for PNG files is .png.

COMPRESSION SCHEMES AND DOWNLOAD TIMES

The more pixels an image contains, the higher its resolution and quality. However, an image that contains more pixels also has a larger file size. As an image's file size increases, so does its download time.

Web designers usually compress image files so they download more quickly in a user's browser. Compression is a process that reduces an image's file size by removing some color information. However, while compression makes files smaller, it can also reduce an image's quality.

Lossless and Lossy Compression Schemes

Graphics are compressed using either lossless or lossy compression schemes.

- ◆ A **lossless compression** scheme means that a graphic file loses no data when it is compressed. However, compressing a file using lossless compression does not gain you any significant download time. GIF files automatically use lossless compression.
- ◆ A **lossy compression** scheme removes data from a graphic file so the file is significantly smaller and downloads more quickly in a Web browser. However, decompressing the image does not restore the data. For this reason, the restored image results in poorer image quality on the screen. JPEG files use lossy compression.

Adjusting Files and Calculating Download Times

To help you manage download times, FrontPage displays the approximate modem download time on the status bar, in the lower-right corner of the window (see Figure 8.6). You can use this estimate to determine how adding images, such as photographs, affects your page download speed.

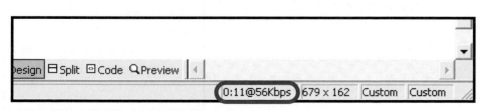

● Figure 8.6
A download time of
0:11 @ 56 Kbps means
the page will require
11 seconds to download
with a 56 Kbps modem.

Low-Bandwidth Alternatives

To reduce download times, you can also create two versions of an image, one in full color and the other with a reduced color palette. You can then tell the Web browser to display the reduced-color image as a placeholder until the full-color version downloads. This allows viewers to quickly see what the image contains before they wait for the better quality image to download.

Converting Graphic Formats

Many graphic applications allow you to open a graphic and save it in another format. For example, you can open a JPEG file in Photoshop and then save the image as a GIF file.

One situation in which you might need to convert an image is when creating animations. If you want to create an animation from a JPEG image, you first must convert it to a GIF since only GIF files can be animated.

When you convert a file from one format to another, the converted image may not look like the original. For example, if you convert a JPEG photograph to a GIF, the resulting image will not have as many colors and may look distinctly different, as shown in Figure 8.7.

Figure 8.7 ●
The left photo is a full-color JPEG image, while the right image shows the same photo saved in GIF format with 256 colors. **For what situations is the GIF format appropriate?**

Section 8.2 Assessment

Concept Check

1. **Define** raster graphic, paint program, vector graphic, draw program, GIF (Graphic Interchange Format), JPEG (Joint Photographic Experts Group), lossless compression, lossy compression.

2. **Compare and Contrast** raster graphics and vector graphics.

Critical Thinking

3. **Evaluate** Why should you consider an image's download time when creating Web pages?

4. **Make Decisions** You are creating a Web site for an art gallery. What issues will you need to consider when choosing graphics for this site?

Applying Skills

Convert File Formats
Open a graphics application, such as Microsoft Paint. Open a JPEG image such as flowers.jpg. Save the image as a GIF file. Compare the quality of the two images and the sizes of the two files.

Section 8.3 Obtaining and Creating Graphics

Guide to Reading

Main Ideas

You can use pre-made graphics, such as clip art, on your Web pages. You can also create original graphics using either input devices or FrontPage toolbars. Always check the terms of use before downloading pre-made graphics.

Key Terms

scanner
dots per inch (dpi)
digital camera
inline graphic
WordArt

Reading Strategy

Identify six ways in which you can obtain or create graphics. Use a web diagram like the one below (also available online).

Ways to Obtain or Create Graphics

Images on Web sites come from many sources. In this section, you will learn about tools and resources you can use to create attractive graphics.

OBTAINING PRE-MADE GRAPHICS

One of the easiest ways to add images to your Web pages is to use pre-made graphics. Pre-made graphics are readily available both online and from other sources.

Locating Pre-Made Graphics

The Web is an excellent source of pre-made graphics. You can use a search engine to locate the exact image you want. Most sites organize their images by category. For example, a site may devote sections to nature, travel, sports, work, and so forth. When you find an image that you want, you can right-click it and select Save Picture As from the menu to save the image to your hard drive.

Many software applications include large image collections that you can insert on your pages. You can also purchase commercial image packages. These packages provide both general image collections and collections built around specific themes or events.

Using Graphics Ethically

It is easy to download a graphic from the Web. However, unless you have specific permission to use someone else's images, doing so could violate copyright laws. These laws apply whether or not you see a copyright statement on the Web site. You also need the owner's consent to use images with a registered trademark.

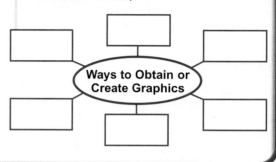

Activity 8.1 Locate Graphics Online Get more ideas for locating images for your Web pages by visiting **webdesign.glencoe.com**.

READ ME!

Jargon Some sites spell "clip art" as one word: "clipart." Try both variations when using a search tool to look for clip art on the Web.

Most Web sites that provide graphics also include instructions as to how you can legally use their images. Be sure you carefully read and follow these licensing and use instructions. Some sites may indicate that specific images are "royalty free." This, however, does not mean that you are free to use the images in any way you want. Follow the site's rules carefully to avoid misusing images. If you are not sure about how you can use an image, send the site's owners an e-mail message, asking for clarification of the policy.

Using Clip Art

Many computers have clip art collections stored on their hard drives. FrontPage also provides a small clip art collection. Clip collections may include illustrations, photos, sound effects, and short video clips. You can use the Clip Art task pane to search for available clip art. If you want to search the Internet, be sure to obtain permission from your teacher first. In the next activity, you will insert a piece of clip art on your Web site's home page.

YOU TRY IT

Student Data File

Figure 8.8
Locate a nature scene such as this for your home page.

ACTIVITY 8E Adding Clip Art to a Web Page

1 Open the CV Walk home in Design (in 2002, Normal) view.

2 Position the insertion point in the upper-left corner of the content area of the home page.

3 On the **Table** menu, select **Insert>Table** to open the Insert Table dialog box. Under Size, type 1 in the Rows text box and 1 in the Columns text box. Under Layout, type 450 in the Specify width text box. Click **In pixels.** Set the Border size to 0. Click **OK.** A narrow, one-line table appears across the entire width of the page.

4 Click anywhere inside the table you just created to position the insertion point. On the **Insert** menu, click **File.** Browse to the DataFile\Ch08\Text folder. Click the **Files of type** drop-down arrow and select **All Files (*.*).** Double-click the **home_page.doc** file to open it. Make certain that the text is formatted according to the Normal style in the Style menu.

5 Position the insertion point in front of the text you just inserted. On the **Insert** menu, select **Picture>Clip Art** to open the Clip Art task pane. In the Search for text box, type nature.

6 Click the **Search in** drop-down arrow and select **Everywhere.** Click away from the drop-down list to close it.

7 Click the **Results should be** drop-down arrow. Clear the check boxes so only the **Clip Art** box is selected. Click away from the drop-down list to close it.

8 Click **Go** (in 2002, **Search**) to start the search process. Locate an image similar to the one shown in Figure 8.8. Double-click the image to insert it on the page. Add alternative text to the image.

9 Close the Clip Art task pane. Save your work. Make certain the embedded file is saved in the images folder (if necessary, create this folder) and click **OK.**

CREATING GRAPHICS USING INPUT DEVICES

To use graphics from print sources, such as photographs or images from magazines, you must convert them into digital images to insert them on your Web pages. You can also create digital images using tools such as digital cameras or Web cams.

Figure 8.9
Flatbed scanners allow you to scan two- and three-dimensional objects. Why do you need a scanner if you want to insert a photograph into a Web page?

Using Scanners

A **scanner** is a tool that converts a printed image into a digital format that can be used on a Web page (see Figure 8.9). A scanner converts an image into a grid of dots, or pixels. The size of the grid a scanner can create defines its resolution, which is stated in **dots per inch** or **dpi.** A scanner with a 600 dpi resolution will give you 600 pixels for every linear inch of the original image. Most new scanners have a resolution of 600 dpi, but some offer 1200 dpi or more. For Web use, a 600 dpi scanner is sufficient.

Using Digital Cameras

With a **digital camera,** you can take a picture and then download the image to your computer. Digital camera prices and capabilities vary widely. Some low-end cameras offer a maximum resolution of 640 x 480 pixels. A resolution of 640 x 480 pixels is acceptable for photographs that are to be placed on the Web.

Web cams are small, low-resolution video cameras, developed primarily for Internet videoconferencing. Although they are video cameras, you can use them to capture a single video frame to use as a still image on a page. Web cams are inexpensive and produce acceptable quality for Web use. However, a Web cam must be attached to a computer system to function, which limits its usefulness.

Importing Pictures into FrontPage

Most input devices have software that allows you to store the image produced on your hard drive in a specified format. Depending on the type of device you have, you may be able to import a picture directly from the scanner or camera into FrontPage. To do this, make sure the scanner or camera is connected to your computer and turned on. From the Insert menu, select Picture and choose From Scanner or Camera to transfer the image onto your Web page.

When you insert a picture file into a Web page, the actual image is not inserted into the page's HTML code. If you look at the page's HTML code, you will see that only the picture's file name appears. An `<img src>` tag will tell the browser where to locate the stored file. The browser must request the graphic file and insert it onto the page. This type of picture is called an **inline graphic.** For example, you can scan a picture, transfer the resulting data from the scanner to your computer, store it as a picture file on your hard disk, and then create an inline graphic by inserting the picture into a Web page.

CREATING GRAPHICS USING FRONTPAGE

FrontPage also provides tools that you can use to create simple graphics for your Web pages.

Using the WordArt Tool

WordArt objects are text objects with special formatting applied. You can choose from 30 basic WordArt styles as shown in Figure 8.10.

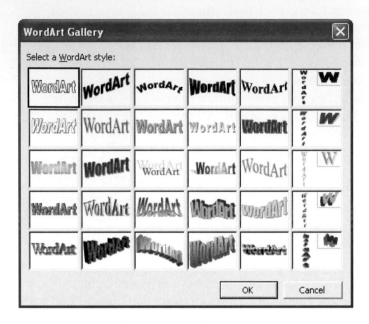

After you select your style, you can then use the WordArt toolbar to format your text. Figure 8.11 identifies these commonly used buttons on the WordArt toolbar:

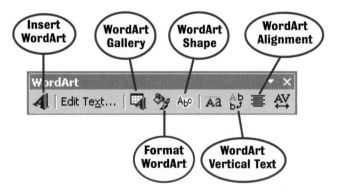

- ◆ **Insert WordArt** allows you to create a new WordArt object.
- ◆ **Edit Text** allows you to format text in your WordArt object.
- ◆ **Format WordArt** lets you change the colors and lines, size, layout, and alternate Web text of your WordArt object.
- ◆ **WordArt Shape** lets you choose your WordArt object's shape.
- ◆ **WordArt Vertical Text** changes the text from the default horizontal alignment to vertical alignment.
- ◆ **WordArt Alignment** allows you to specify the WordArt object's alignment.

In the following You Try It activity, you will use the WordArt tool to create logos for the Our Sponsors page in the CV Walk Web site.

ACTIVITY 8F Adding WordArt to a Web Page

① Open the **sponsors.htm** page in Design (in 2002, Normal) view. Position the insertion point in the content area, immediately below the banner.

② On the Formatting toolbar, click the **Style** drop-down arrow and click **Heading 2.** Type We appreciate the support of our sponsors. Press **Enter** twice.

③ On the **Insert** menu, click **Picture** and choose **WordArt.** In the WordArt Gallery dialog box, select the style in the first column, third row. Click **OK.**

④ In the Edit WordArt Text dialog box, click the **Size** drop-down arrow and click **18.** In the Text box, type Pace Web. Press **Enter.** Type Design. Click **OK** to close the dialog box.

⑤ On the WordArt toolbar, click the **Format WordArt** button. In the Format WordArt dialog box, on the **Colors and Lines** tab, click the **Color** drop-down arrow and click **Fill Effects.** On the **Gradient** tab, under Colors, make Color 1 **dark red** and Color 2 **red.** Click **OK.** On the **Site** (in 2002, **Web**) tab, add alternative text in the Alternative text box. Click **OK** to close the dialog box. The logo should look similar to what is shown in Figure 8.12.

Figure 8.12
Use WordArt to create simple logos.

⑥ Repeat steps 3 through 5 to create logos for the following companies: Einsler Florist and Mountain Sports. Select different WordArt styles for these logos and format them as appropriate.

⑦ Arrange the logos in two rows on the page. Save your work.

Using the Drawing Tool

FrontPage's Drawing toolbar lets you create designs with lines, squares, circles, and other shapes. You can use this toolbar to create simple, Web-ready artwork. The toolbar, shown in Figure 8.13, includes the following buttons:

◆ Use the **Draw** menu to control the grouping and position of objects.

◆ Use the **Select Objects** button to select one or more objects.

◆ Use **AutoShapes** to insert pre-made shapes.

◆ Use the **Line, Arrow, Rectangle,** and **Oval** buttons to draw basic shapes.

◆ Use the **Text Box** button to insert text frames within graphics.

◆ Use the **Fill Color, Line Color,** and **Font Color** buttons to add color to items.

◆ Use the **Line Style, Dash Style,** and **Arrow Style** buttons to format line elements.

Figure 8.13
The Drawing toolbar lets you create basic artwork directly in FrontPage. What tool would you use to fill an oval with color?

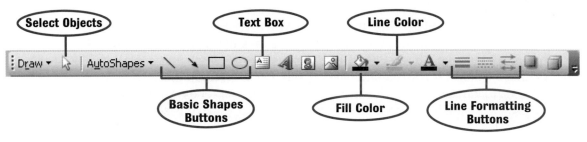

Select Objects — Text Box — Line Color — Basic Shapes Buttons — Fill Color — Line Formatting Buttons

YOU TRY IT

ACTIVITY 8G Adding a Drawing to a Web Page

❶ Open the **Our Sponsors** page in Design (in 2002, Normal) view.

❷ From the **View** menu, select **Toolbars** and choose **Drawing.** The Drawing toolbar appears at the bottom of the screen.

❸ On the Drawing toolbar, select **AutoShapes > Stars and Banners > Horizontal Scroll.** Click to place the image on the page.

READ ME!

Caution FrontPage's Spell Check function will not locate spelling errors in WordArt graphics.

Figure 8.14
Use the Drawing toolbar to create a logo.

❹ Right-click in the image and select **Add Text.** Type The Daily Gazette. Format the text as Times New Roman, 5 (18 pt). Make the text bold and red. Adjust the size of the image as needed to contain the text.

❺ Highlight the text. Select **Fill Color** and click **Fill Effects.** On the **Texture** tab, select **Parchment.** Click **OK.** Leave the text highlighted.

❻ On the Drawing toolbar, select **Shadow Style** and choose **Shadow Style 13.** The logo looks like Figure 8.14. Click away from the image.

7 Position the new logo on the page. Insert a horizontal line between the two rows of logos. To insert the line, position the insertion point where the line should appear. Select **Insert** and choose **Insert Horizontal Line.**

8 Your page should look similar to Figure 8.15. You can place the logos within a layout table (1 row, 1 column, size 0 border) to help keep them in position on the page. Proofread the logos. Save your work.

Figure 8.15
The logos appear on two lines with a horizontal line between them.

Section 8.3 Assessment

Concept Check

1. **Define** scanner, dots per inch (dpi), digital camera, inline graphic, WordArt.

2. **Describe** an advantage that a digital camera has that a scanner does not.

3. **List** the steps in searching for and inserting clip art on a Web page.

Critical Thinking

4. **Make Predictions** How will digital cameras and their features evolve over the next five years? Explain your answer.

5. **Make Decisions** You are designing a Web site for your community theater company. Make a list of instances in which you might use each of the following: a digital camera, a scanner, clip art, drawing tools.

Applying Skills

Create a Logo Select a small business in your community. Use any of the tools you have learned about in this section to create a new logo for this business.

PRESENCE-BASED APPLICATIONS

A presence-based application (PBA) is a program that can determine whether a user is present on a network. PBAs are currently used for computer instant messaging (IM) programs and the "walkie-talkie" feature in some cell phones.

Presence-based applications may someday make cell phones even more useful than they are now.

How PBAs Work

PBAs are fairly simple applications. A PBA on one device uses the Internet or a private network to see if other devices that run the same PBA are online. When the PBA finds another device online, it assumes that device's user is present. It then notifies its own user that someone else is present, and the two devices can interact.

Today's PBAs are limited because they can only communicate with PBAs using the same protocols. For example, someone who uses AOL's IM system can only exchange messages with another AOL user. When PBA users can communicate with anyone, the application will have a chance to reach its full potential.

The Potential of PBAs

PBAs show the greatest promise with wireless devices. Since people usually carry these devices with them, a PBA makes it easy to locate individuals no matter where they are.

Eventually, PBAs might be used to share files and set up last-minute meetings, even videoconferences, among participants in various locations.

Personalizing PBAs

Linking PBAs to databases will allow businesses to offer instant personalized services. For example, airlines may use PBAs to alert travelers to a flight change or to check them in without waiting in line. Hotel reservations could be custom-tailored for frequent visitors at the touch of a button.

Or, imagine you have signed up for a bookseller's mailing list. As you walk past the store, a message arrives on your cell phone, telling you that your favorite author's latest book is now on sale. PBAs may help businesses reach out to customers whenever they are nearby.

Tech Focus

1. Research ways that businesses are currently using instant messenger programs. What are the advantages and disadvantages of IM use in the workplace? What currently emerging PBAs offer more potential?

2. Write an essay describing the social and/or economic impact of presence-based technology. Use research to support your opinions with facts. Cite your sources.

Guide to Reading

Main Ideas

You can use the Pictures toolbar to modify images in FrontPage. A photo gallery is a collection of images. Thumbnails are small images that link to full-size versions of the same image.

Key Terms

resizing
aspect ratio
resampling
cropping
photo gallery
thumbnail

Reading Strategy

Compare and contrast resizing and resampling. Use a Venn diagram like the one below (also available online).

After you have either obtained or created an image, you will probably have to modify this image to make it work on your Web page. You can edit images using either digital imaging software or basic FrontPage tools.

MODIFYING GRAPHICS

To make major changes to images, use a graphic or drawing application. However, you can use FrontPage to make minor modifications, such as changing the size of the image or cropping out distracting elements.

Digital Imaging Software

Popular digital imaging applications (also called graphic applications) include Microsoft Paint, Macromedia Fireworks, Jasc Software Paint Shop Pro, Mac iPhoto, and Adobe Photoshop. These applications vary greatly in price and sophistication. Relatively expensive graphic applications, such as Photoshop, allow you to modify images in a variety of ways. Special tools, called filters, can change an image's appearance, such as making it look like an oil painting. Figure 8.16 shows some examples of filters.

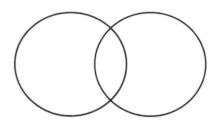

● Figure 8.16
Graphic applications, such as Adobe Photoshop, allow you to manipulate an image in different ways. When might these filters be useful?

Undistorted

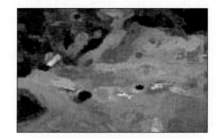

Dry Brush

Twirl

Using the Pictures Toolbar

FrontPage provides tools for making minor edits to images. The Pictures toolbar, shown in Figure 8.17, contains tools that allow you to edit and format images:

◆ The **Rotate** and **Flip** buttons reverse and rotate your picture.

◆ The **Contrast** and **Brightness** buttons increase and decrease the brightness and contrast of the selected picture.

◆ The **Crop** button lets you trim the picture down to a smaller size.

◆ The **Resample** button refines the focus of a picture that has been enlarged or reduced by changing the number of pixels in the picture to match the new screen area occupied by the image.

◆ The **Select** button changes the insertion point to a pointer so that you can select a picture for editing.

◆ The **Restore** button lets you undo any changes that you have made to the picture since you opened the Picture toolbar.

Figure 8.17
The tools on the Pictures toolbar allow you to manipulate pictures. What is the purpose of the Restore button?

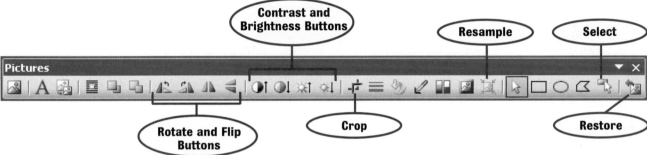

YOU TRY IT

ACTIVITY 8H Manipulating an Image with the Pictures Toolbar

1 Open the CV Walk home page (**index.htm**) in Design (in 2002, Normal) view.

2 On the **View** menu, select **Toolbars** and choose **Pictures** to open the Pictures toolbar. Drag the Pictures toolbar down until it docks at the bottom of the screen.

3 Click the home page image to select it. Click the **More Brightness** and **Less Brightness** buttons and note how the graphic changes. Click the **More Contrast** and **Less Contrast** buttons and note how the graphic changes. When you finish experimenting, click the **Restore** button to return the graphic to its original appearance.

4 Click the **Rotate** and **Flip** buttons and note how the graphic changes. Click the **Restore** button when you finish experimenting.

Resizing Graphics

When you import an image into FrontPage, the picture appears at the exact pixel dimensions with which it was originally stored. After you import it, you will usually want to make the image larger or smaller to fit your page.

Resizing an image refers to changing the size that the image appears to be on the screen. You can resize an image in FrontPage by selecting it and then dragging its sizing handles. Dragging a corner handle keeps the image's **aspect ratio** (the relationship between the image's height and width) constant and in proportion.

You also can use the Appearance tab on the Picture Properties dialog box to resize an image (see Figure 8.18). You can specify the image's width and height in pixels, or select the in percent option to indicate a percentage of increase or decrease in the image's size. You only need to change the width or the height box—the other dimension will change automatically. For example, if you increase an image's width by 10 percent, its height will automatically increase by the same percentage.

When resizing an image, always select the Specify size check box. This option enables the Web browser to correctly position page elements before the picture has completely downloaded, allowing the page to display more quickly. You should also select the Keep aspect ratio option so your image does not become distorted when resized.

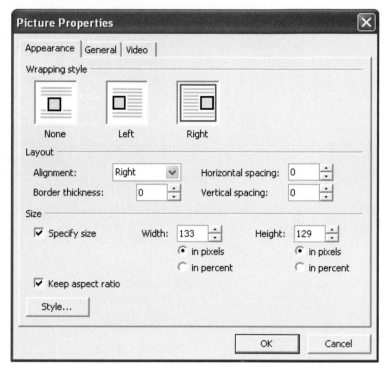

● **Figure 8.18**
The Picture Properties dialog box allows you to modify an image in a variety of ways. How does the "in pixels" sizing option differ from the "in percent" option?

Resampling Graphics

Resizing a graphic changes its appearance but does not change the actual number of pixels in the graphic's file. **Resampling** changes the number of pixels in a graphic's file to match the new screen area occupied by the image's altered size. For example, if you enlarge a 100 x 100 pixel image so that it occupies a 200 pixel square area, resampling adjusts the image so that it is 200 pixels wide and 200 pixels high.

Resampling makes an image's file smaller so that it downloads more quickly. However, resampling also permanently changes your graphic file by changing the number of pixels in that file. If you do not like the change, you can click the Restore button before you save your changes. Since resampling does change the graphic file, use this option with care. You also may want to make copies of your graphic files so you will have the original files if you need them.

Cropping Images

Cropping an image involves removing portions of the image that you do not want to use. This process can significantly reduce the size of a file. In the following You Try It, you will crop, resize, and resample an image.

Activity 8.2 Explore Digital Imaging Applications Find out more about newer digital imaging applications and the advanced features they provide at **webdesign.glencoe.com**.

ACTIVITY 8I Cropping, Resizing, and Resampling a Picture

❶ Open the CV Walk home page in Design (in 2002, Normal) view. Select the home page image.

❷ On the Pictures toolbar, click the **Crop** tool. Drag the pointer to select the area that you want to crop (see Figure 8.19). Click the **Crop** button again to crop the image.

Figure 8.19
Cropping allows you to remove unwanted portions of the picture.

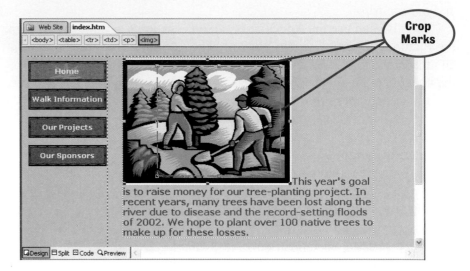

❸ Right-click in the graphic and click **Picture Properties.** In the Picture Properties dialog box, click the **Appearance** tab. Under Wrapping style, click **Right.** Under Layout, change Border thickness to **4.** Under Size, make certain Specify size is selected. In the Width text box, type 250. Click **OK** to close the dialog box.

❹ On the Pictures toolbar, click Resample.

❺ Save your work. Check your page in a browser with a resolution of 800 x 600. The page should look similar to Figure 8.20 (your home page image may be different from the one shown).

Figure 8.20
The cropped graphic takes up less of the page area.

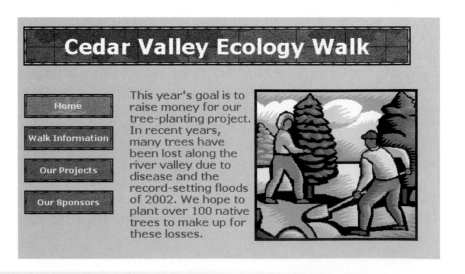

CREATING A PHOTO GALLERY WITH THUMBNAILS

A **photo gallery** is a collection of photographs, typically with a brief description of each image. FrontPage makes it easy to create such a gallery. When you create a photo gallery, FrontPage creates a thumbnail of each image automatically. A **thumbnail** is a small image that links to a larger version of the same image. Thumbnails enable users to decide whether they want to view a larger version of the image (which typically takes extra time to download). In the following activity, you will create a photo gallery that showcases some of the projects funded by the Cedar Valley Ecology Walk.

ACTIVITY 8J Creating a Photo Gallery in FrontPage

YOU TRY IT

1. Open the Our Projects page (**projects.htm**) from the CV Walk site in Design (in 2002, Normal) view.

2. Click anywhere in the content area of the Our Projects page. On the **Insert** menu, select **Picture** and choose **New Photo Gallery** to open the Photo Gallery Properties dialog box.

3. Click the **Add** drop-down arrow and click **Pictures from Files.** In the File Open dialog box, browse to the DataFile\Ch08\Images folder.

4. In the Images folder, hold down the **Ctrl** key and click **eagle.jpg, flowers.jpg, planting.jpg,** and **stream.jpg.** All four JPEG files should be selected. Click **Open.** The four image files are now listed under Add in the Photo Gallery Properties dialog box.

5. Click **eagle.jpg.** In the Caption text box, enter the following caption: Eagles have been flourishing because of increased habitat. Do NOT click **OK.**

6. Repeat step 5 for each of the three remaining photographs, entering the captions shown in Table 8.2.

Photo Gallery File Names and Captions

Photo File Name	Caption
flowers.jpg	We continue to work on naturalizing the upper area of City Park.
planting.jpg	Several hundred native trees are being planted along the Cedar River.
stream.jpg	Extensive cleanup has been completed along Ralston Creek.

Table 8.2
You can assign a caption to each photo in the Photo Gallery Properties dialog box.

7. Click the **Layout** tab. Under Choose a Layout, click **Vertical Layout.** Change Number of pictures per row to **2.** Click **OK.**

8 Save your work. Make sure the images are saved in the images folder. View the photo gallery in **Preview** view. Click one of the thumbnail images. The full-size image will appear, as shown in Figure 8.21.

Figure 8.21
When a user clicks a thumbnail, the full-size image appears.

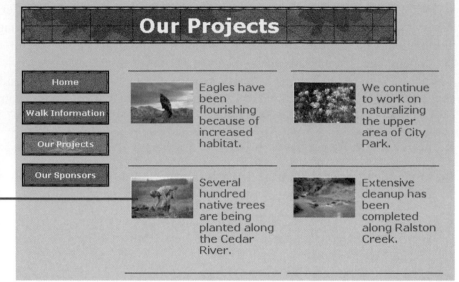

9 Return to **Design** (in 2002, **Normal**) view. Save your work and close the Web site.

The Our Projects page is now complete. In the next chapter, you will further enhance the site by adding multimedia elements to its pages.

Section 8.4 Assessment

Concept Check

1. **Define** resizing, aspect ratio, resampling, cropping, photo gallery, thumbnail.

2. **Describe** how you can resize an image in FrontPage.

3. **Explain** the purpose of resampling an image.

Critical Thinking

4. **Analyze** Why do you think Web designers prefer to modify pictures in a graphics application rather than in FrontPage?

5. **Compare and Contrast** Discuss the difference between cropping a photo and resizing a photo. Give an example of a situation in which each is useful.

Applying Skills

Create a Photo Gallery Obtain at least six digital images of family members or friends. Create a Web page that displays these pictures in a photo gallery. Include one interesting fact about each person pictured.

SECTION 8.1 Using Custom Themes and Shared Borders

Key Terms

external style sheet, 214
embedded style sheet, 214
cascading style sheet, 214
shared border, 215

Main Ideas

- You can modify a pre-made theme to fit the specific needs of your Web site.
- A style sheet applies format and layout settings to all Web pages created with it.
- Shared borders allow page components, such as navigation bars and banners, to appear on more than one page.
- Using shared borders enables you to establish much of your site's basic structure in just a few steps.

SECTION 8.2 Web Graphic Types and File Formats

Key Terms

raster graphic, 219
paint program, 219
vector graphic, 219
draw program, 219
GIF (Graphic Interchange Format), 220
JPEG (Joint Photographic Experts Group), 220
lossless compression, 221
lossy compression, 221

Main Ideas

- There are two basic types of graphics: raster and vector.
- Raster graphics are more common on the Web than vector graphics.
- The GIF graphic file format works best for line art and simple drawings.
- The JPEG graphic file format works best for photographs.
- Compression schemes reduce an image's download time but also diminish its quality.

SECTION 8.3 Obtaining and Creating Graphics

Key Terms

scanner, 225
dots per inch (dpi), 225
digital camera, 225
inline graphic, 225
WordArt, 226

Main Ideas

- You can use the Web to locate pre-made graphics, such as clip art.
- Always make certain you have permission to use a pre-made graphic before placing it on your Web page.
- Scanners enable you to convert a printed image to digital format.
- With a digital camera, you can shoot a picture and download the image file to your computer.
- You can create original images with WordArt and drawing tools.

SECTION 8.4 Editing and Formatting Graphics

Key Terms

resizing, 233
aspect ratio, 233
resampling, 233
cropping, 233
photo gallery, 235
thumbnail, 235

Main Ideas

- You can use the Pictures toolbar to modify images in FrontPage.
- Resizing an image changes the image's appearance on the screen.
- Resampling an image changes the image's graphic file.
- You can crop an image to remove areas that you do not want to use.
- A photo gallery consists of a collection of photos.
- A thumbnail is a smaller version of a larger image.

Reviewing Key Terms

1. What is the difference between a raster graphic and a vector graphic?
2. Which of the following is NOT a graphic file type: PAINT, GIF, JPEG, BMP?
3. What does the abbreviation "dpi" stand for?
4. Identify two input devices that you can use to create images for your Web pages.
5. Rewrite this statement to make it true: *You can use the Resample button on the Pictures toolbar to eliminate the parts of a picture you do not want.*

Understanding Main Ideas

6. **Explain** how you can determine the format of a graphic file by looking at the file's name.
7. **Describe** a situation in which you would create a JPEG file rather than a GIF file.
8. **List** at least four ways you can obtain images to use on your Web pages.
9. **Identify** the functions of buttons on the Drawing toolbar.
10. **Explain** the purpose of the Wrapping style option in the Picture Properties dialog box.
11. **Explain** why it is important to maintain a picture's aspect ratio when you are resizing it.
12. **Discuss** how resizing an image differs from resampling it.
13. **Describe** two situations in which thumbnails would be particularly useful on a Web page.

Critical Thinking

14. **Evaluate Ethics** A friend is creating a Web site to buy and sell trading cards. While making the site, she copies graphics from other Web sites and inserts them on her Web pages. What would you tell your friend to explain why her actions violate copyright laws?
15. **Analyze Design** Think of a situation in which you might not want to use FrontPage's shared borders feature. Explain why shared borders would not be useful in this situation.
16. **Make Decisions** On the Sponsors Web page, you used WordArt and the drawing tools to create logos. Assume that you had created these logos in a graphics application, such as Microsoft Paint. Would you save the logos in JPEG or GIF format? Explain your answer.
17. **Compare and Contrast** How is formatting graphics for the Web different from formatting them for a printed document, such as a magazine? How is it similar?
18. **Analyze Graphics** Summarize the relationship between a graphic's quality, its file size, and its download time. Explain how this relationship might influence you when choosing graphics to include on a Web page.

e-Review

webdesign.glencoe.com

Study with PowerPoint

To review the main points in this chapter, select **e-Review > PowerPoint Outlines > Chapter 8.**

Online Self Check

Test your knowledge of the material in this chapter by selecting **e-Review > Self Checks > Chapter 8.**

Making Connections

Math—Compare Download Times Locate five graphics. At least one should be a GIF (e.g., clip art), and at least one should be a JPEG (e.g., digital photograph). Insert each graphic into a blank FrontPage page (one image per page).

Create a line graph. Place each graphic's type and file size (if known) on the x-axis and the download time of its page on the y-axis. Analyze your findings. Resave a JPEG file as a GIF file and insert it into a new blank page. Compare the quality and download time of the GIF file to the original JPEG file. Analyze your findings.

STANDARDS AT WORK

Students practice responsible use of technology systems, information, and software. (NETS-S 2)

Copyrights and Permissions for Use
A copyright is the exclusive legal right to reproduce, publish, and sell literary or artistic works. The creator of the work owns the copyright regardless of whether it is filed with the government.

Visit three sites that contain clip art or other visual images. Locate the page that discusses the site's terms of use or licensing agreements. Print the information you find. Based on your findings, summarize how each site's images may be used in the following types of media:

1. a report for one of your classes
2. a Web site for a non-profit organization
3. a brochure for a new business in your community
4. a Web site for your school

List the projects that would need permission. Describe how you would obtain permission to use the work.

TEAMWORK SKILLS

Create Images and a Web Site
As a team, select a topic for a Web site. Plan and design a site that has a home page and two additional pages. Use shared borders and a theme to create a common look among the pages.

Find or create images such as photographs, clip art, drawings, and WordArt for your site. Once all the images have been selected, add them to the site. Use all of the following Picture tools as you create the pages for the site: rotate, flip, resize, crop, contrast, brightness, and resample.

Have another team review the site and give you suggestions for improvements. As a team, evaluate these suggestions and make changes that will improve the site.

CHALLENGE YOURSELF

Compare Graphic File Types
Use a paint program to create a simple line drawing. Save the file in each of the formats available in the paint program. Name each file with the type of format being used.

Create a table similar to the one below that compares the file types and the size of the files. If you are using word processing software, you may add a column to display the graphic files in the table. Compare your results. What quality difference can you see among the different files? How do the download times for the various formats compare? Do these results match your expectations? Explain why or why not.

File Type	File Extension	Size
24-bit bitmap	.bmp	3,165 KB
JPEG	.jpg	22 KB

YOU TRY IT

Skills Studio

These exercises reinforce the skills you learned in this chapter's You Try It activities. Refer back to the You Try It activities if you need extra guidance.

1. Customizing a Theme

Create a Web page for an event in your community.

Ⓐ Select an event that will occur in your community in the next three months.

Ⓑ Plan a Web page to announce the event. Gather the information you will need for the page's content. The page should include images.

Ⓒ Choose a theme for the page. Customize the theme by changing colors and inserting a new background picture. You can use resources from the Student Data Files for the background picture or obtain an image from another source.

Ⓓ Create a table similar to the one shown below to record the changes you make to the theme.

ITEM	COLOR	HEXADECIMAL VALUE
Body	Fuchsia	Hex={FF,00,FF}
Heading 1	Maroon	Hex={80,00,00}
Heading 2	Cyan	Hex={00,FF,FF}

Ⓔ Add the content to the page and modify text styles as needed.

Ⓕ Proofread and save your work.

2. Adding Graphics to a Web Page

Add graphics to the community event page.

Ⓐ Select two of the following types of graphics to use in your Web page: clip art, graphics imported from a digital camera or scanner, or graphics created in FrontPage.

Ⓑ Locate or create graphics that will work on the page. Be sure the graphics work with the color and theme you are using for your page.

Ⓒ Insert the graphics into your Web page. Add alternative text. Edit the images as needed to suit your page. If possible, add a picture gallery to your page.

Ⓓ If you acquired images from an outside source, supply permission information as needed.

Ⓔ Save the file. View the page in a browser.

Web Design Projects

1. Create a Virtual Field Trip Web Site

Create a Web site that features virtual trips to the following events or eras:

- The American Civil War
- The Ming Dynasty in China
- The building of the pyramids in Egypt
- The Middle Ages in Europe
- The French Revolution
- World War II

Acquire a graphic for each of the virtual field trips listed above. Edit the images you select so that they are suitable for use on the Web.

Create a site that has a home page and six additional pages (one for each trip). Create a theme and text styles for the site. Use shared borders. Place a page banner in the top shared border and a navigation bar in the left. Layout the home page as illustrated:

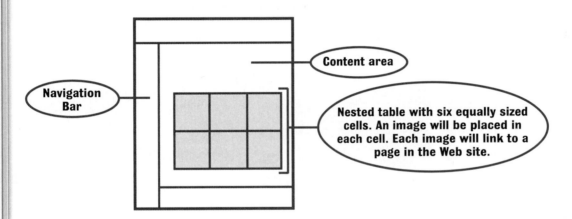

Use your graphics to create an image map on the home page. Each image should link to its corresponding trip page. Add page banners to each page that include the page title (the name of the trip). Do not add content to the trip pages at this time.

2. Create an Art Styles Web Site

You have been asked to create a Web site illustrating different artistic styles from the 19th and 20th centuries. The site will have a home page that links to a page for each of the following styles: Realism, Impressionism, Modernism, and Symbolism.

Select one of the styles and find representative images on the Web or scan them from print sources. Obtain permissions for their use as needed.

In FrontPage, create the home page and a page for each period. Apply a suitable theme (customize an existing theme as needed). Add the navigation from the home page to each of the styles pages. Then build the style page that you have select, placing the images that you have located. Manipulate the images as needed. Provide alternative text for each image. View the Web site in a browser.

Adding Multimedia to a Web Site

WHY IT MATTERS.....................................

People absorb information through all their senses. Sounds and smells make us aware of what is happening in our environment in ways that words cannot. Many recreational activities, such as concerts and video games, use light, images, and sound to enhance the audience's experience. Using sound, video, and animation in your Web site can provide visitors with a more intense, engaging experience by stimulating a variety of senses.

Quick Write Activity

Think of a site with which you are familiar that uses components such as sound, animation, and video. Do you think you enjoy the site more because of these components? Do they make you want to stay longer? Write several sentences explaining your answers to these questions.

WHAT YOU WILL DO..

READ TO SUCCEED

Prepare with a Partner
You might find it easier to work with a partner as you read through a chapter. Before you read, you and your partner can ask each other questions about the topics that will be discussed in the chapter. (Use the section headings or the "You Will Learn to" objectives to identify the topics.) What do you both think is important to know after reading the section? Write down the questions you both have about each section. Keep these questions in mind as you read.

Section 9.1 Multimedia and Web Design

Guide to Reading

Main Ideas

Multimedia elements should never distract visitors from your page's main purpose. Always use multimedia files ethically and legally.

Key Terms

multimedia
audio
video
animation
codec
multimedia authoring tool

Reading Strategy

Identify six multimedia design guidelines. Use a web diagram like the one below (also available online).

Multimedia Design Guidelines

Multimedia is the combined use of different media forms, such as text, graphics, audio, video, and animation. **Audio,** which consists of live, streamed, or recorded sound, can attract visitors' interest and impart information. **Video,** which consists of live or recorded moving pictures, can inform, teach, and entertain. **Animation** uses graphics or text to represent motion, and, because it is relatively easy to use, it is a common feature on the Web.

MULTIMEDIA DESIGN GUIDELINES

Most people like to visit sites that contain audio, visual, and animation. However, videos that take too long to download can frustrate visitors. Some sites are so cluttered with distracting animations that visitors have a hard time reading the text or locating needed information.

Multimedia benefits a Web site when it helps meet the site's goals and purpose. As you plan a site, consider each type of multimedia element and define how you can use it effectively on the site.

Audio Guidelines

For most sites, audio should play for only a short time when the site first loads or when the visitor clicks on a button to listen to the audio clip. Audio that plays the entire time the site is loaded tends to distract visitors and may cause them to move to another site. Here are some examples of effective uses of audio:

◆ An excerpt from a speech on a politician's site
◆ A country's national anthem on a page about the country
◆ Words spoken in another language on a site helping travelers learn basic phrases
◆ The theme song of a new movie on a site advertising the movie

 webdesign.glencoe.com

Video Guidelines

Since video files are large, you should use them to enhance your site—not to convey your main message. When planning video clips, consider the type of connection your typical visitor will have. Well-designed multimedia sites, such as the one shown in Figure 9.1, allow visitors to specify the type of connection they are using and supply a lower resolution presentation for those with slower connections.

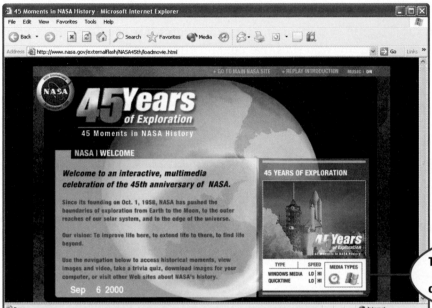

Figure 9.1
The NASA (National Aeronautics and Space Administration) site adjusts the presentation's quality to fit the visitor's connection. What is the graphic in the upper-left corner of this page called?

The video file that visitors see depends on the type of connection they specify

Animation Guidelines

Web designers usually include animations to draw the visitor's attention. Banner advertisements on portal sites, for example, frequently use animations to draw the eye to important content. The type and speed of animations vary, depending on the purpose. If you use animations on an informational site, be careful to keep them subtle so that they do not distract visitors from reading the information you provide.

File Size Guidelines

Always consider download time when using multimedia files. The larger the file, the longer it will take to download. Some audio formats use compression to reduce file size. However, compression generally reduces a file's quality. Before you insert any audio file on a Web page, listen to it to make certain the quality is acceptable.

Streaming media, whether audio or video, reduces the user's waiting time. To stream media, the Web server breaks the transmission into pieces. The user's media player starts playing the first piece of the file as soon as it downloads. As the player receives the remaining pieces, it stores them and plays them in order. The result is a continuous stream of content, where each downloaded piece plays as the rest of the file arrives. Streaming requires the use of a **codec** (compression/decompression scheme) to first compress and then decompress the data.

READ ME!

Caution Not all hosting services will allow you to use streamed data. It is a good idea to check with your service if you want to stream media on your site.

DOWNLOADING MULTIMEDIA FILES FROM THE WEB

The Web can be a rich source of free multimedia files. It is easy to locate and download these files. However, you must be careful to always use downloaded files ethically.

Locating Multimedia Files

You can use search engines to locate online multimedia files. For example, the Dogpile search engine lets you search for specific file types (see Figure 9.2). Many Web sites that contain clip art collections also offer short audio and animation files.

Figure 9.2 The Dogpile search engine lets you request audio files. What other kinds of files does Dogpile let you search for?

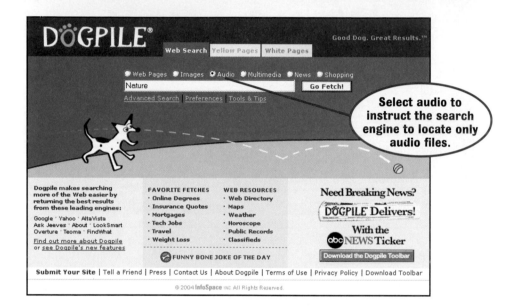

Select audio to instruct the search engine to locate only audio files.

Sources of graphic clip art often provide animation files as well. You can use FrontPage's Clip Art task pane to search for Microsoft animation clip art. When you locate a clip, you can download an animation the same way you would a graphic.

Using Multimedia Files Ethically

Regardless of how you obtain multimedia files, you must have permission to use them. While many clip art collections allow you to use their files on personal sites, they may set limits on their use. Always be sure to read any instructions concerning the legal use of these files. If you download a file from the Web, be sure to follow any rules stated on that Web site. Also be sure to give credit to a file's author if you use someone else's work on your Web site.

You have probably read or heard about the controversy over downloading music online without paying for it. Sites that allow you to download music files for personal use may not allow you to include these same files on a Web site without paying a fee. If the site has usage rules, read and follow them for downloading music. These same rules apply to downloading and using video files on your Web pages.

Activity 9.1 Locate Clips Online Learn more about finding audio, video, and animation clips online at **webdesign.glencoe.com**.

webdesign.glencoe.com

TOOLS FOR CREATING MULTIMEDIA WEB SITES

Designers who create multimedia Web sites use special software packages called **multimedia authoring tools.** The most widely used authoring tool is Macromedia Director, which is shown in Figure 9.3. Director helps you integrate media components, such as audio, video, animation, and photo-quality images, into a seamless whole. Some authoring tools have been developed for special purposes. For example, Macromedia Authorware is designed for creating multimedia training programs, such as interactive tutorials. Authoring tools are expensive and require experience to use successfully.

Numerous applications are available for acquiring and editing audio, including GoldWave, Sound Forge, and Audacity. With these applications, you can create and edit high-quality audio files. Microsoft Windows contains a simple application called Sound Recorder that lets you create and save audio files. While Sound Recorder allows you to make some changes to your file, it does not provide the sophisticated features of commercial audio applications.

Many Windows OSs come with Windows Movie Maker, an application that allows you to perform some basic editing tasks with video clips. When you finish, you can save the file in Windows Media Video (WMV) format. Windows Movie Maker has some drawbacks. It does not allow you to perform sophisticated frame-by-frame editing of your video and it supports only one format, WMV.

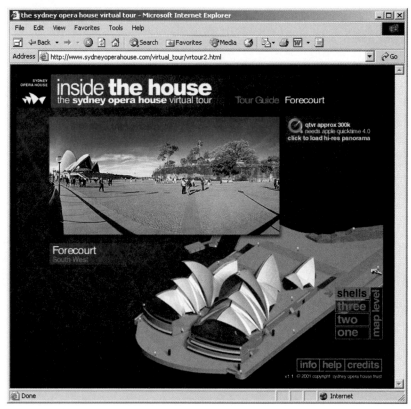

● **Figure 9.3**
Multimedia authoring tools, help you integrate text, graphics, animation, audio, and video. **How is multimedia used to enhance this Web site?**

EVALUATING MULTIMEDIA WEB SITES

When you evaluate or plan a multimedia Web site, ask yourself the following questions:

◆ Do the audio, video, and/or animations support each page's goals?
◆ Are the pages cluttered?
◆ Do any media components distract visitors (for example, do they flash on and off)?
◆ Does the site give you the option to skip lengthy audio or video clips?
◆ Do components such as sound and video work properly?
◆ Do the media components add to your enjoyment of the site?

Figure 9.4
This site uses animation and sound to attract the visitor's attention. How might sound be used effectively on a page such as this?

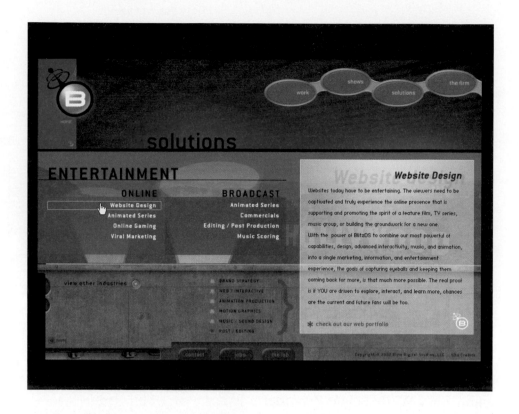

The Blitz Digital Studios Web page shown in Figure 9.4 follows good multimedia design principles. The page contains numerous items, yet it still provides considerable "white space" where the eye can rest. Animated spotlights add interest to the page without distracting the viewer from important content. Animated buttons and audio cues let users know when items have been selected. Visitors also have the option to turn the site's music on or off.

Section 9.1 Assessment

Concept Check

1. **Define** multimedia, audio, video, animation, codec, multimedia authoring tool.

2. **Identify** guidelines for using audio, video, and animation effectively in a Web site.

3. **Summarize** the features of a well-designed multimedia Web site.

Critical Thinking

4. **Analyze** A friend's page contains a flashing banner that makes it hard to read the page's text, and a video with a long download time. How should your friend improve her site?

5. **Make Decisions** Discuss how audio could be used to enhance an educational site about World War II.

Applying Skills

Define Ethical Use
Visit two sites that have clip art, sound, and/or video clips. Print their license and usage pages. Review the printouts and write a summary of how files from these sites may be used on Web sites.

HOW DO WEB SITES MAKE MONEY?

Some Web sites make money by selling goods or services to their visitors. However, this is not the only way for a Web site to support itself.

Web-based advertising can be effective for the advertiser and lucrative for the Web site that carries the ads.

Advertising

Many Web sites make money by displaying advertisements. These include banner ads, which appear somewhere on the screen, and pop-up ads, which appear in a separate browser window. Generally, advertisers pay to place the ads on the site, the same way they pay for an ad on television or in a magazine. Ad rates are usually based on the number of hits the site attracts. The more popular the site, the more expensive it is to place an ad there.

Referrals

Suppose you visit an online newspaper and see a banner ad for a company called BestStuff.com. You click the ad and go to the BestStuff.com site. When you do, the newspaper site earns a small fee, called a referral. Many Web ads work this way because it allows advertisers to pay only when the ad actually attracts someone to their site.

Starting an Online Business

If you would like to start a Web site that sells a product or service online, you must first develop a strong, sensible business plan.

Here are some tactics you might try to make your Web site pay off:

◆ **Look for advertisers** Your ISP, for example, may be interested in placing an ad on your site. So may local businesses. If each advertiser pays only a few dollars each month, the revenue will cover your hosting costs.

◆ **Sell space** For example, if your site includes a page where fellow students can run classified ads, you might charge a small fee per ad. Remember, though, that free Web space is easy to come by, so do not overcharge. Sell space like a service that provides value to your customers, and price it reasonably.

◆ **Get into referrals** Lots of companies will pay you if someone "clicks through" to their site by using a banner ad placed on your site. But be careful. Many personal Web pages include more referral ads than real content, and this approach will drive people away from your site.

Tech Focus

1. Visit five Web sites that display advertisements. Create a chart that describes each site and compares the type, placement, and number of ads on each site. Evaluate the advertising's effectiveness.

2. Select a company and research its approach to e-commerce. How has the Web affected this business and how does it make money on the Web?

Section 9.2 Adding Audio and Video to a Site

Guide to Reading

Main Ideas
You can insert both audio and video into your Web pages. Audio and video files come in a variety of formats.

Key Terms
plug-in
digital video recorder
analog video recorder
video capture card

Reading Strategy
Identify two ways to incorporate audio into a Web site. Use a chart like the one below (also available online).

Ways to Incorporate Audio Files

Many Web sites make extensive use of audio and video. Each audio or video segment used on a Web page is stored in a separate file.

AUDIO AND VIDEO FILES

Every file has a specific format that enables the Web browser to interpret and properly display or play the file's content.

Audio File Formats

Table 9.1 lists the most common audio file formats. Not every OS or browser supports every format. Always test pages containing audio.

Activity 9.2 Evaluate Multimedia Web Sites Learn more about evaluating multimedia Web sites by visiting **webdesign.glencoe.com**.

Table 9.1
The file name extension identifies the audio file format. What type of file would you create using a digital piano?

Common Audio File Formats		
Format	**File Extension**	**Description**
Wave	.wav	Developed jointly by Microsoft and IBM. Mainly used for very short audio clips.
Midi	.mid	Used by synthesizers and electronic instruments.
RealAudio	.ram, .ra	Developed by RealNetworks.
AIFF	.aif, .aifc, .aiff	Developed specifically for the Macintosh.
AU, SND	.au, .snd	The earliest formats for sending sound over the Internet. No longer widely used.
MPEG Audio-Player 3	.mp3	Developed by the Moving Picture Experts Group. Can create very small, highly compressed audio files.

webdesign.glencoe.com

Digital recording devices capture sound by sampling the sound waves. To sample a sound wave means to record fragments of that wave. When played together, these fragments reproduce the entire sound. The sampling rate is the number of times per second a recording device samples sound waves. The higher the sampling rate, the better the audio clip's sound quality. The lower the sampling rate, the lower the sound quality.

Video File Formats

You can insert video as well as audio files on your Web pages. Table 9.2 lists the video file formats commonly used on the Web. Again, some of these formats may not work on some operating systems and Web browsers. Test pages using video under as many different conditions as you can.

Common Video File Formats

Format	File Extension	Description
AVI (Audio Visual Interleaved)	.avi	Used with Windows Media Player. Entire file must download before it can play.
MPEG (Moving Picture Experts Group)	.mpg	Compressed format that can be used for streaming.
QuickTime	.mov, .qt	Developed by Apple, can be used for streaming video. Also known as MOV (Movie) format.
RAM Real Video	.ram, .ra	From Real Networks, can be used for streaming audio and video. Good for low-speed connections.
WMV (Windows Media Video)	.wmv, .asf	Used with Windows Media Player. Can be used for streaming audio and video.

Table 9.2
Video files usually require a browser plug-in to play. Which format would you use if your target audience had low-speed connections?

Each single image in a video clip is called a frame. The quality and resolution of each frame affects the overall quality of the video. Frames appear on the screen at a rate measured in frames per second (FPS). A slow frame rate can result in jerky video. Television, for example, has a frame rate of 30 FPS, which appears to the viewer as smooth video. Internet video generally varies from 10 to 30 FPS, but a rate of at least 15 FPS is recommended. The faster the FPS, the better the video quality, but the larger the video file.

Many audio and video files require a **plug-in.** A plug-in is an application that works with the Web browser to play a particular file format. Common plug-ins include RealNetwork's RealOne Player, Apple QuickTime, and Microsoft Windows Media Player. You can download most plug-ins for free from the company's Web site.

CREATING AND ADDING AUDIO FILES TO A SITE

To play sound, your computer needs a sound card (or sound capabilities integrated into the motherboard) and speakers. To create sound files, you also need a microphone and an audio application, such as Microsoft Sound Recorder, to record audio and save it in a file. Once you store the sound file on your hard disk, you can use audio editing software to modify it.

You can incorporate sound into your Web pages in two basic ways. First, you can create a button and link a sound file to the button. The sound will play when a visitor clicks the button. Second, you can set the sound file to play automatically when the page loads. You can set the file to play once or loop and play repeatedly. Keep the number of loops low to avoid annoying your visitors.

In the following activity, you will insert a sound file into the CV Walk home page.

YOU TRY IT

Student Data File

ACTIVITY 9A Inserting Background Sounds

❶ Open the CV Walk home page (**index.htm**) in Design (in FrontPage 2002, Normal) view.

❷ Right-click anywhere on the page and click **Page Properties.**

❸ In the Page Properties dialog box, under Background sound, click in the **Location** text box. Browse to the DataFile\Ch09\Multimedia folder. Double-click the **birds.wav** file to open it.

❹ Under Loop, deselect the **Forever** check box. In the Loop text box, type 2 (see Figure 9.5). The audio file will repeat twice. Click **OK.**

Figure 9.5
The Page Properties dialog box lets you specify how many times the sound file will repeat.

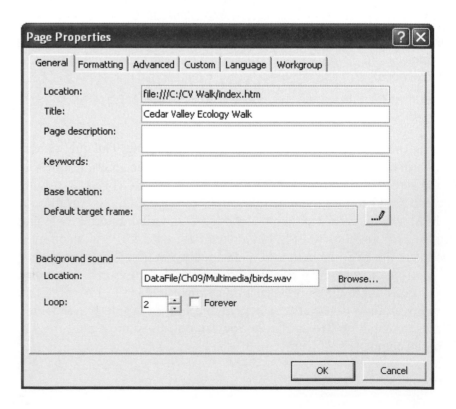

5 Save your page. When the Save Embedded Files dialog box appears, click **Change Folder.**

6 In the Change Folder dialog box, click the **Create New Folder** button. Name the folder multimedia. Click away from the folder, then click **OK.** Click **OK** again to save the embedded file and close the dialog box.

7 Preview the page. You should hear birds chirping as the sound file plays. When you finish, return to **Design** (in 2002, **Normal**) view.

If you create a site that relies heavily on sound, you can insert a short note explaining the purpose of the sound for those that do not have a sound card or have their volume turned down or off.

CREATING VIDEO FILES

You need a video recorder to create your own video. A **digital video recorder,** such as the one shown in Figure 9.6, creates video that a computer can use directly. However, for video created with an **analog video recorder** (or with a VCR), the data must be translated into digital format before a computer can use it. A special circuit board called a **video capture card** can perform this conversion.

Digital video recorders include cables that connect the video recorder to the computer. You can then transfer the video to the computer's hard disk, where it is saved in a file. You can use video editing software to edit this file. The file is then ready to insert into a Web page.

●**Figure 9.6**
Video recorders can capture video and sound that you can transfer to a computer. How might video contribute to a Web site for a high school art class?

ADDING VIDEO FILES TO A SITE

It can be challenging to include video on a Web site. Video clips can require significant download time. Different file formats require different codecs. The Web browser must be able to understand both the file's format and its codec. Because of these challenges, most Web designers do not insert clips directly into Web pages. Instead, they typically provide a link to the video clip. That way, visitors who have the necessary plug-in can decide whether or not they want to access the video and wait for it to download.

In the following activity, you will insert a video clip into the Ecology site's Walk Information page. Visitors will need the QuickTime plug-in (or another plug-in capable of playing video in QuickTime format) to view this clip, so you will tell them how to download this plug-in if they do not already have it installed on their computers.

YOU TRY IT

Student
Data File

READ ME!

Tech Tip In FrontPage 2003, you can use the Layout Tables and Cells task pane to create the table.

Figure 9.7 ●
The Plug-In Properties dialog box specifies the video file to be inserted.

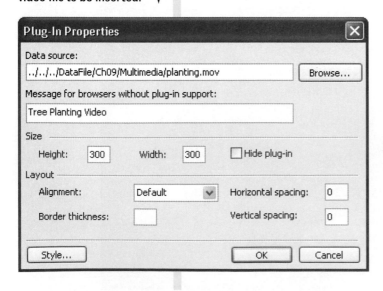

ACTIVITY 9B Inserting a Video Clip

❶ Open the **Walk Information** page in Design (in 2002, Normal) view. Position the insertion point in the upper-left corner of the content area.

❷ On the **Table** menu, select **Insert>Table** to open the Insert Table dialog box. Under Size, type 1 in the Rows text box and 1 in the Columns text box. Under Layout, type 450 in the Specify width text box. Click **In pixels.** Set the Border size to 0. Click **OK.** A narrow, one-line table appears across the entire width of the page.

❸ Position the insertion point inside the table. Type the following text:

Walk is on October 20.
Walk starts at 8 a.m.
All ages are welcome.
Registration fee is $20.
Be sure to pre-register.

Format the text as a bold bulleted list with a font size of 4.

❹ Click after the last line and press **Enter** twice. Type Please support our tree planting project! Center the text. Press **Enter** once.

❺ Click the **Web Component** button on the Standard toolbar. In the dialog box, under Component type, click **Advanced Controls.** In the Choose a control list, click **Plug-In.** Click **Finish** to open the Plug-In Properties dialog box. ▨

❻ Under Data source, browse to the DataFile\Ch09\Multimedia folder. Double-click **planting.mov**. Under Message for browsers without plug-in support, type Tree Planting Video. Under Size, change Height to 300 and Width to 300. The dialog box now appears as shown in Figure 9.7. Click **OK.**

7 Click the video box to select it. Click the **Center** button.

8 Position the insertion point at the right edge of the video box. Press **Shift + Enter.** Select the **size 2** font size. Type The QuickTime plug-in is required to view this video clip. If you do not have the QuickTime plug-in, you can download it at http://www.apple.com/quicktime.

9 Select the text **http://www.apple.com/quicktime.** Right-click on the text and click **Hyperlink.**

10 In the dialog box, click the **ScreenTip** button. In the Set Hyperlink Screen-Tip Text dialog box, type Get QuickTime Plug-in. Click **OK.**

11 In the Address text box, type http://www.apple.com/quicktime. Click **OK.**

12 Save the page. Make certain the video file is stored in the site's multimedia folder. Click **OK.** The page should now look similar to Figure 9.8. Notice that the video is represented by a box containing a graphic of a plug-in and the name of the video clip.

READ ME!

Jargon A Screen Tip is descriptive text that pops up when the mouse cursor hovers over a hyperlink. Using Screen Tips makes your site more user friendly.

● **Figure 9.8**
In Design view, the video is represented by a box containing a graphic of a plug-in and the video clip's name.

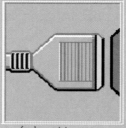

Walk Information

Home

Walk Information

Our Projects

Our Sponsors

※ Walk is on October 20.
※ Walk starts at 8 a.m.
※ All ages are welcome.
※ Registration fee is $20.
※ Be sure to pre-register.

Please support our tree planting project!

.../planting.mov

The QuickTime plug-in is required to view this video clip. If you do not have the QuickTime plug-in, you can download it at http://www.apple.com/quicktime.

⓭ Preview the page and test the video. It should appear similar to Figure 9.9. If possible, test the page in both Internet Explorer and Netscape. When you finish, return to FrontPage.

Figure 9.9 ●
The video clip plays when you open the Walk Information page.

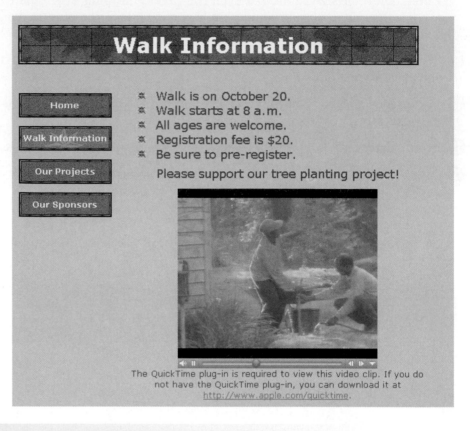

Walk Information

Home

Walk Information

Our Projects

Our Sponsors

✻ Walk is on October 20.
✻ Walk starts at 8 a.m.
✻ All ages are welcome.
✻ Registration fee is $20.
✻ Be sure to pre-register.

Please support our tree planting project!

The QuickTime plug-in is required to view this video clip. If you do not have the QuickTime plug-in, you can download it at http://www.apple.com/quicktime.

Section 9.2 Assessment

Concept Check

1. **Define** plug-in, digital video recorder, analog video recorder, video capture card.

2. **Identify** three audio file formats and three video file formats.

3. **Summarize** at least three ways of obtaining audio files.

Critical Thinking

4. **Analyze Multimedia** You are creating a Web site that presents the history of your school. Discuss how the site might use audio and video. What ethical or legal issues should you consider?

5. **Compare and Contrast** How is a microphone different from a video recorder? How are they similar?

Applying Skills

Evaluate Multimedia Components Visit a site that advertises a movie you have seen in the last few months. Write an evaluation of the multimedia components of the site, using the questions listed on page 247.

Careers & Technology

WHAT DOES A WEBMASTER DO?

If you asked different Webmasters to describe their jobs, they might give many different answers about their responsibilities.

Webmasters often manage teams of designers and programmers.

A Jack of All Trades

When the site's content is simple, the Webmaster's main function is to keep the site up and running. This may involve maintaining the site, which often simply means publishing HTML documents that someone else produces.

However, the Web has become a complicated place. Designers commonly create sophisticated pages using cascading style sheets and nested code. Accordingly, the Webmaster's job has become more complicated and varied. The Webmaster's fundamental responsibility may still be to keep the site running and up to date. However, he or she may also be responsible for:

◆ Server and network management
◆ Site design
◆ HTML coding and programming
◆ Troubleshooting
◆ Monitoring site traffic

Knowledge and Skills

Webmasters should understand network architecture and software, as well as telecommunication technologies. Many Webmasters are also skilled in HTML and other scripting languages.

Some Webmasters have training in graphics or multimedia. Others specialize in database technologies or security, which can be valuable in building secure e-commerce sites. Webmasters with business experience may focus on a site's efficiency and profitability.

Becoming a Webmaster

Many Webmasters start by learning one aspect of the Web, whether it is design, programming, networking, or business. After they receive training in their chosen specialty, they get real-world experience by working on Web design teams.

Organizations such as the World Organization of Webmasters (WOW) have established standards and certifications for Webmasters. WOW certification courses are usually offered through professional schools. A certification can expose you to a wide range of skills that you will need to land a job in the Web field.

Tech Focus

1. Use the Web to find and contact a professional Webmaster. Interview him or her via e-mail or instant messaging. Discuss the job requirements and training. Summarize the interview in a report.

2. Aside from technical skills, what other kinds of skills might be required of a professional Webmaster, especially one who must manage a design team?

Section 9.3 Adding Animation to a Site

Guide to Reading

Main Ideas

Animation provides the appearance of motion. One way of creating animations is to use a series of GIF images, which you can incorporate into a Web page in the same way as a graphic.

Key Terms

Macromedia Flash
Dynamic HTML (DHTML)

Reading Strategy

Compare and contrast Flash and GIF animations. Use a Venn diagram like the one below (also available online).

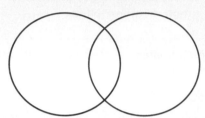

Animation creates the appearance of motion. You can animate both graphics and text. Text or images that appear to bounce across the screen are examples of animations. Interactive buttons, such as hover buttons, are also animated. Animation helps bring your pages to life. Features such as interactive buttons can also make a site more user-friendly.

ANIMATION FILES

The simplest type of animation files are composed of individual GIF images, displayed on the screen one after the other. FrontPage provides some easy ways of animating GIF images. For example, you can have an image zoom in from the left side of the screen, or replace one image with another. You will learn about these animation methods in Chapter 10. In addition, you can use applications specifically designed to create GIF animations.

Another popular animation format is **Macromedia Flash.** The majority of Flash files carry the .swf extension. Flash animations can be much more sophisticated than GIFs and often have a faster download time. To view Flash files, users must have the Flash plug-in, available free at the Macromedia Web site. You can insert Flash files into your pages just as you would other files. However, to create your own Flash animations, you need Macromedia's Flash software or a similar application that supports this format.

CREATING AND USING ANIMATION FILES

When creating a GIF animation, you will store all the images that make up the animation in a single GIF file. This file will also contain instructions that tell the browser the order in which the images should load, the position where each image should appear, and how long each image should appear on the screen. Graphic applications such as Adobe ImageReady and Microsoft PhotoDraw help you to create animated GIFs.

TECH TRIVIA

Customizing Graphics
You can specify a custom color palette for any GIF image you create in Microsoft PhotoDraw. Use the Save As command and click the Options button to uncover the custom palette options.

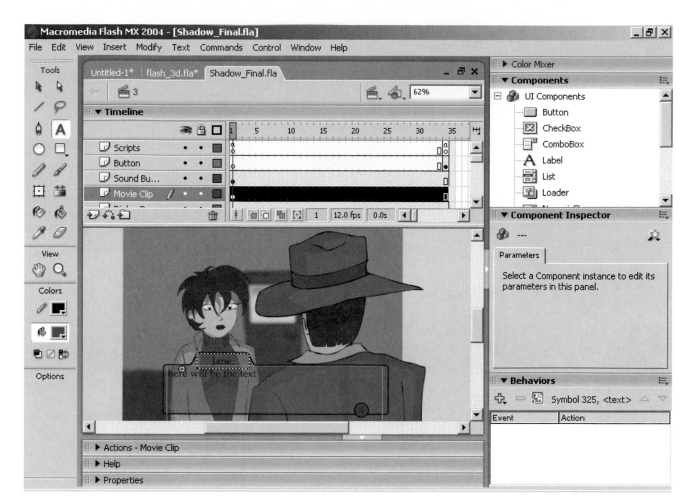

Animation files created with Macromedia Flash can include interactivity. Flash files are thus useful for creating tutorials and similar teaching tools. Figure 9.10 illustrates the use of Flash to create a cartoon-style animation.

INCORPORATING ANIMATION FILES INTO A SITE

FrontPage provides a number of ways to incorporate animation into your Web pages. You insert and resize these files as you would a static GIF. Front-Page also lets you use **Dynamic HTML (DHTML)** to create animations such as lines of scrolling text (called marquees) or page transitions. You will learn about these dynamic effects in Chapter 10.

In the following activity, you will insert an animated GIF into the Walk Information page.

ACTIVITY 9C Inserting an Animation

❶ Open the Walk Information page in Design (in 2002, Normal) view. Position the insertion point in front of the first bulleted item and press Enter. Click in the space you made and delete the bullet (if necessary).

❷ Click the **Insert Picture From File** button. Browse to the DataFile\Ch09\Multimedia folder. Insert the file **leaf.gif** into the page. Add alternative text to the image.

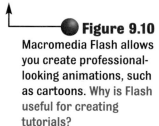

Figure 9.10
Macromedia Flash allows you create professional-looking animations, such as cartoons. Why is Flash useful for creating tutorials?

YOU TRY IT

Student Data File

3 Right-click on the animation and select **Picture Properties.** Under Wrapping style, click **Right.** Under Size, click **Specify size** and change Width to **50.** Make certain that **Keep aspect ratio** is checked. Click **OK.** Save the page. Make certain the animation is saved in the **multimedia** folder and click **OK.** The page now looks similar to Figure 9.11.

Figure 9.11
A GIF animation is inserted into a Web page in the same way as a static (nonanimated) GIF.

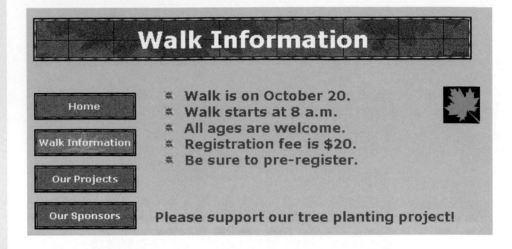

Walk Information

Home
Walk Information
Our Projects
Our Sponsors

* Walk is on October 20.
* Walk starts at 8 a.m.
* All ages are welcome.
* Registration fee is $20.
* Be sure to pre-register.

Please support our tree planting project!

READ ME!
Tech Tip While GIF animation files are not truly movies, that is how they are categorized in Microsoft clip art.

4 Preview the page. The leaf should change from one color to another. Return to **Design** (in 2002, **Normal**) view and save your work.

Section 9.3 Assessment

Concept Check

1. **Define** Macromedia Flash, Dynamic HTML (DHTML).

2. **Identify** at least two ways of obtaining animation files.

3. **Explain** how animation differs from video.

Critical Thinking

4. **Compare and Contrast** Describe an advantage that a Flash animation has over a GIF animation. Describe a disadvantage.

5. **Analyze Animation** Television weather forecasters use radar to generate animated images of weather movement. What does this technique add to the viewer's knowledge?

Applying Skills

Evaluate Animations
Visit a Web portal and locate three examples of animations. What purpose does each animation serve? Why is your eye attracted to this animation? Explain how you would use each animation on a Web page.

SECTION 9.1 Multimedia and Web Design

Key Terms

multimedia, 244   animation, 244
audio, 244   codec, 245
video, 244   multimedia authoring tool, 247

Main Ideas

- Effective audio, video, and animations on a Web page can attract visitors' attention and present useful information.

- You can obtain multimedia files from a variety of sources.

- Multimedia authoring tools help you integrate media components, such as video, audio, and animation, into a seamless whole.

- To evaluate a multimedia site, determine whether the media elements support rather than distract from the site's goals, work properly and play for an appropriate length of time, and add to the viewer's enjoyment without creating clutter.

SECTION 9.2 Adding Audio and Video to a Site

Key Terms

plug-in, 251   analog video recorder, 253
digital video   video capture card, 253
  recorder, 253

Main Ideas

- Audio and video come in a variety of formats.
- A file's extension identifies its format.
- You can incorporate sound into a Web page by linking the file to a button or setting it to play in the background when the page loads.
- To create video, you need a video recorder and hardware and software that lets you transfer the video from the recorder to the computer's hard disk.

SECTION 9.3 Adding Animation Graphics to a Site

Key Terms

Macromedia Flash, 258   Dynamic HTML (DHTML), 259

Main Ideas

- A GIF animation consists of individual GIF images, displayed on the screen one after the other.

- Macromedia Flash can create more sophisticated animations than GIFs.

- Flash files often have faster download times than GIF animations.

- All images that make up a GIF animation are stored in one file, along with instructions that tell the browser the order in which to load the images as well as where and how long to display them.

Reviewing Key Terms

1. What is animation?
2. Rewrite the following sentence to make it true: *Audio files are typically larger than video files.*
3. What is the purpose of a plug-in?
4. What is the purpose of a video capture card?
5. What does FrontPage use to create lines of scrolling text?

Understanding Main Ideas

6. **Summarize** at least three multimedia design guidelines presented in this chapter.
7. **Describe** the purpose of a multimedia authoring tool.
8. **Identify** some of the tools used to create audio and video files.
9. **Summarize** some of the ways in which you can make certain you are using audio, video, and animation files ethically.
10. **Explain** the difference between an analog video recorder and a digital video recorder.
11. **List** the hardware needed to listen to audio. List the hardware needed to create audio.
12. **Identify** three problems that using video clips on Web pages can create.
13. **Discuss** some reasons why animation is a common feature on the Web.
14. **Describe** two ways to insert a sound file into a Web page.
15. **Explain** how an animated GIF file is different from a static (nonanimated) GIF file.

Critical Thinking

16. **Cause and Effect** Some Web sites contain numerous animated advertisements. How might the animations affect your behavior? For example, would you be more likely to click on an animated advertisement than on a nonanimated one? Why?
17. **Analyze** Do you think the saying "If in doubt, leave it out" is appropriate when adding audio, video, and animation to Web pages? Give specific examples in your answer.
18. **Make Decisions** You want to take video of your family's summer vacation and place it on your personal Web site. What hardware will you need? What software?
19. **Evaluate Animations** You are creating a Web site for a local physical fitness center. The manager wants the site to have animated images of people lifting weights. Because she wants these images to be abstract, you cannot use video. Which application do you think would work best for creating these animations? Why?
20. **Synthesize Information** Search the Web for sites that provide free audio, video, and animation files for downloading. Create a list of these Web sites. In general, how would you cite one of these files? How would you cite a file that was not free?

e-Review

webdesign.glencoe.com

Study with PowerPoint

To review the main points in this chapter, select **e-Review > PowerPoint Outlines > Chapter 9.**

Online Self Check

Test your knowledge of the material in this chapter by selecting **e-Review > Self Checks > Chapter 9.**

Making Connections

Language Arts—Summarize a Book or Story
Select a book or story that you have read recently. Write a summary of the plot and make a list of the characters. Read the summary aloud and record it. Listen to the recording and re-record it until you are satisfied with the quality of the recording. Create a Web page to recommend this book or story to another reader. Include the book's title, appropriate graphic or visual elements, the list of characters, and the sound recording of your summary.

STANDARDS AT WORK

Students are proficient in the use of technology. (NETS-S 1)

Use Technology Tools
Assume you are planning a Web site about an upcoming event at your school. Plan and sketch the pages for your site. Identify the multimedia elements you would like to include on each page. Make a list of the technology tools (scanner, digital camera, video recorder, voice/sound recorder, and so forth) available to you. Consider how you can use as many of these technology tools as possible to create your Web site.

Create a three-column chart. List the Web site's pages, the multimedia elements to be included on the page, and the technology tool you will use to create the multimedia element (see below). Using your chart as reference, create your multimedia elements and save them in one folder.

Web Page	Multimedia Element	Technology Tool

TEAMWORK SKILLS

Create a Presidential Web Page
As a team, select one of the American presidents who served during the last half of the twentieth century. Visit his presidential library online and explore the audiovisual resources available. Identify resources that could be used in a Web page honoring the president. Conduct other research as necessary to learn more about the president.

Plan and create a Web page about the president. The page should feature a picture of the president and at least one well-known statement he made. Add other features to the page that note important events in the president's life or career. Either download audiovideo resources from the library or create links to the resources you want to use in your page. Carefully review the site's usage guidelines before downloading and using its materials and cite your sources on your page.

CHALLENGE YOURSELF

Compare and Contrast Plug-ins
Research Windows Media Player and QuickTime Player, two plug-ins for streaming audio and video elements. Your research should focus on answering the following questions:

1. What video file formats will each plug-in read?
2. Besides video, what other types of multimedia does the plug-in play?
3. What is the current version of the plug-in?
4. What company supplies the plug-in?
5. What features does the supplier highlight?

Summarize your findings in a list. Based on your findings, create a Venn diagram to compare and contrast the two plug-ins.

YOU TRY IT

Skills Studio

These exercises reinforce the skills you learned in this chapter's You Try It activities. Refer back to the You Try It activities if you need extra guidance.

1. Adding Sound to a Web Page

Add sound or sound effects to the community event page you created in Chapter 8 (see page 240).

Ⓐ Review the Web page you created in the Chapter 8 Chapter Review. Decide how you could add sound or sound effects to the page.

Ⓑ Either create the sound or sound effect or search the Web for an appropriate sound. For example, you may choose to use a voice recording of people who attended last year's event, or you may add a sound effect related to the event. Save the file.

Ⓒ In FrontPage, add the sound to the page.

Ⓓ Decide if the sound file should loop and how many times it should be repeated.

Ⓔ Save the page, creating a multimedia folder in which the sound file will be stored.

Ⓕ Preview the page in a browser to make sure the sound is working properly.

2. Using an Animation on a Web Page

Build a Web page to display an animation.

Ⓐ Locate an animation file. You can find animations online, or use an animation file from the Student Data Files. Review all usage agreements and get your teacher's permission before downloading any files.

Ⓑ Create a new Web page in FrontPage and select a theme that will work with the animation you are planning to use.

Ⓒ Insert the animation file and save the Web page. Place the embedded animation in a Multimedia folder.

Ⓓ Preview the animation to see what movement occurs.

Ⓔ Write one or two sentences describing the movement. Add this text in FrontPage and make any adjustments needed to display the text attractively.

Ⓕ Proofread and save your work. View your completed page in a browser.

Web Design Projects

1. Create a Web Design Class History

Plan and create a two-page Web site that presents an oral history of your class.

◆ The home page should display information about the class and at least one multimedia element.

◆ Title the second page "A Typical Day in Class."

You want to include several multimedia components in your site. Consider the technology tools available to you. If possible, interview either your teacher about his or her goals for the class, or other class members about important things they have learned. Your interviews can be recorded as digital audio or video files. Edit your audio and video clips so that they are no more than 15 to 30 seconds long. Select an appropriate quality for the clips to minimize file size.

Create the site in FrontPage. Create and insert multimedia elements as appropriate. If you have time, create a third page titled "Projects I Have Completed." On this page, briefly describe your projects and include hyperlinks to your work. Preview your site in a browser.

2. Add Multimedia to the Virtual Field Trips Web Site

In Chapter 8, you created the home page and navigation structure for a Web site that lets visitors explore past events or eras (see page 241).

◆ Select one event or era listed in the site.

◆ Research the event or era.

◆ Develop content based on your research. Your content should identify the event or era and summarize it in one or two paragraphs.

◆ If possible, add hyperlinks to let visitors explore additional information about the event or era.

As you research your topic, consider how to build one multimedia element into the page. Create or obtain the multimedia element (picture, sound, animation, or video) and place it on the page. Cite your sources as needed.

Save your work. Preview the site in a browser to make sure that the multimedia element works properly.

CHAPTER 10 — Adding Interactivity to a Web Site

YOU WILL LEARN TO...

Section 10.1

- Define scripting
- Summarize interactivity design guidelines
- Identify scripting languages
- Compare common scripting languages
- Identify markup languages

Section 10.2

- Apply DHTML effects
- Create a marquee
- Create a banner ad
- Create custom rollover buttons
- Add update information
- Create page transitions

Section 10.3

- Create a form
- Identify different field types
- Place fields and labels into forms

WHY IT MATTERS......................................

Interactivity is a basic component of the Web—users move from one page to another by sending messages to the browser. It is natural to expand on these capabilities to communicate in more sophisticated ways, such as playing online games, using interactive tutorials, and generating online maps. This chapter looks at some ways of creating interactivity.

Quick Write Activity

List five ways in which you have interacted with Web pages in the past week. Then write down how these interactions were useful to you. For example, did they save you time? Did they make the site more interesting or entertaining?

WHAT YOU WILL DO...

ACTIVITIES AND PROJECTS

Applying Skills

You Try It Activities

Chapter Assessment

You Try It Skills Studio

Web Design Projects

IN THE WORKBOOK

Optional Activities and Projects

Guided Reading
Web Design Projects

ON THE WEB

Activities at webdesign.glencoe.com

Reading Strategy Organizers
Go Online Activities
Study with PowerPoint
Self-Check Assessments

READ TO SUCCEED

Managing Time

How much time should you take to read a chapter? The answer depends on many factors. The more difficult the material, the longer it will take to read the chapter. Illustrations can make material easier to understand, but they can also be distracting. Use the main ideas, chapter headings, and section assessment questions to focus your reading. Also, do your reading at a time and in a place where you can concentrate on the material without interruptions. This will increase your speed and understanding.

Main Ideas

Scripting languages make Web pages dynamic and interactive. Examples of scripting languages include JavaScript, Java applets, CGI and DHTML, XML and XHTML are types of markup languages.

Key Terms

script
interactivity
JavaScript
Java applet
Common Gateway Interface (CGI)
markup languages
Extensible Markup Language (XML)

Reading Strategy

Identify four types of scripting languages and a use for each. Use a table like the one below (also available online).

Types of Scripting	Use

You have already added dynamic components, such as rollover buttons and image maps, to Web sites. FrontPage makes it easy to insert dynamic elements without actually understanding the scripting required to create them. In this chapter, you will learn about the scripting needed to create interactive elements on Web pages.

SCRIPTING AND INTERACTIVITY

HTML code creates static Web pages. Inserting scripts makes your pages dynamic. A **script** is a short program that you can insert into the HTML code using special tags. Scripts expand the capabilities of HTML to create dynamic Web pages. There are two common uses for scripts:

Figure 10.1
In this game, the player must react quickly to on-screen images. How is this game interactive?

◆ To insert changing information into a Web page, such as displaying the current date.
◆ To allow **interactivity,** meaning that the user can perform an action that the Web page responds to. Clicking buttons to go to another page is an example of interactivity.

Interactivity allows communication to become a two-way process: you give your visitors information and your visitors send information back to you. This is one way in which the Web is different from static sources of information, such as books or newspapers. You can attract repeat traffic by ensuring that your information is timely and easy to find. You can solicit information from your visitors by providing forms for them to give you feedback.

Entertainment Web sites, such as the one shown in Figure 10.1, typically rely heavily on interactivity.

INTERACTIVITY DESIGN GUIDELINES

Using interactivity requires careful planning. Here are some design guidelines to consider when using interactivity:

◆ Use interactivity only when it enhances the site. For example, having a button change color when clicked tells the user that something is happening.

◆ Maintain simplicity. Too much movement is distracting.

◆ Make certain users understand the response expected of them. If the user needs to fill out and submit a form, clearly label each field.

◆ Check interactive components in all the browsers your visitors are likely to use. Supply alternative text that will appear if a particular component does not function properly.

It is easy to go overboard when adding interactive elements to a Web site. If every item on your page is moving, visitors will quickly become annoyed. Using restraint will help you create Web pages that people will enjoy visiting.

SCRIPTING LANGUAGES

Many different scripting languages can be used with Web pages. Each language is designed for specific types of interactivity. The Web programmer specifies the appropriate scripting language for the Web site.

JavaScript

Netscape Communications and Sun Microsystems designed **JavaScript** to enhance the capabilities of Web programming. JavaScript can create effects such as fading backgrounds, button rollovers, banner displays, and games. A number of sites offer free JavaScript code samples that you can copy and paste into your HTML documents. Figure 10.2 shows a short JavaScript script that is inserted in the body of an HTML document. You will learn more about JavaScript in Chapter 17.

Activity 10.1 Compare Scripting Languages Learn more about the purposes of different scripting languages at **webdesign.glencoe.com**.

┌**READ ME!**┐

Caution Not all browsers fully support JavaScript. Internet Explorer, for example, supports only a subset of JavaScript.

● **Figure 10.2**

The JavaScript code displays the number of days until the year 2006. Why might you insert JavaScript into a Web page?

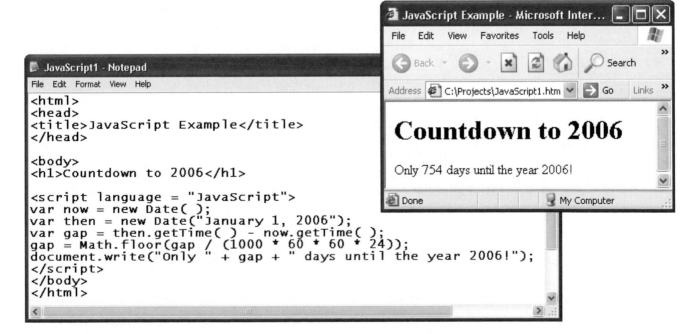

```
<html>
<head>
<title>JavaScript Example</title>
</head>

<body>
<h1>Countdown to 2006</h1>

<script language = "JavaScript">
var now = new Date( );
var then = new Date("January 1, 2006");
var gap = then.getTime( ) - now.getTime( );
gap = Math.floor(gap / (1000 * 60 * 60 * 24));
document.write("Only " + gap + " days until the year 2006!");
</script>
</body>
</html>
```

Countdown to 2006

Only 754 days until the year 2006!

Java Applets

A **Java applet** is a short program written in the Java programming language. Sun Microsystems developed Java and, unlike JavaScript, it is a complete programming language. All major browsers support Java. A Java applet is specifically intended to run in a browser. A Java applet can be dynamic and interactive, and usually occupies a specific portion of the screen. For example, For example, a Java applet can be used to animate a series of GIF images.

Common Gateway Interface

The **Common Gateway Interface (CGI)** provides a link, or interface, between an external application and a Web server. This link allows the Web server to pass a user's request to an application program and then return information to the user. For example, when you enter data into a form, CGI is often used to submit that data to an application, such as a database or spreadsheet, for processing. CGI can be used with any operating system, so it is a dependable way to perform these types of operations.

Dynamic HTML

Microsoft developed Dynamic HTML (DHTML) as an extension of HTML. It allows the user to interact with a Web page. DHTML can create features such as rollover buttons and marquees. In Chapter 9, you used DHTML to create animations in FrontPage.

MARKUP LANGUAGES

A **markup language** is a text file that contains special sequences of characters that function as tags. HTML, XML, and XHTML are three types of markup languages.

HTML Versus XML

As discussed in Chapter 4, HTML is a markup language that defines the appearance of data. HTML tags, however, do not convey any meaningful information about the internal structure or organization of the data they describe. For example, the HTML tag set `<b>  </b>` instructs a Web browser to display the text between the tags in a bold font. However, the tags do not indicate if the text between them is a name, an address, a phone number, or any other type of data.

Unlike HTML, **Extensible Markup Language (XML)** tags impose a specific structure and meaning on data without providing any information about how the data should be displayed. For example, the XML code shown in Figure 10.3 shown on page 271 defines a simple student record that contains a first name, a last name, and a grade point average (GPA). The user-defined XML tags tell the reader exactly what the data items represent, and how they relate to each other. They do not, however, convey any information about how the data items should be displayed on the screen.

You can use XML to create dynamic features. For example, an automobile manufacture's advertisement may show a revolving series of photographs

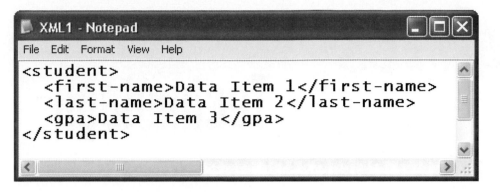

```
XML1 - Notepad
File  Edit  Format  View  Help
<student>
   <first-name>Data Item 1</first-name>
   <last-name>Data Item 2</last-name>
   <gpa>Data Item 3</gpa>
</student>
```

Figure 10.3
XML tags describe the type of data found between the opening and closing tags. What similarity does XML code have to HTML code?

of different vehicles. XML can be used to store these photographs. When the photographs change, the programmer can quickly update the corresponding XML code.

XHTML

The Extensible Hypertext Markup Language (XHTML) is designed to bridge the differences between HTML and XML. It uses the same structures and tags as HTML, but it organizes these tags into modules. Browsers working on different devices such as cell phones and PDAs recognize and run selected XHTML modules. XHTML code can also be written to fit a browser's available memory. Programmers can tailor XHTML code to suit the capabilities and memory of the particular device they are targeting.

XHTML is very much like standard HTML. There are, however, some additional rules that XHTML programmers must follow:

- ◆ The value of all XHTML tag attributes must be enclosed in quotes.
- ◆ All opening tags in XHTML must have a corresponding closing tag.
- ◆ XHTML requires every closing tag to match up with the most recently seen opening tag.

READ ME!

Tech Tip Web developers often use quotes to enclose tag attribute values when writing HTML code as a matter of practice. This avoids having to consider this rule when writing XHTML code.

Section 10.1 Assessment

Concept Check

1. **Define** script, interactivity, JavaScript, Java applet, Common Gateway Interface (CGI), markup language, Extensible Markup Language (XML).

2. **Discuss** how interactivity makes Web pages different from other sources of information, such as books and newspapers.

Critical Thinking

3. **Analyze Scripting** Why was the development of CGI an important step in the development of interactive Web pages?

4. **Compare and Contrast** How is XML code similar to HTML code? How is it different?

Applying Skills

Identify Scripting
View the source code of your favorite entertainment Web site. Identify one or two examples of scripting used in the site. Explain what function the scripting performs on the site.

Ethics & Technology

PROTECTING COMPANY RESOURCES

Misusing the Internet at work can cost a business both money and time.

Personal use of office computers can be very costly for employers.

The Costs of Surfing

Companies lose countless hours of employee productivity to Web surfing. Besides losing productivity, companies face a number of threats from personal Internet use:

◆ In smaller businesses, streaming video or audio downloads takes up broadband space, which slows down the system.
◆ Peer-to-peer file sharing and instant messaging make the company's network less secure and open to viruses and hackers.
◆ Employers can be held liable if employees do anything illegal while using company equipment. They can be sued if a worker downloads offensive material and views it in the workplace. They are also liable if an employee illegally downloads copyrighted material on the company's network.

Keeping an Eye on Employees

Some organizations track and monitor workers' visits to Web sites and their personal use of e-mail. This has become a privacy issue that can be a problem for employers. To avoid "spying," many companies prefer to block offensive Web sites rather than monitor employees' Internet use.

While many companies do not mind occasional personal e-mails, it should not happen often. Employers have the right to monitor Internet use, since employees are using a company-owned system. In fact, an employer has the right to read and permanently keep any data contained on a company computer. The data, as well as the computer, is company property.

If you use a school's or employer's computer, follow these simple guidelines: Always follow your organization's policies and do not do anything that you would not do if your teacher or boss were looking over your shoulder. In fact, your boss may be watching nearly everything you do on your workplace computer.

Tech Focus

1. Research and describe one method employers can use to monitor employees' use of company computer systems. Explain why you think this method should be considered legal or illegal.

2. Find an example of an acceptable use policy. Which types of use are considered objectionable and what are their consequences? Write an acceptable use policy for your class's computer use.

Section 10.2 Adding Dynamic Effects

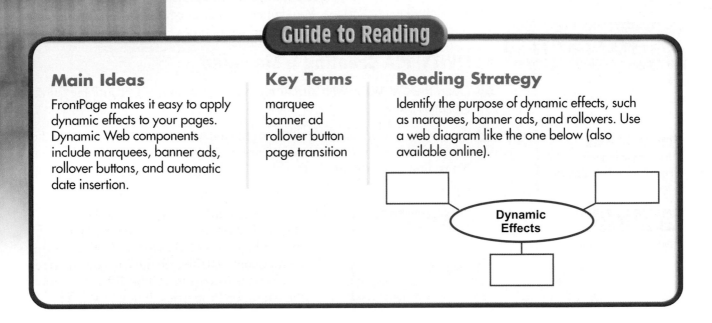

Guide to Reading

Main Ideas

FrontPage makes it easy to apply dynamic effects to your pages. Dynamic Web components include marquees, banner ads, rollover buttons, and automatic date insertion.

Key Terms

marquee
banner ad
rollover button
page transition

Reading Strategy

Identify the purpose of dynamic effects, such as marquees, banner ads, and rollovers. Use a web diagram like the one below (also available online).

Dynamic Effects

Adding dynamic content helps make Web pages interesting. FrontPage makes it easy to add dynamic effects such as marquees, banner ads, and rollover buttons.

USING THE DHTML EFFECTS TOOLBAR

FrontPage automates the process of adding DHTML scripts to Web sites. You can use the DHTML Effects toolbar, shown in Figure 10.4, to create custom effects. This toolbar contains three menus.

◆ The first menu (On menu) allows you to specify the event, or action, that will trigger the effect. For example, the page load option sets the effect to occur when a user asks the Web browser to load the page.

◆ The second menu (Apply menu) allows you to choose the effect you want to add to the page.

◆ The third menu allows you to further refine your request. For example, you can use the third menu to specify that you want an effect to move from right to left on the page.

● **Figure 10.4**
The DHTML Effects toolbar helps you make your page's content dynamic. **What are some user actions that can cause a DHTML effect to occur?**

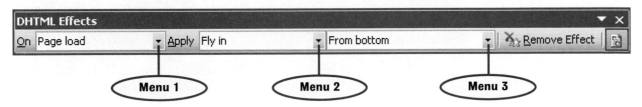

Examples of effects you can create include having a phrase "fly" in from the left side of the page, or "drop" onto the page word-by-word. The Remove Effect button on the toolbar removes the effect from the Web page.

MARQUEES

A **marquee** is a string of text that slides from one edge of the page to the other, much like a tickertape. You can create marquee text that slides in once and then stays put, repeats a specified number of times, or continuously repeats.

ACTIVITY 10A Creating a Marquee

❶ Open the CV Walk Web site home page in Design (in FrontPage 2002, Normal) view.

❷ Position the insertion point at the right side of the page banner inside the top shared border. Press **Enter.** The insertion point should now be on a blank line immediately below the page banner, but still within the top shared border.

Figure 10.5
Fill in the Marquee Properties dialog box as shown.

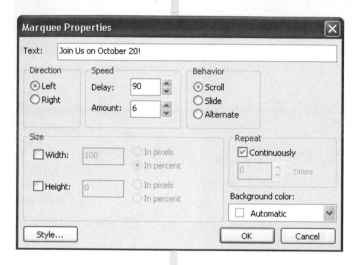

❸ On the Standard toolbar, click the **Web Component** button. In the Insert Web Component dialog box, select **Dynamic Effects** in the Component type box. In the Choose an effect box, select **Marquee.** Click **Finish** to open the Marquee Properties dialog box.

❹ In the Text box, type Join Us on October 20! Leave the default settings as they appear and click **OK** (see Figure 10.5).

❺ Click anywhere in the text you just entered to select it. On the Formatting toolbar, click the **Style** drop-down arrow and select **Heading 1.** Your page should look like Figure 10.6.

Figure 10.6
The marquee moves across the top of the page.

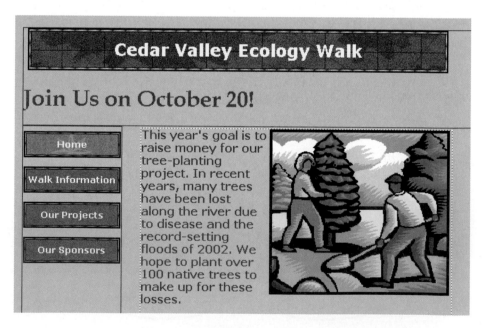

❻ Save your work. Preview the page. Notice that the marquee scrolls across the screen. Return to **Design** (in 2002, **Normal**) view.

BANNER ADS

A **banner ad** is an advertisement that, when clicked, takes the visitor to the sponsor's home page. Banner ads, which are usually rectangular, make it easy for interested consumers to go to the sponsor's Web site. In the following activity, you will create a simple banner ad for the Garden Company Web site. When users position their mouse over the banner ad, it will change from one image to another.

ACTIVITY 10B Inserting a Banner Ad

YOU TRY IT

1 Open the Our Sponsors page (**sponser.htm**) in Design (in 2002, Normal) view. Position the insertion point at the end of the line "We appreciate the support of our sponsors." Press Enter.

2 On the Standard toolbar, click the **Insert Picture From File** button. Then browse to the DataFile\Ch10\Images folder. Double-click **banner1.gif** to insert the image on the page (see Figure 10.7).

3 Right-click the banner image and click **Hyperlink** to open the Insert Hyperlink dialog box. In the Address box, type http://www.gardencompany.com (note that this link will not work since the Garden Company is not a published Web site). Click **OK**.

4 Make certain the banner ad is still selected. From the **View** menu, select **Toolbars** and click **DHTML Effects.** On the DHTML toolbar, select **Mouse over** from the first menu. Select **Swap Picture** from the second menu. Select **Choose Picture** from the third menu.

5 In the Picture dialog box, browse to the DataFile\Ch10\Images folder. Double-click **banner2.gif.**

6 Save the page. Save the embedded files in the **images** folder. Go to **Preview** view. When you move the cursor over the banner ad, the image changes as shown in Figure 10.8. Return to **Design** (in 2002, **Normal**) view.

Student Data File

Figure 10.7
Insert the first banner image on the Our Sponsors page.

Figure 10.8
The banner ad changes when a user touches it with a mouse.

ROLLOVER BUTTONS

A **rollover button** is a button that changes appearance when the mouse pointer passes over it. FrontPage uses DHTML to create a rollover button. You can create a rollover effect by inserting interactive buttons on a site. You did this when you added navigation buttons to the Astronomy Club Web site. In the following activity, you will create a rollover effect by specifying which image should appear initially on the screen, and which image should appear when the user's mouse touches the initial image.

YOU TRY IT

ACTIVITY 10C Creating a Rollover Button

1 Open the Walk Information page in Design (in 2002, Normal) view. Position the insertion point immediately before the line: Please support our tree planting project! Press Enter. Click in the line you created.

2 Click the **Insert Picture From File** button. Browse to the DataFile\Ch10\Images folder. Double-click **button1.gif.**

3 Right-click the button graphic and click **Hyperlink.** In the Insert Hyperlink dialog box, make certain the **Existing File or Web Page** button is selected. In the Address text box, type reg_form.htm. Click **OK.**

4 Open the DHTML Effects toolbar. Select **Mouse over** from the first menu. Select **Swap Picture** from the second menu. Select **Choose Picture** from the third menu. Browse to the DataFile\Ch10\Images folder. Double-click **button2.gif.**

5 Right-click the button and click **Picture Properties.** Under Wrapping style, click **Right.** Add alternative text. Click **OK.** Right-click the leaf animation and click **Cut** to remove the graphic.

6 Save the page. Make certain that the embedded files are saved in the **images** folder.

7 Preview the page. Notice that the Register Now button changes when the mouse pointer touches it (see Figure 10.9). Return to **Design** (in 2002, **Normal**) view.

Figure 10.9
When you roll your mouse pointer over this button, the second image replaces the first image.

Notice how you needed to delete the leaf animation when you added the rollover button to the Walk Information page. The page looked too cluttered and busy with both graphics. You need to constantly evaluate your pages and make similar design decisions as you create your Web sites.

UPDATE INFORMATION

Web developers often use scripting to display the current date. News sites usually display the current date to let you know that the site's content has been updated. In addition, many search engines allow you to search for sites that have been updated within a specific time frame, such as the last six months. In the following You Try It activity, you will add update information to the CV Walk Web site. You will also add text links to the site's footer.

ACTIVITY 10D Adding Text Links and Update Information

YOU TRY IT

❶ Open the CV Walk home page in Design (in 2002, Normal) view.

❷ Position the insertion point in the Shared Bottom Border box. Delete the placeholder text. Press **Enter.**

❸ Type Home | Walk Information | Our Projects | Our Sponsors. Place one space between each item (including the slash marks). Create text links to the four pages you just typed (refer to the You Try It Activity 6H on page 168 for how to add text links). Format the links bold and center them on the page.

❹ Position the insertion point at the end of the text links. Press **Enter.** Select **Insert** and click **Horizontal line.** Press **Enter.**

❺ Select **Style** and click **Address.** Type Last Updated:. Press the **Spacebar** to insert a space after this text.

❻ Select **Insert** and click **Date and Time.** In the dialog box, select **Date this page was lasted edited.** Under Date format, select the date, month, year option shown in Figure 10.10 or a similar option. Click **OK.**

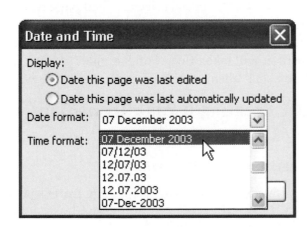

◀——● **Figure 10.10**
You can select how the date and time will display on the page.

7 Press **Enter** twice. Under Font Size, click **2 (10 pt).** Type Copyright © Cedar Valley Ecology Walk Committee.

8 Proofread and spell check your page. The page should look similar to Figure 10.11. Save the page and view it in several browsers.

Figure 10.11
The finished Cedar Valley Ecology Walk home page contains text links, update information, and a copyright notice.

READ ME!

Tech Tip A quick way to insert the copyright symbol is to press Alt + Ctrl + C.

PAGE TRANSITIONS

FrontPage lets you create special effects, called **page transitions,** that the user sees when moving from one page to another. For example, you can make a page's text zoom in or out when a visitor opens the page. You also can specify when a transition will take effect. For example, you can decide that you want the effect to occur when a visitor first enters the page or leaves it.

YOU TRY IT

ACTIVITY 10E Creating a Page Transition

1 Open the CV Walk home page in Design (in 2002, Normal) view.

2 On the Format menu, click **Page Transition.**

3 In the Page Transitions dialog box, select **Page Enter** under Event. In the Duration box, type 3. In the Transition effect box, click **Box out** (see Figure 10.12 on page 279). Click **OK.**

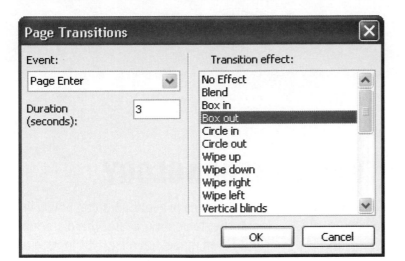

Figure 10.12
Use the Page Transitions dialog box to select different transition effects.

4 Save the page. Preview the site in an Internet Explorer browser. To view the page transition effect, first go to the **Our Projects** page, then click the **Home** button in the Our Projects page. Close the browser and return to **Design** (in 2002, **Normal**) view. Save your work.

READ ME!

Caution Page transitions only work in Microsoft Internet Explorer. Netscape Navigator simply ignores them.

In this section, you added many different effects to the Cedar Valley Ecology Walk Web site. When designing your own Web sites, carefully evaluate the effects you add to a page. Remember that adding too many effects will only distract, and potentially annoy, your visitors.

Section 10.2 Assessment

Concept Check

1. **Define** marquee, banner ad, rollover button, page transition.

2. **Explain** how to use the DHTML Effects toolbar to apply effects to page components.

3. **List** three types of dynamic effects and how they are used.

Critical Thinking

4. **Analyze** You are starting a small Web design business that specializes in banner ads. How might you convince clients to invest in a banner ad rather than a less-expensive static ad?

5. **Draw Conclusions** Why is update information important when you are evaluating a Web site's reliability?

Applying Skills

Apply Dynamic Effects Use the DHTML Effects toolbar to apply various effects to text on a Web page. Identify how different effects change the text. Evaluate why you would or would not want to apply these effects to your Web pages.

EMERGING TECHNOLOGY

THE FUTURE OF TECHNOLOGY

As new technologies emerge, they become the building blocks for the next generation. Researchers constantly look for new technologies to improve products or services.

Cell phones have evolved quickly to keep up with consumer and market demands.

Here are some possible developments that may occur over the next few years:

◆ **Communications** technologies change almost daily. In a few years, people may routinely use the Internet for telephone calls. New wireless technologies may allow wireless PDAs to broadcast real-time streaming content, such as videoconferences.

◆ **The Internet** itself will evolve as greater, possibly unlimited, bandwidth becomes available. This will provide rapid access to huge amounts of information, making the Internet an even more valuable means of communication and research.

◆ **Health care** practitioners can now use the Internet to communicate with distant patients and even make diagnoses without being with the patients. In the future, surgeons will be able to use virtual reality systems and cameras to control surgical robots and perform surgeries remotely.

◆ **Nanotechnology** will lead to the development of tiny supercomputers. Eventually, doctors may be able to treat patients by injecting tiny robots, which will single out and destroy diseased cells. It may also result in paper-thin monitors that roll up and fit in your pocket, and wearable computers built into clothing.

The Technology Life Cycle

There is always a need for new scientific knowledge. Research is motivated by problems with old technologies, competition in the marketplace, and consumer demands. This has created a technology "life cycle" that may never end.

Tech Focus

1. Research the development and evolution of a specific technology product. How and why has the product changed over time? In your opinion, have these changes had positive or negative effects on users?

2. Research developments in one area of technology. What will it be like in five, ten, or twenty years? Write an essay about your predictions. Explain why you think this research will have positive or negative consequences.

Web sites often need to obtain data from visitors. Whenever you order an item online, for example, you typically must enter information such as the item's number, the shipping address, and payment information. Web programmers and designers create forms to allow users to enter and submit these data.

FORMS AND THEIR COMPONENTS

A **form** is structure for collecting data from visitors. Every form contains components called fields. A **field** allows the user to enter information into the form. Each field is identified by a **label.** The label tells the user what type of information (name, address, etc.) should be entered into a particular field. Well-designed forms have clear labels that tell visitors exactly what data (name, address, etc.) to enter in each field. Most forms also contain a Submit and a Reset button. After filling out the fields, visitors click the Submit button to submit the form's contents. They use the Reset button to erase the form's content.

In the next activity you will create a form page that lets participants register online for the Cedar Valley Ecology Walk.

ACTIVITY 10F Creating a Form

❶ Open the CV Walk home page in Design (in 2002, Normal) view. On the **View** menu, click **Navigation.**

❷ Click the **Create a new normal page** button on the Standard toolbar. Click **Save.** In the Save As dialog box, type reg_form.htm in the File name text box. Click **Save.**

❸ If necessary, open the **Folder List.** In the Folder List, right-click **reg_form.htm** and click **Properties.** In the Title text box, type Walk Registration Form. Click **OK.**

❹ On the **View** menu, click **Navigation.** Drag the **reg_form.htm** page from the Folder List to the Navigation pane and link it to the Walk Information page.

GO Online

Activity 10.2 Create Well-Designed Forms **Learn more about designing forms at webdesign.glencoe.com.**

YOU TRY IT

5 Double-click the Walk Registration Form page (**reg_form.htm**) to open it in Design (in 2002, Normal) view.

6 Position the insertion point at the top of the page's content area. On the **Insert** menu, select **Form.** When the Form submenu opens, position the mouse pointer at the top so it turns into a four-way arrow. Drag the submenu to the right to create the Form toolbar, as shown in Figure 10.13.

Figure 10.13
You can drag the submenu away from the menu to create a toolbar.

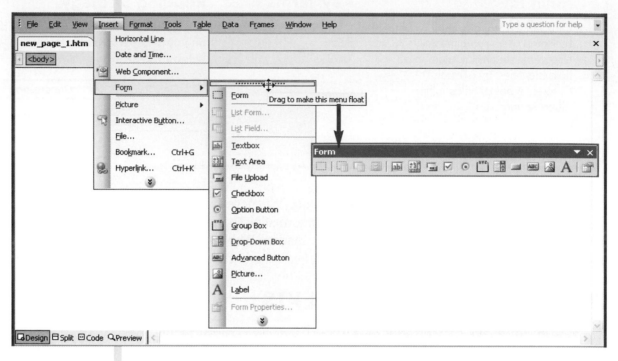

7 Click the **Form** button on the Form toolbar. A small rectangular area marked by dotted lines appears at the top of the page's content area. These lines mark the form's current boundaries. As shown in Figure 10.14, the Submit and Reset buttons are automatically inserted into the form. Press **Enter.** The form's boundaries expand to accommodate the blank line you inserted. Save your work.

Figure 10.14
You have created the foundation for the walk registration form.

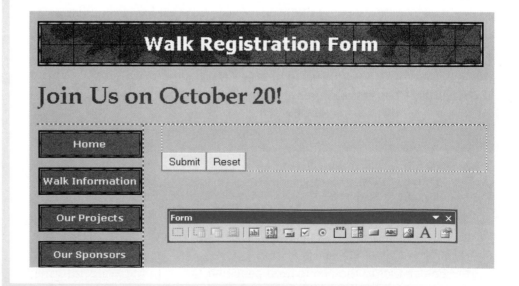

FORM FIELDS

A form can contain different types of fields. Each field type has a specific purpose. For example, a text box lets users enter a relatively small amount of text (such as an address) into a form. A text area, on the other hand, allows users to enter larger amounts of text, such as comments and suggestions.

Limited-option fields, such as option buttons, check boxes, and drop-down boxes, allow users to select predefined choices. Using limited-option fields helps prevent users from entering invalid data. Including predefined choices also allows the form creator to specify exactly what type of information he or she wants from users. Table 10.1 lists commonly used form fields and their purposes.

Common Form Fields

Field Type	Button	Description
Textbox	abl	Allows user to enter a line of text.
Text Area		Allows user to enter many lines of text, such as comments or suggestions. Also called a scroll box.
Option Button		Allows user to select one of two options, such as Yes/No or Male/Female. Also called a radio button.
Checkbox		Allows user to select one or more options from a list of options.
Drop-Down Box		Allows user to select from a list of choices. Also called a pull-down menu.

Table 10.1
Each type of form field has a specific purpose. How would you use a drop-down box on a form?

In the following activity, you will add text boxes, a drop-down box, and a check box to the walk registration form.

ACTIVITY 10G Adding Fields to a Form

YOU TRY IT

❶ Position the insertion point on the blank line at the top of the form. Make certain that the **Normal** style is selected. Type First Name:. Press the **Spacebar** twice. On the Form toolbar, click **Textbox.** A white text box appears.

❷ Carefully select both the label (First Name) and the text box. Click the **Label** button on the Form toolbar.

❸ Right-click the text box and click **Form Field Properties.** The Text Box Properties dialog box opens.

Label	Title
Last Name:	last_name
Address:	address
City:	city
State:	state
E-mail Address	e_mail

Table 10.2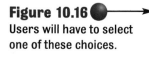
Enter these titles in the Text Box Properties dialog box. All field labels on this table end with a colon.

Figure 10.15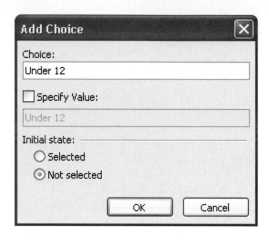
Use the Choice text box to define the choices users can select.

Figure 10.16
Users will have to select one of these choices.

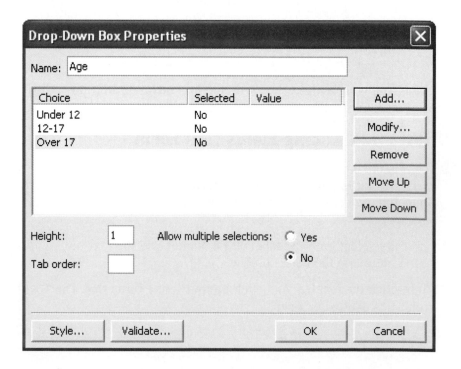

④ In the dialog box, in the Name text box, type first_name. Click **OK.** Position the insertion point immediately to the right of the text box. Press **Enter.**

⑤ Repeat steps 1–4 to create five more fields. Use the labels and titles shown in Table 10.2.

⑥ Since state abbreviations require only two letters, change the field length for the State text box. Right-click the State text box and click **Form Field Properties.** Change the Width in characters text box to 2. Click **OK.**

⑦ Position the insertion point to the right of the e-mail text box and press **Enter.** Type Age: and press the **Spacebar** twice. On the Form toolbar, click the **Drop-Down Box** button. Right-click the drop-down box and click **Form Field Properties.** In the Name text box, type Age.

⑧ Click the **Add** button. In the Choice text box, type Under 12 (see Figure 10.15). Click **OK.**

⑨ Repeat step 7 for the following choices: 12 to 17 and Over 17. The Drop-Down Box dialog box now looks like Figure 10.16. Click **OK.** Select both the text and the drop-down box. Click **Label.** Move down one line.

10 On the Form toolbar, click the **Checkbox** button. Press the **Spacebar** twice. Type Send me more information on the projects supported by the Cedar Valley Ecology Walk. Select both the check box and the text and click **Label.** Right-click the check box and click **Form Field Properties.** In the Name text box, type more_info. Click **OK.**

11 Move down one line. Type Note: Please pay your $20 registration fee when you check in the day of the walk. Format the word "Note" bold.

12 Preview the form. It should look like Figure 10.17. Proofread and spell check the form. Save your work.

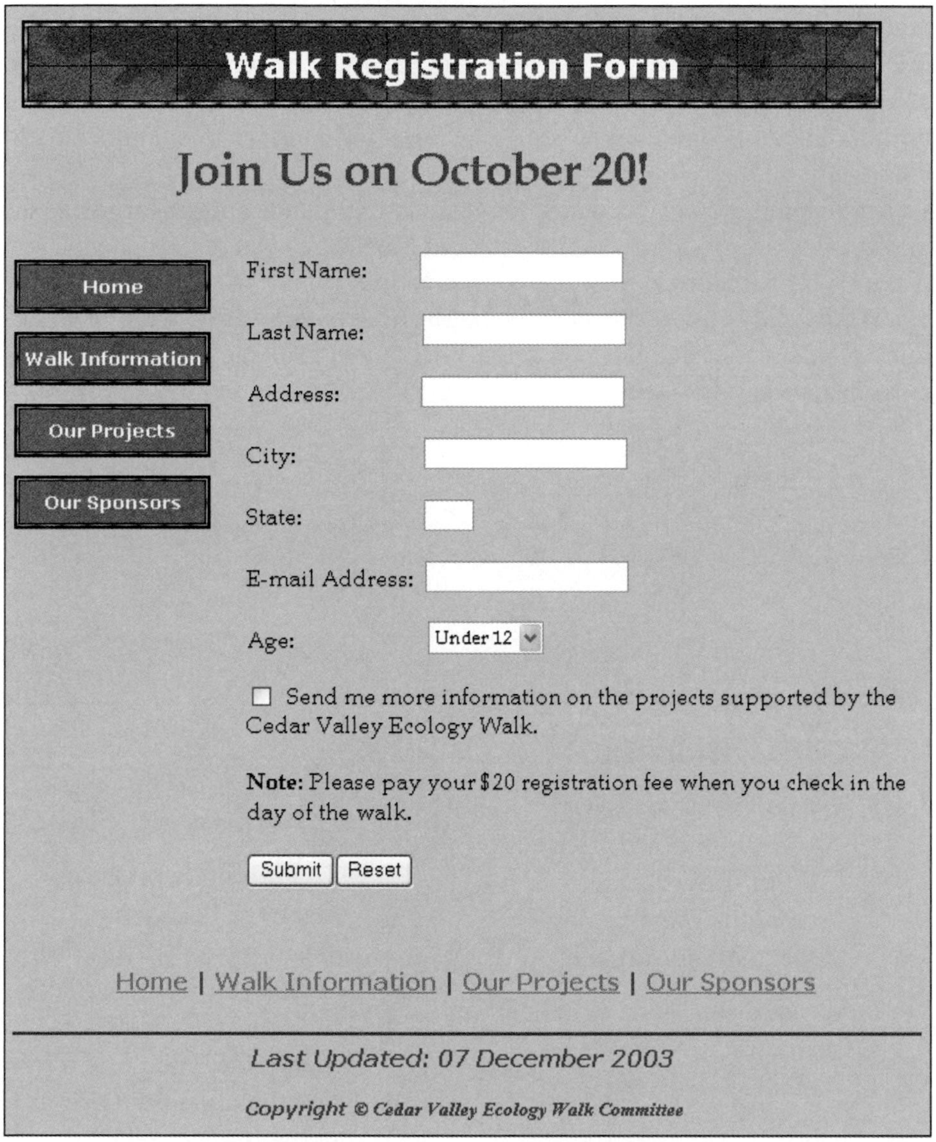

Figure 10.17
Users can complete the form to pre-register for the Cedar Valley Ecology walk.

Walk Registration Form

Join Us on October 20!

Home

Walk Information

Our Projects

Our Sponsors

First Name:

Last Name:

Address:

City:

State:

E-mail Address:

Age: Under 12

☐ Send me more information on the projects supported by the Cedar Valley Ecology Walk.

Note: Please pay your $20 registration fee when you check in the day of the walk.

Submit Reset

Home | Walk Information | Our Projects | Our Sponsors

Last Updated: 07 December 2003

Copyright © Cedar Valley Ecology Walk Committee

13 Go to the Walk Information page (**walk_info.htm**) and click the **Register Now** button to go to the Walk Registration Form page.

14 Practice entering data into the form. Click **Submit.** Notice that you get an error message. The Web site must be published and other actions taken before the form can be processed.

15 Press **Reset** to remove any data that you have entered into the form. Save the page.

You have now created a simple form. However, this form does not do anything with the data that the user enters. To function, a form must be published on a Web server that has the capabilities needed to manage the resulting data.

In a case such as the Cedar Valley Ecology Walk, the form would generate only a small amount of data that would simply be e-mailed to the individual in charge of registration. In cases where forms generate large amounts of data, the server would typically insert the data into databases to be stored and manipulated as necessary. You will learn more about forms in the next unit.

In this unit, you learned how to work with graphics and multimedia elements, and how to add interactivity to your Web pages. All of these items help make Web sites more enjoyable and interesting.

When adding these items to your pages, always follow good design guidelines. Remember that a busy page that is filled with images and motion may overwhelm visitors and cause them to surf elsewhere.

Section 10.3 Assessment

Concept Check

1. **Define** form, field, label.

2. **Explain** why it is important to clearly label each field in a form.

3. **Summarize** how an option button is different from and similar to a check box.

Critical Thinking

4. **Analyze Fields** Could you use a drop-down list to allow users to enter their last names? Explain your answer.

5. **Make Decisions** What kind of form would be needed to let students register for classes online? List possible names for five fields on this form. What field type would best suit each field?

Applying Skills

Identify Form Fields
Select five fields on a printed form that you have used. If you were to create this form for a Web site, identify the type of field you would use for each field you selected.

SECTION 10.1 Overview of Scripting

Key Terms

script, 268
interactivity, 268
JavaScript, 269
Java applet, 270

Common Gateway Interface (CGI), 270
markup language, 270
Extensible Markup Language (XML), 270

Main Ideas

- You can use scripts to make your Web pages dynamic and interactive.
- Interactivity enables a Web site and a user to send information back and forth.
- Limit the amount of interactivity you include on your Web site and keep it simple and easy to understand.
- Scripting languages include JavaScript, Java applets, CGI, and DHTML.
- Markup languages include HTML, XML, and XHTML.

SECTION 10.2 Adding Dynamic Effects

Key Terms

marquee, 274
banner ad, 275

rollover button, 276
page transition, 278

Main Ideas

- The DHTML Effects toolbar lets you apply dynamic effects to page components such as buttons.
- A marquee is a string of text that moves from one edge of the page to the other.
- Clicking a banner ad takes you to the sponsor's Web site.
- Update information lets visitors know when you last made changes to your site.
- Page transitions are effects that users see when they first load or leave a page.

SECTION 10.3 Adding a Form to a Web Site

Key Terms

form, 281
field, 281

label, 281

Main Ideas

- Use forms to let visitors submit information.
- Forms consist of fields for entering specific pieces of information.
- Labels tell users what information to enter into each field.
- Different field types are used to request different types of information.
- Always make certain to clearly label each field.

Reviewing Key Terms

1. Give three examples of interactive Web sites that you have visited. What makes each site interactive?
2. Why is scripting widely used on Web pages?
3. Change the follow sentence to make it true: *A marquee keeps track of the number of visitors to a site.*
4. What is the purpose of a form?
5. How are form fields and labels related to one another?

Understanding Main Ideas

6. **Summarize** interactivity design guidelines.
7. **List** three types of tasks that can be performed with JavaScript.
8. **Describe** some advantages that DHTML has over HTML.
9. **Summarize** the effects that you could create using the DHTML toolbar.
10. **Explain** what would have happened if you had inserted the Ecology Walk marquee ("Join Us on October 20!") immediately below the shared border rather than inside it.
11. **Identify** a situation in which a visitor might want to know when a site was last updated.
12. **Explain** why it is important to provide clearly written labels for your fields.
13. **List** the different types of fields that you used on the walk registration form. Why was each field type appropriate?

Critical Thinking

14. **Analyze** You often visit a Web site that sells books. Each time you visit, the site displays a list of books in which you might be interested. The site personalizes this list to your reading habits. Briefly discuss how a site might use scripting languages to generate this list.
15. **Make Predictions** Do you think the use of interactive Web sites in education will increase or decrease over the next decade? Explain your answer.
16. **Compare and Contrast** In a previous chapter, you inserted business logos into the Our Sponsors Web page. In this chapter, you inserted a banner ad. What advantages does this banner ad have over the business logos? Can you think of a disadvantage?
17. **Analyze Field Types** What are two advantages to using limited option fields? Can you think of a disadvantage?
18. **Evaluate** Why are scripting languages necessary tools for developing dynamic Web pages? How have scripting languages influenced the evolution of the Internet and the way people use Web sites?

e-Review ·················

webdesign.glencoe.com

Study with PowerPoint

To review the main points in this chapter, select **e-Review > PowerPoint Outlines > Chapter 10.**

Online Self Check

Test your knowledge of the material in this chapter by selecting **e-Review > Self Checks > Chapter 10.**

Making Connections

Art—Analyze Your Environment Elements such as banner ads and scrolling marquees are designed to catch a viewer's attention. Over the course of one day, note the items in your environment that catch your attention. These may include

- ◆ billboards
- ◆ televisions commercials
- ◆ print ads
- ◆ non-commercial items

Make a list of the items you have noticed. Then, analyze why these items caught your attention.

STANDARDS AT WORK

Students employ technology in the development of strategies for solving problems in the real world. (NETS-S 6)

Plan Interactivity
You have a friend who owns a clothing store. The store has a Web site that receives about 3,000 hits each month.

Your friend is planning a large sales event for next month and would like to use the Web to advertise the event. You recommend adding interactivity to the site. Your friend asks what that means. Make specific recommendations to add interactive elements about what you would add to your friend's Web site to advertise the upcoming sale.

Assume your friend likes your ideas for interactivity, but would like to see a sample before making a final decision. In FrontPage, create a scrolling marquee that advertises the sale. You do not need to add other elements to the page, because you are simply demonstrating how a marquee catches visitor's attention. Display the marquee in a browser.

TEAMWORK SKILLS

Add Interactive Elements to a Web Site
As a team, review the presidential Web site you created in Chapter 9 (see page 263). Look for opportunities to add interactivity.

Select two types of interactive elements to add to the site. These elements may include:

- ■ scrolling marquees
- ■ rollover buttons
- ■ forms
- ■ update information

Use the FrontPage tools that you have learned about to add the interactive elements to the site.

Test each element in at least two Web browsers. Do they work the same way in both browsers? If they work differently, describe the differences.

Apply three different page transitions to the site. Review each selection in a Web browser. Decide which one of these transitions works best with the site and implement it.

CHALLENGE YOURSELF

Research JavaScripts
Many Web sites offer free JavaScripts that anyone can use in their Web sites. Visit two such sites and review the options that are available. What categories of scripts are available at each site?

On the Web sites you have chosen, find two different JavaScripts for clocks. View and print the source code for each. Compare the two source codes. What similarities do they share? What are the primary differences between the two scripts?

Evaluate what advantages there are in using JavaScripts that others have written. Are there any drawbacks?

YOU TRY IT

Skills Studio

These exercises reinforce the skills you learned in this chapter's You Try It activities. Refer back to the You Try It activities if you need extra guidance.

1. Creating a Drama Club Web Site

The drama club at your school wants to provide a way to order tickets online. In this activity, you will create a Web page for the drama club.

Ⓐ Create a FrontPage Web page for the drama club. Use an existing theme or create a custom theme that works with the play you will be advertising.

Ⓑ Add a scrolling marquee that reads: Buy Your Tickets Now!

Ⓒ Add text to the page announcing an upcoming show. If your school is not planning a play or musical, use the following text:

Our new show is "Our Town" by Thornton Wilder. Performances start at 7 p.m. on Friday, Saturday, and Sunday. Use the easy order form below to buy your tickets early!.

Ⓓ Add a short applause sound that will play upon loading the page.

Ⓔ Add update information to the page.

Ⓕ Save the page. Preview it in a browser to test the marquee and the sound.

2. Adding an Order Form to a Web Site

Add an order form to the drama club Web site you created in Activity #1.

Ⓐ Open the Web page in FrontPage.

Ⓑ Insert a form onto the page. The dotted lines that appear mark the form's boundary. The Submit and Reset buttons appear automatically.

Ⓒ Add two lines above the Submit and Reset buttons.

Ⓓ Create a form similar to the one shown to the right. Use the appropriate type of field for each part of the form.

Ⓔ Proofread and save your work.

Ⓕ View your completed page in a browser.

Order Form

Your ticket will be waiting for you at the ticket window.

First Name _____
Last Name _____
E-mail address _____
Date of Performance [Friday ▼]
Cost of Ticket   ○ Student - $2.00
                 ○ Adult - $6.00

[Submit] [Reset]

Web Design Projects

1. Create a Sandwich Takeout Site

Create a one-page Web site in FrontPage for a sandwich restaurant that takes orders online.

- Add text to the page that includes the current date and time and announces delivery hours of 11 a.m. to 11 p.m. Add other text that advertises the food and guarantees on-time delivery.
- Create a scrolling marquee that reads: Sandwiches To Go: 555-5555.
- Create an order form that asks for the customer's name, address, telephone number, and e-mail address.
- Decide on a menu that includes several sizes of sandwiches and toppings available. For each item, select the best way to make choices (option buttons, check boxes, pull-down menus, and so on).
- The order form should include where and when items should be delivered.
- Proofread and save your work. View the page in a browser and test the fields of the order form. Reset the options before leaving the browser. (Note: The Submit button will not work until the site has been published. You will not publish the site at this time.)

2. Create a Form to Collect Survey Data

You are conducting research to see which books on a school reading list were most popular. Obtain a list of recommended fiction books for 5th and 6th graders from a school librarian or a public library.

Decide what items you need to complete your research. For example, you may want to know which books were most popular with boys and which were most popular with girls. Or you may want to learn which book they would most strongly recommend to a friend.

- Based on what you want to learn, create a form in FrontPage for students to use. Layout the form so it is easy for young readers to understand and follow.
- Only add fields to the form that will help you with your research and do not violate personal privacy guidelines. For example, you do not need students' addresses or phone numbers.
- Proofread and save your work. Preview the site in a browser.

Building 21st Century Skills

Project 1

Civic Responsibility: Create a Web Site for Voters

Student Data File

Create a Web site that encourages people 18 and older to vote.

1. Plan a Web site that includes a home page and two other pages.

   ◆ The home page should include introductory text and a JavaScript that displays famous presidential quotes and slogans.

   ◆ The other two pages should contain information about registering to vote and reasons why it is important to vote.

2. Develop the content for the three pages. Locate a graphic to include on each page. Identify links you can include to send visitors to related sites.

3. Design a custom theme in FrontPage that uses a patriotic motif.

4. Add the text and graphics to the three pages.

5. Browse to the DataFile\Ch10\Multimedia folder. Copy the quotes.htm file's source code and paste it into the body of the home page's source code. Edit the code as needed to be consistent with the site's theme.

6. Preview your site in a browser. Test all navigation and hyperlinks. Spell check and proofread your work. Make any needed changes or improvements to the site.

Project 2

Use Technology Tools: Create an Image Gallery

Create an image gallery about a topic that interests you, such as nature, music, sports, literature, or movies.

1. Plan a Web page with a table that will display your image gallery. The number of cells in the table will depend on the number of images you include in your gallery.

2. Gather the images for your gallery. Use as many of the technology tools you have available, such as the Internet or scanners and cameras, to gather the images. You may use drawings, clip art, photos, and animations. Include at least one piece of WordArt.

3. Place the images in the table. Crop, resize, and resample the images as needed. Add captions to each image.

4. Create a form in which visitor's can submit names and e-mail addresses so you can let them know when you have updated the gallery.

5. Evaluate your gallery in a browser. Make changes as needed.

Building Your Portfolio

Create an Educational Web Site

Create a Web site that provides information about the seven continents. The Web site is targeted at elementary school children. The home page will introduce the site and provide a link to facts about the seven continents.

Ⓐ Africa

Ⓑ Antarctica

Ⓒ Asia

Ⓓ Australia

Ⓔ Europe

Ⓕ North America

Ⓖ South America

When creating your Web site, follow these steps:

1. Conduct research to develop the content for the site.

2. Gather or create multimedia components such as sound, video, and animations to include in the site. For example, you could use an animation of a spinning globe.

3. Remember to use all multimedia images in an ethical manner. Follow copyright guidelines and any Terms of Use agreements from the copyright holder.

4. Use FrontPage to create the Web site. Create the navigation structure for the site. Apply a custom theme.

5. Build the pages by adding the content and multimedia elements you have developed.

6. Find a suitable quote about Earth to include as a scrolling marquee on the site.

7. Use the Web site checklist shown on this page to evaluate your site.

8. Ask a peer to review your finished site and make any needed changes.

9. Optional (with your teacher's permission)—publish the finished Web site on your school or class Web site.

10. For your portfolio, include a screen shot and an electronic copy of your finished product.

Web Site Checklist

INFORMATION DESIGN

☑ The subject of the Web site is clearly identified.

☑ Information is accurate and organized logically.

☑ Text is broken into small blocks.

☑ All content supports the site's purpose and goals.

LAYOUT AND PRESENTATION DESIGN

☑ The design is consistent, uncluttered, and supports the site's goals.

☑ The fonts are easy to read.

☑ Related items are grouped.

☑ Text blocks are separated by white space.

☑ Images are cropped and resized to work well on the Web page.

MULTIMEDIA COMPONENTS

☑ Multimedia elements enhance the content of the page.

☑ All multimedia elements function properly in a variety of Web browsers.

☑ All multimedia elements are properly cited.

☑ Alternative text has been added as needed.

☑ Users understand how to use all multimedia elements.

The Web Site Development Process

Visit *Glencoe Online*

Go to this book's Web site at
webdesign.glencoe.com.

Click on **Unit Activities** and select
Unit 4 Copyright and Fair Use.
Recognize the importance of
understanding copyright policies,
and learn what information you can
and cannot use legally.

Think About It

It Takes Teamwork
It often takes a team of people to create a large Web site. Besides using tools such as FrontPage or HTML, project teams also need to use "soft skills" such as communication and problem-solving skills to get the job done.

Discover Soft Skills Activity
What other soft skills (also called "people skills") do you think you need to have to create a Web site? Name as many as you can think of and explain why the skill is important.

Project Planning

YOU WILL LEARN TO...

Section 11.1

- Identify the stages of the Web site development life cycle
- Identify the responsibilities of project team members
- Use a checklist to evaluate progress
- Explain the use of source control

Section 11.2

- Explain project scope
- Define e-commerce
- Identify types of e-commerce
- Summarize guidelines for developing e-commerce Web sites

WHY IT MATTERS...

Each member of a sports team has a specific assignment. Some members focus on defense while others take shots to score points. Teams win when all members work together. Complex Web sites are often created by teams. Web site development teams create winning sites when all team members contribute their best effort to their assigned tasks.

Quick Write Activity

Think about the qualities that you admire about good teams and team members. In a short paragraph, identify two characteristics of good teams and two characteristics of good team members. Explain why you think these characteristics are important to creating a winning team.

WHAT YOU WILL DO ....

READ TO SUCCEED

Use Notes

When you are reading, you may not want to stop to look up a word or review a difficult concept. To avoid interruptions, keep a note pad handy. Whenever you come upon a section or term you want to go back to, write the word or your question on the note paper and mark the place. After you have finished the chapter, go back to the places you marked. Look up the terms or try to answer your questions based on what you have read.

Main Ideas

Project teams develop many Web sites. The project manager coordinates the work of the team members. Each team member has specific responsibilities and works with other team members to create a site that meets the client's goals and expectations.

Key Terms

client
client liaison
  representative
milestone
project manager
source control

Reading Strategy

Identify one responsibility of six different project team members. Use a table similar to the one below (also available online).

Team Member	Responsibility
Client Liaison Representative	
Project Manager	
Web Author	

Web sites are often developed by project teams. Each project team member has specific responsibilities. In order for people to work well together, they must all understand their specific responsibilities, and the timelines needed to complete the project. Project teams follow the same steps that you have used to create Web sites in the first three units of this book. The primary difference is that, in a team, different people are responsible for different tasks.

OVERVIEW OF THE PROJECT LIFE CYCLE

Web sites developed by teams follow a basic life cycle model, as shown in Figure 11.1. During each stage of the life cycle, the team must complete certain steps before they can start other steps. The amount of time assigned to each stage of the life cycle varies by project. Some overlap may occur within stages. For example, people may begin designing the site's navigation scheme before all of the site's content has been determined. The key is to remember that every Web development project follows this basic pattern.

Figure 11.1

Every Web development project follows the same basic life cycle. Why do you think a circle, and not a straight line, is used to illustrate the Web development process?

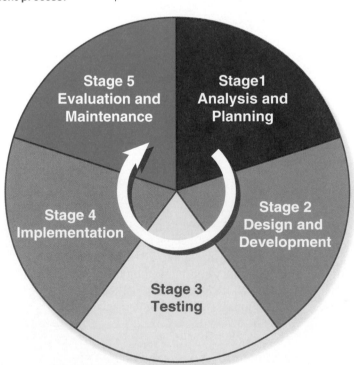

webdesign.glencoe.com

TASKS IN THE PROJECT LIFE CYCLE

The number of people involved in a Web site development project varies by project. Typical team members include a client liason representative, project manager, Web author, Web designer, Web developer, and Webmaster. In some cases, the client liaison representative and the project manager are the same person. The Web developer also may serve as the Webmaster.

All team members work toward the same goal of creating a site that meets the client's expectations. However, members of the project team participate in different stages of the project. As shown in Table 11.1, the client liaison representative and project manager take part in all stages of the project. Other team members participate as needed during the life cycle. All team members should understand the life cycle and know how their roles fit into the model.

Project Life Cycle

Life Cycle Stage	Purpose	Team Members Actively Participating
Analysis and Planning	• Meet with client to determine site's goals, budget, and scope • Research site's audience • Set project milestones	• Client liaison representative • Project manager
Design and Development	• Determine navigation scheme • Develop content • Plan site's layout and visual appearance	• Client liaison representative • Project manager • Web author • Web designer • Web developer
Testing	• Finalize site's beta (final test) version • Evaluate beta version	• Client liaison representative • Project manager • Web author • Web designer • Web developer • Webmaster
Implementation	• Transfer site to Web server • Publicize Web site	• Client liaison representative • Project manager • Web developer • Webmaster
Evaluation and Maintenance	• Evaluate audience reaction to site • Update site information • Maintain site and links	• Client liaison representative • Project manager • Webmaster

Table 11.1
Team members work through a basic life cycle as they create a Web site. Why do certain team members participate throughout the life cycle?

FORMING A WEB DESIGN PROJECT TEAM

Most Web sites are developed for a client. The **client** is the person or organization who pays for the work. Examples of clients include:

- A corporation that wants to develop a corporate presence site
- An organization that needs a convenient way to stay in touch with its members
- A retail store that wants to develop an e-commerce site to sell its products

Client Liaison Representative

The **client liaison representative** maintains contact with the client throughout the Web site development process. Other team members may talk with the client. The client liaison representative, however, is the person responsible for understanding the client's needs and keeping all other team members working toward the client's goals. The client liaison representative asks many questions, including:

- What are the specific goals for the site?
- Who is the target audience?
- What is the budget?
- When does the site need to be published?
- Who will approve the site?
- How often does the client want a status report showing progress on the site's development?

Figure 11.2
The client liaison representative must understand the client's goals in order to communicate them to the Web site development team. Why do you think it would be important to take notes during meetings with the client?

During the analysis and planning stage, the client liaison representative defines the deliverables, which are the actual work that the team will submit. Since a Web site development project may last for many months, the client liaison representative works with the client to set milestones. A **milestone** is a specific step in the Web site development process and a date for its completion. Milestones may include acceptance of the basic design, the content, the navigation, and the images. Figure 11.2 shows a client liaison representative meeting with a corporate client to establish the deliverables and milestones for a corporate presence Web site development project.

Project Manager

The **project manager** oversees the work of all the team members and ensures that team members work together. He or she assigns responsibilities to team members and tracks their progress.

Good project managers assign each team member specific tasks. Strong teams also help each other. For example, the Web author is clearly responsible for the words that go on each page. The Web author may also help the

Figure 11.3
Project managers are problem solvers. What part of project management would you find most rewarding?

Web designer by suggesting photos or graphics that would work well with the text. The project manager encourages team members to work together in these ways.

The project manager focuses on the end goal of delivering a completed Web site on time and on budget. He or she also provides resources and help as needed to achieve this goal, as shown in Figure 11.3.

Web Author

The Web author, also known as the content developer, writes the material that appears on the Web site. Web authors may also select images that support or complement a site's text. Large projects may require several Web authors. When a project has multiple Web authors, a content editor may work with the team of Web authors to gather all the material that will appear on the site.

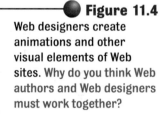

Figure 11.4
Web designers create animations and other visual elements of Web sites. Why do you think Web authors and Web designers must work together?

Web authors use outlines to explain their ideas about the content for each page. As the team decides on the specific pages to include in the site, the Web author begins writing the words. Web site text should:

- Support the site's purpose and goals
- Be presented in an easy-to-read format
- Be appealing
- Be accurate and grammatically correct

Web Designer

The Web designer provides visual direction for the Web site. Based on the site's goals and content, the Web designer selects a color palette, gives shape and definition to each page, and provides a consistent look to the site. The Web designer makes sketches or creates visual prototypes for the site. After the team has approved the prototypes, the Web designer creates the graphics, including navigation buttons, animations, interface layout, and charts. The Web designer creates or obtains photographs, maps, and other visuals to enhance the site. Figure 11.4 shows a Web designer working on a Web site.

Web Developer

Web developers use software applications, such as FrontPage, and authoring languages, such as HTML, to develop or program the Web site. The Web developer's goal is to enable visitors to successfully load the Web site in their browser, navigate within the site, and navigate to external links. To meet this goal, the Web developer explores the Web server that will host the site to learn the technical requirements. He or she also works with the client to identify the types of browsers that the client's audience will be using.

Web developers often use storyboards to present design and navigation ideas. They focus on the interactivity of the site, determining how visitors will move between pages. When they are ready, Web developers create an *alpha,* or first, version of the Web site for team and client review. This version contains placeholder text and graphics. Graphics that are essential to the site (such as logos) are usually included. Basic navigation for the site is also in place.

Based on feedback from the team and the client, the Web developer then creates a *beta,* or final test, version of the site. The beta version includes all of the Web site's elements. Team members and the client thoroughly test this version. Once the team has resolved all issues, the Web developer works with the Webmaster to transfer the files to the Web server that will host the site.

Webmaster

The Webmaster implements and maintains the completed site. He or she posts the site on the Web server, keeps the site up to date, and answers questions from visitors. The Webmaster also adds new content as provided by the project team, tests links on a regular basis, and updates external links as needed.

EVALUATING PROGRESS

When a project starts, the project manager holds a meeting to explain the project and to define team members' roles and responsibilities. Between team meetings, each team member completes specific assignments. Assignments are completed either by individuals or by groups.

During the design and development stage, the team meets periodically to assess team members' progress and resolve outstanding issues. Teams function best when each team member takes responsibility for completing assigned tasks. The project manager holds team members accountable for their work.

FrontPage provides tools you can use to monitor the development of a Web site. Tasks view (available from the View menu) displays a list of tasks that need to be completed in the open Web site. You can create tasks lists for your own Web sites, and assign tasks to different team members when working on team projects. Each task can be categorized as High, Medium, or Low priority. You can also track the status of your tasks, including when they were last modified and whether or not they have been completed.

Using Web Site Checklists

Project teams often use a checklist to evaluate the Web site as they develop it. Using a checklist helps team members evaluate the effectiveness of a site's interaction, information, and presentation design.

Activity 11.1 Explore Web Programming Identify the resources available to Web developers by connecting to the links available at **webdesign.glencoe.com**.

TECH TRIVIA

Tracking Tools
FrontPage's Workflow reports tell you a file's status, the person responsible for developing that file, and whether the file has been published. Access Workflow reports from the View menu (select Reports>Workflow).

Throughout this unit, you will be creating a Web site for an online tee shirt company called WebTee.biz. This company sells various styles of tee shirts to consumers. It also offers custom printing. The company has decided to target its products to individuals who purchase tee shirts in quantity, such as club sponsors, team coaches, and reunion organizers. In the following activity, you will use a checklist to identify the team members responsible for performing specific tasks during the development of the WebTee.biz Web site. You will also identify at which stage of the development life cycle these specific tasks should be completed.

ACTIVITY 11A Identifying Project Team Responsibilities

1 Create a checklist like the one in Table 11.2. This checklist contains a series of questions designed to help you evaluate the different characteristics of the WebTee.biz Web site.

2 Add two columns to the right of your checklist.

3 Label the left column **Team Member(s).**

4 In the left column, next to each question on your checklist, identify the project team member that is responsible for that step. For example, the Web author is responsible for ensuring the accuracy of the site's information. Note that more than one team member may be responsible for evaluating a particular item.

5 Label the right column **Project Stage(s).**

6 In the right column, next to each question on your checklist, identify the stage of the development cycle in which this evaluation step is completed. Again, note that specific items may need to be evaluated at more than one stage of the life cycle. For example, links should be tested in the development, testing, and maintenance stages.

YOU TRY IT

Table 11.2
Checklists enable team members to use consistent criteria for evaluating sites.

The Web Site Progress Checklist

INFORMATION DESIGN
- ☑ Is the information accurate?
- ☑ Is the information concise, clear, and spelled correctly?
- ☑ Does the content support the site's purpose and goals?

LAYOUT
- ☑ Does the site have enough white space?
- ☑ Is important content emphasized?
- ☑ Are related items grouped?
- ☑ Is text aligned consistently?
- ☑ Are all links clearly labeled?

NAVIGATION SCHEME
- ☑ Can you move easily between pages?
- ☑ Can you locate specific information quickly?
- ☑ Do all internal and external hyperlinks work?
- ☑ Can you easily return to the home page?

USER FRIENDLINESS
- ☑ Does the site downloaded quickly?
- ☑ Is the text easy to read?
- ☑ Are both graphic and text links used?
- ☑ Is important information displayed in the safe area?
- ☑ Does the site include accessibility features?

PRESENTATION DESIGN
- ☑ Is the color palette consistent?
- ☑ Does the design support the site's purpose and goals?
- ☑ Are graphics and multimedia used effectively?
- ☑ Do all multimedia features work properly?

Using Source Control

Small Web site development teams have only one Web developer. Larger projects may require several Web developers. The FrontPage source control feature helps teams manage sites when several people are working on the site's programming.

The **source control** feature protects the integrity of the Web site's files. It ensures that only one person at a time can edit a particular file. The feature works like a library that has only one copy of every book. You can check a file out, work with it, and then check it back in. While you have the file, no one else can check it out. They can open the file as "read-only" and look at it, but they cannot make changes to the file. This control avoids the frustration of having one person over-write another's changes.

Source control is disabled in the default installation of FrontPage. You can turn on source control using the Site Settings (Web Settings in FrontPage 2002) on the Tools menu. To activate source control, check the box labeled "Use document check-in and check-out" (see Figure 11.5). To use source control, right-click any file name in the Folder List and click Check Out on the shortcut menu. The green dot beside the file changes to a red check mark to indicate that the file is checked out. When you have completed work on the file, you must check it in before others can make any additional changes.

Figure 11.5
You must activiate source control for each Web site you are developing. How does source control help teams manage Web site development?

Section 11.1 Assessment

Concept Check

1. **Define** client, client liaison representative, milestone, project manager, source control.

2. **Explain** the role of the project manager. Why is it important to have a project manager when developing a Web site as a team?

3. **Describe** how project team members use checklists.

Critical Thinking

4. **Analyze Options** Three team members prefer a hi-tech look for a Web site, while three others prefer a classic look. What should the project manager do to help the team reach an agreement?

5. **Draw Conclusions** Why do you think testing happens before implementation in the life cycle of Web site development?

Applying Skills

Research Team Jobs Select one of the following team roles: project manager, Web author, Web designer, or Web developer. Research the typical educational requirements and experience needed to perform this role. Write two paragraphs summarizing your findings.

Careers & Technology

CERTIFICATIONS AND CAREER PATHWAYS

To improve your chances of getting a job in multimedia and Web development, prepare yourself with the right skills and training.

Microsoft offers a variety of Web-related certifications.

The College Path

If you want a Web-related career, consider pursuing a four-year college degree in computer science or a specialized discipline, such as multimedia or information technology. It is especially useful to have a bachelor's degree in computer science paired with classes related to design, communication, or computer administration.

Computer studies should include comprehensive coverage of markup languages like HTML and XML. It is also important to learn about Web tools, such as Adobe Pagemaker, Microsoft FrontPage, and Macromedia Dreamweaver. Even if you do not want to program, exposure to languages like Java and Visual Basic will help in most Web-related jobs.

The Certification Path

People pursuing careers on the Web may choose from among many kinds of certification programs. Vendor-specific certification programs provide training on specific software products. They may be taught by the developer or a technical school. Some vendor-specific certification programs are:

- **Adobe Systems** offers an Adobe Certified Expert (ACE) certification for Web designers.
- **Macromedia** offers certification in its ColdFusion, Dreamweaver, and Flash products.
- **Microsoft** offers several Internet-related certifications, such as the Microsoft Certified Application Developer (MCAD) credential.

A variety of non-vendor-specific certifications are available as well. The World Organization of Webmasters (WOW), for instance, offers a three-tiered certification program that focuses on a broad range of general skills rather than specific programs.

Mapping a Career Path

On the way to becoming a Web specialist, your career path can take several turns. Many Web developers, for example, enter the field as graphic designers or HTML specialists.

As your experience grows, you may take on a role in project management, interface design, marketing, or some other specialized task. You will need a wide range of skills for a successful career.

Tech Focus

1. Research professional schools and colleges that offer programs for a Web career. Create a multimedia presentation relating one program to your career plans.

2. Research certifications for the career path you are interested in. Describe the courses you would take and who offers them.

Guide to Reading

Main Ideas

The amount of time, money, resources, and people needed to complete a Web site helps to determine the project's scope. E-commerce sites often require significant amounts of time, money, and people to complete.

Key Terms

scope
e-commerce
business-to-business (B2B) e-commerce
business-to-consumer (B2C) e-commerce
target market
budget
instant storefront

Reading Strategy

Identify three items to be considered when designing an e-commerce Web site. Use an organizer like the one below (also available online).

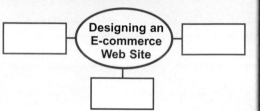

Designing an E-commerce Web Site

One of the first steps in starting a new Web development project is determining how many pages and features a site will include. Identifying the size and complexity of a site helps determine the amount of resources needed to complete that site. Some of the most complex Web sites in development today are e-commerce sites. E-commerce sites will thus be the focus of this unit as we discuss the different stages involved in the Web site development process.

ANALYSIS AND PLANNING

The first stage in the Web site development life cycle involves analysis and planning. During this stage, the client liaison representative meets with the client to identify the site's purpose, goals, and audience.

The Web site's mission statement helps determine that site's content. A list is usually made of all the content and features that people want to include on the Web site. This list of desired items is then balanced against the project's available time, money, and resources. This balancing act defines the project's **scope,** which is the features and content that can be provided with the time and resources available. It is often necessary to omit some content or features to stay within the project's budget and schedule. The project team reviews the project's scope during this initial stage to determine what is and is not essential to the site.

THE BUSINESS OF E-COMMERCE

As noted, developing electronic commerce (commonly referred to as e-commerce) sites often requires a significant amount of time, money, and resources. **E-commerce** is the electronic buying and selling of goods and services. The growth of e-commerce sites has transformed the Internet into a worldwide marketplace.

GO *Online*

Activity 11.2 Explore E-Commerce Identify the growing importance of e-commerce to businesses by connecting to the links at **webdesign.glencoe.com**.

 webdesign.glencoe.com

The Role of E-commerce

Although e-commerce includes all forms of electronic transactions, including access to bank accounts through ATMs, we will limit our discussion of e-commerce to online exchanges. Online e-commerce exchanges include:

◆ Customers researching products online before visiting a retail store to make a purchase.

◆ Customers ordering products online and receiving them through the mail.

◆ Businesses providing online technical product support for a fee.

◆ Educational institutions offering online courses for a fee.

◆ Online events in which subscribers pay to participate.

◆ Government agencies allowing citizens to renew their license plates online.

◆ Nonprofit organizations soliciting donations online.

Some businesses, such as the bookstores Barnes and Noble and Borders, offer online services in addition to a more traditional brick-and-morter shopping experience. Other businesses, such as ebay.com, only do business online (see Figure 11.6).

E-commerce sites provide an alternative to traditional retail shopping. Table 11.3 lists the advantages and disadvantages of traditional and B2C online shopping.

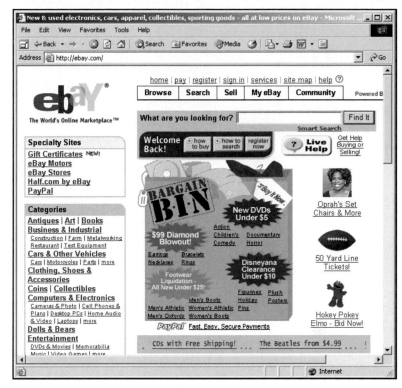

● **Figure 11.6**
Some businesses exist only online. What challenges do online businesses face?

● **Table 11.3**
Consumers can often purchase the same products in retail stores and online. Which advantage of online shopping is most helpful to you?

Traditional Versus Online Shopping

	Traditional Retail Shopping	Online Shopping
Advantages	• You can examine the merchandise. • You can pay with cash, checks, credit cards, or debit cards. • You can take the merchandise home immediately.	• You can shop from home, 24 hours a day, 7 days a week. • You can easily compare prices among different online sources. • You can purchase merchandise that is not available in your local community.
Disadvantages	• You must travel to the store. • You cannot easily compare prices. • Your local stores may not carry the merchandise.	• You cannot examine the merchandise closely. • You usually must pay with a debit or credit card. • You must wait for the merchandise to be delivered.

Types of E-commerce

E-commerce Web sites offer a variety of goods and services to individuals and businesses. The online marketplace can be divided into two main categories: business-to-business (B2B) and business-to-consumer (B2C) e-commerce sites.

Business-to-Business (B2B) E-commerce Electronic exchanges in which both parties are businesses are known as **business-to-business (B2B) e-commerce.** For example, assume that Safety Innovations is a business that manufactures and sells airbags for automobiles. Car manufacturers around the world place online orders with Safety Innovations. The company in turn delivers airbags to the car manufacturers' various assembly facilities.

Business-to-Consumer (B2C) E-commerce Electronic exchanges between businesses and individual consumers are known as **business-to-consumer (B2C) e-commerce.** In B2C e-commerce, businesses sell goods and services to individual consumers.

DESIGNING AN E-COMMERCE WEB SITE

In the early days of e-commerce, some people thought that simply making products available online would bring success. However, businesses soon realized that they must market e-commerce sites for people to visit them.

Determining the Target Market

When you plan an e-commerce site, you must know your target market. Your **target market** is the group of potential customers for the product or service that you are selling. For example, the target market for the air bag manufacturer described in the B2B discussion is car manufacturers.

Businesses often consider the characteristics of market segments when defining their target market. A market segment is a group of people who share common traits or interests and who have money to spend. Businesses often use age to define different market segments.The images, sounds, colors, and text on e-commerce Web sites are frequently designed to appeal to particular age groups, as shown in Figure 11.7. Income, educational background, interests, and activities are other ways of segmenting the market.

Figure 11.7 ●
Businesses target their products to people in specific age groups. How do these two Web sites target different age groups?

Creating the Schedule

It is important to set a realistic schedule when developing a Web site. Project managers are responsible for determining a Web site development project's schedule. The schedule identifies the project's milestones. Project managers often determine these due dates by working backwards from the date the site is scheduled to go live (be published).

As shown in Figure 11.8, some tasks can only begin after other tasks are completed. Other tasks can occur at the same time. For example, content development can begin while planning for the site's interaction and presentation is still taking place.

┌─**READ ME!**─┐

Tech Tip Project managers use software applications such as Microsoft Project to develop complex schedules.

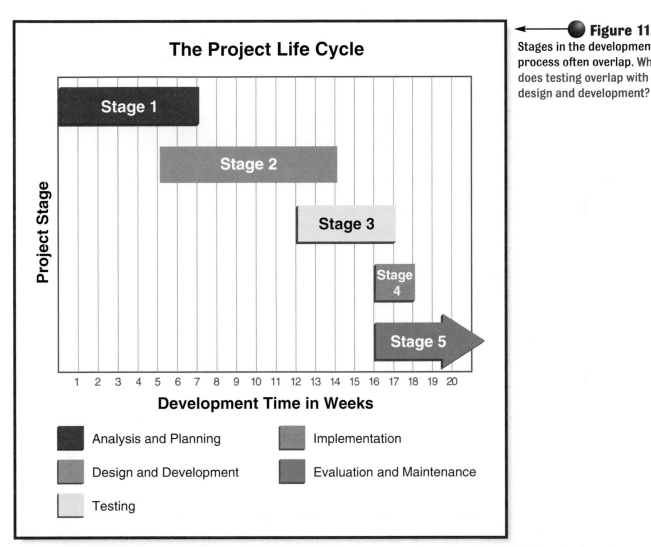

The Project Life Cycle

Stage 1
Stage 2
Stage 3
Stage 4
Stage 5

Project Stage (vertical axis)

1 2 3 4 5 6 7 8 9 10 11 12 13 14 15 16 17 18 19 20
Development Time in Weeks

■ Analysis and Planning   ■ Implementation
■ Design and Development   ■ Evaluation and Maintenance
□ Testing

● **Figure 11.8**
Stages in the development process often overlap. Why does testing overlap with design and development?

ACTIVITY 11B Identifying Tasks and Milestones

YOU TRY IT

❶ Read the proposal from WebTee.biz found in the DataFile\Ch11\Text folder (click **proposal.doc**). WeeTee.biz has prepared this proposal to define the scope of its new Web development project.

❷ As you read the proposal, list the tasks that people on the Web site development team will need to complete.

Student Data File

3 Then list the milestones that the project team will need to meet in order for the site to go live in three months.

4 Develop a schedule for the Web development project. Use the information in Table 11.4 to help you determine how long particular stages of the project will take to complete.

Table 11.4
Schedules help team members stay on task.

Web Site Development Schedule		
Time Frame	**Stage**	**Sample Tasks**
4 to 6 weeks	Analysis and Planning	• Research client's needs. • Define the target market. • Identify available resources and set a realistic budget. • Set milestones for the project.
8 to 10 weeks	Design and Development	• Design interaction. • Design presentation. • Gather information and write content. • Gather visual elements. • Program site.
4 to 5 weeks	Testing	• Debug HTML code as needed. • Test all elements of the site in two browsers. • Fix all problems and retest as needed.
1 week	Implementation	• Transfer all files in the site to the Web server hosting the site. • Test the site after moving it and before going live. • Go live.
Ongoing	Evaluation and Maintenance	• Respond to customer feedback. • Test internal and external links regularly. • Communicate ideas for improvement to project team.

Considering Budget and Human Resources

As businesses seek to establish or expand their presence on the World Wide Web, they must determine what resources they are willing to commit to Web development projects. If a business spends more to develop a site than it will make from sales generated by the site, it will lose money.

Determining Budget A **budget** defines the total financial resources available for site development. Budgets help teams define the scope of the project. For example, WebTee.biz would like to develop a full electronic store for its products. However, it has a limited budget. After considering all the options available, the company decides that the budget is only sufficient to provide product information online and to accept e-mail orders.

When considering budget, businesses also must consider what equipment the e-commerce site will need to function properly. The servers and telecommunications lines that they use must be able to handle the amount of customer traffic that they think their site will receive.

Determining Human Resources When businesses decide that e-commerce will be a primary way to sell to customers, they likely must decide whether to use in-house employees to develop and maintain the e-commerce site. The in-house solution brings together people who already have knowledge of how the company currently sells to customers. They can develop online strategies that coordinate with the company's existing business.

There are potential drawbacks to the in-house solution, including:

◆ A lack of computer expertise among existing employees

◆ Employees who cannot commit time to developing the site

◆ The cost to purchase and deploy the software needed to maintain an e-commerce site

Businesses that do not expect significant sales from e-commerce may choose less costly solutions, such as instant storefronts. An **instant storefront** is a portal site that helps businesses create their own Web sites and begin selling and accepting payments online in a few hours. Some instant storefronts, such as Microsoft's bCentral, also help businesses market their sites.

It generally costs much less to use an instant storefront than it does to develop a site in-house. In some cases, businesses pay a small fee up front and then pay a monthly subscription price to maintain the storefront. Instant storefronts also help businesses through the maze of privacy and security issues that can be difficult for small businesses.

Section 11.2 Assessment

Concept Check

1. **Define** scope, e-commerce, business-to-business (B2B) e-commerce, business-to-consumer (B2C) e-commerce, target market, budget, instant storefront.

2. **Explain** the difference between an in-house solution and an instant storefront.

Critical Thinking

3. **Predict Outcomes** Consider the growth of e-commerce. What effect do you think e-commerce will have in the next ten years on traditional retail stores?

4. **Draw Conclusions** Why do you think you need to consider a budget before you begin working on an e-commerce Web site?

Applying Skills

Compare E-commerce Sites Select two e-commerce sites on the World Wide Web that sell similar products. Compare and contrast the two sites and write two paragraphs summarizing your findings.

STREAMING ONLINE MULTIMEDIA

A few years ago, computer multimedia programs were delivered only on compact disc. Today, streaming technology lets you join a multiplayer action game or watch the latest movie trailers right on your home PC.

Streaming technology works by breaking a media file into pieces and then delivering them in order to the user's computer.

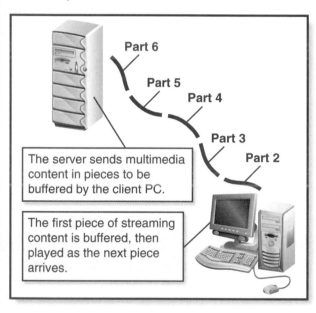

Part 6

Part 5

Part 4

Part 3

Part 2

The server sends multimedia content in pieces to be buffered by the client PC.

The first piece of streaming content is buffered, then played as the next piece arrives.

What Is Streaming Content?

You can download an entire media file from a Web server, and then use player software to play it. But you must wait for the file to download.

Streaming provides a more elegant solution. To stream media, the server breaks the audio or video transmission into pieces. The user's media player starts playing the first piece of the file as soon as it arrives. As the player receives the remaining pieces, it buffers (stores temporarily) and plays them in order. The result is a continuous stream of content, where each downloaded piece plays as the rest of the file arrives.

Uses for Streaming Media

By using streaming technologies, Web sites provide access to information and cultures from around the world. Businesses use streaming media to broadcast speeches and seminars. Streaming technologies are also crucial for activities like teleconferencing, which is an important tool in distance learning as well as in business.

Technical Requirements

Streaming content from a Web site requires special hardware and software:

◆ **Encoder** Streaming content must be specially encoded to work with a specific type of player software, such as RealPlayer or Windows Media.
◆ **Streaming Media Server** This dedicated server delivers the media stream to the user.
◆ **Broadband Connection** Streaming works well only when the server is connected to the Internet (or a LAN) through a broadband link.

Most users have RealPlayer, Windows Media, and QuickTime all installed on their systems, enabling them to play any type of streaming content.

Tech Focus

1. Research the various ways streaming media is used in e-commerce. Analyze the effect of this instant technology on business and how it is changing the nature of business on the Internet.

2. Research the various encoding and player formats used for delivering streaming media. Which format would you choose for an e-commerce site? Explain your choice and the software you would need.

SECTION 11.1 The Project Life Cycle

Key Terms

client, 300
client liaison
    representative, 300
milestone, 300

project manager, 300
source control, 304

Main Ideas

- Project teams often develop Web sites.
- Web site development follows a basic life cycle.
- Teams vary in size, but often include a client liaison representative, project manager, Web author, Web designer, Web developer, and Webmaster.
- Team members have specific assignments that help the team achieve the goal of developing a Web site that meets the client's expectations.
- The client liaison representative works with the client to define deliverables and establish milestones.
- The project manager holds team members accountable for their work and for the team's progress.
- Project teams use Web site checklists to evaluate the effectiveness of the site's interaction, information, and presentation design.
- Source control helps teams manage the files they are creating for a Web site.

SECTION 11.2 Determining Project Scope

Key Terms

scope, 306
e-commerce, 306
business-to-business (B2B)
    e-commerce, 308
business-to-consumer (B2C)
    e-commerce, 308

target market, 308
budget, 310
instant storefront, 311

Main Ideas

- During analysis and planning, the client liaison representative works with the client to identify the site's purpose, goals, and audience.
- E-commerce is the electronic buying and selling of goods and services.
- Business-to-business (B2B) e-commerce involves transactions between businesses, while business-to-consumer (B2C) e-commerce involves businesses selling to individual consumers.
- E-commerce businesses must know their target markets.
- Project managers determine the schedule for all aspects of the site's life cycle.
- Web site developers base their choices on the budget and resources available.
- Businesses with limited resources may use instant storefronts to quickly set up an online presence.

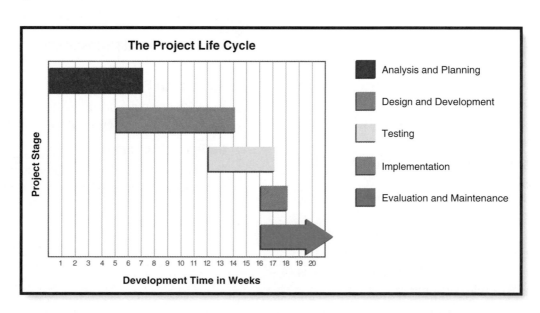

The Project Life Cycle

- Analysis and Planning
- Design and Development
- Testing
- Implementation
- Evaluation and Maintenance

Project Stage

Development Time in Weeks

Reviewing Key Terms

1. Who are typical clients for Web site development teams?
2. What differences exist between the roles of the client liaison representative and the project manager?
3. What FrontPage feature helps teams manage the Web sites they are developing?
4. What is e-commerce?
5. What type of portal site enables small businesses to easily and quickly begin selling products on the Web?

Understanding Main Ideas

6. **Identify** the phases in the Web site development life cycle.
7. **Summarize** the contributions of project managers and Web developers to Web site development teams.
8. **Explain** the major tasks that a Web designer performs.
9. **Describe** how Web site checklists help teams track their performance.
10. **Discuss** the factors to consider when identifying the project's scope.
11. **Explain** the difference between B2B and B2C e-commerce.
12. **Identify** three types of e-commerce transactions.
13. **Explain** why businesses must market their e-commerce sites.
14. **Summarize** characteristics that businesses use to identify a market segment.

Critical Thinking

15. **Make Decisions** The Web designer and Web developer on a project team disagree about who should create the animations for the site. Each thinks the other person should perform this task. As the project manager, what would you do to resolve the disagreement so that the project can move ahead?
16. **Analyze Project Scope** An e-commerce site's mission statement is as follows: "The instant storefront will provide easy access to all products in our catalog. Our products, targeted to buyers from the ages of 15 to 25, will ship within 48 hours of the order." Make a list of items that must be balanced when defining the scope of this e-commerce site.
17. **Draw Conclusions** A small fish market on the West Coast would like to develop an e-commerce site so that it can sell its premium product to other businesses across the country. How would this company identify its target market?
18. **Sequence Steps** During what parts of the development cycle is it important to test your Web site? Why shouldn't you wait until the end of the cycle?

e-Review ⋯⋯⋯⋯

webdesign.glencoe.com

Study with PowerPoint

To review the main points in this chapter, select **e-Review** > **PowerPoint Outlines** > **Chapter 11**.

Online Self Check

Test your knowledge of the material in this chapter by selecting **e-Review** > **Self Checks** > **Chapter 11**.

Making Connections

Math—Conduct a Salary Survey Research online to find salary ranges for the following jobs:

◆ Webmaster
◆ Web designer (may also be called graphic designer)
◆ Web developer (may also be called information architect or information engineer)
◆ Project manager

If possible, find a survey that lists salary ranges from low to high.

Make a bar chart based on the data you collect. Give the chart an appropriate title and label it so that others can easily understand the information you have included.

STANDARDS AT WORK

Students understand the ethical, cultural, and societal issues related to technology. (NETS-S 2)

List Confidential Items

When clients hire companies to create Web sites, they share information about the company that must be kept confidential. Often each member of the project team is required to sign a confidentiality agreement. This agreement tells signers not to discuss any aspects of the project or the information learned about the company with people outside the project team.

Assume you are assigned to a project team that is designing an e-commerce site for a toy store. You sign a confidentiality agreement that states that you may not disclose any information about the company, its employees, or its products. Make a list of things that the team would need to know about the company to develop the site. Place a check mark beside each item that you should not disclose to people who are not on the team.

TEAMWORK SKILLS

Identify Project Team Strengths

Experts have identified different intelligences that affect how individuals learn and work with others. These intelligences include the ability to:

◆ Work well with spoken and written language
◆ Work well with numbers and understand the relationship between objects
◆ Understand how something drawn on paper will look when created
◆ Coordinate the body effectively (for example, dancers and athletes)
◆ Work well with music
◆ Deal well with the behavior, emotions, and motivations of other people
◆ Deal well with one's own emotions and motivations
◆ Work well with one's physical surroundings

Compare these different intelligences to the skills needed by individual members on a project team. Create a two-column table that lists each intelligence and the project team members who should be strong in this type of intelligence.

CHALLENGE YOURSELF

Compare Storefront Solutions

Sites that sell instant storefront solutions explain the services the site offers, the steps you need to take to set up a storefront, and the prices for the services. Some sites also offer a demonstration (demo) of how the storefront works.

Find two instant storefront sites that offer a demo. As you view each demo, make a list of the features that the site offers. Use your lists to create a chart comparing the two storefronts. Based on your comparison, identify which storefront you would you recommend to a friend who wants to create a storefront to sell video games. Explain your reasoning.

YOU TRY IT

Skills Studio

These exercises reinforce the skills you learned in this chapter's You Try It activities. Refer back to the You Try It activities if you need extra guidance.

1. Evaluating Web Sites

Many project teams rely on reviewers to evaluate the usability of a Web site as they develop it. All the reviewers should use the same criteria to evaluate the site. This helps the project team develop sites that most people will find useful.

A With a partner, select three different sites: one e-commerce site, one entertainment-oriented site, and one college or university site.

B With your partner, determine what criteria a site has to meet to be rated 1 (poor), 2 (good), or 3 (excellent). Use the checklist shown in Table 11.2 (page 303) to help determine your criteria and evaluate the sites.

C Use a table like the one on this page to rate each aspect of the three sites. Rate each site separately.

Site URL:
Name of Site:
Type of Site:

Aspect Being Rated	1 (poor)	2 (good)	3 (excellent)
Information Design			
Layout			
Navigation Scheme			
User-Friendliness			
Presentation Design			
Overall Rating			

2. Comparing Evaluations

When reviewers evaluate sites, they bring their personal backgrounds and preferences into the evaluation. Therefore, different reviewers may have very different evaluations of the same site.

A Ask two classmates to evaluate the same sites you reviewed in You Try It Skills Studio Activity 1. They should use the same evaluation tool as in the activity above.

B Compare the similarities and differences among the evaluations. Note any evaluation items that are two or more points different from your evaluation. Ask your classmates to explain their reasoning for these ratings.

C Write a summary of the evaluations and explain what you learned about evaluating Web sites.

Web Design Projects

1. Identify Client Goals

Your company has assigned a new client to you. The client, Outdoor Excursions, sells camping equipment. The client's budget is limited, so it has decided to develop a corporate presence site. Eventually, it plans to develop an e-commerce site to market its products. At your first meeting with the client, you learn the following:

◆ Its customers include people of all ages.
◆ Families often visit the store together to select gear.
◆ The company advertises at local campgrounds and in the telephone book.
◆ Many of its customers recommend the store to their friends.
◆ Their staff members are experienced campers.
◆ The store sells camping clothing and shoes in addition to camping equipment.

Based on this information, prepare a list of recommended pages for the site. You have determined that the budget will only support development of eight to ten pages. Also, prepare a list of follow-up questions that you need to ask the client so that the Web author can begin developing content.

2. Create a Schedule

Carol has been making candles that commemorate a theme or an occasion for friends and family members. Her work has met with great success, and she has decided to broaden her business with an e-commerce site—Candles by Carol. The site will allow people to select a candle that is accompanied by a poem related to the occasion. She has developed candles and poems related to birthdays, weddings, promotions, and so on.

Identify the tasks and milestones needed to create a site for Candles by Carol. Create a Web site development schedule (for help, refer to Table 11.4 from page 310). Assume that Carol would like the site completed within three months.

LIFE CYCLE STAGE	SCHEDULE (time to complete)	TASK LIST (things to do)	MILESTONES (deliverables)
Analysis and Planning			
Design and Development			
Testing			
Implementation			
Evaluation and Maintenance			

Developing a Web Site

WHY IT MATTERS................................

Blueprints help builders and contractors know how to construct a building. As you build sites in FrontPage, your planning serves as the blueprint for your site. Like buildings, many Web sites start small and grow over time. Before a Web site can grow, however, it must be built on a solid foundation.

Quick Write Activity

Review what you have learned about designing Web sites to this point. Write a list of steps you would take to build the home page for a personal Web site. Then compare your list with a classmate's list to see if you both created similar "blueprints."

WHAT YOU WILL DO...

READ TO SUCCEED

Check Your Understanding
Stop often and think about what you are reading. Are you following the ideas? Are you lost? Have you immediately forgotten what you just read? Reread parts when necessary. On a note pad, draw pictures, if necessary. You can also use diagrams to summarize the information. As you complete a section, see if you can connect the ideas. Write down the main idea or concept on your note pad. Then write down supporting information or examples around the main idea. Draw lines or arrows to show the connections.

Examining an E-commerce Web Site

Main Ideas

Many e-commerce sites exist to provide information about a company and its products. Feedback forms allow visitors to share their thoughts about the business, the products, and the site.

Key Terms

feedback form
scroll box
option button
check box

Reading Strategy

Compare and contrast option buttons and check boxes. Use a Venn diagram like the one below (also available online).

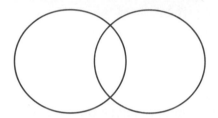

E-commerce sites vary widely in the way they allow consumers to transact business. In this chapter, you will explore some of the factors that are important in creating a usable and secure e-commerce site.

EXAMINING THE WebTee.biz SITE

Many businesses use Web sites to present information about their products and services. While these Web sites may take customer orders, their main function is to provide the business with an online presence. The Web site featured in this unit, WebTee.biz, is such a site. Although it is not large, this Web site performs several important functions:

◆ It gives the company a presence on the World Wide Web.

◆ It showcases the company's products and services.

◆ It gives visitors a chance to contact and interact with the company in various ways, including placing orders and giving feedback.

WebTee.biz Overview

WebTee.biz is a B2C e-commerce site. The business sells custom tee shirts directly to consumers.

The founder of WebTee decided to target consumers who regularly purchase one or more tee shirts at full price from retailers. The target age range is 15 to 25. The company also targets coaches, human resource managers, and event planners who want to create a unique look for their team, employees, or event clients. The company has two sources for sales: its Web site and a new storefront where customers can watch the process that WebTee uses to customize its tee shirts.

Pages in the WebTee.biz Web Site

The WebTee.biz Web site consists of five main pages: Home, Products, FAQ (Frequently Asked Questions), Press Releases, and Contact Us. As shown in Figure 12.1, the site also contains an order form page that is a child of the Products page.

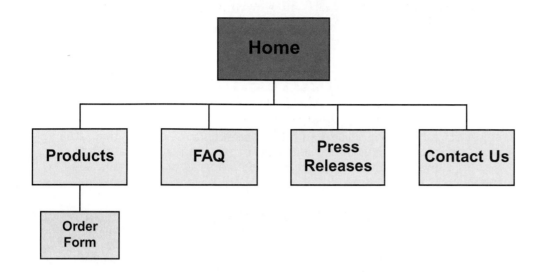

Figure 12.1
The WebTee.biz site contains five main pages and an order form page. Why is the order form page important to the WebTee.biz site?

Although the WebTee.biz site does not have many main pages, each page helps to promote the company and its products. Many of the pages contained on the site are commonly found in e-commerce Web sites.

- ◆ The Home page introduces visitors to the business.
- ◆ The Products page provides an overview of the business's products.
- ◆ The FAQ page answers common questions about the business and its services.
- ◆ The Press Releases page announces what is new in the company.
- ◆ The Contact Us page provides contact information to visitors.

In the next activity, you will visit the WebTee.biz site and become familiar with its pages and features.

ACTIVITY 12A Exploring the WebTee.biz Web Site

YOU TRY IT

❶ Download the **WebTee.biz** files from DataFile\Ch12\Web Examples\ WebTee folder.

❷ Open the Web site in FrontPage. Open the Folder List to see what files make up the site.

❸ Preview the home page (**index.htm**) in a Web browser.

❹ Use the link bar to navigate to each page on the site. Analyze the content of each page. Identify the purpose of each page and describe how the page contributes to the site.

Student
Data File

Figure 12.2
You can link to all other pages on the site from the link bar on the left.

⑤ Return to the home page (see Figure 12.2). Close the browser. Save the site.

READ ME!

Tech Tip A company's contact page should provide e-mail addresses to general locations, such as the customer service department. That way, the addresses do not have to change when company personnel changes.

ENHANCING THE WebTee.biz SITE

The WebTee.biz site has limited e-commerce functionality. It does not, for example, process credit card orders electronically. Instead, the company processes orders by telephone once a day. The plan for the Web site is to expand it gradually by adding more interactivite features. As the site expands, the company plans to start processing online orders. For now, you will focus on adding more ways for a customer to communicate with WebTee.biz.

Creating a Feedback Form

A **feedback form** provides customers with a way to voice their opinions, comments, and suggestions. E-commerce sites especially encourage feedback because it helps cement the relationship between the customer and the business. Customers who take the time to contact the business are also likely to return to the business's Web site.

In the next You Try It Activity, you will add a feedback form to the Contact Us page. The form will include a text area, also known as a **scroll box,** in which visitors can type specific comments to the company.

ACTIVITY 12B Adding a Feedback Form

① Open WebTee.biz in FrontPage.

② Open the Contact Us page (**contact.htm**) in Design (in FrontPage 2002, Normal) view.

③ Position the insertion point after jobs@webtee.biz and press **Enter.** Select **Insert>Form.** Click **Form** to create the Form toolbar. On the toolbar, click the **Form** button. The Submit and Reset buttons automatically appear. The dashed lines indicate the form's boundaries.

④ Select the **Submit** button. Set the pointer before the button and press **Enter** to add a line to the form. Click in this line and type Send us your comments! Format the text bold, font size 3. Press **Enter.**

⑤ Position the pointer on the line above the Submit button. Click the **Textbox** button on the Form toolbar. Double-click the text box to open the Text Box Properties dialog box.

⑥ Type Customer_Name in the Name field, Your name in the Initial value field, and 40 in the Width in characters field (see Figure 12.3). Click **OK.** The words "Your name" appear in the box. Position the insertion point after the text box. Press **Enter** to add a line to the form.

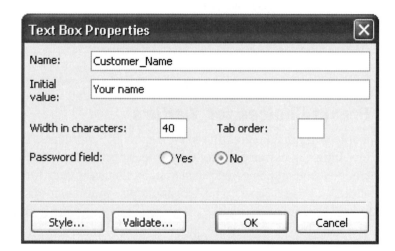

Figure 12.3
Placing text in the text box is an easy way to let visitors know what data to enter in the field.

⑦ Repeat step 5. In the dialog box, type Customer_email in the Name field, Your e-mail address in the Initial value field, and 40 in the Width in characters field. Click **OK.** Position the insertion point after the text box. Press **Enter** to add a line to the form.

⑧ Type Type your comments, ideas, and suggestions in the area below. Format the text bold, font size 2. Press **Enter.**

⑨ Click the **Text Area** button on the Form toolbar. Double-click the box to open the Text Area Box Properties dialog box. Type Feedback in the Name field. Leave the Initial value field empty. Type 60 in the Width in characters field and 5 in the Number of lines field. Click **OK.**

⑩ Select the **Submit** button at the bottom of the form and click **Center** on the Formatting toolbar. Your completed form should appear as shown in Figure 12.4. Save your work.

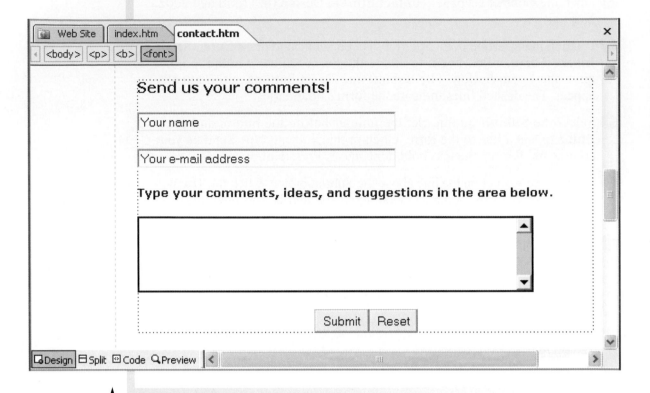

Figure 12.4
A scrolling text box allows visitors to enter more text than the box can display on the screen at one time.

Adding Preset Choices for Visitors

Some people will not take the time to type specific comments. They may, however, be willing to answer questions by selecting from a list of choices. You can include various types of response mechanisms on your forms, such as option buttons and check boxes. The decision to use option buttons or check boxes depends on whether you want visitors to select only one item or multiple items from the list of choices.

Option Buttons An **option button** gives visitors the chance to select one, and only one, choice from a list. In the next You Try It, you will add a feedback question that uses option buttons as preset choices for visitors.

YOU TRY IT

ACTIVITY 12C Adding Option Buttons

① Open the WebTee.biz site. Open the **Contact Us** page in Design (in 2002, Normal) view.

② Add a line between the text area and the Submit and Reset buttons. Make sure the insertion point is left aligned.

③ Type Choose the element of the WebTee.biz site that you like the most. (Select only one.) Format the text bold, font size 2. Press **Enter.**

④ Create the Form toolbar. Click the **Option Button** on the toolbar. Double-click on the button to open the Option Button Properties dialog box.

5 In the Group name field, type Feedback. In the Value field, type Logo. Click **Not selected** in the Initial state line. (If you click Selected in the Initial state line, that option button will appear selected when a user views your page.) The dialog box should look like Figure 12.5. Click **OK.**

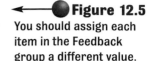
Figure 12.5
You should assign each item in the Feedback group a different value.

6 Position the insertion point after the option button and type the option text Logo. Press **Shift + Enter** to start a new line.

7 Repeat steps 4 and 5 to insert additional option buttons. Use the information in Table 12.1 to create the additional options. Format the option text bold, font size 2(10 pt).

READ ME!

Tech Tip The Group name must be the same for each option button in a series so that the user can select only one option in that group. The value of an option button is not visible to the user.

Value Names and Option Text

Group Name	Value	Option Text
Feedback	Products_page	Products page
Feedback	Feedback_form	Feedback form
Feedback	Order_form	Order form

Table 12.1
Assign each option a unique value.

8 Save your work. Your form should appear similar to Figure 12.6.

Figure 12.6
Visitors choose one of the options to give WebTee.biz feedback about the usefulness of the site.

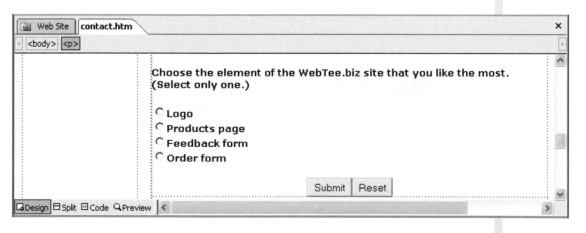

Check Boxes Using **check boxes** allows visitors to select multiple items from a list. WebTee.biz would like to gather information from visitors about ways to improve the site. Since the business wants visitors to select all items that apply, it will use check boxes rather than option buttons. In the next You Try It, you will add a question with check boxes to the feedback form.

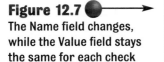

ACTIVITY 12D Adding Check Boxes

① Open the WebTee.biz Contact Us page (**contact.htm**) in Design (in 2002, Normal) view.

② Position the insertion point after the Order form option button. Press **Enter.**

③ Type What can we improve about the WebTee.biz site? (Select all that apply.) Press **Enter.**

④ Create the Form toolbar. Click the **Checkbox** button. Double-click the check box to open the Check Box Properties dialog box. In the Name field, type Order_ease. In the Value field, type ON. Click **Not checked** as the Initial state, as shown in Figure 12.7. Click **OK.**

Figure 12.7
The Name field changes, while the Value field stays the same for each check box item.

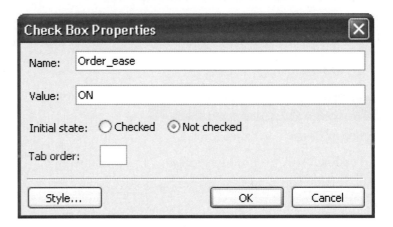

⑤ Position the insertion point after the check box and type Ease of ordering. Press **Shift + Enter** to start a new line.

⑥ Repeat steps 4 and 5 to insert additional check box items. Use the information in Table 12.2 to create the additional items. Format the check box text bold, font size 2 (10 pt).

Table 12.2
Assign each check box a unique name.

Names and Values		
Name	**Value**	**Check Box Text**
Navigation_ease	ON	Ease of navigation
Info_use	ON	Usefulness of information
Contact_us	ON	Ability to contact us

7 Save your work. Your form should look like Figure 12.8.

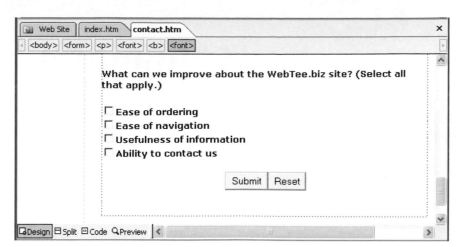

Figure 12.8
Check boxes allow visitors to select as many choices as they desire.

8 Preview the form in a browser. Test all the areas of the form. You should be able to select only one option button and as many of the check boxes as you desire. The Submit button will not work until you publish the site. However, you can use the Reset button to erase all your selections and return the form to its original state.

You have added a form to the Contact Us page that allows visitors to give you feedback. As you start gathering information from customers, you need to consider how to address privacy issues. The next section will discuss these issues, as well as site security.

Section 12.1 Assessment

Concept Check

1. **Define** feedback form, scroll box, option button, check box.

2. **Summarize** the functions of the WebTee.biz pages.

3. **Explain** the difference between option buttons and check boxes.

Critical Thinking

4. **Synthesize Information** Why might a small business choose to create a limited e-commerce site as it learns how to process electronic transactions?

5. **Make a Decision** What type of form component would work best for a business that wants to gather data about its visitor's hobbies? Explain your reasoning.

Applying Skills

Develop a Form
Expand the feedback form to ask for additional information from visitors. Determine the questions you want to ask. Then select the best type of form component to get feedback. Add the information to the WebTee.biz site in FrontPage.

Ethics & Technology

ETHICS IN THE WORKGROUP

More and more businesses are dividing their workforce into teams assigned to specific projects. To be a successful member of a workgroup, you need to understand how to share information and resolve conflicts.

Effective teamwork requires communication skills and the ability to compromise.

Sharing

Sharing ideas, or collaborating, is an important part of being a team member. Suppose you belong to a design team that must update the company's Web site. You have a great idea for a new navigation scheme. Although the idea was yours, the group should get credit for it. And if an idea is bad, the group takes responsibility for that, too.

When group members do not share their resources and ideas, the group becomes less productive. To get the most from a workgroup, each member needs to understand and appreciate the diverse skills and backgrounds of the other members. Successful workgroups combine individual talents to create a strong team.

Reaching Common Goals

It is a constant challenge to balance one's own wishes with those of the group.

For instance, imagine that you are designing the interface of a new Web site. You will look good if the new site includes a lot of graphics. The project manager, however, is worried about budget and time restrictions. The group votes to reduce the number of graphics so that the site can "go live" sooner. Although your personal interests are different from those of the group as a whole, you accept the majority vote.

Negotiating

When you negotiate, you participate with the other group members in considering different points of view. Then the group reaches a compromise that is most acceptable to the whole group.

When your own interests are at odds with the group's, you need to look at your preferences from a business perspective, not a personal one. If you can logically support your position from a business point of view, you will be in a better position to negotiate your differences with the group.

Tech Focus

1. Why is it useful to work in a team with people from diverse backgrounds? What are some benefits and problems that might occur when working out conflicts?

2. In a group, work out the purpose, audience, and elements of a Web page about a popular tourist destination. Describe the processes your group used to share information and work out conflicts.

Section 12.2 Web Site Privacy and Security

Guide to Reading

Main Ideas

E-commerce sites work to maintain the privacy of their customers. They must also try to ensure that business conducted over the Internet is secure.

Key Terms

privacy
cookie
privacy policy
security
data encryption
SSL (Secure Socket Layer)
digital certificate

Reading Strategy

Identify ways to protect privacy and ensure security. Use a table similar to the one below (also available online).

Protecting Privacy	Ensuring Security

E-commerce sites depend on the information they gather from their customers. To protect this valuable data and maintain customer trust, most e-commerce sites spend a lot of time and resources on privacy and security.

WEB SITE PRIVACY

Privacy on the Web is the ethical collection and use of visitors' personal information. Many Web sites use cookies to gather information about visitors.

Cookies

A **cookie** is a small data file that a Web site writes to your hard drive when you visit that site. Cookies contain personal information about you, such as your login or registration information and your preferences. E-commerce sites use cookies extensively. Some sites use the information they have gathered and stored in cookies to welcome customers by name and to display items similar to those the customer purchased in the past. While cookies can make buying online easier and faster, they also pose a potential privacy threat. Cookies can gather data about visitors without their knowledge, and visitors cannot control the use of this data.

Legal Protection of Privacy

Some federal and state laws regulate the information a Web site can collect. For example, the Children's Online Privacy Protection Act (COPPA) regulates the business practices of gathering personal data online from children under age 13. If a Web site knows that a visitor is under age 13, then COPPA requires that site to obtain parental consent before it collects any personal information from that young visitor. Web sites that are likely to attract young visitors must make a reasonable effort to identify the visitor's age.

Activity 12.1 Explore Web Site Privacy **Learn more cookies at webdesign.glencoe.com**.

Privacy Policies

Many Web sites, including e-commerce sites, post privacy policies (also known as privacy statements). A **privacy policy** is a written statement that outlines the information the site is collecting and explains how the organization will use that information (see Figure 12.9). A privacy policy may explain how visitors can control the amount of information they provide to the site. Most policies also describe how customers can review and correct any information the site collects.

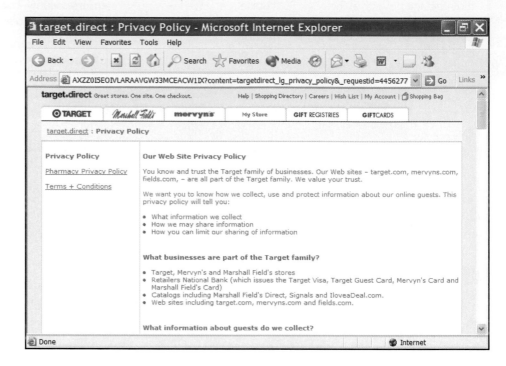

Figure 12.9
Many Web sites post privacy policies. What type of information is provided in the target.direct privacy policy?

WebTee.biz does not currently send out cookies or gather any information about its customers. However, the company wrote a privacy policy in anticipation of adding these features in the near future. In the next You Try It activity, you will add a privacy policy to the WebTee.biz site.

YOU TRY IT

Student Data File

ACTIVITY 12E Adding a Privacy Policy

1 Open the WebTee.biz site in FrontPage.

2 In the Folder List, right-click **index.htm.** On the shortcut menu, click **Copy.** Right-click an empty area of the Folder List and click **Paste.** A copy of the home page will appear.

3 Right-click the **index_copy(1).htm** file in the Folder List and click **Rename.** Rename the file privacy.htm.

4 In the Folder List, double-click **privacy.htm** to open the privacy policy page. Right-click anywhere on the page and click **Page Properties.** Under Title, change the title to Privacy Policy. Click **OK.**

5 On the **View** menu, click **Navigation.** Drag the **privacy.htm** file from the Folder List to the Navigation view window and drop it below the home page, as shown in Figure 12.10 on page 331. If necessary, right-click the box and rename it Privacy Policy.

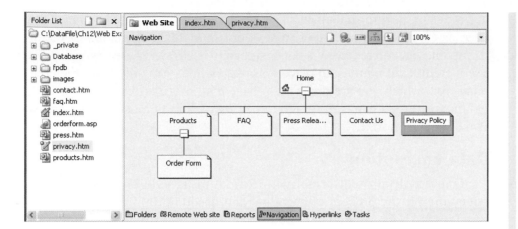

● **Figure 12.10**
The Privacy Policy page can be accessed from the Home page.

❻ Double-click the Privacy Policy box to open the privacy.htm page. Select the text in the main content area (do NOT select the logo or link bar). On the Insert menu, click **File.** Browse to the DataFile\Ch12\Text folder. In the Files of type dialog box, click the drop-down arrow and select **Word 97-2003 (*.doc).** Double-click the **privacy.doc** file to open it.

❼ Format the text to make it consistent with the font and sizes used on the home page.

❽ Proofread and spell check the text. The page should now look similar to Figure 12.11. Save the Privacy Policy page.

● **Figure 12.11**
The privacy policy outlines how WebTee.biz will use customer information.

WEB SITE SECURITY

Security is the protection of data from unauthorized access, both on the Web server and during transmission over the Web. Web businesses try to prevent intruders from stealing or altering sensitive information contained on their Web servers.

Figure 12.12
The padlock in the lower corner of the screen indicates that the site uses SSL to protect data transmitted. How does data encryption provide security to an e-commerce site?

Much of the information available on the Web is open to the public. However, as e-commerce continues to develop, an increasing amount of the information sent and received is not designed to be viewed by everyone. If you use a credit card number to place an order online, you only want the company from which you are ordering to have that information. If other people obtain your credit card information, they may use it to make purchases that you did not authorize.

Data Encryption

One way to protect sensitive information is data encryption. **Data encryption** is the process of encoding and decoding information for security. It uses an algorithm, or set of instructions, that alters the appearance of information before it is transmitted. The receiving computer then applies a decryption algorithm to restore the information to its original state.

The most commonly used data encryption method among Web site publishers is **SSL (Secure Socket Layer)**. SSL uses an encryption algorithm specifically designed to protect data transmitted across the Internet. Because SSL transmits encrypted data, it ensures that only the intended receiver with the proper decryption algorithm can read the information. E-commerce sites rely heavily on SSL to safeguard financial transactions on their sites.

Figure 12.12 shows a Web site protected by SSL. The security lock indicates that the site uses data encryption to send and receive information from its customers. As a consumer, you should look for the SSL icon before providing information that could be misused if the wrong people intercept it.

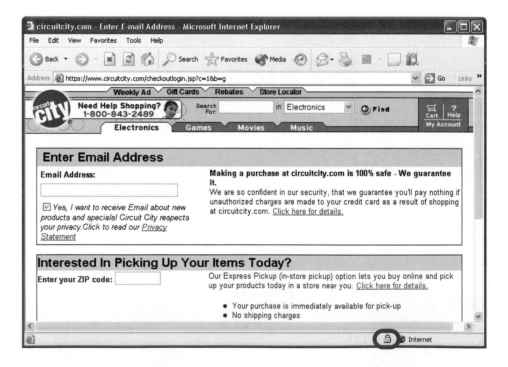

Digital Certificates

Many Web sites purchase digital certificates to ensure visitors that the site is authentic. A **digital certificate** is a document issued by an independent certification authority that confirms a business's credentials. This prevents people from stealing a company's name and using it on their own site for their own purposes. For example, the digital certificate shown in Figure 12.13 confirms that you are visiting the real circuitcity.com, and not another site that is using that name. Since the independent certification authority checks businesses thoroughly before issuing certificates, the presence of such a certificate also tells you that an online business is genuine and not fake.

Digital certificates contain encrypted data such as authorized names, the certificate serial number, expiration dates, and a copy of the certificate holder's public key (used for encrypting and decrypting messages and digital signatures). The certificate also displays the digital signature of the certificate-issuing authority. This signature helps a visitor verify that the certificate is real.

Owning a digital certificate can be an important part of a company's plan to prevent unauthorized access to its online information. Once a business has purchased a digital certificate, it is authorized to display on its Web site the logo of the company that issued the certificate. VeriSign, TRUSTe, and Thawte are examples of businesses that issue digital certificates. When a Web site displays the logo fron businesses such as these, then visitors know that the site meets security standards.

Figure 12.13
Double-clicking on the SSL padlock allows you to view a site's digital certificate. Who issued this digital certificate?

Section 12.2 Assessment

Concept Check

1. **Define** privacy, cookie, privacy policy, security, data encryption, SSL (Secure Socket Layer), digital certificate.

2. **Summarize** the difference between privacy and security.

3. **Explain** the importance of privacy policies for e-commerce sites.

Critical Thinking

4. **Analyze Information** Why is legislation such as the Children's Online Privacy Protection Act (COPPA) necessary to protect Internet users?

5. **Make Predictions** If counterfeiters found a way to forge digital certificates, what effect would this have on e-commerce?

Applying Skills

Research Digital Certificates Visit the site of a company that issues digital certificates, such as VeriSign. Make a checklist of the kinds of information that a business must provide to receive a digital certificate.

THE TALKING WEB

Developers are working on new voice-recognition technology that will make it possible to access the Internet through your phone.

In the future, you may be able to call your favorite Web site no matter where you are.

No Mouse Needed

The "talking Web" will allow users to enter data and select options with their voice and listen to output through a speaker. Eventually, voice-enabled Web sites will be accessible by phone, PDAs, and computers with microphones and speakers.

The Talking Web's Potential

Speech-recognition technology will enable businesses to deliver information to employees and customers more efficiently. For example, off-site workers will be able to send e-mail and complete transactions through a cell phone.

Voice-enabled Web sites can make the Web's content more accessible to people who have trouble seeing or using standard input and output devices.

Programming the Talking Web

Two important technologies are being developed to make the Internet voice- and phone-enabled:

- ◆ **Voice Extensible Markup Language (VoiceXML or VXML)** is a new computer markup language for creating voice-enabled Web content. It supports input by voice or phone keypad. Output is prerecorded audio or synthesized speech.
- ◆ **Speech Application Language Tags (SALT)** will be used with current markup languages such as HTML and XML. These tags will provide multimodal access, which means that users can interact with the Web in a variety of ways. Users can enter information through voice, keyboard, mouse, or phone keypad. They may receive output as text, video, audio, or synthesized speech.

Both VXML and SALT specifications have been submitted to the World Wide Web Consortium (W3C) as part of a larger initiative called the Speech Interface Framework.

Tech Focus

1. Why are researchers interested in creating a "talking" Web? What social or economic effects might it have? How will it affect Web site development?

2. Use the Internet to find ways that voice-enabled Web technologies may be used in the future. Write a short paper describing at least two possible applications for this technology.

SECTION 12.1 Examining an E-commerce Web Site

Key Terms

feedback form, 322
scroll box, 322
option button, 324
check box, 326

Main Ideas

- WebTee.biz is a B2C e-commerce site that sells tee shirts to consumers.
- WebTee.biz targets young customers between 15 and 25, as well as coaches, human resource managers, and event planners.
- Some e-commerce sites mainly exist to provide an online presence for the company and to showcase that company's products.
- Many e-commerce sites expand from accepting online orders to processing electronic payments.
- Feedback forms enable visitors to communicate comments, ideas, and suggestions to the site owner.
- Forms provide various ways for visitors to respond, including scroll boxes, text boxes, option buttons, and check boxes.
- Option buttons and check boxes are preset lists of choices from which visitors may select.
- Option buttons allow visitors to choose only one of the options listed.
- Check boxes allow visitors to select as many choices from the list as they desire.

SECTION 12.2 Web Site Privacy and Security

Key Terms

privacy, 329
cookie, 329
privacy policy, 330
security, 331
data encryption, 332
SSL (Secure Socket Layer), 332
digital certificate, 332

Main Ideas

- Privacy is the ethical collection and handling of personal information by a Web site.
- Many Web sites use cookies to gather and store information about their visitors.
- Legislation regulates the information that sites can gather about young consumers.
- A privacy policy describes the information the site gathers and the way the site owner will use it.
- Security is the protection of data from unauthorized access, both on the Web server and during transmission over the Web.
- Data encryption alters the appearance of information before transmission so that only the intended receiver with the proper decryption program can restore it to readable form.
- SSL is a commonly used data encryption method.
- Digital certificates confirm the validity of online businesses.

Reviewing Key Terms

1. What purpose does a feedback form serve on an e-commerce site?
2. Rewrite this statement to make it true: *Option buttons allow visitors to select as many choices from a list as they desire.*
3. What is the name of a small data file that a Web site writes to a person's hard drive when he or she visits the site?
4. What is the most commonly used data encryption method among Web site publishers?
5. What does a digital certificate tell a visitor about a Web site?

Understanding Main Ideas

6. **Summarize** the functions that give the Web-Tee business an online presence.
7. **Distinguish** between a text box and a text area.
8. **Identify** how the WebTee.biz site sells products to customers online.
9. **Evaluate** how cookies can present a potential security concern.
10. **Explain** why the of privacy of Web site visitors under the age of 13 is protected.
11. **Identify** the types of information that are typically included in a Web site's privacy policy.
12. **Analyze** the reasons why solid Web site security is important for e-commerce businesses.
13. **Explain** how data encryption helps ensure Web site security.

Critical Thinking

14. **Make Recommendations** You are on a Web site development team that is developing an e-commerce site for your employer. The business sells custom-designed calendars to individuals and businesses. In addition to the Home page, what pages would you recommend for this site? Explain your reasoning.
15. **Evaluate Information** The marketing director at a business would like to get feedback from site visitors. Identify what type of form features you would use to gather information about the following: visitor's name, visitor's e-mail address, visitor's age range, products used (assume the company sells six different products), products about which more information is desired, and suggestions for product improvements.
16. **Compare and Contrast** How are Web site privacy and security different? How do they work together to give visitors to e-commerce site confidence to make online purchases?
17. **Make Predictions** As the amount of business conducted online continues to increase, how important will Web site privacy and security issues be in the future?
18. **Evaluate Content** Rewrite the WebTee.biz home page to make it even more online friendly.

e-Review
webdesign.glencoe.com

Study with PowerPoint
To review the main points in this chapter, select **e-Review** > **PowerPoint Outlines** > **Chapter 12.**

Online Self Check
Test your knowledge of the material in this chapter by selecting **e-Review** > **Self Checks** > **Chapter 12.**

Making Connections

Social Studies—Take Part in a Debate Find three examples of American companies that use the Internet to do business globally. Research the following questions:

◆ How have these companies benefited from the Internet?
◆ What economic impact do they have on the countries where they operate?
◆ What impact do they have on the U.S. economy?

Use the information you find to argue for or against the following statement: The Internet has made it possible for international companies to improve the lives of people in developing countries.

STANDARDS AT WORK

Students use technology to locate, evaluate, and collect information from a variety of sources. (NETS-S 5)

Evaluate Home Pages

Select three different e-commerce Web sites in one of the following industries: clothing, entertainment, computer equipment, or travel. Evaluate the home pages of each company. Rate each company's home page based on the following factors:

1. Ease of navigating to product and service information
2. Ease of locating contact information
3. Prominence of special offers
4. Attractiveness of home page

Rate each home page as poor, good, or excellent. Create a chart that contains each home page's URL, its rating, and your explanation for why it received this rating.

TEAMWORK SKILLS

Plan a Web Site

A local CD store wants to redo its Web site. The existing site has a random navigation structure. In researching the site's needs, the team learns that people are most likely to search for CDs in one of three ways: by artist, by CD title, or by musical category.

The store's owner wants to further update the Web site by including a space where customers can rate CDs and submit requests for hard to find items. The store owner also wants to build a list of contacts and to get feedback on the company's products.

Divide the team into two groups:

■ One group should revise the Web site's navigation structure. Research other Web sites that sell CDs to see how they structure their sites.
■ The other group should determine what additional features need to be added to the site. Research other Web sites that sell CDs to see what features they offer.

As a team, create a storyboard for the revised site. The storyboard should reflect both the store owner's goals and the team's research.

CHALLENGE YOURSELF

Research Web Site Security

The local florist has an e-commerce site. The florist would like to add a digital certificate to the site to ensure protection for its customer order form and e-mail. The florist has asked you to research how the digital certificate would work, and how to obtain a demonstration version to try out the process.

Find a company that offers a free download version for personal use. With your teacher's permission, download the demonstration to see how it works. Based on your research, recommend a digital certificate company to the florist. Explain the reasoning behind your recommendation.

YOU TRY IT

Skills Studio

These exercises reinforce the skills you learned in this chapter's You Try It activities. Refer back to the You Try It activities if you need extra guidance.

1. Creating an Order Form

You design and produce mouse pads. Create an order form for your Web site's Products page.

A Create a new Web site in FrontPage. Select a theme that you would like to use for your company.

B Create an order form that looks similar to the one to the right.

C Save your page.

D Preview the page in a browser and test to see that the form works as intended. Make changes as needed.

Mouse Pad Order Form

Contact Information

Name:
Address:
City:
State:
Zip:
E-Mail Address:

Order Information

Style: ○ 9 x 12 rectangle
          ○ 9 x 12 oval

Color: select ▾

Quantity:

Text on Pads:

Submit Reset

2. Adding a Privacy Policy

Add a privacy policy to your mouse pad Web site.

A Locate several privacy policies at e-commerce sites on the Web. Identify the key elements to include in a privacy policy.

B Create a Privacy Policy page. Copy the WebTee.biz Privacy Policy page and paste the page into the Web site you created in You Try It 1.

C Apply the theme you selected to the page.

D Update the content as needed to reflect the mouse pad company.

E Add a link to the order form page that you created in the previous You Try It that directs visitors to the privacy policy.

F Save your work.

G Preview your work in a browser. Test the link to the Privacy Policy page.

Web Design Projects

1. Create a Feedback Form

Outdoor Excursions, which sells camping equipment, has teamed up with a travel agency to offer exciting camping adventures for families. During the initial planning phase of this venture, Outdoor Excursions wants to build its customer list and to get feedback about the type of trips people most want to take.

Create a feedback form in FrontPage. This form is meant to gather relevant contact information, to find out what trips will be most popular, and to help the companies determine the length for the trips. Possible trips are listed in the table below.

Possible Camping Trips

DOMESTIC TRIPS	INTERNATIONAL TRIPS
Badlands National Park	Argentina Tour
Cape Cod National Seashore	Australia Tour
Everglades National Park	Kenya Tour
Grand Canyon National Park	Brazil Tour
Hawaii Volcanoes National Park	Canada Tour
Indiana Dunes National Lakeshore	Germany Tour

2. Plan a Web Site with Feedback

You are a member of a band called *The Speckled Band*. The band's flyer reads: "We play live music for parties, weddings, and other events. If cost is an issue, we also offer a one person DJ service. You choose the type of music you want played. We work in 2-hour time blocks at $250 per hour, plus travel costs. To schedule your event, contact us at 555-5555."

The band wants to develop a Web site that provides information about its services and gathers feedback about the range of services it should offer. Create a new site in FrontPage for the band. The site will have only two pages at this time: the home page and a feedback page. Use the information provided in the flyer to create the home page.

For the feedback page, write 10 short "what we do" sentences that describe services the band does or could offer. Create a feedback form asking each visitor to rate these 10 sentences as extremely interested, very interested, neutral interest, little interest, or no interest. Use option buttons for each of the five ratings. Add basic contact information to the form and a text area for additional feedback.

Adding Web Site Functionality

WHY IT MATTERS.....................................

When selling a house, realtors emphasize the house's best features. These features transform a basic structure into a house that people want to live in. Adding features can also turn a basic Web site into something much more interesting and useful. Guest books, search capabilities, databases, and other features help visitors interact with the site while also collecting useful information for site owners.

Quick Write Activity

Books, such as textbooks, include features that make them more user-friendly. For example, an index helps you locate topics that you want to find. What other features increase a book's usability? What features do Web sites have to make them more user-friendly? How do these features compare to those found in books?

WHAT YOU WILL DO..

ACTIVITIES AND PROJECTS

Applying Skills

You Try It Activities

Chapter Assessment

You Try It Skills Studio

Web Design Projects

IN THE WORKBOOK

Optional Activities and Projects

Guided Reading
Web Design Projects

ON THE WEB

Activities at webdesign.glencoe.com

Go Online Activities
Study with PowerPoint
Self-Check Assessments

READ TO SUCCEED

Organize Information
If you were told to remember the names of everyone in your class on the first day, you would probably find the task difficult. However, what if you grouped people in ways that made it easier? You could remember the names of one row at a time. Grouping information also helps when you have to remember material that you have read. When you take notes, think about how topics relate to each other. Organizing them as a group makes them easier to remember.

Section 13.1 Tracking Visitors to a Site

Guide to Reading

Main Ideas

Hit counters and tracking software track the number of visitors to a Web site. Guest books allow visitors to make comments on the site in a public forum.

Key Terms

hit counter
hits
tracking software
guest book

Reading Strategy

Identify the information provided by hit counters and tracking software. Use a table like the one below (also available online).

Information Provided by Hit Counters	Information Provided by Tracking Software

Organizations that conduct business online need ways to measure the success of their efforts. For e-commerce sites, the total amount sold online is a good indicator of success. However, organizations can measure their site's effectiveness in other ways as well.

HIT COUNTERS

Web developers often use dynamic components to keep track of Web site traffic. One such component, called a **hit counter,** records the number of times visitors have accessed a Web page. A hit counter records the number of **hits,** or number of times browsers request a file from the Web server. The counter number increases by 1 each time someone visits the page.

E-commerce sites often include hit counters to help track Web traffic. Web developers may incorporate either public or hidden hit counters on any page of the Web site. Pages with public hit counters show the hit tally to anyone who views the page. Hidden hit counters, on the other hand, show the hit tally only to people with access to the site's private data, such as the Webmaster or Web site administrator.

YOU TRY IT

ACTIVITY 13A Adding a Hit Counter

1 Using FrontPage, open the WebTee.biz page **index.htm** in Design (in FrontPage 2002, Normal) view.

2 Position the insertion point after the last sentence on the home page ("No questions asked!"). Press **Enter.**

3 Click the **Style** drop-down arrow on the Formatting toolbar and click **Normal.** Click the **Center** button. Type You are visitor. Press **Enter.**

4 Select **Insert** and click **Web Component.** In the Insert Web Component dialog box, select **Hit Counter.**

 webdesign.glencoe.com

⑤ From the Choose a counter style box, select the second counter style, as shown in Figure 13.1. Click **Finish.**

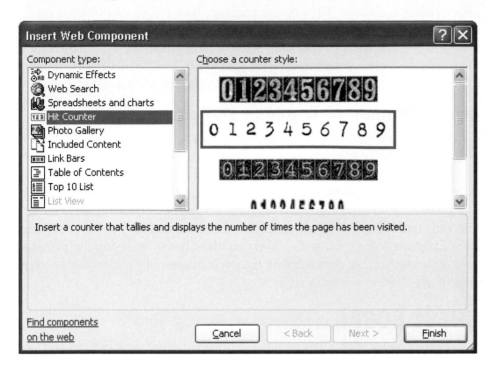

Figure 13.1
The hit counter will display the number of times the Web page has been visited.

⑥ In the Hit Counter Properties dialog box, select **Fixed number of digits.** Type 5. Click **OK.** FrontPage inserts a hit counter.

⑦ Your page should resemble Figure 13.2. Instead of numbers, you may see the words [Hit Counter]. Because the hit counter is a Web component, it will work only after you publish the site later in this section. Save your work and close the Web site.

Figure 13.2
You have added a hit counter to the WebTee.biz home page.

Activity 13.1 Explore Tracking Software Learn more about tracking software at webdesign.glencoe.com.

Hit Counter Limitations

Although hit counters are a convenient way to measure Web traffic, their effectiveness is limited. They do not measure how long a visitor stays on the site, whether he or she visits other site pages, or if this visitor has previously accessed the site. Also, people who use search engines often jump directly to the page that contains the information they want. This visit will not count as a hit unless a hit counter exists on the exact page the visitor downloads.

Other Methods of Tracking Visitors

Many sites, especially e-commerce sites, need more information about visitors than a hit counter can provide. **Tracking software** will help you learn more about the visitors to your site. Often available for free, tracking software records information such as what country visitors are from, how they navigated to your site, and what browser they used. Tracking software can thus help individuals and companies decide where and how to advertise their sites. Tracking software can also help you identify the most popular pages on your Web site. You can then improve the site's structure by making these pages readily available in the site's navigation.

GUEST BOOKS

A **guest book** gives visitors a place to record their experiences with the Web site. Unlike a feedback form, a guest book is a public record of comments made by the site's visitors. Many guest books gather visitors' names, e-mail addresses, and comments. This information is then stored in a log file that other visitors can read.

READ ME!

Caution Given privacy concerns, you should be careful about including your e-mail address in public areas, such as guest book log files.

YOU TRY IT

ACTIVITY 13B Creating a Guest Book

❶ Open the WebTee.biz Web site in FrontPage.

❷ Select **File** and click **New** (in FrontPage 2002, **New > Page or Web**). Click **More page templates** (in 2002, **Page Templates**) in the New task pane.

❸ In the Page Templates dialog box, select **Guest Book.** Click **OK.**

❹ Delete the comment placeholder text from the top of the guest book page. Delete the placeholder text above the comment box and type How do you like our Web site? Please sign our public guest book so we can share your thoughts with other visitors. (Return to the Contact Us page.) Format the text Verdana, 3(12 pt), black.

❺ Select the text **Contact Us.** Click the **Insert Hyperlink** button. Type contact.htm in the Address box and click **OK.**

❻ Save the page. Name the page guestbook.htm.

❼ Choose **View > Navigation.** Drag **guestbook.htm** from the Folder List and place it under the Contact Us page.

❽ Open the **contact.htm** page. Click under the Submit/Reset buttons. Type Please sign our guest book. Format the text Verdana, 2(10pt), bold. Select the text **guest book** and click the **Insert Hyperlink** button. Type guestbook.htm in the address box and click **OK.** Close the page.

9 Return to the **guestbook.htm** page. The page should look like Figure 13.3. Save your work. Preview the page and test the guest book link. Close the Web site.

Figure 13.3
Other visitors to the site can view all comments added to the guest book.

The comment at the top of the guest book template communicates the purpose of the page. Whether you remove this comment or not, it will not appear when you publish the Web site. Note that you can also add form fields to the guest book template, such as a text box for visitors to enter their names or other necessary information.

Section 13.1 Assessment

Concept Check

1. **Define** hit counter, hits, tracking software, guest book.

2. **Summarize** the advantages of using tracking systems to learn about the visitors to a Web site.

3. **Explain** the difference between a feedback form and a guest book.

Critical Thinking

4. **Draw Conclusions** What information can a tracking system provide to help you decide where to place banner ads?

5. **Make Decisions** You are the Webmaster for a teen entertainment site. Should you include text boxes for name and e-mail address in the guest book?

Applying Skills

Explore Tracking Software Conduct Internet research to locate a tracking software application. Search the site to learn what information the tracking software will gather. Categorize the information in list form.

WHAT MAKES A LEADER?

You may not plan to become a manager or the president of a company. Yet, the skills these leaders use are the same skills that would help you on and off the job.

Effective leaders communicate well and understand the value of their co-workers.

Qualities of a Leader

Effective leaders share certain characteristics:

◆ **Communication Skills** Good managers are diplomatic but straightforward when giving directions, offering help, and making evaluations.

◆ **Decision-Making Skills** Managers have to make decisions, and their choices may not always be popular. Decision-making is easier when you learn as much as possible about the organization, its mission, and its resources.

◆ **Trustworthiness** Managing people means motivating and directing them. For this to happen, people must believe they can trust you. Good leaders deliver on promises, keep confidences, and act honestly.

◆ **Accountability** A manager may have to justify decisions, accept responsibility for the outcomes of those decisions, and explain failures. Good leaders accept responsibility without blaming others and give credit to those who deserve it.

◆ **Relationship Skills** Good leaders learn as much as they can about the responsibilities of others. This helps them develop personal connections to colleagues and give appropriate instructions and feedback.

Building Leadership Skills

You can do many things to build leadership qualities. Get involved in classroom or community projects and activities. Find opportunities to practice the skills described in this article. Make a point of taking business, communications, and management courses. These studies will give you insights into business leadership.

Many organizations can help you develop leadership skills. Consider joining a local chapter of the Business Professionals of America and Future Business Leaders of America.

Tech Focus

1. Identify someone who is a good leader. Make a list of that person's leadership qualities. Use the list to identify and assess your own decision-making and leadership skills. Why are these skills valuable?

2. Form a team. Each team member will take a turn as the leader and must direct and motivate other members to do specific tasks, as directed by your instructor. Assess each person's leadership skills.

Main Ideas

Web developers uses tools such as site maps, tables of contents, and bookmarks to help visitors locate information on the site. Site search components enable visitors to find specific words or phrases on the site.

Key Terms

site map
table of contents
frequently asked
  questions (FAQ)
bookmark
search capabilities

Reading Strategy

Identify four ways to make information easy to find on a Web site. Use a web diagram like the one below (also available online).

Ways to Make Information Easy to Find

The Web sites you have created in this text do not have many pages. Visitors to these sites will be able to locate the information they need by simply clicking the links on the link bar. However, Web sites that contain hundreds or thousands of pages often add features that make information easier for visitors to locate. Such features include site maps, tables of contents, frequently asked questions pages, and search capabilities.

READ ME!

Jargon A link bar is often called a table of contents because it provides an overview of the site's content.

SITE MAPS AND TABLES OF CONTENTS

A **site map** organizes a Web site's pages into logical categories. Visitors can target their search by identifying the categories that may contain the information they need. The Web developer must carefully consider how to organize the pages so the groupings make sense to visitors. FrontPage includes a Web component to help developers create site maps.

A **table of contents** on a Web site functions in much the same way as a table of contents in a book. It allows visitors to see the contents and organization of the site in one glance. As shown in Figure 13.4, a table of contents generally lists each main page on the site. Lists of subpages then appear beneath these main pages. The subpage lists are indented so visitors can quickly see the page's level on the site's hierarchy. When you use the Web component to create a table of contents, FrontPage embeds hyperlinks to each item in the table. This makes it easy for visitors to jump quickly to the page that they want to see.

● **Figure 13.4**
Each item in the table of contents links to a page on the Web site. **Why is a table of contents a good way to access books published online?**

FREQUENTLY ASKED QUESTIONS PAGES

A **frequently asked questions (FAQ)** page answers common questions that visitors are likely to have about the site. The WebTee.biz site includes an FAQ page that answers questions about the company's custom design process.

Many FAQ pages include bookmarks. A **bookmark** is a hyperlink to another document or to a specific place within a document. When clicked, the bookmark transports visitors to the marked location. Intrapage bookmarks are useful when you have long pages that are divided into logical sections, or when you want to jump from a central list of links to multiple locations on the page. When used on an FAQ page, bookmarks allow visitors to immediately see the answer when they click a question at the top of the page. In the next activity, you will add bookmarks to the WebTee.biz FAQ page.

YOU TRY IT

ACTIVITY 13C Adding Bookmarks

❶ Open the WebTee.biz **faq.htm** page in FrontPage. Switch to **Page** view (select **View > Page**), if necessary.

❷ Place the insertion point at the end of the Frequently Asked Questions heading and press **Enter.**

❸ Copy and paste each of the four questions from the page. Format them as a bulleted list, as shown in Figure 13.5.

Figure 13.5
Each question in the list will link to a bookmark.

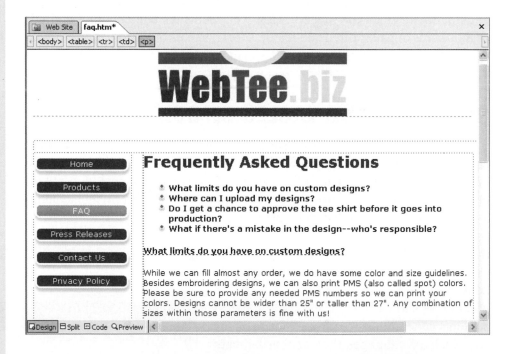

❹ Highlight the text **What limits do you have on custom designs?** (highlight the question in the page, NOT the question in the bulleted list). Select **Insert,** and click **Bookmark.** In the Bookmark name box, type limits in the box and click **OK.** FrontPage inserts a dotted line under the text with the new bookmark (see Figure 13.5).

⑤ Repeat step 4 to create bookmarks for the three remaining questions on the page. Use the names in Table 13.1 as the bookmark names.

FAQ Bookmarks

Question	Bookmark Name
What limits do you have on custom designs?	limits
Where can I upload my designs?	upload
Do I get a chance to approve the tee shirt before it goes into production?	approve
What if there's a mistake in the design—who's responsible?	responsible

←● Table 13.1
Make your bookmark names logical and unique.

⑥ Highlight the first question in the bulleted list. Select **Insert** and click **Hyperlink.** In the Insert Hyperlink dialog box, click **Place in This Document** in the Link to box. In the screen that opens, select **limits,** as shown in Figure 13.6. Click **OK.**

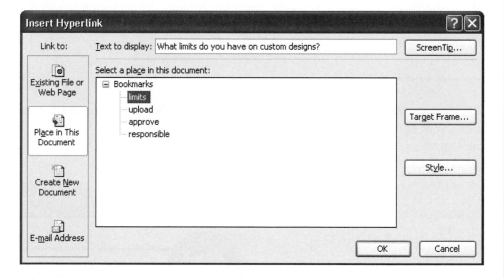

←● Figure 13.6
The hyperlink connects the question at the top of the page to the answer.

⑦ Repeat step 6 for the other three questions in the bulleted list. Make sure each question links to the bookmark name you assigned it in step 5.

⑧ Save your work. Test the bookmarks in a Web browser.

SEARCH CAPABILITIES

Site maps, tables of contents, and bookmarks are tools Web developers use to make the information on a site easy for visitors to find. If they think visitors will want to search for a particular word or phrase on the site, then they will add **search capabilities** to the site. In the next activity, you will add search capabilities to the WebTee.biz site.

ACTIVITY 13D Creating a Web Search Form

1 Open the WebTee.biz **index.htm** page in FrontPage.

2 Place the insertion point at the end of the hit counter and press **Enter.**

3 Select **Insert** and click **Web Component.** In the Insert Web Component dialog box, select **Web Search.**

4 Choose **Current Web** in the Choose a type of search box. Click **Finish.** In the Search Form Properties dialog box, click **OK** to accept the default choices. FrontPage inserts the Web search box on to the WebTee.biz home page (see Figure 13.7). Save your work.

Figure 13.7
The Web search box allows visitors to search the site for particular words or phrases.

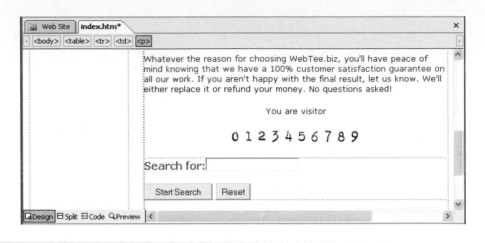

Visitors can use this box to search for words or phrases on the site. Since it is a Web component, this capability becomes active only after you publish the site to a server with FrontPage server extensions.

Section 13.2 Assessment

Concept Check

1. Define site map, table of contents, frequently asked questions (FAQ), bookmark, search capabilities.

2. Explain why it is useful to include a site map and table of contents on a large Web site.

3. Summarize why Web sites post frequently asked questions pages.

Critical Thinking

4. Analyze What types of information should be easy to locate on an e-commerce site? Explain your reasoning.

5. Evaluate Identity two Web sites in which you have used a search form. Explain how this search feature helped you locate information on the site.

Applying Skills

Identify Search Features Visit the Web site of your local newspaper or the site of an "e-zine" that you like to read. Explore the site to learn which of the features described in this section are available. Use each available feature and write a sentence describing the results.

Guide to Reading

Main Ideas

Databases organize information by fields and records. Dynamic Web pages use database information. Database interface pages display database information so that it looks consistent with the Web site's design.

Key Terms

database
record
database driven
database interface page

Reading Strategy

Identify the two main purposes for connecting a database to a Web site. Use a diagram like the one below (also available online).

Purposes for Connecting to a Database

When visitors place online orders or provide feedback, the company must have a way to collect, organize, and store this information. Many companies use databases to maintain the information received through their Web site.

CONNECTING WEB SITES AND DATABASES

A **database** is a collection of information, organized for easy retrieval. Databases are organized by fields and records. A field is one piece of information, such as a first name or last name. A **record** is a group of related fields that contain the information gathered about a particular person or item. For example, the WebTee.biz database record used for information about the long-sleeve tee shirt includes fields for item number, color, size, and price.

There are two main reasons for connecting a Web site to a database:

◆ To allow visitors to access information directly from the database
◆ To provide a way to collect information from visitors and add it to the database

Static Versus Dynamic Pages

Web site developers often use the terms "static" and "dynamic" to distinguish between pages that contain fixed information and those capable of change. On a static page, the information is embedded in the HTML code that makes up the page. It cannot change without changing the code.

Dynamic pages, on the other hand, are shells that contain changing information. The information that changes comes from an external source. When the external source is a database, the Web site is said to be **database driven.** FrontPage provides the Database Interface Wizard to help you create database-driven forms and perform other database-related tasks. Although the database information comes from an external source, you can format the information displayed in these forms to maintain the look and feel of your site.

GO *Online*

Activity 13.2 Explore Databases **Learn more about databases at webdesign.glencoe.com.**

Setting Up a Database Connection

You can link your FrontPage-based Web site to databases created with a variety of applications, such as Microsoft Access and Microsoft SQL Server. You can store the database on the Web server, on a separate file server, or on a separate database server. Because of this flexibility, it is simple to move information from one location to another without your Web site's visitors being aware that anything has changed.

INTERACTING WITH A DATABASE

You must publish the database with your Web site to enable visitors to access its information. (Some companies place the database in the Web site's folder, while others keep it in a separate folder.) Once you make the database accessible, you can create your Web pages to either display information from the connected database or to request information from visitors that is then stored in the database.

Order Forms

A **database interface page** is a Web page that connects to and interacts with a database. An order form is a database interface page that allows visitors to send order information to a database.

An order form must be saved as an active server page (.asp) before it can interact with the database. The order form page (orderform.asp) in the WebTee.biz Web site contains a form that interacts with the orderform.mdb database. Customers fill out this form to place orders (see Figure 13.8).

Figure 13.8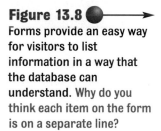

Forms provide an easy way for visitors to list information in a way that the database can understand. Why do you think each item on the form is on a separate line?

The WebTee.biz site must be connected to a database before visitors can submit their orders. In the next activity, you will confirm that a connection exists between the order form file (orderform.asp) and the WebTee database (orderform.mdb).

ACTIVITY 13E Confirming a Database Connection

❶ Open the WebTee.biz site in FrontPage. Open the **Folder List.**

❷ From the Folder List, double-click the **orderform.asp** page to open it in Design (in 2002, Normal) view. Right-click the form and select **Form Properties.** The Form Properties dialog box appears.

❸ Click the **Options** button. Select **orderform** in the Database Connection to Use field, as shown in Figure 13.9.

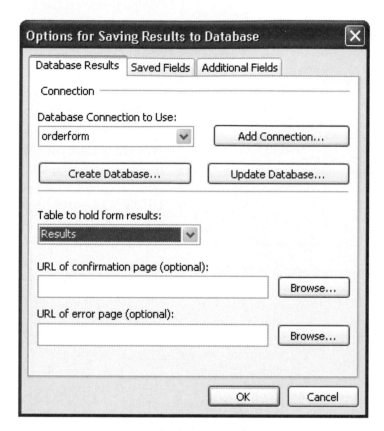

Figure 13.9
You can use the Database Connection to Use field to select the database you want to connect to.

❹ Click **OK** twice. If you do not receive an error message, then the connection from the orderform.asp page to the database is confirmed.

❺ Open the **products.htm** page. Click on an order link. The link should send you to the orderform.asp page.

As shown in Figure 13.9, when you select the orderform database in Step 3, the word "Results" appears in the "Table to hold form results" field. This indicates that a table named "Results" will store the data obtained from the orderform.asp page. When a customer completes the order form and clicks the Submit button, the order goes to the orderform database on the server. Each field on the form connects to a field in the database. The database stores the entire customer order as a new record.

You cannot test the order form at this time. In Chapter 14, you will publish the site to a server. If this server has FrontPage Server Extensions, you will be able to test the functionality of the order form.

Results Pages

Another type of database interface page is a results page. A results page records orders that have been placed. While order forms submit information to a database, results pages extract information from a database for use by the database's owner. Figure 13.10 shows a sample WebTee.biz results page.

While the orderform.asp page on the WebTee.biz site is public and open to visitors, the company set up the results page as a private page. Only qualified WebTee.biz personnel can view this page.

Restricting access to the results page helps to keep personal customer information private. People who work at WebTee.biz use this information for different purposes. Some purposes are immediate, such as fulfilling and shipping customer orders. Other purposes are longer term, such as analyzing what cities and states orders come from and tracking repeat customers.

Order Results Page

first_name	last_name	address1	address2	city	state	zip	phone	email
Tom	Smith	1111 Smith Drive		Smithville	CA	00000	512-000-0000	tsmith@smithvill
Tim	Jones	1111 Jones Way		Jonesville	JA	00000	555-000-1111	tjones@jonesvill

Thanks for visiting WebTee.biz   Last Updated: Monday November 29, 2004

Section 13.3 Assessment

Concept Check

1. **Define** database, record, database driven, database interface page.

2. **Summarize** the reasons that companies connect databases to Web sites.

3. **Explain** the difference between a public database interface page and a private database interface page.

Critical Thinking

4. **Analyze** Why are databases a convenient way to organize data such as customers' names, addresses, and items ordered?

5. **Draw Conclusions** Why do you think it is important to design database interface pages with the same look and feel as the rest of the Web site?

Applying Skills

Plan a Database You work for a company that plans to sell two clothing products online. Look at several catalogs and note the product information they contain. Based on this information, list the fields needed for the database that will collect information for clothing orders placed online.

Real World Technology

ACCESSIBILITY ON THE WEB

Web sites often include elements that can limit their usability for many people.

Operating systems such as Windows provide tools that make computers more accessible.

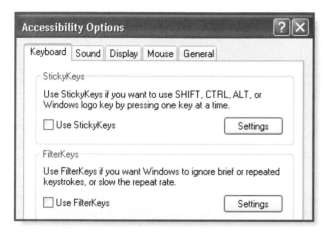

Designing for Different Needs

When the Web first became popular, many developers did not think visually impaired people would use it much. Nor did they consider that flashy visual elements would make downloading difficult for users with older technology. Yet these individuals make up an important part of the online market.

People may not be able to access the information on a Web site for many reasons:

◆ Physical disabilities that prevent users from seeing, hearing, or understanding the graphic or audio elements on the screen
◆ Limited movement that restricts use of input devices
◆ Poor language or technology skills
◆ Old technology, such as out-of-date software, text-only screens, or slow Internet connections
◆ Environments that make it difficult for people to see, hear, or use their hands when using a computer

Accessibility Guidelines

Successful Web sites allow all visitors to get the information they want quickly and easily. The World Wide Web Consortium (W3C) and Section 508 of the United States Rehabilitation Act provide accessibility guidelines to help Web designers create accessible sites. Some guidelines include:

◆ **Text Options** Always provide text versions of graphics or audio, including navigation buttons. For example, if clicking a photo of chili displays a recipe, then the text version might read "Recipe for making chili."
◆ **Cascading Style Sheets (CSS)** Pages designed with CSS allow users to easily change settings, such as colors, text size, etc.
◆ **Multiple Technologies** Web sites should be accessible to individuals using any major browser as well as older technologies.

Always check your pages to make sure users can understand them with graphics or colors turned off. That way you can make sure that all users have a satisfying visit to your site.

Tech Focus

1. Find out what accessibility tools are available on your word processor, operating system, or authoring software. Make a chart listing at least five tools, the disabilities they address, their functions, and how to activate them.

2. Learn more about the accessibility guidelines issued by the W3C or Section 508 of the Rehabilitation Act. Create a checklist to make your site accessible to everyone.

Section 13.4 Frames

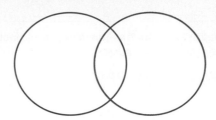
The WebTee.biz site currently uses shared borders.

◆ The top border contains the company's logo.
◆ The left border contains the link bar.
◆ The bottom border contains copyright and date information.

Some sites use frames in place of shared borders. A **frame** is a separate region on a Web page that contains its own Web document. With shared borders, everything on a Web page scrolls together. With frames, different parts of the screen can scroll independently.

Figure 13.11
Each frame has its own scroll bar. What will happen to the right frame when a visitor scrolls the left frame?

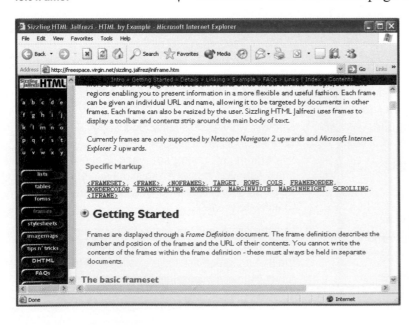

HOW FRAMES WORK

You make a frames page by first creating a single shell page called a **frameset.** This container page includes information about the size and placement of all the separate frames that exist within that single Web page. Many frames pages contain two separate frames—one for navigation, and one for content.

Frames are designed to make navigation easier by keeping part of a site constant. For example, many frame sites place the link bar in a frame on the left side of the page. When a visitor selects any item on the link bar, the frame on the right displays the selected page. The link bar frame itself, however, remains unchanged.

When a visitor to the site shown in Figure 13.11 selects "frames" in the link bar, the page about frames appears in the content frame on the right side of the screen. When the visitor selects "forms," the content page changes and presents information about forms, but the link bar remains the same. As the visitor scrolls through the content page in the right frame, the link bar remains visible on the screen.

GUIDELINES FOR FRAMES PAGES

While useful, frames pages can also cause problems for some viewers. Following certain guidelines will help make your frames pages more user-friendly.

Size Guidelines

In theory, you can create an unlimited number of frames on a page. However, dividing the pages into many small segments can confuse visitors. As you design your site, you should consider the number, placement, and size of the frames.

- ◆ On a site that contains a left and right frame, the Web designer usually defines the pixel width of the left frame. The right frame takes up the remaining space on the page. It is best not to define the pixel width of the right frame since monitor sizes and resolution vary.
- ◆ On a site that contains a top and bottom frame, the designer assigns a pixel width to the top frame. The bottom frame then fills the remaining space on the page.

Usability Guidelines

Many older browsers do not support frames. When creating a frames-based site, be sure to consider your target audience. If this audience mainly uses older browsers, you may not want to create a site with frames.

Frames can also make a site more difficult to navigate for visitors with accessibility issues. People with sight limitations, for example, use devices called screen readers that read aloud the contents of Web pages. These devices have difficulty making sense of pages with frames. For frames to meet the requirements of the Americans with Disabilities Act, you must assign each frame a logical title. You may also choose to reproduce each frames page as a non-frames page to increase your site's accessibility.

FRAMES PAGES AND FRONTPAGE

It is easy to create a frames page using FrontPage. For instance, you can select one of the many FrontPage templates that use frames.

Creating a Frames-Based Page

The Page Templates dialog box contains a Frames Pages tab. This tab displays the templates available to create a frames-based Web site. As shown in Figure 13.12 (shown on the next page), you can preview the layout and number of frames contained in the template's frameset by looking at the lower right corner of the Frames Pages tab.

TECH TRIVIA

Creating Accessible Web Sites It is important to design Web pages so that they are accessible to everyone. An accessible site does not have to be only text. An accessible site is a site that is flexible—a site that offers users different ways of accessing the same information and features.

Figure 13.12
FrontPage includes
templates for frames-
based Web sites. How many
frames does the previewed
template contain?

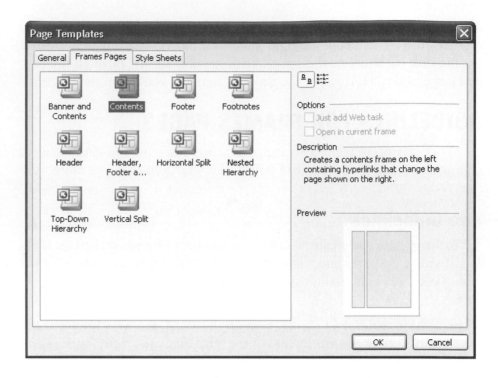

After you select a template, you can add content to a frame in one of two ways:

◆ Selecting the **Set Initial Page button** allows you to link existing content to a frame. Use this button to add an existing page to a frames site.

◆ Selecting the **New Page button** allows you to create new content in the frame. Use this button to create a blank page in which to add content.

Right-click a frames page to access the Frame Properties dialog box. This dialog box allows you to give each individual frame a title, define the height or width of the frame, and decide whether to include a scroll bar with the frame.

Converting a Site into a Frames-Based Site

You can convert a non-frames-based site into a frames-based site. For instance, assume the WebTee.biz marketing group has requested that the company logo always be visible to the customer. When visitors move down the page on the current site, the logo in the top shared border scrolls off the screen. Creating a top frame to hold the company's logo will ensure that customers always know what site they are visiting.

In the next activity, you will convert the existing WebTee.biz site into a frames-based site with top and bottom frames. The top frame will house the company's logo, while the bottom frame will contain all other content.

YOU TRY IT

ACTIVITY 13F Using Frames on a Site

① Browse to where you store your WebTee site. Right-click on the **WebTee** folder and select **Copy.** Press **Ctrl + V** to paste the copy in the same folder. Rename the folder **WebTee_Frames.**

② Open the WebTee_Frames **index.htm** page in FrontPage.

3 Right-click anywhere on the page and select **Page Properties.** In the Page Properties dialog box, click the **Custom** tab. In the User variables box, select **Microsoft Border** and click **Remove.** Click **OK.** This removes the Web site's top shared border, as shown in Figure 13.13. Click **Save.** Repeat the step for each page in the site.

Figure 13.13
Removing the top shared border removes the company's logo from the page.

4 Open the **index.htm** page. Select **File** and click **Save As.** Type base.htm in the File name field. Click the **Change title** button and title the page Base. Click **OK** and then click **Save.**

5 Switch to **Navigation** view. Right-click the **Home** page. Click **Add Existing Page** in the shortcut menu. Click **base.htm.** Click **OK.** Click and drag the **Base** page until it is parallel to the Home page.

6 Select **File** and click **New** (in 2002, **File > New > Page or Web**). Click **More page templates** (in 2002, **Page Templates**). In the Page Templates box, select the **Frames Pages** tab. Select the **Header** template. Click **OK.** FrontPage creates a blank frames page, as shown in Figure 13.14.

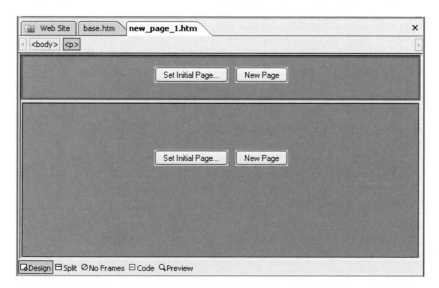

Figure 13.14
You will add information to both the top and the bottom frames.

7 Click the **New Page** button in the top frame. This is the frame that will contain the company's logo. Select **Insert > Picture > From File.** Browse to the DataFile\Ch13\Images folder and select **WebTeelogo.jpg.** Click the **Insert** button. Notice that only part of the logo is visible on your page. Center the logo.

8 Right-click inside the top frame. Select **Frame Properties.** In the Name box, type header. If using FrontPage 2003, type Logo for the title (this option is not available in 2002). Under Frame size, make the height 128 in pixels. Click the **Frames Page** button and uncheck the **Show Borders** check box. Click **OK** twice to return to the frames page.

9 Click the **Set Initial Page** button in the bottom frame to create a link to existing content. Scroll inside the Insert Hyperlink dialog box and double-click the **base.htm** page to link it to the bottom frame, as shown in Figure 13.15.

Figure 13.15
Although the page looks similar to the shared borders version of the site, the logo is now in a frame.

10 Right-click on the bottom frame and select **Frame Properties.** Type Home for the Name. In FrontPage 2003, type Content for Title. Click **OK.**

11 Select the top frame and click **Save.** In the Save as dialog box, name the document header.htm. Change the title to Header. Click **OK** and **Save.** Save the embedded file in the images folder and click **OK.** You are returned to the Save As box. To save the entire frameset, type index.htm in the Save as text box, change the title to Index, and click **Save.** Click **Yes** to replace the existing **index.htm** file.

12 Preview the site in a browser. Notice that as you scroll down any page, the WebTee.biz logo remains visible. Close the browser and close FrontPage.

READ ME!

Caution Use the Change title button in the Save As dialog box to change the page title of each frame. Changing the page titles will help make your site more accessible.

PUBLISHING A WEB SITE LOCALLY

It is possible to publish a Web site locally. Doing this transfers the site's files from where you created them (**local Web site**) to another location on your computer or network (**remote Web site**). This option allows you to test the publishing process, even if you do not have a Web host for the site. You can view sites published in this way in your computer's browser, but a public Internet audience has no access to the sites.

In the following You Try It activity, you will use FrontPage to publish the WebTee.biz frames site locally. Note that publishing a Web site locally will not enable all of your Web components. Some components, such as hit counters, only activate when you publish the site to a server that has FrontPage Server Extensions installed.

ACTIVITY 13G Publishing a Web Site Locally

YOU TRY IT

❶ Open the **WebTee_Frames** site in FrontPage.

❷ From the **File** menu, select **Publish Site** (in 2002, **Publish Web**).

❸ The Remote Web Site Properties dialog box opens (in 2002, the Publish Destination dialog box opens). In 2003, select **File System,** as shown in Figure 13.16.

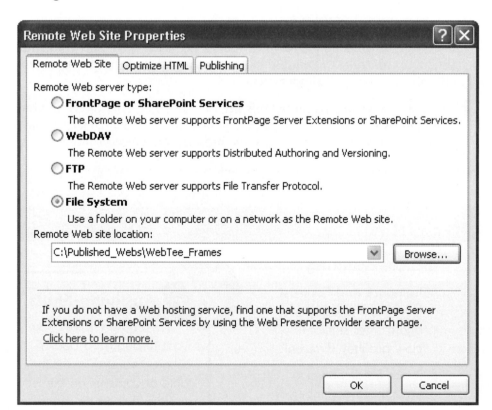

◄───● Figure 13.16
The Remote Web Site Properties dialog box lets you specify server type and location.

❹ In the Remote Web site location box, type the path to the remote location where you want to publish your site (in 2002, type this path into the Enter publish destination box in the Publish Destination dialog box). Your teacher will tell you which path to type. Click **OK.** When FrontPage asks if you want to create a Web site at this destination, click **Yes** (in 2002, **OK**).

⑤ As shown in Figure 13.17, a screen appears that shows your local Web site files on the left and your remote Web site files on the right (in 2002, click the **Show** button in the Publish Web dialog box to reveal the remote files). Click on one of the files in the local Web site list. Click **Ctrl + A** to select all the files and folders in the list.

Figure 13.17 ●——▶

When publishing, you transfer files from your local computer to a another (remote) location.

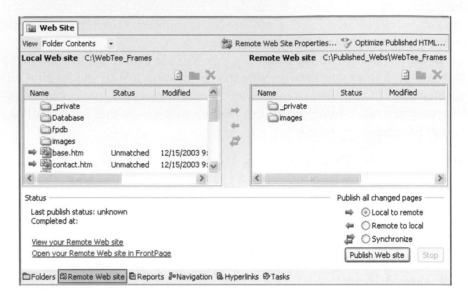

⑥ Click **Publish Web site** (in 2002, **Publish**). FrontPage will transfer all files from the local to the remote Web site. Click **Ignore and Continue** (in 2002, **Continue**) when told that publishing a site locally will not enable all of your site's components.

⑦ Click the **View your Remote Web site** link (in 2002, **Click here to view your published Web site**). Open the published site. Test the site by navigating to the various links. Close the browser and close FrontPage.

Section 13.4 Assessment

Concept Check

1. **Define** frame, frameset, Set Initial Page button, New Page button, local Web site, remote Web site.

2. **Describe** the information contained in a frameset.

3. **Identify** three problems with using frames when designing a Web site.

Critical Thinking

4. **Compare and Contrast** How are shared borders and frames similar? How are they different?

5. **Make Predictions** Do you think the number of new sites created with frames will increase or decrease in the future? Explain your reasoning.

Applying Skills

Evaluate Frames You want to publish a book online. You plan to list the table of contents on the left and the text on the right. The table of contents will list the book's 12 chapters. The text is one long document. Is this book a good candidate for a frames-based site?

SECTION 13.1 Tracking Visitors to a Site

Key Terms

hit counter, 342
hits, 342
tracking software, 344
guest book, 344

Main Ideas

- You may incorporate a public or hidden hit counter on any page on your site.
- Hit counters do not track length of stay or count hits when visitors go directly from a search engine to a page without a hit counter.
- Tracking software can identify the countries where visitors live, how they navigated to your site, and the browsers they used.
- A guest book is a public record of visitors' comments.

SECTION 13.2 Making Information Easy to Find

Key Terms

site map, 347
table of contents, 347
frequently asked questions
  (FAQ), 348
bookmark, 348
search capabilities, 349

Main Ideas

- A site map enables visitors to search for information by category.
- A table of contents lists the main pages with their subpages indented beneath them, usually with embedded links to each page.
- An FAQ page provides answers to common questions about the site.
- Bookmarks enable visitors to jump to marked locations within a long page.
- Search capabilities allow visitors to access site information by searching for a word or phrase.

SECTION 13.3 Collecting and Storing Information from Visitors

Key Terms

database, 351
record, 351
database driven, 351
database interface page, 352

Main Ideas

- Databases collect, organize, and store information in fields and records for easy retrieval.
- A database can change the information on the dynamic Web page to which it is linked.
- After publishing a database with your Web site, you can create pages that display database information or collect and store information in the database.
- You must save an order form as an active server page (.asp) to connect it to a database.
- Order forms submit information to a database, while results pages extract information from a database.

SECTION 13.4 Frames

Key Terms

frame, 356
frameset, 356
Set Initial Page button, 358
New Page button, 358
local Web site, 361
remote Web site, 361

Main Ideas

- Frames enable different parts of the screen to scroll independently.
- A frameset contains information about the size and placement of all frames within a Web page.
- Define the pixel width of the left or top frame. Fill the remaining space with the right or bottom frame.
- Provide a descriptive title for each frame to make your site accessible.
- The Frames Pages tab in the Page Templates dialog box displays the FrontPage templates for creating a frames-based Web site.
- You can publish a Web site locally to test your site without making it available to Internet visitors.

READ TO SUCCEED PRACTICE

Organize to Remember Review the chapter by looking over headings and subheadings. Notice how topics are organized. Are they grouped together in helpful ways? Would you regroup some topics to make the information easier to remember? Find a section that you think is particularly well organized. Read it through once. Then write down all the information you can remember. Did you hit all the main points? How many smaller details did you remember?

Reviewing Key Terms

1. What element provides a space for visitors to submit comments about the Web site?
2. What is a bookmark?
3. What do search capabilities allow a visitor to do?
4. Change the following sentence to make it true: *A record is one piece of information, such as a last name or telephone number.*
5. On a frames site, what is the name of the shell page that includes the information about the size and shape of each frame on the page?

Understanding Main Ideas

6. **Describe** the limitations of hit counters.
7. **Identify** the types of decisions that tracking software can help companies make.
8. **Explain** how a guest book is different from a feedback form.
9. **Evaluate** how search capabilities make a site more user-friendly.
10. **Describe** how intrapage bookmarks can be useful on long pages.
11. **Explain** how databases are organized.
12. **Compare and contrast** static and dynamic pages.
13. **Summarize** the purpose of a database interface page.
14. **Explain** why you might want to publish a site to another location on your computer.

Critical Thinking

15. **Analyze** You are trying to decide how to advertise your e-commerce site that sells your photography. One suggestion has been to place a banner ad on several Web portals. You contact three Web portals and find that all use tracking software to gather information about visitors. You can only afford to place a banner ad on one of the sites. What information about the portal's visitors would be most useful to you in deciding which Web portal to select?

16. **Draw Conclusions** Six of your ancestors were writers. Their writings include short stories, poems, children's stories, and one novel. You have collected all these works and plan to post them on a Web site. What techniques can you use to help visitors easily find the writings of a particular person or to find a specific genre of writing?

17. **Make Recommendations** You are working on a team that is developing a Web site examining the opposing points of view on a community issue. One team member has suggested using a frames site with four frames. The top frame would contain the navigation. The rest of the page would be divided into three equal frames, each containing information about one of the three viewpoints being expressed. What problems, if any, do you see with this approach? Explain your reasoning.

e-Review ·················

webdesign.glencoe.com

Study with PowerPoint

To review the main points in this chapter, select **e-Review > PowerPoint Outlines > Chapter 13.**

Online Self Check

Test your knowledge of the material in this chapter by selecting **e-Review > Self Checks > Chapter 13.**

Making Connections

Language Arts—Design a Table of Contents

Imagine you are planning to post your class notes from all the classes you are currently taking to a Web site. Review your notes from the last month. Then write a table of contents that organizes the material

◆ By class
◆ By appropriate subcategories within that class

Make certain that the subcategories you use will be helpful to people visiting the site. For example, you could use the date the notes were taken as a subcategory. Classmates who missed a particular class could use this subcategory to search for your notes.

STANDARDS AT WORK

Students demonstrate a sound understanding of the nature and operation of technology systems. (NETS-S 1)

Make a Guest Book Entry

Locate a Web site that includes a guest book. Then create a two-column chart. Label one column "Strengths" and the other column "Weaknesses."

1. Navigate through your chosen site. Evaluate the design and content of each page you visit.
2. As you navigate the site, complete the two-column chart.
3. When finished, review your chart. What do you think is the greatest strength of the site? What improvement would you suggest to deal with one of the weaknesses?

Make an entry in the site's guest book. Compliment the site on its specific strengths. In a positive way, suggest an improvement or an additional feature for the site. Visit the site after you have posted your guest book entry to see how the entry appears.

TEAMWORK SKILLS

Design a Database Interface

Your school is developing a Web site where students and faculty can post book reviews. The site will also allow students to buy or trade books. Your team is planning and designing the databases and forms needed to support the site.

1. Plan the review form. Research sites that include book reviews. Note what information is gathered from people posting reviews. Then design and create a form in FrontPage that will gather review information for your site.
2. Choose the database fields needed to manage the book buying and trading. Make a list of all the information needed about the person offering the book for sale or trade. Then list the book information (title, author, price, etc.) that someone would need to make a decision to buy or trade the book. Create a list of field names for the database.
3. Use FrontPage to create the buying and trading form. Name the fields on the form to match the field names in the database.

CHALLENGE YOURSELF

Research Tracking Software

Use a search engine to locate three businesses that sell tracking software. Navigate each of these sites. Make a list of the types of information that the tracking software can gather. Some sites offer online demonstrations of the software. Do not sign up for free trials unless you have your teacher's permission to do so.

Based on your research, create a chart that compares the types of information that can be gathered by each of the tracking software applications. Then write a short report that explains what types of Web sites would find tracking software useful.

YOU TRY IT
Skills Studio

These exercises reinforce the skills you learned in this chapter's You Try It activities. Refer back to the You Try It activities if you need extra guidance.

1. Adding a Hit Counter and Guest Book

Add a hit counter and guest book to the mouse pad e-commerce site.

Ⓐ Open the site you created in the Chapter 12 You Try It Skills Studio (see page 338).

Ⓑ Select a name for the business. Design a simple logo for the site.

Ⓒ Add a home page to the site (make the order form page a child page of the home page). Place the logo on the home page. Add content describing the custom mouse pads offered by your company.

Ⓓ Add a hit counter to the home page.

Ⓔ Add a guest book page. Make the page a second child page of the home page.

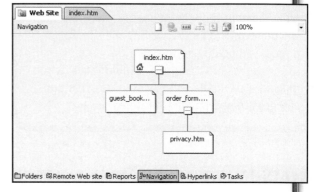

Ⓕ Save your work. Preview the site in a browser. (Note that the hit counter will not work until the site has been published to a server with Microsoft FrontPage Server Extensions.)

2. Converting to a Frames-Based Site

Convert a Web site into a frames-based site.

Ⓐ Select a Web site that you created during this course. Make a copy of the site, if necessary.

Ⓑ Review the pages that are included in the site. Decide which shared border you want to replace with a frame. For example, in the WebTee site, you removed the top shared border. Remove the selected shared border from the site.

Ⓒ Select an appropriate Frames Page template. Create a blank frames page.

Ⓓ Provide a name and title for each of the frames. Adjust the size of the frames as needed. Add or link content to each of the frames.

Ⓔ Save your work. Preview your converted site in a browser. Make sure that the frames work properly.

Ⓕ With your teacher's permission, publish the site to another location on your hard drive. Test the published site in a browser.

Web Design Projects

1. Create Bookmarks for a Résumé

Gather the information you need to create a résumé that includes the following sections:

- Contact Information
- Career Objective
- Education
- Software Proficiency
- Experience
- References

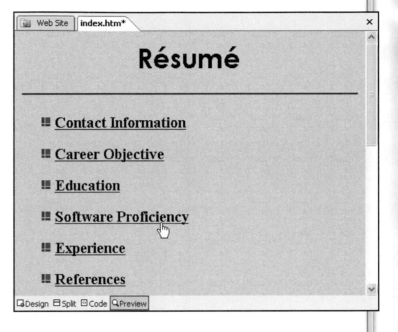

Under software proficiency, you will list specific software applications that you know well enough to use on the job. For your reference section, list the teacher of your FrontPage class and one other teacher or an employer who knows you well.

Create the résumé in FrontPage. Add bookmarks that allow visitors to quickly move to each section of the résumé. Proofread the résumé carefully and make changes as needed. Preview the résumé in a browser. Test the bookmarks to make certain they work properly.

2. Create an Investing for Teens Web Site

Your school has formed a new club called Investing for Teens. The club explores the basics of financial investments and helps students plan future investments. Develop a Web site that contains the following four pages:

- A home page that introduces the club and gives the list of upcoming meetings.
- A membership form page that gathers e-mail addresses from visitors who want to receive a monthly online newsletter.
- An informational page that describes basic financial tips for savings and investing money. The page includes links to other investing sites aimed at teens.
- A glossary page that lists common investing terms and their definitions.

Create the site in FrontPage. Include a hit counter on the home page. Add bookmarks to the glossary page so that visitors can move quickly to the terms.

Preview the site in a browser and make changes as needed. With your teacher's permission, publish the site to another location on your computer. View the published site in a browser.

CHAPTER 14 Publishing a Web Site

WHY IT MATTERS.....................................

Publishing a Web site is similar to publishing a book. Publishing a book involves converting an author's manuscript into a finished print product. Book stores and other businesses then distribute this product to readers. Publishing a Web site involves moving Web page files from the computer where they were developed to a Web server. The last piece of the process is making your audience aware that the product is available.

Quick Write Activity

Think about an item that you purchased recently. Write a short paragraph explaining why you decided to purchase this item. How did this item first come to your attention? Did you see it advertised on television or the Internet? Did you hear about it from friends? Evaluate how important advertising was in your decision to buy this item.

WHAT YOU WILL DO..

ACTIVITIES AND PROJECTS

IN THE WORKBOOK

Optional Activities and Projects

Guided Reading

Web Design Projects

ON THE WEB

Activities at webdesign.glencoe.com

Reading Strategy Organizers

Go Online Activities

Study with PowerPoint

Self-Check Assessments

READ TO SUCCEED

Take Good Notes

The chapters in this book are organized so that main headings describe main ideas and subheadings introduce supporting details. You can organize your notes by this method. Think of main ideas as Level 1 ideas. Supporting details can be Level 2, 3, or 4. Every time you read a main idea, write down a brief Level 1 note. Under that, write down the Level 2 supporting details. Level 2 may also have its own supporting information. Those are Level 3 details. Note those details beneath Level 2. Continue this method as you read through the chapter.

Section 14.1 Web Servers

To **publish** a Web site, you transfer that site's Web page files from the local computer where you created them to a remote Web server. When you publish your Web site, any Internet user may view it. Knowing how to publish a Web site is a crucial part of the overall Web site development process.

THE TECHNICAL NEEDS OF A WEB SERVER

As shown in Figure 14.1, a **Web server** is a powerful computer that maintains a constant connection to the Internet. A server's hardware largely determines its efficiency. Understanding this hardware can help you select an appropriate server when you publish your Web site.

Figure 14.1
Web servers are constantly connected to the Internet. What factors affect a Web server's efficiency?

webdesign.glencoe.com

When choosing a Web server, evaluate the following items:

◆ **CPU Power** A Web server's CPU power determines the number of instructions it can process in a given time period. The maximum processing capability of a server is determined by the number of central processing units (CPUs) it has and the speed (frequency) those processors run at. A high-performance Web server is typically able to process roughly 16 times more instructions per second than a typical desktop computer.

◆ **Hard Drive Speed and Capacity** Many high-capacity Web servers support multiple hard drives. The hard drives in high-end Web servers usually retrieve data at a substantially higher rate than the drives in common desktop systems.

◆ **Communications Channel Bandwidth** Fast CPUs and fast hard drives will not accomplish much if the Web server has a limited communication channel. High-speed digital communication lines such as DSL or T1/T3 lines transfer data quickly between computers.

◆ **Scalability** The term "scalability" refers to a Web server's ability to handle increasing Web traffic. A server that can be easily upgraded to handle a dramatic increase in traffic is said to be highly scalable.

◆ **Reliability** Some servers are more reliable than others. For instance, some servers incorporate dual power supplies so that if one burns out, the other will continue running the system. Other servers will continue to operate if the computer's CPUs malfunction.

● **Figure 14.2**
Companies such as Microsoft offer Web-hosting services. What is a Web host?

WEB HOSTS

Instead of purchasing a Web server, many individuals and companies pay Web-hosting services (also referred to as Web hosts) to store their site for them. A **Web host** provides server space to customers for a fee (see Figure 14.2). Customers post, or transfer, their files to a host. A **host** is the name of the Web server on which a particular Web site resides.

Choosing a Web Host

You should consider several factors when choosing a service to host your Web site.

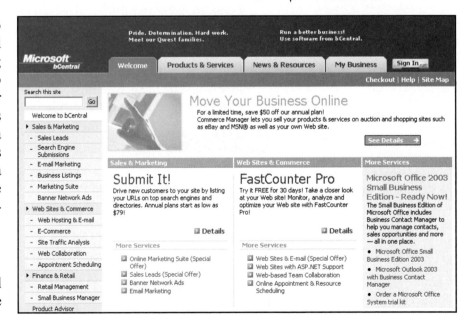

Cost Some Web hosts charge customers an initial setup fee. In addition, many Web hosts charge users a monthly fee to host their Web site. Large hosting companies generally charge higher monthly maintenance fees than smaller companies. While they may cost more, larger companies often can provide superior Web-hosting benefits.

Performance Web site performance is often called "throughput" or "bandwidth." Large Web-hosting companies typically offer much better performance. They have faster CPUs, bigger and faster hard drives, and higher capacity communication lines. These high-performance features are critical for high-traffic sites that must be able to handle millions of hits per day.

Reliability One Web server might provide much greater reliability for your Web site than another. For example, many large Web-hosting companies provide **Web server clusters** that store a given Web site on multiple physical computers that act as a single virtual host. If one computer in the cluster should fail, the other computers in the cluster can continue to service requests without interruption. In addition, large hosting companies maintain backup copies of their clients' Web site data so that they can restore the site quickly in case of computer failure.

Tech Support Different Web hosts offer different levels of support. If you do not feel comfortable troubleshooting your site's problems, you may want to use a Web host that offers a higher level of tech support.

Storage Space and Bandwidth Make sure that the host server or hosting plan you choose has enough room for all your Web files. Also make sure that the server has enough bandwidth to handle your site's traffic.

YOU TRY IT

ACTIVITY 14A Calculating Web Site Size and Bandwidth

❶ Open the **WebTee.biz** home page in FrontPage. Select **Folders View**. Right-click on the folder that contains all the site's files (this folder is usually at the top of the Folder List). Select **Properties** to open the Folder Properties dialog box (see Figure 14.3).

❷ Locate the folder's Size information. The Size number is the total size of your Web site. The Web host you use to publish this site should have at least this amount of space to store your Web page files.

Figure 14.3
Use the Folders Properties dialog box to determine the size of your Web site.

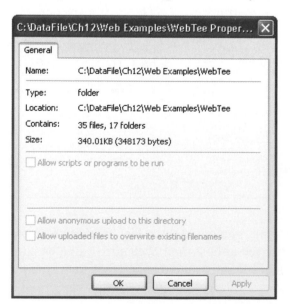

❸ Estimate how many visitors you think will access your site in a month. For example, suppose that the WebTee.biz site will receive approximately 100 visits a month.

❹ Multiply the estimated number of visits per month (step 3) by the site's size (step 2). The result is the site's approximate transfer bandwidth. This is the minimum amount of bandwidth that a Web host should have to effectively administer your site.

FrontPage Server Extensions When you use FrontPage to create a Web site, make sure that your Web host supports FrontPage server extensions. Front-Page server extensions are support programs installed on a server. Various Web components, such as hit counters, search forms, confirmation fields, discussion groups, and user registration features, will not function if the server does not have these extensions installed.

Internal Versus External Hosting

When publishing a Web site, companies must decide if they are going to host the site internally or externally. Cost, performance, and reliability are important factors in the decision to use either internal or external hosting.

Internal Hosting When companies provide their own Web server, they are using **internal Web hosting.** Since many companies already own and operate one or more Web servers, the decision to use internal hosting is generally not determined by cost. Most companies choose internal hosting to achieve greater control over their Web site.

Controlling their own servers also allows companies to determine the content and functionality of their Web sites. They can host Web applications that access large databases or conduct financial transactions (e-commerce sites). Many smaller Web-hosting companies do not support or allow some or all of these capabilities.

External Hosting When companies pay someone else to host their site, they are using **external Web hosting.** Many companies find that an external hosting solution is more cost effective than buying their own Web server. Since Web-hosting companies provide Internet services for many clients, they can afford to maintain more up-to-date computer hardware and communications equipment. The fact that costs are shared across multiple customers also allows larger Web-hosting services to offer prices that individuals and smaller services cannot match.

READ ME!

Tech Tip FrontPage Server Extensions can run on most common Web servers, including Unix, Linux, and Windows NT-based servers.

Activity 14.1 Explore Web Hosts Find out more about Web hosts and the services they provide by visiting **webdesign.glencoe.com.**

Section 14.1 Assessment

Concept Check

1. **Define** publish, Web server, Web host, host, Web server clusters, internal Web hosting, external Web hosting.

2. **Identify** five factors that an individual should consider when choosing a Web host.

Critical Thinking

3. **Compare and Contrast** Explain how internal Web hosting differs from external Web hosting.

4. **Draw Conclusions** How might a Web server that an individual buys differ from a server that a large company buys?

Applying Skills

Evaluate Web-Hosting Services Research two Web hosting companies. Determine their setup costs, monthly fees, and performance and reliability safeguards. Create a chart comparing the two companies.

SECURITY ON THE WEB

Security is a constant concern for e-commerce sites or sites that transfer sensitive data, such as credit information. Sites that are not secure risk losing customers, reputations, and money.

Different security measures are being developed to protect wireless technology.

Threats to Web Sites

Hackers often target Web servers that contain private information such as credit card numbers. Virus writers may infect e-commerce sites and corporate networks and cause billions of dollars' worth of damage.

Firewalls, password schemes, and antivirus programs are still the first line of defense against online criminals. But they must constantly evolve to keep up with new threats from hackers and viruses.

Blended Attacks

An attack that combines hacking and viruses is called a "blended attack." These attacks are carried out by first hacking into a system and then spreading a virus. Fighting blended attacks requires integrated security measures.

Antivirus (AV) vendors are offering a new generation of tools that will tie together security measures such as firewalls, AV software, intrusion detection software, and packet sniffers. When one tool detects a problem, other tools swing into action to defend against it. Coordinating the work of these different technologies further protects networks against attacks.

Wireless Threats

The wireless trend is creating a new layer of threats. Wireless security may improve when the industry adopts the new Wi-Fi Protected Access (WPA) encryption standard. This standard features strong data-encryption techniques and user-validation measures. These features will make it more difficult for intruders to access a wireless LAN or to use its data.

Tech Focus

1. Research current or emerging security measures used to protect e-commerce Web sites. Identify the capabilities and limitations of these systems.

2. Create a presentation about a corporate network or e-commerce site that was victimized by a hacker or a virus. Assess the security the site used and the results of the attack.

Main Ideas

HTTP and FTP are the two main protocols used to transfer Web files to a Web server. Test your published site on different hardware and in different browsers.

Key Terms

InterNIC
case sensitive
directory structure
download
upload
cross-platform testing

Reading Strategy

Identify three guidelines for selecting a Web site name. Use a diagram similar to the one below (also available online).

The process of publishing a Web site involves more than transferring Web files to a Web server. You also need to determine your site's name and make sure that your files and folders are properly named and organized.

NAMING A WEB SITE

Choosing your Web site's name is an important part of the Web development process. In many cases, the Web site name is the same as the site's URL. Before they see any pages, your visitors will first see your site's name. The name you choose should make a good first impression.

Selecting a Name

The name you give your site determines how easily visitors can locate and access the site. Consider the following guidelines when selecting a Web site name:

◆ **Choose a logical name.** Start by making sure your Web site name has a logical relationship with the company, institution, product, or individual it represents. Good examples include ibm.com, microsoft.com, or ucla.edu. Remember that the domain name extension you choose is an important part of the Web site name.

◆ **Keep your site name short.** Keep your Web site name as short as possible without losing clarity. For example, most people would prefer to type NBA.com into their Web browsers instead of NationalBasketballAssociation.com.

◆ **Choose a unique name.** Select a name that will attract users to your site and set your site apart from similar ones.

Registering a Domain Name

You can register a domain name so that no one else can use it. The Internet Corporation for Assigned Names and Numbers (ICANN) assigns Web site names and IP addresses. ICANN provides a Web site called **InterNIC**. This Web site contains information about the Web name registration process and maintains a list of domain registration services. Many of these services also act as Web hosts.

Before you can register a domain name, you must first make sure that the name you want is available. You can type your selected domain name into the WHOIS registration database to see if it is already registered. As shown in Figure 14.4, you can access this database through the InterNIC site. You generally pay a small yearly fee to use domain names that you have registered.

Figure 14.4
You can use the WHOIS registration database to see if the domain name you want is already registered. Why can you not use a domain name that is already registered?

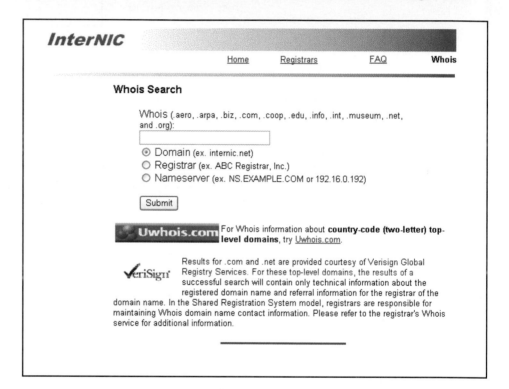

REVIEWING PAGE FILES AND FOLDERS

After you have chosen a server or a Web-hosting service and have selected your site's name, you are ready to publish your Web site. However, you need to consider some issues regarding page file and folder names before you actually transfer your site's files to your chosen Web server.

Maintaining Web Page File Names

When transferring files to a server, make sure to use their exact names. Many servers are **case sensitive**—they distinguish between file names that contain uppercase and lowercase letters and those that contain only lowercase letters.

For example, suppose your home page contains an internal hyperlink to a page called OliverTwist.htm. You, however, mistakenly publish this page as olivertwist.htm. If your Web host uses a case-sensitive server, then users will receive an error message when they click on this link (see Figure 14.5). This error occurs because the link target name does not exactly match the actual file name.

 ## The page cannot be displayed

The page you are looking for is currently unavailable. The Web site might be experiencing technical difficulties, or you may need to adjust your browser settings.

Figure 14.5
Users may receive an error message such as this if you do not publish your Web pages exactly as they are named. What does it mean to be case sensitive?

You can easily correct case-sensitive errors if you publish a Web page incorrectly. First, you can change the hyperlink reference in the first Web page to match the actual name of the target page. The second option is to rename the target Web page so that it matches the hyperlink reference in the first page. Either approach is simple and effective.

Maintaining a Site's Directory Structure

Publishing a small Web site typically does not require great organizational skills. However, suppose you create a Web site for a large library that contains a Web page for every book in its collection. If you stored every Web page in its own folder, you would need a plan to organize those folders. A **directory structure,** sometimes called a folder structure, is a hierarchy used to organize folders and the files the folders contain.

It is difficult to manage many files if they all reside in a single directory or folder. Users will experience slow download times if the server has to scan hundreds of files every time they click a hyperlink on your site. You should instead create multiple folders to contain your Web pages and organize these folders in a logical fashion. A Web site's directory structure should divide Web page files into groups of approximately the same size (see Figure 14.6). For example, you can divide a group of 900 files into 30 groups of 30 folders.

TECH TRIVIA
Directory versus Folder
The terms "directory" and "folder" are often used interchangeably. "Folder" is the preferred name for the Windows OS, and "directory" is used on most other platforms. Both terms refer to the organizational structure of the platform's file management system.

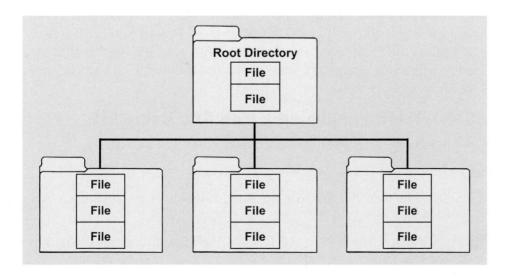

Figure 14.6
To keep track of all the files that may be included in a Web site, you should keep a logical organization to the files and folders on the site. Why do you think such organization is important?

When you publish your site, you must maintain its directory structure on the Web server exactly as it is on the computer used to develop the site. All of the folders must be named exactly the same on the server as on the local computer, and they must maintain the same relative position in the directory hierarchy. If you fail to do this, many of the hyperlinks on your Web site will cease to function correctly when you publish the site.

When you publish a Web site with FrontPage, you must specify only the document root, or top-level, directory on the target Web server. FrontPage will create and name all other folders on the site appropriately during the transfer process, so you need not do this manually. This feature helps avoid the potential problems that occur when folders or files are misspelled or misplaced in the directory hierarchy.

TRANSFERRING FILES TO A SERVER

You can choose from several methods to transfer Web files to a Web server. The two most popular transfer methods are Hypertext Transfer Protocol (HTTP) and File Transfer Protocol (FTP). Web hosting services will tell you the method you should use to upload files to their server.

Transferring Files Using HTTP

You can use Hypertext Transfer Protocol (HTTP) to publish to a Web server that has the FrontPage Server Extensions or Sharepoint Team Services from Microsoft installed. HTTP is the main protocol used to download files over the Internet. The term **download** means to transfer data from a file server to a client (user) machine. Virtually all Web browsers use this protocol to access Web pages. However, HTTP is a two-way protocol, so it can also be used to upload Web pages as well. The term **upload** means to transfer data from a client computer's system to a server.

Transferring Files Using FTP

You can use File Transfer Protocol (FTP) to publish to a Web server that does not have the FrontPage Server Extensions or Sharepoint Team Services installed. To use FTP, you need to know the name of the designated FTP server and have a valid user name and password.

Although there are many commercial and shareware FTP clients available, FrontPage has a built-in FTP client. In the following You Try It activity, you will use the FrontPage FTP client to publish your WebTee.biz site. Your teacher will need to supply the remote Web site location, FTP client address, user name, and password.

Activity 14.2 Explore File Transfers Find out more about transferring files to a server by visiting **webdesign.glencoe.com**.

READ ME!

Caution! Do not use FTP to transfer files to a Web server that has FrontPage Server Extensions installed and enabled. Doing so may disable the extensions.

YOU TRY IT

ACTIVITY 14B Publishing a Web Site Using FTP

Get permission from your teacher before starting this activity!

❶ Open the WebTee.biz Web site in FrontPage.

❷ Select **File** then **Publish Site** (in 2002, **Publish Web**). 2002 users, skip to step 3.

❸ 2003 users, select **FTP** in the Remote Web Site Properties dialog box. Click **OK.**

4 Type the Remote Web site location given to you by your teacher. Then click **OK.**

5 Type the user name and password supplied by your teacher in the Name and Password required dialog box. Click **OK.**

6 Your screen should look similar to Figure 14.7. The window on the left shows the Local Web site. The window on the right shows the files on the Remote Web site. Confirm that you are in the correct directory to publish your site. Otherwise, navigate to the correct directory. 2002 users, skip to step 8.

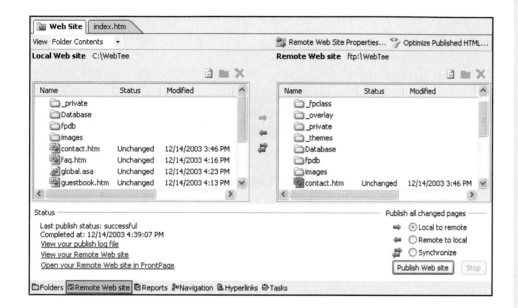

● Figure 14.7
You transfer files from your computer to the remote location.

7 2003 users, select **Local to remote** in the lower right corner.

8 Click **Publish Web site** (in 2002, **Publish**). FrontPage shows you the progress of the published pages.

9 View your published site. Click **View your remote Web Site** (in 2002, **Click here to view your published Web site**).

10 Click on **View your publish log file** (in 2002, **Click here to view your publish log file**) to read the log of all publish events (see Figure 14.8).

● Figure 14.8
The publish log helps you track your file transfers.

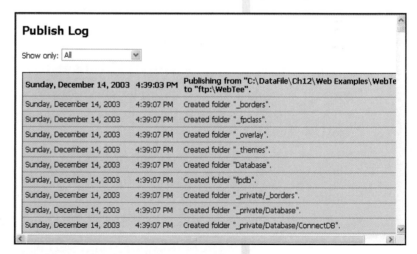

The publish log shows you when files were published. The FrontPage FTP client provides other options you can use when publishing a large Web site. On the Publishing tab of the Remote Web Site Properties dialog box, you can choose to publish only those pages on the Web site that have been changed. The larger a site gets, the more time this option saves.

TESTING A PUBLISHED WEB SITE

It is important to test a Web site after you publish it to ensure that it displays and functions properly on a variety of Web platforms. The process of testing sites on a variety of computer hardware and software configurations is known as **cross-platform testing.**

Testing on Various Hardware

Personal computers running Microsoft Windows are currently the most common hardware/software configuration in use. However, this combination is by no means the only possible Internet platform.

Many individuals and businesses choose to run the Linux operating system on PCs, while others prefer to run the Apple Macintosh.

Many large-scale Web-hosting companies use high-end servers manufactured by IBM, Sun, or Hewlett-Packard. These systems typically run a version of the Unix operating system: AIX, Solaris, and HP-UX, respectively. Any Web developer who wishes to provide a truly cross-platform Web site should ensure that the site's software operates consistently and correctly on all these Internet platforms.

Testing on Different Browsers

As you know, most Web surfers use either Microsoft Internet Explorer or Netscape Navigator to access Web sites. After you publish a site, you must test it in various browsers. Web developers use the most current HTML standards in order to achieve maximum success with different hardware, software, and browser configurations. Pages created in FrontPage comply with most current HTML standards.

Section 14.2 Assessment

Concept Check

1. **Define** InterNIC, case sensitive, directory structure, download, upload, cross-platform testing.

2. **Explain** the importance of developing a logical directory structure for a large Web site.

Critical Thinking

3. **Draw Conclusions** Why is it important to register a domain name?

4. **Compare and Contrast** How are the guidelines for choosing a Web site name similar to and different from the guidelines for choosing a Web page name?

Applying Skills

Create a Directory Structure A local music store asks you to create a site that describes each CD that they sell. Assume that the music store organizes their CDs by genre (Pop/Rock, Classical, Country). Artists are arranged alphabetically within each genre. Create a directory structure that mirrors the music store's CD organization.

Ethics & Technology

THE INTERNET AND THE WORLD

The Internet has given people around the world a window to information and global communication. But this has had both positive and negative results.

The Internet allows people from many different cultures to communicate with each other.

The Positive

The Internet has been positive in many ways:

◆ **Society** People use the Web to voice their opinions about important social issues. They can also communicate with people around the world to learn about their cultures and views.

◆ **Economics** The business world has grown because of the Internet. Both large and small businesses can serve customers anywhere in the world.

◆ **Politics** Voters are better informed than ever. Someday, you may be able to vote via the Internet in state or national elections.

◆ **Education** Students use the Web for research and communication. Distance learning brings the classroom into the home, allowing people to study online from anywhere.

The Negative

The Net also has critics, for many reasons:

◆ **Cultural Differences** The Internet enables different cultures to learn about one another, but this is not considered a benefit everywhere. Some people may object to images and discussions that their children can find online.

◆ **Privacy** Each day, we give away more of our privacy as businesses and government agencies collect personal data online. Criminals can now go online to steal personal information or launch viruses.

◆ **Depersonalization** While the Internet is a great communication tool, some critics argue that spending too much time online actually isolates people from those around them. Many of these critics believe that communication over the Internet is less effective than person-to-person communication.

◆ **Safety** Some individuals use the Internet to lure other users into dangerous situations. It is also easy to access unethical material online. For these reasons, parents should always supervise their children on the Internet.

Tech Focus

1. Research a company that uses the Internet to do business around the world. Discuss how the Internet made it possible for this company to "go global."

2. Describe one positive and one negative aspect of the Internet on society. Explain why you have chosen these examples. Support your conclusions with research.

Section 14.3   Promoting a Web Site

Main Ideas

A published Web site serves little purpose if few people know about it. You can use different methods to promote your Web site.

Key Terms

publicize
spam
link trading
meta tag

Reading Strategy

Summarize the pros and cons of various Web site publicizing methods. Use a table like the one below (also available online).

Publicizing Method	Pros	Cons

Once you have published your site to a Web server, you need to **publicize** that site. Publicizing a site involves letting the general public know about your site and how to access it.

PUBLICIZING WEB PAGES

You can publicize your Web site through a variety of methods. Each technique has advantages and disadvantages.

Advertising a Site

People need to know that a site exists before they can use it. E-mail, print media, and link trading are often used to let people know that a site exists.

E-Mail Advertising Some Web site publishers publish HTML and plain-text e-mail messages to promote their sites or sell products or services. Individuals need only click a hyperlink embedded in the e-mail's body to launch the site. This approach can be cost effective since many Internet accounts allow users to send an unlimited number of e-mail messages for no additional cost.

However, many people do not like receiving unsolicited e-mail messages, commonly known as **spam.** Many ISPs use message filtering technologies to eliminate unwanted spam from their users' e-mailboxes. Some ISPs have even adopted no-spam policies, and they will terminate the accounts of users who violate these rules. In addition, some legislators are drafting laws that would fine the senders of spam.

Print Advertising Some Web site publishers send printed ads through regular mail to promote their site. A printed ad can reach individuals who do not use e-mail services. However, it costs money to print and mail advertisements and to obtain mailing lists. A printed message also lacks the immediacy of an e-mail message since recipients cannot simply click a hyperlink to visit the publicized site.

Link Trading Web sites that share common goals may agree to display a link to each other's site, an arrangement referred to as **link trading.** Trading links can increase a Web site's traffic and attract new visitors who are interested in the site's subject matter. It also costs very little to trade links. While this technique is cost effective, it does not always make sense. For example, a company will not want to link its Web site to a competitor's Web site.

Registering with Search Tools

Perhaps the most effective way to publicize a Web site is to register it with an Internet search engine or directory service. Registering your site exposes it to millions of Internet users who frequently use search tools to locate products, services, or information on the Web.

There are two main disadvantages to registering a site with a search tool. First, users generally receive many hits when making a search request. Depending on the number of hits received, users may or may not visit your site. Second, search tools process so many registration requests that it often takes several days, or even weeks, to include a Web site in their database.

Even with these drawbacks, however, registering a site is an important way to publicize it. In the following activity, you will learn how to register a Web site with a search engine.

ACTIVITY 14C Registering a Web Site with a Search Engine

1 With your teacher's permission, open your Web browser. Go to a search engine such as AltaVista, Google, or Dogpile.

2 Locate the engine's site submission page. For example, on Google, select **Jobs, Press, & Help,** and then select **Submitting your Site** on the All About Google page.

3 To register your Web site, you would type the site's URL into the engine's form and then submit it (see Figure 14.9).

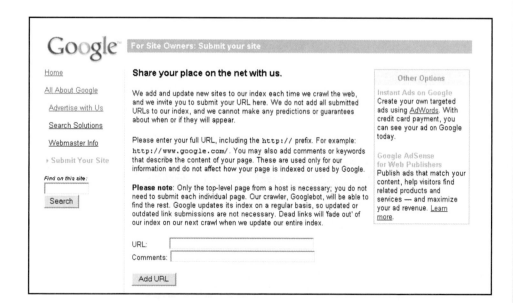

YOU TRY IT

● Figure 14.9
You can help attract visitors to your Web site by registering it with a search engine.

Using Meta Tags

A **meta tag** is a piece of HTML code that the Web author places in the page's file. Meta tags do not affect how the page displays in a Web browser. Instead, they influence how a search tool categorizes the page.

Meta tags provide information about the Web site. The "description" meta tag describes the site's purpose. This description usually displays in a search tool's search results. The "keywords" meta tag contains words or phrases that describe the site's content. Search engines use these keywords to create their databases. Adding the right meta tags to your Web pages can improve how your site displays on a search tool's hit list.

You can see meta tags by viewing a page's source code. Select View and then Source from your browser to open a page's source code in Notepad (meta tag are usually located near the top of the HTML document). The description and keywords meta tags for the Smithsonian Institution are shown below. The description tag describes the Smithsonian and its purpose. The keywords tag lists the keywords that people may use when searching for the Smithsonian site online.

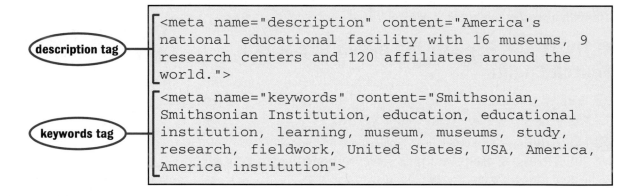

description tag

```
<meta name="description" content="America's national educational facility with 16 museums, 9 research centers and 120 affiliates around the world.">
```

keywords tag

```
<meta name="keywords" content="Smithsonian, Smithsonian Institution, education, educational institution, learning, museum, museums, study, research, fieldwork, United States, USA, America, America institution">
```

YOU TRY IT

ACTIVITY 14D Adding Meta Tags to a Web Site

❶ Open the WebTee.biz home page (**index.htm**) in FrontPage.

❷ Select **File** and then **Properties** to open the Page Properties dialog box. Click the **Custom** tab.

❸ Click the **Add** button that is next to the box labeled System variables. This opens the System Meta Variable (HTTP-EQUIV) dialog box shown in Figure 14.10.

Figure 14.10 ●──►
Search engines use meta tags to create their databases.

4 Type description into the Name box. Type a description of the WebTee.biz site into the Value box. Click **OK.**

5 Repeat step 3. Type keywords into the Name box. In the Value box, type keywords for the WebTee.biz site. Choose words that you think people would use to locate this type of site (for example, tee shirts, custom printing, etc.) Click **OK.**

6 Click **OK** to close the Page Properties dialog box. View the site in **Code** (in 2002, **HTML**) view. The meta tags have been added to the site's source code. Close FrontPage.

INCREASING WEB SITE TRAFFIC

Once a site has established an initial base of visitors, however, most Web site publishers will want to expand their user base over an extended period of time. Some techniques for increasing Web site traffic include:

◆ **Offer periodic sales and promotions.** E-commerce sites use this technique to attract repeat customers. Visitors will return to find out what items are on sale. Many sites also offer other types of promotions, such as gift certificates, referral bonuses or discounts, or free shipping on purchases over a certain amount (see Figure 14.11).

● **Figure 14.11**
Free shipping helps attract more visitors to the Amazon.com Web site. How do you think free shipping helps Amazon.com increase its sales?

◆ **Give away prizes.** Some Web publishers sponsor drawings in which Web surfers can win a prize just by visiting the site.

◆ **Offer recognition.** To some people, the opportunity to win recognition is almost irresistible. For this reason, many Web sites solicit information, suggestions, and articles from their user base, and then publish the names of people who made a significant contribution.

Figure 14.12
Privacy settings can be adjusted to control cookies. How are cookies useful? How might they be harmful?

USING COOKIES FOR TARGETED MARKETING

Advertising is most effective when it is aimed at a highly focused target audience. For example, if your Web site sells jazz CDs, you want to market this site to people who have purchased jazz music in the past.

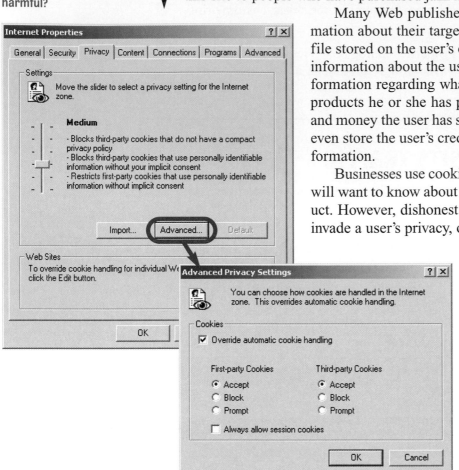

Many Web publishers use cookies to gather information about their target audience. A cookie is a small file stored on the user's computer that contains specific information about the user. Cookies usually contain information regarding what sites the user has visited, the products he or she has purchased, and how much time and money the user has spent online. Some cookies may even store the user's credit card or checking account information.

Businesses use cookies to target users that they think will want to know about a particular promotion or product. However, dishonest people can also use cookies to invade a user's privacy, or they could even use personal information illegally. For this reason, all Web browsers give users the ability to prevent certain types of cookies from being stored on their computer (as shown in Figure 14.12).

Section 14.3 Assessment

Concept Check

1. **Define** publicize, spam, link trading, meta tag.

2. **Describe** the methods commonly used to publicize Web sites.

3. **Explain** what a cookie is and what it contains.

Critical Thinking

4. **Draw Conclusions** Why do you suppose Web sites depend so heavily on repeat visitors?

5. **Compare and Contrast** What similarities and differences do you see in promoting a Web site via e-mail and promoting it with printed media?

Applying Skills

Promote a Web Site
Write a proposal for publicizing an e-commerce Web site that sells extreme sports gear. First, define the objective of the site. Then determine the most effective ways to market the site while minimizing the negative side of the methods you choose.

SECTION 14.1 Web Servers

Key Terms

publish, 370
Web server, 370
Web host, 371
host, 371

Web server clusters, 372
internal Web hosting, 373
external Web hosting, 373

Main Ideas

- Items to consider when selecting a Web server include CPU power, hard drive speed and capacity, communications channel bandwidth, scalability, and reliability.
- When you select a host, consider the costs and benefits of each Web server.
- When a company hosts its own sites, it is using internal hosting.
- When a company uses a hosting service for its sites, it is using external hosting.

SECTION 14.2 The Publishing Process

Key Terms

InterNIC, 376
case sensitive, 376
directory structure, 377

download, 378
upload, 378
cross-platform testing, 380

Main Ideas

- Web site names should be as unique, logical, and short as possible.
- A well-planned directory structure organizes files into groups of approximately the same size.
- When you publish your site, you must maintain its directory structure on the server exactly as it is on the computer used to develop the site.
- HTTP is the most common protocol used to download files.
- FTP is the most common protocol used to upload files to a Web server.
- You should test your published site on a variety of hardware configurations and browsers to make sure that it displays properly.

SECTION 14.3 Promoting a Web Site

Key Terms

publicize, 382
spam, 382

link trading, 383
meta tag, 384

Main Ideas

- Techniques for publicizing Web pages include e-mail, printed ads, link trading, and registering with search tools.
- Meta tags provide additional information about the Web page, including keywords indicating the site's purpose and content.
- Some search engines use meta tag information to associate a site with a particular topic.
- Sites can increase traffic by offering sales and promotions, giving away prizes, or offering recognition.
- Cookies are small files on the user's computer that contain information about the user.
- Businesses often use cookie information to target potential customers.
- Web browsers give users the ability to prevent certain types of cookies from being stored on their computer.

Reviewing Key Terms

1. What is a Web server?
2. What is the difference between internal Web hosting and external Web hosting?
3. Change the following sentence to make it true: *When you download files, you transfer them from a client computer system to a server.*
4. Why is cross-platform testing important?
5. What is InterNIC?

Understanding Main Ideas

6. **Explain** why a Web site must be published before visitors can view the site in their browsers.
7. **Summarize** five factors that affect a Web server's efficiency.
8. **Identify** six factors you need to consider when selecting a Web host.
9. **Explain** how to register a domain name.
10. **Discuss** the reasons that a site's directory structure should be well organized.
11. **Evaluate** the advantages and disadvantages of e-mail advertising.
12. **Identify** five methods that can be used to publicize and promote a new Web page.
13. **Describe** three ways to increase traffic to a Web site.
14. **Summarize** the importance of case sensitivity when transferring Web page files to a server.

Critical Thinking

15. **Compare and Contrast** The chapter identifies scalability and reliability as two important factors in a Web server's efficiency. Distinguish between these two factors.
16. **Analyze Web Hosts** Assume you are helping a small company choose an external Web host. What factors would you tell the company to consider when making its choice? Why would the level of tech support provided by the Web host be a factor in determining which Web host to use?
17. **Draw Conclusions** You are responsible for publishing a Web site that has several hundred pages organized into about twenty folders. How would a log of publishing events be useful to you?
18. **Make Predictions** You publish a site for NB Products. The company sells promotional materials for corporate and school events. The site's meta tags, however, only contain the company's name. Will people using a search engine be likely to find the site during their search for promotional products? Why or why not? What meta tags would you recommend the company use to help people locate its site?

e-Review ··················
webdesign.glencoe.com

Study with PowerPoint

To review the main points in this chapter, select **e-Review > PowerPoint Outlines > Chapter 14**.

Online Self Check

Test your knowledge of the material in this chapter by selecting **e-Review > Self Checks > Chapter 14**.

Making Connections

Language Arts—Conduct a Debate Conduct a classroom debate on the following topic: Cookies should not be allowed because using cookies to collect information is an invasion of a user's privacy.

With your teacher's permission, organize into two teams with each team taking one side. Research the issues involved and be prepared to argue your assigned point of view.

STANDARDS AT WORK

Students use productivity tools to collaborate in constructing technology-enhanced models, prepare publications, produce creative works. (NETS-S 5)

Create a Web Page with Meta Tags

Create a one-page Web page in FrontPage. This page is targeted at families in your community who have children under the age of five. The purpose of the page is to provide an overview of services available to these young children and their families. These services could include health care centers, preschools, day care centers, and local parks, recreation areas, and businesses that cater to children.

List four services or businesses on your page. To keep the amount of text on the page to a minimum, you decide:

◆ to list each service or business.
◆ to include a one-sentence description for each service or business.
◆ to provide a link to the Web site for each service or business.

You want search engines to list your page near the top when users search for services in your community. Consider what meta tags you need to include to make this happen. Add these meta tags to your page.

TEAMWORK SKILLS

Publicize a Web Site

Your team is creating a Web site for a business that offers classes in English as a second language. Your intended audience is recent immigrants to the United States who have limited English skills.

1. Select a name for the business.
2. Select a domain name for the Web site.
3. Explain why this is a good domain name for your site.
4. Research the domain name to see if it is available. If it is not available, select another domain name.
5. Write an advertising plan that describes how you will let people know about the site. Identify and describe at least three ways to advertise the site.
6. List your three choices. Place the method that you think would be most effective at the top of your list. Explain why you think this method would be an effective way to advertise your site.

CHALLENGE YOURSELF

Recommend a "Pay-per-click Service"

You are helping a local bed and breakfast launch their Web site. The owners are interested in the "pay-per-click" service available from some search engines. With this service, a search engine will list your site as a link, a banner, or at the top of the search list for a small fee. Charges are based on the number of people who actually click on your URL.

Research the "pay-per-click" services available from at least three of the following search engines: Google, Lycos, Yahoo, HotBot, and Dogpile. Locate their pricing structures and any other important information about their programs. Based on your research, create a chart that compares pricing structures. Write a paragraph recommending one of the services. State the reasons for your choice.

YOU TRY IT
Skills Studio

These exercises reinforce the skills you learned in this chapter's You Try It activities. Refer back to the You Try It activities if you need extra guidance.

1. Calculating Web Site Size

You are ready to publish the Astronomy Club Web site. In this activity, you will calculate the size of the Web site and estimate the minimum amount of bandwidth that a Web host will need to host your site.

Ⓐ Open the Astronomy Club site in FrontPage in Folders View.

Ⓑ Locate and write down the Web site's size.

Ⓒ Estimate the number of visitors you expect to access your site in a month. Assume that 15 percent of the students in your school will visit the site each month. In addition, you expect about 50 people outside the school to access the site monthly.

Ⓓ Calculate the site's approximate transfer bandwidth by multiplying the estimated number of visitors per month by the Web site's size.

2. Adding Meta Tags and Publishing a Site

Select a site you have created in this course, but have not yet published. Add meta tags to the source code and publish the site.

Ⓐ Find at least two sites on the Web on the same topic as your site.

Ⓑ View the source code for these sites. Identify any meta tags used by these sites.

Ⓒ Use your research of other sites, as well as your own ideas, to create a list of meta tags for your site.

Ⓓ Open the site you want to publish in FrontPage.

Ⓔ Add the meta tags you have selected to your site.

Ⓕ Publish your site using the instructions your teacher supplies. Be sure to ask for your teacher's permission before publishing the site!

Ⓖ View the site in a browser. View the site's source code to check the meta tags you created.

Web Design Projects

1. Organize Web Site Structure

The Tools for Home and Business Company has three stores. The company now wants to offer its products online. The company has completed the design for its Web site. Pages include the following:

◆ A home page (contains company overview and a table of contents with links to all the site's pages)
◆ A contact page
◆ An about us page
◆ A FAQ page
◆ A Tools for Home page (includes information and photos about small power tools, gardening tools, plumbing tools, and first aid kits)
◆ A Tools for Business page (includes information and photos about large tools such as table saws, electric sanders, and routers)
◆ An order form (allows customers to place an order and e-mail it to the business)

Use FrontPage to create the Tools for Home and Business Web site. Use placeholder text for graphics. Organize the site's files using a logical directory structure. Select a consistent naming structure for all files and folders. Use lowercase for all file and folder names.

2. Publish a Site

Using the transfer method your teacher assigns you, upload the Tools for Home and Business Company site to a server (be sure to get your teacher's permission before you publish your site).

◆ Test the site in two browsers to make sure that the site structure has transferred properly. If possible, test the site on different hardware configurations.
◆ Use FrontPage to add a graphic to one of the pages.
◆ Publish only the page that has changed (again, be sure to get your teacher's permission before publishing the changed page).
◆ Test the site again in two browsers to confirm that your changes display properly.

Maintaining a Web Site

YOU WILL LEARN TO...

WHY IT MATTERS.....................................

Most people would welcome the opportunity to live in a beautiful home. Even the grandest house, however, loses its appeal if the roof leaks or the walls are falling down. Most objects require maintenance to keep them attractive and useful. Web sites are no exception. You must repair and update your sites on a regular basis if you want your visitors to return.

Quick Write Activity

Think about the Web sites you have created. What items on these sites might need maintenance? What would happen if you failed to maintain these items? How does maintenance make these items more useful or attractive to visitors?

WHAT YOU WILL DO...

ACTIVITIES AND PROJECTS

Applying Skills

You Try It Activities

Chapter Assessment

You Try It Skills Studio

Web Design Projects

IN THE WORKBOOK

Optional Activities and Projects

Guided Reading

Web Design Projects

ON THE WEB

Activities at webdesign.glencoe.com

Reading Strategy Organizers

Go Online Activities

Study with PowerPoint

Self-Check Assessments

READ TO SUCCEED

Two-Column Notes

Two-column notes are a useful way to organize and study what you have read. Divide a piece of paper into two columns. In the left column, write down main ideas. They can be written as a word, phrase, or question. In the right column, write down supporting details. Use short phrases rather than sentences. For example, for the main idea *types of monitors,* the details could be: *1)CRT (cathode ray tubes) are less expensive. Take lots of power and space. 2) Flat screens use LCD (liquid crystal display). Images may not be as clear as CRT.*

Main Ideas

Web server maintenance is the primary responsibility of a Webmaster. Maintenance includes diagnosing and repairing a server's hardware and software, and backing up critical system data.

Key Terms

hot-swappable hard drives
hard drive mirroring
backup
incremental backup

Reading Strategy

Identify three important tasks required to maintain a Web server. Use a table like the one below (also available online).

Maintenance Task	Purpose of Task

Web server maintenance involves several kinds of tasks. Webmasters must monitor both the Web server's hardware and its software to make sure that they are working correctly. In addition, Webmasters must back up Web server data to preserve the data in case of a malfunction.

Activity 15.1 Explore Web Server Maintenance Find out more about maintaining a Web server by visiting **webdesign.glencoe.com**.

MAINTAINING A WEB SERVER

The Webmaster is responsible for ensuring the smooth, uninterrupted operation of the company's Web servers. Although some Webmasters develop and publish Web sites, most primarily focus on making sure the servers can properly upload, download, store, and back up Web site files.

Maintaining Uploading and Downloading Capabilities

A Web server's primary function is to upload and download Web site files. The server's ability to do this depends on two basic components.

Communication Hardware The first component is the communication lines and equipment that allow the server to "talk" to the outside world. This equipment includes hardware such as network adapters, routers, load balancers, and firewalls. The Webmaster must diagnose and repair this hardware should it fail.

However, individual Webmasters or businesses have little or no control over other types of communication failures. Large telecommunications companies, such as AT&T, MCI, SBC, and Sprint, own and operate most transmission lines (see Figure 15.1 on page 395). If these channels fail for any reason, the Web site host will not be able to fix the problem. For this reason, some Web hosting companies lease high-speed data lines from two or more telecommunications vendors so that they can still service customers if one particular network of lines goes down.

Communication Software The second component that determines a server's ability to upload and download files is the protocol software that controls the flow of data across the communication lines. The HTTP and FTP software that a Web server uses to transfer data may crash or malfunction as the result of a program bug or a power failure. The Webmaster must quickly address any software glitch that causes the server to stop responding to requests. In some cases, the Webmaster can stop and restart the offending service without affecting other programs. However, sometimes the Webmaster may have to reboot the entire server to recover from such an error.

Maintaining Storage

Web hosting services that allow their users to upload files must prepare for the possibility that their storage space will fill up. Once this happens, users cannot upload additional files. Also, the Web server itself may crash because the operating system can no longer create files. To prevent problems, a Webmaster must delete unused or outdated files whenever possible, or upgrade the Web server's storage capacity *before* problems occur.

Webmasters use different techniques for maintaining a Web server's storage devices. Some Web servers use a system of **hot-swappable hard drives** to store information. This type of system typically contains between two and six hard drives. Each drive has a small indicator that glows green when the drive is operating correctly and red when it fails. If a failure occurs, the Webmaster can easily remove the damaged drive from the server and replace it without having to power down the server.

Some Web servers use a third technique called **hard drive mirroring** to maintain storage. Hard drive mirroring means that data written to a primary

● Figure 15.1
Telecommunications companies customize services for businesses and individuals. What type of customer would be most likely to use high-speed data lines?

TECH TRIVIA

Web Server Ports Web servers use ports to connect to the Internet. The Web server that connects to the World Wide Web is typically port 80 and the FTP server is typically port 21. Clients connect to services at a specific IP address and port.

drive are automatically written onto one or more secondary drives in a parallel operation. If the primary drive fails, one of the secondary drives takes over. This switching function occurs automatically, without requiring any manual intervention, so the Web server remains fully functional with zero down time. The Webmaster can then replace the damaged drive when convenient.

As shown in Table 15.1, each storage option has pros and cons. The Webmaster must assess the company's needs when deciding which option to choose.

Table 15.1
Web server storage options vary significantly in complexity and cost. What storage option would a small business probably choose to maintain its server's storage?

Storage Option Pros and Cons		
Storage Option	**Pro(s)**	**Con(s)**
Hot-Swappable Hard Drive	Damaged drives can be replaced quickly and easily without having to power down the server.	Substantially more expensive than standard hard drives.
Hard Drive Mirroring	No down time (the computer works without interruption). Inexpensive to replace drives in system.	Speed at which data are stored may not be as fast as other storage options.

Backing Up Data

The loss of critical information can potentially drive a company out of business. For example, an e-commerce business that loses its customer information database will not be able to fulfill orders and will lose money.

Webmasters protect the company's valuable information by making backups. A **backup** is a copy of a specific set of data. Webmasters can store backups on tapes, CD-ROMs, hard drives, or even floppy disks. Some backup systems can transmit backup data over the Internet to a remote location, thereby protecting that data from any disaster that might occur at the source location.

Sometimes the backup is an exact copy of the original data. Other times, the files are compressed so that they occupy less disk space on the backup device. Nearly all backup devices give users the option of doing a complete system backup or an incremental backup. An **incremental backup** only stores data on the backup device that have changed since the last full backup was performed.

Like most other aspects of Web site maintenance, Webmasters must evaluate various backup solutions as to their overall effectiveness in terms of performance, convenience, and cost. Many companies and individuals will choose a simple, low-cost backup strategy, while others will opt for extra performance and extra data protection at a higher cost.

THE ROLE OF THE WEBMASTER

The Webmaster plays an important role in making sure Web sites function properly. In the next activity, you will examine the skills required to become a Webmaster.

ACTIVITY 15A Becoming a Webmaster

YOU TRY IT

❶ With your teacher's permission, go to a career resource Web site, such as the America's Job Bank (www.ajb.dni.us).

❷ Use the search feature available on your chosen site to locate information about the career of Webmaster. For example, type *Webmaster* into the America's Job Bank's Career Resource Library search engine (see Figure 15.2).

❸ Review the resources available and locate information about the career of Webmaster. For example, the Princeton Review provides salary information, an overview of a typical day in the life of a Webmaster, and an occupational forecast.

❹ Go to a job Web site, such as Monster.com. Use the search feature on your chosen site to locate Webmaster jobs. Note the number of Webmaster positions currently available and the various locations across the country where the openings occur.

❺ View the job description of three advertised positions. Make a list of the various tasks required of the Webmaster. Identify the job skills that you would need to successfully compete for this position.

● **Figure 15.2**
American Job Bank's Career InfoNet provides information about the general job market, the job market in your state, and the skills needed for a specific career.

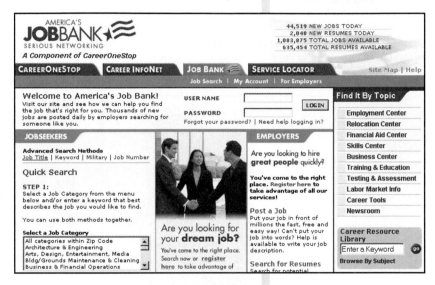

Section 15.1 Assessment

Concept Check

1. **Define** hot-swappable hard drives, hard drive mirroring, backup, incremental backup.

2. **Summarize** the important aspects of maintaining a Web server.

3. **Identify** various strategies for data storage maintenance.

Critical Thinking

4. **Compare and Contrast** Explain the similarities and differences between a complete backup and an incremental backup.

5. **Draw Conclusions** What can you conclude about the value a skilled Webmaster brings to a large company?

Applying Skills

Choose a Data Backup Utility Use the Web to locate information on three backup utilities. Determine the features and cost of each one. Then, recommend the one that you believe provides the best overall value.

STARTING AN E-BUSINESS

Like any business, a commercial Web site has to attract customers. To do this successfully, an e-business has to start with a good business plan.

If your site's message is clear and the design is appealing, potential customers are more likely to become real customers.

Start with a Plan

A business plan lays out the company's mission and outlines issues that managers should address in running the business. Your site's business plan should identify:

◆ The product or service you will sell
◆ The type of customers you expect
◆ The methods you will use to advertise, market, and sell your product or service
◆ The expenses you expect to have and the income you expect to receive

Business Functions

It is important to remember that many basic business rules and functions apply whether your company is online, on the corner, or both. A Web site can provide many of the same functions you will find in a traditional store.

For example, your Web site should provide a way to:

◆ Advertise your business, like a newspaper or radio ad
◆ Market your product or service, like a printed brochure or coupon
◆ Browse products, like a printed catalog or a store's shelves
◆ Place orders, like a customer service counter or toll-free number
◆ Pay, like a check-out counter

The Message Is Everything

Your Web site's main mission is to deliver your company's message to potential clients or customers. Successful sites make it easy for visitors to find the facts they need, without having to click through lots of pages or wait for long downloads.

Create your site's marketing message as if you were a first-time customer. Your site should clearly describe the products or services you offer, prices and availability, ordering and shipping instructions, and so on. Most important, the site should make visitors feel there is an advantage to doing business with you.

Tech Focus

1. Create a checklist to evaluate how well a commercial Web site works as a marketing tool. Compile your guidelines with those of the rest of the class. Then use this group checklist to evaluate three Web sites.

2. Suppose you have started a business that provides a service, such as gardening or photography. Create a plan that explains how you would use a Web site to market that business.

Section 15.2 Updating Information

Guide to Reading

Main Ideas

Published Web sites require regular updating. Webmasters often archive rather than discard the elements they remove. Preparing technical documentation is an important part of Web site maintenance.

Key Terms

file management
direct server update
local client update
archiving

Reading Strategy

Compare and contrast direct server updates and local client updates. Use a Venn diagram similar to the one below (also available online).

Even after publication, a Web site is never really finished. Webmaster are responsible for updating information on the site and fixing errors, such as broken hyperlinks. As the Webmaster of the sites you create, you should also plan to update your sites regularly to make them more useful and interesting to visitors.

GUIDELINES FOR UPDATING A SITE

Visitors return to sites that contain dynamic information. Some sites require constant updating to remain useful. For example, news sources must update their sites frequently to reflect events happening around the world. Webmasters of e-commerce sites, such as the one shown in Figure 15.3, must update their sites to display new merchandise and offers. When updating a site, consider the following guidelines:

- Think about how your changes will benefit your visitors.
- Frequently update content elements such as the site's graphics, text, last-updated date, and recommended links.
- Try to maintain the site's overall structure, navigation bars, logos, color schemes, and contact information. Changing these elements randomly will only confuse repeat visitors.
- Create a schedule for regular updates. Commit yourself to uploading modified pages according to your schedule.

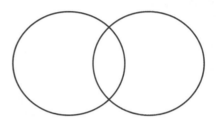

● **Figure 15.3**

Merchandise displays on e-commerce sites change frequently. **What other types of sites do you think should be updated frequently?**

EDITING AND UPDATING WEB FILES

A comprehensive Web site maintenance plan should include a strategy for file management. **File management** refers to creating, naming, moving, updating, and deleting files on a computer system.

Methods of Updating Files

Webmasters can update a Web page in basically one of two ways. They can either perform direct server updates or local client updates.

Direct Server Updates A **direct server update** involves updating the file directly on the Web server where it resides. The Webmaster opens a text editor, such as Notepad, on the server, loads the Web page for editing, makes the desired changes, and saves the file back to the server. Updating a live site (a site that has been published to a server) allows the Webmaster to quickly load, change, and save the file. Changes become visible to visitors immediately.

Local Client Updates You can make a **local client update** by changing a copy of the Web page on a client workstation (for example, on the computer you used to create the Web site). You can then upload the revised page to the server. Web surfers will not see the new version until you upload the file to the server.

YOU TRY IT

ACTIVITY 15B Updating a Web Site Locally

1 Open the WebTee.biz Web site in FrontPage. 2002 users, open the **contact.htm** page and skip to Step 3. 2003 users, select **File>Publish Site.**

2 In 2003, in the Remote Web site folder, select the **contact.htm** file. Notice that the left direction arrow in the middle of the screen becomes active (see Figure 15.4). Click on the left direction arrow to download the contact.htm file to your local computer. Double-click **contact.htm** in the Local Web site box.

Figure 15.4
You can download a page to a client workstation to update that page.

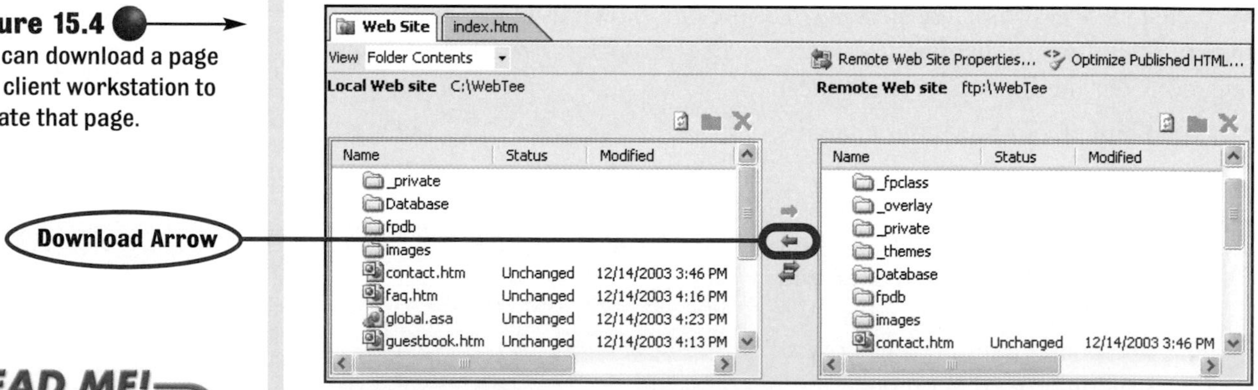

Download Arrow

Web Site	index.htm			
View Folder Contents ▾			Remote Web Site Properties...	Optimize Published HTML...
Local Web site	C:\WebTee		Remote Web site	ftp:\WebTee

Name	Status	Modified
_private		
Database		
fpdb		
images		
contact.htm	Unchanged	12/14/2003 3:46 PM
faq.htm	Unchanged	12/14/2003 4:16 PM
global.asa	Unchanged	12/14/2003 4:23 PM
guestbook.htm	Unchanged	12/14/2003 4:13 PM

Name	Status	Modified
_fpclass		
_overlay		
_private		
_themes		
Database		
fpdb		
images		
contact.htm	Unchanged	12/14/2003 3:46 PM

3 On the contact.htm page, delete the existing phone number, and type Toll-free (800) 555-5555. Save your changes.

4 On the **File** menu, click **Publish Site** (in 2002, **Publish Web**). With your teacher's permission, publish the Web site. Open the Contact Us page and view your changes. Close the Web site.

READ ME!

Caution If you update a live site, viewers may see your half-completed changes as you work on the page. You should only update a live site if you need to make an emergency fix, such as correcting incorrect information, fixing typos, or replacing broken links.

READ ME!

Tech Tip When you publish a site the second time, FrontPage only updates pages that have been changed.

Automated Updates Any Web site that requires frequent changes must use an automated update process. This allows multiple people to generate new Web content on their local workstations, test those pages to ensure that they look right and function correctly, and then submit them for inclusion in the next regular Web site update. An automated tool can then connect to the server (or servers) via HTTP or FTP and post all of the new content files in a single operation. This allows many people to service the never-ending process of updates, while protecting the live Web site from mistakes and/or tampering.

Using FrontPage Reports

FrontPage allows you to generate a variety of reports that can help you monitor the condition of a FrontPage-based Web site. You can access these reports from the View menu on the Standard toolbar. The Site Summary, Files, Problems, and Workflow reports arc useful maintenance tools.

Site Summary Report The Site Summary report summarizes the statistics for the entire site. It provides an overview of each individual report generated by FrontPage. As shown in Figure 15.5, you can use the report to review the number of files and pictures on your site and the size of these files. The report notes slow pages (pages that take longer than 30 seconds to download at 56Kbps), old files (files that have not been modified in over 72 days), and recently added files (files created in the last 30 days). The report also records the number of internal and external links, along with the number of broken and unverified links.

READ ME!

Caution You can generate some reports only after publishing the site to a server that runs FrontPage Server Extensions.

● **Figure 15.5**
The report shows that the WebTee.biz site currently contains 35 files. How can a report showing the number of broken links be helpful to a Webmaster?

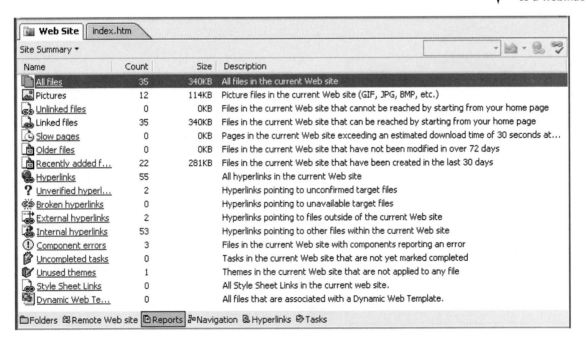

Files Report The Files report allows you to access information about all files on your Web site. The report lists the file's name, title, size, and type along with the folder it is stored in and the date it was last modified. The person who last modified the file is also noted. Different options allow you to view only recently added files, recently changed files, or older files.

READ ME!

Tech Tip You can also use the Recalculate Hyperlinks option from the View menu to check and repair all hyperlinks on your Web site.

Problems Report The Problems report enables you to check for particular issues, such as unlinked files, pages that download slowly, or Web components that do not work properly.

You can also use the Problems report to access the Hyperlinks report. Updating hyperlinks is an essential part of Web site maintenance, since nothing signals a neglected page as clearly as hyperlinks to nonexistent pages. The Hyperlinks report identifies broken links on your site. Unbroken links are marked "OK". A question mark and the label "Unknown" mark internal hyperlinks and external links on pages that have never been published. FrontPage cannot verify whether these links will work until after the page is published. In the following activity, you will check for broken links on the WebTee.biz site.

YOU TRY IT

ACTIVITY 15C Checking for Broken Links

❶ Open the WebTee.biz Web site in FrontPage.

❷ On the **View** menu, select **Reports>Problems>Hyperlinks** (in 2002, **Broken Hyperlinks**). The hyperlinks screen will appear, as shown in Figure 15.6.

Figure 15.6
The hyperlinks report lists broken links first.

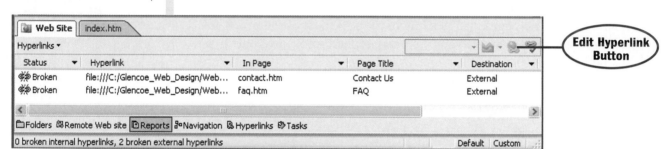

Edit Hyperlink Button

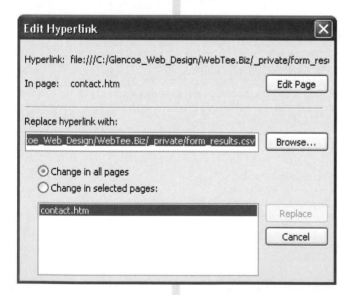

❸ Look for broken hyperlinks under the Status column. Double-click on a broken hyperlink. The Edit Hyperlink dialog box appears, as shown in Figure 15.7.

❹ If possible, enter a new URL into the Edit Hyperlink dialog box to replace your broken link.

❺ Click **Replace** to change the broken hyperlink. If possible, test the new link.

❻ Repeat steps 4–6 to repair any remaining broken hyperlinks.

❼ Save and close the Web site.

Figure 15.7
The Edit Hyperlink dialog box allows you to change the path to any hyperlink at the site.

Workflow Report The Workflow report summarizes the current status of a site under development. You can use this report to review the status of individual files, see who is responsible for developing these files, check whether or not a file has been published, and review source control.

ARCHIVING WEB PAGES

The process of saving old pages is called **archiving.** You can store archived information in several ways. The easiest way is to create a folder named "Archive" and copy old Web page elements into subfolders within that folder. You can store an archive folder and its subfolders in several places, such as on your local computer, on a removable storage device, or on your Web host's server.

When you update a site, do not immediately discard old Web elements. Instead, keep old pages and graphics for at least six months to a year. Old pages can make good templates, and you can reuse old graphics. When archiving an HTML document, remember to archive the document's associated graphics files and folders. Store the graphics in a folder with the same name as the original graphics folder so that your archived page's links will work properly.

DEVELOPING TECHNICAL DOCUMENTATION

Many Web site publishers provide various forms of technical documentation to accompany their software. Such documentation might be intended for Web site users, Webmasters, or even Web site developers. Regardless of its intended readership, documentation can be an essential part of an effective Web site.

Web site user documentation is usually limited to online help files or downloadable PDF files that users can print or view electronically with a "reader" program. Documentation intended for Web site content developers contains instructions for creating content in a form that will flow easily into the Web page design. Other people, such as Webmasters and system administrators, may require additional documentation to help them learn how to execute automated publishing tools and to verify that the updating process runs smoothly.

Section 15.2 Assessment

Concept Check

1. **Define** file management, direct server update, local client update, archiving.

2. **Explain** the importance of archiving Web pages.

3. **Summarize** why it is useful to develop technical documentation.

Critical Thinking

4. **Summarize** Describe the steps you would use to repair a broken hyperlink.

5. **Compare and Contrast** How are direct server updates similar to and different from local client updates?

Applying Skills

Plan Updates to a Site The WebTee business plans to add sweatshirts to their product line. Describe your plan to update the site to include sweatshirts. Explain the reasons for your planned updates.

HOT ZONES AND THE WIRELESS WEB

Every day, new wireless zones (or "hot spots") pop up, allowing people worldwide to access the Web while they are on the move.

The growth of wireless zones may soon allow you to connect to the Internet from nearly anywhere.

What Is a Wireless Zone?

Wireless zones are public wireless LANs that enable people to access the Internet with wireless devices, such as notebook PCs, PDAs, digital pagers, and digital cell phones. Wireless zones are already available in hundreds of locations, such as Internet cafes, hotels, and convention facilities.

McDonald's, for example, provides wireless Internet access at several of its restaurants. Customers with wireless devices can connect to the Internet at the restaurant for a small fee. Many other retailers are following this trend.

Wireless zones are not just for mobile users. In fact, large-scale wireless zones may be the best option for people in rural areas and other places with limited access to wired connections. Large phone-service providers are now setting up wide-ranging wireless zones in such areas, so computers can connect to the Internet without tying up phone lines or running up long-distance fees.

Wireless Advantages

Wireless zones benefit individuals and businesses:

◆ Mobile workers can use a wireless device to connect with their employer's network to check e-mail, share documents, and perform other tasks without being tied to phone lines.
◆ Consumer-oriented businesses, such as retailers and restaurants, can offer wireless Web access to attract customers.

Wireless Dangers

Although they have many advantages, wireless networks also pose unique security risks. Someone with the right equipment can locate a wireless network's signal and tap into it, becoming part of the network. This security threat exists because wireless network transmissions can radiate in all directions.

A new breed of security measures, such as wireless firewalls and encryption schemes, are already being introduced to handle these threats. Still, users of wireless zones will need to be more cautious than wired users for the foreseeable future.

Tech Focus

1. How can businesses use wireless hot spots for profit? Create an imaginary business or describe an actual business that currently uses wireless zones to attract customers.

2. Research the potential impact of wireless zones on areas where Internet access is now limited. What impact could this technology have on people who live in such areas?

Section 15.3 Keeping a Web Site Secure

Guide to Reading

Main Ideas

Many Web sites collect valuable information about the Web surfers who visit it. Part of a Webmaster's job is keeping this personal data secure from unauthorized access.

Key Terms

access control
password
user authentication
global access control

Reading Strategy

Describe three ways to control access to a Web site. Use a web diagram similar to the one below (also available online).

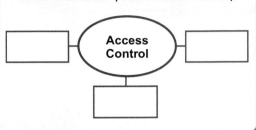

Web servers are specifically designed to transmit information to the general public. If a server can be tricked into thinking that an intruder is a legitimate user, it will provide the unauthorized visitor with any information requested. Such information could include names, addresses, phone numbers, e-mail addresses, credit card information, and other personal data. Safeguarding the confidentiality of users' personal data must be a primary concern for any Web site publisher who collects and stores such information.

CONTROLLING ACCESS TO A SITE

Webmasters are usually responsible for setting up a system that will allow access to users with permission to enter the site and keep out users without permission. Restricting the availability of a site to a specific set of authorized users is known as **access control.** Webmasters can use various techniques to implement this control.

Password Controls

Perhaps the most widely used form of access control among Web sites today is the password. A **password** is a set of letters or numbers that a user enters to gain access to a site. Virtually every Web site that restricts access to a specific group of authorized users will require those users to identify themselves with a user ID and a password. The system will then check the password the user entered to make sure it matches the one assigned to the identified user. This process is known as **user authentication.**

Some sites encourage users to improve the security of their passwords by enforcing various password rules. For example, one site might require passwords to contain a minimum number of characters, while another site might reject all passwords that do not include at least one number. Other sites require users to change their password every 30, 60, or 90 days. All of these rules make it harder for hackers to use other people's passwords.

> **READ ME!**
>
> **Jargon** People skilled at fooling computer systems into granting access to restricted information or performing unauthorized operations are commonly known as hackers.

To enter a protected Web site, users must typically enter their user ID and password into the site's login screen. In the next activity, you will create a login screen using HTML.

ACTIVITY 15D Creating a Login Screen

❶ Open FrontPage. Create a new page.

❷ Switch to **Code** (in 2002, **HTML**) view. Enter the HTML text exactly as shown in Figure 15.8. (Delete any unneeded code that FrontPage automatically provides.)

Figure 15.8 ●⟶
This HTML code creates a login screen.

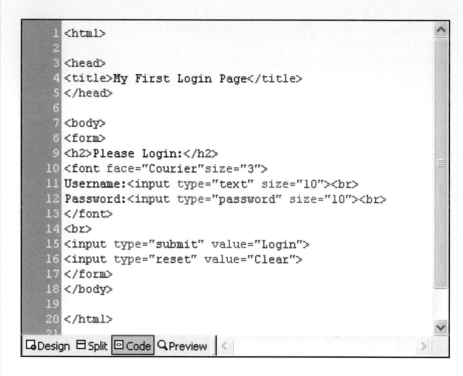

Figure 15.9 ●⟶
The login screen requires the user to enter a username and password.

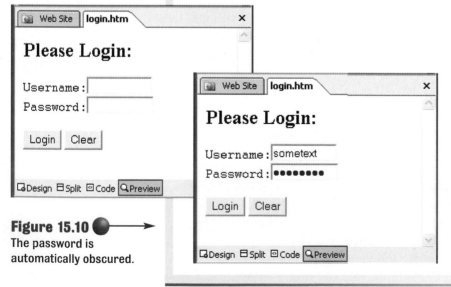

Figure 15.10 ●⟶
The password is automatically obscured.

❸ Save the file as **login.htm**.

❹ Preview the **login.htm** file. It should appear as shown in Figure 15.9.

❺ Type sometext in the Username field. Enter the same text into the Password field. Note that the text does not display the same way in both fields.

❻ Your Web page should now look like Figure 15.10. Close the page.

When you type text into the Password field, dots replace the text. Obscuring text in the Password field helps promote Web site security by keeping the password a secret from other users.

Global Access Controls

Once the site authorizes a user to enter, it may use additional access control mechanisms to safeguard valuable data. Granting or denying access to system data for multiple users is known as **global access control.** Users are assigned to groups, and different groups are given different levels of access to the system. For example, one group of users may be granted rights to view system data but denied the right to change any data. Another group may be given rights to enter new data records into the central database but not to delete an existing record from it.

The administrator group typically has rights to perform any operation to the system. Only a small number of people, such as the Webmaster and the system administrators, have this high level of access. Using global access control can substantially enhance a Web site's security.

MONITORING WEB SITE TRAFFIC

Different tools can help companies or individuals monitor their Web site's traffic. Monitoring traffic can help people know how and when their sites are being used.

Web Page Tracking Systems

Web page tracking systems generate information about which pages visitors are hitting, how often, and from where. Webmasters can use Web traffic monitoring tools to manage Web site security. The reports these tools generate can help Webmasters identify individuals who have accessed the site through unauthorized channels or at prohibited times of the day.

FrontPage Usage Reports

FrontPage generates Usage reports that track how many people have visited a site on a daily, weekly, and monthly basis. As shown in Figure 15.11, the Usage reports also note what operating systems and browsers visitors used. This information can help you determine what types of functionality you should include on your site.

Certain usage reports even let you know how visitors found your site. For example, FrontPage indicates if a visitor clicked a banner ad to link to your site. This information can help you measure the usefulness of different marketing efforts.

Activity 15.2 Explore Global Access Controls Find out more about global access controls by visiting **webdesign.glencoe.com.**

READ ME!

Caution Usage reports are only available for Web sites hosted on Web servers that contain FrontPage Server Extensions.

● **Figure 15.11**
Usage reports can help you track Web site traffic. Why is it important to know what browsers visitors are using to view your site?

Usage Summary		
Name	Value	Description
Date of first data	Monday, February 05, 2001 12:00 AM	Usage data accumulated starting with this date
Date last updated	Saturday, March 17, 2001 11:59 PM	Last time usage processing was run on the server
Total visits	4	Number of pages viewed from external sources
Total page hits	59	Number of hits on all pages.
Total bytes downloaded	0 KB	Number of bytes downloaded
Current visits	4	Number of pages viewed from external sources for this mon…
Current page hits	59	Number of page hits received for this month (Mar-01)
Current bytes downloaded	0 KB	Number of bytes downloaded this month (Mar-01)
Top referrer		Most frequent referrer this month (Mar-01)
Top referring domain		Most frequent referring domain this month (Mar-01)
Top web browser	Microsoft Internet Explorer 5.0	Most frequent browser used to view this web this month (M…
Top operating system	Windows 2000	Most frequent operating system used by browsers this mont…
Top search terms		Most frequent search terms used to find this web this month…
Top user		Most frequent user to view this web this month (Mar-01)

ETHICS AND WEBMASTERING

The need for Web site security is well established, as is the technology to implement such security. However, the question still remains as to how much security any given Web site publisher should be required to provide. For instance, a public school district that provides information about its students' grades should take steps to ensure that such information is not made available to everyone. However, should that district be required to implement passwords, global access controls, and other measures to keep that information as secure as possible? These questions do not yet have a clear legal answer.

Webmasters often must make ethical decisions when monitoring Web sites. For instance, some Web sites allow users to upload images to the server. Web hosting services often store image files in a "holding" directory until a moderator, who may be the Webmaster, can preview them. Once approved, the files are then moved to a "live" directory where anyone can access them. During this process, the Webmaster must make choices regarding what is and is not appropriate material. Along with repairing hardware and software, these ethical choices are sometimes part of the Webmaster's job.

CONCLUSION

Whether you are developing a Web site for a major corporation, or creating a site for your own personal use, many of the same basic steps need to be followed. The projects you have completed throughout this book have given you the fundamental skills needed to create interesting, user-friendly Web sites. In the next unit, you can enhance these skills by learning more about how to use HTML code. As you develop as a Web designer, you will continue to build upon the basic skills learned in this book.

Section 15.3 Assessment

Concept Check

1. **Define** access control, password, user authentication, global access control.

2. **Explain** the need for Web site security.

3. **Summarize** the ethical questions Webmasters encounter.

Critical Thinking

4. **Draw Conclusions** How do global access control mechanisms enhance the security provided by user passwords?

5. **Compare and Contrast** How are access control mechanisms similar to data encryption techniques (see page 332)? How do they differ?

Applying Skills

Analyze Security Visit three online shopping, auction, or banking sites. Identify the means they employ to keep customer data secure.

SECTION 15.1 Web Server Maintenance

Key Terms

hot-swappable
  hard drives, 395
hard drive mirroring, 395
backup, 396
incremental backup, 396

Main Ideas

■ The Webmaster is responsible for maintaining the smooth, continuous operation of the company's Web servers.

■ A server's ability to upload and download files depends on the communication lines and other hardware and on the protocol software that controls the flow of data.

■ Some servers use two-to-six hot-swappable hard drives with indicator lights to report drive failure.

■ Webmasters protect the company's data by making backups.

■ Incremental backups copy only the data that changed since the last full backup.

SECTION 15.2 Updating Information

Key Terms

file management, 400
direct server update, 400
local client update, 400
archiving, 403

Main Ideas

■ A Web site requires regular updating to keep it useful and attractive to visitors.

■ A direct server update is quick and easy, but visitors can see your half-completed changes.

■ To update a page locally, download the page, change it on your computer, preview it in a browser, and upload the modified page to the server.

■ FrontPage provides Site Summary, Files, Problems, and Workflow reports to monitor the condition of a FrontPage-based Web site.

■ After you update a site, archive rather than discard old Web elements.

SECTION 15.3 Keeping a Web Site Secure

Key Terms

access control, 405
password, 405
user authentication, 405
global access control, 407

Main Ideas

■ Most Web sites with access control require users to identify themselves by entering a user ID and password into a login screen to gain access to the site.

■ Global access control mechanisms enable different levels of system access to different groups of users.

■ Web page tracking systems generate information about which pages visitors are hitting, how often, and from where.

■ FrontPage Usage reports track the number of visitors to your site and note the operating systems and browsers they used.

■ Other Usage reports let you know how visitors found your site.

■ The Webmaster must sometimes make ethical choices about what is and is not appropriate material for the Web site.

Reviewing Key Terms

1. How do hot-swappable hard drives help reduce down time for Web servers?
2. What is hard drive mirroring?
3. What do Webmasters use to make backups?
4. Change the following sentence to make it true: *The process of saving old Web pages is called file management.*
5. What is the name of the process that compares the password entered by the user with the password assigned to the identified user?

Understanding Main Ideas

6. **Describe** the primary tasks of Webmasters.
7. **List** two techniques Webmasters use to maintain Web server storage devices.
8. **Summarize** the guidelines for updating a Web site.
9. **Describe** the purpose of the FrontPage Site Summary Report.
10. **Identify** two ways in which documentation may be provided to Web site users.
11. **Describe** the most common way for Web sites to implement access control.
12. **Discuss** how Webmasters can use Web tracking systems.
13. **Identify** the types of information you can learn by accessing the FrontPage Problems report.

Critical Thinking

14. **Make Decisions** As Webmaster, it is your job to choose the backup strategy for your company. Its site is updated several times a week as products are added and removed. What type of backup plan(s) would you develop for this site? Explain your reasoning.
15. **Draw Conclusions** You serve as Webmaster for two sites. One site contains 100 internal hyperlinks and 5 external hyperlinks. The other has 10 internal hyperlinks and 75 external hyperlinks. How frequently should you run the FrontPage Problems Report for each site? Explain your reasoning.
16. **Evaluate Security** As Webmaster for a large e-commerce site, you are setting global access controls for the site and for the database in which all customer and product information is stored. You are assigning access to the following groups: salespeople who gather customer information, product line managers who develop new products, customers, warehouse personnel who fill the orders, and top-level managers. What level of access should each group be given? Explain your reasoning.

e-Review ·················
webdesign.glencoe.com

Study with PowerPoint
To review the main points in this chapter, select **e-Review > PowerPoint Outlines > Chapter 15.**

Online Self Check
Test your knowledge of the material in this chapter by selecting **e-Review > Self Checks > Chapter 15.**

Making Connections

Language Arts—Create an Oral Presentation Assume that you work for a company that sells hardware solutions for Web server storage devices. The company offers each of the storage solutions discussed in the chapter to its customers.

Prepare an oral presentation that you can use on sales calls to businesses. Assume that your customers include both large companies and Web hosting businesses. Your presentation should focus on the features and benefits of each storage device offered by your company and the cost of each option (research options as needed). Be prepared to answer questions at the end of your presentation.

STANDARDS AT WORK

Students us a variety of media and formats to communicate information and ideas effectively to multiple audiences. (NETS-S 4)

Create Technical Documentation

You are the Webmaster for your company's Web site. You are currently completing a round of local client updates to the site, which will be posted to the Web server. However, you have been assigned to a special project team and will not be able to complete the next round of updates to the Web site. You must therefore document your tasks so they can be completed by another person.

- Write a set of procedures for the person who will be doing the updates.
- Explain in words, drawings, or screen shots the updating process.
- Test your procedures by updating the WebTee.biz site that you published in the last chapter. The site should be updated by adding a scrolling marquee that reads: Electronic payments to be accepted beginning next month.

TEAMWORK SKILLS

Update a Web Site

As a team, select a Web site that you have created in this course, but have not yet published. Publish the site, either to your hard drive or to a Web server. Check with your teacher to learn how you should publish the site.

Review the site to identify at least three improvements the team can make to the site. Once you have identified three changes, complete the following tasks. You may want to have different members of the team complete different tasks.

- Make the changes as a local client update.
- Preview the site in a browser to test your changes.
- Publish the site again to the same location.
- View the published site in a browser and verify that your changes appear and work as expected.
- In FrontPage, print the Files report and highlight the files that changed during your update.

CHALLENGE YOURSELF

Identify Security Procedures

Conduct an interview with a Webmaster from your school, school district, or local business. Before the interview, write a series of questions that you would like to ask about the types of security procedures he or she uses to manage access to Web sites.

Write down the Webmaster's answers to your questions and ask additional follow-up questions as needed. Based on the interview, write a two-page report that explains how the Webmaster controls access to all the information contained on the Web site.

YOU TRY IT
Skills Studio

These exercises reinforce the skills you learned in this chapter's You Try It activities. Refer back to the You Try It activities if you need extra guidance.

1. Updating a Web Site

Add an additional question and answer to the WebTee.biz FAQ page.

Ⓐ Open the WebTee.biz **faq.htm** page in FrontPage.

Ⓑ Add the following question to the page: What is your return policy?

Ⓒ Decide whether or not the WebTee.biz site should accept returns of custom designs. Write an answer to the question that reflects your policy.

Ⓓ Include this question in the list at the top of the page.

Ⓔ Add a bookmark to the question.

Ⓕ Proofread your work and save the site.

Ⓖ With your teacher's permission, publish the site. Check the FAQ page carefully to make sure it has been updated.

2. Viewing FrontPage Reports

Use FrontPage reports to check the status of the WebTee.biz site.

Ⓐ Open the WebTee.biz home page in FrontPage.

Ⓑ Select **View>Reports>Site Summary.** Print the Site Summary report.

Ⓒ Use the Site Summary report to identify how many files have been recently added to the Web site.

Ⓓ Click the Recently added files link. Identify the three files that have been added to the site most recently. Identify each file's type and the date each file was created.

Ⓔ Return to the Site Summary report. Identify how many internal and external links are contained in the Web site.

Ⓕ Select **View>Reports>Files>Recently Changed Files.** Identify the files that were modified when the FAQ page was updated.

Ⓖ Select **View>Reports>Problems>Hyperlinks.** Identify how many links in the site are OK, and how many are broken. Close the site.

Web Design Projects

1. Check Web Site Accessibility

Any Web site posted to a public school's Web server must comply with the district's accessibility policy. This policy should comply with the guidelines established in Section 508 of the U.S. Rehabilitation Act (see Appendix E). Following these guidelines, all accessibility problems should be fixed before a site is published.

One common accessibility error is a lack of alternative text for graphics. Screen readers need this information to interpret the site for the visually impaired.

If you are using FrontPage 2003:

◆ Use the FrontPage 2003 Accessibility report to check for Accessibility errors on the WebTee.biz site (select **Tools>Accessibility**). Make sure to check whether the site complies with Access Board Section 508. Add alternative text as needed and run the Accessibility report again.

If you are using FrontPage 2002:

◆ Open the WebTee site. Switch to **HTML** view. Identify images that do not have alternative text. Switch to **Normal** view and add alternative text as needed.

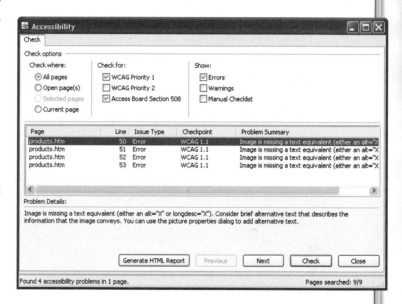

2. Document a Procedure

You are Webmaster for a Web hosting service. The hosting service allows clients to select the backup method for their sites. The least expensive method is incremental backup. The mid-range option is daily incremental backups and monthly complete backups. The most expensive option is a daily complete backup. The service has several clients who have chosen each option.

You will be on vacation next week. The person filling in for you knows little about your job. Write a set of procedures for each of the backup options available. With your procedures, provide a schedule of when backups are done. Let the schedule reflect the fact that you process incremental backups in the early afternoon. You schedule complete backups to run overnight and you check the results the following morning.

Problem Solving: Develop a Commercial Web Site

You are working on the Web site for a furniture store that has just added computer furniture to their inventory. The store owners have decided that they need a new Web site that features the new computer furniture line.

1. Write a mission statement and goals for the site and determine the target market. The computer furniture is high quality and ergonomic, meaning that it is specifically designed for physical comfort and safety. The company plans to sell this line of products for home-office use. As part of your planning process, determine the site's name.

2. Create a storyboard for the site. The site should include information about the business and its products.

3. The home page should explain the benefits of an improved working environment.

4. Each type of product should have its own page. Include pages for desks, chairs, accessories, and storage units.

5. Include a frequently asked questions (FAQ) page.

6. Add an order form that can be accessed from each of the product pages.

7. Design the order form so that it includes all the information the business would need to fill the order. You may want to look at similar product catalogs to see what types of styles, sizes, finishes, and other features you should include in your form. You also may want to research order forms online for ideas of how to structure the form.

8. Be sure to include a privacy policy.

9. Create the Web site in FrontPage. Test the site in a browser after each page has been added.

10. Add search capabilities that will allow users to find information at the site.

11. With your teacher's permission, publish the site to another location on your hard drive or network. Test the site. Make corrections as needed.

Building Your Portfolio

Create an Online Portfolio

In this project, you will create a frames site to house an online portfolio. An online portfolio is a great way to display your best Web site designs.

1. Create a Web site in FrontPage that uses the Contents frames template.

    ◆ The narrow left frame will contain links to the content pages.
    ◆ The content pages will contain your best Web pages.

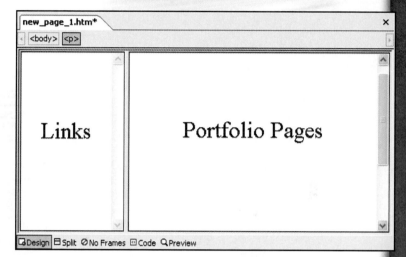

2. Review the sites that you have created during this class. Select pages to include in your portfolio. Try to include pages that demonstrate the various FrontPage skills that you have learned. Aim to include six to eight samples.

3. Create a home page that introduces you and your portfolio. Assume that the visitors to your site will be potential employers.

4. Create blank content pages for each of the Web pages or sites you plan to add to your portfolio.

5. Open the Web pages that you want to include in your portfolio. In **Split** (in FrontPage 2002, **HTML**) view, copy the code from each page and paste it into one of the blank content pages of your portfolio Web site.

6. Create links from the left frame to each of the content pages. Add a copyright statement to the left frame that identifies you as the copyright holder of your work.

7. Add a hit counter to the left frame.

8. Add a guest book to the site to invite visitors to comment on your portfolio.

9. Preview your site in a browser, making changes as appropriate.

10. Optional (with your teacher's permission)—publish the finished Web site on your school or class Web site.

11. For your portfolio, include a screen shot and an electronic copy of your finished product.

12. Ask three classmates to review your portfolio. Have each of them add an entry in the guest book.

UNIT
5

Advanced HTML

Visit *Glencoe Online*

Go to this book's Web site at
webdesign.glencoe.com.

Click on **Unit Activities** and select
**Unit 5 Cyber Manners and
Netiquette.** Take a quiz to check
your knowledge of safe and effective
online communication.

Think About It

Technology of Tomorrow

Even though you may not know exactly how they work, computers and the Internet are part of our daily lives. From telephone networks to bank networks to the Internet, we are connected to the world at home, at school, and at work.

Predict the Future Activity

For many years, telephones affected more people than any other type of communication. Do you think in the next ten years more people will communicate with each other using the telephone, the Internet, or another new kind of technology? Explain your answer.

HTML Tables and Frames

YOU WILL LEARN TO...

Section 16.1

● Create a basic table using HTML

● Define borders

● Merge cells

● Align content in tables

Section 16.2

● Create a frame-based Web page using HTML

● Create a link bar page

● Create a content page

● Create a container page

● Control Web page layout with frames

● Create links between frames

WHY IT MATTERS.....................................

When viewed from above, a football field looks like a giant table or grid. This table defines the boundaries of the playing field. Lines within the table form a grid that tells players where to position themselves during the game. An HTML table on a Web page functions in a similar way. It both defines the layout space and allows Web designers to position items precisely on the page.

Quick Write Activity

Examine the notes you have taken for one of your other classes. Select one day's notes and organize the information into a table. How does a table help you organize and interact with information?

WHAT YOU WILL DO..

ACTIVITIES AND PROJECTS

IN THE WORKBOOK

ON THE WEB

READ TO SUCCEED

Study with a Buddy

It can be difficult to review your own notes and quiz yourself on what you have read. According to research, studying with a partner for just 12 minutes can help you study better. Two-column notes are particularly useful for studying with a buddy. One buddy reads one main idea from the left column of the notes. The other buddy tries to recite all the supporting details in the right column. The first buddy provides any information missed by the second buddy. When you have gone through all the main ideas, switch roles.

Creating Tables in HTML

In Chapter 6, you learned how to use tables in FrontPage. In this chapter, you will learn how to build a table using HTML tags.

DEFINING A BASIC TABLE

Three sets of HTML tags define a table:

◆ The `<table></table>` tag set marks the beginning and end of the table area.

◆ The `<tr></tr>` tag set marks the beginning and end of a table row.

◆ The `<td></td>` tag set marks the beginning and end of a table column.

The simplest table is one that defines a single table cell—that is, a table with one row and one column. Figure 16.1 shows the HTML source code that defines such a table, and illustrates how this table will look when viewed in a Web browser.

Figure 16.1

Notice that you cannot see the boundaries of the cell in the browser. How many rows and columns are in a single table cell?

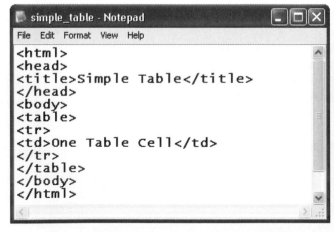

 webdesign.glencoe.com

USING TABLE ATTRIBUTES

It is easy to modify a table's characteristics by using table attributes. The HTML table code defines an area on the Web page where you can place items within a grid. As shown in Figure 16.1, this grid is invisible.

Creating Table Borders

To outline a table grid and make it visible on the screen you need to use the `border` attribute. In addition, you can use the `bordercolor` attribute to specify the table border's color. Figure 16.2 shows the HTML code used to create a blue border. The number 1 defines the width of the border. The higher the number you use, the thicker the border. The `bordercolor` attribute uses a hexadecimal number or one of the 16 standard colors to define the border color.

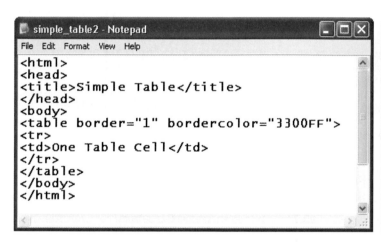
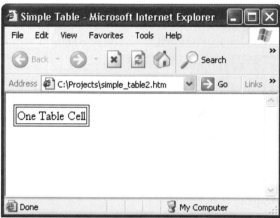

Figure 16.2
The `border` attribute creates a boundary around the cell. What defines the width of the border?

Notice that two blue rectangles actually appear around the table cell in Figure 16.2. The browser draws a border around each cell in the table, and then another border around the entire table. The space between the outer border and the cell border is the **cell spacing.** You can adjust this spacing with the `cellspacing` attribute.

The space between a cell border and the cell's content is the **cell padding.** You use the `cellpadding` attribute to adjust this spacing. Figure 16.3 shows the Figure 16.2 table with cell padding and only one border.

Figure 16.3
Set the cell spacing to 0 if you only want to see one border. What does a cell padding of 5 do?

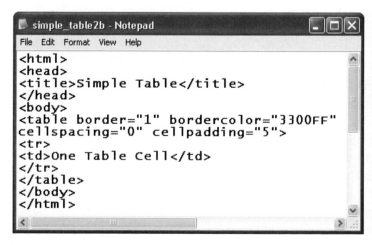
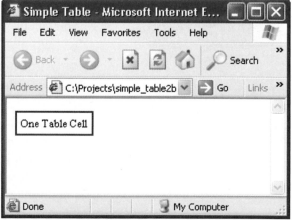

Merging Cells

Most tables contain more than one cell. The code used to create a cell is also used to create a table with multiple rows and columns—you just use more row and column tags.

You can combine, or merge, two or more table cells to make one larger cell. You can merge cells horizontally by grouping multiple columns in a row. By merging columns, you create a header row. A **header row** contains titles for each column in a table. As shown in Figure 16.4, you place the colspan attribute within a <td> tag to merge cells horizontally. The number after the attribute (2) indicates the number of columns to be merged.

Figure 16.4
You add the colspan attribute within the <td> tag. What information often appears in a header row?

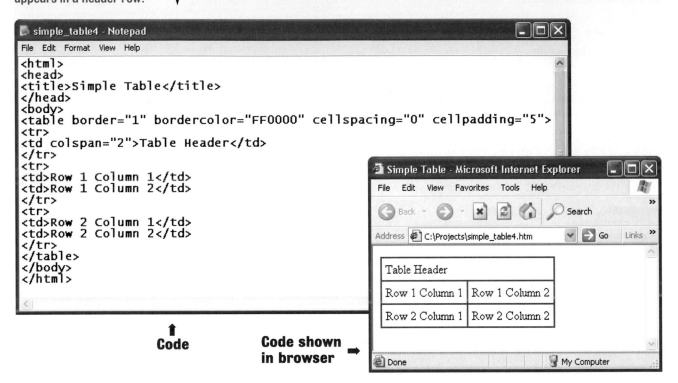

Code

Code shown in browser ➡

You can also merge cells vertically by grouping multiple rows in a column. By merging rows, you can create a header column. A **header column** contains titles for each row in the table. You use the rowspan attribute to merge cells vertically.

Activity 16.1 Explore Table Attributes Learn more about table attributes at **webdesign.glencoe.com**.

Controlling Table Alignment

You can use the align attribute to:

◆ Align a table on a page
◆ Align items in a cell

The possible values for the align attribute are left, center, and right.

When used in the <table> tag, the align attribute affects the horizontal alignment of the entire table. When used in the <tr> tag, the align attribute will align the contents of all the cells in that row. When used in the <td> tag, the align attribute defines how the contents of one particular table cell will align. If the align attribute is not present, the default alignment for tables and table cells is left.

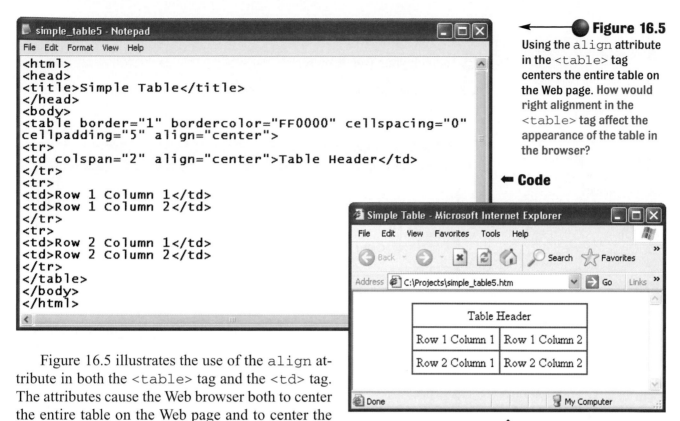

Figure 16.5

Using the `align` attribute in the `<table>` tag centers the entire table on the Web page. How would right alignment in the `<table>` tag affect the appearance of the table in the browser?

← **Code**

Code shown in browser

Figure 16.5 illustrates the use of the `align` attribute in both the `<table>` tag and the `<td>` tag. The attributes cause the Web browser both to center the entire table on the Web page and to center the table heading within the first row of the table.

Creating a Table

In the following activity, you will create a table using HTML. You will add a border to the table and adjust its cell spacing and cell padding. You will also align items and create a header column.

ACTIVITY 16A Creating a Table Using HTML

❶ Open a text editor such as Notepad or use FrontPage as an HTML editor.

❷ Enter the HTML source code shown in Figure 16.6.

YOU TRY IT

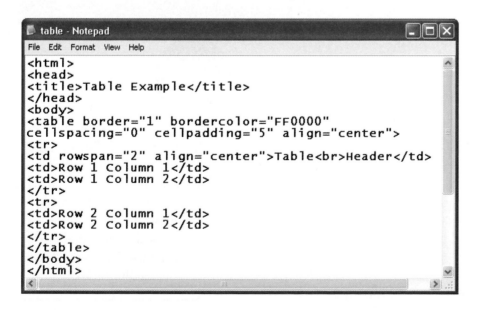

Figure 16.6

Enter the source code to create an HTML table.

③ Save the file as **table.htm.**

④ Launch your Web browser.

⑤ Open the file that you just created in the browser. Your results should look like Figure 16.7

Figure 16.7
Using `rowspan` creates a header column.

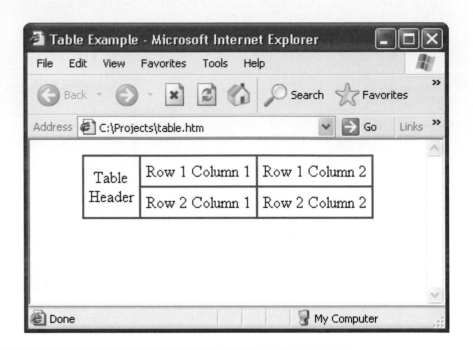

As you can see, it is easy to create a basic table using HTML. By defining a sufficient number of table cells within a given Web page, a Web designer can position elements on the user's screen very precisely.

Section 16.1 Assessment

Concept Check

1. **Define** cell spacing, cell padding, header row, header column.

2. **Summarize** the ways in which tables can be used for page layout.

3. **Identify** the HTML tags and attributes that define tables.

Critical Thinking

4. **Compare and Contrast** Explain how using the `align` attribute in the `<table>` tag is different from using the `align` attribute in the `<td>` tag.

5. **Draw Conclusions** Identify a scenario where you would need to use a header column.

Applying Skills

Merge Cells Review the HTML source code in Figure 16.5. Revise the table structure so that the table heading appears on the left side of the table rather than on the top. Make the table cell that holds the header text two rows high.

Ethics & Technology

PRIVACY ISSUES AND THE INTERNET

People voluntarily give out all sorts of personal information over the Internet. When they do that, however, they may unknowingly be letting others track their online activities.

Some operating systems provide tools for blocking cookies.

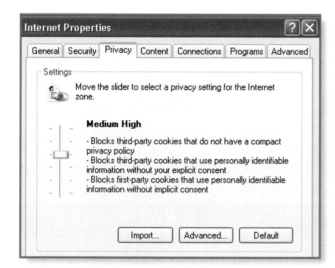

Site Registration

Many Web sites ask visitors to provide information about themselves. You may need to register to set up an account with an online store, to enter a sweepstakes, or to join a site's chat area.

Web sites often use this information to improve their services. For example, a Web portal service might use the information to customize the page you see whenever you visit the site, so it always matches your interests.

However, many sites sell or share users' personal information. To avoid this problem, check the site's privacy statement to see how it will handle your information.

Cookies and Web Bugs

Cookies are text files that a Web site can place on your computer. A Web bug is a GIF-format file used to gather information from your system; Web bugs are harder to track than cookies. For example, you can easily find a collection of cookies on your hard drive, using tools in your browser. To find Web bugs, you need to view a Web page's underlying code.

Taking Precautions

Here are some other steps you can take to guard your privacy online:

◆ Never use your primary e-mail address in transactions that might lead to spam. Some people get a second address (such as a free Web-based e-mail account) to access sites that require registration.
◆ Be careful in areas such as newsgroups and chat rooms. You are not anonymous there. If you post a message, a knowledgeable user can find your IP address and use it to track you.
◆ Use a cookie management program with Web bug controls to keep Web bugs off your system and reject the types of cookies you do not want.

Tech Focus

1. Research a potential threat on the Internet to individual privacy. What measures can users or organizations take to overcome this problem? Share your findings with the class.

2. Is it worth giving up your privacy for the convenience of using the Internet? Write a short essay that analyzes this conflict.

Guide to Reading

Main Ideas

HTML frames give you the ability to display more than one Web page on the screen at the same time. You can customize hyperlinks to support frames.

Key Terms

frame
container page
left-hand navigation
content page
top navigation

Reading Strategy

Compare and contrast content pages and container pages. Use a Venn diagram similar to the one below (also available online).

Figure 16.8

In this Web page, the frame on the left moves independently of the frame on the right. What advantage is there to creating a Web page that contains frames?

As you learned in Chapter 13, some Web designers find it useful to divide Web pages into two or more rectangular regions. Each region is called a **frame,** and each frame contains its own Web page. These Web pages can operate completely independently of each other, or they can interact with each other. For example, Figure 16.8 shows a Web page that contains two frames. The photograph in the left frame slowly changes while the bar along the right side scrolls. Both of these frames, however, move independently of each other.

© 2003 Smithsonian Institution.

webdesign.glencoe.com

CREATING FRAME PAGES IN HTML

A Web page with two frames is composed of three separate HTML documents (see Figure 16.9). One document defines the Web page that will display in frame 1. This Web page is usually the site's link bar. The second document contains the code for the page that will display in frame 2. This second page usually contains the Web site's content. The third HTML document, called a **container page,** defines the characteristics of the frames that contain the other two documents. All of these documents together are referred to as a frame set.

Activity 16.2 Explore Frames
Learn more about frames at
webdesign.glencoe.com.

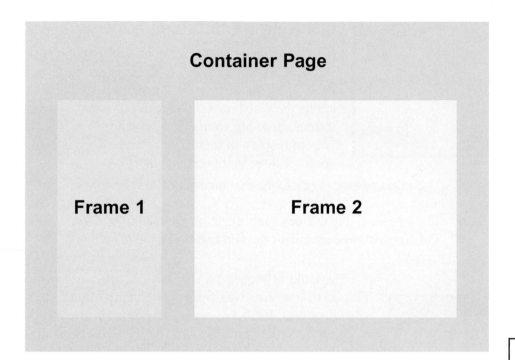

Container Page

Frame 1   **Frame 2**

● **Figure 16.9**
The container page directs the browser to display the other two HTML documents in frames. How many HTML documents would be needed to create a Web page with three frames?

● **Figure 16.10**
The file name for this page is linkbar.htm. What type of list is created in this document?

Creating a Link Bar Page

Most HTML frame sets contain a link bar (also called a navigation bar). As you learned earlier, a link bar is a set of buttons containing hyperlinks to other Web pages on the site. The HTML code shown in Figure 16.10 uses different levels of heads and a bulleted list to create a very simple link bar.

A link bar can appear virtually anywhere on the screen. Most Web designers, however, choose to place it on the left side. A frame-based Web site with a link bar on the left side of the screen is often said to have **left-hand navigation.**

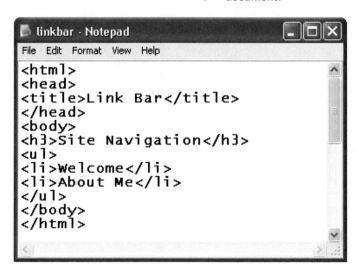

```
linkbar - Notepad
File  Edit  Format  View  Help
<html>
<head>
<title>Link Bar</title>
</head>
<body>
<h3>Site Navigation</h3>
<ul>
<li>Welcome</li>
<li>About Me</li>
</ul>
</body>
</html>
```

Figure 16.11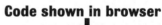
The file name for this page is welcome.htm. How do you know that this page is a complete HTML document?

Creating a Content Page

The link bar page is usually designed to occupy as little screen space as possible. This is to save room for the **content page,** which should be the site's main focus. The purpose of the content page is to capture the user's attention and fulfill the primary purpose of the Web site. In many frame-based Web sites, clicking the link bar will cause the main content page to change to present new information, a new message, or a new product. Figure 16.11 contains HTML code that displays a simple content page.

```
welcome - Notepad
File  Edit  Format  View  Help
<html>
<head>
<title>Welcome Page</title>
</head>
<body>
<center>
<h1>Welcome</h1>
<br>
<h3>to my</h3>
<br>
<h2>Web Site</h2>
</center>
</body>
</html>
```

Creating a Container Page

Once you create the link bar page and the content page, you can tie them together with a container page. The container page has the responsibility of telling the Web browser where to position the page's frames, how big to make them, and what HTML files to display in them. A container page is composed of three main commands:

- The `<frameset></frameset>` tag set defines the container page.
- The `<frame>` tag defines each frame on the container page.
- The `src` attribute identifies the file name that will display in the frame.

The code in Figure 16.12 creates a container page. This page contains two frames as defined by the two `<frame>` tags. Each `frame` tag contains an `src` attribute. This attribute identifies the file name that will display in the frame. As shown in Figure 16.12, the first frame displays the linkbar.htm file, while the second frame displays the welcome.htm file.

Code ↓

```
frameset - Notepad
File  Edit  Format  View  Help
<html>
<head>
<title>Named Frameset</title>
</head>
<frameset cols="200,*">
<frame src="linkbar.htm">
<frame src="welcome.htm">
</frameset>
</html>
```

Code shown in browser ↓

Figure 16.12 ●——→
The code shown above creates a left frame that displays a link bar and a right frame that displays the content page. How is the `<frame> src` attribute similar to the `src` attribute you used in Chapter 4?

Laying Out Frames Vertically While the `<frameset></frameset>` tag set supports a variety of attributes, one of the most important is the `cols` attribute. This attribute instructs the browser to place the frames in columns, giving the page a vertical layout.

The `cols` attribute also specifies the width of each column. In a two-column site, the width of the first column is usually defined with a number, and the width of the second column is usually defined with an asterisk. The asterisk character (*) represents the remaining space on the screen. In the code in Figure 16.12, the first column is 200 pixels wide, and the second column covers the remaining width of the screen.

Laying Out Frames Horizontally The frame set shown in Figure 16.11 uses left-hand navigation. Some Web sites, however, place link bars along the top or bottom of the page (also called **top navigation**). The `rows` attribute defines a Web page that is organized in rows instead of columns. The number assigned to the attribute defines the height, rather than the width, of the frames. Web developers usually specify the height of the top frame and use an asterisk (*) for the bottom frame. In the following activity, you will use HTML to create a frame page with a horizontal layout.

ACTIVITY 16B Creating a Frame-Based Web Page

❶ Open your text editor. Enter the HTML code listed below. When finished, save the file as **header.htm.**

```
<html>
<body bgcolor="FF0000">
<center>
<h2>Header Frame</h2>
</center>
</body>
</html>
```

❷ Enter the HTML code listed below. Save the file as **content.htm.** Save it in the same folder as header.htm.

```
<html>
<body bgcolor="FFFFFF">
<center>
<h1>Main</h1>
<h1>Content</h1>
<h1>Frame</h1>
</center>
</body>
</html>
```

❸ Enter the HTML code listed below. Save the file as **footer.htm.** Save it in the same folder as the other two files.

```
<html>
<body bgcolor="3399CC">
<center>
<h2>Footer Frame</h2>
</center>
</body>
</html>
```

TECH TRIVIA

Resizing Frames The `noresize` attribute can be used to prevent users from dragging a frame's border and changing the size of the frame.

YOU TRY IT

READ ME!

Caution Many Web sites use frames. However, the Americans with Disabilities Act discourages the use of frames because they are difficult for people with various disabilities to navigate. This is especially true for people who use voice-activated instructions to access the Internet.

4 Enter the HTML code listed below. Save the file as **frameset.htm.** Save it in the same folder as the other three files.

```
<html>
<head>
<title>Three Row Frameset</title>
</head>
<frameset rows="60,*,60">
<frame src="header.htm">
<frame src="content.htm">
<frame src="footer.htm">
</frameset>
</html>
```

5 Launch your Web browser. Open **frameset.htm** in the browser. Your results should look like Figure 16.13.

Figure 16.13 ●——→
The three frames display in rows across the page.

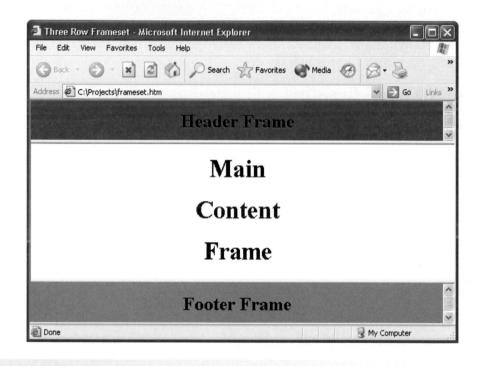

CREATING LINKS BETWEEN FRAMES

Whenever a user clicks a hyperlink, the Web browser's default behavior is to load the specified target page (the page to which the hyperlink points). When using frames, a Web designer may want the browser to behave differently. For example, when the user clicks a hyperlink in the link bar, the designer may want the content page to change, while the link bar itself remains unchanged.

To keep the link bar from changing, include the `target` attribute in the link's anchor tag. This attribute tells the browser to load the target Web page into a specified frame (the content frame) rather than into the current frame. For example, the `target` attributes shown in Figure 16.14 on page 431 tell the browser to load both the welcome.htm and the about_me.htm pages into the content frame when a user clicks the corresponding link in the link frame.

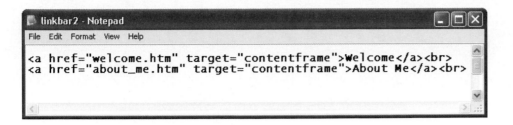

Figure 16.14
The `target` attribute is added to a hyperlink's anchor tag. What is the purpose of the `target` attribute?

For the target attribute to work, you must also add the `name` attribute to the `<frame>` tag found on the container page (see Figure 16.15). If you do not include this attribute, then the browser will not know which frame you want a page to load in.

Figure 16.15
Both the Welcome and About Me pages are loaded into the content frame when their link is clicked in the link bar. What is the purpose of the `name` attribute?

Section 16.2 Assessment

Concept Check

1. **Define** frame, container page, left-hand navigation, content page, top navigation.

2. **Explain** the purpose of a container page.

3. **Summarize** the attributes needed to change the behavior of hyperlinks on a frame page.

Critical Thinking

4. **Draw Conclusions** Why do you think left-hand navigation is more common on frame-based sites than top navigation?

5. **Analyze Links** Why is it common for the link bar on a frame page to remain constant as the content page changes?

Applying Skills

Explain Frame Placement A friend is building a Web site using frames and has decided to place the navigation bar on the right. Explain to your friend why you think it would be better to place the navigation bar on the left.

THE HOME AND WORKPLACE OF THE FUTURE

At the dawn of the computer age, futurists dreamed of "intelligent homes" that had kitchens smart enough to prepare meals and appliances that fixed themselves. These visions largely remained science fiction. But in many ways, smart houses and workplaces are becoming real.

Today, many workers carry a laptop PC, a cell phone, and a PDA. In the future, a single small device may do the work of all three.

Smart Appliances

Today's smart homes often have networks that monitor and automatically adjust lights, temperature, and TV or stereo volume in any room of the house. Newer gadgetry will soon make it possible for your house to assist you even more.

An emerging breed of Internet-enabled appliances will make future homes smarter than ever. Next-generation refrigerators will warn you when the milk is about to expire, order more eggs for you, or schedule their own service when they need repair. You might be able to look up a recipe using a browser on your microwave oven's built-in computer screen.

Smart Houses

Beyond those features, imagine a home for an elderly or disabled resident with doors that open automatically or motion sensors to track movement. Such a house might be able to call for help if it detects no motion for a certain amount of time, in case the person has fallen or lost consciousness.

Smart homes can also help the occupant lead a more independent life. Programmable appliances and fixtures can be controlled automatically. Others can be controlled by voice or breath rather than by hand.

Smart Workplaces

Visions of tomorrow's workplace abound, but most agree that wires will not be part of it. With the advent of wireless networks and widespread, broadband Internet access, workers in the future will not be tethered to a desk. In fact, the "office of tomorrow" may be anyplace you want—the kitchen table, a park bench, or a lounge chair by a hotel pool.

As workers gain mobility, they will continue to demand ever-smaller and more integrated devices.

Tech Focus

1. Research current and emerging smart-house technologies. Discuss the positive or negative impact of smart houses on individuals and on society.

2. Consider the ways in which people rely on technology, both at home and at work. In your view, what are the key advantages and disadvantages of this reliance? Share your opinion with the class.

SECTION 16.1 Creating Tables in HTML

Key Terms

cell spacing, 421
cell padding, 421
header row, 422
header column, 422

Main Ideas

- Tables organize data into rows and columns.
- The `<table>` and `</table>` tags define a table's area.
- The `<tr>` and `</tr>` tags define rows.
- The `<td>` and `</td>` tags define columns.
- Table attributes define the table grid, the alignment of the table on the page, and the alignment of text in the cells.
- You can merge cells to make larger cells.
- The `colspan` attribute is used to create a header row.
- The `rowspan` attribute is used to create a header column.

SECTION 16.2 Creating Frames in HTML

Key Terms

frame, 426
container page, 427
left-hand navigation, 427
content page, 428
top navigation, 429

Main Ideas

- Frame-based sites use at least three separate HTML documents to display a Web page.
- Common pages in a frame set include the link bar page, the content page, and the container page.
- The container page tells the browser how to display the link bar and content pages.
- If your page has two frames, specify the width (or height) of one frame and use an asterisk (*) to let the other frame fill the remaining space.
- You can use the `target` and `name` attributes to tell the browser to load the target Web page into a specified frame.

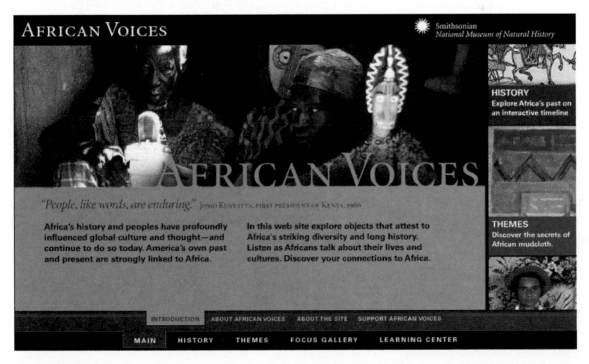

© 2003 Smithsonian Institution.

Reviewing Key Terms

1. What is the difference between cell spacing and cell padding?
2. Where are column titles placed in an HTML table?
3. Where are row titles placed in an HTML table?
4. What is the name of the HTML document that defines the characteristics of the frames in a frame-based Web site?
5. Where does the navigation frame usually appear in a vertical frame layout?

Understanding Main Ideas

6. **Identify** a table cell.
7. **Summarize** how to create a table border using HTML code.
8. **Summarize** how you would create a heading that spans several columns.
9. **Explain** the ways in which tables and items in cells can be aligned on a Web page.
10. **Identify** the attributes commonly used with the table tag.
11. **Explain** the HTML documents needed to create a Web page using frames.
12. **Explain** how you control the width of the frames on a Web page.
13. **Describe** what generally happens when a user selects an item from the link bar in a frame-based Web site.
14. **Identify** how the `target` attribute is used in a frame-based Web site.

Critical Thinking

15. **Synthesize Information** You have been asked to create an HTML page. This page will contain a header with a logo, a link bar, a main content area, and a footer with copyright information and text links. The main content area will contain a photograph and a list of individuals that states the individual's name, where he or she was born, and where he or she attended college. Describe how you would use tables to both organize the page's layout, and to organize the page's main content.

16. **Make Recommendations** You have been asked to create a frame-based Web site for a small business in your community. The owner insists that the link bar should be placed on the right-hand side of the page and the content on the left. How would you convince the owner that left-hand navigation would be a better choice?

17. **Draw Conclusions** What advantages and disadvantages do you see in building a frame-based Web site? What types of issues should you consider before deciding to use frames in a Web site? For example, if your Web site targets an older audience, why might you decide *not* to include frames in this site?

e-Review ·················

webdesign.glencoe.com

Study with PowerPoint

To review the main points in this chapter, select **e-Review > PowerPoint Outlines > Chapter 16.**

Online Self Check

Test your knowledge of the material in this chapter by selecting **e-Review > Self Checks > Chapter 16.**

Making Connections

Art—Create a Table Many artists such as Piet Mondrian have created highly-structured paintings based on square and rectangle shapes. If possible, view examples of Mondrian's work on the Web or at the library. Think of a place or event in your community that you could describe using only squares, rectangles, and colors. Then, use HTML table code to create this work of art. View it in a browser and make changes as needed to express your ideas.

STANDARDS AT WORK

Students use technology to locate, evaluate, and collect information from a variety of sources. (NETS-S 5)

Explore Accessibility
Section 508 of the Americans with Disabilities Act includes a number of specific standards that Web sites should meet to be accessible to people with disabilities. The law mandates that government and education sites comply with its rulings.

Research the specific standards listed in Section 508. Select one of the standards (other than the one shown below). Then, write an HTML code sample that does not meet the provision and an HTML code sample that does meet the provision.

For example, one standard states "A text equivalent for every non-text element shall be provided." HTML code that does *not* meet this standard is:

```
<img src="images/books.gif" width
="40" height="30">.
```

HTML code that does meet the standard is:

```
<img src="images/books.gif"
alt="Books" width="40" height=
"30">.
```

TEAMWORK SKILLS

Create a Frame-based Web Site
Your school has decided to create a frame-based site featuring its faculty. The site will have two frames. The left frame will be the link bar frame and will contain a list of the school's faculty members. The right frame (or content frame) will display a picture and text about each faculty member. Your task is to set up this site and create a content page for one teacher at your school.

First create the HTML code for the link bar. Then, decide as a group what information you will give about the teacher. Gather the information needed from the teacher you have selected. Create the HTML code for the content page for the teacher. Finally, write the HTML code for the container page. Test your work in a browser, making revisions until you are satisfied with the results.

CHALLENGE YOURSELF

Create a Nested Table
A table that is entirely contained within a cell of another table is called a nested table. Nested tables help you accomplish particular tasks. Suppose, for example, that you want to place a thick blue border around the following table.

Row 1 Column 1	Row 1 Column 2
Row 2 Column 1	Row 2 Column 2

An easy way to accomplish this is to place the code used to create the table inside another table. Use HTML to create the table shown above and test the results in a browser. Then add a blue border around the entire table. Do this by nesting your table code inside another table that has one row and one column. Adjust cell spacing and cell padding as needed. View the table in a browser and make any necessary adjustments.

YOU TRY IT

Skills Studio

These exercises reinforce the skills you learned in this chapter's You Try It activities. Refer back to the You Try It activities if you need extra guidance.

1. Creating a Table

Make a list of local trees for a nature group's Web site.

Ⓐ Compile a list of the different trees found in your community. Write the common name of the tree in the left column of a table similar to the one shown below. Research to find the information needed to complete the table.

COMMON NAME	SCIENTIFIC NAME	BRIEF DESCRIPTION
Red maple		
Burr oak		
White pine		

Ⓑ Use a text editor to create the HTML code for this table. Add cell spacing and cell padding as needed to make the table readable. Specify an appropriate border color.

Ⓒ Add a header row to the table that spans the entire width of the table. Use the title: The Trees Around Us.

Ⓓ Save your work and preview it in a browser.

Ⓔ Make changes, as needed, to the HTML code to improve the look of the table.

2. Creating Frames

A local park would like to include your table as part of a frame-based Web site about the park.

Ⓐ Write the HTML code for a link bar frame that will include links to the following content pages: About the Park, Trees in Our Community, Coming Events, and Contact Us.

Ⓑ Using HTML, create a content page for the Trees in Our Community page. The content should include the title and table created in the previous activity.

Ⓒ Using HTML, create the container page needed to make the frames work together.

Ⓓ Preview the site in a browser. Test the site to make sure that all pages work properly. Make changes as needed to get the frames to display properly.

Web Design Projects

1. Create an Inventory Table

You want to organize the CDs, videos, or DVDs that you own. You decide to create a table to manage this information. Select one of your collections (CDs, videos, and so on). Plan the type of information that you would like to track. For example, you may decide to classify your CDs as music CDs and data CDs. For your music CDs, you may want to list the title of the CD, the artist(s) performing, and your favorite track.

◆ Once you plan the information to include, sketch a table that would organize this information is a useful way.

◆ Based on your sketch, write the HTML code to create the table. You do not need to create a row for every item in your collection. You simply need to enter several items from your collection to test how your table is functioning.

◆ Proofread and save your work.

◆ View the table in a browser and make any changes needed to improve the look of the table.

◆ Add one more row to the table and enter the information for a newly acquired item. View the table in a browser again to make sure that your insertion is properly displayed.

2. Create a Frame-based Recipe Index

You are learning to cook and you have begun collecting easy-to-follow recipes. You decide to display these recipes in a frame-based site. Find a recipe that you can use for this project.

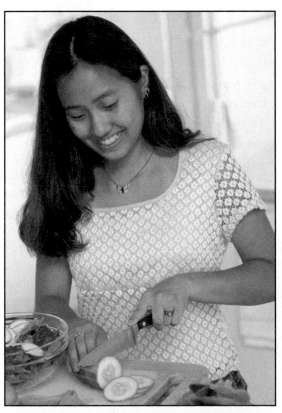

◆ Create the link bar frame listing just one recipe. You will expand the link bar as you add new recipes.

◆ Create the content page which will display the recipe. The recipe should have a title, a table listing the ingredients, and an ordered list of the steps required to complete the recipe (see Appendix B for the tags needed to create an ordered list).

◆ Create the container page needed to display the link bar frame and the content frame.

◆ Proofread and save your work. Preview the site in a browser and make changes to the HTML code as needed so that the frames display properly.

HTML, Scripting, and Interactivity

WHY IT MATTERS......................................

Actors read scripts to learn what they must do and say while on stage. Similarly, programmers include scripts in HTML pages to make specific actions occur on a Web page. While HTML can be used to create interesting and useful Web pages, neither HTML nor any other markup language can provide all the features and functionality that every Web developer might want. For this reason, HTML lets you add other technologies such as scripts to Web pages. These supplemental technologies can add useful functions to the Web site.

Quick Write Activity

HTML can be used with various technologies. How does its versatility make it more likely that HTML will be around longer than if it did not work with other programming languages?

WHAT YOU WILL DO..

ACTIVITIES AND PROJECTS

Applying Skills

You Try It Activities

Chapter Assessment

You Try It Skills Studio

Web Design Projects

IN THE WORKBOOK

Optional Activities and Projects

Guided Reading

Web Design Projects

ON THE WEB

Activities at webdesign.glencoe.com

Reading Strategy Organizers

Go Online Activities

Study with PowerPoint

Self-Check Assessments

READ TO SUCCEED

How Can You Improve?
What do you do after you take a test on the material you have studied? If you do well, your study strategies were successful. If you do poorly, think about how to improve your studying for the next test. It can be very helpful to think about the process you use to learn material. How can you improve your understanding? Discuss study techniques with classmates. But remember, what works for one person might not work for you. Pay attention to your study methods and find out how you learn best.

Guide to Reading

Main Ideas
You can use HTML code to insert multimedia elements into a Web page. Other HTML tags allow you to create forms.

Key Terms
animated GIF
radio button
pull-down menu
text area

Reading Strategy
Identify four HTML tags used to add features to a form. Use a table like the one below (also available online).

HTML Tag	Function

In Chapters 9, 10, and 12, you learned how to use FrontPage to insert multimedia elements and forms into a Web site.

ADDING MULTIMEDIA ELEMENTS

In this section, you will learn how to insert multimedia elements into your Web pages using HTML.

Inserting Audio Files Using HTML

Adding an audio file to a Web page is very similar to adding an image file. You use the `<a href></a>` tag set to identify the location of the audio file. (You can use the same tag set to insert video as well.) As with a graphic, you can create a text link by including text within the anchor tag set.

YOU TRY IT

ACTIVITY 17A Adding an Audio File Using HTML

Student Data File

Figure 17.1
Enter this HTML code to insert an audio file into a Web page.

```
birds - Notepad
File  Edit  Format  View  Help
<html>

<head><title>Audio</title></head>

<body>
<p>Click to hear the sound of
<a href="multimedia\birds.wav">
birds chirping.</a></p>
</body>
</html>
```

Figure 17.2
Click the text link to start the audio file.

Click to hear the sound of birds chirping.

❶ In the folder where you are storing your Web sites, create a folder named **audio**. In the audio folder, create a folder called **multimedia**. Copy **birds.wav** from the DataFile\ Ch17\Multimedia folder into the multimedia folder.

❷ Open a text editor, such as Notepad. Enter the HTML source code listed in Figure 17.1.

❸ Name the file **birds.htm** and save it in the audio folder.

❹ Open the **birds.htm** file in a Web browser. The results should look like Figure 17.2.

Adding Animated GIFs Using HTML

An **animated GIF** is a sequence of GIF images that are all stored together in a single file along with an image transition delay value. This value determines the amount of time each image will remain on the screen before the next image replaces it. As with other graphics, you use an <img> tag to insert animated GIFs into a Web page.

CREATING A REGISTRATION FORM

In Chapter 10, you used the FrontPage Form toolbar to create a registration form. In this section, you will create a similar form using HTML.

Text Boxes

An HTML text box allows visitors to enter limited amounts of text on a Web page. The <input> tag indicates where a text box should appear on a page. The <input> tag has a type attribute that takes different values, depending on the type of element you are creating. When creating a text box, the type attribute should equal "text".

ACTIVITY 17B Adding Text Boxes Using HTML

❶ Open a text editor, such as Notepad. Enter the HTML source code listed in Figure 17.3.

❷ Save the file as **text_box.htm.**

❸ View **text_box.htm** in a Web browser. The results are shown in Figure 17.3. Save your work. You will build upon this file throughout this section.

Activity 17.1 Explore HTML Resources Learn more about advanced HTML at **webdesign.glencoe.com.**

YOU TRY IT

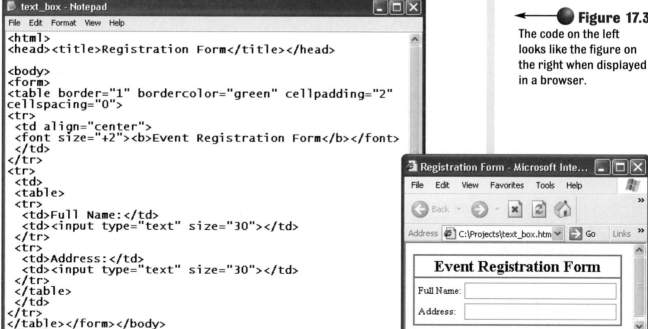

● **Figure 17.3**
The code on the left looks like the figure on the right when displayed in a browser.

Preset Options

A **radio button** (also referred to as an option button) is an interactive control that allows the user to select only one item from a list. Like text boxes, radio buttons are defined with the `<input>` tag. When creating a radio button, however, the `type` attribute should equal `"radio"`.

Like radio buttons, check boxes are defined in HTML with the `<input>` tag. To create a check box, set the `type` attribute to equal `"checkbox"`.

YOU TRY IT

ACTIVITY 17C Adding Radio Buttons and Check Boxes Using HTML

1 Open **text_box.htm** in your text editor. Click after the last `</tr>` tag you entered in Activity 17B and press **Enter** twice.

2 Enter the HTML source code listed in Figure 17.4.

Figure 17.4
Enter this code to add radio buttons and check boxes to the form.

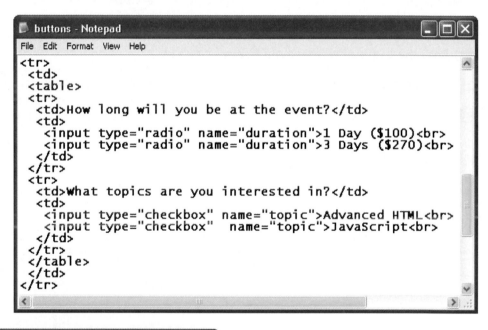

```
<tr>
 <td>
 <table>
 <tr>
  <td>How long will you be at the event?</td>
  <td>
   <input type="radio" name="duration">1 Day ($100)<br>
   <input type="radio" name="duration">3 Days ($270)<br>
  </td>
 </tr>
 <tr>
  <td>What topics are you interested in?</td>
  <td>
   <input type="checkbox" name="topic">Advanced HTML<br>
   <input type="checkbox"  name="topic">JavaScript<br>
  </td>
 </tr>
 </table>
 </td>
</tr>
```

Figure 17.5
Radio buttons and check boxes provide visitors with preset options.

3 Save the revised file as **buttons.htm**.

4 View the **buttons.htm** file in a Web browser. The results should look like Figure 17.5. Save your work.

Pull-Down Menus

A **pull-down menu** (also referred to as a drop-down menu) is an interactive element that gives users a list of options to choose from. Users may select only one of those options at a time. Pull-down menus are defined with the `<select></select>` tag set. Options in the menu are defined by the `<option></option>` tag set.

ACTIVITY 17D Adding a Pull-down Menu Using HTML

YOU TRY IT

1 Open **buttons.htm** in your text editor. Click after the last `</tr>` tag you entered in Activity 17C and press **Enter** twice.

2 Enter the HTML source code listed in Figure 17.6.

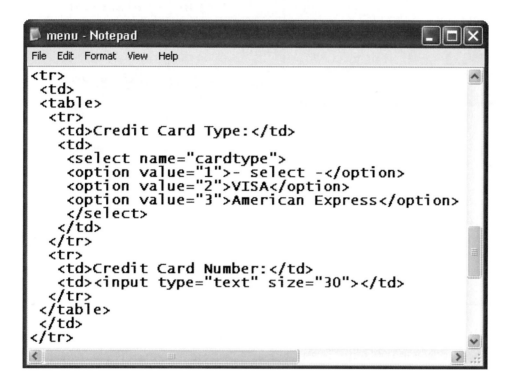

Figure 17.6
Enter this code to add a pull-down menu to the form.

Figure 17.7
Visitors can choose only one option from the pull-down menu.

3 Save the revised file as **menu.htm**.

4 View **menu.htm** in a Web browser. The results should look like Figure 17.7. Save your work.

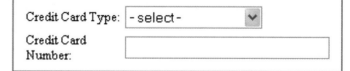

Text Areas

A **text area** (also referred to as a scroll box) allows the user to enter more information than a text box. If the amount of text the user enters exceeds the space provided in the text area, the control will automatically display a scroll bar that allows the user to scroll the text up and down or left and right. The `<textarea></textarea>` tag set defines a text area.

In the next You Try It, you will use HTML to create a text area. You will also use HTML to add Submit and Reset buttons to the registration form (note that the Submit button is not functional).

ACTIVITY 17E Adding a Text Area Using HTML

❶ Open **menu.htm** in your text editor. Click after the last `</tr>` tag you entered in Activity 17D and press **Enter** twice.

❷ Enter the HTML source code listed in Figure 17.8.

❸ Save the revised file as **final_form.htm**.

❹ View **final_form.htm** in a Web browser. The results should look like Figure 17.8.

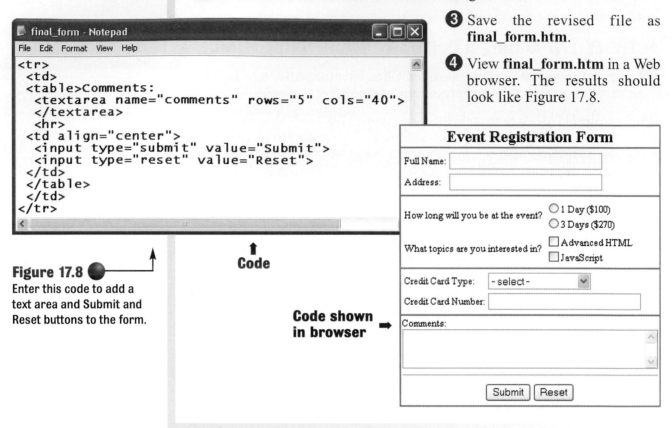

Code

Code shown in browser ➡

Figure 17.8
Enter this code to add a text area and Submit and Reset buttons to the form.

It is not difficult to create a form using HTML. Knowing which HTML tags to use can help you adjust form elements when you create a form in FrontPage.

Section 17.1 Assessment

Concept Check

1. **Define** animated GIF, radio button, pull-down menu, text area.

2. **Explain** how radio buttons and pull-down menus are similar.

3. **Summarize** the HTML tags needed to create a pull-down menu.

Critical Thinking

4. **Drawing Conclusions** How might a company use the information that visitors submit in a registration form?

5. **Compare and Contrast** In what ways are radio buttons similar to check boxes? In what ways are they different?

Applying Skills

Use HTML Attributes Under appropriate supervision, locate a Web site that provides advanced HTML reference information. Identify optional attributes that you could use to affect the appearance of text boxes, pull-down menus, and text areas.

Careers & Technology

DEVELOPING PROFESSIONAL SKILLS

Successful professionals understand that their behavior and appearance can be just as important as the quality of their work.

Your professional skills may be just as important to employers as your technical skills.

The Professional Résumé

If you want to present yourself as a professional, start with your résumé. While your first résumé may not include much work experience, you can still focus on your relevant skills. A good résumé is:

◆ **Neat and Orderly** Your résumé should be free of errors. It should list experience in a logical sequence, establishing a complete timeline of your work and educational history.

◆ **Accurate** Many employers will check your background and may discover your errors (or false statements).

◆ **Tailored** Target each résumé to the specific job for which you are applying. This means focusing on the skills and experiences that relate to that job and omitting any that do not.

Interview Guidelines

Preparation is the key to successful interviewing. Keep the following guidelines in mind:

◆ **Appearance** Dress professionally.

◆ **Communication Skills** Speak clearly, look at the other person when you talk, and listen carefully to what he or she says.

◆ **Body Language** Remember that body language can say as much as words. Look interested, sit or stand straight, and smile when appropriate.

◆ **Job Qualifications** Relate your skills, experiences, and interests to the job.

◆ **Goals** Think of your career goals and how this job fits into your career path.

Becoming a Professional

To give yourself a head start before you enter the workforce, follow these tips:

◆ **Focus on the Future** Start thinking like a professional now. Notice the way you interact with others and show responsibility.

◆ **Get Practice** Join an organization that helps young people develop professional and business skills.

◆ **Look for Experience** Apply for apprenticeships or internships that fit your career path.

Tech Focus

1. Prepare 10 questions you would expect an interviewer to ask you and 5 questions you might ask an interviewer. Conduct a mock interview with a classmate.

2. Find out about internships in your chosen field. Explain how these programs might fit into your own career plan.

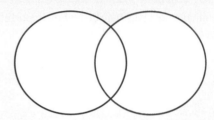
As discussed in Chapter 10, a script is a small program that a Web developer can add to an HTML document to make a static page dynamic. Scripting languages allow Web developers to write small programs that give them greater control over Web site functionality.

CLIENT-SIDE SCRIPTS

Different scripting technologies interact with HTML-based Web sites in different ways. Some scripting languages are designed to be transferred to the user's computer along with the HTML code. Once on the user's computer, these scripts are then executed by the user's Web browser. This type of program is known as a **client-side script.**

JavaScript

JavaScript is a scripting language that Web developers commonly use for developing client-side scripts. You can incorporate JavaScript code into a standard Web page by using the `<script></script>` tag set. Everything between these tags must conform to the rules of the JavaScript language. For example, JavaScript is case sensitive, so you must enter the code exactly. Everything contained between the two tags must be JavaScript. If you try to include an HTML command, you will generate an error message.

JavaScript code contains different elements that come together to make the script work. These elements are described as follows:

◆ JavaScript treats each element in a browser window as a unit called an **object.** An object can have properties that define it. For example, if a page contains a graphic, then the `<img>` tag defines that object, and the graphic's height is one of the object's properties.

GO Online

Activity 17.2 Explore Scripts
Learn more about different types of scripts at **webdesign.glencoe.com**.

READ ME!

Tech Tip Including `<!--` and `//-->` tags in your code tells browsers that cannot read JavaScript to skip the code. Browsers that can read JavaScript will still process the code.

 webdesign.glencoe.com

- An **event** is something that causes an effect to occur. An event may be triggered by a user action, such as pressing a key or clicking a button, or by the computer system itself.
- The part of the JavaScript that responds to an event is called an **event handler.** The event handler code defines the action that will occur when an event takes place.
- A **function** is code that performs a specific task. While the event handler code defines the action, the function code is what performs the action.
- JavaScript uses **variables** to identify values that will change when the script is executed.
- **Conditional statements** are commonly used in JavaScript to allow the script to react differently depending on the user's actions.

Web developers can use JavaScript for a variety of programming tasks. In the next activity, you will use JavaScript to create a rollover button.

ACTIVITY 17F Creating a Rollover Button Using JavaScript

YOU TRY IT

① Open a text editor, such as Notepad. In the folder where you are saving your Web sites, create a folder named **rollover**. In the rollover folder, create a second folder named **images**. Copy the **button1.gif** and **button2.gif** files from the DataFile\Ch17\Images folder into the images folder.

② Enter the source code listed in Figure 17.9.

Figure 17.9
Enter this JavaScript code to create a rollover button.

```
File  Edit  Format  View  Help
<html>
<head>
<title>Rollover Buttons</title>

<script language="javascript">
<!--
var image1=new Image;
var image2=new Image;
image1.src="images/button1.gif";
image2.src="images/button2.gif";
function swapImage(type)
{
   if (type == 1)
   {
     document.rollover.src=image1.src;
   }
   else
   {
     document.rollover.src=image2.src;
   }
}
// -->
</script>
</head>

<body>
<p><b>You can use JavaScript to create
rollover buttons.</b></p>
<img name="rollover" src="images/button1.gif"
   onMouseOver="swapImage(2)"
   onMouseOut="swapImage(1)">
</body>
</html>
```

Variable → *Objects*

Function → *Conditional Statement*

Event → *Event Handler*

③ Name the file **rollover.htm** and save it in the rollover folder.

❹ View **rollover.htm** in a Web browser. The results should look like Figure 17.10. Test the button by touching it with your mouse.

Figure 17.10
The button image changes when the user's mouse touches it.

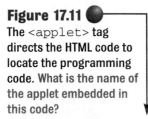

Figure 17.11
The `<applet>` tag directs the HTML code to locate the programming code. What is the name of the applet embedded in this code?

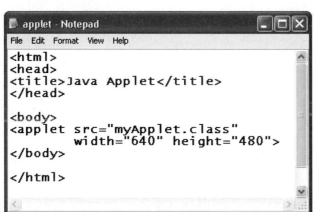

```
applet - Notepad
File  Edit  Format  View  Help
<html>
<head>
<title>Java Applet</title>
</head>

<body>
<applet src="myApplet.class"
        width="640" height="480">
</body>

</html>
```

Java Applets

Java applets are small programs written in the Java programming language. These client-side programs can also be embedded in a Web page. However, unlike JavaScript, the actual Java source code is not included with the HTML file. Instead, the Web developer may simply include an `<applet>` tag that tells the Web browser where to locate the applet program. The applet then downloads over the Internet and executes within a specified area on the Web page. Figure 17.11 shows the code used to insert a small applet into a Web page.

SERVER-SIDE SCRIPTS

Other scripting languages execute on the Web server and transfer the output to the user's computer as a Web page. A program such as this is called a **server-side script.**

Common Gateway Interface (CGI)

The Common Gateway Interface (CGI) is a standard set of rules that allows Web pages to interact with server-side scripts. Web developers often use CGI to create Web-based forms that users fill out and then submit to the server. The information the users provide passes through the CGI to a server-side script that then processes the information in some way. The script typically saves such information in a database and sometimes generates a confirmation or notification e-mail message as well. The details of creating server-side scripts that utilize CGI are beyond the scope of this book.

TECH TRIVIA

Creating CGI Scripts CGI scripts can be written in a variety of languages including Java, C, or C++. On Linux Web servers, the Perl scripting language is one of the most popular choices for implementing CGI scripts.

Dynamic Content

HTML pages are generally static. Once a server has transferred an HTML page to a user's browser, the information on that page does not change. Server-side scripts, however, can be used to change static content into dynamic content. "Dynamic content" is a generic term that refers to information that changes based on a user's action. For example, some forms will offer different options depending on the information submitted by the user. Server-side scripts help make this feature possible. A server-side script retrieves data based on the user's input and then generates a Web page that displays in the user's browser. While it looks like a typical HTML document, the information on this page has been changed to suit that particular user.

DEBUGGING CODE

Since Internet-based programming is relatively new to the software industry, there are not as many sophisticated debugging tools available as there are for many other programming environments. One way to identify potential problems is to include an alert statement in your code. An alert statement tells you when a particular action is not occurring as specified. Alert statements are useful to Web developers during the testing phase. They are not helpful, however, to visitors to the Web site. Therefore, alert statements should be removed before the site is published.

Error messages, such as the one shown in Figure 17.12, also identify problems in your code. This message tells you that, in line 18 of the source code, "image2" is undefined. Using this information can help you locate and fix your error.

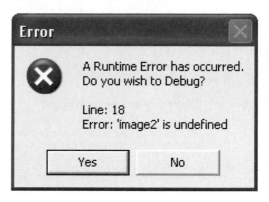

Figure 17.12
Error messages help you debug your HTML code. How does this error message work?

Section 17.2 Assessment

Concept Check

1. **Define** client-side script, object, event, event handler, function, variables, conditional statements, server-side script.

2. **Explain** the difference between client-side scripts and server-side scripts.

3. **Summarize** the various HTML tags used to create interactive elements.

Critical Thinking

4. **Draw Conclusions** Why do many Web developers copy scripts written by other people into their own pages?

5. **Make Recommendations** What types of dynamic content would you recommend adding to a site that provides historical information about your city?

Applying Skills

Explore HTML Web Sites Under appropriate teacher supervision, search the Internet to locate one or more Web sites that contain JavaScript tutorials. Review the information and write a paragraph summarizing one new fact or technique you have learned.

Real World Technology

SPAM

Spam will soon make up more than 50 percent of all e-mail sent. That is trillions of messages clogging the Internet!

Web-based e-mail services, such as Hotmail, let you decide how strictly to filter e-mail.

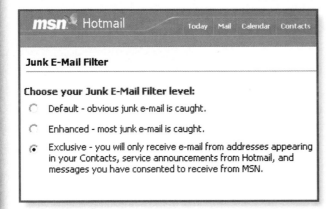

msn Hotmail Today Mail Calendar Contacts

Junk E-Mail Filter

Choose your Junk E-Mail Filter level:

- Default - obvious junk e-mail is caught.
- Enhanced - most junk e-mail is caught.
- Exclusive - you will only receive e-mail from addresses appearing in your Contacts, service announcements from Hotmail, and messages you have consented to receive from MSN.

What Is Spam?

The word "spam" is used to describe unwanted e-mail messages of all kinds. Spam can include advertisements, sales pitches, and chain letters.

Spammers commonly send out thousands of messages at a time. They may use legitimate mailing lists gathered from sources such as marketing agencies. Some spammers steal e-mail address lists. Spammers also may use software that makes up user names and attaches them to an ISP's address, such as *yourname@isp.net*. Although many of these fake addresses may not work, some will reach users.

Spam is so common because it is cheap and profitable. There is no charge to send e-mail messages. Spam, however, is anything but cheap and profitable for users who receive it each day. Users waste a lot of time deleting spam from their inboxes. Fighting spam costs businesses billions of dollars each year in lost productivity.

Reducing Spam

There are a number of ways to reduce spam:

- **Client Filters** E-mail programs often provide special tools called "filters." These block mail coming from certain addresses or users. Filters can be effective. However, since many spammers use different return addresses each time they send messages, they may be difficult to block. Filters may also block messages you want to receive, such as newsletters you requested from a Web site.
- **ISP Filters** Many ISPs offer server-based filters. These programs automatically block messages from known spammers, so they never reach your inbox.
- **Software** Inexpensive spam-blocking programs, such as SpamKiller or SpamCatcher, block mail from known spammers. These programs can be customized or can automatically update their built-in lists of spammers.

A number of states now have anti-spam laws on the books. To avoid this problem, many spammers have moved their operations to countries that have no anti-spam laws.

Tech Focus

1. Write a report about the threat that spam poses to individuals, businesses, and the Internet. What do you think is the best way to fight spam?

2. Open your e-mail program and learn about its built-in filtering tools. How easy are they to use, and how effective do you think they would be against spam?

SECTION 17.1 Adding Interactivity Using HTML

Key Terms

animated GIF, 441
radio button, 442
pull-down menu, 443
text area, 443

Main Ideas

- You can use the `<a href></a>` tag set to insert an audio or video file.
- An animated GIF is a sequence of GIF images stored together in one file along with an image transition delay value.
- The `<input>` tag has a `type` attribute that takes different values, depending on the type of element you are creating.
- The `type` attribute for a text box should equal "`text`". For a radio button, it should equal "`radio`". For a check box, it should equal "`checkbox`".
- The `<select></select>` tag set defines a pull-down menu.
- The `<textarea></textarea>` tag set defines a text area.

SECTION 17.2 Adding Interactivity Using Scripting

Key Terms

client-side script, 446
object, 446
event, 447
event handler, 447
function, 447
variables, 447
conditional statements, 447
server-side script, 448

Main Ideas

- Scripts executed by a user's browser are known as client-side scripts.
- JavaScript is widely used for client-side scripting applications.
- JavaScript events are triggered by user action or by the computer system.
- A JavaScript event handler responds to events.
- Web developers can use JavaScript for a variety of common programming tasks.
- Java applets are client-side programs that download and execute when browsers encounter their reference tag in the HTML code.
- Server-side scripts execute on a Web server and transfer the results to the user's browser.
- CGI is a server-side scripting language used to process information, often saving the information in a database.
- CGI enables Web pages to interact with server-side scripts.
- Dynamic content is customized information generated by a Web server.
- An alert statement in your code tells you when an action is not occurring as specified.

Find Your Study Method Consider your reading weaknesses and strengths. Think about recurring problems you have when you study and test. Then go back over the Read to Succeed features at the beginning of each chapter in this book. Determine which suggestions would be most useful to you. Try using one or more Read to Succeed methods when you read through this chapter and review the material.

Reviewing Key Terms

1. Which interactive element allows users to select only one item from a list, where all the items in the list are viewed at the same time?
2. Which interactive element uses the `<select></select>` tag set?
3. How does a text area allow a user to move up and down to review what they have typed?
4. Which types of scripts are transferred to the user's Web browser with the HTML code?
5. Rewrite this statement to make it true: *Objects are triggered by a user's action or by the computer system.*

Understanding Main Ideas

6. **Describe** the benefits of having interactive elements in a Web site.
7. **Explain** how an animated GIF works.
8. **List** the HTML tag and `type` attribute used for radio buttons, check boxes, and pull-down menus.
9. **List** the types of scripts used as client-side scripts and the types used as server-side scripts.
10. **Distinguish** between an event and an event handler.
11. **Describe** the similarities and differences between a JavaScript and a Java applet.
12. **Describe** a common use of a CGI scripts.

Critical Thinking

13. **Analyze Multimedia** You are planning a Web site to announce a new soft drink. What types of sound files might you use? Also, describe an animated GIF that could be used at the site.
14. **Make Decisions** You are creating an online form. One of the questions that users must answer is "Which conference will you attend?" The conference will be held in 10 cities. What type of interactive control would you use? Explain your decision.
15. **Draw Conclusions** Some e-commerce sites include wish lists that allow a visitor to select items that they may want to purchase in the future. Is the script that supports the wish list feature a client-side script or a server-side script? Explain the reasons for your choice.
16. **Analyze Languages** Identify ways in which scripting languages are similar to and different from HTML or other markup languages. How has the development of scripting languages changed how users interact with the Internet?
17. **Evaluate Languages** How does dynamic content transform database information into a user-friendly Web page?

e-Review ·················

webdesign.glencoe.com

Study with PowerPoint

To review the main points in this chapter, select **e-Review > PowerPoint Outlines > Chapter 17.**

Online Self Check

Test your knowledge of the material in this chapter by selecting **e-Review > Self Checks > Chapter 17.**

Making Connections

Social Studies—Create a Survey Form Your psychology class is exploring birth order and personality traits. Use a psychology textbook or library book to find a list of personality traits. Then create a survey form that asks people to identify their birth order (oldest, middle, youngest, and so on) and select the traits that apply best to them. Create the survey form using HTML and test it in a browser.

STANDARDS AT WORK

Students use productivity tools to collaborate in constructing technology-enhanced models, prepare publications, produce creative works. (NETS-S 3)

Debug Scripts
Work with a partner to research the advanced options that FrontPage provides for debugging scripts and HTML code.

After reviewing the information, you and your partner should use FrontPage to create separate Web pages that contain a JavaScript. You may download the JavaScript from a Web site (with your teacher's permission).

- Test the page in a browser to make sure that the script works correctly.
- Remove one line of the script.
- Write down the exact code removed and the placement of that code.
- Have your partner debug the code using the FrontPage debugging options or other debugging resources. See if your partner identifies the correct place where the code has been removed.

TEAMWORK SKILLS

Converting a Printed Form into an Electronic Form
With your teacher's permission, form a team. Have each team member find three printed forms that they have seen or used.

- As a team, select one form.
- Plan how to convert the printed form into an electronic form.

Beside each field on the printed form, write the type of field that should be used. Use text areas only when the information truly cannot be selected in some other way. For example, many printed forms include a line or box to list the state. However, the list of states is known, and therefore should be included as a pull-down menu.

Create the form in HTML. Test it in a browser and make changes and modifications as needed.

CHALLENGE YOURSELF

Create a Dictionary of Terms
The World Wide Web Consortium provides an HTML validator that can check HTML code and report errors. This tool is free of charge, but the results are not always easy to understand.

- Go to the World Wide Web Consortium's Web site.
- Review the documentation provided about the validator.
- As you read the material, write down at least five words or phrases that you do not clearly understand. For example, the word *parse* is used frequently in the documentation.
- Find a definition or description of each word or phrase you have written down.
- Create a Web page using HTML code that displays these words or phrases and definitions or descriptions.
- With your teacher's permission, use the HTML validator to check the page you have created.

YOU TRY IT
Skills Studio

These exercises reinforce the skills you learned in this chapter's You Try It activities. Refer back to the You Try It activities if you need extra guidance.

1. Creating a Web Page with Audio in HTML

Build a Web page in HTML that contains two audio files.

Ⓐ Locate two audio files that are related in some way.

Ⓑ Write a short story or poem that incorporates these two audio files.

Ⓒ Create a folder named **Skills_17.** In this folder, create a second folder named **multimedia.** Copy the two audio files into the multimedia folder.

Ⓓ Open Notepad or another text editor.

Ⓔ Create an HTML document that includes links to the two audio files within the text you have written. Use HTML to format the document.

Ⓕ Proofread your work carefully.

Ⓖ Save the file as an .htm document in the Skills_17 folder.

Ⓗ Open the file in a Web browser. Test the links to the audio files.

Ⓘ Make any changes or improvements needed and test the file in the browser again.

2. Creating a Ticket Order Form

To avoid long lines at tickets counters, the local sports team has placed order kiosks around the city.

Ⓐ On paper, plan the order form. The form should include game dates, type of payment information, customer information, and the number of tickets desired (use the form on this page as a model).

Ⓑ Open Notepad or another text editor.

Ⓒ Use HTML to create the form.

Ⓓ Save the form as an .htm document.

Ⓔ Open the file in a Web browser and test the form.

Ⓕ Make any changes or improvements needed and test the form in the browser again.

Sports Tickets Order Form

Full Name:

Address:

Phone Number:

Which game do you want to attend?
☐ Tigers vs. Bears
☐ Tigers vs. Sox

Where would you like to sit?
○ A Section ($10.00)
○ B Section ($20.00)
○ C Section ($30.00)

How many tickets do you want to purchase?

Credit Card Type: - select -

Credit Card Number:

Expiration Date:

Total amount of purchase:

Submit   Reset

Web Design Projects

1. Create a Survey Form

A summer day camp staff is planning programs for next summer. They want to survey parents about what camps they would like to see offered. The possible types of camps include: art camp, soccer camp, baseball camp, bird watching camp, animal care camp, music camp, mystery adventure camp, swimming camp, and gardening camp. The staff is also open to ideas from the parents about other types of camp experiences.

Use HTML to create a form that parents can complete online. You want to gather contact information from the parents, as well as their preferences for camp types. Test the form in a browser, making any changes or improvements as needed.

2. Use JavaScript to Add a Submit Button

You will now add a Submit button to the form you created in Project 1 above. This Submit button will include a JavaScript function that will allow people to verify their information.

◆ Add the HTML code below to create the Submit button. Place this code after the last row in the community form.

← HTML Code

```
submit_button - Notepad
File  Edit  Format  View  Help
<tr><td align="center">
<label>
<input name="Submit" type="submit"
onClick="MM_callJS('processForm()')" value="Submit">
<input type="Reset" name="Submit2" value="Reset">
</label>
</td></tr>
```

JavaScript

◆ Add the JavaScript shown at right to the head of your form code. This script will add interactivity to the Submit button.

◆ Test the HTML code in a browser. Make corrections as needed.

```
submit_button - Notepad
File  Edit  Format  View  Help
<script language="javascript">
<!--
function processForm( )
{
  if (document.forms[0].elements[0].checked)
  {
    alert('Yes');
  }
  else
  {
    alert('No');
  }
}
function MM_callJS(jsStr)
{ //v2.0
  return eval(jsStr)
}
//-->
</script>
```

Building 21st Century Skills

Project 1

Problem Solving: Use HTML and JavaScript

You are part of a customer service group. People who need help may call or e-mail questions to your company. A representative is available 24 hours a day, seven days a week to respond. Create a Web page that advertises these services.

1. Create an HTML document that includes the JavaScript code (shown below) in its `<head>` section.

2. Customize the script by replacing "INSERT text here." with your own messages.

3. Write HTML code for the `<body>` section of the page. The page should list the services you are offering in an unordered list.

4. Create a table that contains three answers to common customer problems.

5. Carefully proof your code. Test your site in at least two browsers. Make any needed changes.

```
greetings - Notepad
File  Edit  Format  View  Help
<html>
<head><title>Customer Greeting</title>
<script language="javascript">
<!- -
today = new Date()
  if ((today.getHours()>6 && (today.getHours() <=12))
  {
    document.write("Good morning! INSERT text here.")
  }
  if ((today.getHours() >12 && (today.getHours() <=18))
  {
    document.write("Good afternoon! INSERT text here.")
  }
  if ((today.getHours() >18 && (today.getHours() <=23))
  {
    document.write("Good evening! INSERT text here.")
  }
  if ((today.getHours() >=0 && (today.getHours() <6))
  {
    document.write
    ("It's late, but we're still here! INSERT text here.")
  }
// -->
</script></head>
<body>
```

Project 2

Communication Skills: Create a Community Services Web Site

Create a frames-based Web site that provides information about services available in your community, such as libraries, parks, hospitals, and community events.

1. Use a text editor to create the link bar page that will display in the left frame. The list of pages will include the home page, a community services page, a community connections page, and a parks and recreation page.

2. Create the content page for the home page (content pages will display in the right frame). Use WordArt or drawing tools to create a simple community logo. The page should also welcome visitors and describe what can be found at the site.

3. Create the container page that describes how the link bar page and the content page will display.

4. Create the links between the link bar and each of the content pages.

5. Create content pages for the remaining pages. The other content pages should contain brief descriptions of services available in your community, including contact information.

6. Proofread your HTML code carefully. Test your site in a browser. Make changes as needed.

Building Your Portfolio

Create a Feedback Form

Select a Web site that you have created for your Web design class and add a feedback form to the site. In this project, you will use your HTML skills to create the feedback form.

1. Create a feedback form page that will link to the home page of the site you have selected. Use FrontPage to create the new page and to add it to the site's navigation scheme.

2. Switch to **Code** (in FrontPage 2002, **HTML**) view. Create the form using HTML coding. Title the form "Help Me Improve the Web Site".

3. Create the following statements and check boxes for responses:

What did you like about this Web site?

☐ Site design   ☐ Color scheme   ☐ Information structure

☐ Navigation   ☐ Ease of use   ☐ Content

☐ Hyperlinks

What did you NOT like about this Web site?

☐ Site design   ☐ Color scheme   ☐ Information structure

☐ Navigation   ☐ Ease of use   ☐ Content

☐ Hyperlinks

---

4. Create the following statement with radio (option) buttons for the response:

Rate my site:

○ Excellent   ○ Good   ○ Needs improvement

---

5. Create a text area labeled "Comments" that people can use to write specific suggestions and ideas.

6. Include a statement at the bottom of the form that thanks visitors for responding.

7. Add code to make the form page consistent with the rest of the Web site. For example, you may want to add a background color or specify a particular font.

8. Test the form in a browser. Make sure that you can navigate to the form from the site's home page.

9. Optional (with your teacher's permission)—publish the finished Web site on your school or class Web site.

10. For your portfolio, include a screen shot and an electronic copy of your finished product.

Microsoft® FrontPage® Reference Guide

Use this reference guide to identify FrontPage page views and toolbars.

FRONTPAGE PAGE VIEWS

FrontPage lets users look at an individual page in different ways when the page is open in Page View mode. Page views vary depending on the version of FrontPage being used.

Page View Options

In FrontPage 2002	In FrontPage 2003	Function
Normal	Design	Lets you modify a page
HTML	Code	Lets you examine the HTML code for the page and make changes to it, if necessary.
View Not Available in 2002	Split	Shows Code View at the top of the screen and Design View at the bottom. Allows you to compare the actual page with the HTML code used to create it.
Preview	Preview	Lets you see the page approximately as it will appear in a Web browser.

2002 Page Views   **2003 Page Views**

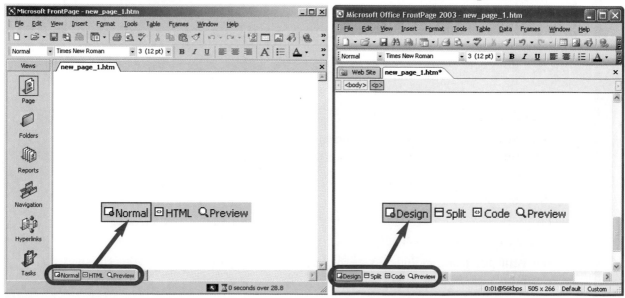

COMMON FRONTPAGE TOOLBARS

FrontPage provides toolbars to help users complete different tasks. These toolbars are similar to those found in other Microsoft applications.

1. Standard Toolbar

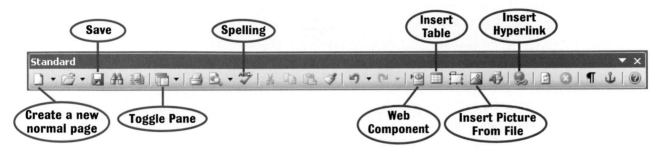

- Use the **Create a new normal page** button to create a new Web page.
- Use the **Save** button to save your work.
- Use the **Toggle Pane** button to switch between the Folder List and the Navigation Pane.
- Use the **Spelling** button to spell check your work.
- Use the **Web Component** button to insert a Web component into a page.
- Use the **Insert Table** button to create a table.
- Use the **Insert Picture From File** button to insert a graphic into a page.
- Use the **Insert Hyperlink** button to insert a hyperlink into a page.

2. Formatting Toolbar

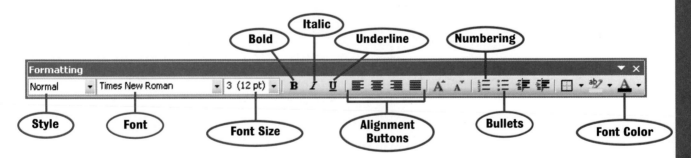

- Use the **Style** menu to format text with predefined styles.
- Use the **Font** menu to select different font types.
- Use the **Font Size** menu to select font sizes.
- Use the **Bold, Italic,** and **Underline** buttons to make selected text bold, italic, or underlined.
- Use the **Alignment** buttons to align text left, centered, right, or justified on a page.
- Use the **Numbering** button to create numbered lists.
- Use the **Bullets** button to create bulleted lists.
- Use the **Font Color** menu to select font colors.

3. Pictures Toolbar

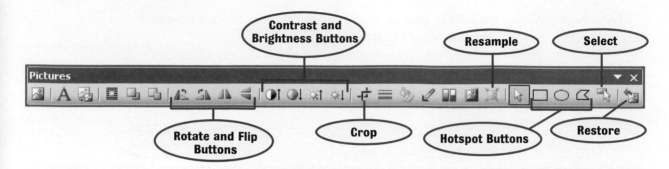

- ◆ Use the **Rotate** and **Flip** buttons to reverse and rotate pictures.
- ◆ Use the **Contrast** and **Brightness** buttons to increase and decrease a picture's brightness and contrast.
- ◆ Use the **Crop** button to trim a picture down to a smaller size.
- ◆ Use the **Resample** button to refine the focus of a picture that has been enlarged or reduced.
- ◆ Use the **Hotspot** buttons to create hotspots with different shapes.
- ◆ Use the **Select** button to select a picture for editing.
- ◆ Use the **Restore** button to undo recent changes to a picture.

4. WordArt Toolbar

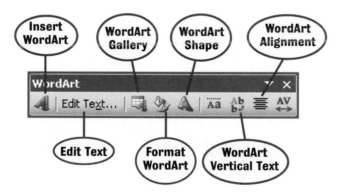

- ◆ Use the **Insert WordArt** button to create a new WordArt object.
- ◆ Use the **Edit Text** button to format text in a WordArt object.
- ◆ Use the **WordArt Gallery** button to select different WordArt styles.
- ◆ Use the **Format WordArt** button to change the colors, lines, size, layout, and alternate Web text of a WordArt object.
- ◆ Use the **WordArt Shape** button to choose a WordArt object's shape.
- ◆ Use the **WordArt Vertical Text** button to change text from a horizontal to a vertical alignment.
- ◆ Use the **WordArt Alignment** button to specify the WordArt object's alignment.

5. Drawing Toolbar

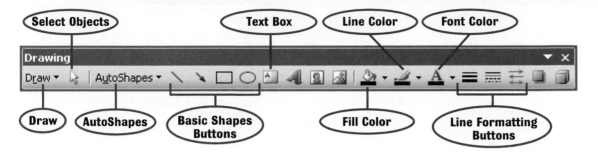

- ◆ Use the **Draw** menu to control the grouping and position of objects.
- ◆ Use the **Select Objects** button to select one or more objects.
- ◆ Use the **AutoShapes** menu to insert pre-made shapes.
- ◆ Use the **Line, Arrow, Rectangle,** and **Oval** buttons to draw basic shapes.
- ◆ Use the **Text Box** button to insert text frames within graphics.
- ◆ Use the **Fill Color, Line Color,** and **Font Color** buttons to add color to items.
- ◆ Use the **Line Style, Dash Style,** and **Arrow Style** buttons to format line elements.

6. Form Toolbar

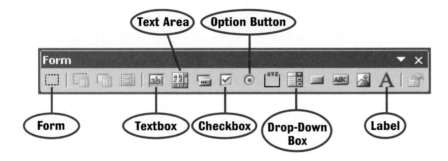

- ◆ Use the **Form** button to create a new form.
- ◆ Use the **Textbox** button to create a box where users can enter a line of text.
- ◆ Use the **Text Area** button to create a box where users can enter many lines of text.
- ◆ Use the **Checkbox** button to create a list in which users can select one or more options.
- ◆ Use the **Option Button** button to create a list in which users can select one of two options.
- ◆ Use the **Drop-Down Box** button to create a menu in which users can select from a list of choices.
- ◆ Use the **Label** button to identify what type of information needs to be entered into a form field.

HTML Reference Guide

The tables in this appendix contain common HTML tags (as used in Chapter 4) and advanced HTML tags (as used in Chapters 16 and 17).

How to Use the Tables

◆ Attributes associated with a tag are listed under the tag.

◆ "*Italic text*" that appears between quotes represents values such as numbers and colors that are selected by the programmer.

◆ "Non-italic text" that appears between quotes indicates specific values that the programmer cannot change.

Common HTML Tags and Attributes

Tags and Attributes	Description
`<a></a>`	Tag set that marks the anchor, or clickable, portion of a hyperlink. Anchor content is specified between the anchor tags and can include text or an image.
`href="`*URL or file name*`"`	Attribute that specifies the URL or file being linked to. Can also be used to create links to audio and video files.
`target="`*name of frame*`"`	Attribute that tells the browser to load the target Web page into a specified frame (see advanced HTML table).
`<b></b>`	Tag set used to display text between tags in boldface.
`<blockquote></blockquote>`	Tag set that offsets a paragraph from the regular body text, usually by indenting the paragraph's left and right margins. Useful when formatting quotes or citations.
`<body></body>`	Tag set that marks the start and end of the Web page's displayable content.
`bgcolor="`*selected color*`"`	Attribute that specifies a page's background color.
`text="`*selected color*`"`	Attribute that specifies the text color for an entire Web page.
` `	Empty tag that inserts a line break.
`<font></font>`	Tag set that lets you specify the enclosed text's characteristics.
`color="`*selected color*`"`	Attribute that defines the font color used.
`face="`*selected font type*`"`	Attribute that defines the font type (e.g., Arial) used.
`size="`*selected font size*`"`	Attribute that defines the font size used. Possible numbers range from 1 to 7, where 1 is the smallest font size.

Common HTML Tags and Attributes (cont.)

Tags and Attributes	Description

`<h1></h1>`
`<h2></h2>`
`<h3></h3>`
`<h4></h4>`
`<h5></h5>`
`<h6></h6>`
	Tag set used to specify heading levels. 1 (`<h1>`) is the largest heading and 6 (`<h6>`) is the smallest heading.

`align="selected alignment"`	Attribute used to define a heading's alignment. Alignment values include: `left`, `right`, or `center`.
`<head></head>`	Tag set that defines the header area of an HTML document. Header information is not displayed on the Web page.
`<hr>`	Empty tag that inserts a horizontal line.
`<html></html>`	Tag set that marks the start and end of an HTML document.
`<i></i>`	Tag set used to display text between tags in italics.
`<img>`	Empty tag that displays an image on a Web page.
`src="image file name"`	Attribute that specifies the image's source location. This attribute must be included in all image tags.
`alt="alternative text"`	Attribute that gives the browser an alternative text message to display in place of a missing image. This attribute should be included in all image tags to make a site accesible.
`align="selected alignment"`	Attribute used to wrap text around an image or to align an image on the page.
`border="selected number"`	Attribute that specifies the pixel size of an image's border.
`height="selected height"`	Attribute that specifies an image's height in pixels.
`width="selected width"`	Attribute that specifies an image's width in pixels.
`<li></li>`	Tag set that identifies a list item within an unordered (bulleted) or an ordered (numbered) list.
`<ol></ol>`	Tag set used to specify an ordered, or numbered, list.
`<p></p>`	Tag set that indicates the start and end of a paragraph.
`align="selected alignment"`	Attribute used to define a paragraph's alignment. Alignment values include: `left`, `right`, or `center`.
`<title></title>`	Tag set that defines the Web page's title, which is displayed in the Web browser's title bar.
`<ul></ul>`	Tag set used to specify an unordered, or bulleted, list.
`type="selected bullet type"`	Attribute used to specify the type of bullet used to display each list item. Type values include: `disc`, `square`, and `circle`.

Advanced HTML Tags and Attributes

Table Tags and Attributes	Description
`<table></table>`	Tag set that marks the start and end of the table area.
`align="`*selected alignment*`"`	Attribute that defines the horizontal alignment of the entire table. Possible alignments include: `left`, `center`, and `right`.
`border="`*selected width*`"`	Attribute that creates a table border. The higher the border width number, the thicker the border.
`bordercolor="`*selected color*`"`	Attribute that specifies the table border's color.
`cellpadding="`*selected number*`"`	Attribute that adjusts the space between a cell's border and the cell's content.
`cellspacing="`*selected number*`"`	Attribute that adjusts the space between the outer border and a cell's border.
`width="`*selected number*`"`	Attribute that specifies a table's width. Number can be in pixels or a percentage of the document's width.
`<td></td>`	Tag set that marks the start and end of a table column.
`colspan="`*selected number*`"`	Attribute used to merge cells horizontally. The number indicates the number of columns to be merged.
`rowspan="`*selected number*`"`	Attribute used to merge cells vertically. The number indicates the number of rows to be merged.
`align="`*selected alignment*`"`	Attribute that defines how the contents of one particular table cell will align. Possible alignments include: `left`, `center`, and `right`.
`<th></th>`	Tag set that defines a table header.
`<tr></tr>`	Tag set that marks the start and end of a table row.
`align="`*selected alignment*`"`	Attribute that aligns the contents of all the cells in a selected row. Possible alignments include: `left`, `center`, and `right`.

Frame Tags and Attributes	Description
`<frame>`	Empty tag that defines each frame on a container page.
`noresize`	Attribute used to prevent users from resizing the frame.
`src="`*name of document*`"`	Attribute that specifies the file name that will display in the frame.
`name="`*name of frame*`"`	Attribute on the container page that works with the `target` attribute to tell the browser which frame to open a page in.
`<frameset></frameset>`	Tag set that defines the container page.
`cols="`*selected sizes*`"`	Attribute that defines a frame page organized in columns. Number specifies the width of each column in pixels or as percentages. An asterisk (*) can be used to represent the remaining space on screen (e.g., `cols="45, *"`).
`rows="`*selected number*`"`	Attribute that defines a frame page organized in rows. Number specifies the height of each row in the page.

Advanced HTML Tags and Attributes (cont.)

Frame Tags and Attributes	Description
`<noframes></noframes>`	Tag set that establishes an alternative layout for browsers incapable of supporting frames.
`<form></form>`	Tag set that defines the start and end of a form.
`<input>`	Empty tag that defines a form element.
`name="selected name"`	Attribute that defines the name of the form element.
`type="checkbox"`	Attribute that defines a check box.
`type="radio"`	Attribute that defines a radio button.
`type="text"`	Attribute that defines a text box.
`type="submit"`	Attribute that defines a Submit button.
`type="reset"`	Attribute that defines a Reset button.
`size="number"`	Attribute used to define the size of a text field.
`<option></option>`	Tag set that creates individual options in a form menu. Must be placed within the `<select></select>` tag set.
`value="selected number"`	Attribute that specifies the initial value of a menu option.
`<select></select>`	Tag set that defines a pull-down menu.
`name="selected name"`	Attribute that defines the menu's name.
`<textarea></textarea>`	Tag set that defines a text area.
`cols="selected number"`	Attribute that defines a text area's width.
`name="selected name"`	Attribute that defines the text area's name.
`rows="selected number"`	Attribute that defines a text area's height.

Script Tags and Attributes	Description
`<!— and //-->`	Tag set that tells browsers that cannot read JavaScript to skip the code. Browsers that can read JavaScript still process the code.
`<applet>`	Empty tag that inserts an applet into an HTML document.
`height="selected number"`	Attribute used to define the applet's height.
`src="name of program"`	Attribute used to define location of applet.
`width="selected number"`	Attribute used to define the applet's width.
`<script></script>`	Tag set that inserts a script into an HTML document.

Web-safe Color Reference Guide

USING COLORS ON THE WEB

As discussed in Chapter 7, not every monitor displays color in the same way. To avoid complications, you should select colors from the 216-color Web-safe color palette when formatting text, choosing backgrounds, and creating basic graphics for your site. Using this limited color palette (shown on the next page) helps ensure that colors will display properly no matter what computer system, monitor settings, or Web browser people use to view your pages.

THE 16 NAMED COLORS

You can also use the World Wide Web Consortium's 16 named colors to maintain color consistency across various platforms, monitors, and Web browsers. These 16 colors can be used by name in an HTML tag in place of a hexadecimal number. For example, both the `<font color="green">` tag and the `<font color="#008000">` tag can be used to define a green font color. The 16 named colors and their corresponding hexadecimal values are shown in the table below. These colors may appear differently on your monitor than they do here in print.

16 Named Colors

Color Name	Hexadecimal Value	Example
Aqua	#00FFFF	
Black	#000000	
Blue	#0000FF	
Fuchsia	#FF00FF	
Gray	#808080	
Green	#008000	
Lime	#00FF00	
Maroon	#800000	
Navy	#000080	
Olive	#808000	
Purple	#800080	
Red	#FF0000	
Silver	#C0C0C0	
Teal	#008080	
White	#FFFFFF	
Yellow	#FFFF00	

THE WEB-SAFE COLOR PALETTE

Colors in the chart are notated in both their hexadecimal values for use in Web design programs and their RGB (red, green, blue) values for use in graphics programs.

- The first number/letter combination shown represents the color's hexadecimal value. You can use hexadecimal values to select colors when creating HTML documents or when using FrontPage.
- The second set of numbers shown represents the color's RGB value. Each of these numbers correlates to an intensity value of red, green, and blue as displayed on a monitor. For example, an orange color would have the RGB color designation of: red 255, green 102, and blue 51.

FFFFFF R=255 G=255 B=255	FFFFCC R=255 G=255 B=204	FFFF99 R=255 G=255 B=153	FFFF66 R=255 G=255 B=102	FFFF33 R=255 G=255 B=51	FFFF00 R=255 G=255 B=0	66FFFF R=102 G=255 B=255	66FFCC R=102 G=255 B=204	66FF99 R=102 G=255 B=153	66FF66 R=102 G=255 B=102	66FF33 R=102 G=255 B=51	66FF00 R=102 G=255 B=0
FFCCFF R=255 G=204 B=255	FFCCCC R=255 G=204 B=204	FFCC99 R=255 G=204 B=153	FFCC66 R=255 G=204 B=102	FFCC33 R=255 G=204 B=51	FFCC00 R=255 G=204 B=0	66CCFF R=102 G=204 B=255	66CCCC R=102 G=204 B=204	66CC99 R=102 G=204 B=153	66CC66 R=102 G=204 B=102	66CC33 R=102 G=204 B=51	66FF00 R=102 G=204 B=0
FF99FF R=255 G=153 B=255	FF99CC R=255 G=153 B=204	FF9999 R=255 G=153 B=153	FF9966 R=255 G=153 B=102	FF9933 R=255 G=153 B=51	FF9900 R=255 G=153 B=0	6699FF R=102 G=153 B=255	6699CC R=102 G=153 B=204	669999 R=102 G=153 B=153	669966 R=102 G=153 B=102	669933 R=102 G=153 B=51	669900 R=102 G=153 B=0
FF66FF R=255 G=102 B=255	FF66CC R=255 G=102 B=204	FF6699 R=255 G=102 B=153	FF6666 R=255 G=102 B=102	FF6633 R=255 G=102 B=51	FF6600 R=255 G=102 B=0	6666FF R=102 G=102 B=255	6666CC R=102 G=102 B=204	666699 R=102 G=102 B=153	666666 R=102 G=102 B=102	666633 R=102 G=102 B=51	666600 R=102 G=102 B=0
FF33FF R=255 G=51 B=255	FF33CC R=255 G=51 B=204	FF3399 R=255 G=51 B=153	FF3366 R=255 G=51 B=102	FF3333 R=255 G=51 B=51	FF3300 R=255 G=51 B=0	6633FF R=102 G=51 B=255	6633CC R=102 G=51 B=204	663399 R=102 G=51 B=153	663366 R=102 G=51 B=102	663333 R=102 G=51 B=51	663300 R=102 G=51 B=0
FF00FF R=255 G=0 B=255	FF00CC R=255 G=0 B=204	FF0099 R=255 G=0 B=153	FF0066 R=255 G=0 B=102	FF0033 R=255 G=0 B=51	FF0000 R=255 G=0 B=0	6600FF R=102 G=0 B=255	6600CC R=102 G=0 B=204	660099 R=102 G=0 B=153	660066 R=102 G=0 B=102	660033 R=102 G=0 B=51	660000 R=102 G=0 B=0
CCFFFF R=204 G=255 B=255	CCFFCC R=204 G=255 B=204	CCFF99 R=204 G=255 B=153	CCFF66 R=204 G=255 B=102	CCFF33 R=204 G=255 B=51	CCFF00 R=204 G=255 B=0	33FFFF R=51 G=255 B=255	33FFCC R=51 G=255 B=204	33FF99 R=51 G=255 B=153	33FF66 R=51 G=255 B=102	33FF33 R=51 G=255 B=51	33FF00 R=51 G=255 B=0
CCCCFF R=204 G=204 B=255	CCCCCC R=204 G=204 B=204	CCCC99 R=204 G=204 B=153	CCCC66 R=204 G=204 B=102	CCCC33 R=204 G=204 B=51	CCCC00 R=204 G=204 B=0	33CCFF R=51 G=204 B=255	33CCCC R=51 G=204 B=204	33CC99 R=51 G=204 B=153	33CC66 R=51 G=204 B=102	33CC33 R=51 G=204 B=51	33CC00 R=51 G=204 B=0
CC99FF R=204 G=153 B=255	CC99CC R=204 G=153 B=204	CC9999 R=204 G=153 B=153	CC9966 R=204 G=153 B=102	CC9933 R=204 G=153 B=51	CC9900 R=204 G=153 B=0	3399FF R=51 G=153 B=255	3399CC R=51 G=153 B=204	339999 R=51 G=153 B=153	339966 R=51 G=153 B=102	339933 R=51 G=153 B=51	339900 R=51 G=153 B=0
CC66FF R=204 G=102 B=255	CC66CC R=204 G=102 B=204	CC6699 R=204 G=102 B=153	CC6666 R=204 G=102 B=102	CC6633 R=204 G=102 B=51	CC6600 R=204 G=102 B=0	3366FF R=51 G=102 B=255	3366CC R=51 G=102 B=204	336699 R=51 G=102 B=153	336666 R=51 G=102 B=102	336633 R=51 G=102 B=51	336600 R=51 G=102 B=0
CC33FF R=204 G=51 B=255	CC33CC R=204 G=51 B=204	CC3399 R=204 G=51 B=153	CC3366 R=204 G=51 B=102	CC3333 R=204 G=51 B=51	CC3300 R=204 G=51 B=0	3333FF R=51 G=51 B=255	3333CC R=51 G=51 B=204	333399 R=51 G=51 B=153	333366 R=51 G=51 B=102	333333 R=51 G=51 B=51	333300 R=51 G=51 B=0
CC00FF R=204 G=0 B=255	CC00CC R=204 G=0 B=204	CC0099 R=204 G=0 B=153	CC0066 R=204 G=0 B=102	CC0033 R=204 G=0 B=51	CC0000 R=204 G=0 B=0	3300FF R=51 G=0 B=255	3300CC R=51 G=0 B=204	330099 R=51 G=0 B=153	330066 R=51 G=0 B=102	330033 R=51 G=0 B=51	330000 R=51 G=0 B=0
99FFFF R=153 G=255 B=255	99FFCC R=153 G=255 B=204	99FF99 R=153 G=255 B=153	99FF66 R=153 G=255 B=102	99FF33 R=153 G=255 B=51	99FF00 R=153 G=255 B=0	00FFFF R=0 G=255 B=255	00FFCC R=0 G=255 B=204	00FF99 R=0 G=255 B=153	00FF66 R=0 G=255 B=102	00FF33 R=0 G=255 B=51	00FF00 R=0 G=255 B=0
99CCFF R=153 G=204 B=255	99CCCC R=153 G=204 B=204	99CC99 R=153 G=204 B=153	99CC66 R=153 G=204 B=102	99CC33 R=153 G=204 B=51	99CC00 R=153 G=204 B=0	00CCFF R=0 G=204 B=255	00CCCC R=0 G=204 B=204	00CC99 R=0 G=204 B=153	00CC66 R=0 G=204 B=102	00CC33 R=0 G=204 B=51	00CC00 R=0 G=204 B=0
9999FF R=153 G=153 B=255	9999CC R=153 G=153 B=204	999999 R=153 G=153 B=153	999966 R=153 G=153 B=102	999933 R=153 G=153 B=51	999900 R=153 G=153 B=0	0099FF R=0 G=153 B=255	0099CC R=0 G=153 B=204	009999 R=0 G=153 B=153	009966 R=0 G=153 B=102	009933 R=0 G=153 B=51	009900 R=0 G=153 B=0
9966FF R=153 G=102 B=255	9966CC R=153 G=102 B=204	996699 R=153 G=102 B=153	996666 R=153 G=102 B=102	996633 R=153 G=102 B=51	996600 R=153 G=102 B=0	0066FF R=0 G=102 B=255	0066CC R=0 G=102 B=204	006699 R=0 G=102 B=153	006666 R=0 G=102 B=102	006633 R=0 G=102 B=51	006600 R=0 G=102 B=0
9933FF R=153 G=51 B=255	9933CC R=153 G=51 B=204	993399 R=153 G=51 B=153	993366 R=153 G=51 B=102	993333 R=153 G=51 B=51	993300 R=153 G=51 B=0	0033FF R=0 G=51 B=255	0033CC R=0 G=51 B=204	003399 R=0 G=51 B=153	003366 R=0 G=51 B=102	003333 R=0 G=51 B=51	003300 R=0 G=51 B=0
9900FF R=153 G=0 B=255	9900CC R=153 G=0 B=204	990099 R=153 G=0 B=153	990066 R=153 G=0 B=102	990033 R=153 G=0 B=51	990000 R=153 G=0 B=0	0000FF R=0 G=0 B=255	0000CC R=0 G=0 B=204	000099 R=0 G=0 B=153	000066 R=0 G=0 B=102	000033 R=0 G=0 B=51	000000 R=0 G=0 B=0

These colors may appear differently on your monitor than they do here in print.

Style Sheets

USING STYLE SHEETS

Web designers often use style sheets to determine how their pages will display on screen. For example, imagine that you want a site's body text to be Arial and its font color to be light green. An easy way to implement this is to use a cascading style sheet (CSS).

Cascading Style Sheets

A cascading style sheet consists of code that defines formatting and layout settings for a Web site's HTML tags. Cascading style sheets are usually either embedded or external. An embedded style sheet is contained in the Web page to which it is applied.

An external style sheet is a separate file with a .css extension that can be linked to multiple Web pages. When you modify a style sheet file, all of the pages attached to that sheet are automatically changed to reflect your modifications. Using CSS thus allows you to:

◆ change the formatting for an entire Web site by changing only the style sheet.
◆ keep the formatting within a site consistent.

The term "cascading" refers to the fact that multiple style sheets can be attached to one Web page. If there is a conflict between style sheets, the format specified in the last style sheet linked to the site will be the format used. Style sheets can be applied to any Web page, whether it was created in Microsoft Notepad, Microsoft Front-Page, or in another Web development application such as Macromedia Dreamweaver.

CSS and Browser Compatibility

Style sheets are published along with the site. Some older browsers do not support CSS. Although most newer browsers will support CSS, it is a good idea to check whether your target audience's browsers will support any style sheets that you may be using.

Most newer browsers support both level 1 (CSS1) and level 2 (CSS2) Cascading Style Sheets. CSS2 are style sheets that allow Web sites to be customized to work with specific equipment. This equipment can include aural devices, Braille devices, and other devices used by people with accessibility needs. Select Tools>Page Options and the Authoring (in 2002, Compatibility) tab to enable CSS1 and CSS2 features in FrontPage.

STYLE SHEETS AND FRONTPAGE

FrontPage provides pre-made style sheets that you can attach to your Web sites. You can select these style sheets from the Style Sheets tab in the Page Templates dialog box.

Each pre-made style sheet provides a different type of text, header, hyperlink, and background style and color. For example, as shown below, the Street style sheet contains navy Verdana text, Comic Sans MS headers, and a light cyan background.

You can use the Page Templates dialog box to select pre-made style sheets.

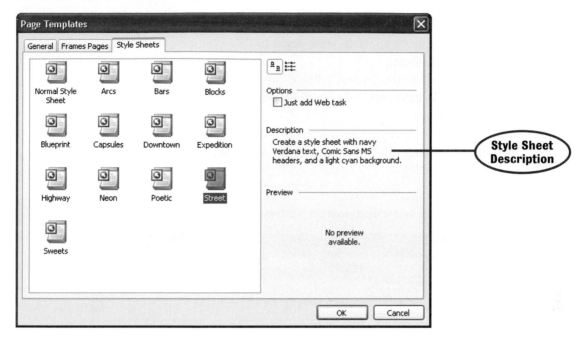

Style Sheet Description

Reading a Style Sheet

The code for each style sheet is divided into sections. These sections include links (items that begin with `a:`), body, table, and six levels of headings. The information contained in each section defines how that item or items will display on screen. For example, the body section in the Street style sheet (shown right) contains the following line:

```
font-family: Verdana, Arial, Helvetica;
```

This line tells the Web browser that body text should be placed in Verdana. However, if Verdana is not available, then Arial should be used instead. If neither Verdana nor Arial are available, then the browser should use Helvetica. By letting Web designers specify the order in which font substitution should take place, cascading style sheets provide them with more control over how a page will appear on different systems with different browsers.

You can edit pre-made style sheets to meet the particular needs of your site. If none of the pre-made style sheets work, then you can use the Normal Style Sheet template to create your own customized external style sheet.

Style sheets determine the formatting for different items on a Web page.

```
a:link
{
    color: rgb(0,102,102);
}
a:visited
{
    color: rgb(0,153,153);
}
a:active
{
    color: rgb(255,102,0);
}
body
{
    font-family: Verdana, Arial, Helvetica;
    background-color: rgb(204,255,255);
    color: rgb(0,0,102);
}
table
{
    table-border-color-light: rgb(102,204,204);
    table-border-color-dark: rgb(0,102,102);
}
h1, h2, h3, h4, h5, h6
{
    font-family: Comic Sans MS, Arial, Helvetica;
}
h1
{
    color: rgb(153,0,0);
}
```

Attaching a Style Sheet in FrontPage

To attach an external cascading style sheet to a Web site, follow these steps:

1. Open your site in FrontPage.
2. On the Standard toolbar, click the **Create a new normal page** drop-down arrow and click **Page.**
3. In the Page Templates dialog box, click the **Style Sheets** tab. Double-click the style sheet you want to apply to your page. In this example, we will select the **Street** style sheet.
4. Click the **Save** button. In the Save As dialog box, type a name for your style sheet in the File name text box. In this example, we will use the name street.css. Click **Save.**
5. Open a page in your site. If you want to link your style sheet to a particular page, then open that page. In this example, we will open the **skills2.html** page, as shown below.

This figure shows the Web page before the style sheet is attached.

6. On the **Format** menu, click **Style Sheet Links.**
7. In the Link Style Sheet dialog box, select All pages. (Even if there is only a single page in your site, you will want the style sheet to be linked to any new pages that may be added to the site.) Click Add to open the Select Style Sheet dialog box. Make certain that the Look in text box contains the address of your Web site.

8. Double-click the name of your style sheet (in this example, **street.css**) to add that file to the Link Style Sheet dialog box, as shown below.

The style sheet file you select is added to the Link Style Sheet dialog box.

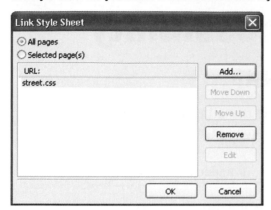

9. Click **OK** to close the Link Style Sheet dialog box. (If the Confirm Format Style Sheet Links dialog box appears, click **Continue.**) The Web page changes to reflect the new style sheet's formatting, as shown below.

This figure shows the Web page after the style sheet is attached.

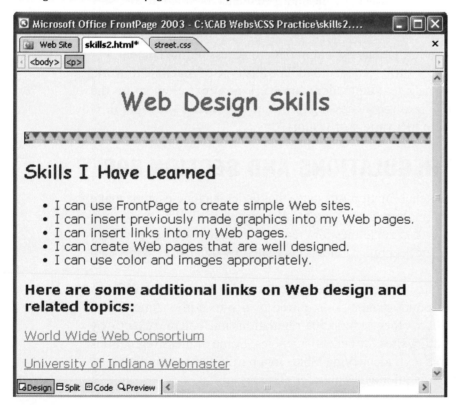

Removing a Style Sheet

To remove a style sheet from a Web site, follow these steps:

1. On the **Format** menu, select **Style Sheet Links.**
2. In the dialog box, select the style sheet that you want to remove.
3. Select either **Selected page(s)** or **All pages.** Click **Remove.**

Web Sites and Accessibility

WHAT DOES ACCESSIBILITY MEAN?

Making a Web site accessible involves making sure that all types of people can access and use its content. As a Web designer, it is important to understand that people who visit your Web pages have different needs.

◆ Some users may have difficulty seeing, hearing, or understanding text, graphic, or audio elements.

◆ Web users with limited mobility may have difficulty using a mouse or keyboard.

◆ Some users may be using old technology or out-of-date software.

To make your site accessible, you should try to present information in as many different ways as you can. For example, to accommodate people with hearing limitations, you should provide text that describes the audio elements included in your site. That way, people who have difficulty hearing can still understand how you are using audio on your page.

Many people with vision limitations use equipment to access online content. For example, screen readers read a site's content aloud. For this type of machine to work, a Web designer must provide a text equivalent for every non-text element on the screen. Providing alternative means of accessing information makes a site more flexible and thus more accessible to a variety of visitors.

ACCESSIBILITY REGULATIONS AND SECTION 508

Section 508 of the U.S. Rehabilitation Act states that Federal agencies must make their public information technology accessible to all visitors, including those with disabilities. Section 508 provides guidelines for creating accessible Web sites. These guidelines are based on the accessibility guidelines issued by the World Wide Web Consortium (W3C).

Many of the 508 guidelines encourage designers to make it easier for all users to understand, scan, and respond to the tasks required by a site. While some guidelines are open to interpretation, other Section 508 regulations must be met exactly by Web designers who are creating sites for Federal agencies. Some of these regulations include providing alternative text, identifying tables in a particular way, and making information conveyed through color accessible for all users.

Alternative Text

Section 508 states that alternative text must be provided for every non-text element on a Web page.

◆ Every visual on a Web site including graphical buttons, symbols, and image maps must have a text equivalent. When creating HTML documents, every `img` tag should include an `alt` attribute.

◆ Alternative text and text captions should also be provided for all multimedia elements such as animations, videos, and audio items. Provide transcripts of audio segments and descriptions of video to increase accessibility.

◆ Graphs and charts need to include alternative text that summarizes their content. If a longer description is required, use the `longdesc` attribute to link to the description.

◆ Alternative text or some type of equivalent must be provided for dynamic content such as scripts and applets. This alternative text or equivalent must be updated if the dynamic content changes. Visitors should still be able to use pages even if dynamic content is not supported by their browsers.

◆ Each frame in a frames-based site should be titled. The `<noframes>` tag should be used so people with browsers that do not support frames can still view the site.

Alternative text should give a brief description of the information or functionality provided by the element being described. Think about how your visitors will respond to your alternative text. For example, using "Blue button" to describe a blue Submit button will not make as much sense to a visitor as the alternative text "Submit button." Also make sure that your alternative text can be understood when it is read aloud by a machine such as a screen reader.

If it is difficult to provide access through alternative text, you can supply text-only pages (pages that contain the same information as your site, but present that information only through words). Include a link on your Web site's main page that will direct the user to the text-only page.

The Section 508 Web site provides information about accessibility regulations and guidelines.

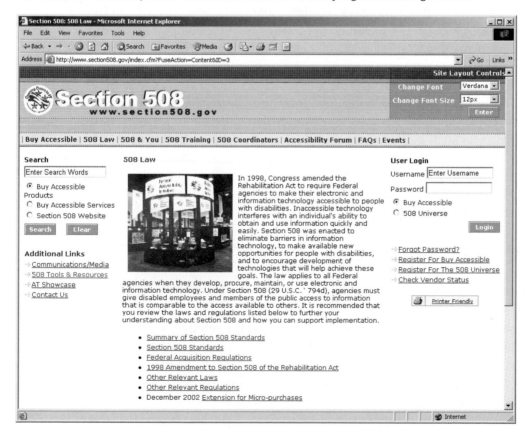

Tables and Accessibility

Screen readers read tables cell by cell. If row and column headers are not properly identified and labeled, then a table may not make sense to the user when its contents are read aloud by a screen reader. For example, considering the following table:

NAME	COLLEGE	MAJOR	GRADE POINT AVERAGE
Madeline	Yale	English	3.5
Josh	Auburn	Communications	3.0

If this table is designed to be read by a screen reader, it will be interpreted as:

◆ Name: Madeline; College: Yale; Major: English; GPA: 3.5
◆ Name: Josh; College: Auburn; Major: Communications; GPA: 3.0

If is it not properly designed, then the screen reader may, for example, read the columns as:

◆ Name: Madeline, Josh
◆ College: Yale, Auburn

A person who is listening to this information will not understand how the names and colleges relate to each other. To learn more about designing accessible tables, go to the W3C Web site.

Color and Accessibility

Many people are color-blind, and have problems distinguishing various shades of red and green. Other users may have problems seeing light blue colors clearly. Because of this, all information on a Web page that is communicated with color should also be available without color.

There are a variety of visual cues that you can use to organize and display information that do not depend on color. For example, format text to illustrate degrees of importance. Major headings should be formatted larger and bolder than body text. Visual cues such as this can help all users scan and understand information on a Web page.

Most users also find it easier to read a screen when there is a high contrast between the text's background and the text itself. Web designers should use colors that provide a high-contrast between text and its background.

CASCADING STYLE SHEETS AND ACCESSIBILITY

The W3C recommends using cascading style sheets (CSS) to make Web sites more accessible. CSS can increase accessibility in the following ways:

◆ Pages designed with CSS allow users to easily change settings, such as colors and text size. For example, to increase a page's readability, a user can change the page's background to white, and its text to black.
◆ Voice properties such as volume control and the ability to say or spell a specific word can be included on a page to provide information to people with vision limitations.

FRONTPAGE 2003 ACCESSIBILITY TOOLS

FrontPage 2003 provides an Accessibility report that you can use to check your Web site. As shown below, you can check to see whether your site complies with the Section 508 guidelines, or with the Web Content Accessibility Guidelines (WCAG) developed by the W3C. When checking for WCAG compliance, you can choose to see whether your site meets the Priority 1 checkpoints (points that **must** be satisfied for a site to be fully accessible), or the Priority 2 checkpoints (points that **should** be satisfied to make a site even more accessible to different groups).

You can use the FrontPage Accessibility report to see if your site complies with 508 and WCAG regulations.

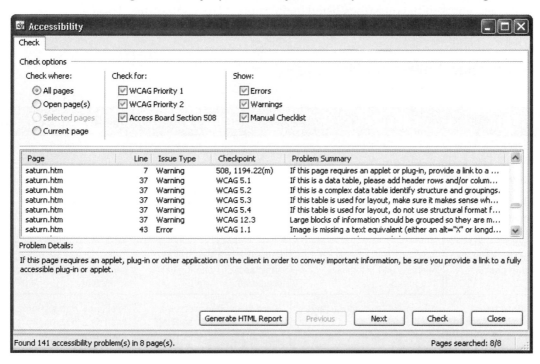

To check your site for accessibility, follow these steps:

1. On the **Tools** menu, select **Accessibility.** The Accessibility dialog box appears.
2. In the Check options section, under Check where, select the page(s) you want to check in your Web site.
3. Under Check for, select the guidelines you want to check your site against. It is a good idea to select all three guidelines so you can identify all possible problems on your pages.
4. Under Show, select the type of items you want included in your report.
   ◆ **Errors** are items that must be changed for the Web site to comply.
   ◆ **Warnings** are suggested changes.
   ◆ The **Manual Checklist** provides additional suggestions and allows you to create a checklist that you can use to track your changes.
5. Click **Check** to generate your report. To create an HTML version of your report, click **Generate HTML Report.** You can use this printable report to locate and correct accessibility errors in your HTML code.

The report shows where problems are located and whether those problems count as errors or warnings according to the 508 or WCAG guidelines. Correct all errors to ensure that people with different needs can use and enjoy your site.

APPENDIX F

Web Design Rubric

A rubric is a tool that you can use to evaluate Web pages and Web sites. The rubric in this appendix lists criteria that you can use to assess various aspects of Web site design.

You can use the rubric to evaluate existing sites, or to evaluate your own sites. As you create a site, ask yourself the questions listed in the rubric. Then determine if your site rates as excellent, good, or poor. Revise your site as needed to improve its rating.

Web Site Evaluation Rubric

CRITERIA	EXCELLENT (3)	GOOD (2)	POOR (1)
Information Design			
Is the site's purpose clearly stated?	The site's purpose is clearly stated.	The site's purpose is understood but not strongly stated.	The site's purpose is unclear.
Is all content current, accurate, and properly cited?	All content is current, accurate, and properly cited.	Some content is current, accurate, and properly cited.	None of the content is current, accurate, or properly cited.
Is the text logically organized and presented in short sections?	Text is presented in short sections and is logically organized.	Some text is presented in short sections and logically organized.	Text is presented in long sections and its organization is unclear.
Has all the content been proofread and spell checked?	All content is proofread and spell checked.	There are minor problems with grammar and spelling.	Problems with grammar and spelling are strongly noticeable.
Presentation Design			
Does the site's content, formatting, and color scheme support its purpose?	The site's content, formatting, and color scheme supports its purpose.	Some of the site's content, formatting, and color scheme supports its purpose.	None of the site's content, formatting, and color scheme supports its purpose.
Is the site's color scheme, layout, and formatting consistent?	The site's color scheme, layout, and formatting is consistent.	The site's color scheme, layout, and formatting is inconsistent in some pages.	The site's color scheme, layout, and formatting is inconsistent in every page.
Does the page contain sufficient white space?	The page contains sufficient white space.	The page contains some white space.	The page contains insufficient white space.
Is text readable against the background?	Text is readable against the background.	Text is difficult to read against the background.	Text is unreadable against the background.
Is formatting used to emphasize important text?	Formatting is used to emphasize important text.	Formatting is sometimes used to emphasize important text.	Formatting is not used to emphasize important text.
Is important information displayed in the safe area?	Important information is displayed in the safe area.	Some of the important information is displayed in the safe area.	None of the important information is displayed in the safe area.

CRITERIA	EXCELLENT (3)	GOOD (2)	POOR (1)
Interaction Design			
Do all internal and external hyperlinks work properly?	All internal and external hyperlinks work properly.	Not all internal and external hyperlinks work.	None of the internal and external hyperlinks work.
Can users move easily between all pages?	Users can move easily between all pages.	Users can move easily between some pages.	Users cannot move easily between pages.
Can users locate specific information quickly?	Users can locate specific information quickly.	Users can locate specific information with some searching.	Users cannot locate specific information.
Can users easily return to the Web site's home page?	Users can easily return to the Web site's home page.	Users can easily return to the Web site's home page from some pages.	Users cannot easily return to the Web site's home page from any page.
Multimedia and Interactivity			
Does every element enhance the site and promote usability (i.e., buttons change colors to let users know when something is clicked)?	All elements enhance the site and promote usability.	Some elements enhance the site and promote usability.	None of the elements enhance the site and promote usability.
Do users clearly know how to use all interactive elements?	Users clearly know how to use all interactive elements.	Users know how to use some interactive elements.	Users do not know how to use any interactive elements.
Are all form elements and links clearly labeled?	All form elements and links are clearly labeled.	Some form elements and links are clearly labeled.	None of the form elements or links are clearly labeled.
Does every multimedia and interactive element work properly in a variety of browsers?	All multimedia and interactive elements work properly in a variety of browsers.	Some multimedia and interactive elements work properly in a variety of browsers.	None of the multimedia and interactive elements work properly in a variety of browsers.
Usability and Accessibility			
Does the site display properly in a variety of different browsers at different resolutions?	Site displays properly in a variety of different browsers at different resolutions.	Site displays properly in some different browsers at different resolutions.	Site does not display properly in different browsers at different resolutions.
Are both graphic and text links included?	Both graphic and text links are included.	Some text links are included.	No text links are included.
Does a frames site offer alternatives to help users whose browsers do not support frames?	Frames site offers the `<noframes>` option to help users whose browsers do not support frames.	Frames site offers some alternative to help users whose browsers do not support frames.	Frames site does not offer any alternative to help users whose browsers do not support frames.
Does every frame in the frames-based site have a logical title?	All frames in the frames-based site have a logical title.	Some frames in the frames-based site have a logical title.	None of the frames in frames-based site have a logical title.
Is alternative text provided for all non-text items?	Alternative text is provided for all non-text items.	Alternative text is provided for some non-text items.	Alternative text is not provided for any non-text items.
Does every page download quickly for the target audience?	All pages download quickly for the target audience.	Some pages download quickly for the target audience.	None of the pages download quickly for the target audience.

GLOSSARY

absolute link A type of link that contains the complete URL or path of the file being linked to. (p. 105)

access control A security measure in which a site's availability is restricted to a specific set of authorized users. (p. 405)

accessibility option A feature that allows differently abled individuals to access and use Web pages. (p. 70)

active button A clicked button that is in the process of doing something, such as transferring the user to another Web page. (p. 166)

alignment The position of text on a page, such as left, right, or centered. (p. 188)

analog video recorder A device that creates analog video. This video must be translated into a digital format before a computer can use it. (p. 253)

anchor tag An HTML tag used to create hyperlinks. The tag identifies what is clicked on and where it links to. (p. 104)

animated GIF A sequence of GIF images that are all stored in a single file along with an image transition delay value that controls the time each image will stay on the screen. (p. 441)

animation The movement of text and graphics; a common feature on the Web. (p. 13)

application software Computer programs that allow users to perform a specific task on the computer; also referred to as *applications*. (p. 41)

applications See *application software*. (p. 41)

archiving The process of saving and storing old Web pages and their components. (p. 403)

aspect ratio The relationship between an image's height and width. (p. 233)

attribute An HTML instruction that is included in an HTML tag to specify a characteristic of a Web page element. (p. 98)

audio Live, streamed, or recorded sound; often used on Web pages to attract visitors' interest and to impart information. (p. 13)

backup A copy of a specific set of data, usually stored in a different place such as a tape, CD-ROM, or another hard drive. (p. 396)

bandwidth Determines the amount of data that can be transmitted at the same time over a broadband connection. (p. 44)

banner ad An advertisement that, when clicked, takes the visitor to the sponsor's home page. (p. 275)

basic input/output system (BIOS) Small program that performs basic startup activities, such as activating the computer's operating system. (p. 40)

bitmapped graphic See *raster graphic*. (p. 219)

body Part of an HTML document that contains a Web page's content; content placed in the body is viewed in the browser window. (p. 97)

bookmark A hyperlink to a specific document or another place in the same document; often used as intrapage links on long pages. (p. 348)

Boolean search A type of search that combines keywords in specific ways to locate specific pages. (p. 72)

border A visual break on the page that is used to add interest and to separate elements. (p. 113)

budget The total financial resources available for a Web site's development. (p. 310)

bulleted list See *unordered list*. (p. 100)

business-to-business (B2B) e-commerce Electronic exchanges in which both parties are businesses. (p. 308)

business-to-consumer (B2C) e-commerce Electronic exchanges between businesses and individual consumers. (p. 308)

cascading style sheet A style sheet that consists of code that defines formatting and layout settings for HTML tags. (p. 214)

case sensitive Distinguishing between file names that contain uppercase and lowercase letters and those that contain only lowercase letters. (p. 376)

cell Each individual square within a table; the intersection of a column and a row. (p. 163)

cell padding The space between a table cell's border and its content. (p. 421)

cell spacing The space between the outer border of a table and the cell border. (p. 421)

central processing unit (CPU) The part of the computer where data is processed; sometimes referred to as the "brain" of the computer. (p. 34)

check box A form field option that allows visitors to choose as many items from a list as they desire. (p. 326)

client In a network, the individual computers that are part of that network. (p. 45) In a Web site development team, the person or organization that contracts and pays for the work. (p. 300)

client liaison representative The project team member who maintains contact with the client throughout the Web site development process. (p. 300)

client-side script A script that is executed by the user's Web browser. (p. 446)

closing tag See *ending tag*. (p. 92)

codec Compression and decompression scheme used with streaming media; the Web server breaks the transmission into pieces, allowing the media to display more quickly on the user's screen. (p. 245)

color scheme A set of selected colors used consistently for a Web site's interface elements, such as title graphics, navigation buttons, and background. (p. 184)

column Cells in a table that are arranged vertically. (p. 163)

commercial software Software that is developed and distributed with the intention of making a profit. (p. 81)

Common Gateway Interface (CGI) A type of script that provides a link, or interface, between an external application and a Web server. This link allows the Web server to pass a user's request to an application program and then return information to the user. (p. 270)

conditional statement A type of code that allows a script to respond differently depending on the action taken by the user. (p. 447)

configuration How a system of computers is arranged or set up. (p. 43)

consistency A logical coherence among parts; rule that encourages designers to use similar design elements throughout a site. (p. 178)

container page Page that defines the characteristics of each page in a frames-based site. (p. 427)

content The text and graphics included on a Web page. (p. 150)

content page The page that contains the main information on a frames-based site and fulfills the site's main purpose. (p. 428)

cookie A small data file that a Web site writes to a visitor's hard drive containing personal information such as login or registration information. (p. 329)

copyright Asserts that only the copyright's owner has the right to sell his or her work or to allow someone else to sell it. (p. 82)

cropping To remove portions of an image that you do not want to use. (p. 233)

cross-platform testing The process of testing Web sites on a variety of computer hardware and software configurations to make sure that the site will function properly for different users. (p. 380)

D

data encryption Security measure in which sensitive information is encoded and decoded as it is transferred across the Internet. (p. 332)

database A collection of information that is organized by fields and records for easy retrieval. (p. 351)

database driven Dynamic page that uses a database for its source of information. (p. 351)

database interface page A Web page that connects to and interacts with a database. (p. 352)

debugging The process of locating and correcting errors in a Web site's HTML code. (p. 107)

DHTML See *Dynamic Hypertext Markup Language*. (p. 259)

digital camera A photographic device that saves images in a digital format so they can be easily used on the Web. (p. 225)

digital certificate A document issued by an independent certification authority that confirms a business's credentials. (p. 332)

digital video recorder A device that creates digital video that a computer can use directly. (p. 253)

direct server update The act of updating or revising a Web site's files directly on the Web server where the site resides. (p. 400)

directory structure A hierarchy used to organize folders and the files contained in the folders; also called folder structure. (p. 377)

domain name Part of a URL that identifies the entity (such as a university, individual, or business) that sponsors the Web site. (p. 68)

domain name extension Part of the URL that tells users what type of organization uses the address. (p. 69)

dots per inch (dpi) A definition of resolution that states the number of pixels created for every linear inch of an image, such as 600 dpi. (p. 225)

download To transfer data from a file server to a client (user) machine. (p. 378)

draw program A type of software application that is used to create vector graphics. (p. 219)

drop-down box An interactive element that looks like a text field, but operates like a set of option buttons in that users can choose only one item from a list of options; also known as a *pull-down menu.* (p. 283)

dynamic button See *interactive button.* (p. 166)

Dynamic HTML (DHTML) Available in FrontPage as a tool to create animations such as scrolling text (marquees) and page transitions. (p. 259)

E

e-commerce The electronic buying and selling of goods and services. (p. 306)

e-mail Abbreviation for electronic mail, the most common way to send messages and communicate over the Internet. (p. 65)

embedded file File that you add to the FrontPage document from other applications. (p. 113)

embedded style sheet A style sheet that contains format and layout settings that only apply to the current Web page. (p. 214)

empty tag An HTML tag that requires only an opening tag; also known as an *orphan tag.* (p. 93)

ending tag The last of a pair of HTML tags; also known as a *closing tag.* (p. 92)

event Anything that causes an effect to occur; often triggered by a user's action. (p. 447)

event handler The part of the script that responds to an event and defines the action that will occur when the event takes place. (p. 447)

Extensible Hypertext Markup Language (XHTML) A markup language that is designed to bridge the differences between HTML and XML. (p. 271)

Extensible Markup Language (XML) A markup language whose tags impose a specific structure and meaning on data without providing any information about how the data should be displayed. (p. 270)

external hyperlink A hyperlink that takes a user to a page on a different Web site. (p. 77)

external style sheet A style sheet containing format and layout settings that is stored in a separate file. (p. 214)

external Web hosting When a company pays another business to host its Web sites. (p. 373)

extranet A type of network that can be accessed by outside or remote users who are authorized to use the network. (p. 66)

F

fair use doctrine Allows for small portions of a copyrighted work to be used for educational purposes. (p. 82)

feedback form A form that allows customers to voice their opinions, comments, and suggestions, and can help to cement a relationship between the customer and the business. (p. 322)

field A form component that allows the user to enter information into the form. A form field often corresponds to a field database. (p. 281)

file Contains information, such as text, graphics, video, or animation, that is stored on computer hardware. (p. 6)

file management The process of creating, naming, moving, updating, and deleting files on a computer system. (p. 400)

file name The name of the HTML document that makes up the Web page itself. (p. 139)

file name extension The three or four characters after a period in a file name that tell the computer system what type of file it is reading. (p. 97)

File Transfer Protocol (FTP) Provides a standardized method of uploading and downloading files on the Internet. (p. 64)

folder An item that helps the user organize files. (p. 48)

Folder List Part of FrontPage that displays the folders and files that you can access in the current Web site. (p. 23)

folder structure See *directory structure.* (p. 377)

font A family of letters, numbers, and other symbols that share a consistent style. (p. 51)

footer The bottom portion of a Web page; usually contains date information, copyright information, contact information, and text links. (p. 168)

form A structure that includes fields for collecting data from visitors to a Web site. (p. 281)

frame A separate region on a Web page that contains its own Web document. (p. 356)

frameset A shell page in a frames-based site that contains information about the size and placement of the frames within the site. (p. 356)

freeware Software that can be freely copied and used for any legal purpose. (p. 81)

frequently asked questions (FAQ) A list of questions and answers to questions that visitors are likely to have about the Web site, the business, or a company's products. (p. 348)

FTP See *File Transfer Protocol.* (p. 64)

function In JavaScript, code that performs a specific task or action. (p. 447)

G

gateway An Internet server that allows the LAN to communicate with the Internet. (p. 63)

GIF (Graphic Interchange Format) A graphic file format that can save only a maximum of 256 colors. (p. 220)

global access control A security measure in which groups of users are granted or denied access to computer system data; different groups of users are often given different levels of access to system data. (p. 407)

graphic A drawing, chart, diagram, painting, or photograph stored in a digital format. (p. 12)

graphic link A type of link in which users click on an image to activate the link. (p. 105)

graphical user interface (GUI) Type of interface that allows users to interact with software by selecting words, symbols, or graphics from a desktop. (p. 41)

guest book A public record of comments from visitors to a Web site. (p. 344)

GUI See *graphical user interface.* (p. 41)

H

hard drive mirroring Storage method in which data are written to more than one hard drive at the same time; helps keep Web servers fully functional at all times. (p. 395)

hardware The physical components of the computer. (p. 34)

header Part of an HTML document that provides information such as the page's title to the browser; information contained in the header is not visible on the Web page. (p. 97)

header column Column in a table that contains the titles for each row. (p. 422)

header row Row in a table that contains the titles for each column. (p. 422)

hierarchical navigation scheme Type of navigational plan in which pages are arranged in levels from top to bottom, with the topmost level being the Web site's home page. (p. 132)

hit counter A dynamic Web component that records the number of times visitors access a Web page. (p. 342)

hits The number of times a browser requests a page from a Web server. (p. 342)

home page The main page on a Web site which contains general information about the site, such as an introduction and a list of the other available pages; generally the first page a visitor sees. (p. 7)

host The name of the Web server on which a particular Web site resides. (p. 371)

hotspot A graphic link to a related page or another area on the current page. (p. 197)

hot-swappable hard drives Storage system used by some Web servers that contains multiple hard drives; allows a Webmaster to replace one drive for another in case of failure of the drive. (p. 395)

hover button A navigation button that changes appearance when touched by a mouse pointer. (p. 166)

HTML See *Hypertext Markup Language.* (p. 92)

HTML editor See *text editor.* (p. 74)

HTML tag Text contained between two angle brackets (< >) that tells the Web browser how to display a page's content. (p. 92)

HTML validator An application developed to debug HTML code. (p. 107)

HTTP See *Hypertext Transfer Protocol.* (p. 64)

hyperlink A way to link Web pages together and allow users to move from one online location to another. Link may consist of text or a graphic. (p. 14)

Hypertext Markup Language (HTML) The code used to create Web pages. (p. 92)

Hypertext Transfer Protocol (HTTP) Used to transfer files from a Web server to a Web browser. (p. 64)

I

image map A graphic with clickable areas called hotspots that link to another page or to another area on the same page. (p. 197)

image tag An empty HTML tag that finds an image from a specified location and displays it in a browser. (p. 103)

incremental backup Copies only the data that have changed since the last full backup to the backup device. (p. 396)

information design Part of Web site design process in which you determine the content that will appear on each page. (p. 18)

inline graphic Created by storing a graphic in an electronic format on a hard drive and inserting the graphic into a Web page. (p. 225)

instant storefront A portal site that provides easy-to-use screens that walk businesses through the process of creating their own Web sites. (p. 311)

intellectual property Creative works created and owned by individuals such as authors, software developers, and musicians. (p. 82)

interaction design Part of Web site design process in which you determine how the user is likely to navigate through the site. (p. 17)

interactive button Type of button that changes to let users know that an action has taken place; also called a *dynamic button.* (p. 166)

interactivity Allows communication between the visitor and the Web page; the user can perform an action that the Web page responds to. (p. 268)

interface Means by which a user interacts with a computer or a computer program. (p. 22)

internal Web hosting When a company uses its own Web server to host its Web site. (p. 373)

Internet Hardware, such as computers, cables, and telephone wires, that is connected to create a massive worldwide network. (p. 6)

Internet service provider (ISP) A business that provides a network to customers that they use to access the Internet. (p. 63)

Internet Use Agreement Used by organizations such as schools and businesses to regulate online use; also called *Acceptable Use Policies* or *AUPs.* (p. 80)

InterNIC A Web site providing information about the Web name registration process. (p. 376)

intranet A LAN or WAN that is designed to make it easy to share information within an organization, such as a business or a school. (p. 66)

inverted pyramid A type of narrative structure that places the most important information at the beginning of a story, where it will best catch the reader's attention. (p. 152)

ISP See *Internet service provider.* (p. 63)

J

Java applet A short Java code program that runs in a browser. (p. 270)

JavaScript A scripting language used to enhance the capabilities of Web programming by allowing the creation of special effects such as fading backgrounds and button rollovers. (p. 269)

JPEG (Joint Photographic Experts Group) A graphic file format that can support millions of colors; preferred format for saving photographs. (p. 220)

K

keyboard An input device that lets you enter text into the computer. (p. 35)

keyword An important word related to the specific topic you are trying to locate. (p. 72)

L

label Text that tells the user what type of information to enter into a form's field. (p. 281)

left-hand navigation A frames-based Web site with a link bar on the left side of the screen. (p. 427)

linear navigation scheme Type of navigational plan in which every page exists at the same level; each page in the site is accessed from the one before it. (p. 133)

link bar A related group of horizontally or vertically aligned links; also known as a *navigation bar* or *table of contents.* (p. 166)

link trading An agreement between Web site publishers to display a link to each other's sites; inexpensive way to publicize Web sites. (p. 383)

local area network (LAN) Type of network that connects computers in a single location, such as a single department within a company. (p. 43)

local client update The process of revising Web pages by copying the files from the Web server to a local (client) workstation, updating the files on the local workstation, and uploading the revised files to the Web server. (p. 400)

local Web site A Web site that resides on the hard drive or network drive where the site's files were originally created. (p. 361)

logo A symbol used to represent a business or an organization. (p. 162)

lossless compression A compression scheme in which a graphic file loses no data when it is compressed. (p. 221)

lossy compression A compression scheme that removes data from a graphic file so that the file is significantly smaller and downloads more quickly in a Web browser than one saved with lossless compression. (p. 221)

M

Macromedia Flash A popular animation formation, usually carrying a .swf extension. (p. 258)

markup language A text file that contains special sequences of characters that function as tags, such as HTML, XML, and XHTML. (p. 270)

marquee A string of text that moves from one edge of the page to the other. (p. 274)

meta tag A piece of HTML code that the Web author places in the page document to help search engines categorize the page; does not affect how the site is displayed. (p. 384)

microprocessor In most PCs, the name for the single chip that is the computer's CPU. (p. 34)

milestone A specific step in the Web site development process and the date for its completion. (p. 300)

mission statement A statement that describes the purpose and audience of a Web site. (p. 126)

modem Hardware device that enables a computer to send and receive signals through telephone wires or cable. (p. 45)

monitor The part of the computer that shows the output in a quick, readable form; also known as a display screen. (p. 36)

mouse The most common pointing device used to enter commands into the computer. (p. 35)

multimedia The integration of elements such as graphics, text, audio, video, animation, and interactivity by means of computer technology. (p. 13)

multimedia authoring tool Special software applications used by Web site designers and developers to create multimedia Web sites. (p. 247)

multitasking Working with more than one application or document at a time. (p. 41)

N

navigation bar See *link bar.* (p. 166)

navigation link A button that users click to locate additional information and to navigate to other Web pages. (p. 166)

Navigation Pane Part of FrontPage that displays the page titles of all the files that have been added to the navigational structure of the current Web site. (p. 23)

navigation scheme The plan that determines how Web pages will relate to each other within a Web site. (p. 131)

nested tag An HTML tag that is enclosed within another set of tags. (p. 93)

netiquette General guidelines that have developed over the years to guide Internet interactions. (p. 81)

network A system in which communication lines or wireless connections are used to connect computers together. (p. 43)

network interface card (NIC) Provides the place to plug the network cable into the computer, and it creates and sends the signal from one network component to another. (p. 45)

network operating system (NOS) Software that is responsible for managing network resources, controlling who can access different network components, and keeping the network running smoothly. (p. 46)

New Page button FrontPage tool that allows you to create new content in a frame. (p. 358)

numbered list See *ordered list.* (p. 100)

O

object In JavaScript, an element in a browser window; it can have properties that define it. (p. 446)

opening tag See *starting tag.* (p. 92)

operating system (OS) Software that specifies how the computer receives and processes input; acts as an interface between a user and the computer hardware. (p. 40)

option button A type of form field that allows visitors to choose only one option from a list of available options; also known as a *radio button.* (p. 324)

ordered list A type of list that contains items, usually numbered, that must appear in a particular sequence. (p. 100)

orphan tag See *empty tag.* (p. 93)

OS See *operating system.* (p. 40)

P

page banner Page element that contains graphics and/or text, such as a site's logo and title graphic; helps users identify where they are in a Web site. (p. 181)

page name The name that appears in the title bar when the page is displayed in a browser. (p. 139)

page title See *page name.* (p. 139)

page transition Special effects that the user sees when moving from one page to another. (p. 278)

paint program A type of software application that is used to create raster graphics. (p. 219)

parent-child relationship In a hierarchical navigation scheme, a page that is connected to another page on a different level; the page that is on the level above is the parent, and the page that is on the level below is the child. (p. 132)

password A set of letters or numbers that a user enters to gain access to a Web site. (p. 405)

path Identifies the drive, folder, and subfolder to which a Web site is being saved. (p. 48)

peer-to-peer relationship In a hierarchical navigation scheme, two or more child pages that have the same parent page. (p. 132)

photo gallery A collection of photographs with brief descriptions. (p. 235)

pixel A single point in a graphic image; short for **pi**cture **el**ement. (p. 155)

placeholder text Text often included in templates to indicate the type of content the user can put in a particular location. (p. 49)

plug-in An application that works with a Web browser to play a particular file format, such as an audio or video file. (p. 251)

point A traditional unit of type measurement. (p. 188)

presentation design Part of Web site design process in which you determine the physical appearance of the site's pages. (p. 18)

printer A hardware device that produces hard copy, or output that is permanent. (p. 37)

privacy The ethical online collection and use of visitors' personal information. (p. 329)

privacy policy A written statement that outlines what information the Web site collects about visitors and explains how that information will be used. (p. 330)

project manager The project team member who oversees the work of all the team members and ensures that team members work together. (p. 300)

protocol A set of rules and procedures that specify how data are formatted and transmitted between computer systems. (p. 64)

proximity The closeness of elements on a page that can cause readers to make assumptions about how elements relate to each other. (p. 158)

publicize The process of letting the general public know that your Web site exists and telling them how to access it. (p. 382)

publish To transfer files from a local computer to a remote Web server so that the Web site can be viewed over the Internet. (p. 370)

pull-down menu See *drop-down box*. (p. 443)

R

radio button An interactive control that allows a user to select only one option from a list of options; also known as an *option button*. (p. 442)

random-access memory (RAM) Where the computer stores data that it is currently processing. (p. 35)

random-access navigation scheme A type of navigation plan in which a site's pages are not organized in any particular order. (p. 133)

raster graphic A graphic made up of pixels; also known as a *bitmapped graphic*. (p. 219)

record A group of related fields in a database that contain all the information gathered about a particular person or product. (p. 351)

relative link A type of link that is used when linking to a local file, such as one within the same Web site. (p. 105)

remote Web site A Web site that exists on a hard drive or network drive that is different from the location where the Web site was created. Transferring files from a local to a remote Web site allows you to test the publishing process. (p. 361)

repetition Design rule that encourages designers to duplicate specific elements on all (or most) of a site's pages to make the site more user-friendly. (p. 178)

resampling Changing the number of pixels in a graphic file to match the new screen area occupied by the image; this changes the size of the graphic file. (p. 233)

resizing Changing the size of the image as it appears on the screen without changing the file size of the graphic. (p. 233)

rollover button A button that changes appearance when the mouse pointer passes over it. (p. 276)

row Cells in a table that are arranged horizontally. (p. 163)

S

safe area Amount of space available on every Web browser and system combination; generally defined as 640 x 480 pixels, the size of the smallest monitor available. (p. 155)

sans serif A font that does not have special adornment at the end of letters or numbers. (p. 190)

scanner A hardware device that converts a printed image into a digital format that can be used on a Web page. (p. 225)

scope In a Web site development project, the features and content on a Web site that can be provided with the time and resources available. (p. 306)

screen resolution The amount of pixels that a monitor can display; measured by width and height such as 640 x 480. (p. 155)

script A short program that you can insert into HTML code using special tags; expands the capabilities of HTML to create dynamic Web pages. (p. 268)

scroll box A form field that includes a text area that will expand to allow visitors to enter lengthy comments; also known as a *text area*. (p. 322)

search capabilities A Web site feature that allows visitors to find specific words or phrases in the site's content. (p. 349)

search engine An application that locates information about Web pages and then stores this information in searchable databases that you can access from your browser. (p. 72)

secondary storage Device such as a hard drive or a CD-ROM needed to save data long-term. (p. 37)

security The protection of data from unauthorized access, both on the Web server and during transmission over the Web. (p. 331)

serif Font that has an extra line or curve on the ends of certain letters or numbers. (p. 190)

server A powerful central computer that manages files and services for a network. (p. 45)

server-side script A script that is executed on the Web server, with the output transferred to the user's computer as a Web page. (p. 448)

Set Initial Page button FrontPage tool that allows you to link existing content to a frame in a frames-based site. (p. 358)

shared border An area that remains the same on all (or some) of the pages in a Web site. (p. 215)

shareware Copyrighted software that an author allows to be freely distributed. (p. 81)

site map A list of categories that organizes the content of large Web sites. (p. 347)

software The set of instructions that tells the computer what to do. (p. 34)

source code The text and HTML commands used to create the Web page. (p. 94)

source control A FrontPage feature that protects the integrity of the Web site's files by ensuring that only one person at a time can edit a particular file. (p. 304)

spam Unsolicited e-mail messages. (p. 382)

SSL (Secure Socket Layer) Data encryption method commonly used by Web site publishers because its algorithm is specifically designed to protect data transmitted across the Internet. (p. 332)

starting tag The first of a pair of HTML tags; also known as an *opening tag.* (p. 92)

storyboard A visual representation of a Web site and its pages. (p. 137)

subfolder A folder contained within a folder; used to further organize files. (p. 48)

subpage A page that is a child of another page. (p. 195)

T

table An item consisting of columns and rows that is used to organize a Web page's content. (p. 163)

table of contents A Web site element that allows visitors to see the contents and organization of the site in one glance; similar to the table of contents of a book. (p. 347)

target audience The main group of people that you want to visit your Web site. (p. 127)

target market The potential customers for the product or service that you are selling; often defined by characteristics such as age, income, and interests. (p. 308)

task pane Part of FrontPage that provides quick access to the typical tasks performed when creating a Web site. (p. 23)

template A reusable pattern that helps you place information quickly and efficiently on a Web page. (p. 49)

testing The process of repeatedly checking the Web page and site to make certain that elements display as designed. (p. 107)

text Consists of words, letters, numbers, and other symbols. (p. 12)

text area Form element that allows the user to enter as much text as desired; also known as a *scroll box.* (p. 443)

text box Form element that allows the user to enter a relatively small amount of text into a form (p. 283)

text editor An application used to enter and edit the HTML code in a Web page. (p. 74)

text link A type of link in which users click text to activate the link. (p. 105)

theme A collection of design elements, graphics, and colors that help maintain a consistent image throughout the Web site. (p. 51)

thumbnail A small image that links to a larger version of the same image; lets users decide if they want to view the larger image, which takes longer to download. (p. 235)

title graphic An image that appears at the top of every page on a Web site. (p. 162)

top navigation A frames-based Web site with a link bar at the top of the screen. (p. 429)

top-level page The highest level in a hierarchical navigation structure; usually the home page. (p. 132)

tracking software Records information about Web site visitors such as what browser they used, how they navigated to the site, and what country they are from. (p. 344)

Transmission Control Protocol/Internet Protocol (TCP/IP) Basic Internet protocol that contains the specific information that allows computers to identify each other and exchange data. (p. 64)

typography The style, arrangement, and appearance of text. (p. 187)

U

uniform resource locator (URL) A unique address that enables a browser to locate specific page files on the Web. (p. 68)

unordered list A list that contains items that can appear in any order. (p. 100)

upload To transfer data from a client (user) computer to a server. (p. 378)

URL See *uniform resource locator.* (p. 68)

user authentication The process of checking the password the user enters against the one assigned to the user. (p. 405)

V

variable Used by scripts to identify a value that will change when the script is executed. (p. 447)

vector graphic A graphic composed of simple lines defined by mathematical equations. (p. 219)

video Live or recorded moving images. (p. 13)

video capture card A circuit board that can convert analog video to digital video. (p. 253)

W

Web author Person who writes the text that will appear on each Web page. (p. 19)

Web browser Software application that interprets files to display Web pages on the user's computer. (p. 7)

Web design The process of determining a Web site's content, appearance, and navigational scheme. (p. 20)

Web designer Person who develops the look and feel of the Web site. (p. 19)

Web developer Person who uses programming skills to develop Web sites. (p. 20)

Web development The entire process of determining a Web site's goals, and designing, publishing, and maintaining the site. (p. 20)

Web directory Search tool that catalogs Web sites (not pages) by topic or category. (p. 72)

Web host A business that provides Web server space to customers for a fee. (p. 371)

Web hosting service Service that sells Web server space, usually for a monthly fee. (p. 77)

Web page A single file within a Web site that has a unique name. (p. 7)

Web server A powerful computer that maintains a constant connection to the Internet; stores Web pages and makes them available on the Internet. (p. 370)

Web server cluster System that stores a Web site on multiple physical computers that act as a single virtual host. (p. 372)

Web site A group of related files organized around a common topic; the files may include Web pages, graphics, audio, and video. (p. 7)

Web site development application Sophisticated application package that some Web developers use to create Web sites. (p. 74)

Webmaster Person who manages and maintains Web sites. (p. 20)

Web-safe color The 216 colors that display consistently from computer to computer, giving Web designers some control over their pages' appearance. (p. 184)

white space An area on a Web page without any content. (p. 158)

wide area network (WAN) Network that connects computers across a wide geographical area, such as a region of the United States. (p. 43)

WordArt Text objects with special formatting applied. (p. 226)

World Wide Web Software that sends information that is stored in files along the Internet's hardware. (p. 6)

WYSIWYG Applications that allow you to create Web pages so that what you see on the screen is very similar to the appearance of the final page; stands for "what you see is what you get." (p. 74)

X

XHTML See *Extensible Hypertext Markup Language.* (p. 271)

XML See *Extensible Markup Language.* (p. 270)

INDEX

IMAGE CREDITS